The Postwar Transformation of Germany

The Postwar Transformation of Germany
Democracy, Prosperity, and Nationhood

EDITED BY
JOHN S. BRADY,
BEVERLY CRAWFORD,
and
SARAH ELISE WILIARTY

Ann Arbor
THE UNIVERSITY OF MICHIGAN PRESS

Copyright © by the University of Michigan 1999
All rights reserved
Published in the United States of America by
The University of Michigan Press
Manufactured in the United States of America
⊗ Printed on acid-free paper

2002 2001 2000 1999   4 3 2 1

No part of this publication may be reproduced, stored in a retrieval system, or transmitted in any form or by any means, electronic, mechanical, or otherwise, without the written permission of the publisher.

A CIP catalog record for this book is available from the British Library.

Library of Congress Cataloging-in-Publication Data

The postwar transformation of Germany : democracy, prosperity, and
    nationhood / edited by John S. Brady, Beverly Crawford, and Sarah
    Elise Wiliarty.
      p. cm.
    Includes bibliographical references (p.   ) and index.
    ISBN 0-472-10993-6 (alk. paper)
    ISBN 0-472-08591-3 (pbk. : alk. paper)
      1. Democracy—German. 2. Political culture—Germany. 3. Germany—
Economic conditions—1945–1990. 4. Germany—Social policy.
5. Germany—Politics and government—1945–1990. 6. Political
participation—Germany. 7. Social change—Germany. I. Brady, John,
1969– II. Crawford, Beverly. III. Wiliarty, Sarah Elise, 1968–
JN3971.A91 P695 1999
306.2′0943′09049—ddc21   99-6174
                                                                                     CIP

Acknowledgments

We gratefully acknowledge the permission to reprint the following:

Ernst Haas's chapter, "The Late Flowering and Early Fading of German Nationalism" from Ernst B. Haas, *Nationalism, Liberalism, and Progress,* vol. 1, *The Rise and Decline of Nationalism.* Copyright © 1997 by Cornell University. Used by permission of the publisher, Cornell University Press.

Portions of Ludger Lindlar and Carl-Ludwig Holtfrerich's chapter, "Germany's Export Boom at Fifty — An Enduring Success Story?" were previously published in Ludger Lindlar and Carl-Ludwig Holtfrerich, "Geography, Exchange Rates and Trade Structures: Germany's Export Performance since the 1950s," *European Review of Economic History,* vol. 1 (1997), 217–46. Used by permission of the publisher, Cambridge University Press.

Portions of Thomas U. Berger's chapter, "The Burdens of Memory: The Impact of History on German National Security Policy were previously published in Thomas U. Berger, "The Past in the Present," *German Politics* 6, no. 1: 39–59, published by Frank Cass & Company, 900 Eastern Avenue, Ilford, Essex, England. Copyright © Frank Cass & Co Ltd 1997.

Contents

Germany Transformed? A Framework for Analysis   1
*Beverly Crawford, John S. Brady, and
Sarah Elise Wiliarty*

Building Democracy: The Institutions and Political Culture of German Democracy

The German Response to the Challenge of
Extremist Parties, 1949–1994   35
Peter H. Merkl

Building Democracy and Changing Institutions: The
Professional Civil Service and Political Parties in
the Federal Republic of Germany   63
Gregg O. Kvistad

Building Democracy: Judicial Review and the
German *Rechtsstaat*   94
Donald P. Kommers

From State Culture to Citizen Culture: Political
Parties and the Postwar Transformation of
Political Culture in Germany   122
Michaela Richter

The Challenge of Prosperity: The Foundations of the German Economy and Challenges of the Future

Germany's Export Boom at Fifty — An Enduring
Success Story?   163
Ludger Lindlar and Carl-Ludwig Holtfrerich

The German Welfare State: Principles,
  Performance, Prospects   202
  Claus Offe

Norms, Ideology, and Institutions: (En)Gendered
  Retrenchment of *Modell Deutschland?*   225
  Patricia Davis and Simon Reich

**The Question of Nationhood: The Evolution of
National Identity in the Federal Republic**

The End of Longing? (Notes toward a History of
  Postwar German National Longing)   271
  Charles S. Maier

The Late Flowering and Early Fading of
  German Nationalism   286
  Ernst Haas

The Federal Republic as a Nation-State   339
  Peter Krüger

Immigration and Nationhood in the Federal
  Republic of Germany   357
  Christhard Hoffmann

Two Discourses of Citizenship in Germany:
  The Differences between Public Debate and
  Administrative Practice   378
  Jost Halfmann

Germany's Place in the World

The Enduring Transformation of Postwar German
  Foreign Policy   401
  Thomas Banchoff

Germany's Place in the World   420
  Wolfgang Krieger

The Contemporary Power of Memory: The
  Dilemmas for German Foreign Policy   439
  Andrei S. Markovits and Simon Reich

The Burdens of Memory: The Impact of History
  on German National Security Policy   473
  Thomas U. Berger

Conclusion

From the Bonn to the Berlin Republic and
  Beyond: Critical Junctures and the Future of the
  Federal Republic   503
  John S. Brady and Sarah Elise Wiliarty

Contributors   519

Index   521

Germany Transformed?
A Framework for Analysis

Beverly Crawford, John S. Brady, and Sarah Elise Wiliarty

The recent wave of political and economic liberalization spreading over much of the globe has unleashed a flood of scholarly speculation about the sources of successful democratic consolidation and economic development in societies that have broken from an illiberal past. The exact sources of success are still unknown. The search for historical analogies and the keys to a successful transition to democracy and markets has drawn scholars to a reexamination of the founding and evolution of postwar Germany. Indeed, the Federal Republic of Germany is probably the most prominent case of a political and economic transformation in the postwar period. The transformation that was required of the Federal Republic of Germany in the aftermath of World War II is also what is required of postcommunist states today: nothing less than the destruction of illiberal and traditional economic, political, and social practices and the creation of a liberal society, polity, and economy.

Yet, exactly when the attraction of market capitalism and liberal democracy for countries of the East and the South is stronger than ever, the market and democratic institutions of the West have come under increasing international and domestic pressure, clouding their future. In the last 22 years, over 40 countries have attempted to make the transition from various forms of autocracy and central economic planning to something approaching liberal democratic political systems and market economies. While the East and the South are desperately seeking to develop market and democratic institutions, the advanced capitalist societies are experiencing widespread dissatisfaction with those very institutions. The postcommunist world wants nothing more than to imitate the existing practices of the industrial democracies; and yet the process of economic globalization seems to be a threat to democracy and a harbinger of economic inequality leading to rising xenophobia and the practice of ethnic and sectarian "identity politics" that strike at the heart of liberal democracy. Ironically, at the very moment when Germany became a historical model for the "transition" to liberal markets and democracy, the liberal system that it so carefully built after the war was under stress from both international and domestic pressures.

The essays collected in this volume address this conundrum by tracing the paths of the Federal Republic of Germany's "transition" to a liberal capitalist democracy and evaluating the sources of Germany's success and the causes of its difficulties.[1] They look to the period between 1945 and 1990 to examine how Germany's transition evolved. In addition, they look to the period after unification, to see if successes have been consolidated or whether they are currently being undermined by the stresses of unification, economic globalization, and, ironically, Germany's growing power position in the international arena. Such an evaluation is crucial and long overdue if we are to assess the validity of the German model of liberalization for other societies — including that of the former German Democratic Republic — undergoing similar changes in the present period.

Four issues define the content of any democratic and market "transition":

> the task of building democracy,
> the challenge of prosperity,
> the question of nationhood,
> the nation's place in the world.

This volume examines each of these issues in Germany's postwar and postunification development. Has Germany been able to build a solid liberal democracy, a stable and prospering market economy, a liberal concept of nationhood, and a successful and peaceful foreign policy that will withstand the vicissitudes of a multipolar world and a globalized economy? How has the development of democracy, prosperity, nationhood, and foreign policy weathered the challenges of the postwar period: the crises of the Cold War, the rise of radicalism, the growing requirements of economic competitiveness, and large-scale immigration?

Explaining Germany's "Transition": Institutions and Culture

There are two alternative explanations for what conditioned Germany's success and triggered its weaknesses. The first rests on the assumption that new institutions have the power to transform society. From this perspective, institutions are constitutive of social practices and cultural norms. Where for an economist, "getting the prices right" is essential to a host of other economic changes, for the political scientist, "getting the institutions right" is essential to a positive future trajectory of social and cultural transformation. This approach suggests that new institutions can be crafted that will shut out the negative influences of the past.

The concept of institutions is indeed a contested one. We follow Douglass North's rather broad definition:

> Institutions are a set of rules, compliance procedures, and moral and ethical behavioral norms embedded in those rules and compliance procedures designed to *constrain* the behavior of individuals in the interests of maximizing wealth, social order, and the well-being of a society. Institutions establish the cooperative and competitive *incentives* in society by virtue of their norms, rules, and procedures.[2]

By constructing the norms and the rules for membership, distribution, accountability, and participation, institutions shape actor preferences by rewarding some choices and punishing others. They not only constrain some behaviors and encourage others, but they provide power resources to some social actors and deny them to others. They thus shape the strategies of political elites, both inside and outside government, and structure the relations of power among social groups.[3] As such, institutions embody the "social contract" between state and society, and they shape the broad political culture and social understandings of political identity with the incentives and constraints that they provide.

An institutional perspective on postwar Germany would suggest that the conclusion of World War II lopped off the head of fascism, leaving space for the development of new forces to structure the political arena and social identities. New institutions would fashion politics, economics, society, and national identity according to the more or less universal rules of liberal capitalist democracy. These institutions, created under the tutelage of the United States as the victor of the war, transformed Germany into one of the world's most stable democracies and prosperous capitalist economies. Thus, the lesson we can learn is that the "right" institutions can transform other countries now emerging from a totalitarian or authoritarian past.

As an alternative mode of analysis, the cultural approach claims that culture and a nation's history matter more than institutions and carry more weight in explaining outcomes.[4] In this view, culture is conceived of as the result of collective beliefs and attitudes that have evolved over a long historical period and reflect the broad collective consciousness of the nation. Shaping the relationships among institutional actors, culture comes to shape the very identity of the institutions themselves. Cultural arguments make the claim that they can explain why institutions change as a result of struggles among various social actors representing divergent beliefs, values, and interpretations of reality. A cultural approach, the argument runs, explains the emergence, shape, and content of institutions and thus provides more powerful explanations of outcomes.

This cultural approach was popular among German historians of the 1960s and 1970s who attempted to explain the phenomenon of Nazism through the by now familiar concept of the German *Sonderweg*.[5] Arguments in this school of thought suggested that German culture in the nineteenth century had developed differently from the culture of other European countries. As a result, it developed pernicious traits that then were reflected in Germany's political and economic institutions, making Hitler's seizure of power almost a foregone conclusion. A more general statement of the *Sonderweg* argument and its extension to the present suggests that entrenched cultural practices cast a long shadow on the present and shape the identity of new institutions. What is more, these practices can ultimately undermine the liberalization process. Arguments from this perspective, for example, suggest that skinhead violence and the fragmentation of the political party system in Germany may demonstrate the weakness of its postwar institutions and the dominance of an essentially authoritarian, racist, and antidemocratic culture.

Another, more optimistic strand of the cultural approach suggests that cultures are not monolithic; indeed, they are diverse and in a constant state of flux. Core cultural beliefs emerge from conflict and competition among social actors who wish to realize their interests and who are able to press their understanding of reality upon the rest of society. At times, however, competing values and beliefs characterize a particular culture, and "core" cultural beliefs cannot be easily identified. Furthermore, culture interacts with international and domestic social forces to affect the core set of beliefs that shape a nation's collective consciousness. Normally, once this core set of beliefs is formed, it changes very slowly, if at all; nonetheless, cataclysmic events such as defeat in war can discredit old cultural values and make way for the emergence of new beliefs, norms, and values, or the reemergence of old cultural traits that may have once lost power to shape society and institutions but have nonetheless remained alive.

From this set of assumptions, one could argue that cultural developments in the prefascist period of German history created the conditions for a successful democracy and prosperous economy once fascism was destroyed and space was opened for the emergence of new core cultural beliefs. Germany's late development with its advantages of backwardness, Bismarck's unification and the creation of the welfare state, and even certain unintended modernizing tendencies under fascism all created a set of values, norms, beliefs, and social understandings that presaged a successful transformation to democracy and a particularly "German" form of capitalism after World War II.[6] Those cultural features were enhanced and promoted by new institutions throughout the postwar period, and a culture of liberal capitalist democracy has come to dominate German society today.

The contributions to this volume participate in this lively debate between institutionalists and cultural theorists in a joint effort to both explain the sources of Germany's transformation since 1945 and predict its robustness. The central theoretical questions underlying all of the essays assembled here are these: has a liberal political and economic culture "stuck" in Germany? Or have illiberal politics begun to play a significant role there, particularly after unification? In a broader sense, how have institutions, culture, and history interacted to shape the transformation of the Federal Republic? Further, the contributors look to the forces — particularly the forces of globalization and their manifestation in growing international economic competition and migration — that might dramatically change both German culture and institutions in the century to come. Has the German political and economic system, created in a setting much different from the current one, been outstripped by changes in the international system, changes in economic and political pressures, and the related evolution of the political culture itself? It is to a consideration of these questions in the four issue areas under evaluation here that our discussion now turns.

Germany as a Consolidated Liberal Democracy?

Establishing and stabilizing democracy in Germany is one of the main achievements of the West since 1945. Despite this postwar-era success, the failings of the first German republic have not been forgotten. Bonn is not Weimar, but Weimar has haunted Bonn and will likely haunt Berlin as well. Throughout the postwar period, but particularly since unification, observers have questioned the stability of (West) German democracy.

Germany has faced several challenges to democracy in the postwar period, including the rise of radical right-wing parties, a major antiestablishment, nonparliamentary challenge from the left in the 1960s, and radical left-wing terrorism. More recently, unification and the incorporation of eastern Germany, high and lasting unemployment, the end of the postwar economic boom, and, more recently, *Politik-* and *Parteiverdrossenheit* (moroseness about politics and parties) have placed strain on Germany's democratic fabric. The contributors to this section on democracy examine both the sources of Germany's democratic stability and Germany's ability to meet these new challenges.

Theories of democratic transitions often focus either on the elite bargaining process involved in becoming democratic or on preconditions that a country needs for democracy to work. Because Germany's democracy was imposed on the country following World War II, the preconditions school is more appropriate for understanding its democratic stability.[7] The extensive literature on what preconditions are necessary for a country to become democratic has focused on economic development, a society's class configuration, and the presence or absence of revolution, as well as institutions and culture. Indeed, this problem is far too large to be treated thoroughly in one section of this volume. Rather than tackle the entire theoretical spectrum, the authors seek to discover what we can learn about the contributions of culture and institutions to democracy from the German case.

The cultural approach to understanding democratic transition argues that a country's political culture affects its potential to become democratic. Culture may promote self-reliance and social trust (thereby increasing democracy's chances) or obedience to and reliance on the upper classes (thus hurting democracy's chances).[8] In Germany, cultural theorists argued that the traditional authoritarianism of the political culture needed to be eliminated before democracy would be feasible. Changes of this magnitude are not easy, although they may be possible, particularly following the extreme disruption of social organization after the war. Because political culture is difficult to change, the cultural approach is quite open to the idea that an incomplete democratic transition has occurred and that remnants of the antidemocratic tradition remain.

According to the cultural perspective, this incomplete transformation of political culture is exactly what happened in Germany. By the 1950s, democracy appeared to have taken root, but the population had not adopted democratic norms.[9] The stability of the German political system critically depended on that system's continued successful performance, especially economically. In other words, democracy was not valued for itself, but only for the material benefits it apparently brought. Although a majority of Germans were well informed about politics and viewed government positively, most Germans did not take pride in their political institutions. Germans talked less about politics, participated less, and were more alienated from their political parties than the citizens of other democracies. Despite outward appearances, German political culture had not become truly democratic by the 1950s. In the late 1970s, however, new culturally based theories argued that while Germany's political culture may not have been democratic by the 1950s, by the 1970s it was at least as democratic as the political cultures of some older democracies such as the United States and Great Britain.[10] The level of pride in and support for the political system had increased significantly in Germany. Despite periodic economic recessions, Germany had remained a stable democracy.

Because political culture changes slowly over time, it is critical to have strong democratic institutions in place, particularly during the period of adjustment while a country's citizens are learning democracy through participation. What is needed, therefore, is a critical examination of the institutions that helped Germany maintain its democracy during the initial difficult years. An examination of these institutions is critical from the perspectives of both the institutionalists, for whom they are all that matter, and the culturalists, who believe the institutions gave Germany the necessary breathing space for its political culture to change and arrive at a point where it can itself help stable democracy.

Merkl's chapter provides just such an explanation. Arguments about the potential breakdown of German democracy often rely, at least implicitly, on the assumptions that the political culture in Germany has remained undemocratic and that German political institutions are too weak to combat a real extremist challenge, should one occur. Merkl examines this possibility in detail and reaches a cautiously optimistic conclusion about Germany's democratic future. Looking first at Germany's most fundamental political institutions, the Basic Law and the electoral system, Merkl notes that these were created under the assumption that Germany's political culture was undemocratic. Hence, the Parliamentary Council included provisions designed to ensure stability and moderation, such as the constructive vote of no confidence, the regulation of political parties, and the ability of the Federal Constitutional Court to ban extremist parties. Provisions for any kind of referenda were excluded, as the Parliamentary Council did not trust the population with such power. The electoral law, with a 5 percent hurdle and a mixed system combining aspects of majoritarian voting and proportional representation, was meant to encourage the emergence of a two-party system and discourage the splinter parties seen under the Weimar Republic.

In addition to institutions meant to secure German democracy, Merkl examines the strategies employed by political parties, particularly the Christian Democrats, to limit extremism. The Christian Democratic Union under Adenauer maintained a policy of not allowing any party to emerge to its right and of reintegrating former Nazis into the political system in an attempt to prevent the emergence of a new radical right-wing party. Economic recovery and Adenauer's efforts to end Germany's international isolation through Western integration increased support for the Federal Republic, which made a successful extremist challenge unlikely. Indeed, when Germany did experience political extremism from both the left and the right in the 1960s and 1970s, the Federal Republic's democracy was never seriously at risk. Merkl notes that while unification and the potential difficulties of integrating East and West Germany could represent a real challenge to German democracy, the founding institutions and strategies used by the parties have acted not just to maintain democracy, but to foster a political culture that is now also democratic, as seen in both the demonstrations opposing violence against foreigners and the failure of the Republikaner to clear the 5 percent hurdle in the 1994 elections. In closing, Merkl notes that the very myth of Weimar that haunts Germany also serves as a reminder of the dangers of extremism and thereby contributes to democratic stability.

The strong democratic institutions put in place in Germany after World War II helped the country remain democratic and stable until the political culture evolved to the point where it could potentially support a democracy even with fewer protective measures. Once Germany reached this point, however, its citizens began to have less tolerance for certain of these institutions that had been designed to protect democracy, but that were now viewed as hindering the development of a deeper democracy. What happens when a country's political culture "outgrows" its democracy-protecting institutions? Kvistad, Kommers, and Richter examine this dilemma in their essays on the German civil service, the Federal Constitutional Court, and political parties.

Kvistad notes that the historical role of the German civil service, forming the political will of the people, has been taken over by the political parties in the postwar period. Despite the pleas of the Allies, the postwar civil service did not differ much from the traditional civil service, either in attitude or in membership. Because of its more traditional orientation, Kvistad views the latent conflict between the Basic Law and the civil service as a time bomb. The stated goal of the civil service was to defend order, while the Basic Law is a document that values individual rights above all else (perhaps including order). This conflict was played out in the 1960s when the question arose of whether the individual rights secured in the Basic Law applied to civil servants in the context of a process of political mobilization that included increas ingly wider segments of the population. Kvistad sees the real change in Germany occurring when the various social movements entered politics with the stated goal of increasing democracy. The institutional change in the civil service — the Anti-radicals Decree of 1972 — was an ultimately failed attempt to reinforce the traditional civil service and to protect the state from the potentially hostile population. Although the Radicals Decree is still officially on the books, it is no longer strictly enforced. An uneasy truce has been declared between institutions and political culture.

Kommers and Richter address a similar issue in the context of their studies. Kommers, in his study of the Federal Constitutional Court (FCC), and Richter, in her essay on Germany's political parties, both note that these institutions were created (or empowered) immediately following World War II, when the German political culture was antidemocratic. Thus, these institutions were made extremely powerful so that they would be able to resist and change popular opinion. Kommers and Richter fear that in the 1990s, the FCC and the political parties may have too much power, considering that German political culture is now much more democratic than it was in the 1950s.

After noting that the FCC is well respected and actually more active than the U.S. Supreme Court, Kommers asks what has contributed to the success of judicial review in Germany. He argues that Germany's political culture between 1945 and 1965 was underdeveloped, while the legal culture was that of a traditional *Rechtsstaat*. The activity level of the court has created a "constitutional culture" that, through its review of the Basic Law, allows the FCC to have a say on almost every major political issue. The FCC has ruled on party funding and the electoral law, abortion, and asylum. In some cases, such as the postunification change in the abortion law, the FCC laid out all the details of the law it expected the Bundestag to pass. In closing, Kommers notes that while the FCC has both liberated and restricted German democracy — setting guidelines not just for the rules of the political game, but sometimes for particular policies — this institution is not accountable to anyone. He questions whether this arrangement is appropriate for a country that now has a clearly democratic political culture.

Richter notes that while prior to the founding of the Federal Republic German political culture was antiparty, both Adenauer and Schumacher worked hard to foster sentiments supportive of political parties. For the most part, they were successful. Richter highlights three intervals in the postwar period in which antiparty sentiment has been especially high: the period of occupation, the 1970s and 1980s, and the early 1990s. After providing a rich history of the three intervals, Richter finds that the "moroseness" about parties may not be hurting the parties as much as expected. Indeed, when viewed in comparative perspective, the party system actually looks remarkably stable. Instead, she argues that the parties have become "cartel" parties, which are dependent on the state and not really accountable or punishable. Because of their extraordinary connection to the state, the two large parties are unlikely to lose much influence even when they are defeated electorally. Like Kommers, she notes that the strong connection to the state was originally given to the parties because of fears of an undemocratic citizenry.

In short, Germany's steadfast democracy in the postwar period is largely due to its strong democratic institutions, which were mostly implemented immediately following the war. The country's political culture, however, has undergone a serious transformation. While some authoritarian or extremist tendencies may remain, the authors here are in agreement that these tendencies do not exceed those in other countries. The aspect of Germany's democratic transformation that remains interesting is the institutions designed to protect democracy during the early years that are still in place. The political culture may now be more democratic than the institutions. What will happen in this situation? Will the political culture influence the institutions as it was once influenced by them? Will the democratic content of these institutions be further called into question? Similar questions can be posed with regard to economic institutions.

Can Prosperity Continue?

The development of Germany's postwar economy has until recently been an unqualified success story. West Germany emerged from the trauma and destruction of World War II to become one of the strongest economies in Europe, if not the world. Compared to other European countries, Germany did well not only during the boom years of the 1950s and 1960s, but also in the more difficult economic times that followed. Only recently has Germany's economy begun to show signs of difficulty under the combined strains of globalization and unification. The contributors to this volume examine both the sources of Germany's long period of economic success and the extent of the current challenges from both cultural and institutional perspectives.

One explanation for German prosperity lies in German culture. Michel Albert, for example, sees the key to understanding Germany's economic success in its shared norms of compromise, egalitarianism, and putting collective interests before individual interests.[11] Through the defeat of World War II, Germans became aware of their country's vulnerability. Like the Japanese, the Germans perceived their postwar democracy and economic prosperity as fragile, and thus they did not raise contentious issues that might call into question the social compromise — at least not until recently.

While not denying the importance of certain institutions, the cultural explanation holds that German institutions only work because they are based on the shared norms discussed above. Because Germany's culture fosters mutual responsibility and cooperation, Germany's powerful unions (unlike Britain's or France's) are also responsible. Unions cooperate with employers to run the apprenticeship system that keeps Germany's workforce well trained, and they do not make unreasonable wage demands. For example, the largest union, IG Metall, voluntarily dropped its demand for a 35-hour workweek when the country unexpectedly had to cope with reunification. According to theorists in the cultural tradition, Germany's cooperative trade unions help make the economic environment stable, which encourages growth.

The cultural emphasis on group interests over individual interests also influences the economy in positive ways. For example, firms are viewed as social communities working to benefit all members, both workers and management.[12] An awareness of the need to work for the general good encourages both a high personal savings rate — which provides funds for investment — and a focus on the high-end export market, which provides numerous well-paid jobs for skilled workers, as well as solid profits for firms. The historical German focus on education and innovation contributes to excellent training programs and research and development centers.

While the German model has been remarkably successful during the postwar period, some analysts fear it will break down as American business culture spreads across the ocean to Europe. The "neo-American" model brings with it many potential disadvantages, including conspicuous consumption and a loss of the work ethic.[13] American-style "casino capitalism" values the individual entrepreneur who makes profits fast, not the well-organized company with a long-term perspective. Thus, the sometimes slower, but steady success of Germany's firms may not suffice in a changed corporate culture. As borders become more permeable, Germany may have to adopt the American focus on short-term profit and extreme competitiveness in order to attain continued economic success. Instead of focusing on the shared norms that were fundamental to Germany's prior economic success, German firms may shift their attention to the quarterly profit statement. In the long run, cultural analysts fear that this change will hurt Germany's economy.

The institutional approach offers an alternative to the cultural explanation; it holds that Germany's institutions are the source of the country's economic success.[14] Several institutions are thought to have contributed to Germany's prosperity. For example, Germany's investment banks have provided large amounts of capital on a long-term basis, since the late nineteenth century. Because of the extent of their investment, banks have worked closely with management, both providing technical advice and to some extent limiting competition in an effort to advance an industry as a whole.[15]

Germany's central bank, the Bundesbank, has provided another anchor of Germany's institutional framework with its control over macroeconomic policy. The remarkably independent Bundesbank at times acts against the wishes of both the government and the powerful commercial banks to meet its primary goal of fighting inflation. At times it has even tightened the money supply during a recession to achieve this aim. Because of the political independence of the Bundesbank and the close relationship between financial and industrial capital, Germany has been able to pursue policies that favored exporters.[16] These actors were strong enough to prevent revaluation of the mark even when it was recommended by economic officials in both major parties and the unions. The policy of long-term undervaluation strengthened export industries. The countercyclical effects of a consistently strong currency also allowed Germany to avoid the stop-go cycles experienced in Britain and the inflation-producing devaluations of the French.

The institutions of Germany's labor market were also designed to produce economic growth. The apprenticeship system ensures that workers receive quality training and that firms have incentives to provide that training.[17] Because Germany's unions are highly centralized and organized by industry, it is easier to negotiate and enforce wage agreements, and unions are less likely to bid against each other competitively, as occurs in Britain. This form of union organization has allowed workers and management to make agreements that usually last two to three years. It has ensured long periods of labor peace and nearly eliminated inflation caused by a wage-push spiral.[18] Furthermore, the "dual system" that provides workers with representation at the industry level through unions and at the plant level through works councils gives German workers and firms the necessary flexibility to negotiate agreements satisfactory to both labor and management.[19]

Germany's institutions, both those discussed above and others that encourage research and development, create an economic environment in which the best strategy for firms to pursue is what Streeck terms "diversified quality production": manufacturing high-quality products with a focus on the export market.[20] Because the institutions discourage competition based on price but encourage competition based on quality, Germany is able to maintain a high-wage, egalitarian society.[21]

Like the cultural approach, the institutionalist approach recognizes the potential economic challenges facing Germany. Changes in the international economy—such as increased trade and capital mobility—are exerting pressure on states to liberalize their economies in order to make their products more competitive and their countries more attractive to investors. Some analysts argue that in the face of such pressures all countries, including Germany, will have to liberalize their economies.[22] Institutionalists fear that liberalization would radically alter the institutions that make up the foundation that has enabled Germany to succeed economically by focusing on the high-end export market.

While institutionalists agree that it is institutions that matter, there are two camps regarding how serious the current challenge is. One camp believes Germany's institutions will hold up against the globalization onslaught. Germany's institutions, such as the dual system of labor representation and the apprenticeship system, provide industry with a high-skilled, flexible labor force, the asset that is most necessary in a highly competitive system. Germany's institutions may even have been strengthened and revitalized through unification.[23] The other camp argues that German institutions will not be able to withstand the pressure of globalization and unification.[24] The German system's failure to adapt to this problem manifests itself most clearly in high, persistent unemployment. The pessimistic institutionalists fear that high unemployment may cause breakdown of collective bargaining, especially if employers quit employer organizations.[25] If Germany is unable to maintain its corporatist economic system, wages will sink, and Germany will begin to look like Great Britain or the United States.

The three political economy essays in this volume dive directly into the debate over the continued health of the German economic model. In the most optimistic of the contributions, Ludger Lindlar and Carl-Ludwig Holtfrerich focus on sources of Germany's economic success and ask whether they are being challenged. Because Germany's export orientation is a primary contributor to the country's economic success, Lindlar and Holtfrerich attempt to account for Germany's ability to export and examine whether Germany's export chances are declining. As evidence of a potential decline, they note that Germany's domestic costs, particularly for labor, are comparatively high, that Germany is attracting less foreign direct investment than previously, and that Germany does not export many high-tech products. Their essay examines the importance of Germany's geographical location, its product specialization, and domestic and international monetary institutions.

In looking at the importance of Germany's geographical location, Lindlar and Holtfrerich find that institutions of regional integration such as the Organization for European Economic Cooperation (OEEC), the European Payments Union (EPU), and the European Economic Community (EEC) played a critical role in reestablishing and deepening trade within Western Europe, especially in the 1950s. By the 1960s, market forces were more important in spurring Germany's export economy. Institutions established a critical foundation that then allowed the market to play a gradually increasing role.

Lindlar and Holtfrerich find that while Germany has not specialized in high-tech products (as the United States and Japan have), neither is the country falling behind. Instead, Germany has specialized in "medium-tech" products, including electrical machinery, chemicals, and transportation equipment. Furthermore, regardless of whether the product is high-tech, medium-tech, or low-tech, Germany's specialization in production of very high quality products has contributed to Germany's economic success. Lindlar and Holtfrerich argue that both market forces and institutions contributed to Germany's international specialization, which in turn has led to Germany's export success. Domestic demand led to specialization in both high-quality automobiles and environmental technology, while institutions provided a well-educated workforce and top-of-the-line research and development.

To examine the effect of international and domestic monetary institutions on Germany's strength as an exporter, Lindlar and Holtfrerich divide the postwar era into pre- and post–Bretton Woods periods. Under Bretton Woods, international institutions shaped Germany's monetary policy, and as a result, growth was viewed as preferable to stability. Since Bretton Woods, Germany has been able to pursue a more independent monetary policy, and economic policymakers have generally pursued stability over growth. This policy has led to an appreciation of the Deutschemark. The authors blame Germany's current employment difficulties primarily on the Bundesbank's unwillingness to reorient its policies from controlling domestic inflation to looking at ways to relieve the recession and unemployment problems that have recently plagued most countries in Europe. If the Bundesbank were to loosen the money supply, that would allow Germany's export-oriented economy (and perhaps other European economies) to recover. The different goals of international and domestic actors illustrate how institutions have played a critical role in shaping Germany's monetary policy.

Claus Offe represents the pessimistic institutionalists. He argues that while the welfare state helped to consolidate the Federal Republic, unification, European integration, and globalization are challenging the welfare state. Offe describes the institutional architecture of the German welfare state as a building with four floors: the first floor represents the regulation of labor at work (worker protection); the second represents the social insurance system; the third represents the rules on collective agreements; and, in a somewhat unusual interpretation of the term *institution,* the fourth floor represents macroeconomic policy, especially the policy of full employment. The institutions of the welfare state work together to create a solid "building." Unlike a traditional building, however, Offe's welfare-state building has its foundation in the roof with the policy of full employment. If that policy has changed (as seems to be the case), then the rest of the building may not hold. He finds it unlikely that economic winners will continue to be able to support the increasing number of economic losers.

Offe accounts for Germany's high unemployment partially by pointing to the increased openness of borders, due to both globalization and European integration, which has strained Germany's institutions. The open economy has allowed foreign labor and goods in while also allowing investment and jobs to flow out. Additionally, more women are seeking employment, further increasing the labor supply. Unification and the transfer of West German institutions to the new *Länder* have driven up both wages and unemployment in the East. Taken together, these changes have made the "institution" of full employment too difficult to sustain. While political parties have suggested a variety of policies to alleviate German unemployment, most have involved reductions in the welfare state. What is more, many of these policy suggestions would reorganize and weaken the other institutions of the welfare state, particularly those Offe finds on the second and third floors.

While Davis and Reich's approach is similar to Offe's, they do not believe that the German welfare system is near collapse. Their investigation of who the "outsiders" are reveals that they are predominantly women. Davis and Reich argue that the much-admired German model will endure exactly *because* of both the institutional limits built into it and the cultural bias that allows discrimination against women. They predict that the social welfare benefits will remain, but that fewer people will benefit from them. Because welfare institutions reflect the discriminatory political culture of the Germany they were created in, women will be the primary losers in these economic changes. In a detailed analysis of German welfare institutions, Davis and Reich find gender bias in a wide range of policies. For example, mandatory protection for pregnant women means they are required to take time off both before and after delivery. Because the amount of social welfare benefits one receives often depends on how much one has paid into the system, women generally have less access to these benefits than men. Furthermore, at least partially because of restricted store hours, limited day care, and half-day schools, many women who do work do so only part-time. Because much part-time work does not count as paying into the social welfare system, these workers (mostly female) do not receive the benefits that made the German model famous. Thus, political culture allows bias in institutions, which creates a safety valve to allow for perpetuation of those institutions, even in difficult economic times.

The authors in this volume contribute to the ongoing debate on sources of Germany's past economic success and the likelihood that that success will continue. Because of the turmoil the German political economy is currently experiencing, this debate probably will not be resolved soon. The theoretical questions raised by these authors will continue to be critical: Are culture or institutions more relevant to economic success? Or is it the interaction of culture and institutions that really matters? How robust are national differences — whether cultural or institutional — at a time when the international economy is becoming increasingly open? What kind of an impact will these international forces have on Germany domestically? These are the central questions that will occupy scholars of German political economy in the years to come.

Is Germany's National Identity "Liberal"?

Doubts regarding the meaning of German nationhood have a long tradition. As early as 1796, Friedrich Schiller asked, "Germany? But where is it? I don't know how to find such a country."[26] The subsequent answers given to Schiller's question, whether the liberal nationalism proposed in the early nineteenth century by German republicans, the antidemocratic and imperialist nationalism of the Bismarck era, or the racist and antisemitic nationalism propagated by the National Socialist regime, shaped not only the course of German history but also the social and political conflicts in the modern West.

In the postwar period the force of nationalism in German politics was weakened. For most Germans, the experience of National Socialist domination discredited the idea of nationalism as a legitimate basis for social integration. Moreover, the partition of Germany in the Potsdam Accord destroyed any semblance of the unity of culture, state, and nation[27] and thus laid the groundwork for the development of two separate traditions of nationhood. In the West, Germans seemingly abandoned the *völkisch* idiom of national identity propagated by the National Socialists in favor of a more liberal, democratic understanding of nation. German politicians complemented this development with the successful attempt to integrate Germany into the European Union and develop a European identity.

By contrast, the leaders in the East attempted to sow the seeds of a socialist nation among the general populace. According to official rationale, the German nation had been split and had "given way to two new nations which were not based on cultural identity, social communication, shared values or any other traditional criterion, but solely on social class."[28] This state-led attempt to create a new national identity never took root.

The fall of the Berlin Wall and the subsequent unification of the two German states have initiated a new period in the evolving definition of German national identity. In their efforts to create one German nation-state, the political leaders and citizens of the new Federal Republic are again faced with the question of what it means to be German. In the wake of unification, Germany has taken its place as a united, sovereign nation-state among the other nation-states of Europe. Where the German nation is, is no longer a question. Yet other questions remain. What is the content of Germany's new self-understanding: does Germany possess an ethnocultural or a political, liberal definition of nation? Has Germany broken with its nationalist past, or are there important continuities between past and contemporary conceptions of German nationhood? And finally, and most importantly, what role does the German understanding of nation play in German politics?

An important step in coming to terms with these questions entails exploring the sources of German national self-understanding. Two alternatives present themselves as possible sources: culture and institutions. From the cultural perspective, German nationhood is conditioned by cultural traditions and historical legacies. These traditions and legacies—for example, the tradition of defining the German nation as a community of descent—influence the political behavior of individuals, the dynamic of political debates, and even policy outcomes. Given the power of past habits of national understanding in the present, the proponents of the cultural perspective view the future with a certain amount of trepidation; for these scholars, the possibility that at certain historical conjunctures Germany's negative nationalist past will play a significant political role should not be dismissed.

In the second perspective, that of the institutionalists, contemporary notions of German nationhood have their origins in the political and social institutions of the Federal Republic: the constitution, the institutions of the social market economy, Germany's pluralist, democratic civil society. These and other institutions are the foci for national identification in the Federal Republic. As long as they remain viable, there is reason, according to the institutionalists, to be cautiously optimistic about the Federal Republic's future.

The contributors to this volume explore the influence of both cultural and institutional factors in their discussions of the various facets of German nationhood. In their analysis they demonstrate the power of cultural traditions, for example in the formation of immigration policy, and the continuing influence of historical legacies of German nationhood on politics in the Federal Republic. But they also illustrate the manner in which institutions, for example the Basic Law (*Grundgesetz*), have also decisively shaped the politics of nationhood. In the end, they suggest we have reason to be cautiously optimistic about Germany's future.

Before discussing the relative roles of culture and institutions in the development of German national identity, we briefly touch on the ethnocultural and liberal political components of German self-understanding. In the political tradition of nationhood, the nation's identity is constructed in relation to the institutional and territorial frame of the state. It is political unity and not shared culture that constitutes the nation.[29] In the European context, France is the quintessential example of the political nation. By contrast, in the ethnocultural tradition, the nation exists prior to the institutional frame of the state. The nation is not the bearer of universal political values but is rather an organic, cultural, linguistic or racial community.[30] Again in the European context, Germany, with its *völkisch* conception of nationhood, is one of the best examples of the ethnocultural tradition; the nation consists of the German people, the *Volk,* a unique pre-political community united by the ethnic spirit of Germanness.[31]

In their analyses of the German tradition of nationhood, most scholars focus on the tradition's *völkisch* and ethnic components. Charles Maier, in his contribution to this volume, shifts the focus to reveal a further component of this tradition, namely, the element of longing. For Maier, German political culture is saturated with longing. As a category of German national consciousness, longing has consisted simultaneously in the yearning for the integration of places beyond German state borders and a desire for the creation of political community within those same borders.

This yearning for a common German home, a yearning that continued into the Cold War and that was present in both the East and the West, has not been conditioned by the lack of a national framework, as conventional wisdom might lead us to suppose. After all, as Maier notes, the Czechs also lacked a national framework, and they did not yearn. Rather, the decisive factor in the development of German longing has been the fragmented nature of the German people. In response to their fragmentation, the Germans hankered for a common German home, which has been created by unification. What role, then, does longing play in a democratic political culture like that of the Federal Republic? While Maier does not posit the end of longing, he feels that Germans in the postwar period have substituted for longing more liberal, cosmopolitan orientations.

One of the most decisive changes in the study of national identity and nationalism over the last years has been the turn toward a political-structural perspective. From this perspective, national identity is not a pre-political given, but rather is the result of a process conditioned by such factors as social modernization and changes in intercultural and international relations.[32] For example, in the German case nationalism was at its peak—during the Napoleonic era, the founding years of the Bismarckian Reich, World War I, and the National Socialist regime—when Germany was undergoing fundamental social changes, including the creation of an industrial economy, the centralization of the German state, and the political mobilization of the masses. During such periods, the positing of the German nation as a homogenous entity helped to compensate for the stresses of modernization. The larger the strains of modernity, the more comfort, protection, and security the imagined unity of the nation provided.[33]

The contributors to the section on nationhood in this volume all work from a political-structural perspective in which they begin with the assumption that German nationhood is the result of a political process. They disagree, however, regarding the role played by institutions and cultural legacies in this process. Both Ernst Haas and Peter Krüger underline the importance of institutions for the development of German national identity. In an essay rich in historical detail, Haas examines the role played by nationalism and nationalist ideologies in the rationalization of the German polity across three time periods: 1880–1917, 1918–45, and 1945 to the present. Three groups of variables are decisive in determining the outcome of rationalization: social processes such as urbanization and industrialization; institutional factors; and the actions of elites. It is through institutions that the rival claims of elites can be addressed in a manner accepted by all; viable political and economic institutions are thus an important ingredient in the successful rationalization of a polity. For Haas, the Federal Republic's success in establishing a liberal nation-state is partly due to the "right" institutional framework.

The West German Parliamentary Council, as Peter Krüger notes, was not conceived of as a national constituent assembly. Indeed, the delegates to the council were strictly against seeing the deliberative body as such. They did not want to be seen as having deepened the rift in an already divided Germany. Yet despite their best intentions, as Krüger argues, the delegates writing the *Grundgesetz* produced a complete constitution and founded a Western-type nation-state. The *Grundgesetz* institutionalized the principles of self-determination, human and civil rights, adaptable political institutions, and the sovereignty of the people as the new political basis of the German nation. In the course of the postwar period, these political institutions provided the basis for the development of constitutional patriotism in the Federal Republic.

In perhaps no other area of German politics is the influence of cultural legacies seemingly more apparent than in immigration policy. The definition of German citizenship as a community of descent anchored in the principle of *jus sanguinis* remains the centerpiece of German citizenship and naturalization policy. Recent work by Rogers Brubaker and Hermann Kurthen has demonstrated how the maintenance of the *jus sanguinis* principle continues to shape the politics of citizenship in Germany and is primarily responsible for the Federal Republic's low rate of naturalization. As Kurthen notes, the exclusive definition of membership expressed by the *jus sanguinis* principle coexists alongside more liberal, inclusive definitions of membership in law, rhetoric, and political practice. This has been the source of much political confusion and political polarization surrounding the issues of citizenship, immigration, and asylum in the wake of unification.[34]

In his contribution, Christhard Hoffmann traces the influence of both cultural legacies and institutional factors on the Federal Republic's immigration policy. Like Kurthen, he notes the continued use of an ethnocultural definition of citizenship and the problems this caused for the politics of immigration. However, he departs from Kurthen's and Brubaker's analysis insofar as he sees the maintenance of this notion of nationhood not as a result of the desire to maintain a *völkisch* definition of German identity, but as a function of the postwar split of the two Germanys. Though the principle of descent continues to influence immigration and citizenship policy, Hoffmann also notes important sources of change in the institutional realm. Changes in the legal realm, as well as the provision in the Basic Law regarding universal human rights, provided a counterbalance to the restrictive practices of governmental agencies. Thus, both historical legacies and institutional factors must be considered if we are to adequately understand Germany's politics of citizenship.

Jost Halfmann also tackles the issue of citizenship. Focusing on the asylum and integration debates of the late 1980s and early 1990s, Halfmann points out that while the German public and the German legal administration both agreed that an immigration crisis was brewing, they disagreed not only about potential solutions, but about the content of the crisis. The public debates mainly focused on Germany's Nazi past and whether the obligation to provide asylum to all those seeking it was still practical in light of the huge numbers of refugees and still desirable in light of debatable accusations that many refugees were seeking economic, not political, asylum. The tone of the public debates was moralistic, focusing on the *jus sanguinis* citizenship definition, potential links to the Nazi past, and fears of a new aggressive German nationalism.

Debates within Germany's administration, on the other hand, took a much more technical approach to the immigration crisis. State officials worried that Germany had lost control of its borders through a combination of the liberal asylum law and the influx of *Aussiedler* (Germans living outside of Germany but having a claim to citizenship). Furthermore, because of the difficulty of becoming a naturalized German citizen, the population was becoming increasingly split between residents without citizenship and citizens. The state regarded these issues as technical problems, while the populace viewed them primarily in moral terms. The policy solution—stricter regulations for both asylum seekers and *Aussiedler* combined with somewhat more liberal naturalization rules—was sufficient to end the debate temporarily, but it did not constitute a permanent solution.

What does the future hold? At the end of his essay, Charles Maier forecasts the continued salience of longing in German and European politics. All electorates, he feels, will long for communities that will be increasingly harder to achieve, namely, ethnically homogenous ones. In the modern period, the nation has been the dominant form of political community into which citizens have been organized. The development of the German national community has been tied to aggressive, antidemocratic politics, virulent racism and antisemitism, and the Holocaust, but also, as our authors demonstrate, to the evolution of liberal, democratic institutions and a modern, pluralist political culture in the postwar period.

The arguments presented here suggest that the developments of the last 50 years will continue. We can, however, cite a number of potentially troublesome developments in contemporary German politics that suggest caution in our analysis of the future. German political culture remains marked by the presence of racist and discriminatory practices. Although attacks against minorities in the Federal Republic have decreased, discriminatory practices remain part and parcel of German everyday life. Furthermore, two new studies, the first of the German police and the second of university students in Hessen, have found the presence of significant levels of anti–immigrant and nationalist attitudes. In the policy arena, the restrictive naturalization and citizenship policy suggests the continuing influence of an exclusive, ethnocultural definition of German identity in immigration policy.[35] While these examples do not document the return of Germany's nationalist past, they suggest that our optimism must be tempered by the knowledge that the Federal Republic, like most other nation-states, still has strides to make in fulfilling its liberal, democratic potential.

What Is Germany's Place in the World?

During the Cold War, Germany was integrated tightly into Western institutions under the tutelage of the United States. Despite the fact that its international commitments were largely shaped by the preferences of the winners of World War II, alternatives to tight integration—the revival of four-power diplomacy and reunification within a four-power framework—were clearly available, but they were not chosen. Then, in the decade before reunification and sovereignty, the Federal Republic of Germany grew as an economic power, capable of eastward expansion, yet its foreign and security policies continued to be shaped by Germany's membership in the European Community and NATO. And Germany continued to maintain its tight integration in Western institutions after 1989, when, as the most powerful country in Europe, it achieved full sovereignty.

Germany's foreign policy behavior, both during the Cold War and in the wake of unification, presents a puzzle. Since 1949, it has accepted limits on its sovereignty and military capabilities in a way that is perhaps unique in world history for an important European power. Contrary to many expectations, there has been little evidence of a pernicious German nationalism in foreign policy behavior either of a right-wing or of an anti–integrationist variety. Indeed, in its international behavior since 1949, Germany appears to have made a radical break with the traditional hallmarks and "normal" practices of national sovereignty so common in other European democracies.[36] Why?

The four chapters on foreign policy in this volume address this question. And they disagree on the answer. The central debate among them focuses on whether this historically puzzling military reticence, hesitance about sovereignty, and lack of self-assertion can be found inside Germany or in Germany's external environment. Further, the contributors engage in a debate over the role of the "rational actor": Are German decision makers rational, basing their preferences on a calculation of net gains from a particular policy choice? Or do decisions have a more unconscious and nonrational source in affect and emotion — pride, shame, fear, revenge, comfort, or "longing," all tightly bound with historical memory? Does the source of German foreign policy lie in rational calculations based on structural or institutional constraints and incentives, or does it lie in the deeper recesses of domestic culture?

Wolfgang Krieger argues that external forces have historically shaped Germany's policy preferences and continue to do so. He argues that decisions to tightly integrate with the West and limit Germany's military capability are rational responses to international constraints. In the early postwar period, the Western powers tightened the shackles on German power when they saw the results of the 1949 election, in which the major parties received small percentages of the vote and a variety of nationalist-oriented parties seemed to enjoy high levels of support. The Western allies did not want to see a group of well-intentioned but weak democratic politicians fail. Thus, Krieger argues, Adenauer opted for tight integration that allowed greater sovereignty for the Federal Republic at the expense of unification. He also chose integration over unification because it allowed "the German question" to be removed from the mercy of four-power diplomacy.

After 1990, Krieger argues, similar international constraints prevail. Decision makers fear an "international ganging up" against the new Germany. They fear that growing German power will make others feel insecure and thereby fuel nationalism around Europe. Rising nationalism will translate into trade protectionism, and German exports will be endangered. In Krieger's view, decision makers accept limits on German power in order to prevent rising nationalism among Germany's neighbors and protect trade; those limits provide for German security and reduce external threat. Thus, in game-theoretic terms, Germany is enhancing cooperation and attenuating the security dilemma by reducing its own appearance of threat and therefore inducing others to cooperate. Domestic support for continued multilateralism is easy because no anti-integration party has emerged in Germany to sway public opinion away from its integrationist stance.

Krieger's argument goes against the conventional "realist" predictions of the directions of German foreign policy in the current period. Realists argue that international constraints have changed after 1989 in ways that would indeed lead to a "ganging up" on Germany: because the Soviet Union dissolved and the United States retreated from Europe, power positions are fluid, and uncertainty about the source of threat is potentially high. With multiple "poles," states feel unprotected from one another and perceive fewer gains from cooperation, both because power is more evenly distributed and because they are unsure about their neighbor's power capabilities. They are therefore likely to rush to protect themselves, and they defect from cooperative efforts that do not protect their interests.

Membership in international institutions, however, structures incentives against "ganging up." This is because, first of all, institutions provide the necessary transparency and information to relieve heightened fears that arise in a multipolar world. By mitigating the uncertainty of multipolarity, these institutions — such as NATO and the European Union — reduce the fear that others will act unilaterally or gang up on one of their members. All members are then more reluctant to rush to unilateral action or "ganging up" themselves.[37] Second, international institutions create the expectation that all participants will interact indefinitely, and a defection will be punished by another member's noncooperation in the future.[38] Institutions help cement expectations that a common future exists. Finally, members of international institutions calculate reputational gains from cooperation; a defection counts as a reputational "loss," and the prospect of loss increases the willingness to cooperate. Taken together, these arguments suggest that strong international institutions both shape substantive preferences of their members and enhance a preference for cooperation.

If international institutions are indeed as powerful as this description implies, then Germany's traditional commitment to them would explain why Germany chooses to reduce threats to its partners and why it wishes to further institutionalize economic, political, and military relations among European states to prevent ganging up. Indeed, Krieger shows that institutional limitations created in the 1954 Paris treaties linked German unification to European integration. Linking European integration to German unification then channeled German national feelings toward European integration, and over the next several decades, politicians from both major parties chanted the mantra that unification could only occur as a result of the integration process. Although the order of events was shifted somewhat, the mantra paid off, and the tight linkage explains the outcome.

Tom Banchoff disagrees. In his essay for this volume, he argues that the international environment, though important, was and continues to be much more ambiguous than Krieger's description would allow, leaving more room for alternative choices. Similarly, international institutional norms and rules left room for alternative interpretations and alternative policy choices. He argues against the claim that a rational calculation of net gains from a particular policy choice shaped German preferences. The roads not taken — the choice to integrate within the four-power framework rather than within exclusively Western institutions in the early period, or the choice to pursue a more vigorous Ostpolitik in the current period than is currently being pursued—were certainly as rational as the choices actually made. For Banchoff, neither an international structural nor an institutional argument explains actual policy choices.

He thus looks to domestic political culture, specifically to what he calls the "historical memory" of decision-making elites, to find the source of German policy preferences. He argues that Adenauer's negative memories of German *Schaukelpolitik* between the wars pushed him to forge tight institutional links with the West. Kohl's historical memory focused on the unstable balance of power politics of the past, and, Banchoff argues, Kohl's memory of the legacy of nationalism and balance of power politics made it imperative that western institutions, NATO, and the EC remain the focal point of German foreign policy. Markovits and Reich make a similar point: the powerful historical memory of Nazism among all of Germany's neighbors, as well as within Germany itself, made it unacceptable to express German nationalist sentiments, and thus the only acceptable strategy was for Germany to develop into a good European. It is these memories, then, that explain actual choices between two rational alternatives.

Markovits and Reich are in Banchoff's camp, but their approach is much more sweeping and conceptual in scope, and their level of analysis is not focused on the historical memories of key decision makers but on what they call "collective memory." Collective memory operates at the level of culture, and at the level of political competition and mobilization. Thus, to the extent that collective memory is a determinant of policy choice, the source is internal, and the choice is not necessarily "rational" in the sense of a preference calculated upon the basis of net gains.

Under what conditions do collective memories lead to one policy preference and under what conditions do they lead to another? If we see a particular policy outcome on the one hand and a store of multiple historical memories on the other, it is tempting to pick the memory that fits the outcome. Indeed, almost any foreign policy decision can be traced to one memory or another. For example, Markovits and Reich point out that both French and German collective memories of their relationship have been negative since the French Revolution. And at times those memories have pushed both into war. But why did those memories lead to a strong French-German alliance in the postwar period? What was the role of historical memory in shaping that new relationship, and why didn't it simply lead to new animosities, friction, and discord?

This dilemma suggests that there is a need to specify the conditions under which some memories and not others shape policy preferences and the conditions under which collective memory leads to one outcome and not its opposite. Institutions can provide those conditions. Peter Katzenstein has argued that institutions create a set of *norms* that become self-perpetuating in the domestic political culture. That culture defines a dominant worldview that then constrains available choices. Particularly in times of uncertainty, actors rely on the worldview they have acquired over time.[39] But it is social institutions that cement some worldviews and not others and explain why some norms arise and not others.

Thomas Berger's essay here links institutions and culture in a causal relationship. He argues that memories may not directly give rise to policy choice, but powerful memories and the intersubjective web of meanings attached to them are embedded in powerful institutions. Collective historical memories and their social interpretations are at the heart of institutions. They are anchored in institutions and reproduced there. The most powerful institutions embody the most powerful memories and thus keep some historical memories alive and squelch others.

In uniting both institutional and cultural explanations in a "constructivist" rather than a rational choice approach, Berger offers an explanation for the "puzzle" of Germany's nonassertive security policy and hesitancy about the exercise of its sovereignty. He shows that initial electoral victories in the early postwar period allowed one party platform embodying one set of historical memories and one set of social understandings of Germany's security needs to be institutionalized, thus weakening alternative memories, interpretations, and intersubjective understandings. The key social understanding that guided German security policy was "reassurance and deterrence." In practice, this meant a strong defense anchored in the Western alliance in conjunction with efforts to minimize and subdue East-West hostilities. Although this policy of "reassurance and deterrence" has gone through many phases and incarnations, it has guided German policy up to the present day, explaining Germany's policy in the aftermath of the Gulf War and the Bosnian war and vis-à-vis the Partnership for Peace.

In sum, Berger's synthesis suggests that most of the dominant explanations for German foreign policy today—external constraints or domestic imperatives, rational calculations or the less calculated historical memories embedded in political culture—separately provide incomplete and unsatisfying explanations for Germany's foreign policy puzzle. Constraints—whether imposed by the international system or by multilateral institutions—are not deterministic; and memories come and go, are multiple and contradictory. We might therefore unite cultural and institutional explanations with the following proposition: international constraints will determine — in the broadest sense — which memories are allowed to be institutionalized both in international institutions and in domestic political culture. Thus, for example, pro-Nazi memories are not allowed to be institutionalized and are repressed by laws, norms, and dominant practices.

Institutions themselves are sticky, that is, they create norms and principles and new foreign policy traditions and culture. Taken together, then, these four essays suggest that institutions modify constraints and cement some memories, thus weakening those that have little institutional legitimacy. Institutions define the logic of the foreign policy game and keep memories alive.

Conclusion

The synthesis proposed by Berger of institutions and culture could characterize the overall analysis of the other issues under investigation here. By abandoning one set of "core beliefs" after the trauma of World War II, by adopting the dominant institutions of liberal capitalist democracy and the "core beliefs" that lie at their heart, by adapting those institutions to those aspects of Germany's particular cultural context that did not overtly clash with liberalism, and by choosing most of the features of a liberal national identity, Germany appears to have abandoned its *Sonderweg*.

The essays collected here agree that a democratic political culture has become institutionalized in the postwar period; that culture is likely to persist as long as democratic institutions remain strong, but ironically, the culture has "outgrown" the institutions created in the early part of the Federal Republic's history. It may now be time for the institutions to change, to become more accountable to a public that has now adopted their democratic values. Similarly, economic institutions designed to facilitate growth have depended on and created an entrepreneurial culture and a tamed but politically powerful labor force. Those institutions, however, may have become constraining to entrepreneurship in an age of economic globalization, and voices from that culture are demanding change. Future research needs to specify the conditions under which German economic institutions will adapt and the conditions under which they are able to withstand the challenges of globalization better than those of other industrial capitalist countries. And finally, although Germany has adopted most of the values of a liberal national identity, its institution of citizenship has retained the values of ethnonationalism that facilitate discriminatory practices in everyday life. If the arguments in this volume are correct in their thrust, a change in that institution could result in an important change in values and in the concept of nationhood in Germany.

NOTES

1. We are not the first to undertake this task. See, for example, Kendall Baker, Russell J. Dalton, and Kai Hildebrandt, *Germany Transformed: Political Culture and the New Politics* (Cambridge, Mass.: Harvard University Press, 1981). This was the first major work to document Germany's changing political culture in the postwar period.

2. Douglass C. North, *Structure and Change in Economic History* (New York: Norton, 1981), 15.

3. See Mark Granovetter and Richard Swedberg, *The Sociology of Economic Life* (Boulder: Westview Press, 1992); Walter W. Powell and Paul J. DiMaggio, eds., *The New Institutionalism in Organizational Analysis* (Chicago: University of Chicago Press, 1991); James G. March and Johan P. Olsen, "The New Institutionalism: Organizational Factors in Political Life," *American Political Science Review* 78 (1984): 734–49; and Sven Steinmo, Kathleen Thelen, and Frank Longstreth, eds., *Structuring Politics: Historical Institutionalism in Comparative Analysis* (Cambridge: Cambridge University Press, 1992).

4. See, for example, Kathleen Thelen and Richard Locke, "The Shifting Boundaries of Labor Politics: New Directions for Comparative Research and Theory," draft, 25 August 1993; and Gunnar Grendstad and Per Selle, "Cultural Theory and New Institutionalism," *Journal of Theoretical Politics* 7, no. 1 (January 1995): 5–28.

5. See, for example, Karl Dietrich Bracher et al., *Deutscher Sonderweg— Mythos oder Realität?* (Munich: Oldenbourg Press, 1982); Jürgen Eiben, *Von Luther zu Kant: Der deutsche Sonderweg in die Moderne: Eine soziologische Betrachtung* (Wiesbaden: Deutscher Universitäts Verlag, 1989); Hans Ulrich Wehler, *Aus der Geschichte lernen? Essays* (Munich: C. H. Beck Verlag, 1988); and Hans Ulrich Wehler, *Entsorgung der deutschen Vergangenheit? Ein polemischer Essay zum "Historikerstreit"* (Munich: C. H. Beck Verlag, 1988).

6. Jürgen Habermas argues a variation on this theme: he suggests that the postwar Federal Republic finally embraced the liberal principles of the French Revolution, after that project had failed miserably in Germany in 1848. And it was the horror of the fascist period that finally made that embrace possible. See Jürgen Habermas, *The Past as Future,* ed. Max Pensky (Lincoln: University of Nebraska Press, 1994).

7. Theories focusing on the bargaining process assume that authoritarian elites must be convinced to give up their power. In postwar Germany, this was clearly not the situation. For process-based theories, see Guillermo O'Donnell, Philippe Schmitter, and Laurence Whitehead, eds., *Transitions from Authoritarian Rule,* 4 vols. (Baltimore: Johns Hopkins University Press, 1986); and Alfred

Stepan, *Rethinking Military Politics: Brazil and the Southern Cone* (Princeton: Princeton University Press, 1988).

8. See, for example, Robert D. Putnam, with Robert Leonardi and Raffaella Y. Nanetti, *Making Democracy Work: Civic Traditions in Modern Italy* (Princeton: Princeton University Press, 1993), and Reinhard Bendix, *Nation-Building and Citizenship: Studies of Our Changing Social Order,* 2d ed. (Berkeley: University of California Press, 1969, first published 1964).

9. Gabriel Almond and Sidney Verba, *The Civic Culture* (Princeton: Princeton University Press, 1965).

10. David P. Conradt, "Changing German Political Culture," in *The Civic Culture Revisited,* ed. Gabriel Almond and Sidney Verba (London: Sage, 1989).

11. Michel Albert, *Capitalism vs. Capitalism* (New York: Four Walls Eight Windows, 1993).

12. Ibid., 124.

13. Ibid., 171.

14. Many West German institutions predate the founding of the Bonn Republic and did not fit well with the free-market liberal doctrine pushed by Ludwig Erhard, the finance minister and later chancellor. For example, although the overarching industrial association, the Bundesverband der Deutschen Industrie, was established in 1949, it was based on the industrial federations set up during the Nazi era. While the cartels and price-fixing that took place under Hitler were eschewed, many of the leaders of these organizations continued in their positions and continued to collaborate with each other. Government consultations with the *Verbände,* which began under the Weimar Republic, were embedded in the postwar constitution. See Andrew Shonfield, *Modern Capitalism* (Oxford: Oxford University Press, 1969).

15. Alexander Gerschenkron, *Economic Backwardness in Historic Perspective* (Cambridge, Mass.: Harvard University Press, 1962).

16. Peter A. Hall, *Governing the Economy: The Politics of State Intervention in Britain and France* (Oxford: Oxford University Press, 1986).

17. David Soskice, "The Institutional Infrastructure for International Competitiveness," in *The Economics of the New Europe,* ed. A. B. Atkinson and R. Brunetta (London: Macmillan, 1992).

18. Peter Hall, "Central Bank Independence and Coordinated Wage Bargaining: Their Interaction in Germany and Europe," *German Politics and Society,* no. 4 (spring 1994): 1–23.

19. Kathleen Thelen, "The Politics of Flexibility in the German Metalworking Industries," in *Bargaining for Change,* ed. Miriam Golden and Jonas Pontusson (Ithaca: Cornell University Press, 1992), 215–46.

20. Wolfgang Streeck, "On the Institutional Conditions of Diversified Quality Production," in *Beyond Keynesianism: The Socio-Economics of Production and Full Employment,* ed. Egon Matzner and Wolfgang Streeck (Worcester: Edward Elgar, 1991), 21–61.

21. Lauk and other scholars in the neoclassical economics tradition strongly disagree with the institutional analysis. Lauk believes that Germany's over-regulated economy, and particularly its powerful unions, will suffocate economic

growth. The extensive welfare state and the short working hours create a drag on productivity, which makes German products less competitive internationally. This argument turns the institutional analysis on its head by claiming that Germany's institutions have become its problem. See Kurt Lauk, "Germany at the Crossroads: On the Efficiency of the German Economy," *Daedalus* 123 (winter 1994): 57–83.

22. Martha Derthick and Paul Quirk, *The Politics of Deregulation* (Washington, D.C.: Brookings Institution, 1985); Jeffrey Frieden and Ronald Rogowski, *The Impact of the International Economy on National Policies: An Analytical Overview*, paper prepared for the Project on Internationalization and Domestic Politics, September 1994.

23. See the contributions in Kirsten S. Wever and Lowell Turner, eds., *The Comparative Economy of Industrial Relations* (Madison: Industrial Relations Research Association, 1995).

24. In addition to Offe's contribution to this volume, see Suzanne Berger and Ronald Dore, eds., *National Diversity and Global Capitalism* (Ithaca: Cornell University Press, 1996); and Kathleen Thelen, "Beyond Corporatism: Toward a New Framework for the Study of Labor in Advanced Capitalism," *Comparative Politics* 27, no. 1 (October 1994): 107–24.

25. See Thelen, "Beyond Corporatism."

26. Peter Alter, "Nationalism and Liberalism in Modern German History," in *Nationality, Patriotism, and Nationalism in Liberal Democratic Societies*, ed. R. Michener (St. Paul, Minn.: Paragon House, 1993), 88.

27. John Borneman, "State, Territory, and Identity Formation in the Postwar Berlins, 1945–1989," *Cultural Anthropology* 7, no. 1 (February 1992): 45.

28. Alter, "Nationalism and Liberalism," 100–101.

29. William Rogers Brubaker, "Immigration, Citizenship, and the Nation-State in France and Germany: A Comparative Analysis," *International Sociology* 5, no. 4 (December 1990): 386.

30. Ibid.

31. Lutz Hoffmann, "Das 'deutsche Volk' als Integrationsideologie und seine historische Entwicklung," in *Die Wiedergeburt des nationalistischen Denkens: Gefahr für die Demokratie*, Friedrich Ebert Stiftung, Gesprächskreis Arbeit und Soziales Nr. 52 (Bonn: Friedrich Ebert Stiftung, 1995); Brubaker, "Immigration, Citizenship, and the Nation-State," 391.

32. Heinrich Haferkamp, "Nationen und Nationalismus—Zur Konstitution eines folgenreichen Prinzips politischer Legitimität," *Politische Vierteljahreszeitschrift*, no. 2 (1993): 27; Ernst B. Haas, "What Is Nationalism and Why Should We Study It?" *International Organization* 40, no. 3 (1986): 714.

33. Hoffmann, "Das 'deutsche Volk' "; and Cecelia Applegate, *A Nation of Provincials: The German Idea of Heimat* (Berkeley: University of California Press, 1990).

34. Hermann Kurthen, "Germany at the Crossroads: National Identity and the Challenges of Immigration," *International Migration Review* 29, no. 4 (winter 1995): 934.

35. Ibid., 928.

36. An excellent review of the German academic and policy discourse on foreign policy can be found in Gunther Hellmann, "Goodbye Bismarck? The Foreign Policy of Contemporary Germany," *Mershon International Studies Review* 40 (1996): 1–39.

37. Charles A. Kupchan and Clifford A. Kupchan, "Concerts, Collective Security, and the Future of Europe," *International Security* 16 (summer 1991): 130–33.

38. See Robert Axelrod, *The Evolution of Cooperation* (New York: Basic Books, 1984); Kenneth A. Oye, ed., *Cooperation under Anarchy* (Princeton: Princeton University Press, 1986); and Helen Milner, "International Theories of Cooperation among Nations: Strengths and Weaknesses," *World Politics* 44 (April 1992): 474–75.

39. Peter Katzenstein, "Coping with Terrorism: Norms and Internal Security in Germany and Japan," paper prepared for delivery at APSA, Washington, D.C., August 29–September 1, 1991, 3–4.

Building Democracy: The
Institutions and Political Culture of
German Democracy

The German Response to the Challenge of Extremist Parties, 1949–1994

Peter H. Merkl

From the first day, and especially in the occupation years, a specter was haunting the reestablishment of democratic government in the Western zones of Germany, the specter of the fall of the Weimar Republic. And even though the causes of this catastrophe included other factors too, such as unfavorable international and economic developments, or civil-military and church-state relations,[1] the quest for democratic stability naturally focused on the extremist challenges from the left and the right. In 1932–33, the Nazi (NSDAP) and Communist (KPD) parties had a combined majority of the vote even before the deeply divided officials and defenders of the republic began to abandon ship in the gathering storm from the right. After the fall of the Third Reich, the democratic politicians of West Germany—many of them former Weimar politicians—were consequently preoccupied with the ways in which such a lethal antidemocratic assault on a new democratic system could be avoided.

This essay particularly deals with the deliberate measures, for example in the constitution and electoral law, by which democratic West German leaders sought to forestall a recurrence of the Weimar predicament. But it will also concern itself with such general aims as the emphasis on creating a robust political system and strong economy on the premise that Weimar extremist movements had flourished upon economic and political weakness and crisis. The essay will stress the early plans and arrangements since most of them began in the fifties and continued, with varying emphasis, through later years of crisis. In the process, the reader needs to keep in mind that the definitions of who was or was not "extremist" tended to be controversial[2] and to change in the public perception in accordance with the politics of the day. In the heyday of Soviet ultimatums, for example with regard to West Berlin, and during the terrorist scare of the seventies, the odor of red herrings could be politically damaging. During the recurrent waves of right-wing extremism, most recently during the era of neo-Nazi and skinhead violence against foreigners, many a conservative, or conservative position, became suspect as allegedly linked to electoral challenges from the extreme right.

Inoculations against the Right-Wing Virus

At the most general level of postwar awareness of the mistakes of Weimar, there was a new political activism — in the midst of the *Ohne-Mich* (count me out) generation — that led many bourgeois notables to feel guilty about their political noninvolvement that had facilitated the rise of Hitler. To quote the late Carlo Schmid of the Social Democratic Party of Germany (SPD): "Whose fault was it that power could fall into the hands of monsters? Whose responsibility is it that [our] people were so deceived and overwhelmed? . . . Mine, and that of people like me who thought we were too good [for politics]."[3] This new activism also led many young Christian Democrats, such as Helmut Kohl, into politics to forestall extremist developments by the default of respectable if unpolitical elements of society. Some of them also felt, like the late Franz Josef Strauss, that their new party, the Christian Democratic Union/Christian Social Union (CDU/CSU), should never leave any free space for another party on its right. In other words, Christian Democratic leaders should always make a determined effort to appeal also to the old Nazis and potential neo-Nazi recruits before this clientele might fall into the hands of demagogues of the extreme right. As we shall see below, this advice has characterized the politics of CDU/CSU leaders from Adenauer to Kohl. And its pendant has been the efforts of the Social Democratic leadership over the years not to leave any breathing space to its left for a revival of a viable communist party.[4]

It goes without saying that the democratic parties and their leadership also emphasized the positive messages of democratic values as against those of German nationalism and national socialism, as indeed had been done by the Western occupation through their programs of licensing German parties, media, and politicians, and of "reeducation." The licensing process, of course, included the rejection of neo-Nazi parties and of German would-be politicians and journalists with a Nazi background, which dovetailed with the denazification programs of the occupying powers. Surprisingly, denazification and reeducation were fairly popular outside of the circles that found themselves punished or disqualified from political or journalistic activities.[5] The punishment of war criminals—in 1949 almost four-fifths of adults in the American zone approved of the Nuremberg trials—and of Nazis before denazification tribunals (two-thirds approved) found broad agreement in principle even though particulars of its application raised pointed criticisms. The positive popular reaction to democratic reeducation under the occupation and to the democratic parties after 1949 is particularly surprising when we consider the large minorities of German postwar opinion expressed on a host of issues related to the Third Reich, the war, and German nationalism throughout the late forties and the fifties in polls of the occupation and, later, West German polling institutes.[6] Knowledgeable readers get the impression that West German adults in that period in large numbers tended to continue to hold the nationalist and Nazi views of the war years while exhibiting a gratifying willingness to accept democracy for the present and future.[7]

In view of these unsettled and uncertain views of those days, it was extremely important that the democratic leadership firmly took control and imposed its own opinions and choice of institutions rather than wait for a diffident popular opinion to find its way to stable, democratic government. Let us turn now to the particular measures by which the democrats—SPD, CDU/CSU, FDP (Liberal Democratic Party),[8] and some leaders of smaller groups—attempted to secure the future, autonomous West German government against extremist challenges that, they were sure, would arise sooner or later.

Suspicion of Popular Passions

Their first opportunity to create their own framework of government on a large scale—the writing of *Länder* constitutions had been under far more limiting circumstances—was the drafting of the West German Basic Law by the Parliamentary Council in 1948–49. The council had been convoked by the minister presidents of the Western *Länder* at the instigation of the Allies, who subsequently interfered very little in the details of the writing of the constitutional documents, especially not in details affecting the ability of the government to defend itself against extremist challengers.[9] It was not a popularly elected body, nor did the German public pay much attention to its work, evidently unaware that this constitution would last for the foreseeable future and farther. The Basic Law was also never ratified by the people, but only by the *Länder* diets, which had elected the members of the Parliamentary Council according to a prearranged formula: its 65 voting members balanced Christian and Social Democrats (27 each), adding five FDP and two each from the (Lower Saxonian) German Party (DP), the Catholic Center (Z), and the KPD.

This council fought hard over some issues of marginal bearing on extremist challenges.[10] But there was little discussion over the bill of basic democratic rights (Article 1–19) — except for the issue of "parents' rights" to choose the religious denomination of local schools — and on making democracy (without further specification) an "unalterable part" of the Basic Law (Article 20). Most significantly for our topic, there was broad agreement for instituting structural supports for a bipolar party system. The major parties were agreed that Weimar multi-partyism and executive instability above all had doomed the Weimar Republic before the onslaught of the extreme right and left, and they resolved to forestall these tendencies in any way they could. The underlying assumptions appear to have been that (*a*) the German electorate was not a reliable foundation for democratic stability; (*b*) a strong partisan government therefore had to be created that in times of political crisis — usually envisioned like the Weimar debacle of 1932–1933 — could take decisive action to cope with the crisis at hand; (*c*) this strong executive had to be at least temporarily shielded from the threat of a parliamentary no-confidence vote; and (*d*) it had to have at its disposal tough emergency powers to use against parliamentary paralysis and against extremist challengers.

To quote council member Georg August Zinn (SPD, Hesse): "we cannot rely on the masses."[11] Zinn and others would have preferred to vest these powers in an American-style presidential regime, although Weimar had fared poorly with presidents such as Paul Hindenburg, who, in response to multiple pressures, appointed Adolf Hitler chancellor in 1933. Instead, the framers of the Parliamentary Council settled on a strong chancellor and a British-style system of *party government* à la Walter Bagehot, which gives the parliamentary majority and its partisan head, the prime minister and cabinet, a powerful mandate until the next election.[12] But there was no mistaking the same distrust of the masses and their "sudden passions" that had inspired the Philadelphia Convention of 1787. Zinn and his fellow members of the Parliamentary Council looked upon Weimar as a period of multiparty near-anarchy during which weak institutions and scattered authority had fallen too much under the sway of the moods of the multitude.[13]

Barriers to Fragmentation

Unfortunately, it is almost impossible to remold a party system at will, say from a multiparty base into a two-party, or at least two-bloc, system. Imitation and transfer of political traditions and arrangements from one country to another often produce equivalents that are as dissimilar as, say, British and French parliamentary government in the Third and Fourth Republics of France. French adaptations of British parliamentary democracy have always produced a very different system. And it must be a very slow process to reeducate a whole people toward responsible self-government. But in the meantime the council could attempt to devise constitutional structures and procedures that might create the preconditions for a German version of British party government. To this end, they built into the Basic Law four features that have continued to this day, although it is debatable whether they alone have accomplished the purposes they were intended to. They are the basis of the democratic guardianship by the major parties and the Federal Constitutional Court.

1. Constructive no-confidence (Article 67), a device from the Württemberg-Baden constitution that makes a no-confidence vote of the legislative assembly against the chancellor (or minister president) contingent on a majority vote for a successor. The underlying assumption was that the future equivalent of the Nazis and Communists of 1932–33 would have to agree on a new chancellor before they could overthrow the government in office.[14] The chancellor's office was also given an exalted position above that of the other cabinet members by prior investiture and the express power to set guidelines (*Richtlinienkompetenz*) for the cabinet. Both features are not typical of British practice.
2. Careful avoidance of popular initiative and referendum, except for territorial changes (Article 29), a conscious effort to avoid the divisive plebiscites of Weimar politics, for example on the national flag, on the Young Plan of reparations, and on the expropriation of aristocratic estates. Again, there was the unmistakable intention to keep the public from interfering with the political enterprise of the elected politicians.[15]
3. The regulation of the nature and internal organization of political parties together with procedures for suppressing (extremist) parties hostile to the "democratic basic [constitutional] order" (Article 21). The Federal Constitutional Court was entrusted with the responsibility of deciding which parties were anticonstitutional and outlawing them. The details of this article were spelled out further in a law on parties and in the organic law establishing the court in 1951. In spite of serious questions regarding the political wisdom and civil liberties aspects of suppressing a political party,[16] the procedure was invoked by the Adenauer government in 1951 against the neo-Nazi Socialist

Reich Party (SRP) and in 1956 against the Communists (KPD) and led to their suppression.

4. The council was quite aware of the importance of the electoral law for discouraging splinter parties and encouraging the dominance of the largest parties but refrained from casting its electoral preferences into the constitution. The subsequent debate over the electoral law, a modified version of proportional representation, continued until 1956, producing a minimal hurdle of 5 percent for representation and the two-ballot system (1953) — with the first ballot a voter selects a "direct" candidate for the Bundestag, who wins representation with a plurality in the district; the second ballot determines the partisan representation in the Bundestag, drawn from *Länder* lists for each party. The first, or "personality," ballot was expected to make for a trend toward a two-party system,[17] while the minimal threshold would discourage split-offs from the major parties and new parties. The actual emerging party system, however, was a three-party system, with the FDP alone surviving the deadly impact of the 5 percent clause until 1983, when the Greens became the first party to break the triopoly of Bonn parties. In the meantime, the Party of Democratic Socialism (PDS), too, has found its way into parliament (1990).

The Aftermath of the First Elections (1949)

The first election to the parliament of the new FRG produced a major shock to the democratic leadership in that it seemed to re-create much of the appearance of Weimar multi-partyism: next to the three major parties (CDU/CSU, 31.0 percent; SPD, 29.2; and FDP, 11.9), there were representatives of five further parties (German Party, 4.0 percent; Center Party, 3.1; Bavarian Party, 4.2; German Right Party, 1.8; and Economic Reconstruction Union [WAV], 2.9), plus the KPD (5.7 percent) and independents (6.2 percent). Two "Trojan horse" Nazis (F. Dorls and F. Richter-Roessler) also were elected. Economic conditions in 1949–50 were still far from settled and were light-years away, it seemed at the time, from the "economic miracle" to come. In fact, there were two million unemployed, not to mention millions of survivors of war casualties, the injured of the war, and about 10 million German refugees from the East.

To make matters even more ominous, the German refugees began to form a large new party with the grandiloquent name Bund der Heimatlosen und Entrechteten (BHE). The large pool of refugee voters and the traditionally irredentist and pro-Nazi attitudes of ethnic Germans in the East in World War II made the BHE, in the minds of German and Allied observers, a major extremist menace to West German democracy. The BHE soon began to enter local councils and state diets. At the national level, however, the BHE was soon tamed by Adenauer's administration with a clever mixture of concessions and gestures to refugee interests coupled with the resolute takeover of the party itself by the CDU/CSU. Refugee voters also turned out to be far more interested in material aid and credit—as indeed they had been at lower levels under the occupation—than in nationalist ideology. A sweeping program to tax the natives for the benefit of the refugees (*Lastenausgleich*) facilitated their social and economic integration into West German society. The last remaining BHE political leaders were brought into the next Adenauer government (1957) as Christian Democrats and soon disappeared from the political limelight at the Bonn level, if not from the *Länder* governments. Only a small core of right-wing refugee politicians and organizations remained to flirt with neo-Nazism in the sixties and later. This was the first demonstration of the Adenauer/Strauss prescription not to leave any political vacuum to the right of the CDU/CSU.

More revealing still of the approach of the democratic leadership of the day was the treatment of ex-Nazis and neo-Nazis. On the one hand, the Adenauer era effectively defused the danger of a huge mass of alienated ex-Nazis—there had been some 10 million NSDAP members at the end of the war—in the midst of the fledgling phase of democracy. If the occupation campaign of denazification had been far too inclusive of little ex-Nazis screened and pilloried,[18] its slowing pace and growing leniency led to its near-abandonment after 1949. Left to their own preferences, German authorities changed from the natural (and customary international) law basis of Nuremberg for prosecution to one of positive law violations. They no longer asked if accused persons had served a criminal regime, but whether they had violated German laws against homicide, false arrest, and inflicting bodily harm that were in effect at the time of the offense. Regarding tens of thousands of denazified and dismissed ex-Nazi civil servants and professional military personnel, moreover, a 1951 law in pursuance of Article 131 of the Basic Law reinstated them or granted them pensions while at the same time pledging them to loyalty toward the state.

Militant Democracy (*Streitbare Demokratie*)

At the same time, the barriers and disqualifications of the licensing system of the occupation were allowed to lapse, triggering a flood of attempts to launch extreme-right political careers and several new parties, including the Socialist Reich Party (SRP) and the German Right Party (DRP). The SRP, it will be remembered, became the first test case of suppressing an "anticonstitutional party" for the newly established Federal Constitutional Court, as soon as the party had received 11 percent of the popular vote in the 1951 Lower Saxonian Landtag elections and 7.7 percent in the Bremen elections of the same year. What made the SRP seem more dangerous than the national-conservative rightist groups that had dominated extreme rightism until then was its populism and deliberate pitch to the working-class elements that had found the NSDAP of yesterday so attractive.

Furthermore, as Eckhard Jesse has demonstrated persuasively, the spirit of "militant democracy" of the democratic leadership expressed itself in efforts to place the barriers of defense of the democratic state ahead of the points at which neo-Nazi political parties might grow from social movements of the extreme right. In particular, the Bundestag in 1959 amended the German criminal code to threaten swift punishment for treason, high treason, and conspiracies against the state in ways that Weimar had never attempted. Instead of waiting for outbreaks of political violence, the legislation already criminalized the advocacy of violence and the publication of materials hostile to the constitutional order. In 1953 alone, over 1,600 people were found guilty of thus "endangering the state" (*Staatsgefährdung*), a charge applied particularly to persons associated with the extreme left.[19] Actually, both the KPD, which could boast voting percentages in excess of 10 percent and participation in the cabinets of several *Länder* in 1946–47, and the radical right *were* doing rather poorly in the fifties; the KPD was associated in the voter's mind with the grim communist dictatorship in the GDR and, especially by the Social Democrats, with the forced merger of the SPD and KPD in 1946.[20]

The KPD had already been hobbled considerably by the consolidation of the trade unions into one confederation, the DGB (Deutsche Gewerkschaftsbund), under determined Social Democratic domination against communist bridgeheads. The final blow of being outlawed came in 1956 for the KPD, after years of acute shrinkage of the membership (from 324,000 in 1947 to 78,000 in 1956) and the suppression of the Free German Youth (FDJ), as well as the erosion of the KPD press. The extreme right likewise suffered from association with the Nazi debacle. Both extremes therefore tended toward infiltration and front organizations whenever they found it difficult to be accepted on their own merits.[21] This made it much harder to prosecute and fight them than the laws for suppression of extremist activities suggest.

Success and Party Government

However useful both the constitutional provisions and the beginning practices of militant democracy initiated in the fifties may appear, there can be little doubt that the preeminent role in securing German democracy against extremist challenges was played by the economic and political consolidation of the new regime in all its aspects. First of all, there were the conspicuous successes of the economic recovery, which, by the mid-fifties, turned into the "economic miracle" and, throughout the following decade, raised German prosperity to two and three times the prewar levels. To the extent that the breakdown of Weimar democracy had also been the result of successive economic crises — the dislocations and great inflation of the first four years and from 1929 on the Great Depression — Bonn democracy got off to a far more promising start. But there were also the great triumphs of diplomacy of the Adenauer administration, which overcame West Germany's isolation and pariah status and, in the first 10 years, gave the country security from the expansive Soviet threat. The war and the disclosure of German war crimes against humanity had left Germans in an outcast role in the world. The integration of the FRG in the Western alliance and family of nations and its active involvement in the movement toward European integration became major assets of pride and satisfaction with the performance of democratic government.

Less obvious, if possibly of greater long-term significance, was the political consolidation of *party government* on the basis of a working bipolar political system. The framers of the Basic Law had hoped for such political concentration with two dominant parties, but it required the cooperation of the voters, who, at the first Bundestag election, had shown little inclination to abandon their Weimar multiparty ways. Already in 1953, however, owing to the new electoral law and the conspicuous successes of the Adenauer administration abroad and in very recent economic growth, the CDU/CSU surged from a level of 31 percent of the popular vote to a spectacular 45.2 percent (and 50.2 percent four years later), a majority in the Bundestag and a veritable revolution in the historical development of the German party system.

At this point, moreover, Christian Democratic monopolizing of the sources of private campaign finance for the smaller parties right of center began to take most rival parties into an iron embrace that resulted in the co-optation of their leaders and the absorption of their voters into the great CDU/CSU machine.[22] Only the FDP managed to survive this process, which assured Christian Democratic hegemony for 20 years and still casts a shadow today. The concentration on the right, moreover, had a profound impact on the SPD, which likewise embarked on the determined pursuit of additional voters — about 3 percent more every federal election — until it actually caught up with the CDU/CSU in 1972. This rise of the SPD vote from a share of 29.2 percent in 1949 to 45.8 percent in 1972 involved a wrenching 1959 reform in program and attitudes in which this second major party jettisoned most of its old ideological and sectarian heritage. After the congress at Bad Godesberg (1959), the SPD turned from a Marxist "class party" into a "people's party" eager to appeal to all walks of life.[23]

From 1961 until 1983, consequently, a bipolar party system established itself in which either of the largest parties alternately had the support of the small FDP as a coalition partner. The FDP, moreover, felt compelled to pledge before each election which of the major parties it would join after the elections, thereby giving the voters a clear choice between the two alternatives. There was a brief lapse in 1966–69 when a grand coalition interrupted what soon became an alternating system: in 1969, the SPD (with the FDP) took over from the long-reigning CDU/CSU and stayed in power for 13 years, followed again by the Christian Democrats under Chancellor Helmut Kohl. As bipolar systems have done in other democracies such as Britain and the United States, this West German development completed German democracy by placing the major decisions in the hands of the voters rather than leaving them to the wheeling and dealing among several parties, as in multiparty systems such as postwar Italy, Weimar, or the Fourth Republic of France. The centrism and relative de-ideologization characteristic of a bipolar system also manifested themselves in the amazing commonalities in the elections programs of the SPD and the CDU/CSU in the early sixties — for example, in security and European policies — which further narrowed the voter's choice to one between Tweedledee and Tweedledum, quite similar to U.S. Democrats and Republicans in those days.

The Resurgence of Extremist Challenges

The consolidation of democratic party government soon faced major challengers, beginning in the mid-sixties. A downturn in the economy, a weaker chancellor (Erhard), and a resurgence of extreme right and left set the stage for what many saw as the first uncertain moments of the FRG. The second wave of extreme-right agitation, prejudicial incidents, and voting[24] began with the foundation of the National Democratic Party (NPD) by DRP politicians — in particular Adolf von Thadden, a conservative nationalist—in 1964. During the *Länder* elections of 1966–68, the NPD succeeded in surmounting the 5 percent hurdle and entering Landtage in seven of the eleven *Länder* of the old FRG. It barely missed the 5 percent mark (with 4.3 percent of the popular vote) in the Bundestag elections of 1969 and has since declined to insignificant levels.[25] According to the reports of the Constitutional Protection Service (*Verfassungsschutz*), right-wing legal offenses such as racist or antisemitic insults and violent acts also fluctuated toward much higher levels (200–500 incidents annually) in the NPD years. But curiously, the militants became even more violent as the NPD declined, and in the late seventies and the eighties, the number of right-wing incidents reached considerable heights, while right-wing voting was negligible.[26]

What did the democratic leadership do to cope with this acute extremist challenge from the right? The Constitutional Protection Service had begun to publish its annual reports on extremism in the winter of 1959–60, when a series of antisemitic incidents had alarmed the public with slogans and swastikas painted on the outside of several synagogues. In a dramatic manifestation of militant democracy, an instantaneous alliance of major-party spokespersons, the media, the churches, and the trade unions thereupon pounced upon the DRP, even though it had publicly disavowed these terrorist actions.[27] The rise of the NPD in the mid-sixties, similarly, triggered a grand alliance against the new party and led to serious discussions about suppressing it. However, unlike in the early fifties, the democratic leadership of the FRG now was much surer of itself and far less inclined to "shoot with cannons at mere sparrows."

There were also renewed discussions about introducing an American-style electoral law to choke off the development of smaller parties, but they produced no result. The NPD's efforts to clear itself by fighting the "slanderous" label of "neo-Nazis" in court, moreover, turned into a rout when the court held that there were enough old Nazis on the NPD's board to justify such an accusation. The party's protestations of loyalty to the "basic democratic order" were taken to be mere lip service. And indeed, there appeared to be a core of Nazi revivalist populism replete with solidaristic (*Volksgemeinschaft*), anticapitalist-egalitarian appeals barely veiled under the traditional, conservative nationalism of NPD chief von Thadden.[28] While there was a substantial element of protest voters from the major parties—CDU/CSU, SPD, and FDP—behind it, the overwhelming impression was of a radical-right movement that had developed while the Christian Democratic ability to integrate all political forces to the right of center had waned with Adenauer's resignation (1963) and retirement from politics.

Challenge from the Left

Some of the challenges to the political stability of the FRG also came from the left, where the transformation of the SPD after Bad Godesberg had left a great deal of left-wing alienation over such a "betrayal" of the original character and mission of the party. The grand coalition of SPD and CDU/CSU of 1966, which was brought on by the refusal of the FDP to continue in coalition with the Christian Democrats,[29] further aggravated the dismay of left-wing Social Democrats with this renewed "betrayal" by their own party leadership. Several circumstances combined to make this an explosive mixture. One was the foreign policy angle of the SPD change in course, which committed the party to the Western alliance and thereby against the Soviet orbit and away from its remaining ties to the SED (Sozialistische Einheitspartei Deutschlands) and GDR at a time of increasing détente and East-West dialogue.[30]

Factionalism within the SPD also took on extreme forms, not only with the opposition of the old left socialists to the party leaders, but especially with the progressive alienation of young and particularly New Left radicals. Over the years, the SPD had repeatedly expelled or censured its university student affiliates, in particular the Socialist German Student Federation (SDS) in 1961, but also its successor, the Socialist University Federation (SHB). At the height of the upheaval in 1969, the entire "youth section" of the SPD, the Young Socialists (Jusos), carried on in radical subgroups ranging from the extreme-left Stamokap faction,[31] over the "nonrevisionists" — signifying their opposition to the transformation of the SPD since Bad Godesberg — the "ethical socialists," and a structural reformist group. They fought *each other* and the party leadership with torrents of invective and mutual excommunication. The SPD under Chancellors Willy Brandt and Helmut Schmidt responded with a mixture of conciliation, inviting the young radicals to "work within the system," jawboning (especially Schmidt), and expulsion, as with the SDS.

The SDS was also deeply involved with the rebellious student movement, to which it gave a pronounced "red" coloration, and with the Extraparliamentary Opposition (APO), a broad coalition of trade union, student, and party radicals who for a decade had battled against a draft of the Emergency Laws (*Notstandsgesetze*) that had been under discussion in the Bundestag.[32] While the APO could hardly be considered a left-wing equivalent of the NPD, the SDS certainly was.[33] The reemergence of a West German communist party (DKP) in 1968, with open links to the Communist Party (CP) of the USSR and the SED in East Berlin, further clarified the alignments even though the new party never rose beyond the most modest electoral support. Again the Bonn government chose not to apply the instruments of suppression against the DKP[34] — doing so would also have disturbed the new spirit of détente with the Soviet bloc and the GDR — although the rebellious students did not escape the wrath of local law enforcement, for example in West Berlin. On the other hand, a rush of new, militant groups of the extreme left emerged in the seventies that made the SDS and DKP look like choirboys, even though their actual threat to the stability of Bonn democracy was rather small.

First among these were a number of very small Marxist-Leninist student groups (K-groups), as well as a new KPD/ML party (1968) and, eventually, a renewed KPD (1980) and a West German Communist Federation (KBW). More significant for our topic, left-wing terrorist groups such as the RAF (Baader-Meinhof group), Revolutionary Cells, and June Second Movement arose in the seventies who, despite a rather low count of casualties among their victims — as compared to the Italian Red Brigades, the Basque ETA, or the Provisional IRA — brought about a climate of public hysteria in the FRG that in itself raised fears of overreaction at the expense of democratic procedure. The principals of the Baader-Meinhof group were captured by 1972 and tried in 1977, but offshoots of the movement continue to surface with terrorist actions to this day. In the meantime, however, the FRG strengthened its security apparatus in terms of funding and personnel to levels that would have been commensurate with a much larger threat.[35] The understandable desire to get at the few terrorists led to the restriction of democratic rights and immunities for everybody.[36] The insecurities of the SPD-FDP governments of the early seventies somehow produced in them a fear of "radicals" in the public service, which generated witch hunts and prohibitions against job applicants with a background of youthful participation in left-wing student protest. The Anti-radicals Decree of 1972 sought to stop the student radicals' "long march through the institutions" by barring such "radical" mail carriers, truck drivers, and elementary school teachers from becoming civil servants. "No freedom for the enemies of freedom" was a typical slogan behind this so-called *Berufsverbot*. In some SPD *Länder* that had attempted drastic educational reforms, for example in Hesse, the CDU opposition also contended that left-wing radical schoolteachers and educational administrators had to be kept from brainwashing schoolchildren with their new methods.[37]

Assessing the Turbulent Seventies

While the problems of the late sixties and the seventies were considerable, especially in economic, social, and educational policy, there was never any Weimar-type crisis of stability of the government. The system established in the fifties and later improved clearly held the challengers at bay. The grand coalition in its time had tackled problems requiring large parliamentary majorities, such as the Emergency Laws, which by themselves established further instruments for dealing with extremist challenges. After 1969, the Brandt administration (SPD-FDP) firmly took control, enlarged its majority in 1972, and governed through the two energy crises of the seventies without a lapse. Even the change of socialist chancellors in 1974, from Brandt to Helmut Schmidt, was not accompanied or caused by a lapse of control.[38] Party government German-style was obviously working well, and the challenges from the extreme right and left were no threat to executive stability. Militant democracy, too, had risen to the challenge of terrorism without fail, although in the end it tended to go overboard.

As the files of the Constitutional Protection Service mushroomed, its net of informers and contact persons grew to an estimated 20–30,000, and its methods included covert surveillance and photography, violations of the privacy of mail and telephone, and the cooperation of administrative agencies and the criminal police (BKA). Small wonder that civil libertarians and political critics compared this inflated apparatus of internal security to the Gestapo and the East German Stasi, and that many people began to worry about its potential threat to the very rights and freedoms it was supposed to protect. The spread of data banks with collated information about individuals from the census and from police files conjured up further fears of an Orwellian "dossier society" and in the early eighties even caused the national 10-year census to be aborted.[39] The threats from terrorism and from extremist groups simply did not warrant such an overblown apparatus, although there were some political reasons for this excess: On the SPD-FDP government's side, there was a great deal of defensiveness motivated by the détente policies of Ostpolitik, that is, the rapprochement with the governments of the GDR and Soviet bloc nations. On the side of the CDU/CSU opposition, there was a concerted smear campaign to link the social-liberal government with extreme-left groups or, at least, to show that it was "soft on terrorism," or on communism.[40] The improbable consequence of all this was the buildup of internal security as an alibi, and acrimonious debates about whether these measures were, or should have been, directed more against the extreme left or the extreme right.[41]

The Quiet Eighties

The decade of the 1980s witnessed a general dying down of the passions of earlier decades, which is not to say that the extremist movements of various colors died down too. On the right, in fact, there was now a newspaper of broad appeal to veterans and neo-Nazis alike, the *Deutsche Nationalzeitung* of right-wing Munich publisher Gerhard Frey, whose German People's Union (DVU) achieved modest success in the early 1990s. At the same time, an intellectual *nouvelle droite* resurfaced, and there were a number of new action groups that were eventually outlawed, as I indicated earlier.[42] In the mid-eighties, moreover, a new populist right was founded, the Republikaner (REP) — named after the American Republicans under Reagan — who by the end of the decade spearheaded the third wave of the German radical right. Headed intermittently by an old SS officer and television talk show host, Franz Schoenhuber, the REP succeeded in attracting, in particular, the anti-foreigner protest vote, which had accumulated resentments toward the Turkish and other guest workers, the growing stream of German ethnic "resettlers" (*Aussiedler*), and the first massive waves of asylum seekers from Third World countries. In 1989, the REP surprised everyone by winning more than 7 percent of the popular vote in Berlin and in the European elections of midsummer 1989, months before the fall of the Berlin Wall.

In the meantime, the radical left in West Germany was stagnating, with a DKP vote so low in national elections that it did not even add up to the number of members of DKP-related organizations, well under 1 percent of the popular vote. Its traditional social base was eroding, except for an element of foreign workers, and its membership declined steeply by the end of the decade. The new reform impulses from Gorbachev's CP (USSR) only aggravated internal tensions between SED-oriented communist traditionalists and the glasnost reformers. The collapse of the SED regime in the end brought about the organizational and financial collapse of the DKP in the West.[43]

The successor groups of the RAF continued to engage attention in the eighties, although their terrorist actions took a different direction, away from the "terrorist coups to free the jailed terrorists" and toward attacks on NATO installations and personnel. They planted a series of bombs and car bombs at U.S. bases in 1981 and 1982 — the Revolutionary Cells claimed credit especially for anti-U.S. actions — tried to assassinate the U.S. army commander Frederick Kroesen, and attempted to involve themselves in the big pacifist campaign of 1981–83 against the refurbishment of NATO missiles. There were some efforts also to coordinate anti-NATO actions with the Red Brigades of Italy and terrorist

50 The Postwar Transformation of Germany

groups in other European countries during 1983–85. In 1986, a banner year of Middle Eastern terrorism — and retribution by air strikes on Libya — the RAF returned to domestic targets, a Siemens executive, a diplomat, and the annual hunger strikes among incarcerated comrades. They closed the decade with an attempt to invade a Berlin World Bank–International Monetary Fund meeting in 1988 and the assassination of the president of the Deutsche Bank (right after the fall of the Wall) and of the Treuhand president, Detlev Rohwedder (1991), who had been in charge of privatizing East German state enterprises.[44]

If we ask whether these right-wing and left-wing extremist actions of the eighties destabilized West German democratic government, the answer is obviously no. Party government German-style sailed through the minor extremist challenges and the major upheaval of the anti–NATO missile pacifist campaign. It even weathered the change of government of 1982, after Chancellor Schmidt lost a "constructive vote of no-confidence" to Kohl, a change caused by the walkout of the FDP. It is interesting to relate, in the context of party government, that the victorious new CDU/CSU–FDP coalition believed it necessary, or at least desirable, to obtain popular confirmation of its parliamentary victory by means of an election in early 1983.[45] By the end of the eighties, both of the extremes were in the rather ironical position cast upon them by the great surprise of November 9, 1989, the fall of the Wall. The Republikaner were at least temporarily overwhelmed by the reality of what they had agitated for, German unification, while the RAF terrorists were shown up to have been materially aided and sheltered for decades by the GDR government and Stasi.

The Test of Unification

The most severe test of Germany's democratic stability since the 1950s has probably been the unification of West and East Germany since 1990. It changed the national constituency, adding another 16 million people — with backgrounds of drastically different orientation — and piling enormous economic burdens on the shoulders of both West and East Germans. Nevertheless, as far as we can tell half a decade later, the new FRG seems to have survived the momentous transition with *something rather similar to the old Bonn design*. There appears to be a broad consensus on democratic institutions in East and West. Initial enthusiasm for democracy, in fact, was very high in the former GDR, even though it has been declining in recent years. Party government continues with the prevalence of the two major parties, even though the FDP now seems to be kept alive only with ticket-splitting by CDU/ CSU voters.[46] The Greens may be close to taking up a similar role of the kingmaker, but they still appear somewhat to lack the posture of political maturity and pragmatism that used to distinguish the FDP in its best moments.[47]

The biggest problem in the arena of party politics is the Party of Democratic Socialism (PDS), the successor party of the GDR's SED, which drew 36.6 percent in East Berlin in the last city election (1995) and one-fifth of the East German vote in the last Bundestag elections (1994). The PDS has also picked up the old DKP vote in the West, but that element is so small that the PDS, with 4.4 percent nationwide, would have failed to clear the hurdle for representation in the Bundestag had it not received four direct mandates in 1994, all in East Berlin.[48] In the context of a united Germany, the PDS still represents an East Germany that resists unification. The party has so far avoided speech and behavior, such as agitation or violent demonstrations, that we normally associate with extreme parties. But until recently there has been no serious effort by any of the other parties to draw the PDS into a coalition. The gulf between them and the PDS seems to be too large for coalition-building,[49] although in the last years several SPD leaders have hinted that they might consider such an alliance in spite of the longstanding SPD taboos. If the PDS should collapse tomorrow, its votes might make the SPD a stronger rival to the CDU/CSU. Christian Democratic election propaganda frequently accuses the SPD of following the "red socks," that is, of collaboration with the PDS. There are voices in the CDU/CSU, moreover, especially in the CSU, that would like to apply the practically defunct old Anti-radicals Decree of 1972 to ex-SED applicants for public service from the GDR.

Behind the strong support in the former GDR for the party whose predecessor was the communist state party, the SED — a trend similar to the return of neocommunists to political prominence in Poland, Russia, and Hungary — stand the very real, unresolved problems of German unification, but also subjective beliefs that East Germany has become an "internal colony" of West German business and government.[50] The high unemployment and economic inequality of the five new *Länder* will eventually yield to the relentless, massive transfers of public investment that have maintained East German growth rates in excess of 10–12 percent for the past several years. It is much harder to argue with questions of identity and subjective distortions such as are evident with the responses to *Politbarometer* questions contrasting a respondent's assessment of the "general economic situation in East Germany" with that respondent's "own economic situation." For the fifteen months until the beginning of 1996, for example, East German respondents gave the following responses, with minor fluctuations:[51]

Oct. 1994–Dec. 1995:

Assessment	General economic situation, East	Own economic situation
bad	27–39%	8–14%
partly bad / partly good	49–63%	35–50%
good	5–14%	38–56%

The difference in assessments is striking and hardly logical. The alienation between East and West, or the "wall in the minds," is likely to be perpetuated by the special pleadings of East German spokespersons such as the PDS. There is still a great deal of nostalgia for the "good old days of the GDR": 34 percent of East Germans—60 percent of PDS adherents—admit to such nostalgic feelings even today.[52]

Once More, the Radical Right

The radical right Republikaner and other right-wing parties of the third wave (1989–92) experienced a renewed surge once the initial euphoria of unification had worn off and major economic problems surfaced in East and West. Although they fell far short of the 5 percent clause (with 2.1 percent) in the first Bundestag elections of unified Germany[53] and did poorly in the *Land* elections of that eventful year (1990), they nearly made it into the Hamburg Assembly in 1991—the REP received 4.8 percent and the DVU 2.8 percent, which could have added up to 7.6 percent for a combined extremist right. The following year, while antiforeign opinion crested all over Western European countries, the REP achieved 10.9 percent and 15 seats in the Baden-Württemberg elections, and the DVU received 6.2 percent in Bremen and 6.3 percent in Schleswig-Holstein. In the local elections of Hesse in 1993, again, the REP gained a toehold of 8.3 percent. In anticipation of further right-wing gains, observers then ignored the notably unremarkable REP performance in all the other Landtag races and overlooked their steep decline, for example in Bavaria, where they had scored 14.6 percent of the popular vote (admittedly with a very low turnout) in the European elections of 1989.[54] Many knowledgeable people expected a large right-wing wave to wash into the Bundestag in 1994 and, quite probably, block the formation of a majority government coalition of either the CDU/

CSU–FDP or the SPD and the Greens, leaving only a grand coalition as an alternative.

In the meantime, however, the leadership of the major parties had found a way out of years of bitter haggling over immigration policy and, in particular, over the stream of foreign asylum seekers, who numbered close to half a million in 1992 alone. Against determined resistance from their own internal fringe groups, they worked out a compromise toward the end of 1992 and promptly enacted a constitutional change of the asylum paragraph (Article 16) the following May.[55] Perhaps even more important, the economy seemed to have passed the worst of a recession that had generated three to four million unemployed in 1992–93. Suddenly, the popularity of the Kohl administration began to pick up again, and respondents in public opinion polls credited it once more with "economic competence." The pollsters were still predicting 4–5 percent of the vote for the REP early in 1994. But the actual vote received by the REP that year was only 1.9 percent. The Mannheim election researchers have estimated that there is no more than a core vote of 2 percent of real right-wing extremists in Germany. The rest seem to be temporary protest voters who rise up, abandoning their usual parties, when certain issues are rife: economic uncertainty, unemployment, seeming political weakness. After some free-floating talk about the formation of a possible grand coalition — if the voters did not behave — the CDU/CSU and FDP were back in the saddle, trying to claim all right-wing voters for themselves. Adenauer's and Strauss's old policy toward the far right had won, and party government was still intact.

If there had been no pressing need to suppress the REP as an electoral threat, another aspect of right-wing activity was widely perceived as crying out for suppression: from 1991, the great waves of asylum seekers who were housed in makeshift quarters all over small German towns — to the consternation of unhappy townspeople — had triggered waves of antiforeign mayhem by skinheads and neo-Nazis all over Germany, beginning in the East. The ever-increasing ferocity of such attacks on foreign individuals aggravated partisan polarization over the asylum issue to a fever pitch, shedding far more heat than light and leading to considerable hyperbole among the media, in German papers — they often heated fear and loathing of foreigners to a white-hot point — and foreign ones as well. Pundits in prominent newspapers, such as the *New York Times* and *Los Angeles Times* in this country, falsely compared the anarchic forces at work — most of the skinheads were not politically oriented or affiliated with any political party — with the marching storm troopers of another day. Academics ponderously pronounced German democratic stability in danger, usually without explaining exactly how and why.[56] Were the neighborhood gangs of skinheads going to seize power in the country? Could they demonstrate, as the police had not been able to, that the nocturnal skinhead and other assailants were commanded by an extreme-right conspiracy or party? The thousands of violent incidents, as I have analyzed elsewhere, of course differed considerably from each other. Some were regular neighborhood pogroms, such as the ones in Hoyerswerda and Rostock-Lichtenhagen, others "merely" night riders carrying out the presumable ire of local neighbors who had complained for weeks about the asylum hostels and found authorities deaf and unresponsive.[57] It was an ugly story in any case, and some of the incidents are still going on, evidently beyond effective control of the German police.

Was this a threat to the German state, or to democratic stability? Probably not, or no more than the levels of juvenile crime in American cities — including hundreds of lethal drive-by shootings, a certain percentage with racial overtones, for example black versus Chicano — have endangered American democracy. And once again, a response of militant democracy materialized in Germany: the responsible media and democratic organizations such as the trade unions and parties promptly formed a united front denouncing the anti-foreign mayhem and conjuring up the ghosts of the Nazi past, for better or for worse. Indeed, the orgy of anti-foreign violence of 1991–93 at times even exceeded the high levels of extreme-left violence of the seventies, according to the official statistics and to the reports of the Constitutional Protection Service. Subsequently, police efforts and organization were reinforced — especially in East Germany, where the police had hardly been capable of significant countermeasures — and court sentences made more severe. Most significantly, hundreds of thousands of antiracist demonstrators formed chains of light and had rock concerts against the violence in many major cities. Demonstrative actions and gestures by prominent individuals and companies further advertised the fact that most Germans wanted to take sides with the victims and with foreigners in general against the prejudices of other Germans.

Concluding Remarks

As we look back toward 1949, or in some instances even earlier, we see an unmistakable pattern that has carried the new democracy through occasional lapses and through major crises. The postwar German leadership clearly saw and feared a return to Weimar conditions. They made special efforts to block or obviate the extremist challenges from right and left that had contributed to the demise of Weimar. They designed a constitution and electoral laws that were likely to frustrate extremist challengers from right and left. They tried to meet their challenges, depending on the situation before them, both with positive measures — building up a democratic consciousness, a centrist, bipolar party government, and economic and political strength — and with the instruments of governmental repression and militant democracy, such as the procedures for surveillance and suppression of extremist groups.[58]

It may be well, at this point, to ask whether some of these prescriptions against the challenge of extremism worked better than others. The institutional contrivances, such as the electoral law, the emphasis on executive stability, and the powers of courts and executive to stop extremist organizations, obviously had to be installed first, before the first serious challenges occurred. But what good would they have done if the economic and political circumstances had not provided a propitious setting for the electorate to support democracy? Militant democracy in the narrower sense of the word, deliberate policies to win over the little Nazis and communists of yesterday while closing ranks against the extremist challenges of today, seems to have developed fully only at a more advanced stage, say with the sixties and seventies, although its antecedents — such as leniency for old Nazis and absorption for the German ethnic refugees — go back to the first days of the republic. By the seventies and eighties, the sheer accumulation of successful defenses against political extremism could be taken for granted. By today, on the other hand, there may be new problems, such as partisan polarization, that are quite capable of creating new extremist challenges if the political adversaries cannot seem to find common grounds for action — witness the asylum issue.

At times the militant democrats may have gone overboard, too, as in the days of antiterrorist hysteria, with measures against former student radicals, or in exaggerated perceptions regarding the radical left or right. Whether they did or not, in these as in other instances, of course is a question enmeshed in partisan controversy so heated that it may be hard to tell. In the end, the most recent wave of electoral right-wing radicalism may also have succumbed to the best kind of militant democracy at the popular level, as an estimated two or three million Germans demonstrated against anti-foreign violence and racism. It is far from clear what the Republikaner had to do with that violence, though few would doubt that they were anxious to recruit some of the skinheads themselves and that they expressed anti-foreign prejudices. Evidently, everyone assumed that there was a direct nexus, and the ensuing backlash seems to have cut down the right-wing phalanx at the polls in 1994 in punishment for what apparently they strove to avoid.[59] No doubt, in time there will be another right-wing wave, and then we can pontificate once more about such challenges.

To return to the first sentence of this essay, will the specter of the fall of the Weimar Republic always have to haunt the Germans, or will it become obsolete in time with growing democratic maturity? With circumstances and environment so very different today, is it really needed? There are many powerful founding myths that have helped other nations find democratic stability. The Germans too have experienced other founding myths, including that of the foundation by Bismarck more than a hundred years ago and, more recently, the horrible ghosts of the Third Reich. In this context, the legend of the Weimar experience as a warning to contemporaries has made a positive contribution and will continue to do so in the foreseeable future.

NOTES

1. For a complete catalogue, see, for example, Karl Dietrich Bracher, *The German Dictatorship* (New York: Praeger, 1970), chaps. 1–4; or idem, *Die Aufloesung der Weimar Republik* (Villingen: Ring-Verlag, 1955).

2. Disagreements on whether certain conservative issues or public figures were "really Nazi-like" or whether certain left-wing crusades or personages were "really communist"—especially during the Cold War—have continued to this day.

3. Carlo Schmid, *Erinnerungen* (Bern, Munich, Vienna: Scherz, 1979), 149–54, 217. See also the Schmid quote in my *The Origin of the West German Republic* (New York: Oxford University Press, 1963), 25–26. Schmid speaks eloquently about the gullibility of many decent "average citizens" in the face of Nazi propaganda in Weimar days.

4. The recent resurgence of the East German communist state party, the PDS (Party of Democratic Socialism), poses a major new challenge to the SPD, which might grow to rival the CDU/CSU in size if only the PDS were to wither away.

5. The popularity of and broad support for democratic reeducation have in recent years been obscured by German left-wing, anti-American critics, who mostly belonged to the 68er generation and younger cohorts, and who rarely know much about the occupation period.

6. See especially the polls of American occupation reported by Anna Merritt and Richard Merritt, *Public Opinion in Occupied Germany* (Champaign-Urbana: University of Illinois Press, 1970); and in Elisabeth Noelle-Neumann, *The Germans* (Westport, Conn.: Greenwood Press, 1980).

7. Merritt and Merritt, *Public Opinion*, 39–43.

8. It should be recalled that these parties sometimes held rather different views from those later adopted and that the rising partisan rivalries of 1948–

49—after years of all-party coalitions at the *Länder* level—tended to exaggerate their profiles: in the heat of the battle, the FDP, for example, was considered rather right-wing, part of the CDU/CSU old "reactionaries" or even "clerical fascists," and the SPD's "democratic reliability" was frequently questioned by its adversaries.

9. On this subject, too, subsequent commentators have sometimes distorted the record, claiming that the constitution was "imposed" by the Western Allies, or that the latter compelled the Germans to adopt certain features against their will. There was minor interference in the German design of intergovernmental fiscal relations, and the Allies reserved to themselves a number of powers relating to foreign and defense policy and the status of West Berlin, as well as residual emergency powers, including the right to intervene if the Federal Republic was threatened from within. See Merkl, *Origin,* 114–28, 172–75.

10. Chief among these was the federal system, which divided the council between centralizers (SPD) and states'-rights advocates (CDU/CSU). The latter claimed that Weimar democracy had been overwhelmed from the center and weakened by excessive centralization. The former pointed to the extremist challenges to Weimar that had been hiding under the assertion of autonomy of certain *Länder.* Ibid., 66–79.

11. Heinz Medefind, "Für starken Bundespräsidenten," *Neue Zeitung,* 11 January 1948, 2. This "distrust of the people of the small parties" of course also found its critics among the younger generation in the council and outside.

12. Under a system of disciplined large parties, cabinet solidarity, cabinet government, and the prime minister's right to pick the time of the election (within the parliamentary term), this *party government* provides a strong basis for dealing with the crisis at hand. At the next election, however, the government has to accept the verdict of the voters on what it has wrought. See, for example, Peter Pulzer, "Responsible Party Government in the German Political System," in *Party Government and Political Culture in Western Germany,* ed. Herbert Doering and Gordon Smith (New York: St. Martin's, 1982), 9–37; and Rudolf Wildenmann, "The Party Government of the FRG: Form and Experience," in *Party Governments: European and American Experiences,* ed. Richard S. Katz, The Future of Party Government Series, vol. 2 (New York and Berlin: de Gruyter, 1987), 78–117.

13. See also the formulation of Theodor Heuss (FDP), a council member and the first president of the FRG, in U.S. Office of Military Government, Civil Administration Division, *Documents on the Creation of the German Federal Constitution,* 1949, 85. He blamed the illusion of the "fairness of the Germans" and "nationalistic fantasies" for the breakdown of the Weimar constitution.

14. This procedure has never been tested as intended, and indeed it produced rather unexpected results—for example, when Chancellor Willy Brandt in 1972 wanted to dissolve the Bundestag to ask for a new electoral mandate. He had to persuade his own party to abstain so that the opposition CDU/CSU could vote him down and a new election could be called.

15. The rejection of direct democracy and of presidentialism have in common the distrust of the popular will, or "general will." Merkl, *Origin,* 39–40, 80–

84. This feature has long been under critical scrutiny and may well become a casualty of the postunification efforts at constitutional reform. Some of the new East German *Länder* constitutions already include initiative and referendum.

16. Although there has been recurrent clamor for outlawing various neo-Nazi groups, the German government has been most reluctant to use this power for extremist parties involved in bona fide electoral campaigning. This does not prevent their surveillance through the Constitutional Protection Service and, in several recent cases of "neo-Nazi action groups," their dissolution and suppression, a fate visited for example on the Wehrsportgruppe Hoffmann (1980), the People's Socialist Movement (Busse) and Action Front of National Socialists (Kuehnen) in the 1980s, and several groups in the 1990s.

17. To represent regionally concentrated minorities, such as the Danes in Schleswig-Holstein, the electoral law also gives full representation to a party that gains three such "direct" mandates. More recently, this rule permitted the PDS, for example, to enjoy full representation even though its percentage in the 1994 Bundestag elections was only 4.4. It gained four direct mandates in East Berlin, where many former members of the SED (Sozialistische Einheitspartei Deutschlands) apparat are concentrated.

18. In the U.S. zone of occupation alone, some 13 million ex-members went through the process, which, because of its sheer size and unwieldiness, soon acquired the reputation that "the little ones got punished while the big ones got away." The inevitable passage of time, while the anger over Nazi crimes waned and the anticommunist Cold War emerged, created enormous disparities between the standards of denazification justice in the early as compared to later years.

19. See E. Jesse, *Streitbare Demokratie in der Bundesrepublik Deutschland* (Habilitation thesis, University of Trier, 1989); and idem,"Extremismus und streitbare Demokratie in der Bundesrepublik Deutschland von der Gründung bis zur Vereinigung," in *Jahrbuch Extremismus und Demokratie,* vol. 2, ed. Uwe Backes and E. Jesse (Bonn: Bouvier, 1990), 5–36.

20. See Schmid, *Erinnerungen,* 284; and *Wehner: Beitraege zu einer Biographie* (Cologne: Kiepenheuer & Witsch, 1976), especially Peter Bender, "Herbert Wehner und die Deutschlandpolitik," ibid., 39–50.

21. The KPD was particularly active trying to infiltrate pacifist groups such as Deutsche Friedensunion (DFU). Old Nazis, on the other hand, frequently attempted to hide their cause in local voters' associations of a "nonpartisan" sort.

22. The concentration of right-of-center campaign finance occurred through the so-called sponsor societies (*Förderergesellschaften*), which strong-armed donors into giving funds only through them and not directly to the various parties on the right. The strength of the CDU/CSU led to anguished protest about Adenauer's *Demokratur,* a German neologism combining the words *Demokratie* and *Diktatur.*

23. For details, see Gerald Braunthal, *The West German Social Democrats, 1969–1982* (Boulder: Westview Press, 1983), 9–11.

24. For materials and analysis of the second wave, see especially Ekkart Zimmermann and Thomas Saalfeld, "The Three Waves of West German Right-

wing Extremism," in *Encounters with the Contemporary Radical Right,* ed. Peter H. Merkl and Leonard Weinberg (Boulder: Westview Press, 1993), 50–74.

25. Its membership, too, dropped from a high mark of 28,000 in 1967 to under 6,000 by the early eighties. Like earlier right-wing parties, the NPD had gathered some remaining elements also from the old refugee party (GB/BHE), the DP, and the DRP organization. Its best vote was 9.8 percent in Baden-Württemberg, and its greatest achievement the expansion of the right-wing appeal to the southern *Länder.*

26. See the cumulative chart in Zimmermann and Saalfeld, "Three Waves," 63. Violent incidents reached an annual level around 100 between 1979 and 1989 (the beginning of the third wave), while nonviolent offenses rose to between 1,500 and 2,000.

27. On that occasion, administrative measures against the radical right suppressed the DRP organization of Rhineland-Palatinate as a spin-off of the outlawed SRP. Later in 1967, the Justice Minister called the "political criminal law" of the fifties exaggerated and proposed to scale back its repressive aspects. See Federal Press and Information Office, *Leistung und Erfolg 1967* (Bonn), 34. In the same publication, the Interior Ministry argued in favor of a purely majoritarian electoral law on the grounds that it would produce majority governments capable of governing, a message certain to be noticed by the FDP and by all smaller parties.

28. See especially Jesse, "Extremismus und streitbare Demokratie," 17–19; but also Peter Dudek and Hans-Gerd Jaschke, *Entstehung und Entwicklung des Rechtsextremismus in der Bundesrepublik* (Opladen: Westdeutscher Verlag, 1984), 1:349–55. See also John D. Nagel, *The National Democratic Party: Right Radicalism in the FRG* (Berkeley: University of California Press, 1970), 69–122; Nagel also discusses alternative ways of coping with the NPD.

29. The falling-out began in 1966 with the rebellion of the "Young Turks" of the FDP against the CDU in North Rhine–Westphalia, which brought about the fall of the CDU-FDP state government and new elections in this large state. The CDU suffered a notable defeat, which was taken as a bellwether of the fortunes of the national CDU/CSU.

30. There was a notable increase, according to public opinion polls, in West German willingness to recognize the Oder-Neisse border and even the GDR as a separate state.

31. According to the party statute, all SPD members under 36 years of age are Jusos, some 250,000 at the time under discussion, but only about 40,000 of them were actively involved. *Stamokap* is an abbreviation of "state monopoly capitalism," which was the interpretation of FRG capitalism in the eyes of Stamokap and of many communists. See, for example, Peter H. Merkl, "Factionalism and the Limits of the West German Party State," in *Faction Politics: Political Parties and Factionalism in Comparative Perspective,* ed. F. Belloni and D. Beller (Santa Barbara: Clio Press, 1978), 245–64, especially 250–54.

32. These Emergency Laws were meant to carry out the constitutional mandate (Articles 7, 11, 91, and 110–13) anticipating a state of emergency

brought on by revolutionary attempts from the extreme right or left. Early drafts had alarmed the democratic forces on the left, including the trade unions, and it took a large parliamentary majority of the grand coalition, in 1968, finally to bring a decade of debate to a conclusion. See especially Michael Schneider, *Demokratie in Gefahr? Der Konflikt um die Notstandsgesetze* (Bonn: Neue Gesellschaft, 1986).

33. See Jesse, "Extremismus und streitbare Demokratie," 19–21. The SDS and the core of the student rebellion tended toward anarchism and antiauthoritarian revolution in its public statements and, after the death of a student protester at the hands of the Berlin police in June 1967, toward violent confrontations with the police.

34. At its highest point the DKP boasted 40,000 members. Financial support for it came from the GDR.

35. See also Peter H. Merkl, "West German Left-Wing Terrorism," in *Terrorism in Context,* ed. M. Crenshaw (University Park: Pennsylvania State University Press, 1995), 160–210, especially 173ff.

36. See, for example, Tatjana Botzat, Elisabeth Kiderlen, and Frank Wolff, *Ein deutscher Herbst: Zustaende, Dokumente, Berichte, Kommentare* (Frankfurt, Verlag Neue Kritik 1978). See also Gerard Braunthal, "Public Order and Civil Liberties," in *Developments in West German Politics,* ed. Gordon Smith et al. (London: Macmillan, 1989), 308–22, especially 310–13, 318; Braunthal points out that right-wing radicals were rarely kept from public service.

37. Much of the educational controversy dealt with methods introducing social conflict didactically into the classroom and asserting children's rights to disagree with their parents.

38. See also the essays on German party government in the seventies in Doering and Smith, *Party Government and Political Culture,* 59–76, 130–53. The reasons for the change to Helmut Schmidt were a spy scandal involving the chancellor's secretary, G. Guillaume, and a general weariness of office on the part of Chancellor Brandt, who apparently preferred the role of party leader and chair of the Socialist International to the rough-and-tumble of the chancellorship.

39. For details, see Braunthal, "Public Order and Civil Liberties," 313–16. Polls had also shown that one out of three citizens threatened to refuse cooperation with the far too nosy census takers. The Federal Constitutional Court eventually ruled that the census questions were excessively intrusive. The use of data banks is now under the supervision of *Land* Commissioners for Data Protection and controlled by regulatory legislation, an upshot of the controversies of the early eighties.

40. There was also considerable public animus toward antinuclear and environmental protest by groups ranging from local initiative groups to traveling groups of left-wing anarchists or "chaotics," some of them quite violent.

41. See the complaints in Backes and Jesse, *Jahrbuch Extremismus* that left-wing extremists found many defenders among the media and in the literature whereas the extreme right was left to fend for itself.

42. On the DVU, see Heinrich Sippel, "NPD und DVU," in Backes and

Jesse, *Jahrbuch Extremismus,* 174–84. Frey acquired the *Deutsche Soldatenzeitung,* a bimonthly predecessor, in 1959 and renamed it *DNZ* in 1968. The administrative measures to suppress the Wehrsportgruppe Hoffmann and others were not motivated by any concern that these groups endangered the democratic order. They were merely gestures of a right-of-center government eager to show it was "not soft on neo-Nazis." See Jesse, "Extremismus und streitbare Demokratie," 29–30; and Armin Pfahl-Traugher, "Das Verbot der Nationalen Sammlung," in Backes and Jesse, *Jahrbuch Extremismus,* 218–27.

43. See Patrick Moreau, "Der westdeutsche Kommunismus in der Krise — Ideologische Auseinandersetzungen und Etappen des organisatorischen Verfalls," in Backes and Jesse, *Jahrbuch Extremismus,* 170–206.

44. See *International Terrorism in the 1980's: A Chronology of Events,* 3 vols. (Ames: Iowa State University Press, 1989–92); and Merkl, "West German Left-Wing Terrorism," 164–73. See also Egon Bauer, "Hungerstreik und Mordanschlag auf Alfred Herrhausen — Die RAF im Jahre 1989," in Backes and Jesse, *Jahrbuch Extremismus,* 207–17.

45. Party government had also been pronounced healthy in the sixties and seventies by Gordon Smith, *Democracy in Western Germany: Parties and Politics in the FRG* (London: Heinemann, 1982), 62–68; and William E. Paterson, "Problems of Party Government in West Germany — A British Perspective," in Doering and Smith, *Party Government and Political Culture,* 101–15. See also Kenneth Dyson, "Party Government and Party State," ibid., 77–100.

46. In the polls, "general satisfaction with democracy" hit a low point in 1993 but has recovered since, especially in East Germany. See *Einstellungen zu aktuellen Fragen der Innenpolitik 1995 in Deutschland* (Mannheim: IPOS, 1995), 29–33. By now, the FDP has practically faded in the five new *Länder* and shows stability and lasting support only in Baden-Württemberg.

47. The Greens went into a complete eclipse in the 1990 elections when they failed to win 5 percent of the popular vote but have since returned in strength at the federal and *Länder* levels. Since their fundamentalist wing lost its battle for control of the party, its "Realo" wing is now in a position to negotiate coalitions with the SPD, or other parties.

48. Large numbers of persons and functionaries formerly associated with the SED regime are still concentrated in East Berlin districts. As far as campaign finance is concerned, the PDS may be one of Germany's richest parties — it took over the huge SED holdings, including foreign investments and real estate.

49. With 4.4 percent PDS and 7.3 percent Greens, the task of rallying a majority of the Bundestag without them has become much more difficult than it was before 1983. On the other hand, some of the leadership of the CDU/CSU, FDP, and SPD made it clear in 1994 that they would consider another grand coalition if the results of the Bundestag elections of 1994 frustrated the normal operation of the two-bloc system.

50. See, for example, Thomas A. Baylis, "Leadership Change in Eastern Germany: From Colonization to Integration," in *The FRG at 45,* ed. Peter H. Merkl (New York: New York University Press, 1995), 243–62.

51. This was computed from the monthly *Politbarometer* releases from October 1994 through December 1995. In September, the positive assessments of the general economic situation in the East rose to 14 percent and of the respondent's own situation to 55 percent.

52. See *Politbarometer,* October 1995, where 54 percent of East Germans also expressed the belief that the "federal government is not doing enough to help East German living conditions reach West German levels."

53. Helmut Kohl won that first election handily with 44 percent for the CDU/CSU and an impressive 11 percent for the FDP, his coalition partner. After the December 1990 elections, however, an acute hangover seemed to seize the nation, and there was no end to recriminations and attacks on Kohl for his rash promises that the East would "blossom" and there would be no new taxes to pay for the West.

54. Having benefited from substantial CSU defections in 1989, the REP dropped to 4.9 percent in the Bavarian *Land* elections of 1990 and 3.9 percent in 1994 in their home state (in unified Berlin, too, they dropped to 3.1 percent). In the midst of acrimonious partisan debate over the German asylum law, even well-informed politicians and journalists expected the REP to make it into the next (1994) Bundestag, possibly with as much as 15 percent of the national vote.

55. The constitutional amendment passed under virtual conditions of siege to the Bundestag in Bonn, and although it may still be hard to tell the long-range significance of the change, it was evidently perceived by the frustrated populace to have "solved" the problem. The number of asylum seekers also declined steeply in the following year, while their entry into Germany was made far more difficult.

56. For details, see Peter H. Merkl, "Are the Old Nazis Coming Back?" in Merkl, *The FRG at 45,* 427–86.

57. See Helmut Willems, *Fremdenfeindliche Gewalt: Einstellungen, Täter, Konflikteskalation* (Opladen: Leske & Budrich, 1993), 211–36, 242–46. See also Tore Bjørgo and Rob Witte, eds., *Racist Violence in Europe* (New York: St. Martin's Press, 1993); and Bjørgo's special edition of *Terrorism and Political Violence,* vol. 7 (spring 1995).

58. In the end, even the Republikaner came under Constitutional Protection Service surveillance as an extreme rightist organization when, in 1994, they tried to enter a close alliance with the DVU, which was already so labeled. Up until that point, and under much criticism, the REP had evidently been officially considered a populist right-wing group that did not merit the close attention given the more extreme organizations of the day.

59. There were some other reasons for the decline of the REP vote, such as the alliance with the extremist DVU and the new attention to the REP by the Constitutional Protection Service, or the notorious leadership squabbles of the party.

Building Democracy and Changing Institutions: The Professional Civil Service and Political Parties in the Federal Republic of Germany

Gregg O. Kvistad

After World War II, West Germany under Allied tutelage had no option but to adopt some form of Western-style liberal democracy. Yet Western German political elites, especially local and regional party leaders, appear to have been extraordinarily willing participants in the process of political transformation between 1945 and 1949.[1] The constitution that was ratified in May 1949, marking the birth of Germany's second democracy, was a German affair. It has been called a home-grown "reactive" document looking backward not only to the disasters of Nazism and the failed Weimar Republic, but further, according to Kielmansegg, to the more amorphous and problematic German "above-parties ideology of the authoritarian state."[2] The new institutional order in the Federal Republic secured a prominent place for rehabilitated political parties — both as agents of societal interest representation and as participants in the exercise of state power. Plebiscites and the direct election of the German head of state, regarded as two of the most problematic institutional artifacts of the Weimar Republic, were rejected, and Article 21 of the Basic Law defined for political parties the role of "forming the political will of the people."[3] Political parties, the pejorative "societal" actors of the 1848 revolution and the early Weimar years, were thereby constitutionally elevated in the new regime to a role that had more or less been occupied by civil servants in Germany's nineteenth-century ideology of the authoritarian state.

This chapter will investigate the question of whether the ideology of the authoritarian state was entirely transcended by the political-institutional arrangement of the Federal Republic laid down in the Basic Law, or whether that project more complexly involved a political-social transformation both within and outside of the Federal Republic's "reactive" institutional arrangement. Specifically, the chapter will address the professional civil service, the institution that survived in the Federal Republic that is most closely tied to Germany's nineteenth-century ideology of statism. The institutional role of the professional civil service in the Federal Republic can be considered, however, only by simultaneously addressing the Federal Republic's rehabilitation of political parties. Following March and Olsen, the ideology of the authoritarian state to which the Basic Law is said to have "reacted" will be understood as a shared "logic of appropriateness" defining criteria for membership in Germany's political institutions as well as their proper arrangement.[4] As such, the logic of appropriateness of German statism, at least historically, defined criteria for what might be called "rational" political membership in Germany's political institutions — a membership that a person may acquire, but into which one is not "naturally" born — specifically, membership in the professional civil service and Germany's political parties.

The "above-parties ideology of the authoritarian state" to which Kielmansegg referred, or what will be called here German statism, first consolidated in *Vormärz* Prussia during the development of a nascent mass politics. Seventy years later it was challenged by, but largely survived, the tragic experience of the Weimar Republic. This logic dichotomized the realms of state and society and posited the state as a site of hortatory political agency in which a public interest could be discerned and implemented. Only in the state realm, protected from the vicissitudes of the market for the satisfaction of needs, could the universal good of the entire community and not the partial good of individuals or groups be articulated and properly pursued. State actors, who were mainly professional civil servants, were suggested by this logic to be experts skilled at the maintenance of public order and civil life in the face of the threat of an economically motivated, conflictual, and proto-anarchic civil society of ordinary citizens organized in particularistic interest groups and political parties.[5]

Political Parties and the *Parteienstaat*

After 1945, the "vertical" pull of German statism that had historically relegated political parties to the status of, at best, semi-legitimate pur veyors of particularistic interests was said to have dissipated and been replaced by a constitutionally sanctioned, pluralistic, "horizontal" calculation of party advantage.[6] Commentators suggested that this change was encouraged by the postwar power vacuum in Western Germany created by the collapse of other public institutions such as the civil service and the military, and by the ability of political parties to "create the impression, whether or not true, that they were persecuted from the beginning [of the Nazi era]."[7] This new, rehabilitated hortatory role for Western Germany's political parties was buttressed by the rapid electoral consolidation of a two-and-one-half-party system, which by the second federal election in 1953 had already awarded the CDU/CSU, the SPD, and the FDP a combined 84 percent of the vote. A number of other factors furthered this transformation process, including the Federal Republic's new 5 percent hurdle, which prohibited parliamentary representation for minor parties receiving less than 5 percent of the vote or failing to win three mandates outright, and the transformation of Western German political parties in the 1950s and 1960s, led by the CDU, into pragmatic, broadly based agents of multiple interest intermediation and mass integration. By the mid-1960s, large Western German parties had even become models for a European party type, the "catch-all party," formulated by Otto Kirchheimer. Unlike the divisive and particularistic parties of Germany's past, the "catch-all party," or *Volkspartei,* which the CDU became under the early tutelage of Adenauer and which the SPD became after its Godesberg Program in 1959, was marked by a reduction in the party's ideological baggage, a strengthening of top leadership groups, and a de-emphasis on class and denominational clientele.[8] The business of West Germany's new parties by the 1960s was to attract voters, win elections, and pragmatically govern. The effectiveness of the regime's political parties had apparently removed the rationale for other political institutions in the Federal Republic to appeal to some ultimate political value residing "above parties."[9]

As this development proceeded, Western German politicians and commentators rescued the term *Parteienstaat,* or party state, from its Weimar usage, when it connoted ineffective and divisive parliamentary wrangling, to apply now to the Federal Republic's new, positive role for political parties.[10] Yet the redefinition of West German parties as constituent elements of the Federal Republic's rehabilitated *Parteienstaat* occurred against the backdrop of Germany's pre-democratic dichotomization of state and society and the positing of parties as societal agents of particularistic interest representation. This historical legacy produced a *Parteienstaat* in the Federal Republic that essentially bridged and accommodated the two parts of the traditional German political dichotomy of state and society, but that did not completely leave that dichotomy behind. The bridging involved redefining the nature of membership in and relationships between the state civil service and political parties in the new Federal Republic. Not only did party success in policy-making right after the war demonstrate to senior civil servants that the Federal Republic's political parties were legitimate political actors, but party membership was frequently sought among postwar Germans desiring entrance into the civil service to demonstrate that they had the requisite democratic value commitment.[11] The rehabilitation of the *Parteienstaat* in the Federal Republic meant, in other words, that "rational" political membership in the German professional civil service after the war partly hinged on membership in the political parties that nineteenth-century German statism had previously rejected as politically illegitimate agents located in the "lower" societal realm. So dramatic was this evident institutional shift that some commentators argued in the 1960s that the German state had completely "dissolved" into German society; while the state/society dichotomy was important for understanding nineteenth-century German politics, they suggested, it had become completely "obsolete" and "inappropriate" for the modern Federal Republic.[12]

This rather hopefully expressed Western-liberal "normalization" of postwar German politics via the *Parteienstaat,* however, quite seriously overstated the obvious. The Federal Republic was indeed a liberal democratic regime built on much firmer foundations, with better institutions and constitutional safeguards, than the ill-fated Weimar Republic. But it was not a regime marked in all regards by a "zero hour," or totally clean slate. To be sure, the complete defeat of the Hitler regime in 1945 and the subsequent occupation of Germany by the Allied powers created a more conducive context for the Federal Republic's founding and democratic consolidation than what Weimar experienced. That did not completely translate, however, into a totally new political discourse for the new regime with completely new institutional role assignments and value attachments. Clear vestiges of old German political discourses and practices were discernible within the Federal Republic's much-vaunted *Parteienstaat.* Careful observers noted the retention of statist elements in the Federal Republic's party politics by identifying them as "heirs to state norms" and "institutional reference points of the state" in postwar Germany.[13] It was suggested somewhat more subtly that political parties became the "bearers" of the German state with the new *Parteienstaat,* and that necessitated a "new interpretation" of society as a realm no longer controlled and contained by the state, as was traditional in German political ideology, but rather as a realm occupied by "those forces within [society] which have successfully established a claim to embody the state in virtue of their ability to express the political will of the majority."[14] The traditional *ideological* role of the German state had thus not completely disappeared in the Federal Republic but rather had been partly incorporated in the catch-all parties of the *Parteienstaat*. Indeed, it is argued that the "political will" that these parties formed, in keeping with Article 21 of the Basic Law, reflected the will of "party elites who speak the moralistic language and adopt the didactic style of leadership of the state tradition of authority." The Federal Republic's political parties thus embodied — and certainly not problematically, according to many commentators — a moral sense of mission, a shared responsibility for the whole, and a high-minded view of politics as a collaborative effort among qualified elites.[15] The *Parteienstaat* concept still retained, after all, the word *Staat*. The professional civil service in the new Federal Republic had a quite different historical legacy to sort out.

The Professional Civil Service and Its Traditional Principles

If political parties were reconceptualized in the early years of the Federal Republic to constitute a hortatory *Parteienstaat* "forming the political will" of the people, did the professional civil service experience a similar institutional redefinition? Did it become, for instance, a less esteemed Anglo-American pragmatic institution of neutral administration and implementation? To answer this question requires first turning to the legacy of the collapse of the Weimar Republic on the institutional politics of the Federal Republic. As Kurt Sontheimer observed, "Other comparative cases from the standpoint of democratic orders are not available in German history." In the early postwar period, the political debate in Western Germany was suffused by the "fear . . . that what happened to the republic of Weimar could happen once more."[16] According to Dolf Sternberger, writing in 1949,

> In hundreds of political, state, and constitutional discussions, one witnesses so often a sensitive and fearful . . . fixation: what must be done in order to avoid the "mistakes of the past"? This question appears much more frequently than the more natural and healthy question: what must be done in order to make it good?[17]

The attempt to avoid these "mistakes" left the Federal Republic's political elites engaged in a broad discussion of the new regime's institutional order.[18] The professional civil service — the key institution for understanding the nature of "rational" political membership in Germany's statist ideology — became the focus of much of that attention.

In their effort to remake German politics, West German policymakers first determined that political institutions and their composition were relatively more pliable than the German population's political attitudes.[19] Very quickly, a consensus developed among West German political elites that Weimar's demise was due to the regime's institutional "value-neutrality," weakness, and resulting inability to defend itself from its "enemies."[20] In response, the Federal Republic was to be founded on what Donald Kommers has called an "objective order of values" that was to inform all aspects of German political institutions and their activity. Expressed as the "unity of the [Federal Republic's] Constitution as a logical-teleological entity," the regime's

> framers are said to have arranged these values in a hierarchical order, the most important of which is a "free democratic basic order" crowned by the principle of "human dignity." . . . These principles, or values, are "objective" because they have an independent reality under the Constitution. As a consequence, all organs of government must affirmatively enforce these values.[21]

In short, all institutions in the Federal Republic were to be "value-laden." In contrast to Weimar, which was celebrated by one of its contemporaries as having "the most democratic constitution in the world" but criticized in the early postwar period as too liberally and tolerantly opening its political institutions to the subversion of "enemies" of its democracy, the Federal Republic's institutions would be governed by a meta-legal requirement to uphold the "free democratic basic order" at all times. The Federal Republic's civil service, as the new regime's foremost "rational" political institution, had a central role to play in upholding the Federal Republic's "objective order of values."

At this level of abstraction, we might predict that the Federal Republic's civil service after 1945, as an important value-laden institution constructed on the "lessons" of Weimar and charged with protecting the free democratic basic order from its enemies, would have been especially sensitive to the continued employment of former Nazis in the new regime. As Peter Katzenstein observed, however,

> Despite Allied Occupation and the program of de-Nazification, after 1945 continuity in civil service personnel was as great as it had been in the transition from the Second Empire to the Weimar Republic in 1919 and from the Weimar Republic to the Third Reich in 1933. A decade after the collapse of Nazi Germany, about two-thirds of the senior civil servants held positions in the Federal Re-

public comparable to those in the administrative structure of Hitler's Germany.[22]

This "complete failure" of the denazification of the state civil service was acknowledged in 1948, when it ground to a virtual halt.[23] Between 1945 and 1948, 53,000 officials lost their positions; an article in the West German constitution (Article 131), however, ensured the reinstatement of all but 1,004 of those officials.[24] What explains this generous political accommodation in the new value-laden institutional order of the Federal Republic?

The lingering power of the statist logic of political membership continued to suggest after 1945 that the institution of the professional civil service, as such, was "always the most secure support of the state," and that remained true for the new West German democracy as well.[25] The institution of the German civil service is explicitly mentioned in Article 33 of the Federal Republic's constitution, where it was stated that "Civil service law is to be regulated under the consideration [*Berücksichtigung*] of the traditional principles [*hergebrachte Grundsätze*] of the professional civil service." Because of the performance of the civil service in both the Weimar and Nazi regimes, a few participants in West Germany's constitution-drafting Parliamentary Council joined the Allies in questioning the wisdom of constitutionally securing the "traditional" civil service in Germany's new democracy.[26] Those voices were outnumbered, however, by the many defenders of the institution who pointed both to the functional requirements of the modern state and to the proud institutional tradition of the German professional civil service — a tradition grossly violated, it was argued, but not destroyed by Hitler's instrumentalization for genocidal ends.[27] In short, the institutional ideology of the civil service was powerful enough in the early years of the Federal Republic to allow the Nazi practice to be rationalized away as institutionally aberrant. When the Allies challenged the retention of the institution, West German political elites — including Social Democrats — virtually unanimously closed ranks around the need to preserve the German professional civil service and its "traditional principles." In keeping with Germany's surviving statist logic of appropriateness in this period, Bernd Wunder characterized the German reaction to the Allies' demand for civil service reform as "completely uncomprehending." West German democratic elites utterly rejected Allied proposals to neutralize the institution politically, to eradicate the special status of *Beamten,* and to establish a civil service commission with independent personnel officers.[28]

Observers have argued that the Parliamentary Council and other West German elites supporting the professional civil service were not intransigently trying to link the West German bureaucracy to "reaction and traditionalism" at this time, but rather attempting to preserve the "core of the structural principles of the German civil service" that was necessary for the "functioning of the state."[29] Identifying the "core of the structural principles" of this institution, however, is difficult. Legal scholars have suggested that they reach "at least as far back as the Weimar constitution," which evidently includes the Nazi period, but that they cannot refer to the absolutist or constitutional monarchies of the nineteenth century; others make direct reference to tenth-century feudal law, the Prussian General Code of 1794, Bavarian law of 1805, imperial law of 1873, and Weimar law of 1919.[30] The Federal Constitutional Court itself cited legal commentary published in 1876, 1885, 1928, 1930, 1956, and 1967 in its discussion of the traditional principles, which, the court claimed, dictate: "If the civil service is not dependable, then society and the state are 'lost' in critical situations."[31] A civil service reform commission argued in the Federal Republic that the traditional principles involve some rights of the individual civil servant, such as free speech and free assembly, but refer primarily to the civil servants' duties of political loyalty, including the necessity loyally to "intervene on behalf of the state and its constitutional order at all times"; the civil service relationship, in short, involved the "entire personality" of the civil servant.[32] The one "rational" political institution regarded as existentially crucial for the survival of the free democratic basic order of the Federal Republic was thus acknowledged to be grounded in a logic of appropriateness that predated by decades, if not centuries, the advent of democratic politics on German territory. By early 1952, the Allies gave up their efforts to effect a substantial reform of the civil service, the traditional nineteenth-century logic of membership of which the Federal Republic had unambiguously inherited and strenuously defended.[33]

This preservation of the German professional civil service in the Federal Republic nevertheless existed in tension with another aspect of the value-ladenness of the new democratic political order: the priority of the individual fundamental rights located in the first 19 articles of the Basic Law dedicated to protecting the "dignity of man." The collision was not realized until the early 1970s, but the potential was inherent in the constitution's simultaneous inclusion of a pre-democratic institution wholly dedicated to the upholding of the political order, on the one hand, and the prominence of a catalogue of democratic rights and liberties for individual citizens, on the other. Those rights included protections of free speech, equal treatment, and assembly, as well as prohibitions of discrimination by sex, origin, race, language, belief, religion, or political perspective. According to Carl Friedrich, writing in 1949, the appearance and location of these fundamental rights in the constitution marked an important break with Germany's past: "Man is thereby put above the state, and all state authorities are specifically enjoined to respect and to protect the dignity of man."[34]

The preservation of the professional civil service in the Federal Republic, however, modified Friedrich's essentially accurate description. Man was "put above the state" only if that man was not *part* of the state. If a man was part of the state, that is, if he was employed in the state civil service, then he enjoyed a *Sonderstatus* relative to ordinary German citizens. This status, according to both Federal Constitutional Court decisions and legal commentary, dictated that the catalogue of civil and political protections accorded German citizens by the first 19 articles of the Basic Law was not entirely applicable to state civil servants.[35] What intervened between German civil servants, as "rational" members of the German political community, and the fundamental rights of German citizens were the "traditional principles" of the German professional civil service appearing in Article 33. The rationale for the continued applicability of these traditional principles, and their absolute precedence for German civil servants relative to their fundamental civil and political liberties as German citizens, remained an institutional logic of appropriateness that held the state and its agents as existentially necessary protectors of a proto-anarchic civil society. Without the guarantee of civil servants' political loyalty at all times, state authorities would not be in a position reliably to protect the "dignity of man" that was one of the value-laden cornerstones of the new political order.

By the early 1950s, Germany's professional state civil service and its traditional principles were bent to respond to what Richard Löwenthal called the "deep impact that a wide anti-Communist and anti-Soviet current had during the regime's formative years."[36] The Cold War in this period rationalized vigilance about the possible infiltration of West German political institutions — particularly political parties and the state civil service — by East German and Soviet-sponsored functionaries.[37] The Communist threat was regarded by West German elites to be much more menacing in the early 1950s than the Nazi "small fry" reinstated into the civil service; indeed, it was suggested that the expertise of the old officials would be useful for consolidating the new Federal Republic.[38] Adenauer responded by issuing a decree in September 1950, which built not only on the constitutional requirement implicit in Article 33 to uphold the free democratic basic order, but also on recent federal and *Land* civil service law calling for civil servants to "acknowledge" (*bekennen*) the democratic state order at all times.[39] Adenauer explicitly listed 13 organizations, 10 of which were Communist or leftist in orientation, "the support of which is inconsistent with official duties." The decree's anti-Communist colors were revealed by the statement that "especially serious offenses to duty" are those committed by civil servants who support the "resolutions of the Third Party Convention of the [Communist] Social Unity Party and the so-called 'National Congress.' "[40] Adenauer's decree, which was part of a broad effort to secure the Federal Republic in the Western alliance, appeared within a domestic context of political apathy, if not outright fear of politics. His explicit demand on the political loyalty of West German civil servants met with virtually no critical reaction in either the German public or legal commentary.[41] This was to change dramatically by the 1970s.

Democracy and Its "Militancy"

The Federal Republic's new political order thus combined a liberal-democratic institution of party governance with a pre-liberal institution of bureaucratic political agency. Article 21 of the Basic Law gave political parties in the Federal Republic the right and duty to form the political will of the people, while Article 33 reserved for the professional civil service a protective and exclusive political role vis-à-vis civil society. Party governance via the *Parteienstaat* was said at least to bridge—if not to transcend—the nineteenth-century German dichotomy of state and society. But bureaucratic political agency via surviving aspects of the civil service tradition retained a clear dichotomy between the rights and duties of state actors, on the one hand, and the rights and duties of citizens, on the other. This unique combination of liberal party politics and pre-liberal bureaucratic politics in the Federal Republic is captured in the idea of "militant democracy," or what is referred to in German political and legal commentary as *streitbare Demokratie, wehrhafte Demokratie, wertgebunde Demokratie,* and *militante Demokratie.*[42] Discussions of militant democracy in the Federal Republic reflect some of the long-standing tensions within German liberalism as well as concerns about the "normalcy" of German political development. Some German commentators boasted in the 1970s that the Federal Republic was one of the "most liberal" orders in the world, while others warned against the "unenlightened liberalism" of the Anglo-American tradition.[43] Some argued that militant democracy was present in virtually all liberal state forms, while others argued that militant democracy was a "specifically German affair" because of Germany's past and its international security exposure.[44] None of these particular views disputed the legitimacy of the construct, but the meaning of militant democracy has been difficult to ascertain in the Federal Republic, even among the construct's defenders.[45] What is clear, however, is that militant democracy—involving the *Parteienstaat* and the professional civil service — became by the late 1950s the main political instrument in the Federal Republic for upholding the new regime's "objective order of values."

Militant democracy posed "rational" rules for inclusion and exclusion in the Federal Republic's political community. Included were those forces that either would not threaten or would positively uphold the free democratic basic order at all times. Excluded — and *excludable* — were both the direct political participation of a mobilized German citizenry and political actors whose efforts would undermine the free democratic basic order. According to Article 21 of the Basic Law, "Parties which, by reason of their aims or the behavior of their adherents, seek to impair or abolish the free democratic basic order or endanger the existence of the Federal Republic of Germany shall be unconstitutional." The first systematic usage of the term *streitbare Demokratie,* or militant democracy, appeared in the 1956 Federal Constitutional Court decision banning the KPD (Communist Party of Germany), which came four years after the banning of the right-wing SRP (Socialist Reich Party). The court argued:

> The Basic Law represents a conscious effort to achieve a synthesis between the principle of tolerance with respect to all political ideas and certain inalienable values of the political system. Article 21 (2) does not contradict any basic principle of the Constitution; it expresses the conviction . . . based on concrete historical experience, that the state could no longer afford to maintain an attitude of neutrality toward political parties. [The Basic Law] has in this sense created a "militant democracy," a constitutional [value] decision that is binding on the Federal Constitutional Court.[46]

Protecting the "inalienable values of the political system" was the paramount goal of militant democracy. The court continued, "if limitations on the political freedom of opponents [*Gegner*] of the political order are necessary for this defense, then so be it."[47]

Militant democracy thereby legitimized the "rational" political exclusion of even "natural" members of Germany's political community, that is, German citizens. As long as German citizens did not, by their individual actions or participation in a political party, endanger the free democratic basic order, their fundamental political and civil liberties prominently guaranteed in the first 19 articles of the Basic Law were secure. This so-called enlightened German position differed from what Roman Herzog — the later Federal President — saw as the naive and "simplified worldview" in "America and also in Europe" that posited "only the state . . . endangers freedom."[48] Eckart Bulla similarly argued that

" 'reason of state' [*'Staatsräson'*] and spheres of freedom for citizens are not constitutionally opposite ends of a continuum."[49] The catch-all parties of the Federal Republic's rehabilitated *Parteienstaat* were regarded as bridging *Staatsräson* and individual freedom. As long as political parties and their citizen members did not endanger the free democratic basic order, they were free politically to believe and act as they saw fit. State civil servants in the Federal Republic's militant democracy, however, were to guarantee a positive willingness actively to uphold the free democratic basic order at all times.

The institutional role of state civil servants in the Federal Republic's militant democracy was — as it had been in German political ideology since the early nineteenth century — to constitute the state's primary "rational" capacity to protect against the illegitimate and potentially destabilizing political interventions of German society. Ludwig Raiser claimed that "the principle of militant democracy . . . requires civil service loyalty to the constitution."[50] Martin Kriele, somewhat more pointedly, suggested that the most important question to ask in the Federal Republic's militant democracy was, "In which direction will the civil servant shoot?"[51] Consistent with traditional German statism, the "rationality" of the state civil servant's membership in the political community of the Federal Republic was thus heightened relative both to the "rationality" of political party participation in the construction of the will of German people and to that of ordinary citizens engaging in legal political activity. Civil servants had a special constitutional obligation not just to avoid endangering the free democratic basic order, as did political parties and their members in the Federal Republic, but moreover to demonstrate a positive willingness and capacity to defend that order at all times. Institutionally, the role of the Federal Republic's professional civil service thus remained informed by the nineteenth-century idea that state institutions (the civil service) must protect German society from its inherent anarchistic self-destructiveness. The Federal Republic renamed this basic institutional arrangement a militant democracy, thereby nominally and in object "democratizing" the traditional statist logic of "rational" political membership inherited by the Federal Republic from the nineteenth century, but statism as a "logic of appropriateness" by no means disappeared from the new regime.

An Institutional Arrangement Collides with a Mobilized Citizenry

The institutional arrangement of the postwar Federal Republic may have been informed by aspects of the nineteenth-century ideology of

German statism, but it was nonetheless the product of an extraordinarily conscious attempt by political elites to establish the means by which democracy could take root and successfully consolidate on German territory. Entrance into much of the political order was controlled by "rational" membership criteria, by performance requirements that, if met, sanctioned participation but, if unmet, rationalized exclusion. In this institutional arrangement, state employees in the professional civil service had the role of positively protecting the free democratic basic order from its enemies at all times; catch-all political parties had the role of forming the political will of the German public consistent with the free democratic basic order; and ordinary citizens had the role of not endangering the free democratic basic order with acts hostile to the constitution. Nonperformance of these roles—which were hierarchically arranged in order of existential importance for the survival of the democratic regime and, not accidentally, hierarchically arranged consistent with the nineteenth-century ideology of German statism—earned exclusion, in some form or another, from the Federal Republic's political community. This was exclusion, however, with the preservation of democracy on German soil as its goal and rationale. Estimable in the eyes of the Allies and the rest of the world watching Germany's second experiment in democracy, it nonetheless collided, beginning in the 1960s, with the "revolutionary" democratization and mobilization of the lowest factor in the Federal Republic's "rational" institutional arrangement: the German citizenry.[52]

Karl Jaspers, the noted philosopher, published a book in the spring of 1966 titled *Wohin treibt die Bundesrepublik?* or *Where Is the Federal Republic Going?* Jaspers's provocative thesis was that the country was spiraling from a "party oligarchy" to an "authoritarian state" and would end in a new "dictatorship."[53] Jaspers's polemic was bad social science, but it became an immediate best-seller in the Federal Republic, which had just left the Adenauer era behind.[54] The book argued that responsibility for the prevention of dictatorship in the Federal Republic rested not with the institutional structures discussed here, with the *Parteienstaat* and the *Berufsbeamtentum* (Professional Civil Service) that constituted the *militante Demokratie*. Instead, "it depends," according to Jaspers, "decisively on the people . . . even the best institutions do nothing when the people fail to use them."[55] He criticized West Germans for having

> respect for the government as such . . . ; a need to honor the state in the form of representative politicians as replacements for the emperor and the king; the feelings of being a subject [*Untertan*] in relation to authority in all of its forms, down to the last counter of the

bureaucratic clerk's office; a readiness for blind obedience; the trust that the government will make it right; . . . In short: state consciousness is for us frequently subject consciousness, not the democratic consciousness of free citizens.[56]

Jaspers's polemic directly challenged the statist logic of appropriateness that survived in the Federal Republic. Whereas West Germany's political elites had structured the new regime's institutions to preserve democracy through "rational" means, Jaspers called for German citizens to wake up and mobilize themselves. Jaspers called for a "real revolution," which, he claimed, was to be led by "free citizens" who "do not want power, but rather [want to] convince," and who act "from below and are nonviolent."[57]

Jaspers's call to action in 1966 in the Federal Republic coincided with the formation of the "Grand Coalition" government, a move that catapulted the post-Godesberg, reformed SPD into governmental responsibility and left the small, middle-class FDP as the only parliamentary opposition in the Bundestag. Many intellectuals, left-wing Social Democrats, and trade unionists regarded the new government with considerable unease and began to explore other avenues of political representation, especially as the government began parliamentary deliberations on proposed "Emergency Laws" in 1967. Not only was the Grand Coalition led by a chancellor who, as a former member of the Nazi Party, according to the Social Democratic writer Günter Grass, "has already once acted against all reason and served criminals," but the government was also debating the reinstitution of emergency laws that reminded many of the infamous Article 48 of the Weimar Constitution, a constitutional anomaly that virtually allowed governance by emergency decree.[58] Coming together in what they called an "extraparliamentary opposition," or APO (*Außerparlamentarische Opposition*), these new activists in the Federal Republic also rejected the adequacy of the "economic miracle" and Ludwig Erhard's corporatist call for a "formed society" (*formierte Gesellschaft*) constructed by what they regarded as statist elites.[59]

Overlapping with the activism of the APO in the late 1960s in the Federal Republic was the mobilization of West German university students.[60] The early days of the student movement saw the demand to "open up" West German institutions. According to Jürgen Habermas,

> The worldview of these students is shaped by the impression that social institutions have coalesced into a relatively closed, conflict-free and self-regulating, yet violent apparatus. Enlightenment and

opposition can be provided only by uncorrupted individuals on the margins of the apparatus. Whoever assumes a function within it, however unimportant, becomes integrated and neutralized.⁶¹

Though the worldview of mobilized students in the Federal Republic in the late 1960s was very diffuse and by no means settled on a conscious rejection of Germany's traditional statist logic of appropriateness, a counter-discourse of democratic political emancipation "from below" began to appear in this period among Western German activists. At a conference in 1967 after the police killing of a student in Berlin at a demonstration protesting a visit by the Shah of Iran, Rudi Dutschke, the intellectual force behind the West German student movement, argued,

> We are no longer represented by the institutions in this system. Therefore, these institutions are not an expression of our interests. Therefore, we must take a position against these institutions. . . . Our only chance for a genuine democratization from below is not from within the established organizations, but from within the centers of action that we have created, which really produce actions, and actions are the only requirement for democratization from below.⁶²

A noted historian has described the mobilization of 1967–68 as producing in the minds of many West Germans a sense that, unlike at the beginning of the Federal Republic, "now one stood before a genuine 'hour zero.' "⁶³

Occurring virtually simultaneously with the "revolution in the way of thinking" called for by Jaspers, and "silently" occurring in the broader West German public, were two developments that prompted concern for institutionalized politics in the Federal Republic. First, the Communist Party of Germany, or KPD, which had been banned by the Federal Constitutional Court in 1956 as antithetical to the *Parteienstaat* and the value order of the Federal Republic, was refounded in 1968 as the DKP, or German Communist Party; second, in the late 1960s and early 1970s, a violent leftist terrorism appeared on the West German scene that first targeted property and then people, particularly political and economic elites.⁶⁴ Unlike the mass of "silent revolutionaries" growing in the Federal Republic at this time who were organized in various interest groups and "citizens' initiatives," the DKP and the terrorist groups were interested in a more active confrontation with the institutional arrangement of the Federal Republic and were suspected of having—and later proved to have had—close financial and logistical support from the GDR and the Soviet Union.⁶⁵ Throughout the 1970s and early 1980s, these developments were perceived as substantial threats to the institutional order of the Federal Republic. That perception was informed, however, not only by the Cold War logic of anticommunism, which was ubiquitous in the West generally and not just in the Federal Republic, but also by the much older political tradition of German statism, which regarded, as we have seen, the realm of disorganized civil society as threatening to the rational politics of the German state. Indeed, in early 1969, Chancellor Kurt Kiesinger stated,

> Communism is not the danger. . . . The real danger to our present society and order is not Communists and their agents; the real danger, which grows from the depths of a people that has a difficult history to overcome, is nihilism and anarchism. If we do not deal with these with the necessary means, then one day they could become dangerous for us.[66]

Kiesinger's invocation of the familiar threat of civil society, where the "depths of the people" produce "nihilism and anarchism," carried with it the implicit invocation of the strong and reliable German state, the role of which was to contain these threats to the Federal Republic's free democratic basic order.

The Reassertion of Institutions in the Face of Popular Mobilization

Willy Brandt, a Social Democrat, became Chancellor of the Federal Republic in the autumn of 1969. Regarded as a *Machtwechsel,* implying regime change, and not just a *Regierungswechsel,* or change of government, Brandt's government came to power only months after Gustav Heinemann, another Social Democrat, was chosen to be Federal President. Heinemann was said to represent the "absolute antipode of the state understanding of the CDU/CSU."[67] The Federal President's inaugural address to parliament contained words, he said, that "some will not want to hear," especially those who "continue to cling to the authoritarian state [*Obrigkeitsstaat*] that was for a long enough time our misfortune to have." He stated,

> we stand only at the beginning of the first really free period of our history. Free democracy must finally be the life element of our society. . . . Not less, but rather more democracy — that is our requirement, that is the main goal which we all, and especially the youth, have prescribed.[68]

With German society's mobilization in the 1960s, Heinemann saw a "spring breeze" wafting through the Federal Republic's institutions, earning him the title of "radical in the civil service" from the author Heinrich Böll.[69]

Federal Chancellor Willy Brandt's first speech before parliament four months later echoed Heinemann's new political discourse. He stated, "we wish to dare more democracy . . . each citizen will have the possibility of participating in the reform of state and society." Brandt concluded by saying,

> In a democracy, government can only be successful if it is supported by the democratic engagement of the citizenry. We have as little need for blind assent as our people have need for stilted dignity and grand sovereign distance. . . . We stand not at the end of our democracy; we are, rather, only now really beginning.[70]

In an earlier interview, Brandt argued that democracy was less an "organizational form of the state" than a "principle that must influence and inform the entire societal being of the people."[71] Clearly, the election of new federal political leaders with a self-proclaimed new "democratic" political discourse, following on the heels of the most intense political mobilization of German society since the Weimar Republic, appeared directly to challenge the statist logic of appropriateness of rational political membership that had survived the Federal Republic's founding. The "rationalism" of state institutions — including the *Berufsbeamtentum* and the *Parteienstaat* constituting the *militante Demokratie* — that in the Federal Republic was to exclude the participation and influence of non-democratic forces appeared to be challenged by a discourse of "more democracy" and an unprecedented call for the political mobilization of German citizens "from below." On the streets and now in federal government offices, a sea change appeared to be occurring in the Federal Republic at the end of the 1960s that would displace or at least diminish the political centrality of state institutions, particularly the professional civil service, with democratically mobilized German citizens. But politics in the Federal Republic, as it is everywhere else, was much more complicated than what appeared in the rhetoric of its new political leaders.

Two days after Brandt's inaugural address to parliament, his foreign minister, Walter Scheel, met the Soviet ambassador in Bonn to discuss a possible treaty based on the mutual renunciation of force. Within the next three months, the Brandt government established further bilateral talks with Poland and East Germany on the normalization of relations.

This extraordinarily rapid "third cycle" of the Federal Republic's *Ostpolitik* resulted in separate signed treaties with Moscow and Warsaw in 1970.[72] Willy Brandt's call for "more democracy" at home was thus put on the back burner while his government engaged in the boldest foreign policy initiative in the Federal Republic's history. Yet critical observers, especially from the very agitated CDU/CSU, posited a link between the "leftist" societal mobilization that SPD rhetoric was calling for at home and the normalization of relations with East Germany's patron state, the Soviet Union. Arnulf Baring attempted to capture the mood of the right wing of the CDU/CSU with this sketch of the SPD leadership:

> Had not Willy Brandt already once turned his back on Germany and adopted a foreign citizenship? Had not Herbert Wehner, that old Communist, as everyone knew, worked in Moscow in the 1930s for the Comintern? That sounded secretive, yes, it seemed threatening. . . . And now Egon Bahr [Brandt's negotiator in Moscow], again in Moscow, had for months been shut behind closed doors in conference with the Soviet Foreign Minister, and, from what one heard, not even the Foreign Office in Bonn had learned exactly what was discussed by the two men.[73]

The image of "leftist" foreign policy intrigue merged with attributions of Social Democratic "sympathizing" with anti–institutional politics and leftist terrorism that began to erupt in the Federal Republic in the summer of 1970.[74] Had not, it could be asked further, the Social Democratic Federal President and Chancellor both endorsed the "engagement of the citizenry" and the "prescriptions" of the Federal Republic's politically mobilized student movement? How different, in fact, was leftist terrorism from leftist street demonstrations? Both had forsaken the protective institutions of the Federal Republic's militant democracy and replaced them with direct action. Furthermore, the SPD's rebellious youth organization, the Jusos, not only supported the party's *Ostpolitik,* but also called for policy collaboration between the SPD and the DKP, the reconstituted Communist Party.[75] Regardless of the fact that the refounding of the DKP in 1968 was not constitutionally challenged by the CDU when the Christian Democrat Kurt Kiesinger was Chancellor, the CDU asked the SPD in June 1971 what it planned to do about the DKP, hinting that it might begin banning proceedings against the party.[76] The Social Democrats were put on the defensive.

With checkered success, Willy Brandt attempted to distinguish in this period between what he saw as a primitive anticommunism that would prevent forward movement in *Ostpolitik* and the SPD's rejection of the DKP's repeated offers of electoral and policy collaboration.[77] This took the form of an explicit Social Democratic *Abgrenzungsbeschluß*, or demarcation decree, written by the academic Richard Löwenthal and issued by the party leadership in November 1971. It stated:

> Free democracy on one side, Communist party dictatorship on the other: no policy of peace and no foreign policy of *rapprochement* can overcome the contradictions between these systems. . . . A reduction in conflict between states requires that every state respects the domestic order of others. . . . Social Democracy accepts once more the challenge of defending this order without compromise against the false teachings of Communism.[78]

Foreign policy normalization with neighboring Communist states, including East Germany, would thus be joined by a continued domestic policy "containment" of Communist influence within the Federal Republic. Militant democracy mandated keeping an eye on the DKP and its electoral strength and holding the possibility of banning (via Article 21 [2] of the Basic Law) at the ready. Not actually banning the DKP unless absolutely necessary, however, was argued to serve democracy's consolidation in the Federal Republic because elections were seen as more effective weapons against political extremism than state fiats. At the same time, it was suggested that not actually banning the DKP also served the interest of the government's *Ostpolitik* in this period — a position denied by Willy Brandt in 1976 but partly affirmed by him in 1986.[79] Willy Brandt allegedly told the Soviet leader, Leonid Brezhnev, in September 1971 that to promote success in *Ostpolitik*, his Social Democratic government would not pursue a banning of the DKP.[80]

In any case, the *Parteienstaat* was challenged by the appearance of the DKP in the late 1960s, and militant democracy had the institutional means to remove it from the party landscape, but the partly "societal" location of the Federal Republic's *Parteienstaat* argued for a bit of tolerance. In 1971, the same could not be said for alleged threats to the professional civil service, the foremost "rational" institution in the Federal Republic for protecting the free democratic basic order as an "objective order of values." In the context of a continued questioning of the Social Democrats' anti-Communist credentials — exploited with skill by the CDU/CSU — the Brandt government issued what could be called a second *Abgrenzungsbeschluß* in early 1972. Following on the heels of moves in Bremen and Hamburg (both under SPD control) to ban DKP members and other activists in "right- or left-radical groups" from public employment in the educational sector, this came to be known as the

Radikalenerlaß, or Radicals Decree, which called for the consistent implementation of standing civil service law to prohibit the employment of people who are "hostile to the constitution" (*verfassungsfeindlich*) and unable to "guarantee" a readiness to uphold the Federal Republic's free democratic basic order at all times.[81]

Issued by the *Länder* minister presidents and the federal chancellor in January 1972, the *Radikalenerlaß,* or "Basic Principles regarding the Question of Anti-constitutional Elements in the Civil Service," required state employees to (1) guarantee that they would intervene on behalf of the free democratic basic order at all times, (2) avoid all organizations that pursued goals hostile to that order and that would establish doubt about that guarantee, and (3) demonstrate their positive attachment to the free democratic basic order with their entire conduct.[82] The stated intentions of the policy participants in the Radicals Decree were simple and direct: to make consistent the implementation of standing civil service law in the *Länder* and at the federal level in the face of new applicants — some radicalized by the leftist political mobilization of German society in the 1960s — to the *Berufsbeamtentum* of the Federal Republic's value-laden *militante Demokratie*.[83] Indeed, it has been suggested that if student activist Rudi Dutschke had never uttered his infamous call to "march through the institutions" of the Federal Republic, the Radicals Decree never would have appeared.[84] Built on the "traditional principles of the professional civil service" mandated by Article 33 of the Basic Law, the Radicals Decree was, essentially, "no new law," as Federal Chancellor Willy Brandt argued. But that was precisely part of what made the political fight over the civil service that ensued in the next nearly two decades the most divisive political battle that the Federal Republic had experienced.[85] The old law, more or less unconsciously applied in a newly transformed political context — constituted by an unprecedented popular mobilization of citizens in German society, a new Social Democratic government rhetorically promising "more democracy," and an attempt to "normalize" relations with Communist Eastern Europe — no longer rested on an unambiguously "appropriate" logic of political membership for the institution of the professional civil service. The nineteenth-century idea of a state institution politically protecting and acting for an unreliable and particularistic German citizenry located in an "antipolitical" society was rejected by Germans on the street, in the proliferation of interest groups and "citizens' initiatives," and in political and social commentary throughout the Federal Republic.[86]

The legal and political wrangling over the Radicals Decree in the 1970s and early 1980s was legendary and filled volumes of commentary. It addressed the attempt to establish the means by which the "special status" of the civil servant vis-à-vis the ordinary West German citizen could be both determined and adequately demanded and measured;[87] it discussed the nature of the object against which the civil servant was to protect the free democratic basic order of the Federal Republic;[88] and it treated the civil and political rights of the civil servant with respect to the fundamental rights located in the Basic Law and the intensity and breadth of the civil servant's demanded loyalty.[89] Each of these disputes revealed the unsettling of the institutional logic of appropriateness for the German civil service—a logic uncontested at the Federal Republic's founding but profoundly challenged by the political mobilization of German society in the 1960s and 1970s. A Constitutional Court decision in 1975 attempted to clarify the legal issues at stake, concluding that the traditional principles of the institution, including the loyalty demand, superseded the freedoms of belief and expression for the individual civil servant.[90] But even that decision remained legally contested, and it did hardly anything to end the political conflict.

In the 1970s, the SPD, FDP, and CDU/CSU engaged in endless polemics and sometimes serious legislative efforts—all failed—to resolve their differences over the Radicals Decree and its implementation. These political battles involved whether party membership (e.g., in the DKP) or an "individual case test" would indicate the civil servant's required political loyalty;[91] whether a functional security differentiation among roles in the civil service would rationalize differentiated demands on political loyalty;[92] whether all applicants for civil service should undergo an "automatic check" with the Office for the Protection of the Constitution;[93] and, self-referentially, how the continuing controversy over the Radicals Decree was affecting the general political climate in the Federal Republic.[94] By the end of the 1980s, the decree had produced over 350 organizations in the Federal Republic dedicated to its removal.[95] Reformers found it difficult to exit from the decree's strictures without violating constitutional law or engaging in a fundamental institutional overhaul that no one was seriously interested in attempting. Regret and frustration beset particularly the SPD, with Willy Brandt declaring in 1986 that he "had not imagined that the decree would have the effect that it did."[96] Ten years earlier Brandt essentially acknowledged the collapse of the institutional logic of appropriateness for the civil service that the Federal Republic was experiencing: "What I mean is the following: one always proceeded from the idea of the civil service as totally unified and homogeneous. But that is absolutely not the case. . . . A somewhat differentiated way of looking at things is appropriate here."[97] By the time the SPD was forced out of government in 1982 and Helmut Kohl of the CDU took over as Federal Chancellor, a good part of the party-political debate over the decree had become more tactical than substantive. Minor liberalizations of the implementation of the decree were asserted by some *Länder* during the 1970s and early 1980s and by the federal government in 1979, but most of these were posited as "refinements" or "corrections."[98] By the end of the 1980s, the decree had in fact suffered an incremental death, though one not all political elites in the Federal Republic wanted to acknowledge; never wholly and explicitly repudiated, its most restrictive implementation had disappeared not just from SPD-governed *Länder*, but from Union-governed jurisdictions as well.

The unification of the two German states in 1990 provided the occasion for revisiting the traditional role of the civil service that the Federal Republic had inherited as part of its institutional arrangement in 1949, but that it had struggled with mightily in the two decades before. In March 1990, the first freely elected democratic East German government explicitly rejected the Federal Republic's civil service and its "traditional principles." The Western-oriented outcome of that election, however, which essentially mandated the quick accession of the GDR to the Federal Republic via Article 23 of the Basic Law without a constituent assembly, put this institution in the GDR's immediate future.[99] The State Unification Treaty that was signed in August 1990 explicitly posited the introduction of the professional civil service and its traditional principles into the former GDR.[100] But this institution and what was understood as its role in German society in 1990 were quite different from what they had been when the Federal Republic was founded in 1949 or when the Radicals Decree appeared in 1972. Though the political loyalty of former East Germans remained a crucial consideration for policymakers at this time, that did not rationalize a blanket "cleansing" of East German officials from the unified civil service: only Stasi members and human rights violators, but not former Communist Party members, were explicitly banned from the institution. Even that less stringent concern for the political reliability of the institution was mediated by worries about the need for integration and an "internal reconciliation and a new beginning" for the GDR; by European Union law that would alter the "Germanness" of the institution with the inflow of foreign nationals into the German civil service; and by fiscal constraints posed by high unemployment rates and the future massive costs of unification.[101]

Last but not least, memories of nearly two decades of struggling with the institutional identity of the German civil service that began with the Radicals Decree importantly framed the unification deliberations. The CDU/CSU took the more accommodationist position of the "individual case" test that they had rejected in the battle over the Radicals

Decree, in the process arguing that their tougher party membership criterion of the 1970s and early 1980s was no longer appropriate.¹⁰² Likewise, by 1991 the Union parties had dispensed with the "automatic check" with the Office for the Protection of the Constitution for candidates in all of the *Länder* it governed — the very issue that had prevented cooperation with the SPD in the early 1980s — thereby lifting what many commentators regarded as the heart of the decree.¹⁰³ For its part, the SPD did not want to repeat what party leader Hans-Jochen Vogel called in 1989 "the loss of credibility among the German youth" and "damage to the psychological climate in the Republic" that the Radicals Decree controversy had unleashed.¹⁰⁴ During the unification debate, the SPD rejected the decree and its provisions as a "political absurdity" that could not be allowed to reappear.¹⁰⁵

Conclusion

The history of the professional civil service in the postwar Federal Republic thus reveals an institution with an extraordinarily powerful political identity reaching back to the early nineteenth century. That identity was rescued in 1949 from both the taint of Hitler's crimes and the efforts of the Allies to engage in substantial institutional reform. Only with the political mobilization of German society that began in the 1960s did the traditional "logic of appropriateness" of the civil service as a state institution with the role of protecting society from its own political self-destructiveness begin to lose meaning. The loss of meaning was spurred — but not caused — by the Radicals Decree and the opposition generated by it in the 1970s and 1980s, and it continued to dwindle as the Federal Republic faced the complicated challenges of European political integration, a shrinking fiscal capacity, and the profound challenges of German state unification. The professional civil service and its "traditional principles" continued to survive in name in the Federal Republic in the mid-1990s. But its underlying institutional "logic of appropriateness" had been redefined by a German citizenry no longer willing to occupy the nonpolitical role of "subject" that had been relegated to them by a century and a half of German statism.

The result of this successful popular challenge to Germany's traditional statist logic of political membership has not been the institutional collapse and political anarchy that German statism had promised. Instead, the collapse of this logic of membership removed some of the last substantive (though not electoral) political rationales for maintaining the institutional status quo of the professional civil service as a primarily protective and not service-providing entity. At the same time, this collapse has not yet produced anything resembling a broad-based, fundamental reform of the institution. That fact, perhaps now more than ever before in the Federal Republic's history, is more directly attributable to the policy style of incrementalism that characterizes reform in most other policy arenas in the Federal Republic than to any substantive political rationale.[106] The protective political identity of the institution no longer functions as an effective impediment to institutional reform, as it had for the Federal Republic's first four decades.

German society, in turn, has channeled a major part of its mobilization in the 1990s into the catch-all parties of the Federal Republic's *Parteienstaat*. The Cassandra warnings of the death of the Federal Republic's *Parteienstaat* notwithstanding, German political parties continue to survive—though in somewhat different form from their heyday two decades ago—as the most successful and widespread media of political interest intermediation for citizens in the Federal Republic.[107] Moreover, the domestication and coalition-willingness of the *Fundi-frei* Greens in the 1990s, a party that has even occasionally courted the CDU, unambiguously signals the successful consolidation of a differentiated parliamentary regime in the Federal Republic. That consolidation shifted political power from statist institutions once hypostasized "above" ordinary German citizens to political organizations of mobilized and instrumentally rational actors located in German society. In the process, the institutional identity of Germany's professional civil service has shifted from protecting and acting for politically weak if not dangerous citizens, to serving and acting with politically astute and differentiated members of the German political community.

NOTES

1. Peter Merkl, *The Origin of the West German Republic* (New York: Oxford University Press, 1963), 3–22.

2. Peter Graf Kielmansegg, "The Basic Law—Response to the Past or Design for the Future?" in *Forty Years of the Grundgesetz* (Washington, D.C., Research Fellows of the German Historical Institute 1989).

3. Donald P. Kommers, *The Constitutional Jurisprudence of the Federal Republic of Germany* (Durham: Duke University Press, 1989), 39–40.

4. James G. March and Johan P. Olsen, *Rediscovering Institutions* (New York: Free Press, 1989), 160–61.

5. For a general discussion of German statism, see Kenneth H. F. Dyson, *The State Tradition in Western Europe: A Study of an Idea and Institution* (New York: Oxford University Press, 1980), 25–78.

6. David Southern, "Germany," in *Government and Administration in Western Europe,* ed. R. Ridley (New York: St. Martin's, 1979), 54.

7. Eckhard Jesse, "Parteien in Deutschland," in *Parteien in der Bundesrepublik Deutschland,* ed. Heinrich Oberreuter and Alf Mintzel (Munich: Olzug, 1990), n. 103; Merkl, *Origin,* 83; Kenneth Dyson, "Party Government and Party State," in *Party Government and Political Culture in Western Germany,* ed. Herbert Döring and Gordon Smith (New York: St. Martin's, 1982), 84.

8. Otto Kirchheimer, "The Transformation of the Western European Party Systems," in *Political Parties and Political Development,* ed. Joseph LaPalombara and Myron Weiner (Princeton: Princeton University Press, 1966), 190–91.

9. M. Rainer Lepsius, "Institutional Structures and Political Culture," in Döring and Smith, *Party Government,* 118.

10. Kenneth H. F. Dyson, *Party, State, and Bureaucracy in Western Germany* (Beverly Hills: Sage, 1977), 6–7, 10.

11. Nevil Johnson, *State and Government in the Federal Republic of Germany: The Executive at Work* (Oxford: Pergamon Press, 1983), 187; John Herz, "Political Views of the West German Civil Service," in *West German Leadership and Foreign Policy,* ed. H. Speier and W. P. Davison (Evanston, Ill.: Row, Peterson, 1957), 106.

12. Dyson, *Party, State,* 11; Klaus von Beyme, *Das politische System der Bundesrepublik Deutschland nach der Vereinigung* (Munich: Piper, 1991), 138, 152.

13. Dyson, "Party Government," 88–90.

14. Dyson, *Party, State,* 6–10; Nevil Johnson, "Parties and the Conditions of Political Leadership," in Döring and Smith, *Party Government,* 160.

15. Dyson, "Party Government," 87–98.

16. Kurt Sontheimer, *Die verunsicherte Republik* (Munich: Piper, 1979), 7.

17. Dolf Sternberger, "Demokratie der Furcht oder Demokratie der Courage?" *Die Wandlung* 4 (1949): 8.

18. Karl Dietrich Bracher, *The German Dilemma: The Relationship of State and Democracy* (New York: Praeger, 1975), 50.

19. Note the warnings about the dangers of too much concern with state institutions and not the citizenry's democratic consciousness in Bracher, *German Dilemma,* 130.

20. Ernst-Rainer Hönes, "Beamte als Verfassungsfeinde?" *Der öffentliche Dienst* 12 (1972): 222; Hermann Borgs-Maciejewski, "Radikale im öffentlichen Dienst," *Aus Politik und Zeitgeschichte: Beilage zur Wochenzeitung Das Parlament,* 1973, no. B27/73:9; Egon Plümer, "Mitgliedschaft von Beamten und Beamtenanwärtern in verfassungsfeindlichen Parteien," *Neue juristische Wochenschrift,* 1973, no. 1:5; Hella Mandt, "Grenzen politischer Toleranz in der offenen Gesellschaft: Zum Verfassungsgrundsatz der streitbaren Demokratie," *Aus Politik und Zeitgeschichte: Beilage zur Wochenzeitung Das Parlament,* 1972, no. B1–2/72:4; Eckhart Bulla, "Die Lehre von der streitbaren Demokratie: Versuch einer kritischen Analyse unter besonderer Berücksichtigung der Rechtssprech-

ung des Bundesverfassungsgerichts," *Archiv des öffentlichen Rechts* 98 (1973): 343; Friedrich Fuchs and Eckhard Jesse, "Der Streit um die 'streitbare Demokratie': Zur Kontroverse um des Beschäftigung von Extremisten im öffentlichen Dienst," *Aus Politik und Zeitgeschichte: Beilage zur Wochenzeitung Das Parlament,* 1978, no. B3/78:18; Andreas von Schoeler, "Liberalismus und Extremismus," *Liberal,* 1978, no. 4:277.

21. Kommers, *Constitutional Jurisprudence,* 53–54.

22. Peter Katzenstein, *Policy and Politics in West Germany: The Growth of a Semisovereign State* (Philadelphia: Temple University Press, 1987), 256–57.

23. See, however, Merkl, *Origin,* 83, 177.

24. Herbert Jacob, *German Administration since Bismarck: Central Authority versus Local Autonomy* (New Haven: Yale University Press, 1963), 10, 158.

25. Hönes, "Beamte," 223.

26. Ibid.

27. Martin Broszat, *The Hitler State: The Foundation and Development of the Internal Structure of the Third Reich* (London: Longman, 1981), 257–58.

28. Bernd Wunder, *Geschichte der Bürokratie* (Frankfurt am Main: Suhrkamp, 1986), 153–55.

29. Konrad Kruis, "Berufsbeamtentum — Ärgernis oder Forderung der freiheitlichen rechts- und sozialstaatlichen Demokratie?" *Politische Studien,* 1979, no. 3:189–201.

30. Klaus Stern, *Das Staatsrecht der Bundesrepublik Deutschland,* vol. 1 (Munich: C. H. Beck'sche Verlagsbuchhandlung, 1977), 270; Ulrich Battis, "Rechtssprechung zur Radikalen-Frage," *Juristische Arbeitsblätter,* 1979, no. 2:73; Anke Warbeck, "Die hergebrachten Grundsätze des Berufsbeamtentums im Wandel der Zeiten und ihre Bedeutung," *Recht im Amt* 37 (1990): 296.

31. *Entscheidungen des Bundesverfassungsgerichts* (Tübingen: J. C. B. Mohr, 1975), 39:374.

32. See Stern, *Staatsrecht,* 270–71.

33. Wunder, *Geschichte,* 162–63.

34. Carl J. Friedrich, "Rebuilding the German Constitution, II," *American Political Science Review* 18 (1949): 707–8.

35. Stern, *Staatsrecht,* 270, 285–86; Borgs-Maciejewski, "Radikale im öffentlichen Dienst," 9; Gottfried Arndt, "Zur Vereinbarkeit der Mitgliedschaft in nicht verfassungsfeindlichen Parteien und Vereinigungen mit Beschäftigung im öffentlichen Dienst," *Zeitschrift für Beamtenrecht,* 1974, no. 4:123–24; Plümer, "Mitgliedschaft," 6; Hönes, "Beamte," 224; Ulrich Matz, "Extremisten im öffentlichen Dienst," *Die öffentliche Verwaltung* 13 (1978): 468; Carl Hermann Ule, *Die Grundrechte: Handbuch der Theories und Praxis der Grundrechte* (Berlin: Duncker & Humblot, 1962), 573; *Entscheidungen des Bundesverfassungsgerichts,* 39:350–51.

36. Quoted in Sontheimer, *Die verunsicherte Republik,* 19.

37. Merkl, *Origin,* 105–8.

38. Gerard Braunthal, *Political Loyalty and Public Service in West Ger-*

many: The 1972 Decree against Radicals and Its Consequences (Amherst: University of Massachusetts Press, 1990), 15; Merkl, *Origin,* 3; Jacob, *German Administration,* 158.

39. Reinhard Böttcher, *Die politische Treuepflicht der Beamten und Soldaten und die Grundrechte der Kommunikation* (Berlin: Duncker & Humblot, 1967), 30.

40. "Beschluß der Bundesregierung vom 19 September 1950," in *Die politische Treuepflicht,* ed. Edmund Brandt (Karlsruhe: C. F. Müller Juristischer Verlag, 1976), 138–39.

41. Sontheimer, *Die verunsicherte Republik,* 18–19; Fuchs and Jesse, "Streit," 26; Wunder, *Geschichte,* 156.

42. Mandt, "Grenzen," 16; Johannes Lameyer, *Streitbare Demokratie: Eine verfassungshermeneutische Untersuchung* (Berlin: Duncker & Humblot, 1978), 173.

43. E. von Löwenstern, "Kein Überwachungsstaat," *Die Welt,* 12 October 1978; Martin Kriele, "Die Gewähr der Verfassungstreue," *Frankfurter Allgemeine Zeitung,* 25 October 1978.

44. Hartmut Maurer, "Das Verbot politischen Parteien," *Archiv des öffentlichen Rechts* 96 (1971): 206–7; Peter Graf Kielmansegg, "Ist streitbare Demokratie möglich?" *Frankfurter Allgemeine Zeitung,* 7 May 1978; Matz, "Extremisten," 466.

45. For a critique, see Martin Kutscha, *Verfassung und "streitbare Demokratie"* (Cologne: Pahl-Rugenstein Verlag, 1979).

46. Quoted in Kommers, *Constitutional Jurisprudence,* 228.

47. Quoted in Klaus Stern, *Zur Verfassungstreue der Beamten* (Munich: Verlag Franz Vahlen, 1974), 11.

48. Roman Herzog, "Recht und Schutz des Einzelnens," *Die politische Meinung,* 1976, no. 166:8.

49. Bulla, "Lehre," 341.

50. Ludwig Raiser, "Der 'Radikalen-Erlaß': Prüfstein eines demokratischen Rechtsstaates?" *Zeitschrift für Evangelische Ethik,* 1979, no. 2:116.

51. Martin Kriele, "Der rechtliche Spielraum einer Liberalisierung der Einstellungspraxis im öffentlichen Dienst," *Neue juristische Wochenschrift,* 1979, no. 1–2:4.

52. Among the many studies suggesting that "revolution" is the correct characterization of the mobilization and subsequent reform of West German society in the late 1960s and early 1970s is Dennis L. Bark and David R. Gress, *A History of West Germany,* 2 vols. (Oxford: Basil Blackwell, 1989).

53. Karl Jaspers, *Wohin treibt die Bundesrepublik?* 2d ed. (Munich: Piper, 1988).

54. Kurt Sontheimer, "Einführung zur Neuausgabe, 1988," in Jaspers, *Wohin,* i.

55. Jaspers, *Wohin,* 141.

56. Ibid., 146.

57. Ibid., 185–86.

58. Arnulf Baring, *Machtwechsel: Die Ära Brandt-Scheel* (Stuttgart: Deutsche Verlags-Anstalt, 1982), 39–40; Klaus Hildebrand, *Von Erhard zur Großen Koalition,* vol. 4 of Hildebrand, *Geschichte der Bundesrepublik Deutschland* (Stuttgart: Deutsche Verlags-Anstalt, 1984), 369.

59. Eckhard Jesse, *Die Demokratie der Bundesrepublik Deutschland,* 7th ed. (Berlin: Colloquium Verlag, 1986), 29.

60. Wilfried Röhrich, *Die Demokratie des Westdeutschen: Geschichte und politisches Klima einer Republik* (Munich: Verlag C. H. Beck, 1988), 77–78.

61. Jürgen Habermas, *Toward a Rational Society,* trans. Jeremy Shapiro (Boston: Beacon Press, 1970), 25.

62. Quoted in Baring, *Machtwechsel,* 84.

63. Ibid., 363.

64. On the shift in attitudes in the Federal Republic beginning in the late 1960s, see Ronald Inglehart, *The Silent Revolution: Changing Styles among Western Publics* (Princeton: Princeton University Press, 1977); Ronald Inglehart, "New Perspectives on Political Change," *Comparative Political Studies* 17 (1984): 485–532; David Conradt, "Changing German Political Culture," in *The Civic Culture Revisited,* ed. Gabriel Almond and Sidney Verba (Boston: Little, Brown, 1980), 212–72; and Kendall Baker, Russell Dalton, and Kai Hildebrandt, *Germany Transformed: Political Culture and the New Politics* (Cambridge, Mass.: Harvard University Press, 1981).

65. Hildebrand, *Geschichte,* 372–73.

66. Quoted in Hildebrand, *Geschichte,* 374.

67. Ibid., 399.

68. Gustav Heinemann, "Ansprache vor dem Deutschen Bundestag und dem Bundesrat in Bonn, 1 Juli 1969," in *Präsidiale Reden* (Frankfurt: Suhrkamp, 1975), 25–32.

69. Wolfgang Jäger, "Die Innenpolitik der sozial-liberalen Koalition, 1969–1974," in *Republik im Wandel, 1969–1974, Die Ära Brandt,* vol. 5/I of Karl Dietrich Bracher, Wolfgang Jäger, and Werner Link, *Geschichte der Bundesrepublik Deutschland* (Stuttgart: Deutsche Verlagsanstalt, 1986), 159.

70. Willy Brandt, "Regierungserklärung vor dem Bundestag am 28 Oktober 1969," in *Reden und Interviews,* vol. 1 (Bonn: Presse- und Informationsamt der Bundesregierung, 1971), 13–30.

71. Quoted in Jäger, "Die Innenpolitik," 25.

72. Baring, *Machtwechsel,* 251–53; Gordon Smith, *Democracy in West Germany* (New York: Holmes & Meier, 1979), 172–73.

73. Baring, *Machtwechsel,* 89.

74. Ibid., 382.

75. Michael Balfour, *West Germany: A Contemporary History* (New York: St. Martin's, 1982), 241.

76. Baring, *Machtwechsel,* 389.

77. Franz Osterroth and Dieter Schuster, *Nach dem Zweiten Weltkrieg,* vol. 3 of *Chronik der deutschen Sozialdemokratie,* 2d ed. (Berlin: Verlag J. H. W. Dietz, Nachf., 1978), 419–504.

78. Quoted in Baring, *Machtwechsel,* 358.
79. Willy Brandt and Helmut Schmidt, *Deutschland 1976—Zwei Sozialdemokraten im Gespräch* (Reinbek bei Hamburg: Rowohlt, 1976), 48; Willy Brandt, *"Wir sind nicht zu Helden geboren . . .": Ein Gespräch über Deutschland mit Birgit Kraatz* (Zurich: Diogenes Verlag, 1986), 132.
80. Baring, *Machtwechsel,* 394.
81. See Komitee für Grundrechte und Demokratie, ed., *Ohne Zweifel für den Staat* (Reinbek bei Hamburg: Rowohlt, 1982), 43; "Grundsätzliche Entscheidung des (Hamburger) Senats, 23.11.1971," in Brandt, *Die politische Treuepflicht,* 162; and Braunthal, *Political Loyalty,* 29–30.
82. See Erhard Denninger, ed., *Freiheitliche demokratische Grundordnung,* vol. 2 (Frankfurt: Suhrkamp, 1977), 518–19.
83. Brandt and Schmidt, *Deutschland 1976,* 48; see also Peter Graf Kielmansegg, "Von der Notwendigkeit und den Schwierigkeiten streitbarer Demokratie," in *Verfassungsfeinde als Beamte?* ed. Wulf Schönbohm (Munich: Günter Olzog Verlag, 1979), 52–53.
84. Sontheimer, *Die verunsicherte Republik,* 27.
85. "Demokratie und Sicherheit: Interview des Bundeskanzlers," *Bulletin,* 1972, no. 55:773; Kielmansegg, "Basic Law."
86. P. C. Mayer-Tasch, *Die Bürgerinitiativbewegung* (Reinbek bei Hamburg: Rowohlt, 1976), 13–15; Jürgen Habermas, ed., *Observations on "The Spiritual Situation of the Age"* (Cambridge: MIT Press, 1985).
87. See, for example, Helmut Lecheler, "Die Treuepflicht des Beamten— Leerformel oder Zentrum der Beamtenpflichten?" *Zeitschrift für Beamtenrecht,* 1972, no. 8:232; Hönes, "Beamte," 224; Matz, "Extremisten," 468; Hans-Walter Scheerbarth and Heinz Höffken, *Beamtenrecht: Lehr- und Handbuch,* 3d ed. (Siegburg: Verlag Reckinger, 1979), 113; Stern, *Zur Verfassungstreue,* 20; Hans-Dietrich Weiss, "Die Verfassungstreuepflicht des Beamten im Spiegel der Rechtssprechung—Eine Dokumentation zum 'Radikalen-Problem,' " *Zeitschrift für Beamtenrecht,* 1974, no. 3:81; Otthein Rammstedt, "Zur Vermessung des Beamten," *Frankfurter Hefte,* 1975, no. 10:5; Kriele, "Der rechtlichen Spielraum," 1; Borgs-Maciejewski, "Radikale im öffentlichen Dienst," 20–21; and Erich Heimeshoff, "Bemerkungen zur Extremisten-Problematik," *Deutsche Richterzeitung,* 1979, no. 3:81.
88. See, for example, Jürgen Habermas, " 'Verteufelung kritischen Denkens'—Briefwechsel zwischen Kurt Sontheimer und Jürgen Habermas," *Süddeutsche Zeitung,* 26–27 November 1977; Helmut Ridder, " 'Berufsverbot'? Nein, Demokratieverbot," *Das Argument,* 1975, no. 7–8:581; Helmut Krüger, "Verzicht auf die Gewähr der Verfassungstreue?" *Zeitschrift für Rechtspolitik,* 1978, no. 12:274; Peter Frisch, *Extremistenbeschluß* (Opladen: Heggen-Verlag, 1975), 79–80; and Richard Löwenthal, "Wer ist ein Verfassungsfeind?" *Die Zeit,* 23 June 1972.
89. See, for example, Bernhard Blanke, " 'Staatsräson' und demokratischen Rechtsstaat," *Leviathan,* 1975, no. 2:154; Ernst Martin, "Extremistenbeschluß und demokratische Verfassung," *Aus Politik und Zeitgeschichte: Beilage zur*

Wochenzeitung Das Parlament, 1973, no. B50/73:8–12; Kurt Frederking, "Das außerdienstliche Verhalten des Beamten aus beamtenrechtlicher Sicht," *Die Polizei,* 1980, no. 2:61; Wulf Damkowski, "Radikale im öffentlichen Dienst," *Recht im Amt,* 1976, no. 1:6; Karl-Otto Konow, "Grenzen der schriftstellerischen Betätigung der Beamten," *Zeitschrift für Beamtenrecht,* 1972, no. 1:49; Georg Berner, " 'Radikalenerlaß' und Rechtssprechung," *Politische Studien,* 1977, no. 233:290; Johannes Gerlach, *Radikalenfrage und Privatrecht: Zur politischen Freiheit in der Gesellschaft* (Tübingen: J. C. B. Mohr, 1978), 25–26; Bulla, "Lehre," 351; and Stern, *Zur Verfassungstreue,* 19.

90. *Entscheidungen des Bundesverfassungsgerichts,* 39:350–51, 366–67.

91. See, for example, Hans Koschnick, *Der Abschied vom Extremistenbeschluß* (Bonn: Verlag Neuer Gesellschaft, 1979); and *24. Bundesparteitag der Christlich Demokratischen Union Deutschlands, Niederschrift, Hannover, 24.– 26. Mai 1976* (Bonn: Christlich Demokratischen Union Deutschlands, 1976), 204–5.

92. See, for example, Klaus-Henning Rosen, "Ärgernis und Mahnung: Seit Zehn Jahren wirkt der Ministerpräsidentenbeschluß," *Sozialdemokratischen Pressedienst* 37 (26 January 1982): 5; and "Beschluß E 12, Verfassungstreue im öffentlichen Dienst," in *27. Bundesparteitag der Christlich Demokratischen Union Deutschlands, Niederschrift, Kiel, 25.–27 März 1979* (Bonn: Christlich Demokratischen Union Deutschlands, 1979).

93. See, for example, "No. 42: Protokoll über die Sitzung des Parteivorstandes am 29. Mai 1978," in *Sitzungen des Parteivorstandes Protokolle, 1978* [SPD] (Bonn: Friedrich Ebert Stiftung, 1978), 6–7; and Hans Klein, " 'Eine verantwortungslose Politik,' 138. Sitzung des 8. Bundestages am 15. Februar 1979," *Das Parlament,* 24 February 1979.

94. See, for example, Karl Liedtke, *Informationen der Sozialdemokratischen Bundestagsfraktion,* 1979, no. 184:1; and *26. Bundesparteitag der Christlich Demokratischen Union Deutschlands, Niederschrift, Ludwigshafen, 23.–25. Oktober 1978* (Bonn: Christlich Demokratischen Union Deutschlands, 1978), 72.

95. See "Die GEW will Extremisten den Zugang zum Staatsdienst öffnen," *Frankfurter Allgemeine Zeitung,* 14 October 1978.

96. Brandt, *"Wir sind nicht . . . ,"* 131–32.

97. Brandt and Schmidt, *Deutschland 1976,* 49–50.

98. Braunthal, *Political Loyalty,* 93–137.

99. Walter Leisner, "Verfassungsreform des öffentlichen Dienstrechts?" *Aus Politik und Zeitgeschichte: Beilage zur Wochenzeitung Das Parlament,* 1991, no. B49:33; Franz Kroppenstedt, "Der öffentliche Dienst der Zukunft," *Zeitschrift für Beamtenrecht,* 1990, no. 7:198.

100. Bundesministerium für innerdeutsche Beziehungen, ed., *Texte zur Deutschlandpolitik, Reihe III/Band 8b—1990* (Bonn: Deutscher Bundesverlag, 1991), 7–17.

101. Gregg O. Kvistad, "Accommodation or 'Cleansing': Germany's State Employees from the Old Regime," *West European Politics* 17 (1994): 65–69.

102. "Der Bundesminister des Innern teilt mit: 'Ansprache von Staats-

sekretär Franz Kroppenstedt,' " 8 January 1991, mimeo; *Deutschland-Union-Dienst* 43 (3 August 1989).
103. *DDP,* no. 200 (3 December 1991).
104. *Presseservice der SPD,* no. 656/89 (18 October 1989).
105. "Hetzjagd auf unbescholtene Genossen," *Süddeutsche Zeitung,* 10 November 1990.
106. Katzenstein, *Policy and Politics,* 3–82.
107. Gunter Hofmann and Werner A. Perger, eds., *Die Kontroverse: Weizsäckers Parteienkritik in der Diskussion* (Frankfurt am Main: Eichborn, 1992); Hermann Schmitt and Sören Holmberg, "Political Parties in Decline?" in *Citizens and the State,* ed. Hans-Dieter Klingemann and Dieter Fuchs (Oxford: Oxford University Press, 1995), 95–133.

Building Democracy: Judicial Review and the German *Rechtsstaat*

Donald P. Kommers

In 1949 German leaders in the three western zones of occupation embarked upon a bold venture in constitutional engineering. With the adoption of the Basic Law they created a new *Rechtsstaat,* which in time would blossom into one of the world's most durable and stable democracies. Whether German democracy owes its impressive durability and stability to constitutional engineering or to the prosperity of Germany's postwar social economy is a question likely to remain unresolved. Weimar's constitution might well have survived under the social and economic conditions of the Federal Republic of Germany (FRG), much as the Basic Law might have failed under the political and socioeconomic realities of the Weimar Republic.

Yet constitutional engineering, as this essay demonstrates, does matter. Judicial review in particular has functioned much as the Basic Law's founders intended it to operate. Indeed, the institution of judicial review was an essential component of the freshly minted *Rechtsstaat.* The purpose of this essay is to measure the influence of this institution upon the development of German democracy, to examine its capacity to deal with crucial issues such as abortion, asylum, and citizenship in the light of the democratic values the Federal Constitutional Court has sought to define and vindicate, and finally to assess the role that constitutional values and institutional structures play in explaining the successes and difficulties associated with the resolution of these issues. The main thesis of this chapter is that the tradition of the *Rechtsstaat* has been maintained under the Basic Law, but at the same time has been transformed in the light of Germany's modern representative democracy.

I. Background

In rebuilding their political system, the founders of the Federal Republic resurrected the tradition of the German *Rechtsstaat* but adapted it to the new constitutionalism of the Basic Law. In restoring the *Rechtsstaat,* the authors of the Basic Law recalled its theory and practice under the constitutions of 1871 and 1919. The traditional *Rechtsstaat,* a concept with no exact equivalent in Anglo-American law,[1] sprang from the womb of early-nineteenth-century German liberalism. (Loosely translated as "law state," or even more freely as a "state based on the rule of law," the *Rechtsstaat* is more partial toward the state than its understanding in Anglo-American law.) Associated at first with a state based on reason, it evolved later into a form of juridical positivism crowned by the supremacy of statutory law (*Gesetz*).[2] So conceived, the *Rechtsstaat* was designed to protect the liberty and natural equality of all citizens by means of fixed and general laws. In its distinctive German incarnation it identified itself with the control of administrative power manifested institutionally by a system of administrative courts separated from the regular judiciary and entrusted with the faithful execution of law as written down in formal statutes.[3] In short, the *Rechtsstaat* sought to limit the power of the centralized state by means of law and relied on the state to create the foundations of a civil society.

The constitutionalism of the historical *Rechtsstaat,* however, did not assume the presence of political democracy, as in England, or the practice of judicial review, as in the United States. It was perfectly compatible, for example, with the monarchical conservatism of the Bismarckian Constitution of 1871. In addition, and relatedly, as already suggested, statutes (*Gesetze*) did not take precedence over the constitution (*Verfassung*). Under the Weimar Constitution of 1919, the *Rechtsstaat* did finally come to rest in a parliamentary democracy founded on the principle of popular sovereignty. Yet German constitutional scholars such as Richard Thoma and Gerhard Anschütz theorized popular sovereignty in terms of a procedural democracy based on the rule of law.

In the prevailing jurisprudence of Anschütz and Thoma, democracy was quintessentially a *method* for translating the popular will into law. Their approach to law, like that of democracy, was purely formal (i.e., positivist). If truly representative of the popular will and obedient to the formalities of the legislative process, parliament could claim that its laws embodied the will of the state. The duty of courts was to carry out these laws as written; judges were not permitted to submit the content of law to the judgment of suprapositive ethical norms.[4] In this radically democratic view of the Weimar Constitution, no institution save parliament itself, in the form of yet another duly enacted law, could gainsay the state's will as reflected in law. In short, the *Rechtsstaat* controlled the constitutional state, which is to say that constitutionalism remained subordinate to the Constitution's democratic elements.

II. The Basic Law and Judicial Review

The Basic Law, by contrast, differs radically from the Weimar Constitution.[5] First, the Constitution is the supreme law of the land, just as its bill of rights represents paramount law.[6] Second, the Basic Law in its most essential parts is unamendable, thus freezing these parts in perpetuity so long as the Federal Republic of Germany (FRG) shall last.[7] Finally, the Basic Law is a value-oriented constitution, embracing an ensemble of rights and norms applicable and enforceable throughout the entire legal order, one that establishes human dignity as its master value and makes it the state's duty to respect and protect it at all times.[8]

In addition to these features of supremacy, permanence, and normativity, the Basic Law creates a "democratic and social federal state" bound by the "constitutional order" and subject to both "law *and justice*" (emphasis added).[9] These words appear as *Gesetz* and *Recht* in Article 20 (3), indicating the extent to which the transition from 1919 (Weimar Constitution) to 1949 (Bonn Constitution) involved both continuity and change. *Gesetz,* which refers to statutes, represents the will of the people (i.e., the democratic will), whereas *Recht* suggests a normative "law state" that imposes limits on the will of the majority. As with the 1919 Constitution, the Basic Law weds the liberal *Rechtsstaat* to the social welfare state (*Sozialstaat*), but it transposes the traditional "law state" into a "just state." Democracy, too, changes color under the Basic Law. It would now be a material — not a formal — democracy bound by the values of the constitutional order and committed to the militant defense of the "free democratic basic order."[10] Thus the restored *Rechtsstaat* would be a constitutional democracy in which the rival principles of democracy and constitutionalism would lock themselves into a new and uneasy embrace, with the Basic Law's constitutionalist blades poised to cut short the reach of its democratic shoots.

The crowning achievement of this new system of constitutional justice — and its boldest institutional innovation — is the Federal Constitutional Court. Armed with extensive authority to decide constitutional disputes among levels and branches of government and to hear the constitutional complaints of ordinary citizens, the Court proceeded to shape the content and character of German public life, evolving in time into one of the world's most powerful and respected constitutional tribunals. This is not the place for any full description of the Court's role in Germany's governmental system.[11] It is sufficient to suggest that the Court's influence has been felt in nearly every sphere of German law and politics. It has reviewed the constitutionality of laws covering subjects ranging from foreign policy to university admission standards, touching areas of life and politics over which the United States Supreme Court exercises no comparable guardianship.[12]

The interesting question posed by this reality is why the Constitutional Court itself has evolved into the durable and stable institution it has become within the framework of German politics. However controversial some of its decisions have been, the Court's legitimacy is accepted by all of Germany's major political actors, and public opinion polls continue to show, as they have throughout the life of the Federal Republic, that German citizens exhibit more confidence in this tribunal than in any other public or private institution. With the possible exception of the recent Bavarian Crucifix Case,[13] the Court's decisions have met with a degree of compliance and support across the political spectrum that must be the envy of constitutional tribunals in other countries.

This chapter will suggest that the legal culture of the traditional *Rechtsstaat,* with its heavy emphasis on legality—construed here as a highly formalized way of presenting and deciding legal or constitutional disputes—together with the underdeveloped political culture of the German people, at least in the Federal Republic's first two decades, accounts, at least in part, for the impact and acceptance of judicial review in Germany. By the same token, the following discussion will show that the Constitutional Court has done its part in creating a constitutional culture that draws the Basic Law into almost every major political controversy in and out of parliament. As the daily reading of any major German newspaper will show, legislators in Bonn can hardly proceed with their work without casting their eyes in the direction of Karlsruhe, where the Court resides. That the Basic Law has become such a vital part of political debate in Germany is one measure of the extent to which the *Rechtsstaat* has legalized Germany's political culture.

III. The Constitutional Court and Political Democracy

As the principal guardian of the Basic Law, the Court has played an enormously important role in defining the scope and limits of political democracy. That role includes policing the operation of the electoral system, securing the parliamentary rights of minor parties, laying down rules for the admission of parties into legislative bodies, limiting the amount and use of public funds in electoral campaigns, and declaring — or refusing to declare — political parties unconstitutional. In each of these areas, the Constitutional Court has produced a vibrant, copious, and controversial jurisprudence.

Parliamentary Representation

Almost every phase of the electoral system and parliamentary politics has been subject to judicial review in furtherance of the democratic values that the Constitutional Court has found in the Basic Law.[14] Two articles of the Basic Law figure prominently in most of the constitutional cases discussed in this and the next subsection on party democracy. Article 21, in contrast to the Weimar Constitution, recognizes parties as important agencies of political representation and requires them to be organized on "democratic principles"; Article 38 provides that members of parliament be freely chosen in "direct and equal" elections, and that they represent the "people," remain "unbound by any instructions," and act only in accord with "their conscience." These two provisions embrace clashing visions of political representation, and many of the judicial decisions mentioned below can be seen as an effort to reconcile the two visions.

Constitutional cases illustrative of these principles dictated higher salaries for legislative representatives, imposed severe limits on the ability of the executive to dissolve parliament, and invalidated a parliamentary ruling depriving a representative unaffiliated with a political party of his speaking rights on the floor of the Bundestag.[15] In a series of cases, the Court has also vindicated the legislative rights of minority parliamentary parties outside regnant governing coalitions,[16] affirming in one important case the right of such parties to form committees to investigate charges against the incumbent government, largely on the theory that in modern parliamentary democracies the principle of separation of powers manifests itself most effectively not in the checks and balances between governmental units but in the duty of opposition parties to confront the dominant coalition in control of both legislature and executive.[17] In addition, the Court has insisted on virtual mathematical equality in the apportionment of legislative districts.[18]

Together with insisting on equally populated single-member districts, the Court has placed the imprimatur of its approval on proportional representation (PR),[19] coming close to suggesting, although not as yet mandating, the adoption of PR as necessary constitutionally if political parties are *effectively* to represent all the people. Yet the Court has also sustained the validity of the 5 percent rule—the rule conditioning a party's entry into a parliamentary body on winning 5 percent of the total vote—a constant feature of German electoral law since 1949. In the interest of stable parliamentary government as well as *effective* political representation, the Court has upheld the application of the 5 percent rule to local, national, and European elections.[20] But the Court has also served notice that it will tolerate no higher barrier than 5 percent.[21]

The 5 percent rule was struck down only within the context of reunification politics. The National Unity Election Case arose when several minor parties—the far-right Republicans, the Greens, and the Party of Democratic Socialism (PDS) (East Germany's old communist Socialist Unity Party [SED])—contested the application of the 5 percent rule to the first all-German election in 1990, and won. The case is important not only because it represents still another effort to protect minor parties, but also because in this instance the Court would act as a bridge between the two parts of Germany, advancing a constitutionalism of reconciliation and serving as a force for political integration in the nation as a whole.[22] The Court ruled that political parties in the eastern *Länder* would be severely handicapped if the normal rule were to apply nationwide. Accordingly, and on the Court's recommendation, the 5 percent clause in this first all-German election would apply separately in east and west, thus enabling the PDS and the eastern Greens to win representation, as they did, in the new all-German parliament. It would be difficult to overestimate the impact of the Court's decision. By clearing the 5 percent barrier in the old GDR, the PDS and the eastern Greens acquired a national platform on which to increase their visibility, to highlight issues that might otherwise have remained dormant, and to set the stage for their electoral victories in 1994, this time under the 5 percent rule as applied to all of Germany.[23]

In the court's vision of democracy, there is a direct and immediate relationship between direct elections, parliamentary representation, and the law state. Electoral majorities must of course observe the limits imposed on majority rule by the Basic Law, but valid law—and its administration—must also flow, directly and inexorably, from the will of the majority as expressed in parliamentary elections. Recently, for example, in the aftermath of a titanic constitutional controversy that drew the entire country into its vortex, the Federal Constitutional Court declared that any deployment of German military forces outside of NATO must be approved by a parliamentary majority if the principle of popular sovereignty on which the Basic Law is based is to be preserved.[24] And yet, early on in the FRG's history, the Court invalidated state and local advisory referenda on whether Germany should arm itself with atomic weapons. The real meaning of the Atomic Weapons Case, however, resides in its subtext, which is that national policy, like the popular will, is to be determined *indirectly* through parliament and not directly by means of plebiscitary institutions.[25]

The Maastricht and Foreign Voting Cases, both highly controversial, constitute the most recent decisions on the meaning of popular democracy. European leaders rejoiced when the Court upheld the constitutionality of the Maastricht Treaty, but what the Court had to say about the meaning of national sovereignty and the voting rights of German citizens set off alarm bells well beyond Germany's borders.[26] For present purposes the case may be reduced to these propositions: Article 38 (1) confers on German citizens the right to vote for members of the Bundestag; in the act of voting, German citizens participate in the exercise of "public authority," which under the terms of Article 20 "emanates from the people"; the people are therefore the sole source of democratic legitimacy; the Bundestag has only so much power as the people give to it; and thus the "sovereign power" vested in Germany's parliament may not be transferred to an international organization unless there is a clear line of democratic legitimation running from the people to the Bundestag and from the Bundestag to the European parliament. The Court found that in its current development, the European Union (EU) satisfies the *minimal* conditions of democratic legitimation, but warned that in the future, as the EU's authority expands, it will have to take steps to remove its democratic deficit.[27] In this bold assertion of authority, the Court not only circumscribed the power of the national legislature to transfer its powers, but went on to limit the power of an international organization by the standards of Germany's Basic Law.

In the current version of the *Rechtsstaat,* however, the "people" within the meaning of Articles 20 (2) and 28 (2) do not include legally resident aliens for purposes of voting in county and local elections. Accordingly, the Foreign Voting Cases invalidated *Land* and municipal statutes allowing resident aliens the right to vote in such elections.[28] The people (*das Volk*), said the Court, means the *German* people, for only these people are capable of "legitimating democratic state authority." In brief, the Basic Law creates a particular body politic, one composed of German *citizens,* and it is only from this body politic that all state authority emanates.[29] As we shall see later on, these decisions limit the ability of the *Rechtsstaat* to deal effectively — and perhaps fairly — with the twin problems of asylum and citizenship.

The Neutral State versus the Party State

In 1977, in the highly controverted Official Propaganda Case, the Constitutional Court put more gloss on its definition of political democracy. Over the vigorous dissent of Justice Joachim Rottmann, the Court ruled that an incumbent coalition government — in this case, a coalition consisting of the Social Democratic Party (SPD) and the Free Democratic Party (FDP) — could not validly use public funds to advertise its accomplishments during the course of an election campaign without undermining the "free self-determination" of all voters "to participate with equal rights" in the process of shaping the popular will. The state must remain neutral, said the Court, in the interest of protecting the "dignity and freedom" of all citizens so that the political process can be oriented toward "social justice" and the "common good."[30] Justice Rottmann, in dissent, charged the majority with undermining the "privileged position" that the Court itself has bestowed on political parties within the meaning of Article 21.[31]

Justice Rottmann was referring to a long string of judicial cases dealing with the role of political parties in Germany's restored *Rechtsstaat*. With its interpretation of Article 21 (1), which recognizes the role of political parties in shaping "the political will of the people," the Court mounted a revolution in German constitutional theory. The traditional German *Rechtsstaat* insisted on a strict separation between state and society; the latter was a source of fragmentation and division; the state, by contrast, represented a higher unity. Staffed by impartial public servants committed to the general interest, it alone had the capacity to govern creatively within the context of ordered liberty. Article 21 as interpreted stands this theory on its head. Now parties would participate in the process of governance, but under the terms of Article 21 such parties must be democratic in both structure and ideology and "publicly account for the sources of their funds."

Out of this sparse language the Constitutional Court transformed the *Rechtsstaat* into a *Parteienstaat* (party state), representing "a unique synthesis of Western parliamentarism and the German state tradition."[32] In the Court's idealized conception of democracy, the purpose of elections is to determine the will of the people and then to translate that will into public policy. But if the popular will is to be discerned in its pristine purity, the state must retain its neutrality during elections, as the Official Propaganda Case declared. By the same token, Article 38 (1) envisions legislators as representatives of the "whole people" subject only to their "conscience" and "unbounded by instructions of any kind." On the other hand, under the judicially imposed logic of Article 21, modern mass democracies cannot do without political parties; they are essential for mobilizing voters and expressing the popular will. When therefore parties engage in electoral campaigns, they function as "integral units of the constitutional state." In short, according to an early judicial ruling, political parties are "constitutional organs." As such, they are empowered, along with other official organs of the state, to vindicate their institutional rights before the Constitutional Court.[33]

The party-funding cases represent the most striking effort to determine the shape of the *Parteienstaat*. These cases bear witness once again to the power and influence of judicial doctrine. They have triggered a process of interplay between law and politics that resembles the thrust and riposte of a fencing match. The narrative begins in 1958, when the Court struck down a federal law permitting citizens and corporations to deduct from their taxable income a portion of their donations to political parties.[34] According to the Court, this practice violated the equality rights of political parties unable to rely on large donors for their funding. Recognizing the financial plight of political parties and their need for funds, the Court suggested in its opinion that the state might constitutionally fund political parties as a means of insuring effective competition among them and diminishing their reliance on special interests.

The Bundestag took the hint and passed the Party Finance Act of 1959. The act authorized the public funding of parties, which by 1964 reached the astronomical sum of DM 38 million—equal to one German mark per voter. This sum was divided among the parties in the Bundestag proportionate to the number of parliamentary seats won. In 1966, the Court's Second Senate invalidated this law because it limited funding to the parliamentary parties. In the interest of equality, ruled the Court, minor parties failing to win 5 percent of the national vote are also entitled to share in the funding. In addition, the Court ruled that Article 21 forbids the *general* funding of political parties. State funds may only be used, declared the Court, to defray the expenses incurred by the parties during an election campaign, for it is only during this time that the parties function as constitutional organs of the state.[35]

The Party Finance Case of 1966 represented a compromise between traditional and modern views of the relationship between parties and the state. In the ideal *Parteienstaat,* according to the modern view, parties must be not only competitive but also unified, program-oriented organizations of active citizens capable of educating the electorate and shaping the popular will. The *Parteienstaat* is the opposite of the *Verbändestaat,* a system in which special interests dominate the political process and undermine majority rule. Thus parties must be liberated from these interests so that they accurately reflect the popular will, and the state must do the liberating by way of public funding. The older view is that parties are voluntary associations with roots in society; they are independent of the state. Here one sees the influence of Article 38 (1), which obligates legislators who now as representatives of the *state* must reflect the interests of the "whole people." The state is an independent entity devoted to the public interest, one that does not depend on parties for its articulation or implementation.

The 1966 decision also prompted the Bundestag, at long last, to pass the Political Parties Act of 1967,[36] a comprehensive statute that codified many of the rulings on political parties and elections laid down by the Court over the years. The act generated another round of litigation as various minor parties challenged nearly all of its funding provisions. In an important ruling, the Court invalidated statutory provisions limiting funding eligibility to parties securing at least 2.5 percent of the total vote. In holding that this limit violated the principle of equality (*Chancengleichheit*) as well as that of equal suffrage under Article 38 (1), the Court instructed the legislature to lower the eligibility figure to 0.5 percent of the vote. Acting as a virtual legislative body, the Court also established the threshold above which corporations would be required to disclose their financial gifts to political parties. In still another leading case, the Court for the first time affirmed the right of an independent candidate to receive funding.[37] The tension here between Articles 21 and 38 was very clear, and it reflected a deeper conflict between competing conceptions of democracy. In this case, the logic of the *Parteienstaat* had to be subordinated to the *independence* — that is, a legislator unbound by instructions — of candidates running in single-member constituencies.

The parliamentary-judicial scuffle continued for another 16 years as the Bundestag tightened the definition of political parties, increased steadily the public funding of parties — about 500 million marks in 1990 — and amended the tax laws to maximize party income from private sources, and all this against the backdrop of major scandals in party finance and dwindling party membership.[38] Once again the Court proceeded to strike down provisions limiting the financing of small parties, as well as tax-deductible donations deemed to violate the principle of equality.[39] Through it all, the Court adhered to its seminal 1966 ruling that permitted state funding of electoral campaigning but not of general party activity, even as the justices began to reveal signs of uneasiness over the feasibility of this distinction.

In the face of judicial admonitions, the Bundestag amended the Parties Act for the fifth time in 1988, now to increase state subsidies still again, to relax certain disclosure rules, and to allow generous tax deductions to individuals and couples who donate to the parties. In addition, and for the benefit of smaller parties, the Bundestag established a flat base payment (*Sockelbetrag*) for parties receiving at least 2 percent of all second-ballot votes, a reform that would place millions of marks in the hands of certain minor parties, encouraging their proliferation. The Greens, as often before in these cases, challenged the constitutionality of these amendments. On 9 April 1992, the Court struck down all of them, and in a rare reversal of one of its precedents, unanimously rejected the core of its 1966 decision — that is, the distinction between general party expenditures and expenditures incurred during election campaigns. From now on, the Court declared, state funding may not exceed the total amount raised by the parties themselves, and in its parting shot the Court directed the Bundestag to change the Parties Act accordingly by January of 1993.[40] Once again, the Bundestag obediently complied.

The classic tension between state and society referred to earlier surfaced again in the 1992 case. After the 1990 election the parties received nearly 500 million marks in state funds. The Court seemed worried that the established parties were becoming too entrenched and comfortable, reinforcing their internal bureaucracies at the state's expense, thus widening the distance between themselves and their voters. Now *Staatsfreiheit* — that is, freedom *from* the state, as opposed to private interest groups — was being emphasized as the Court sought to impose a constitutional policy that would send the parties back into society, where they would have to depend much more than in the past upon their own resources and fund-raising capabilities.

IV. Abortion, Citizenship, and Asylum

In turning to the issues of abortion and citizenship, we find that the Court binds itself once again to a jurisprudence of values as well as to the constitutionalism of the *German state people,* with the curious result that the Court adheres to a constitutionalism of integration with respect to the former but not to the latter. Judicial review, however, plays a more crucial role in determining abortion policy. In the Constitutional Court's understanding of the Basic Law, all abortion laws must be reviewed with strict scrutiny to ensure that they reflect and foster the immutable value of human dignity. Less clear is how the Court would deal with a new citizenship law given its understanding of the term "people" within the meaning of the Basic Law. The problem facing judicial interpreters is that they confront a constitutional text that enshrines the values of both universalism and particularism.

Abortion

The German abortion decisions of 1975 and 1993 were extraordinary assertions of judicial power not unlike the 1973 and 1992 decisions of the United States Supreme Court.[41] On 18 June 1974, West Germany's parliament, controlled by an SPD-FDP coalition, enacted a liberalized abortion statute that decriminalized abortion during the first trimester of pregnancy if performed by a physician with the consent of the pregnant woman. The law required the woman to undergo compulsory counseling before procuring an abortion, but it empowered her to make the final decision within the 12-week period. Christian Democratic members of the Bundestag and the governments of three *Länder* under Christian Democratic control immediately challenged the law's constitutionality.[42]

In one of its most notable decisions, the Court invalidated the new law, holding that fetal life constitutes human "life" within the meaning of the Basic Law (Article 2 [2]), that the life of the fetus preempts the woman's right to personal self-determination under Article 2 (1), and that the state is obligated, at every stage of pregnancy,[43] to defend and protect the life of the unborn fetus. Yet, as if to parry its own thrust, the Court held that the constitutional "right to life" does not always triumph over the woman's constitutional right to self-fulfillment. Both rights, said the Court in a 6–2 decision, must be interpreted in the light of the *value* of human dignity that the state is also obligated to protect and defend under Article 1 (1).

Accordingly, even while describing an abortion as "an act of killing" — and the law must make this reality unambiguously clear — the Court held that a woman could end her pregnancy in the presence of a duly certified medical, genetic, or criminological indication for which under the invalidated statute a woman was permitted to procure an abortion in the second trimester. The Court itself added "extreme social hardship" to this list of conditions under which an abortion would remain unpunished. Apart from these exceptions to the general rule that favors the life of the fetus over the contrary wishes of the pregnant woman, the Court directed parliament to reinstate the criminal penalty for abortion and mandated the adoption of counseling procedures and other measures designed to discourage women from having abortions, especially for "social" reasons. Parliament complied, and the new law, adopted in response to the Court's directives, remained unchanged until reunification.

On the day of German unity, 18 million East Germans found themselves subject to the FRG's legal order, including the Basic Law. Abortion policy, however, was a bone of contention between GDR and FRG leaders. The protection of the fetus at all stages of pregnancy remained valid law in the FRG, whereas abortion on demand within the first trimester of pregnancy was permitted by law in the GDR. The unity talks might have foundered on this division had not the two sides agreed to retain their respective laws on their own territory until an all-German parliament elected in a unified Germany could work out an acceptable compromise. The agreement required a constitutional amendment specifically allowing the five new states of the old GDR to "deviate" temporarily from the provisions of the Basic Law with respect to abortion.[44] The Unification Treaty itself specified 31 December 1992 as the deadline for the adoption of an all-German abortion law.

After long and painful negotiations stretching over many months, a majority of a severely fractured Bundestag worked out a settlement that commanded the support of the SPD, FDP, and most east German Christian Democrats. Known as the Pregnancy and Family Assistance Act, the new law legalized abortion in the first trimester of pregnancy, leaving the abortion decision up to the woman after required counseling and a three-day waiting period. In addition, the new law amended sections of laws dealing with social security, medical insurance, child support, vocational training, job placement, welfare assistance, housing, and rent control, all for the purpose of producing a package of socioeconomic guarantees that would make it easier for women to carry their pregnancies to term.[45]

Christian Democratic representatives in the Bundestag, together with the Bavarian *Land* government, wasted no time in challenging the statute. In response to their petitions, the Constitutional Court enjoined the law's implementation pending a final judgment on the merits. That judgment came down 10 months later, on 28 May 1993. In a 6–2 vote on the principal issue, the Court nullified the statute and instructed the legislature to adopt a package of social legislation designed once again to discourage abortion and to protect the fetus at all stages of pregnancy. For the Court this was a complex case, torn as it was between the felt necessity of adhering to its 1975 ruling and its desire to reconcile the opposing values crying out for judicial recognition. By the same token, the Court was aware of the crucial role it could — and wished to — play in reconciling the tensions between east and west.

The principle of *Rechtsstaatlichkeit* was crucial here, and in resolving this second major abortion case, the Court reverted to time-honored principles of constitutional interpretation and to a constitutional theory that sets limits to majoritarian power. Earlier in this chapter, we spoke of the Basic Law as a unity of rights and values. In this respect, the Constitutional Court has given constitutionalism a meaning that rings as strange to American ears as it is different from the traditional German understanding of the rule of law. The most salient feature of the constitutionalism that the Court has read into the Basic Law is the theory of an "objective order of values." These values are arranged in a hierarchical order topped by the principle of human dignity. Each guaranteed right in the Basic Law also represents a corresponding value—one that reinforces and clarifies the meaning of the guaranteed right—and as a *value* it may obligate the state to create the conditions necessary for the effective exercise of the right.[46] These values are thus a part of the general legal order, constituting an objective morality that social and political reality must mirror.[47]

The Constitutional Court has conceptualized the Basic Law as a "logical-teleological entity,"[48] from whence the notion of an objective value order has been derived. The unified structure of principles and values represented by the Basic Law means that each principle and each value must be informed by related and competing principles and values and interpreted in the light of the Constitution as a whole. The concept of a constitution as a structural unity has also given birth to the interpretive principle of "practical concordance" (*praktische Konkordanz*), according to which constitutionally protected values and rights must be harmonized with one another in the event of their conflict. One may not be realized at the expense of the other; both are to be preserved in creative tension with one another. Or, in German constitutional parlance, the principle of the constitution's unity requires that the two values be "optimized" to the fullest extent possible.[49] To sacrifice a value or a right in the interest of the competing value or right would undermine the Constitution's unity.

These interpretive principles informed the abortion decision of 1993; the core of the decision may be summarized as follows: In the order of values laid down by the Basic Law, human dignity is paramount, and that dignity indwells in all human life. Unborn life is human life and thus worthy of the protection that respect for human dignity requires. Abortion is a fundamental wrong at any stage of pregnancy, and the law must reflect the reality of this wrong. To legalize abortion is therefore unconstitutional. Moreover, the Basic Law constitutionally requires parliament to enact a law that declares abortion illegal as a general principle. The state may legalize abortion only for serious reasons specified by law. Finally, the legal system as a whole, informed as it is by the *Sozialstaat* principle, must statutorily provide for a social environment conducive to the protection of unborn life.

The foregoing propositions constitute the core of the 1975 case, a core rooted in the universal principle of human dignity. The 1993 Court, staffed by justices none of whom participated in the first case, obviously felt constrained by the earlier case, much as the United States Supreme Court felt constrained in 1992 to sustain the essential core of *Roe* v. *Wade*. In the United States, human dignity — to the extent that dignitarian arguments are present — is understood to limit the role of the state. American constitutionalism is *rights*-oriented. German constitutionalism, by contrast, is often described as *value*-oriented, and despite the vigorous judicial protection of individual rights under the Basic Law, the logic of German constitutionalism may require that in a particular instance the right give way to the value.

Yet to speak of the triumph of one value or right over the other is to misunderstand the nature of Germany's constitutional *Rechtsstaat*. The principles of proportionality and balance are at the heart of German constitutionalism. German constitutional scholars tell us incessantly, as does the Court, that one of the functions of the Basic Law is the integration of society around a common core of shared values.[50] From this perspective, as German constitutionalists understand it, the object of constitutional adjudication, as already suggested, is to optimize competing rights and values to the extent possible in the light of the universal principle of human dignity. Accordingly, in the 1993 case, the pregnant woman's right to physical inviolability and self-determination under Article 2 (2) of the Basic Law could not be ignored. And so, in a major departure from its 1975 ruling, the Court held that while the state is required to condemn abortion as illegal — except for those instances where an abortion may be justified for serious reasons specified by law — the illegal act of abortion need not be punished in the first trimester of pregnancy so long as the state adopts protective measures proportionate to the value of unborn life under the Basic Law.

It might be suggested that in the 1993 case, the Constitutional Court yielded to a jurisprudence of pure pragmatism. There seems to be no doubt that the Court struggled to accommodate the interests of both east and west Germany. By requiring the *Rechtsstaat* to adopt measures designed to discourage women from having abortions, the Court bowed to certain western interests; in holding that first-trimester abortions need not be punished, it conceded points to eastern interests. But the Court was also balancing and, in its self-understanding of the function of judicial review, optimizing competing values. Whether it succeeded or not, the Court tried to build a bridge between people of opposing views rather than handing total victory to one side. In this way, the Court sought to honor the competing values on both sides of the abortion debate.

Still, the 1993 decision is one manifestation of Germany's highly legalized political culture. In directing the state to adopt prolife counseling, to amend laws in such a way that women would not lose their jobs or suffer other disabilities by giving birth to their children, to criminalize third-party efforts to persuade women to have abortions, and to ban abortion under state-supported medical insurance programs and at the same time to insist that state welfare funds be used to pay for abortions that poor women after counseling insist on having in the first trimester, the Court left very little to chance — or politics. What is remarkable about the German political debate over abortion is that all the mainstream parties responsible for the passage of the law agreed that the state has a duty under the Basic Law to protect the fetus at all stages of pregnancy. Court and parliament, however, disagreed over the means to this end.

Asylum and Citizenship

Asylum and citizenship have been issues of major public importance in Germany — asylum because nearly a million persons fleeing from their native lands sought refuge in Germany between 1988 and 1993; citizenship because millions of foreign residents who have lived in Germany for decades have been denied rights enjoyed by citizens. The problems were — and are — both political and constitutional and stem in part from the meaning historically attached to the concept of the *German* people.[51]

Until 1993, the Basic Law granted the right to asylum to "persons persecuted on political grounds." Article 16 (2) was a powerful expression of Germany's political morality in the light of the nation's past. Under this article, together with its statutory supports, any person claiming asylum on the ground of a well-founded fear of political persecution was entitled to have that claim adjudicated, during which time the person claiming the right to asylum would be entitled to free housing and other benefits under German law. This is not the place to describe the detailed and complicated procedures for handling asylum claims. It suffices to remark that in the event of a denial of the claim, the asylum seeker had the right of appeal to the administrative courts and ultimately to the Federal Constitutional Court, adjudicative procedures that often took months, even years, to exhaust, thus placing a heavy strain on Germany's social welfare system, not to mention the xenophobia that the presence of these people was beginning to cause in certain native quarters.

Against this background and after months of debate, the crisis, such as it was, ended with an amendment to the Basic Law. The new Article

16a retained the general right to political asylum but rendered this right unavailable if an alien entered Germany from a member state of the European Union or arrived by land through neighboring countries designated by statute as safe third states in which there is no justified fear of political persecution. The "third-state" clause forces aliens to apply for asylum in designated safe countries through which they must pass to reach Germany; if they fail to seek asylum in these countries, they forfeit their right to apply for asylum in Germany and thus can be summarily turned back at the border or at an international German airport. In addition, paragraph 3 of Article 16a authorized parliament, after examining all reliable sources of information, to identify and specify "safe states of origin," with the consequence that the courts are bound by such legislative determinations unless an asylum seeker is able satisfactorily to rebut the presumption that he or she does not face political persecution or degrading treatment in that person's home country. Article 16a (4), finally, substantially curtails the power of administrative courts over deportation proceedings. They may suspend an order terminating an asylum claim only where "serious doubt exists as to the legality of the measure." While the amendment appeared to have had its intended political effect, having rendered Germany far less hospitable to asylum seekers than before, the constitutional issues raised by paragraphs 2, 3, and 4 were serious. The constitutionality of the "third-country" clause was a central issue in cases involving an Iraqi national who had come to Germany by way of Athens and an Iranian national who had traveled from Hungary to Austria to Germany. Both claimants were denied asylum because they entered Germany from safe third countries.

On 14 May 1996, the Constitutional Court handed down its long-awaited consolidated decision. It unanimously sustained the constitutionality of the third-state clause if the third state has been duly found to apply the Geneva Convention on the Status of Refugees and the European Convention on Human Rights in the face of a further legislative finding that the state in question poses no threat of political persecution or degrading treatment. The Court ruled further that a person coming to Germany through a safe third state could be denied asylum and summarily deported unless the asylum seeker is able to overcome with concrete evidence the presumption that political persecution or degrading treatment does not occur in the third country.[52]

In two companion cases, however, the Court handed down divided opinions. By a 5–3 vote, the Second Senate sustained the constitutionality of Article 16a (3) and (4). In the first case, the Court sustained a deportation order returning an asylum seeker to his home country, namely, Ghana. Since Ghana was legislatively declared a "safe home country," the deportation order could be revoked only in the presence of compelling evidence to the contrary. In the second case, the Court upheld Article 16a (4), which allows the Federal Authority for Refugee Affairs to detain asylum applicants without a valid passport from safe countries of origin in an area of the airport considered extraterritorial pending a decision on whether the application is "manifestly ill-founded." Under Article 16a (4), as already noted, an administrative court may not interfere with such a finding unless there is serious doubt about the measure's validity.[53]

Finally, the Court has placed its stamp of approval on limiting the right of asylum only to persons claiming political persecution by the state.[54] Accordingly, the right of asylum does not extend to persons threatened by private violence or to persons fleeing the ravages of civil wars, or to persons seeking refuge from the perils of economic injustice. Parliament, however, is making some attempt to deal with nonpolitical refugees on humanitarian grounds. The political solution to this problem is likely to be one worked out multilaterally within the framework of the European Union.

More critical is the problem of German citizenship. As Gerald Neuman notes, "The central problem in German nationality law is the emergence of multiple generations of alien residents as a consequence of the *jus sanguinis* rule, and the resulting division of the resident population of the Federal Republic into two hereditary classes with differing sets of rights."[55] The principle of *jus sanguinis* governed the definition of German citizenship until 1993. Naturalization of immigrants was permitted under the Citizenship and Nationality Act of 1913, but citizenship was conferred entirely at the discretion of administrative officials, and then only after a compelling showing of cultural assimilation. Amendments to the Citizenship and Nationality Act in 1993 narrowed the discretion of state officials and granted certain categories of immigrants a right to become naturalized citizens, but these reforms are unlikely substantially to increase the rate of naturalization in the light of strong German resistance to both multiculturalism and a policy of dual citizenship.

Denizens need not be naturalized to enjoy the benefits of full membership in the national community. The Basic Law, however, is part of the problem; it conditions certain benefits and rights on citizenship. In addition, the Constitutional Court itself has tended to confer restricted meaning on the term "people" as used in the Basic Law. This was dramatically illustrated in the Foreign Voting Cases. The "people" subsumed in the notion of "popular sovereignty" are the people of the state (*Staatsvolk*). In linking political rights to persons "who are permanently subject to a particular sovereignty,"[56] the Court seemed legitimately concerned with the integrity of the nation-building process. But a deeper and largely unjustified fear penetrates the decision, for the Court appears to presume that loyalty to the "free democratic basic order" cannot be assumed in the absence of citizenship.

The Foreign Voting Cases continue to apply to national and state parliamentary elections and to citizens of states that are not members of the European Union. The Maastricht Treaty and a subsequent amendment to the Basic Law's Article 28 establishes the right of EU nationals to vote in county and municipal elections. But these elections are subject to the legislative control of the *Länder*. As of this writing, only Berlin and Lower Saxony have extended the right to vote to EU nationals in their local elections. Even so, confining the vote to EU nationals denies this important political right to most resident aliens. And all resident aliens, whether or not EU citizens, lack admission to national and statewide political communities.

A powerful and influential jurisprudence informs the Foreign Voting Cases. Under the prevailing theory of German statehood, as the Constitutional Court has emphasized time and again, the Basic Law did not create a new state; rather, it reorganized a partial area of the old German state; the reorganized area — the FRG — represented a continuation of the German Reich within its 1937 borders. For this reason, Article 116 of the Basic Law defines German citizenship largely in ethnocultural terms. It extends automatic citizenship to German nationals who do not live in the FRG but who lived in the German Reich as it existed on 31 December 1937, as well as to refugees or expellees of German national origin, including their spouses or descendants.[57] The original preamble reinforced this view of German nationhood; it called upon "the entire German people . . . to achieve national unity in "free self-determination."[58]

The preamble and Article 116, however, were transitory provisions that assumed the continued existence of the German people.[59] But now that the German people are together again, the way would seem clear for a definition of citizenship based on broader grounds than the principle of *jus sanguinis*. Social forces and countervailing constitutional principles, however, are changing the terms of the German citizenship debate. First, the preamble and Article 116 were designed to hold together an involuntarily separated people. Now that the German people are back together again, the way would seem clear for a definition of citizenship based on political rather than ethnic grounds. The heated debate over multiculturalism and the basis of citizenship currently taking place is a major sign of change.

Second, the issue of citizenship is being linked to the universal values of the Basic Law and particularly to the principle of human dignity.

Dignitarian arguments can be expected increasingly to inform the debate on both asylum and citizenship. The principle of "optimization," mentioned earlier in the abortion context, requires that all constitutional provisions — and indeed the entire legal order — be assessed in the light of human dignity.

Finally, whether Germany can build an integrated national community — a major goal of German constitutionalism — without extending citizenship to millions of its permanent residents seems highly problematical. The older, conventional view that Germany is not a land of immigrants is fast collapsing under the weight of the Federal Republic's immigrant population. Resident aliens account for 8.5 percent of Germany's total population, and they constitute from 15 to 25 percent of the inhabitants in major metropolitan centers. In the face of these realities, the Court may eventually recognize that the building of trust among all persons permanently resident in Germany is one of the preconditions of a viable democracy.

V. Conclusion

As this essay has tried to show, judicial review has evolved into an important aspect of the modern German *Rechtsstaat,* just as the Basic Law has functioned as a standard for the growth and development of German democracy. The creation of a vigorous and thriving culture of constitutional interpretation is one of the conditions for building and maintaining a constitutional democracy. One measure of the success of the Federal Constitutional Court has been its ability to engender public trust in itself as a legal institution and to render its decisions a major focal point of legal argumentation and political discussion in Germany. In brief, the Court has been a major factor in the creation of a constitutional culture that has served as an incubator of Germany's liberal democracy.

Constitutionalism, however, has limited the reach of Germany's democracy. The Constitutional Court has guided democracy's development along certain lines, ones that are both liberating and restrictive. For example, as we have seen, the Court has defended the rights of minor parties while curbing the expansion of the electorate. With its funding cases, it has also encouraged the development of minor parties while ratifying the 5 percent clause as a condition of entry into the legislatures of both state and nation. Similarly, it has celebrated the concept of popular sovereignty while insisting on a limited view of the German people.

In conferring such vast powers on an electorally unaccountable institution, the founders of the Basic Law created no less than a *juridical* democracy, one that has tended to judicialize almost every aspect of politics. The party funding and abortion cases dramatically illustrate the extent of judicial control over the evolution of public policy, often in a direction that some critics regard as democratically retrogressive. Again, the abortion case is paradigmatic. The control exercised here over the details even of social relationships stems in part from the Court's interpretation of the Basic Law as a constitution of values as well as rights. The constitution of rights has helped to promote political change, but the constitution of values has often favored stability over change, a balance that at least in the beginning seemed appropriate to the culture of the law state and the apoliticism of the German people. For the Germans, constitutional stability was no less important than monetary stability. They sought both by creating institutions—the Federal Constitutional Court and the Bundesbank—largely removed from popular control.

In the last 45 years, the Constitutional Court has evolved into a durable legal institution of the German *Rechtsstaat* even as the civil and political culture has evolved into one of the most democratic in the Western world. For this, too, the Court can take some credit, even as it blunts the full development and blossoming of democratic politics. The asylum issue, for example, has been resolved politically but not constitutionally, whereas the abortion issue has been resolved constitutionally but not politically, and to this extent there continues to be a gap between constitutional normativity and political reality that it is the purpose of the Basic Law to close.

Several paragraphs ago we remarked that the constitutional *Rechtsstaat* has served as an incubator of German democracy. At the same time, German democracy has matured within the framework of enormous economic prosperity and a highly developed civil society based on the right to property and on welfare capitalism. The experience of constitutionalism around the world also seems to confirm that judicial review works best as a limit on majoritarian politics—and as a defender of human dignity—within a context of economic stability, political pluralism, and a culture of civic trust and responsibility. And thus, under the social and economic conditions of postwar Germany, constitutionalism and democracy have been mutually reinforcing.

NOTES

I am grateful to James McAdams and Peter C. Caldwell for their helpful comments on an earlier draft of this chapter.

1. At the risk of oversimplification, the state in the German public mind is the source and principal guarantor of liberty, whereas in the Anglo-American public mind it represents the major threat to liberty. By the same token, German political theory (*Staatsrecht*) has tended to idealize the state, whereas Anglo-American political theory has tended to demonize it.

2. The meaning of the German *Rechtsstaat* cannot be captured in a single sentence. Having gone through many permutations, the history of the concept is complicated and convoluted, embracing as it does versions that may be described as Kantian and Hegelian, formal and material, liberal and illiberal, and moral and amoral. The best, short treatment of the concept's history is Ernst-Wolfgang Böckenförde, "Entstehung und Wandel des Rechtsstaatsbegriffes," in *Festschrift für Adolf Arndt,* ed. Horst Ehmke, Carlo Schmid, and Hans Scharoun (Frankfurt, Europäische Verlagsanstalt 1969), 56ff. Böckenförde treats the development of the concept from its origins in early-nineteenth-century political thought through the Weimar Republic and the Basic Law. See also Gottfried Dietze, *Two Concepts of the Rule of Law* (Indianapolis: Liberty Fund, 1973).

3. See Mahandra P. Singh, *German Administrative Law* (Berlin: Springer-Verlag, 1985), 5–6. See pp. 102–15 for a detailed description of the Federal Republic's current system of administrative courts.

4. To say this is, once again, to ignore many of the nuanced arguments and substantial conflicts among leading constitutional scholars of the Weimar Republic. Sharp images of these conflicts emerge with the mere mention of names such as Herman Heller, Rudolf Smend, Hugo Preuss, Erich Kaufmann, Gerhard Leibholz, Heinrich Triepel, Carl Schmitt, Hans Kelsen, and Ernst Rudolf Huber. Organic, historicist, and integrationist theories of the state engaged in open conflict with liberal and positivist versions. For an extended treatment and comparison of these theorists and theories, see Peter C. Caldwell's superb study, *Popular Sovereignty and the Crisis of German Constitutional Law: The Theory and Practice of the Weimar Constitution* (Durham, N.C.: Duke University Press, 1997), especially chaps. 3 and 4.

5. The Basic Law did not break completely with the past. A large number of its provisions were copied word for word from the Weimar Constitution. In addition, the Basic Law re-creates many of the political structures established in the Weimar Constitution but eliminates those crippling defects *thought* to have facilitated Hitler's destruction of Weimar's democratic political system. See John Golay, *The Founding of the Federal Republic of Germany* (Chicago: University of Chicago Press, 1956). See also Donald P. Kommers, "German Constitutionalism: A Prolegomenon," *Emory Law Journal* 40 (1991): 845–47.

6. For example, unlike the guaranteed rights laid down in the Weimar Constitution, almost all of which could be limited or jettisoned by ordinary law, the bill of rights in the Basic Law, which include all the individual rights associated with liberal constitutionalism, absolutely binds "the legislature, executive, and judiciary as directly enforceable law." The Basic Law (*Grundgesetz* [cited hereafter as GG]), art. 1 (3). Article 19 (4) backs up the binding character of these rights by guaranteeing a judicial remedy for their enforcement.

7. The so-called eternity clause (Article 79 [3]) prohibits any constitutional amendment that would erode the principle of federalism or the values laid down in Articles 1 and 20.

8. GG art. 1 (1).

9. These governing principles, including those of popular sovereignty, separation of powers, and representative government, are set forth in Article 20 of the Basic Law. They also apply to local government. Article 28 (1) — the only place in the Basic Law where the term *Rechtsstaat* appears — requires the *Länder* to adopt "the principles of the republican, democratic and social *law state* [*Rechtsstaat*] governed by the rule of law within the meaning of this Basic Law." For a brief history of this provision and the meaning of its terms, see Ingo von Münch, *Grundgesetz-Kommentar* (Munich: C. H. Beck'sche Verlagsbuchhandlung, 1983), 2:196–206.

10. The Constitutional Court would in time refer to the "militant democracy" of the Basic Law. Germany's militant democracy would refuse to tolerate the enemies of democracy. The concept of "militant" democracy finds its sharpest expression in Articles 18 and 21 of the Basic Law. Under Article 18, persons can be made to forfeit certain basic rights such as freedom of press, assembly, and association, if they use these rights to "undermine the free democratic basic order." Under Article 21 (1), political parties seeking to abolish democracy "shall be unconstitutional." See Helmut Steinberger, *Konzeption und Grenzen freiheitlicher Demokratie* (Berlin: Springer Verlag, 1974).

11. For a fuller account of the Constitutional Court's role in Germany's political system, see Donald P. Kommers, "The Federal Constitutional Court in the German Political System," *Comparative Political Studies* 26 (1994): 470–91. See also David P. Currie, *The Constitution of the Federal Republic of Germany* (Chicago: University of Chicago Press, 1994).

12. The decisions of the Court are now encompassed in nearly 100 volumes of official reports. By the end of 1994, the Court had invalidated nearly 500 provisions of law and administrative regulations, exceeding by far the so-called judicial "activism" of the United States Supreme Court. The formal reports of the Court's decisions, however, fail to tell the full story of the Court's impact on German life and law. By the end of 1994, the Court had disposed of more than 100,000 constitutional complaints filed by ordinary citizens, a procedure that has done more to create a constitutional consciousness among Germans generally than any other activity of the Court. Finally, the Court's work-product has generated a constitutional literature in Germany the volume and sophistication of which fully matches that produced in the United States. In addition, Germany's leading newspapers follow the Court's work in great detail. While much of the reportage is severely critical of particular decisions, it reflects the Court's pervasive presence in Germany's system of government, as well as its popular support in the public at large. See Kommers, "The Federal Consitutional Court."

13. See 93 BVerfGE 1 (1995).

14. Several of these decisions, including the recent — and earthshaking —

Maastricht Case, have also poured specific meaning into the term *democracy,* limiting it to certain norms and procedures with far-reaching consequences for the operation of the political system. See 89 BVerfGE 155 (1993).

15. See, respectively, 40 BVerfGE 296 (1975); 62 BVerfGE 1 (1983); and 80 BVerfGE 188 (1989). But see 70 BVerfGE 324 (1986) (excluding the Green Party from representation on a parliamentary committee dealing with national security).

16. For a list and discussion of some 30 constitutional cases dealing with the rights of parliamentary parties (*Fraktionen*), see Gerald Kretscher, "Selbständige Rechtspersonen des Parlamentsrechts," *Das Parlament,* 22–29 May 1992, 12–14.

17. See Schleswig-Holstein Investigative Committee Case, 49 BVerfGE 70 (1978). Constitutional cases have also invalidated laws restricting the rights of start-up parties and independent citizen groups seeking first-time access to the ballot and forbade parties from changing the order of precedence on party lists or adding persons to such lists after an election has taken place. See, respectively, 3 BVerfGE 19 (1953) and 7 BVerfGE 77 (1957).

18. 16 BVerfGE 130 (1963).

19. The German electoral system is a mixed system of single-member districts and proportional representation. One-half of the current 656 members of the Bundestag are elected in single-member districts, and the other half by proportional representation. Each voter receives two ballots: the first is cast for a specific candidate running in a district, the second for a party list. The number of parliamentary seats allocated to a party is determined by second-ballot, or list, votes, the result being that each party is entitled to a total number of parliamentary seats proportionate to its total of list votes.

20. See, respectively, 1 BVerfGE 208 (1952); 6 BVerfGE 84 (1957); and 51 BVerfGE 222 (1979).

21. Already in 1952, after surveying all the electoral laws adopted by various units of government, the Court invalidated Schleswig-Holstein's imposition of a 7 percent rule, holding that only a compelling reason would justify a rule "exceeding the common German value of 5 percent." See 1 BVerfGE 208, 260 (1952).

22. The electoral law that was to apply to the first all-German election on 2 December 1990 contained the usual 5 percent clause. East German leaders, accustomed to a system of pure proportionality, accepted the clause after the two sides worked out a "piggyback" arrangement that would permit smaller parties or groups in East Germany to field candidates in alliance with other, larger parties in the west. This plan, however, favored some small parties at the expense of others. For example, the strength of Bavaria's Christian Social Union (CSU) would carry its sister party, the GDR's German Social Union (DUS), into the Bundestag, whereas the old communist Socialist Unity Party (SED), now dressed up as the Party of Democratic Socialism (PDS), was unlikely to find a willing partner in the FRG to help it win the needed 5 percent of the national vote.

23. See Andrei S. Markovits and Russell J. Dalton, "Spin Doctors and

Soothsayers: The Bundestag Elections of October 16, 1994," *German Politics and Society* 13 (1995): 1–11.

24. See 90 BVerfGE 286 (1994).

25. See 8 BVerfGE 105 (1958) and 8 BVerfGE 122 (1958).

26. It is important to note that the Maastricht Case arose out of several constitutional complaints all but one of which were found inadmissible, including the Green Party's call for a national referendum on the Maastricht Treaty. The admissible complaint was filed by a German citizen who claimed that the treaty violated his right to vote under Article 38 (1) of the Basic Law. This momentous decision thus hinged on the Court's construction of the meaning of the right to vote under the Basic Law. 89 BVerfGE 155 (1993).

27. The Court declined to characterize the European Union as a "supranational organization" but called it a "Staatenbund," that is, a confederation of states in the process of development. In the end, as noted, the Court sustained all of the treaty's provisions, but laid down the following conditions for German participation: that any power transferred to the Union must be clearly defined by the act of ratification; that the Union be subject to democratic control with respect to its legislative and administrative rules; and that out of respect for the principle of subsidiarity, significant legislative powers remain with the national parliament. Finally, to ensure that these conditions are met, the Court declared its readiness to review further challenges to the execution of the Maastricht Treaty. For an excellent analysis of the Maastricht Case, see Kevin D. Makowski, "*Solange III:* The German Federal Constitutional Court's Decision on Accession to the Maastricht Treaty on European Union," *University of Pennsylvania Journal of International Business Law* 16 (1995): 155–80.

28. See 83 BVerfGE 37 (1990) and 83 BVerfGE 60 (1990).

29. 83 BVerfGE 37, 51 (1990). Article 28 (1) of the Basic Law was amended in 1992, however, to allow citizens of member states of the European Community to vote in local elections. Article 28 (1) was amended in response to the Maastricht Treaty, one of whose provisions commits each member nation to guarantee to the nationals of other member nations the right to vote in local elections.

30. 44 BVerfGE 125, 142–43 (1977).

31. Ibid., 182.

32. Michaela Richter, "The Basic Law and the Democratic Party State: Constitutional Theory and Political Practice," in *Cornerstone of Democracy: The West German Grundgesetz, 1949–89* (Washington, D.C.: German Historical Institute, Occasional Paper No. 13, 1995), 37. The theory of the *Parteienstaat* traces its origin to the work and advocacy of Gerhard Leibholz, a justice of the Federal Constitutional Court from 1951 to 1971. See Gerhard Leibholz, "Die moderne Parteienstaat," in Leibholz, *Verfassungsstaat—Verfassungsrecht* (Stuttgart: Kohlhammer Verlag, 1973), 68–94. For a more up-to-date, critical overview of the jurisprudence of political parties, see Philip Kunig, "Parteien," in *Handbuch des Staatsrechts,* ed. Josef Isensee and Paul Kirchhof (Heidelberg: C. F. Müller Juristischer Verlag, 1987), 103–43.

33. See 1 BVerfGE 208, 225 (1952).

34. 8 BVerfGE 51 (1958).
35. 20 BVerfGE 56 (1966).
36. Gesetz über die politischen Parteien in der Fassung der Bekanntmachung vom 31 Januar 1994 (BGBI. I: 149).
37. 41 BVerfGE 399 (1976).
38. For an extensive treatment of these events and measures, see Göttrik Wewer, ed., *Parteienfinanzierung und politischer Wettbewerb* (Opladen: Westdeutscher Verlag, 1990), 164–94. See also Arthur Gunlicks, "The New German Party Finance Law," *German Politics* 4 (1994): 101–21.
39. See, respectively, 24 BVerfGE 300 (1968) and 73 BVerfGE 40 (1986).
40. 85 BVerfGE 264 (1992). The new law entered into force on time. For a discussion of this statute and the events leading up to it, see Gunlicks, "The New German Party Finance Law."
41. In 1975 the Constitutional Court nullified a federal law that liberalized the FRG's abortion statute; in 1993, more than two years after reunification, the Court reaffirmed the essential core of its 1975 ruling. See, respectively, 39 BVerfGE 1 (1975) and 88 BVerfGE 203 (1993). The comparable American cases are *Roe* v. *Wade,* 410 U.S. 113 (1973) and *Planned Parenthood of Southeastern Pa.* v. *Casey,* 505 U.S. 833 (1992). *Roe* struck down state laws banning abortion. In 1992, although rejecting much of the reasoning of *Roe* and its immediate progeny, the Supreme Court, like Germany's Constitutional Court, reaffirmed the "essential core" of its earlier ruling.
42. In Germany certain petitioners may invoke the Constitutional Court's jurisdiction without presenting a case or controversy, as required by American law. Under German law, a state, or *Land,* government or one-third of the Bundestag's members may test a statute's constitutionality in what is known as an "abstract judicial review" proceeding. The power of judicial decision in such cases is enormous because the Court's holdings have the force of law and are absolutely binding on all governing institutions. See Bundesverfassungsgerichtsgesetz [Federal Constitutional Court Act], sec. 31 (1) in *Grundgesetz,* 53d ed. (Munich: C. H. Beck'sche Verlagsbuchhandlung, 1996), 196.
43. The German justices employed biological reasoning in defining the beginning of life. "Life in the sense of the historical existence of a human individual," declared the Court, "exists according to definite biological-physiological knowledge, in any case, from the 14th day after conception [i.e., at implantation]." See 39 BVerfGE 1, 37 (1975).
44. Article 143, a transitional amendment that the Unification Treaty itself put into the Constitution, reads: "[East German law] may deviate from provisions of this Basic Law for a period not extending beyond 31 December 1992 in so far as and as long as no complete adjustment to the order of the Basic Law can be achieved as a consequence of the different conditions. Deviations must not violate Article 19 (2) and must be compatible with the principles set out in Article 79 (3)." See 6G, art. 143(1), based on Unification Treaty, art. 4.
45. The act's provisions reflected the spirit of the Unification Treaty, Article 31 of which directed the all-German parliament to "ensure [the] better protection of unborn life" and to adopt social policies that would "provide a better

solution" to the problem of pregnant women in distress "than is the case in either part of Germany at present." Unification Treaty, art. 31, sec. 4.

46. Values and rights differ in that an individual can vindicate a right, usually through a lawsuit, whereas only the state can ensure the realization of a value. Although rights are fundamental, they may and often do conflict with their corresponding values. In these situations, the value may trump the right. For example, under the Basic Law's value structure the state may be required to break up a newspaper monopoly—thus encroaching on the subjective right to freedom of the press—in the interest of the social and political pluralism that the institution of a free press was designed to bring about.

47. Value theory gives the Basic Law a longer reach than the U.S. Constitution, for constitutional values—as opposed to negative rights against the state—affect the outcome of disputes under private law. The primary purpose of guaranteed rights in the Basic Law is to protect the liberties of the individual against state interference, but they also influence legal disputes involving private parties (*Drittwirkung*). The influence is indirect, which means that provisions of private law under which a dispute between third parties takes place must be interpreted in such a way as to conform to the constitution's basic values. See 7 BVerfGE 198, 205 (1958); 34 BVerfGE 269, 280 (1973); 49 BVerfGE 89, 142 (1978); and 52 BVerfGE 131, 165 (1979).

48. See, for example, Church Construction Tax Case, 19 BVerfGE 206 (1965).

49. See Klaus Stern, *Das Staatsrecht der Bundesrepublik Deutschland,* 2d ed. (Munich: C. H. Beck'sche Verlagsbuchhandlung, 1984), 133.

50. Ibid.

51. This section relies heavily on the published and unpublished papers of Gerald L. Neuman of the Columbia University School of Law, in particular "Buffer Zones against Refugees: Dublin, Schengen, and the German Asylum Amendment," *Virginia Journal of International Law* (1993); "Asylum Reform in Germany: An Interim Report" (unpublished and undated); and "Nationality Law in the United States and the Federal Republic of Germany: Structure and Current Problems" (unpublished, January 1995).

52. The full text of the Asylum Case appears in *Europäische Grundrechte Zeitung* 23 (May 1996): 237–56.

53. See, respectively, the Judgment of 14 May 1996 (Ghanaian Asylum Case), ibid., 256–68; and Judgment of 14 May 1996 (Nigerian Asylum Case), ibid., 271–88.

54. 80 BVerfGE 315 (1989).

55. Gerald L. Neuman, "Nationality Law in the United States and the Federal Republic of Germany," 22.

56. 83 BVerfGE 37, 52 (1990).

57. This provision was incorporated into the Constitution to extend automatic citizenship to citizens of East Germany as well as to ethnic Germans in other parts of eastern Europe.

58. In an important citizenship case decided on 21 October 1987, the Constitutional Court said: "The duty to safeguard the concept of reunification in the

Basic Law also commands the lasting maintenance of the unity of the German people as the bearer of the right of self-determination in international law as far as possible, with an orientation to the future." [Die im Wiedervereinigungsgebot des Grundgesetzes enthaltene Wahrungspflicht gebietet es auch, die Einheit des deutschen Volkes als des Trägers des völkerrechtlichen Selbstbestimmungsrechts nach Möglichkeit zukunftsgerichtet auf Dauer zu bewahren.] 77 BVerfGE 137, 151 (1987).

    59. East-West Basic Treaty Case, 36 BVerfGE 16, 29ff (1973).

From State Culture to Citizen Culture: Political Parties and the Postwar Transformation of Political Culture in Germany

Michaela Richter

The process by which political parties were incorporated into constitutional thought, institutions, and practices was nowhere easy or automatic.[1] But only in Germany did antipathy toward parties and government become a cultural tradition sufficiently powerful and pervasive first to preclude a peaceful democratic transition and then to undermine the first democratic experiment. Against this background, the emergence in the Federal Republic of a broadly supported "democratic party state," the mass and elite legitimation of its principal founding parties, and the absence of a principled opposition to political parties and government by them amounted to a dramatic cultural and political transformation. Critical to this successful transformation, this chapter argues, were the aggressive push for preeminence by the Federal Republic's founding parties during occupation; the constitutional recognition extended to them in the Basic Law; the role of the Federal Constitutional Court; and the self-confidence of the dominant parties armed with a powerful self-legitimating doctrine.

Yet toward the end of the 1970s and throughout much of the 1980s, opinion polls and voting data pointed to growing evidence of mass disaffection with the main parties, politicians, and the way the political system performed (*Parteien-, Politik-,* and *Staatsverdrossenheit*). The sudden change in public outlook prompted proclamations of a party crisis and fears for German democracy. While some analyses emphasized social-structural explanations (modernization or a fundamental reorientation in values), others increasingly blamed the established parties and the Federal Republic's distinctive form of democracy for the electorate's new antiparty mood. Unification, rather than reversing these trends, only intensified them. Both the opinion and voting patterns and the mounting criticisms of the Bonn parties and the party state gave rise to speculations that Germany's traditional antiparty culture had reemerged.

I contend, however, that neither opinion and voting data nor contemporary antiparty critiques amount to a fundamental reversion to an earlier cultural climate hostile to parliamentary democracy or government by parties. Nevertheless, it is worth noting how much of the literature critical of the parties and party state rejects modern pluralistic democracy. More important, the antiparty mood at both mass and elite levels reveals strains in Germany's democratic culture that the Federal Republic's principal parties must address if the Berlin Republic is to enjoy the same success and stability as did the Bonn Republic.

Section I of this essay provides a historical survey of Germany's antiparty tradition. Against this background, the next section traces how the principal features of the Federal Republic's distinctive "democratic party state" emerged during the occupation. This development I attribute to a conscious strategy pursued most rigorously by Konrad Adenauer of the CDU and Kurt Schumacher of the SPD. Because of them, the new West German constitution (Basic Law) formally recognized political parties and made them integral parts of the constitutional order. Yet even the Basic Law never fully acknowledged the dominant position parties had already achieved by that time.

Section III shows how this gap between the formal constitution and political reality was ultimately bridged by the Federal Constitutional Court. Its constitutional theory and supportive rulings helped not only to consolidate the party state but also to legitimize the ever-expanding influence of the Federal Republic's founding. Because political parties, so legitimized, provided stable and effective government, by the 1960s a "party-supportive" democratic culture was in place. Section IV charts the appearance of a new "cultural strand" in the late 1970s hostile to and sharply critical of the parties. The focus of section IV is on both the empirical data used to demonstrate the new antiparty mood and on elite interpretations blaming the main parties and their "party state" for popular disaffection.

Section V questions whether such cultural trends amount to a revival of Germany's traditional antiparty culture. It concludes that voting and electoral data show unease with, but no fundamental repudiation of, the Federal Republic's major parties and government. Unlike past opponents of parties and party government, contemporary critics of the Federal Republic's party state wish to make it more responsive to new issues, groups, and forms of citizen participation rather than to supplant it with an "above-party" authoritarian state. In this respect, the present debate about parties and the party state itself reflects the successful democratization of German political culture. But in the last section of this chapter, I point to grounds for concern about the potentially adverse long-term implications of a persisting antiparty climate in united Germany. Both the parties and their critics must prevent existing disaffections from undermining Germany's hitherto stable and successful democracy.

As for the use of the concept of political culture in this chapter, several clarifications are in order. First, I focus on a particular substrand of German political culture, namely, negative attitudes toward political parties and government by them. Such antipathies have had a major impact on Germany's political development. Because past hostility to political parties had impeded and undermined German democracy, overcoming that legacy became the primary objective for the founders of West Germany's parties and democratic state. The reemergence and persistence of antiparty views thus justify renewed concern for the continued viability of democracy in united Germany. By so placing contemporary attitudes within a broader historical perspective, both changes from and continuities with past patterns may enable us to avoid potentially fallacious analogies with the Weimar Republic.

Second, as Karl Rohe has pointed out, we need to distinguish "sociopolitical culture" (*politische Sozialkultur*) from interpretations of political reality (*politische Deutungskultur*). The first term refers to attitudes, orientations, assumptions, and codes of behavior of ordinary citizens. These, in turn, often form the basis of interpretations of political reality made by intellectuals, politicians, or "cultural managers." In Germany, public opinions and voting trends frequently have been "reinterpreted" into a fundamental critique of the main parties and the party state. For this reason, I treat such critiques as indicators of cultural traits with implications for German democracy as significant as the patterns of voting and opinion they interpret.[2]

Third, this chapter views political parties both as institutional agents of cultural transformation and as objects of cultural orientations. In Germany's distinctive political development, political parties, although important actors in practice, never achieved a cultural acceptance during the Weimar Republic comparable to other Western democracies. Seeking to overcome this antiparty legacy, the Federal Republic's founding parties took steps that initially created a political culture supportive of political parties. Subsequently, however, some unanticipated consequences of these steps produced a mutant type of "antiparty" culture demanding a shift of power from the main parties to citizens. Thus the German case again demonstrates that the relationship between political institutions and political culture is itself subject to continuous and dynamic changes.

I. State Culture and the Origins of the Antiparty Tradition

West German parliamentary democracy after 1949 has been described as a distinctive constitutional form, the democratic party state. A more precise but less easily translated concept is *parteienstaatliche Demokratie* — a democracy that is a state by parties. This notion registers an altogether new relationship of political parties to society and the state, both in constitutional theory and in political practice.

During the nineteenth century and throughout the Empire, the concept of a party state would have seemed an "abominable hybrid."[3] Central to the "state culture"[4] of the Empire were two distinctions. First, conservative constitutional and political theorists of the Empire presupposed a fundamental dualism between society and the state. Society, composed of jostling, fragmented, selfish, transient interests, was said to be incapable of common purpose and action. Only the state possessed the permanence, unity of direction, concern for the general interest, impartiality, and creative energy necessary to ensure the orderly functioning of society. Since political parties embody society's particularistic interests and conflicts, party participation in its governance would undermine that unity and impartiality. To quote Lorenz von Stein: "The parties serve to make an objective policy impossible. Their influence, indeed, the influence of society on the state and in the state is not legitimate."[5] Giving parties and parliament more power was thus seen as tantamount to sacrificing rational, unified, and impartial state action to party squabbling *(Parteiengezänk)*.[6]

No less important was the distinction between the "whole" and its "parts." Reflecting Germany's belated national unification and the persistence of regional, confessional, and socioeconomic divisions, the Empire's "state culture" emphasized the subordination of partial identities and interests to the whole. Only the state could embody the general interest, while parties merely represented partisan concerns. As Bismarck insisted: "Seen through party lenses, the whole shrinks to the interests of party. The party representative loses what is general or universal. The party lens obscures the common interest."[7]

Inherent in these dualisms were a fear of conflict and the desire to resolve it by "synthesis" in the form of a rational, fair, efficient state. Indeed, in both the Empire and the Weimar Republic, the strength of regional, confessional, and political "milieus" and the absence of a common and shared "civil culture" may have contributed to the belief that the control of a society as large, divided, and complex as Germany "required formal juridical norms monitored by the authority and power of the state."[8]

Although the Weimar constitution established a parliamentary system in which political parties played a decisive role, it continued to reflect the Empire's ambivalence toward political parties. Its one reference to them (Article 130) was negative, warning civil servants against partisan commitments. Legal and constitutional theorists in the Weimar Republic continued to treat political parties as "extra-constitutional" rather than as integral to the constitutional order.[9] Finally, the republic's constitution contained several mechanisms designed to limit party and parliamentary power. The independently elected president with emergency powers was to provide a symbol of unity and a center of power above parties. Referenda and plebiscites were to counteract the "stultifying effect" of party politics by giving citizens a direct voice in legislation.[10]

During the Empire and the Weimar Republic, aversion to political parties extended beyond conservative elites and jurists and became a major component of German political culture. German parties during the Wilhelmine Empire were characterized by ideological polarization, doctrinal rigidity, social and regional particularism, and obstructionism within parliament. These flaws, encouraged by the denial of any governmental responsibility under the 1871 Constitution, reinforced the antidemocratic ideal of a "neutral," nonpartisan (*überparteilich*) state as guarantor of social order and stability. During the Weimar Republic, the parties were both inexperienced in governing and captives of their own past experiences, rigid doctrines, and inflexible organizations. They proved to be incapable of dealing with the combined impact of economic collapse, social deterioration, and political crises. In the end, a culture hostile to government by parties, reinforced by the negative experiences with party government during the Weimar Republic, greatly facilitated popular and elite support for the NSDAP's antidemocratic vision of a *Führer state*.[11]

II. Antiparty Tendencies during the Occupation, 1945–49

Ostensibly, the military defeat and collapse of the Third Reich provided preconditions far more favorable to democratic party government than had accompanied the formation of the Weimar Republic. Collaboration with the Third Reich had destroyed the moral authority and power of the army and civil service, together the most prestigious and important opponents of democracy in the Empire and the Weimar Republic. By contrast, having been banned within weeks of the Nazi seizure of power, political parties were untainted by ties to that regime. Moreover, the combined impact of Nazi social and economic policies and the upheavals created by military defeat and occupation had eroded the social foundations of Germany's polarized milieu parties. Finally, shared experiences of persecution, exile, or concentration camps during the Third Reich had helped to forge, for the first time in German history, a common commitment by the main parties to a democratic, constitutional order.

Yet in 1945, political parties faced serious obstacles: resistance to party government by the occupation authorities, the favored status of the minister presidents and their ambivalence toward political parties, and a public indifferent or hostile to party politics. By the end of 1945, the Western Allies had followed the Soviets in licensing the Social Democrats (SPD), the Communists (KPD), the Christian Democrats (CDU/CSU), and the liberals (LDP in the East and FDP in the West). But these parties were both constrained by rigorous licensing rules and denied access to any real powers and responsibility.[12]

Given the enormous tasks confronting them, the Western Allies wanted problems dealt with efficiently, uniformly, and without lengthy partisan debates or attacks by a parliamentary opposition on occupational authority and policies. Hence the Western Allies limited the powers of the elected parliaments and insisted on all-party governments or grand coalitions within their respective zones. Parity among parties on key bodies became the rule, as was the inclusion of interest groups (i.e., "corporatist" representation). Allied press and broadcasting laws, as well as proposed civil service reforms, sought to curtail party influence over public opinion and administration.[13]

The Western Allies clearly preferred to work with "nonpolitical" German administrators and "nonpartisan" minister presidents. These administrators and minister presidents shared Allied fears about a premature return of conflictual party politics. Especially the South German minister presidents showed an antipathy to political parties reminiscent of the older state tradition. They often distinguished between a "higher form of politics" and "partisan politics" and dismissed parties as "partial spokesmen for the interests of different groups," incapable of those "common efforts" by which "the German nation and the German people [can] be guided toward a normal, healthy life."[14] The South German minister presidents saw federalism as indispensable to checking all-powerful central party organizations. Although committed to democracy, their yearning for nonpartisan governance and distaste for the conflicts and competition at the heart of pluralistic democracy revealed the persistence of conservative antiparty thinking at the elite level.[15]

This was all the more worrisome in the absence of any mass support for democratic parties and government. After 13 years of totalitarian rule, the surveys conducted by the American military government between 1946 and 1949 (i.e., the OMGUS [Office of Military Government, United States] surveys) revealed a political culture ill-suited to the return of democratic government. Most people were politically uninformed and apathetic toward elections and referenda held between 1946 and 1949. Between 1946 and 1949, 60 percent of OMGUS survey respondents preferred a government providing economic security to one guaranteeing democratic freedoms. Toward political parties, popular attitudes ranged from indifference to hostility.

Overwhelmingly, respondents expressed no interest in joining or voting for any of the licensed parties. Asked which rights they were most ready to give up, about half cited the right to vote for a political party. Three-quarters of the respondents questioned between 1946 and 1947 rejected politics as a suitable career for their son. As late as May 1949, two-thirds of the respondents felt that political parties pursued only their own rather than the voters' interests.[16]

No political leaders did more to attack the constraints on and sentiments against party politics during the occupation than Kurt Schumacher and Konrad Adenauer. By 1946, they were the undisputed leaders (respectively) of the SPD and CDU in the British zone. From their perspective, both Allied efforts to minimize party politics and the call for nonpartisan politics among important German public officials signaled the revival of the very hostility toward party government that had destroyed the Weimar Republic. Despite other differences, Schumacher and Adenauer concurred in the belief that constructing a democratic Germany required not nonpartisan bodies or leaders but strong, disciplined political parties, with the will and institutional capacities to provide the unity of purpose and direction once associated with the older conception of the state.

Undoubtedly, power and partisan considerations played a role as well. Schumacher was convinced that, given its opposition to and persecution during the Third Reich, the SPD had earned the "right" to govern Germany. For that role, both a strong party organization and a position of ensured powers for his party in the state were necessary prerequisites. As chancellor, Adenauer liked to project an "above-party" stance. But during the occupation he was committed to denying the SPD the predominant role it was claiming. Hence he was intent on transforming the CDU into a coherent, disciplined party able to match any of the SPD's claims and advantages. Yet while both leaders had a direct stake in creating strong political parties, they also recognized the potential danger of denying the parties real power and responsibility while a future democracy was being constructed.

Working against both the Allies and German "antiparty" forces, these two party leaders pursued a broad and largely successful strategy to secure the primacy of political parties. In the course of the occupation, they increasingly marginalized the minister presidents. Although the Western Allies had commissioned them to lay the constitutional foundations for the new West German state, Schumacher and Adenauer made sure that the Parliamentary Council that was to draft the constitution, or Basic Law, was an "assembly of party men."[17]

Both leaders opposed zonal institutions that excluded or marginalized political parties. These included the British Zonal Council (*Zonenbeirat*), in which parties as well as interest groups and minister presidents were represented; the Minister President Council (*Länderrat*) in the American zone, which excluded parties altogether; and the original model of the Bizonal Economic Council (*Wirtschaftsrat*), which originally was to be administered by experts. To Schumacher, such "unpolitical" bodies were dangerous because they had in the past been "the breeding ground of German nationalism and militarism."[18] For Adenauer, their threat lay in the revival of an authoritarian "leadership principle [*Führergedanken*] in which the *Länder* chiefs, surrounded by large coteries of civil servants, feel free to act and do as they please."[19] Schumacher and Adenauer succeeded in turning both the *Zonenbeirat* and the *Wirtschaftsrat* into exclusively party-dominated bodies. Indeed, to the consternation of the Allies, Schumacher's decision to go into opposition unilaterally ended the practice of all-party governments.

Both leaders insisted that all elected public officials (including minister presidents) follow their party's positions. Both leaders reasserted full control over their party's local organizations and all party functionaries. Both pushed for absolute party discipline in *Länder* parliaments, bizonal structures, and the Parliamentary Council.[20] Finally, both leaders subverted Allied policies designed to keep political parties out of public administration and societal institutions, including the media.

Adenauer and Schumacher were equally committed to the reconciliation of the civil service and political parties, of critical importance to the future party state. On both sides, this rapprochement was guided by tactical considerations and the desire not to revive the antagonisms of the past. Civil servants had early on sought membership in one of the democratic licensed parties as a form of rehabilitation, a way to demonstrate democratic commitments.[21] Without a party cover, moreover, civil servants had been reluctant to administer unpopular occupation policies.[22]

Leaders from the main licensed parties were no less eager to welcome civil servants into their ranks. Lacking well-trained people to take over positions in local and *Land* governments, they depended on "politically reliable" civil servants. Party leaders also saw in the civil service a strong potential base of support. This was true not only of the CDU/CSU and the FDP, but of the SPD as well. Although in theory most open to reforms, for tactical reasons the SPD leadership refused to challenge the traditional civil service and its rights.[23]

Common opposition to Allied civil service reform plans cemented this alliance between the parties and the civil service. These reforms proposed to denazify and to democratize the civil service as well as to depoliticize it by making civil service employment incompatible with any political activity.

The professional civil service resented the mass dismissals entailed by denazification as well as Allied measures to reduce its privileged status. The civil service could defeat or block Allied proposals only by working with the parties. The political parties in turn perceived Allied plans to create a "depoliticized" civil service as likely to revive the very division between parties and the state that had weakened democracy in the past. The parties believed that democracy required a civil service committed to it and under control of democratically elected governments. Neither the civil service nor the parties thus had much use for the "incompatibility principle."[24] In defeating the Allied reforms, they had struck a tacit bargain. Henceforth, the parties would defend the interests of the professional civil service, which, in turn, would accept democratic control and the political appointments this implied.[25]

With this alliance began the "fusion" of the parties and the state apparatus now seen as the defining feature of the Federal Republic's party state. Already during the occupation, many civil servants were members both of the licensed parties and of elective bodies.[26] During this time, too, both the SPD and the CDU began to push for political appointments in public administration at the local and *Land* level, as well as in the Bizone. This use of patronage by one party stimulated the "patronage interests" of the other.[27] In a pattern continued after the establishment of the Federal Republic, if neither of the main parties was strong enough to control such appointments, the SPD and CSU worked out interparty agreements for sharing important patronage posts. In North Rhine–Westphalia, for example, the main parties agreed to parities or quotas for allocating local political posts, ministerial appointments, and all key positions in the Northwest German Broadcasting Service (NWDR).[28]

In short, the conditions and practices subsequently associated with the Federal Republic's party state in fact had already emerged in the four years of occupation. Yet the Basic Law failed to acknowledge these developments. This is because in the course of drafting the constitution, the proponents of strong party government were ultimately forced to reconcile their differences with the opponents of an exclusively party-dominated democracy. In the end, the Basic Law made significant concessions to both sides.

Most decisive for the subsequent development of the Federal Republic's party state was the unprecedented constitutional recognition of political parties in Article 21. By assigning them a constitutional role, the Basic Law made them integral components of the constitutional order. The framers of the Basic Law also rejected extraparliamentary devices used in the Weimar Republic to curb the power of parties, such as a strong, independent presidency and direct forms of participation such as plebiscites.[29]

But the Basic Law also contains provisions designed to check an all-powerful legislature dominated by political parties. Given strong support for the Federal Constitutional Court with its power of judicial review, the SPD was forced to accept it. It also had to agree to the principle of the independent mandate, which the FDP insisted on as a necessary protection for individual deputies against excessive party pressures.[30] Allied insistence on a Bundesrat based on *Länder* representation was in effect a victory for the South German delegates to the Parliamentary Council. They had all along favored such a chamber as the most effective "bulwark" against the party-dominated lower house.[31]

In the end, the distinctive parliamentary system created by the Basic Law reflected German experiences and traditions. The successful resolution of two competing views of democratic government also meant the disappearance of antiparty sentiments from public discourse for the next 30 years. Beyond the constitutional negotiations and compromises, however, lay the reality of increasingly powerful parties. By creating "facts on the ground," Schumacher and Adenauer had secured the continuation and expansion of the pervasive influence of the parties in the state and society.

III. From "State Culture" to "Party State Culture"

By giving constitutional recognition and hence legitimation to political parties, the framers of the Basic Law sought to eliminate the contempt in which parties had been traditionally held. Article 21 thus constitutes, in Wilhelm Hennis's witty phrase, a form of reparation (*Wiedergutmachung*) vis-à-vis the parties.[32] But the Basic Law did not address the gap between the form of parliamentary government adopted in the Basic Law and the existing realities of party power. For better or for worse, this gap was bridged by the Federal Constitutional Court.

The Court's contribution was both theoretical and practical. Especially under the influence of Justice Gerhard Leibholz, the Federal Constitutional Court developed a distinctive constitutional theory. Its central thesis was that universal suffrage, political democratization, the emergence of mass parties, and their participation in government have transformed the classical parliamentary system of representation into what he called the "democratic party state." Because in this form of democracy parties both represent civil society and shape state action on its behalf, the old dualisms of state and party as well as of state and society are transcended.[33]

Leibholz and the Federal Constitutional Court held that Article 21, by acknowledging the constitutional role of parties, "in effect legalized the modern democratic party state" in the Federal Republic.[34] By making parties "integral components of the constitutionally ordered political life," the Basic Law also transformed them from "political" and "sociological" organizations into "constitutionally necessary instruments for the formation of the political will of the people" — indeed, into a "constitutional institution" (*Verfassungsorgan*).[35] In this capacity, political parties were allowed to defend their rights directly before the Court, as may other constitutional organs.[36]

Armed with this new and potent constitutional doctrine, the Federal Constitutional Court has consistently legitimated many features and practices of the "party state" that had first emerged between 1945 and 1949. Thus were recognized the constitutional status of the parties' parliamentary organizations (*Fraktionen*) and their right to enforce party discipline despite the constitutional guarantee of the independent mandate.[37] The Court has upheld public service laws that encouraged the participation of parties within the system of state institutions and the concomitant right of civil servants to be active in parties and to pursue a parliamentary career. Since 1958, while periodically altering the methods and scope of funding political parties (most recently in 1992), the Court has remained committed to the principle of state support for them.[38]

In line with the party-state doctrine, the Federal Constitutional Court has also consistently strengthened the founding parties, and especially the two large *Volksparteien* (i.e., the SPD and CDU/CSU). The purpose of elections, in the view of the Court, is to produce governments with "clear parliamentary majorities conscious of their responsibilities to the public weal." Because only large, integrative parties (*Volks-*

parteien) can provide such governmental majorities, it has insisted that the need for stable government must at times take precedence over the constitutional principle of equal chances for competing parties (*Chancengleichheit*).[39] Further reinforcing the political and electoral hegemony of the principal founding parties, the Court has used the principle of "militant democracy" to ban political groups and parties that oppose or violate "the basic democratic order."[40]

The Federal Constitutional Court's constitutional doctrine and supportive rulings did much to overcome the negative connotations of the "party state" in the Weimar Republic. By establishing and demonstrating the possibility of a positive relationship between political parties and the democratic state, both the Court and the founding parties contributed to the acceptance of the "democratic party state" among conservative opponents of parties and the mass public alike. There thus emerged in the Federal Republic what the Weimar Republic had lacked, a political culture that accepted democratic government based on competitive parties.

By the late 1970s, public opinion surveys convincingly demonstrated that the "output-oriented, detached, politically passive" subjects revealed by the OMGUS surveys and Almond and Verba's first civic culture study had finally been transformed into model democratic citizens.[41] Between 1959 and 1978, the proportion of those who cited the country's political institutions as a source of pride went from 7 percent to 31 percent. By 1972, we find a broad acceptance of the importance of parliament irrespective of satisfaction with its output. More significantly, between 1950 and 1980, the proportion of citizens who felt that the parties in the Bundestag represented the public's interests rose from 35 percent to 70 percent. An even larger percentage of voters (79 percent, according to a 1978 survey) had come to see political competition as essential to democracy, and 90 percent of those questioned believed it to be operative in the Federal Republic. The positive popular orientations toward the democratic parties and the new party state also helped create a popular consensus for the Basic Law itself. Whereas in 1955 only 30 percent viewed the Basic Law positively, by 1972 that figure had risen to 52 percent, and by 1978 to 71 percent. Finally, such positive political orientations were accompanied by a sharp rise in the levels of citizen interest and participation in politics.[42]

No less significantly, the Court's constitutional legitimation and consolidation of the democratic party state encouraged new and distinctive cultural self-understanding on the part of the main party actors. Central to what may be termed a "party-state culture" are assumptions and claims that diverge significantly from Anglo-American ideas of democratic party government.

The Bonn parties have adopted an extraordinarily expansive view of their constitutional role and mission. Nowhere is this made clearer than in Article 1 of the 1967 Party Law (retained in the revised 1994 Party Law). In language reminiscent of Justice Leibholz, it states: "Political parties form an integral part of the free democratic basic order. Their free and continuous participation in the formation of political opinions among the population enables them to discharge the public tasks incumbent upon them pursuant to the Basic Constitutional Law."[43] So fortified, Article 1 of the Party Law (in both the 1967 and 1994 versions) delineates functions to be performed by political parties that far exceed the modest role of "participating in the formation of the public will" assigned to them in the Basic Law.

Thus the original modest constitutional function of "participating in the formation of the public will" now encompasses not only participating in elections, but also influencing public opinion, deepening of political education ("leading people toward political life"), training able citizens to take over public offices, influencing the formation of the "state's will," and working toward "a close relationship between the people and the organs of the state." As Wilhelm Hennis remarked sardonically, the Party Law seems to presuppose "a somewhat stupid population that must be pushed into the path of political virtue by their party handlers" and a "political Germany as an eternal pedagogic province."[44] In other words, whereas the Anglo-American idea of parties centers on their representative function, party-state culture assigns parties a paternalistic or tutorial role in popular education and guidance.

Increasingly, the *Volksparteien* define their task less as representing diverse social interests than as furthering social and political *integration* and *cooperation*. Although the main parties continue to differ sharply on specific policy issues, the prevailing interparty consensus meant that policy differences were no longer treated as fundamental clashes of ideologies. Public clashes notwithstanding, in their working relationships "pragmatism became the pervasive political culture of the governing class."[45]

The party-state culture has also encouraged a fundamental reconception of the opposition's role. At the beginning of the Federal Republic's existence, Kurt Schumacher still envisioned an adversarial (though loyal) opposition. Its purpose was "the permanent attempt to force the positive creative will of the opposition in concrete instances and with concrete propositions on the government and its parties."[46] A decade later, Willy Brandt offered a considerably more benign view of the opposition's role. "In a sound developing democracy," he argued, "it is the norm rather than the exception that the parties put forward similar, even identical demands in a number of fields. The difference arises in their priorities, in the rank order of tasks to be solved, and in the methods and accents chosen."[47] In effect, as opposition parties, both the SPD and CDU have viewed their role as sharing responsibility for government, rather than as advancing sharply delineated alternatives to government policies.[48]

Reinforcing this attenuation of opposition has been the tendency of parties to work out reciprocal quota (*Proporz*) arrangements for sharing public resources and patronage positions in state administration, the public sector, quasi-public institutions, and even private associations. While competitive and majoritarian principles still play a major role in the Federal Republic, they are counterbalanced by numerous "concordance" mechanisms for managing interparty and even intraparty rivalries.[49] The mutual accommodation of interests has become so extensive that to some analysts, "party-state culture" has come to mean "Proporzkultur," or "quota culture."[50]

Finally, within the political discourse defined by the party-state culture, discussions of democracy in the Federal Republic have become increasingly circular. Democracy is defined by and limited to the constitutional and political order established by the Basic Law; its rules are set forth by the main parties who had founded and dominated it; disagreements are settled not in the political arena but by recourse to the Federal Constitutional Court, which then reaffirms the "free and democratic basic order" and the "democratic party state" as the standard for assessing groups, parties, and ideas as "democratic."

Party-state culture, moreover, claims a perfect identity of the "Bonn parties" and the Federal Republic's democratic order. The survival of the former is viewed as indispensable to the continued existence of the latter. Hence attacks on the party state and the Bonn parties are often too quickly treated by the principal *Volksparteien* as fundamental challenges to the Federal Republic's democracy. This pattern may be seen in two responses to party critics: one made by Willy Brandt in 1977 and the other by Chancellor Kohl in his reply to the critique of the Bonn parties offered by President Richard von Weizsäcker in 1992.[51]

Writing for the SPD's newspaper *Vorwärts,* Brandt reminded his readers how difficult the acceptance of political parties has been in Germany, and how conservative antiparty views and demands for an above-party state had facilitated mass support for the Nazis' vision of the *Volksgemeinschaft*. Against this background, Brandt insisted, the decision of the Parliamentary Council to grant constitutional recognition to political parties had been essential to overcoming traditional German opposition to parties. Citing the Federal Constitutional Court, Brandt further reminded his readers that "in the modern state the popular will can be represented only in political parties." That political parties are playing a strong role in both the state and society is thus normal in democracies today. Consequently, he concludes, "to attack this normal situation is to attack the normality of the constitutional order itself."[52]

Replying to Weizsäcker's criticisms 15 years later, Kohl offered a spirited defense of the party state along much the same lines as had Brandt. Kohl stressed how crucial had been the rejection of the "unholy tradition of contempt for political parties" by the Federal Republic's founders. They had understood correctly that "strong political parties [are] the precondition for democratic stability" and the "decisive factors in the life of the state." Measured by "the economic and political stability they achieved," Kohl insisted, "the Federal Republic's political parties can look at themselves with considerable self-confidence." Moreover, "they can take credit for consolidating the second democracy and ensuring its stability." Populist attacks offer no constructive alternatives to the role that democratic parties must play today.[53]

Together these responses reveal both how deeply the *Volksparteien* have internalized Leibholz's theory of the party state and how useful it has been for defending their pervasive influence in state and society. This commitment to the party state was further demonstrated by the failure of the Constitutional Commission (established jointly by the Bundestag and Bundesrat) to introduce reforms in the Basic Law. Despite strong public support for incorporating referenda and citizen initiatives into the Basic Law and pleas by President Weizsäcker and other prominent East and West German public figures to modify Article 21, the members of the commission (made up exclusively of party representatives under strict party discipline) reaffirmed the "democratic party state."[54]

Through setting the parameters of political discourse, the "party-state culture" has reinforced the constitutional consensus that had been the major achievement of the Federal Republic's founders. And by providing the governmental effectiveness and stability needed for West Germany's postwar social, political, and economic transformation, the Bonn parties demonstrated that a well-managed state can be directed by strong parties. By the 1970s, a generation of citizens had matured that was no longer "burdened" by the memory of Weimar. But at just the time when public opinion polls and voting data had demonstrated the vitality of the Federal Republic's democratic culture, a new and antithetical cultural strand appeared. A growing number of citizens, especially among the young, began to show dissatisfaction with the efficient governance and the "cheerless pragmatism" offered by the *Volksparteien* and the democratic party state.

IV. The Democratic Party State under Attack: Antiparty Tendencies since the 1970s

Much as analyses of the Federal Republic's party and political systems in the first 30 years emphasized their stability, those since the late 1970s have resounded with diagnoses of crises. Similar proclamations in the 1960s and early 1970s (such as the alleged governability or legitimacy crisis) proved unwarranted in the face of unwavering voter attachment to and support for the main Bonn parties. But by the end of the 1970s, empirical studies of public attitudes and voting behavior suggested considerable popular disaffection with the established parties. Unification and the addition of voters from the five new *Länder* deepened rather than reversed this trend. Empirical data on voter disaffection, in turn, has fueled an enormous body of books and articles that blame this development on the failings of the *Volksparteien* and the democratic party state. Such accusations are generally accompanied by predictions (or warnings) of an impending crisis of German democracy and recommendations for systemic changes.

Both these tendencies were a marked departure from the democratic culture that had solidified in the first three decades of the Federal Republic's existence. This cultural change raises important questions about the future of democratic governance in united Germany. To what extent do these trends signify a return of the older antiparty tradition in both the popular "sociopolitical" and the elite, or "interpretational," cultures? Does the reemergence of sentiments critical of or hostile to political parties amount to a "crisis" of the parties and the party state? What are the long-term implications of this change for Germany's democratic culture?

Opinion and voting data are often cited by those arguing that there has been a general reversion to hostility against parties. What, then, is the empirical evidence for waning popular attachment to the established parties? In the decade before unification, opinion polls revealed a public that overwhelmingly believed that political parties were only interested in winning votes but didn't care what ordinary citizens really think or want, and that everything was really settled behind the scenes and not by citizens' choices. In these polls, most voters further expressed the belief that the main parties were unwilling or unable to do anything about significant issues such as the environment, employment, housing, energy, and peace. About three-quarters of those questioned expressed their willingness to support a new party.[55]

Initially, unification brought some respite for the main parties, but a year later public opinion polls registered yet another sharp surge in antiparty sentiments, this time among both East and West German publics. By early 1992, 81 percent of West German voters and 59 percent of East German voters felt that on key issues, the main parties did not represent their interests. The same respondents also were convinced that parties settle everything behind the scenes and are not influenced by voters' preferences. By January of 1993, 57 percent of voters in both parts of the country expressed "disappointment" with all parties. Indeed, voter cynicism toward political parties has reached levels not seen since the opinion surveys of the immediate postwar years.[56]

Another indicator of weakening voter attachment to the main parties has been the decline in party membership. Already evident in the old Federal Republic since the 1980s, this drop has increased even more since unification. In the five new *Länder,* defections have reduced the CDU's membership in 1996 to half of what it had been in 1990, the FDP's to one-third.[57] In the old *Länder,* the CDU has become a party of senior citizens, the SPD a party of the middle-aged. Electoral data furnish yet more empirical evidence for voter dissatisfaction with the main Bonn parties. Since the mid-1980s, voter turnout has persistently fallen. In the 1987 federal election, non-voting had reached 16 percent, the highest level since 1949.

Again, unification did little to stem this trend. Although turnout was slightly higher than in 1990, in the 1994 federal election, nonvoters constituted 22.2 percent of the eligible electorate. Some analysts now call this group the third *Volkspartei.*[58] Voter turnout in the *Land* elections of 1996 continued to decline and reached levels not seen since the late 1950s.[59]

Equally serious has been evidence of declining party identification. Whereas in 1972, 55 percent of West German voters identified strongly or very strongly with a political party, by 1994 only 36 percent did so. In the five new *Länder,* the percentage of those identifying strongly or very strongly with any political party reached only 26 percent in 1990 and dropped by 1 percent in 1994.[60] Weakening party attachments, in turn, have eroded electoral support for the *Volksparteien.* Their core voters fell from 60 percent of eligible voters at the beginning of the 1980s to 48 percent by the end of the decade. During the same period, party switches and ticket splitting (or, more accurately, the use of the second ballot to support another party) rose substantially. Again, unification continued rather than halted these trends. In the 1990 federal election, the combined share of the vote for three Bonn parties was down to 66.9 percent. By the 1994 federal election, it had dropped to 66.1 percent. Support for the two principal *Volksparteien* has been falling to the low levels of the first postwar elections, while the FDP struggles to survive. Voter volatility is up, though less dramatically in the West than in the East. The lowest level of voter trust and interest in the main parties is found among the youngest segments of the electorate.[61]

Yet another type of evidence cited to demonstrate citizen unhappiness with the established parties has been the extraordinary proliferation of citizen initiatives. By the end of the 1970s, approximately 50,000 initiatives had mobilized more people than all the political parties put together.[62] Three times as many citizens expressed willingness to join a citizen action group as to enter a political party.[63] Nor has this trend changed since unification. By 1990, only one-fifth of the young found working for a party to be meaningful. By contrast, especially at the local level, enthusiasm for civic action groups is undiminished. In 1993, Hamburg alone counted over 500 citizen initiatives, mini-parties, and ad hoc action groups.[64] In a 1994 public opinion poll, respondents in both the five new and the old *Länder* placed citizen initiatives and social movements seeking greater popular participation in politics far ahead of all parties (including the Alliance 90/Greens) in terms of defending voter interests.[65]

The final evidence of public unhappiness with the Bonn parties has been the readiness of voters to look for new alternatives beyond the stable tripartite party structure that had long underpinned the Federal Republic's party state. In 1983, the Greens, proclaiming themselves as "antiparty" and "anti-establishment," overcame the 5 percent threshold and entered the federal parliament. The new postmaterialist/materialist divide centered not only on a new political agenda dominated by "quality of life issues," but also on a concept of democracy that put citizen movements and direct forms of participation above conventional party and parliamentary politics.

Beginning with the 1988 municipal election in Berlin, disaffected voters also turned to parties of the right, notably (but not exclusively) to the Republikaner. Polling well in a number of municipal elections throughout the spring of 1989, this right-wing party won an astounding 14 percent of the vote in the European parliamentary elections of that summer. After unification, support for right-wing parties has fluctuated with the salience of the immigration issue. But, as recent Landtag elections have shown, the potential of support for them remains important. In Schleswig-Holstein's 1996 Landtag election, the right-wing Deutsche

Volksunion (DVU) only barely missed the 5 percent threshold (4.3 percent). In the 1997 Hamburg elections, which had centered on crime, the DVU missed getting into the legislature by only 238 votes.[66]

Unification produced yet another alternative for disaffected voters in the form of the PDS, the (reformed) successor to East Germany's former Communist ruling party (the SED). Appealing primarily to East Germans disappointed with the social and economic consequences of unification, the PDS (rather than the Social Democrats or the Greens) has become the party of choice for those unhappy with the policies of the Bonn coalition. The PDS emerged from the 1994 federal elections as the third-largest party in the five new *Länder*. At the *Land* and local levels, the strength of PDS support (and the virtual disappearance of the FDP and Alliance 90/Greens) has helped the election of PDS mayors or else has forced both the CDU and the SPD to consider more or less formal arrangements with the PDS for its support.

How has this body of empirical evidence been interpreted? For the past three decades, a substantial number of intellectuals, academics, and publicists — that is, what Rohe calls the *Deutungskultur* (the culture of those shaping interpretation) — have blamed the Federal Republic's *Volksparteien* and party state for an increasingly alienated electorate. These critics see existing evidence of disaffection as severe enough to constitute a crisis — defined variously as a crisis of political representation, as a crisis of the party system, as a crisis of democracy itself.[67]

According to this body of critics, voter disenchantment with the main parties stems from their inability to perform two key functions: that of responding to new issues of concern to voters, and that of representing voter interests. As to party responsiveness, until unification the new issues and concerns said to be ignored by the main parties have been attributed to the "postmaterialist" revolution. Voter defections to citizen initiatives and the Greens were accounted for by the unwillingness of the *Volksparteien* to address what postmaterialists regarded as the critical "problems of the future": environmental disasters, the limits of growth, the threat of new technologies, the danger of nuclear war, and pollution.

Since Germany's unification, voter discontent has allegedly centered on the unexpected social and psychological upheavals produced by this momentous development, its economic costs, and its political ramifications. The main *Volksparteien* are seen as either unwilling or incompetent to deal with these new challenges. By persisting with status quo policies in the face of mounting problems, the *Volksparteien* are accused of having created an increasing sense of immobility, stagnation, and decline.[68]

The increasing inability of the main parties to "represent" ordinary voters and their interests, in turn, has been blamed both on the unanticipated effects of the party state and on the characteristics of the main *Volksparteien*. To critics of the party state, one of its unexpected outcomes has been the "etatization" of the Federal Republic's established political parties. One effect has been the large number of civil servants among party members and parliamentary deputies.[69] This is said to have produced the conflation of state and party outlooks. Thus party representatives pay more attention to official expertise and technical competence than to the political wishes and interests of voters.[70] Another sign of etatization is the level of public financing the parties now receive. As "crypto-organs" of the state, they benefit from state resources. Party functions have become "state activities."[71] Above all, etatization is said to have extended political appointments within the state so far as to abolish the distinction between party and state. Such appointments (*Ämterpatronage*) are described as not limited to the state administration, but as extending as well to ostensibly nonpolitical constitutional organs such as the Federal Constitutional Court or the Office for the Protection of the Constitution.[72] In this view, the growing dependence of the main parties on state funding and patronage appointments has made political parties more concerned with maintaining control over the state than with meeting their representative responsibilities.[73]

Such critics further charge the main parties with having used the constitutional party-state doctrine and the 1967 Party Law to gain ever-greater influence over all society. The *Volksparteien* are said to have done so through patronage appointments to all state-supported "social" institutions—from media, universities, and theaters to savings banks, hospitals, and state-organized lotto. But increasingly, the parties have entered as well private industry (through appointments to boards of directors) and private associations from volunteer groups to sport clubs. Although the parties claim that such activities on their part bring them closer to voters, their critics describe the parties as "strangling civil society."[74]

Other items included in this indictment are the scale of resources and patronage opportunities provided by the party state at all levels of government. Such arrangements have been depicted as encouraging interparty "cartel" arrangements to share the privileges of the party state rather than to risk losing them through electoral competition. At the federal level, such interparty arrangements have been identified as ranging from cross-party support for public funding of the parties to salaries and benefit packages for parliamentarians, as well as quota deals for positions in all key administrative and political institutions.

Such cartel agreements are said to be equally common at the *Land* and local levels.

In short, critics of the party state charge it with having contributed to a "goal displacement" among the main parties. Party leaders are described as primarily concerned with secretive accommodations of their own interests. In this view, the "undesirable intimacy" among the established parties, state bureaucracy, public institutions, and private interest organizations, moreover, reinforces public impressions of an all-powerful, increasingly corrupt "cartel of power" closed to ordinary citizens and immune to reform through conventional electoral politics. Unable to have their interests represented within parliament and without a real alternative among the established parliamentary parties, citizens had no choice but to seek new channels of representation and new modes of influence outside parliament.[75]

The undesirable features of the party state, critics maintain, have been reinforced by the characteristics of its main pillars, the two principal *Volksparteien*, the SPD and the CDU/CSU. As these have evolved into "catch-all" parties with a broad, nonideological, pragmatic approach to voters, they have become more distant for ordinary voters.[76] Seen initially as a force of stability, by the 1980s the catch-all parties, or *Volksparteien*, came to be attacked as undemocratic, unrepresentative, vote-maximizing machines. They have been condemned for avoiding controversy and settling instead for the "minimum consensus." Instead of providing genuine programmatic choices, as democratic parties are meant to do, they offer voters superficial "product differentiation."[77]

The *Volksparteien* are further accused of failing to create emotional bonds with voters or to integrate new social groups. Instead, as parties out to achieve maximum electoral support, they opted for universal appeal. They have become "generalists of public opinion."[78] So similar did some critics find the two main parties that they likened the Federal Republic to a "one-party state."[79] Rejecting such programmatic blandness, voters opted increasingly for alternative forms of expressions and participation outside the established party system through the new social movements and citizen initiatives.[80]

The *Volksparteien* have also been attacked for their reliance on quotas to manage intraparty conflicts. This had become necessary because the main parties have become so fragmented in their social base and organization as to resemble a "loosely coupled anarchy."[81] To minimize the centrifugal tendencies inherent in this fragmentation, the *Volksparteien* have found it useful to divide positions within the party, parliament, state administration, or public institutions among the various factions according to formally negotiated quotas. Indeed, the use of quotas

(*Proporz*) is said to be the "glue" that holds the main parties together, especially at the *Land* and local levels.[82] Intraparty quotas discourage citizens from joining or participating in the main parties since such arrangements reduce the influence of ordinary members in party affairs and contribute to organizational inertia.

Perhaps the most telling charge is that the Federal Republic's founding parties have refused to acknowledge and respond to the positive changes in the German electorate. The politically indifferent, cynical, passive citizenry of the immediate postwar years had been transformed by the 1980s into a politically involved and active one. It is no longer willing to submit to being administered by technocratic and administrative experts or to having its political will formed by and in the image of the main parties. Instead, German voters are eager to broaden their participation beyond periodic trips to the polling booth. The proliferation of citizen initiatives and alternative forms of political and social agency in the late 1970s and 1980s was, above all, a redefinition of the German citizenry's relationship to politics.[83] Since the main parties do little more than fortify their own positions and organizations, citizens are themselves seeking new forms of public involvement through decentralization, direct forms of participation and influence in policy-making, policy-oriented citizen initiatives at the local level, and grassroots parties with nonprofessional citizen-representatives. Such innovations are seen as necessary for revitalizing existing parliamentary and party institutions.[84]

Unification not only continued all these criticisms of the party state and the *Volksparteien* raised in the previous decade but also added new dimensions. For the first time, East German commentators, including prominent members of the citizen movement and East German party politicians, added their views. Less concerned with the failings of the (West) German party-state, their complaints focused primarily on the mistakes made by the Bonn parties during the process of unification; on their failure to deal with the socioeconomic and psychological problems of integration; and on their unwillingness to undertake necessary reforms in the West, as had been done in the East. East German critiques also emphasized the inability of the West German parties to transcend partisan divisions and deal with important problems in an objective, nonpartisan way.[85]

No less novel after unification was the entry into the party debate by the Federal Republic's highly respected president, Richard von Weizsäcker. He not only reconfirmed pre-unification criticisms, but concurred in East German attacks on the responses of the West German parties to unification. Having underestimated the challenges presented by unification, he argued, the *Volksparteien* then failed to prepare East and West German voters for the initial hardships unification might entail. They had neither argued its long-term benefits nor emphasized the importance of solidarity in a common endeavor. He also chided the main parties for their failure to adopt constitutional reforms that incorporated such East German contributions as the Roundtable or the participation of citizen initiatives in elections.[86]

V. Return of the Antiparty Culture?

At least on the surface, the empirical evidence of persisting voter disaffection with the *Volksparteien* and elite critiques of them and the party state suggest that 40 years of democratic government have not entirely succeeded in eradicating the "antiparty gene" from German political culture. But do these recent trends in the "sociopolitical" and "interpretational" culture really signify the resurgence of the older antiparty tradition? In terms of the empirical evidence, there is a general consensus that for the past two decades, voting and opinion data have revealed a worrisome erosion in the support of the Federal Republic's main parties. Yet there is much less agreement on the extent to which contemporary voter attitudes and behavior amount to a fundamental and massive repudiation of the *Volksparteien* or the democratic party state.

One problem is that many of the measures used as empirical indicators of voter sentiments are themselves flawed. The concepts of alienation from the parties, politics, and the democratic state (*Parteien-, Politik-,* and *Staatsverdrossenheit*) are rarely clearly (or uniformly) defined, distinguished, and operationalized. Furthermore, the public opinion and voting trends they measure are open to a variety of conflicting interpretations. Nor do existing voting and opinion data reveal much about the contents, forms, and depth of alleged voter alienation.[87]

Furthermore, those who use empirical data to point to a fundamental *Parteien-, Politik-,* or *Staatsverdrossenheit* in the German population often downplay evidence to the contrary. Longitudinal studies have shown no fundamental antiparty mood, nor a long-term antiparty trend. Throughout the past two decades, moreover, far more German voters had declared themselves satisfied with the democratic system and its parties than alienated from it. This was as true before as it was after unification and applies to West as much as to East German voters.[88]

Moreover, voter disaffection toward political parties fluctuates considerably with perceived trends in the overall economic picture. Thus, in the immediate postunification period, voter disaffection rose sharply in 1991, as the economic downturn hit both the eastern and western parts of the country. With signs of economic improvements in early 1994, levels of public disappointment with the parties declined: in the West, from 57 percent in 1992 to 27 percent by September 1994; in the five new *Länder,* from 54 percent in January 1993 to 30 percent by September 1994.[89]

Nor does support for citizen initiatives or more participatory politics necessarily signify either alienation from politics in general or a rejection of conventional forms of participation. Until the mid-1980s, at the height of the citizen initiatives in West Germany, the established parties experienced a massive growth in their membership. Hans Rattinger has further shown that an affective loss of trust in parties may nonetheless lead to heightened political involvement, based on eminently rational motives. Supporters of citizen movements do not drop out of the active electorate but continue with both conventional and unconventional forms of participation.[90]

The electoral evidence, too, is far less conclusive than is claimed by those who assert that there is a crisis of the party state or a reversion to old antiparty views. In the 1994 Bundestag election, the two main parties actually attracted previous nonvoters. Turnout in that election had slightly increased, to 79 percent of the eligible electorate from 77.8 percent in 1990. While overall support for the main Bonn parties was down, it remained high in the East. Party loyalty, as measured by ticket splitting, remained also surprisingly high. Thus in the 1994 federal election, 95 percent of the CDU/CSU voters cast both ballots for their party, as did 91 percent of the SPD supporters.

Another notable feature of that election was the poor showing of extremist and protest parties. Despite high levels of voter discontent and three years of recession, the combined national protest vote only reached 6.1 percent. Most of it came from support for the PDS in the five new *Länder,* where the party is viewed not as "extremist" but as a legitimate, democratic party representing East German interests. Although the 1994 federal and *Land* elections showed a clear East and West cleavage, its political implications may be no more serious for the German party system than the materialist/postmaterialist divide turned out to be.[91] Seen from a comparative perspective, moreover, Germany's "dealigning" trends are neither unique nor unusual in scale.

Finally, analysts have differed in their explanations of these antiparty tendencies. Rather than pointing to a fundamental alienation from the *Volksparteien* and the party state, the voting and opinion trends of the 1980s have been diagnosed as revealing an electorate more critical, more sophisticated, and more demanding.[92] Alternatively, these movements of voting and opinion have been analyzed as reflecting changes produced by more general processes of modernization and secularization.[93] Still other theories emphasize cyclical patterns of voter participation and voter withdrawal. Indeed, Andreas Schedler has challenged much of the "empirical evidence" for mass alienation from the parties as little more than a demoscopic construct that created the phenomenon it claims to investigate.[94] In the same vein, Peter Haungs and Eckhart Jesse have seen in much of the party-crisis literature merely the typical penchant of West German analysts to see in every shortcoming (real or perceived) a "crisis."[95]

In short, empirical measures reveal an electorate that is certainly less stable in its political loyalties, less content with main parties, and more independent or critical in its partisan responses than was the case in the first three decades of the Federal Republic. At the same time, this electorate shows few signs of fundamental hostility to the Federal Republic's party and political system. At the level of the sociopolitical culture, then, there is little basis for those who worry about a revival of the antiparty and antidemocratic past. What of the "interpretational" culture itself? Do the criticisms launched against the established parties and party state reveal continuities with Germany's antiparty tradition in the public discourse? Here the evidence is more mixed.

On the positive side, contemporary critics show little interest in above-party alternatives to the present constitutional order. Parties are criticized not for furthering social disunity but for failing to represent the diverse, pluralistic interests of society. Similarly, for today's party critics, the key issue is not whether a party-based democracy threatens the proper constitutional order. Rather, the problem is whether the parties themselves in practice abide by democratic principles either in terms of their own organization or in terms of their relationship to the citizenry. Much of the criticism against the *Volksparteien* centers on their "representational" deficit, which derives from their preoccupation with the state rather than with citizens. By contrast, the rhetorical staples of past antiparty critiques have all but disappeared from public discourse.[96]

Yet while critics of the Bonn parties and the "democratic party state" emphasize their commitment to political democracy (if not necessarily to the Federal Republic's version of it), some of their arguments are difficult to reconcile with pluralistic democratic politics. In fact, the antiparty rhetoric of the *Deutungskultur* shows certain continuities with the modes of arguments found in the older antiparty culture. Earlier opponents of parties feared they might bring into the state the diverse, conflicting interests of society. Contemporary critics worry about the penetration and impact of "statified" parties on civil society. In either case, political parties are viewed as subverting or perverting the purity of whatever sphere they enter.

Once again we find a distinction made between political parties and movements reminiscent of the antiparty culture in the past. While social movements are viewed positively, as dynamic, active, vital, forces of change, parties are depicted as rigid, stultifying, soulless, bureaucratic institutions of the status quo.[97] Equally reminiscent of past antiparty attacks is the denigration of parliamentary or representative democracy. Assertions of its inadequacy are derived not from its incapacity to govern but from its distance from the democratic ideal of genuine popular sovereignty. More democracy is equated with less party, as if the two were bound together in some fundamental zero-sum logic.[98]

No less problematic from a pluralist perspective is the rhetoric of crisis in much of the literature on citizen movements or party crisis. On the one hand, the proliferation of crises (of values, civilization, orientation, modernity, acceptance, representation) conveys the image of a society in a state of total upheaval. More ominously, these crises are depicted as dramatic either-or choices between the politics of the status quo and the survival of the planet and/or German democracy. Fundamental crises obviously require radical solutions. At such extreme moments, it is argued, "the demand of citizens to shape political decisions must take precedence over the requirement of effective party government precisely because the whole value base on which effective democratic politics rests must be newly created."[99] In effect, the crisis rhetoric denigrates traditional representative institutions and procedures in favor of untried modes of decision making.

Furthermore, contemporary party critics all too often place demands on political parties that go far beyond their functions of representation, mediation, and governance. Political parties are called upon by their adversaries to provide "spiritual meaning," orientation, identity, societal visions. The parties are thus expected not just to satisfy the basic needs of individuals but to offer them affection, spiritual and intellectual stimulation, "justice of needs" (*Bedürfnisgerechtigkeit*).[100] Such expectations are clearly more suitable for churches than for modern parties.

Some themes introduced by Weizsäcker are no less problematic. They often resemble arguments against party government heard in the early postwar years. Thus Weizsäcker stresses that postunification Germany is a society in "need of orientation." At such times, party politicians should "take on seriously the great questions of the day" and deal with them in the interests of everyone. In the face of such existential problems, "partisan positions become irrelevant. . . . The only important thing is which answers are suitable to the problems confronting unified Germany and not which party supplies them." In his view, "the best thing the parties can do to retain the respect of the population is to . . . overcome their ever-present defensiveness against nonpartisanship."

Finally, Weizsäcker clearly favors reintroducing mechanisms designed to minimize the "stultifying" effects of parties: the direct elections of top political leaders, such as mayors and minister presidents; primaries; and the elimination of list candidates for the federal parliament. Disinterring proposals rejected in the Basic Law, he suggested the "need to rethink the introduction of more plebiscitary elements" and the role of the president as "representing and expressing nonpartisan positions." Similarly, Weizsäcker supports enforcing the independent mandate stipulated in Article 38 as well as revitalizing parliament as an arena for debate and decision making by reducing party discipline and thus the power of the parliamentary parties. He further called for curtailing state funding of political parties, giving ordinary members a greater voice within the parties, and providing more opportunities for outsiders and nonprofessional politicians (*Seiteneinsteiger*) to serve as candidates.[101]

All too often, such proposals to end voter disaffection with the parties and the party state reveal the same ambivalence toward "politics" in general and "party politics" in particular found in the antiparty culture of the past. Common to such calls for change is a view of politics that assumes or desires some natural harmony, some common good, or ultimate truths distorted by partisan competition and conflict. A further assumption is that of a distinctive, discernible public interest inaccessible to political parties but readily determined by ordinary citizens, nonpartisan public figures (such as the federal president), or above-party institutions (Roundtables or Enquete Commissions). Often, misgivings about partisan competition stem from a fundamental discomfort with the pluralist clash of opinions and with the need to arrive at compromises among parties representing divergent electorates and interests.

Nor do party critics acknowledge the complexity of contemporary social, economic, and political problems that parties are called upon to resolve but for which there are no single or simple solutions. Equally ignored are the constraints under which the *Volksparteien* must operate. These include a complex, decentralized institutional structure, which limits room for maneuver and requires bargaining accommodation; a divided electorate whose conflicting demands must be reconciled; domestic and international economic pressures and actors who must be accommodated; and external obligations (to the EU, NATO, the UN).[102]

Although the criticisms of the *Volksparteien* and party state have (in contrast to the Weimar Republic) failed to destabilize the Federal

Republic, there are good reasons to be concerned about the long-term impact of a persistent antiparty trend in the interpretative culture. Such critiques have dominated public discussions of parties for the past 20 years. "Lamentations" over the state of the parties and the party state have become so persistent and pervasive as to have created a "discourse of disaffection" (*Verdrussdiskurs*). Moreover, as Peter Lösche has pointed out, this discourse, quite apart from the evidence supporting it, is increasingly capable of producing genuinely destructive effects on the polity.[103]

By obscuring the very real achievements and strengths of the Federal Republic's party system and state, constant complaints about the sins of the *Volksparteien* and the shortcomings of the democratic party state may re-create a political culture in which antipathy to parties once again becomes the norm. A whole generation has been continuously exposed to antiparty criticisms. Will their commitment to the Federal Republic's democratic state withstand a major crisis? Although not an issue in the present generation, such "inherited" distrust of parties may pose a problem for the future.

Thus, in the absence of any positive reinforcements, future voters may be turned off by party politics to a degree where the oft-proclaimed "crisis of democracy" may become a self-fulfilling prophecy. Such a possibility cannot be dismissed given the close identity between the Federal Republic's principal parties and the democracy they have helped to found and maintain. As Peter Glotz put it: "The Federal Republic of Germany is a party state. The German parties are in a crisis. If the crisis of the parties is not to turn into a crisis of the democratic state, we must act quickly."[104]

A further ground for concern is the evident "bifurcation" in Germany's democratic culture. Increasingly, this encompasses two distinctive and conflicting strands. The first is a "citizen" culture represented by demands for more citizen participation, more citizen voice in decision making, more citizen-oriented grassroots politics. The other is the "party-state culture," represented by the main Bonn parties, who rely on Leibholz's constitutional theory both to legitimate their political and cultural hegemony and to ward off demands for greater citizen participation.

Thus far, the antiparty mood evident at both the mass and elite level has not produced a fundamental repudiation of the Federal Republic's distinctive party state. But the new citizen culture, with its ambivalence about (if not hostility to) the all-pervasive power and influence of the established parties, presents a potential danger for the Berlin Republic. In the long run it will be difficult to maintain the party state in a nonsupportive political culture.

Yet the problem is altogether different from that confronting the Weimar Republic, where a democratic system was implanted in a culture ill-suited to it. By contrast, the *Volksparteien* can take pride in having helped to create a democratic or civic culture in which citizens respond critically to those in power, expect parties to be responsive and responsible, and demand more involvement in the political process. Consequently, rather than forever invoking memories of the Weimar Republic's destruction by forces hostile to political parties, the *Volksparteien* need to respond constructively to legitimate criticisms of the party state as it functions in practice and to demands for less party-dominated forms of social and political activities. The point is not to supplant the democratic party state but to adapt it to an altogether new environment by devising constitutional and political solutions that incorporate the lessons of the Bonn Republic rather than those of its ill-fated predecessor.

Conclusion

Since the early postwar years, there has been an ongoing debate about the relationship of political parties and German democracy. The first such debate occurred in the period of occupation. At the time, Konrad Adenauer and Kurt Schumacher persistently fought antiparty currents evident in public opinion, in the statements of German public figures worried about party influence in government, and in efforts by the Western Allies trying to keep the lid on partisan politics while managing the problems of occupation. The major democratic parties developed successful strategies for extending party influence and thereby laid the foundations of Germany's democratic party state. The Federal Constitutional Court both provided constitutional and legal legitimacy and strengthened the party state in practice. For the first time there emerged in Germany a stable democracy and a democratic culture supportive of political parties and government by them.

But the 1970s gave rise to a new party debate. Evidence of erosion in voter attachments to the main parties produced a massive literature critical of the party state and its pillars, the *Volksparteien*. Out of this debate a new division emerged in the German electorate, between conventional party politics and participatory citizen politics. Yet, prior to unification, the Bonn parties proved remarkably successful in integrating the new groups and agenda into the existing party and political system. While a new antiparty culture had emerged, it was not antidemocratic, nor did it supplant the dominant party-state culture. Germany's unification, however, reignited the party debate. With mounting evidence of the difficulties and costs entailed by merging two such different societies, opinion and voting data showed once again widespread disaffection with the established Bonn parties. Predictably, such signs of voter unhappiness produced yet another wave of analyses critical of the *Volksparteien* and the party state. This time, criticisms focused on the manner in which unification had been carried out as well as its impact on the old and new *Länder*. Despite voter restiveness and pervasive criticisms, however, efforts to reform the party-dominated constitutional order were defeated. The party-state culture, while not uncontested, nonetheless continues to be dominant.

As long as the main parties continue to perform reasonably well at the governmental level, the persistence of a strand in the democratic culture critical of them may not matter. In the long run, however, merely insisting on the tried and true may not suffice. Having contributed to the emergence of a citizenry politically more mature and self-confident than any in the past, the main parties now need to provide mechanisms for involving it in resolving the increasingly complex issues facing united Germany.

In the founding period of the Federal Republic, the *Volksparteien* had arrived at workable and successful solutions to the older antiparty tradition. They must now follow up this success by adapting the constitutional order they had created to the participatory or citizen culture that resulted from it. Yet critics of the Federal Republic's *Volksparteien* and party state must also accept that whatever their alleged faults, they have provided five decades of stable and democratic government and thereby contributed to the emergence of a vital and resilient democratic culture. Those are major achievements that could not have been predicted in 1945.

NOTES

My thanks are due to the College of Staten Island for its support by providing me with release time and with a Faculty Incentive Award.

1. For a comparative survey, see Erwin Faul, "Verfemung, Duldung und Anerkennung des Parteiwesens in der Geschichte des politischen Denkens," *Politische Vierteljahresschrift* 5 (1964): 61–94.

2. Karl Rohe, "The State Tradition: Changes and Continuities," in *Political Culture in Germany,* ed. Dirk Berg-Schlosser and Ralf Rytlevski (New York: St. Martin's Press, 1993), 216.

3. Gordon Smith, "West Germany: The Politics of Centrality," *Government and Opposition* 11 (1976): 398.

4. For this term, see Rohe, "State Tradition," 223.

5. Quoted in Gordon Smith, *Democracy in Western Germany,* 2d ed. (New York: Holmes & Meier, 1982), 9.

6. For an excellent historical survey of the concept of party in German political and legal thought, see Klaus von Beyme, "Partei, Fraktion," in *Geschichtliche Grundbegriffe: Historisches Lexicon zur sozialen und politischen Sprache in Deutschland,* ed. Otto Brunner, Werner Conze, and Reinhardt Koselleck, 8 vols. (Stuttgart: Klett-Cotta, 1972–96), 4:677–733.

7. Quoted in Waldemar Besson, "Regierung und Opposition in der deutschen Politik," *Politische Vierteljahresschrift* 3 (1962): 228.

8. Rohe, "State Tradition," 221.

9. For Weimar constitutional thought concerning political parties, see Werner Conze, "Die deutschen Parteien in der Staatsverfassung vor 1933," in *Das Ende der Parteien 1933,* ed. Erich Matthias and Rudolf Morsey (Düsseldorf: Athenäum/Droste Taschenbücher, 1979), 3–28.

10. For the "antiparty" elements of the Weimar constitution, see Michael Stürmer, "Der Unvollendete Parteienstaat," *Vierteljahreshefte für Zeitgeschichte* 2 (1973): 119–26.

11. For the Weimar Republic's antiparty culture and its manipulation by the Nazis, see Thomas Nipperdey, "1933 und die Kontinuität der deutschen Geschichte," in *Die Weimarer Republik: Belagerte Civitas,* ed. Michael Stürmer (Meisenhain a. G.: Verlag Anton Hain, 1980).

12. An excellent and detailed account of the licensing policies of the Western Allies is Daniel E. Rogers, *Politics after Hitler* (New York: New York University Press, 1995).

13. For a highly informed and comprehensive analysis of Allied constraints on party politics, see Ilona Klein, *Die Bundesrepublik als Parteienstaat: Die Mitwirkung der politischen Parteien an der Willensbildung des Volkes, 1945–1949* (Frankfurt a. M.: Peter Lang, 1990).

14. Quoted in Klein, *Bundesrepublik als Parteienstaat,* 59ff.

15. For the federalist views of the South German minister presidents, see Wolfgang Benz, "Föderalistische Politik in der CDU/CSU: Die Verfassungsdiskussion im 'Ellwanger Kreis': 1947/48," *Vierteljahreshefte für Zeitgeschichte* 25 (1977): 776–820; also Klein, *Bundesrepublik als Parteienstaat,* 56–74.

16. For details, see Anna J. Merritt and Richard L. Merritt, *Public Opinion in Occupied Germany: The OMGUS Surveys, 1945–1949* (Urbana: University of Illinois Press, 1970).

17. For this description, see Volker Otto, *Das Staatsverständnis des Parlamentarischen Rats* (Düsseldorf: Droste, 1971), 41ff.

18. Kurt Schumacher, *Reden, Schriften, Korrespondenzen, 1945–1952,* ed. Willy Albrecht (Bonn: Verlag J. H. W. Dietz, 1985), 370.

19. Remarks made at a CDU conference in Bad Godesberg, 14 December 1946, quoted in *Der Parlamentarische Rat 1948–1949: Akten und Protokolle,* 3 vols. (Boppard am Rhein: Boldt, 1974–85), 1:1137 (hereafter cited as *Akten*).

20. For Adenauer's efforts to control the CDU within and outside the British zone, see Helmuth Pütz, ed., *Konrad Adenauer und die CDU der Britischen Besatzungszone* (Bonn: Eichholz Verlag, 1975), especially pp. 87–98; for Schumacher's defense of party discipline in the Parliamentary Council, see

his "Speech to the SPD Executive, Länder Parties, and SPD Delegates to the Parliamentary Council on April 20, 1949," in Schumacher, *Reden,* 637.

21. Kenneth Dyson, *Party, State, and Bureaucracy* (Beverly Hills: Sage, 1977), 22.

22. For arguments to this effect in the British zone, see Raymond Ebsworth, *Restoring Democracy in Germany: The British Contribution* (London: Stevens & Sons, 1960), 146ff; for similar arguments by members of the bizonal administration, see *Akten* 1:963.

23. For the SPD's position on the civil service, see Wolfgang Langhorst, *Beamtentum und Artikel 131 des Grundgesetzes* (Frankfurt a. M.: Peter Lang, 1994), 37ff.

24. For the Allied civil service reforms and German responses, see especially Wolfgang Benz, "Versuche zur Reform des Öffentlichen Dienstes in Deutschland, 1945–1952," *Vierteljahreshefte für Zeitgeschichte* 29 (1981): 216–45; for the effects of denazification on the civil service, see especially Justus Fürstenau, *Entnazifizierung* (Neuwied and Berlin: Hermann Luchterhand Verlag, 1969).

25. The predominance of civil servants in the Parliamentary Council (61 percent) virtually ensured that the Basic Law not only constitutionally legitimated the professional civil service (Article 33), but also incorporated its substantive demands (Articles 33, 75, 131, 132, 133). For the civil service's role in the drafting of the Basic Law, see John Ford Golay, *The Founding of the Federal Republic of Germany* (Chicago: University of Chicago Press, 1958), 66–74.

26. After the *Land* elections of 1946, for instance, roughly half of the deputies in the Hessian and Württemberg-Baden parliaments were also members of the *Land* civil service; see Ebsworth, *Restoring Democracy,* 147.

27. Hartmut Pietsch, *Militärregierung, Bürokratie und Sozialisierung: Zur Entwicklung des politischen Systems in den Städten des Ruhrgebiets* (Duisburg: W. Braun, 1978), 199.

28. For such agreements, see Curt Garner, "Zerschlagung des Berufsbeamtentums," *Vierteljahreshefte für Zeitgeschichte* 39 (1991): 95–98; for similar interparty agreements on sharing positions in the NWDR, see Theodor Eschenburg, *Jahre der Besatzung: Die Geschichte der Bundesrepublik Deutschlands* (Stuttgart: Deutsche Verlagsanstalt, 1983), 138.

29. For arguments in favor of a strong, independently elected president, see Golay, *Founding of the Federal Republic,* 125. Ironically, the greatest defenders of plebiscitary mechanisms were the "conservative" South German federalists, who saw them as a way to "dam the party spirit" by enabling minorities to appeal directly to the population. For the debate over these mechanisms, see Otmar Jung, *Grundgesetz und Volksentscheid: Gründe und Reichweite der Entscheidungen des Parlamentarischen Rats gegen Formen der direkten Demokratie* (Opladen: Westdeutscher Verlag, 1993).

30. It was included as Article 38 of the Basic Law. For the debate over the independent mandate, see *Akten* 3:105.

31. For the debate on the second chamber, see especially *Akten* 2:132–46.

32. Wilhelm Hennis, "Parteienstaat," *Süddeutsche Zeitung,* 12 November 1985, Feuilleton.

33. The most comprehensive statement of his theory is found in Gerhard Leibholz, *Strukturprobleme in der modernen Demokratie* (Karlsruhe: Verlag C. F. Müller, 1958). For critiques of Leibholz's theory, see Kenneth Dyson, *Party, State, and Bureaucracy,* 8–9; and Richard Saage, "Zum Begriff der Parteien und des Parlaments bei Carl Schmitt und Gerhard Leibholz," in his *Zurück zum starken Staat?* (Frankfurt a. M.: Suhrkamp Verlag, 1983), 156–80.

34. Leibholz, *Strukturprobleme,* 123ff.; 1 BVerfGE 223 (1952); 2 BVerfGE 11 (1952). For the Court's arguments to this effect, see Gerhard Leibholz, Hans-Justus Rinck, and K. Helberg, eds., *Grundgesetz für die Bundesrepublik Deutschland: Kommentar an Hand der Rechtsprechung des Bundesverfassungsgericht* (Cologne: Verlag Dr. Otto Schmidt, 1968), 276–77.

35. 1 BVerfGE 208, 240–41 (1952); for other cases reflecting this interpretation, see especially Leibholz, Rinck, and Helberg, *Grundgesetz,* 308–9.

36. 4 BVerfGE 27 (1954).

37. For Leibholz's view on the relationship between Article 21 and Article 38 of the Basic Law, see Gerhard Leibholz, "Parteienstaat und repräsentative Demokratie," *Deutsches Verwaltungsblatt* 66 (1951): 1–8; for the Federal Constitutional Court's contradictory rulings, see Manfred Abelein, "Die Rechtssprechung des Bundesverfassungsgericht," in *Um Recht und Freiheit. Festschrift für Friedrich August Freiherr von der Heydtte,* 2 vols., ed. Heinrich Kipp et al. (Berlin: Duncker & Humblot, 1977), 2:777–92.

38. For the Court's 1958 ruling, see 8 BVerfGE 51 (1958); for party finance rulings since then, see Donald Kommers, *The Constitutional Jurisprudence of the Federal Republic* (Durham, N.C., and London: Duke University Press, 1989), 201–15.

39. For quotes and a general analysis of the Court's ruling in favor of the *Volksparteien,* see Hans-Justus Rinck, "Der verfassungsrechtliche Status der politischen Parteien in der Bundesrepublik," in *Die moderne Demokratie und ihr Recht,* ed. Karl Dietrich Bracher, Christopher Dawson, Willi Geiger, and Rudolf Smend (Tübingen: J. C. B. Mohr [Paul Siebeck], 1966), 310–28.

40. For the relevant rulings, see Kommers, *Constitutional Jurisprudence,* 224–28.

41. Gabriel Almond and Sidney Verba, *The Civic Culture* (Princeton: Princeton University Press, 1963).

42. For these data, see David Conradt, "The Changing German Political Culture," in *The Civic Culture Revisited,* ed. Gabriel Almond and Sidney Verba (Boston: Little, Brown, 1980), 224–25; also Kendall L. Baker, Russell J. Dalton, and Kai Hildebrandt, *Germany Transformed* (Cambridge, Mass.: Harvard University Press, 1981), 38–58.

43. The Law on Political Parties (*Parteiengesetz*), 1967 and 1994, in *Documents on Politics and Society in the Federal Republic of Germany* (Bonn: Federal Ministry of the Interior, 1978, 1995).

44. Wilhelm Hennis, "Der 'Parteienstaat' des Grundgesetzes: Eine gelun-

gene Erfindung," in *Die Kontroverse: Weizsäcker's Parteienkritik in der Diskussion,* ed. Gunther Hofmann and Werner Perger (Frankfurt a. M.: Eichborn Verlag, 1992), 45.

45. Gordon Smith, "The German *Volkspartei* and the Career of the Catch-All Concept," in *Party Government and Political Culture in West Germany,* ed. Herbert Döring and Gordon Smith (New York: St. Martin's Press, 1982), 66ff.

46. William Paterson and Douglas Webber, "The Federal Republic of Germany: The Re-emergent Opposition," in *Opposition in Western Europe,* ed. Eva Kolinski (New York: St. Martin's Press, 1987), 92.

47. Ibid., 146.

48. To be fair, cooperative opposition is reinforced by the complexity of the Federal Republic's decentralized and fragmented decision-structure. For this point, see Paterson and Webber, "Re-emergent Opposition?" 151.

49. For an excellent discussion of the Federal Republic's "mix" of adversarial/majoritarian and "concordance" democracy, see Oskar W. Gabriel, "Das lokale Parteiensystem zwischen Wettbewerbs- und Konsensdemokratie," in *Parteien und regionale Traditionen in der Bundesrepublik Deutschland,* ed. Dieter Oberndörfer and Karl Schmitt (Berlin: Duncker & Humblot, 1991), 371–96.

50. For the historical origins of "Proporzkultur," or quota culture, and its resurgence in the Federal Republic, see Thomas Kühne, "Zur Genese der deutschen Proporzkultur im Wilhelminischen Preussen," *Politische Vierteljahresschrift* 36 (1995): 222–42.

51. Gunther Hofmann and Werner A. Perger, *Richard von Weizsäcker im Gespräch* (Frankfurt a. M.: Eichborn Verlag, 1992).

52. Willy Brandt, "Was soll das Gerede vom Parteitagsstaat," *Vorwärts,* 13 October 1977, reprinted in Ulrich Sarcinelli, "Etablierte Parteien und 'Parteienverdrossenheit' – Reflexionen von Politikern zur Parteiensystemkritik," in *Handbuch des deutschen Parteiensystems,* ed. Heino Kaak and Reinhold Roth (Opladen: Westdeutscher Verlag, 1980), 1:310–16.

53. *Die Welt am Sonntag,* 19 July 1992. Kohl's defense of the party state was taken up as well by other prominent politicians in all the major parties. For their responses, see *Die Zeit,* 3 July 1992 and 31 July 1992; also *Frankfurter Allgemeine Zeitung,* 20 June 1992 and 25 June 1992.

54. For the debate over the constitutional reforms, see especially the essays by Henning Voscherau, "Verfassungsreform und Verfassungsdiskurs"; Wolfgang Fischer, "Formen unmittelbarer Demokratie im Grundgesetz"; and Rupert Scholz, "Die gemeinsame Verfassungskommission: Auftrag, Verfahren, Ergebnisse," all in *Aus Politik und Zeitgeschichte,* B52 (1994).

55. For details, see Manfred Küchler, "Staats-, Parteien-, oder Politikverdrossenheit?" in *Bürger und Parteien,* ed. Joachim Raschke (Opladen: Westdeutscher Verlag, 1982), 39–54.

56. Renate Köcher, "Auf einer Woge der Euphorie," *Aus Politik und Zeitgeschichte,* B51 (1994): 16–17.

57. Geoffrey K. Roberts, *Party Politics in the New Germany* (London: Pinter, 1997), 174.

58. Jürgen Falter and Siegfried Schumann, "Nichtwahl und Protestwahl: Zwei Seiten einer Medaille," *Aus Politik und Zeitgeschichte*, B11 (1993).

59. For the Landtag elections of 1996, see *Berichte der Forschungsgruppe Wahlen e. V. Mannheim*, Nr. 84 (Baden-Württemberg); Nr. 85 (Rhineland-Palatinate); Nr. 86 (Schleswig-Holstein) (Mannheim: Forschungsgruppe Wahlen e. V., 1996).

60. Russell J. Dalton, "A Divided Electorate?" in *Developments in German Politics*, ed. Gordon Smith, William E. Paterson, and Stephen Padgett (Durham, N.C.: Duke University Press, 1996), 46–47.

61. Roberts, *Party Politics*, 129–30.

62. Udo Kempf, "Bürgerinitiativen — Der empirische Befund," in *Bürgerinitiativen und Repräsentatives System*, 2d ed., ed. Bernd Guggenberger and Udo Kempf (Opladen: Westdeutscher Verlag, 1984), 295–317.

63. Jutta Helm, "Citizen Lobbies in West Germany," in *Western European Party Systems*, ed. Peter Merkl (New York: Free Press, 1980), 576.

64. *Der Spiegel*, 52 (1993): 28.

65. *Der Spiegel*, 10 (1994): 41.

66. Thomas Dürr, "Doppeltes Dilemma," *Die Woche*, 26 September 1997.

67. Representative of the pre-unification literature are Rupert Scholz, *Krise der parteienstaatlichen Demokratie?* (Berlin and New York: Walter de Gruyter, 1983); Christian Graf von Krokow and Peter Lösche, eds., *Parteien in der Krise* (Munich: C. H. Beck, 1986); Jürgen Dittberger and Rolf Ebbighausen, eds., *Parteiensystem in der Legitimationskrise* (Opladen: Westdeutscher Verlag, 1973); Michael Stolleis, Heinz Schäfer, and René A. Rhinow, *Parteienstaatlichkeit: Krisensymptome des demokratischen Verfassungsstaat?* (Berlin and New York: Walter de Gruyter, 1986); Joachim Raschke, ed., *Bürger und Parteien* (Opladen: Westdeutscher Verlag, 1982); and Bernd Guggenberger and Udo Kempf, eds., *Bürgerinitiativen und Repräsentatives System*, 2d ed. (Opladen: Westdeutscher Verlag, 1984). For postunification analyses of voter disaffection as manifestations of crisis, see Richard Stöss, "Parteikritik und Parteiverdrossenheit," *Aus Politik und Zeitgeschichte*, B21 (1990); Hildegard Hamm-Brücher, "Wege in die und aus der Politik(er)verdrossenheit," *Aus Politik und Zeitgeschichte*, B31 (1993); Warnfried Dettling, "Parteien im eigenen Saft? Von der Krise zur Reform," *Aus Politik und Zeitgeschichte*, B31 (1993); Gunter Hofmann and Werner A. Perger, eds., *Die Kontroverse: Weizsäcker's Parteienkritik in der Diskussion* (Frankfurt a. M.: Eichborn Verlag, 1992); J. Buchholz, ed., *Parteien in der Kritik* (Bonn: Bouvier Verlag, 1993); and Thomas Jäger and Dieter Hoffmann, *Demokratie in der Krise?* (Opladen: Westdeutscher Verlag, 1995).

68. For recent analyses blaming the main parties for the Federal Republic's growing "immobility" and "reform blockade," see, e.g., Dieter Buhl, "Schluß mit der Harmonie?" *Die Zeit*, 14 February 1997; also Christoph Bertram, "Die neue deutsche Lethargie," *Die Zeit*, 15 August 1997; and "Standort Deutschland: Nichts geht mehr," *Der Spiegel*, 32 (1997).

69. In the 1980s, civil servants constituted 10 percent of the SPD's member-

ship, 12.4 percent of the CDU's, 12.5 percent of the CSU's, and 14 percent of the FDP's. By the mid-1970s, 49 percent of members of the Bundestag were civil servants, while 15 percent of federal public officials had had political careers. See Wolfgang H. Lorig, "Parteipolitik und öffentlicher Dienst: Personalrekruitierung und Personalpatronage in der öffentlichen Verwaltung," *Zeitschrift für Parlamentsfragen* 1 (1994): 105.

70. Werner Frotscher, "Die parteienstaatliche Demokratie — Krisenzeichen und Zukunftsperspektiven," *Deutsches Verwaltungsblatt* 17 (1985): 919ff.

71. Ibid., 920; for details on the scale of party financing, see Hans Herbert von Arnim, *Die Partei, der Abgeordnete und das Geld* (Mainz: v. Hase & Koehler, 1990).

72. On proportionate sharing of judicial posts, see Werner Schmidt-Hieber and Ekkehard Kieswetter, "Parteigeist und politischer Geist," *Neue Juristische Woche* 29 (1992): 1791. For the details of 1992 appointments to the Federal Constitutional Court, see *die tageszeitung,* 9 September 1995. For recent maneuverings in appointing the heads of the Office for the Protection of the Constitution and the external intelligence agency, the BND *(Bundesnachrichtendienst),* see *Der Spiegel,* 8 (1995): 16.

73. For details and criticisms to this effect, see especially Herbert von Armin, *Der Staat als Beute* (Munich: Knaur/Droemersche Verlagsanstalt, 1995).

74. Raschke, introduction to *Bürger und Parteien,* 17; for a similar critique, see Hofmann and Perger, *Weizsäcker im Gespräch,* 146–48.

75. Raschke, introduction to *Bürger und Parteien,* 12.

76. For the concept of the catch-all party, see Otto Kirchheimer, "The Transformation of Western European Party Systems," in *Political Parties and Political Development,* ed. J. LaPalombara and Myron Weiner (Princeton: Princeton University Press, 1966), 177–200.

77. Bernd Guggenberger, " 'Wirken bei der Willensbildung mit': Mitwirkung oder Monopol der Parteien," in Krokow and Lösche, *Parteien in der Krise,* 125–33.

78. Raschke, introduction to *Bürger und Parteien,* 12.

79. Wolf-Dieter Narr, *Auf dem Weg zum Einparteienstaat* (Opladen: Westdeutscher Verlag, 1977).

80. Bernd Guggenberger, "Wie repräsentativ ist die repräsentative Demokratie?" in Guggenberger and Kempf, *Bürgerinitiativen,* 175–80.

81. See, e.g., Peter Lösche, " 'Lose verkoppelte Anarchie': Zur aktuellen Situation von Volksparteien am Beispiel der SPD," *Aus Politik und Zeitgeschichte,* B43 (1993): 35; also Elmar Wiesendahl, "Zu einigen vernachlässigten Aspekten der Organisationswirklichkeiten politischer Parteien," in *Politische Willensbildung und Interessenvermittlung,* ed. Jürgen Falter et al. (Opladen: Westdeutscher Verlag, 1984).

82. For the centrality of quotas for the CDU, see Josef Schmid, *Die CDU: Organisationsstrukturen, Politiken, und Funktionsweisen einer Partei im Föderalismus* (Opladen: Leske & Budrich, 1990), 263ff; for the SPD's use of quotas, see Lösche, "Lose verkoppelte Anarchie," 43–44.

83. I am grateful for Gregg Kvistad's comment to this effect when he read an earlier draft of this chapter.

84. See, e.g., Horst Zillesen, "Bürgerinitiativen und repräsentative Demokratie," in Guggenberger and Kempf, *Bürgerinitiativen,* 116–21.

85. For East German criticisms, see the essays by Wolfgang Ullmann, Bärbel Bohley, Friedrich Schorlemer, and Wolfgang Thierse in Hofmann and Perger, *Die Kontroverse;* also Wolfgang Hardtwig and Heinrich Winkler, *Deutsche Entfremdung: Zum Befinden in Ost und West* (Munich: C. H. Beck, 1995).

86. Hofmann and Perger, *Weizsäcker im Gespräch,* 135–76.

87. For this critique, see Küchler, "Staats-, Parteien-, oder Politikverdrossenheit?" 40.

88. For a less pessimistic assessment of recent opinion trends, see especially Dieter Fuchs, "Trends of Political Support," in Berg-Schlosser and Rytlevski, *Political Culture in Germany,* 232–70; also Oscar Gabriel, "Institutionsvertrauen im vereinigten Deutschland," *Aus Politik und Zeitgeschichte,* B31 (1993).

89. Köcher, "Euphorie," 16–17.

90. Hans Rattinger, "Abkehr von den Parteien? Dimensionen der Parteienverdrossenheit," *Aus Politik und Zeitgeschichte,* B11 (1993).

91. For details on the voting patterns in the 1994 elections, see the essays by Andrei Markovits and Russell J. Dalton, "Spindoctors and Soothsayers: The *Bundestag* Election of 1994"; Russell J. Dalton and Wilhelm Bürklin, "The Two German Electorates: The Social Bases of the Vote in 1990 and 1994"; and Robert Rohrschneider and Dieter Fuchs, "A New Electorate? The Economic Trends and Electoral Choice in the 1994 Federal Election," all in "The *Bundestagswahl* 1994: The Culmination of the *Superwahljahr,*" ed. Russell J. Dalton and Andrei Markovits, special issue of *German Politics and Society* 13 (1995).

92. For this point, see Bettina Westle, "Zur Akzeptanz der politischen Parteien und der Demokratie in der Bundesrepublik," in *Wahlen und Wähler: Analysen aus Anlaß der Bundestagswahl 1987,* ed. Max Kaase and Hans-Dieter Klingemann (Opladen: Westdeutscher Verlag, 1990), 253–96.

93. For the impact of "modernization" on voter support for the *Volksparteien,* see Elmar Wiesendahl, "Volksparteien im Abstieg," *Aus Politik und Zeitgeschichte,* B34–35 (1992).

94. Andreas Schedler, "Die demoskopische Konstruktion von 'Politikverdrossenheit,' " in *Politische Vierteljahresschrift* 34 (1993): 415ff.

95. Peter Haungs and Eckhard Jesse, eds., introduction to *Parteien in der Krise? in- und ausländische Perspeletiven* (Cologne: Verlag Wissenschaft und Politik, 1987), 13.

96. For a comparison between the older and the recent antiparty critiques, see especially Hartmut Jäckel, "Parteienverdrossenheit—Kein Krisensymptom," in Haungs and Jesse, *Parteien in der Krise?* 182–87.

97. Peter Haungs, "Probleme der parlamentarischen Demokratie," in Guggenberger and Kempf, *Bürgerinitiativen,* 167ff.

98. For examples of such thinking, see Bernd Guggenberger, "Bürgerinitiativen: Krisensymptom oder Ergänzung des Systems der Volksparteien?" in Raschke, *Bürger und Parteien,* 190–214; also Bernd Guggenberger and Claus Offe, "Politik aus der Basis," in *An den Grenzen der Mehrheitsdemokratie,* ed. Bernd Guggenberger and Claus Offe (Opladen: Westdeutscher Verlag, 1984), 8–19.

99. Raschke, introduction to *Bürger und Parteien,* 26.

100. See, e.g., Katrin Lederer and Peter Knoepfel, "Menschliche Bedürfnisse und Parteipolitik," in Raschke, *Bürger und Parteien,* 69–86.

101. For Weizsäcker's remarks and recommendations, see Hofmann and Perger, *Weizsäcker im Gespräch,* 117–64; for similar suggestions, see Hans Herbert von Arnim, "Parteien in der Krise," *Die Zeit,* 3 July 1992; or Hildegard Hamm-Brücher, "Wege in die und aus der Politik(er)verdrossenheit."

102. For excellent critiques of the recent antiparty literature, see especially Peter Lösche, "Parteienverdrossenheit ohne Ende? Polemik gegen das Lamentieren von Politiker, Journalisten, Politikwissenschaftler und Staatsrechtler," *Zeitschrift für Parlamentsfragen* 3 (1995): 149–59; also Wolfgang Zeh, "Deutsche Parteienprüderie in neuen Kleidern," in *Staat und Parteien: Festschrift für Rudolf Morsey,* ed. Karl Dietrich Bracher, Paul Mikat, Konrad Repgen, Martin Schumacher, and Hans-Peter Schwarz (Berlin: Duncker & Humblot, 1992), 1009–27.

103. The term *Verdrussdiskurs* is Lösche's; for these points, see his "Parteienverdrossenheit ohne Ende?" 154–59.

104. Peter Glotz, "Die Krise des Parteienstaats," *Neue Gesellschaft/Frankfurter Hefte* 39 (1992): 514.

The Challenge of Prosperity: The Foundations of the German Economy and Challenges of the Future

Germany's Export Boom at Fifty — An Enduring Success Story?

Ludger Lindlar and Carl-Ludwig Holtfrerich

In a nutshell, West Germany's postwar economic prosperity can be characterized as export driven. From 1949 onward, exports grew consistently faster than domestic product. Germany's world market share increased from the end of the 1940s to the beginning of the 1970s from 2 percent to well above 10 percent and, until recently, maintained that level. Germany's economic strength became increasingly identified with its ability to compete successfully on the world market. From the very beginning, domestic economic policies were oriented toward creating that success story. During the subsequent decades of slower growth, the importance of exports even increased as the German economy became more and more integrated into the Western European and the world economy.

But Germany's ability to generate an ever increasing income via production for the world market is no longer taken for granted. In the wake of the 1992–93 recession, a *Standortdebatte* erupted, questioning more vigorously than before Germany's "international competitiveness."[1] Three problems were identified: Germany's domestic costs are considered to be much too high, labor costs in particular; Germany has lost attractiveness as a location for foreign direct investment; and Germany is said to export too few high-tech products. Additionally, it is claimed that German firms have as yet failed to take full advantage of the growth dynamics in the Asia/Pacific region. The unexpected slowdown in 1995–96 and the failure of the unemployment rate to decline have intensified the debate.

This essay places the *Standortdebatte* into a historical perspective, without fully addressing each of the points raised therein. Three topics will be dealt with: the role of geographical location for Germany's external trade (section II), Germany's international specialization as a supplier of investment and chemical goods for the world market (section III), and the role of domestic and international monetary arrangement for Germany's export performance (section IV). The essay starts with an overview (section I).

I. Overview

The export boom of West Germany's economy started in autumn 1949 and proceeded, even after 1973, nearly uninterrupted until unification. Between 1949 and 1994, exports of goods grew consistently faster than domestic commodity production, accounting in 1989 for 30 percent of total output, while it was less than 10 percent at the beginning of the 1950s. Only in 1975, 1983, and 1993 did exports decline in absolute terms, and only in 1951 and 1980 did the balance on current account become negative. On average, exports grew by 9.5 percent p.a., GDP by 4.2 percent.

Four phases can be distinguished.

Phase One: Reconstruction, 1949-58
The sustained recovery of the German economy was initiated by the currency reform in 1948, but export demand did not have a major impact on the German economy until autumn 1949, when the Western occupational powers abolished the requirement to pay for German imports with U.S. dollars.[2] During the following years, exports directly contributed to more than a quarter of the overall demand expansion. The export expansion was made possible and facilitated by the reintegration of Germany into the Western world economy. Indeed, the Organization for European Economic Cooperation (OEEC) and the European Payments Union (EPU) were the first international organizations in which Western Germany was allowed to become a member. Export growth was extremely rapid until the European recession in 1958. An average annual rate of 23.5 percent — in real terms — over the time span of nearly a decade was never experienced before in German history and probably will remain unique. The export boom was mainly caused by a tremendous demand for German goods as the European economy entered into the postwar boom and by the ability of the Germany economy to respond to these market signals.

Phase Two: The Sustained Boom, 1959-74
After 1959, the export boom consolidated. Two reasons can be found: (i) International trade and payments were further liberalized, on a multilat-

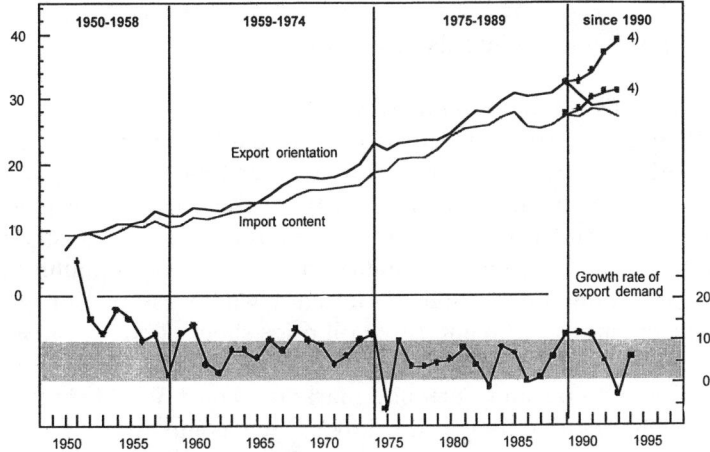

Fig. 1. Export orientation of domestic production,[1] import content of domestic supply,[2] and growth rate of export demand[3] in West Germany, 1950–94 (in percent). (Data from Statistisches Bundesamt, *Volkswirtschaftliche Gesamtrechnungen, Wirtschaft und Statistik, Statistisches Jahrbuch,* various issues; calculations by the authors. *Comments:* 1 Share of exports in domestic commodity production. 2 Share of imports in domestic commodity supply (domestic commodity production plus imports minus exports); commodity production refers to agriculture, mining, and manufacturing. 3 Goods and services, in constant prices; 1950–59 without trade with Berlin and the Saarland; 1949 was excluded because of the extreme increase in exports. Including trade with East Germany.)

eral basis within the framework of the GATT (General Agreement on Tariffs and Trade) and the Bretton Woods system and on a rather discriminatory basis within the newly founded European Economic Community (EEC). Exports to the other EEC member states accounted for more than a quarter of the total increase of Germany's export demand, compared to 10 percent in the decade before. (ii) Economic growth in Western Europe continued to be high; in many countries, growth rates even accelerated compared to the 1950s. Since rapid growth also meant booming import demand and, via increasing incomes per capita, a greater potential for intra-industry trade, international trade boomed too. West Germany liberalized its capital account, and monetary authorities found it increasingly difficult to isolate their economy from world inflation. Foreign direct investment and other technology imports contributed to West Germany's process of catching up to the United States, and substantial immigration from southern Europe released at least some of the pressure on an extremely tight labor market. Overall, exports grew at an average annual rate of 8.2 percent. This remarkable decade ended as the Western world entered into its first postwar recession.

Phase Three: The Adjustment to Slower Growth, 1975–89
In the 1970s and 1980s Germany experienced a further globalization, as did the other OECD (Organization for Economic Cooperation and Development) countries. For the first time, the openness of Germany and other Western European economies went beyond that level already achieved in 1913.[3] The enlargement of the European Community deepened the economic integration of Germany with Western Europe. But times became more turbulent: three oil price shocks (two negative ones in 1973 and 1979 and a positive one in 1986), substantial instabilities on international capital and currency markets (Third World debt crises, the big swing of the dollar in the 1980s), new competitors from newly industrializing countries—just to name a few. In real terms, Germany's exports grew at an average annual rate of 4.0 percent, which still compares well in long-run[4] and international comparisons. Many observers claimed that exports grew too fast because in the second half of the 1980s, Germany's surplus on the current account climbed to a remarkable 6 percent of GDP. However, since Germany had a well-established reputation of being an open market economy, its economic policymakers never faced an international critique similar to that directed against Japan's trade surplus.

Phase Four: Unification and After
Unlike in other Western European countries, the export boom in West Germany continued well into 1992. In 1990 and 1991 together, exports increased by nearly 25 percent in real terms. The overwhelming share of those additional exports went to the eastern part of Germany, which, however, paid a high price: the collapse of its economy. The economic and social union between the Bundesrepublik and the GDR rendered East Germany's manufacturing sector uncompetitive virtually overnight; the impact of the unfavorable exchange rate of the East German mark upon entering the currency union and the general problems of the transformation process were magnified by too rapidly rising wages. During the second half of 1992, the West German economy followed the rest of Western Europe into the recession, Germany's deepest since the war. In 1993, exports declined. The recent upswing is, as in other European countries, disappointingly weak. In 1995, Germany's GDP increased by less than 2 percent instead of the originally projected 3.5 percent. Companies find themselves in a difficult situation because the overshooting appreciation of the German mark invalidated much of their efforts at

cost reduction. The impact of the European Single Market, introduced in 1993, is yet difficult to assess. Overall, exports grew at an average annual rate of 6.3 percent in real terms, which compares well with the previous period.

II. Geography, Regional Trade Structures, and Institutions

Germany is the largest natural trading partner in continental Europe by virtue of size, degree of industrialization, and geographical location. For the entire postwar era, Germany has also been at the center of the institutional integration of the European economy. The opening of the East is likely to strengthen this position. How did the close integration of Germany into the European economy evolve during the postwar decade? What impact did the market-driven and the institutional integration of Western Europe have on West Germany's postwar export boom? What impact does it have today, in an increasingly globalized world economy? In order to answer these questions, we first analyze the regional trade structures of the leading OECD economies from the 1950s to the 1990s. Next, we look at regional institutions and their impact on the economic integration of Western Europe since the war. Finally, we test a gravity model for Germany's external trade in order to distinguish between market-driven and institution-driven trade integration.

Regional Export Integration

There are several methods of measuring foreign trade integration between countries;[5] we find the following method, which we call *relative export integration* between country i and j (rei_{ij}), to be most useful for our purposes:

$$rei_{ij} = r_{ij}/i_{ij} \quad \text{with } r_{ij} = x_{ij}/X_i$$
$$i_{ij} = M_j/(M - M_i)$$

where
- x_{ij} = Exports of country i to country j
- X_i = Total exports i
- M_j = Total imports of country j
- $M - M_i$ = World imports without imports of country i

This measure normalizes the regional trade structure of a country by the relative size of the respective trading partner.[6] We choose exports since we are interested in the demand side interdependence of countries and its impact on economic growth. The measure takes the value 1 if a country i distributes the same share of its total exports to country j as country j's share in world imports; it is larger than 1 if country j has a greater importance for country i's trade than what can be explained by its world market share alone. A regional agglomeration of trade flows is indicated by neighboring or proximate countries all having relative export integration values well above 1.[7] We analyze the relative export integration for the 1950s, the late 1960s, and the early 1990s.

1953–59

Four trade blocs can be distinguished: (i) the continental European core (CEC) and the associated colonial empires; (ii) the Sterling bloc, centered around the United Kingdom and overlapping with Scandinavia; (iii) North America; and (iv) the Communist state trading countries in Eastern Europe. Generally, neighboring countries achieved a higher relative export integration, Western European countries in particular. Already in the 1950s, the United States and Japan had a regional preference for trade with each other. West Germany was more integrated with the CEC than any other economy;[8] it had values of relative export integration well above 1 with all countries or country group of the CEC. With the exception of Finland, all continental European economies also had a pronounced relative export integration with West Germany. Indeed, West Germany was the *only* country having both values above 1.3 in all rows and columns of the upper left side bloc. Because of its size, Germany was also the most important trading partner of the CEC: more than 30 percent of intraregional exports originated in Germany, 25 percent in the Benelux countries, 16 percent in Scandinavia, 13 percent in France, 9 percent in Austria and Switzerland, and 7 percent in Italy. Apparently, Germany had already in the 1950s become — again — the most important trading partner of Western Europe.

1967–73

Germany remained, unchallenged, the center of the CEC. The relative export integration of the EEC members increased; all values were at that time at least as high as 1 but in most cases above 2. On the other hand, the relative export integration of the EEC countries with respect to the EFTA (European Free Trade Association) countries declined. With the exception of the Benelux countries, which already in the 1950s had founded a small customs union, the integration of the natural trading partners increased, most strongly between Austria and Switzerland and the Scandinavian countries.

TABLE 1. Relative Export Integration of Leading OECD Countries, 1953–59 (bilateral exports relative to the adjusted world import share of the trading partners)

From/To	Contin. European Core[a]	West Germany	France	Italy	Benelux	Austria, Switzer- land	Scandi- navia	U.K.	Western Europe's Periphery	Eastern Europe	USA, Canada	Japan, Australia[b]	Devel- oping Countries
West Germany	**2.3**	—	**1.5**	**1.8**	**2.4**	**4.1**	**2.5**	0.4	**1.5**	0.3	0.5	0.3	0.8
France	**1.4**	**1.6**	—	1.3	**1.5**	**1.9**	0.8	0.6	1.0	0.3	0.4	0.1	**1.5**
Italy	**1.6**	**2.2**	1.2	—	0.7	**4.2**	0.9	0.7	**2.3**	0.4	0.6	0.2	1.0
Belgium-Lux.	**2.2**	**1.8**	**2.0**	0.8	**6.3**	**1.4**	**1.4**	0.6	0.8	0.3	0.7	0.2	0.7
Netherlands	**2.2**	**2.9**	1.0	0.8	**5.0**	1.3	**1.9**	1.1	0.6	0.2	0.4	0.1	0.8
Austria	**2.2**	**4.0**	0.6	**5.9**	0.8	**3.0**	0.7	0.3	**1.9**	1.3	0.3	0.1	0.4
Switzerland	**1.9**	**2.8**	**1.4**	**2.8**	1.2	**3.4**	1.3	0.6	1.3	0.5	0.8	0.5	0.7
Denmark	**1.6**	**2.9**	0.5	**1.5**	0.6	0.8	**3.3**	**3.2**	0.4	0.4	0.5	0.1	0.4
Norway	**1.7**	**2.0**	0.8	0.9	1.1	0.7	**4.3**	**2.0**	0.9	0.6	0.6	0.1	0.5
Sweden	**2.0**	**2.2**	1.0	1.1	**1.6**	0.8	**5.7**	**1.8**	0.8	0.4	0.4	0.1	0.6
Finland	0.9	1.3	0.9	0.4	1.0	0.3	1.1	**1.8**	0.5	**2.1**	0.3	0.1	1.0
U.K.	0.8	0.5	0.5	0.7	0.8	0.6	**1.7**	—	0.7	0.2	0.7	0.2	**1.7**
U.S.	0.5	0.6	0.4	0.8	0.7	0.5	0.4	0.4	0.7	0.0	**3.6**	**1.5**	**1.5**
Canada	0.3	0.4	0.2	0.3	0.4	0.3	0.3	**1.6**	0.1	0.1	**4.9**	0.8	0.3
Japan	0.2	0.2	0.1	0.2	0.3	0.2	0.3	0.3	0.3	0.2	**1.5**	—	**2.0**

Source: UN, *Yearbook of International Trade Statistics*, various issues; calculations by the authors.

Note: All values above 1.3 are set in bold.

[a] West Germany, France, Italy, Benelux, Austria, Switzerland, Scandinavia.
[b] Including New Zealand.

TABLE 2. Relative Export Integration of Leading OECD Countries, 1967–73 (bilateral exports relative to the adjusted world import share of the trading partners)

From/To	Contin. European Core[a]	West Germany	France	Italy	Benelux	Austria, Switzerland	Scandinavia	U.K.	Western Europe's Periphery	Eastern Europe	USA, Canada	Japan, Australia[b]	Developing Countries
West Germany	2.0	—	1.9	1.7	2.2	3.1	1.5	0.6	1.1	0.4	0.6	0.3	0.7
France	1.8	2.1	—	2.3	2.1	1.8	0.6	0.7	1.2	0.3	0.3	0.2	1.1
Italy	1.7	2.3	2.2	—	1.1	2.1	0.6	0.6	1.4	0.4	0.6	0.2	1.0
Belgium-Lux.	2.3	2.5	3.2	1.0	4.7	0.9	0.8	0.6	0.6	0.2	0.4	0.1	0.5
Netherlands	2.2	3.4	1.7	1.1	3.8	0.9	1.0	1.1	0.7	0.2	0.3	0.2	0.6
Austria	1.8	2.5	0.4	2.7	0.6	5.4	1.7	1.0	0.3	1.2	0.3	0.1	0.6
Switzerland	1.5	1.6	1.4	1.9	0.6	4.8	1.4	1.1	1.3	0.5	0.6	0.6	0.9
Denmark	1.5	1.4	0.5	0.9	0.5	1.3	6.4	2.9	0.8	0.3	0.5	0.2	0.5
Norway	1.5	1.5	0.5	0.6	0.7	0.6	6.3	2.7	1.4	0.2	0.4	0.2	0.6
Sweden	1.7	1.2	0.8	0.7	1.0	1.4	8.2	2.0	0.9	0.4	0.5	0.3	0.6
Finland	1.4	1.1	0.7	0.5	0.9	0.8	5.0	2.7	0.8	1.5	0.3	0.2	0.4
U.K.	1.0	0.6	0.7	0.6	1.1	1.2	1.9	—	2.1	0.3	0.9	0.9	1.4
U.S.	0.5	0.5	0.4	0.5	0.6	0.4	0.3	0.6	0.6	0.1	3.9	1.2	2.0
Canada	0.2	0.2	0.1	0.2	0.3	0.1	0.2	1.1	0.2	0.1	5.2	0.8	0.4
Japan	0.2	0.3	0.1	0.2	0.3	0.3	0.2	0.4	0.5	0.2	1.9	2.1	2.2

Source: UN, *Yearbook of International Trade Statistics*, various issues; calculations by the authors.

Note: All values above 1.3 are set in bold.

[a]West Germany, France, Italy, Benelux, Austria, Switzerland, Scandinavia.
[b]Including New Zealand.

1992-94
For the 1990s, we observe a declining integration of Germany with the CEC but an increasing integration with the United Kingdom, the Western European periphery, and, strongly, with Eastern Europe. Today, Germany is more than ever before *the* core of the European economic system (all rows and columns with European countries or country groups are set in bold). Britain has lost its special role and is now fully integrated into the Western European economy. We also observe closer regional and subregional blocs like Scandinavia and North America. Only the United States and Japan still have a pronounced relative export integration with developing countries.

Regional Institutions

Three regional economic institutions have shaped West Germany's and Western Europe's external economic development after the war: the Organization for European Economic Cooperation (OEEC), founded in 1948; the European Payments Union (EPU), created shortly thereafter; and the European Economic Community (EEC), created by six continental European countries in 1957, whose predecessor was the European Community for Coal and Steel, founded in 1952. All three institutions had one belief in common: regional economic integration is a better means to promote postwar economic reconstruction than the solutions provided by the GATT (multilateral, nondiscriminatory trade policy) and the Bretton Woods agreement (return to convertibility as soon as possible) alone. While the OEEC and the EPU were explicitly intended as intermediate steps toward an open, nondiscriminatory world economy, this was not clear with the EEC. For this reason, it did not remain undisputed, in West Germany as well as in many other Western European countries.

The Organization for European Economic Cooperation and the European Payments Union
In 1947, the institutional framework for a multilateral, nondiscriminatory world economy faced difficult times. The tariff cuts agreed upon in Geneva were ineffective because of mounting quantitative restrictions in Europe.[9] The British currency crisis made clear that convertibility was, at the early stage of reconstruction, an elusive goal. Western Europe was in extremely short supply of U.S. dollars, which forced many countries to tighten their trade and payments restrictions. The German economy was badly needed as a supplier of intermediate and investment goods and as a market for the neighboring countries' exports, but political

TABLE 3. Relative Export Integration of Leading OECD Countries, 1992–94 (bilateral exports relative to the adjusted world import share of the trading partners)

From/To	Contin. European Core[a]	Germany	France	Italy	Benelux	Austria, Switzer-land	Scandi-navia	U.K.	Western Europe's Periphery	Eastern Europe	USA, Canada	Japan, Australia[b]	Developing Countries
Germany	**1.7**	—	**2.2**	**2.1**	**2.1**	**3.6**	**2.2**	**1.4**	**1.6**	**2.2**	0.7	0.4	0.3
France	**1.5**	**1.9**	—	**2.5**	**1.9**	**1.4**	0.8	**1.7**	**2.2**	0.7	0.4	0.3	0.7
Italy	**1.5**	**2.2**	**2.4**	—	0.9	**2.0**	0.8	1.2	**2.1**	**1.6**	0.4	0.4	0.7
Belgium-Lux.	**2.0**	**2.3**	**3.3**	**1.5**	**3.3**	1.1	1.1	**1.5**	1.1	0.6	0.3	0.2	0.5
Netherlands	**2.1**	**3.1**	**1.9**	**1.4**	**4.1**	1.0	**1.5**	**1.7**	1.2	0.9	0.2	0.2	0.4
Austria	**2.1**	**4.3**	0.8	**2.1**	0.7	**3.4**	1.1	0.6	0.8	**3.8**	0.2	0.3	0.3
Switzerland	**1.7**	**2.6**	**1.6**	**2.0**	0.8	**2.8**	1.2	1.2	1.0	0.7	0.5	0.7	0.7
Denmark	**1.9**	**2.6**	1.0	1.1	0.9	0.9	**8.2**	**1.7**	1.0	1.2	0.3	0.6	0.4
Norway	**1.6**	**1.4**	**1.4**	0.7	**1.6**	0.3	**6.8**	**4.3**	0.9	0.5	0.5	0.3	0.2
Sweden	**1.8**	**1.6**	1.0	1.0	**1.4**	1.1	**10.3**	**1.8**	0.9	**1.7**	0.5	0.6	0.3
Finland	**1.6**	**1.5**	1.0	0.9	1.0	0.9	**7.0**	**1.9**	**2.0**	**1.5**	0.4	0.4	0.5
U.K.	**1.5**	**1.4**	**1.7**	**1.3**	**1.7**	0.8	**1.9**	—	**2.4**	0.6	0.7	0.5	0.7
U.S.	0.5	0.5	0.5	0.4	0.7	0.5	0.4	1.0	0.6	0.4	**6.0**	**1.8**	**1.4**
Canada	0.2	0.1	0.1	0.1	0.2	0.2	0.2	0.3	0.1	0.1	**5.3**	0.7	0.2
Japan	0.4	0.6	0.3	0.2	0.5	0.3	0.4	0.6	0.4	0.2	**1.7**	**1.8**	**1.6**

Source: IMF, *Direction of Trade Statistics* database; calculations by the authors.
Note: All values above 1.3 are set in bold.
[a]West Germany, France, Italy, Benelux, Austria, Switzerland, Scandinavia.
[b]Including New Zealand.

circumstances prevented an early recovery. U.S. policymakers realized that new solutions had to be found, the more so as the relationships with the Soviet Union rapidly deteriorated. The Marshall Plan was at the center of these solutions: its funds allowed the Western European countries to continue their reconstruction even in the face of balance of payments difficulties; it paved the way toward the reintegration of the western part of Germany into the European economy; it allowed the United States to put pressure on the Western European countries in order to reduce their trade and payments restrictions; and it created the preconditions for economic cooperation between the Western European countries.

The OEEC and the EPU, both created by the United States as part of its Marshall Plan program, played a key role in the liberalization of European trade and payments. The United States decided to bring up the question of import controls on the agenda of the OEEC, the European counterpart to the U.S. Marshall Plan administration, the Economic Cooperation Administration (ECA). In dire need of financial support from the Marshall Plan, the Western European partner countries agreed to the U.S. demands for a swift removal of most quantitative restrictions by the early 1950s. The EPU replaced the network of bilateral payments agreements, which since 1945 were created between the Western European countries, by a general clearing mechanism.[10] Under the bilateral clearing system, countries tended to balance their bilateral trade because they did not have enough U.S. dollars to pay for a bilateral trade deficit, or they were not willing to credit a bilateral surplus by the trading partners' inconvertible currency. Under orderly market conditions, trade between two countries is seldom balanced. Hence the European division of labor, already hampered by quantitative controls and high tariffs, was further constrained by the payments mechanism. Under the EPU, every country opened up an account with the EPU's legal agent, the Bank for International Settlements in Basle. At the end of each month, the bilateral trade balances between the member states were added to a total balance for each country; a trade deficit with one country could therefore be cleared by a trade surplus with another country. Even if the total trade balance was negative, the deficit could be financed up to a specified limit, either by the surplus of other countries or by the start-up capital, provided by Marshall Plan funds. Hence, the EPU could also support a country in the face of a deteriorating current account, which was the case with Germany in 1951. The EPU made the currencies of Western Europe de facto convertible with each other. In doing so, it discriminated against the rest of the world, the United States in particular, because the dollar shortage still required the trade of many

EPU members to be balanced with nonmember countries. The EPU was dissolved in 1958 as all Western European currencies became convertible externally.

Frequently, it has been claimed that the GATT and the Bretton Woods institutions were responsible for the extraordinarily rapid growth in world trade after the war.[11] This is only partly true. Historical evidence suggests that the GATT and the Bretton Woods agreement would have failed without any substantial progress in the liberalization of trade and payments in Western Europe. This progress was achieved by the OEEC and the EPU. Both regional institutions were designed to solve the reconstruction problems of a traditionally highly integrated regional economic space,[12] where a mutual removal of import controls and payments restrictions would have a strong impact on export growth and reconstruction without straining the currency reserves. However, in the absence of an institutional framework including the former war enemies West Germany, Austria, and Italy, progress in regional economic integration would have been slow. It was the United States and its financial leverage, the Marshall Plan, that speeded up Western Europe's regional economic integration and in doing so gradually released the GATT and the Bretton Woods agreement from its infancy.

The European Economic Community
The European Economic Community of 1957 with its original six member states—Germany, France, Italy, Belgium, Luxembourg, and the Netherlands—has developed into the historically most profound and stable institution for economic and political integration in Europe. Only a few envisaged this development. The main intention behind the founding treaty of the EEC was the political integration of Germany by economic means. This was particularly in the interest of France. Economically, the treaty of Rome had five goals: the abolition of all trade restrictions on industrial goods and services between the member states; the free movement of capital and labor within the community; the creation of a common market for agricultural goods; the introduction of a common external tariff; and, to some extent, the harmonization of economic and social policies. Those goals were intended to be achieved within a time span of 12 years, which in case of difficulties could be extended. The common tariff was introduced in 1959. By the end of the 1960s the common agricultural market was completed. The abolition of tariffs on industrial goods proceeded even faster than intended. As early as 1968, all tariffs between the EEC members were removed. When completed, the EEC customs union accounted, at that time, for 13 percent of world trade and 45 percent of the members' external trade.

However, the realization of the treaty's remaining program proved to be far more difficult. The member states did not agree to realize these goals until the Single Market was implemented in 1993.

A customs union has a trade-creating and a trade-diverting impact: it creates trade if a country starts to import a good from the other member countries that has previously been produced at home; it diverts trade if imports from nonmember countries will be replaced by imports from member countries. One way to distinguish between trade creation and trade diversion is to look at the import content of domestic supply. If the import content increases with respect to the customs union's members, trade is created. If the import content decreases with respect to the rest of the world, trade is diverted. The overall effect of a customs union is positive, if the total import content rises after the customs union becomes realized. For our purpose, it is useful to look only at the impact of the EEC trade policy on Germany's external trade with the other EEC members and the EFTA members. Overall, the economic integration of Germany with both country groups strongly increased from 1950 to 1992, but with a different time profile. Generally, trade liberalization had a strong *immediate* impact on the import content as well as on the export orientation. At the beginning of the 1950s, Germany's trade integration with the eventual EEC and EFTA countries was similar. From 1959 to 1972, import demand from the EEC countries increased much more than total domestic demand, while the import demand of the EFTA expanded in line with it. Hence, the EEC was in Germany's case strongly trade-creating but, overall, not trade-diverting. That is, even for Germany, the EEC did not only have a political logic, but also an economic one.

The removal of trade restrictions within the original EEC created trade to a substantially greater extent than the eventual removal of trade restrictions with the second-round member states of the EEC and the remainder of the EFTA in the 1970s. To some extent, this can be explained by the rapid growth of their domestic products, which increased from 1959 to 1973 by 875 billion U.S. dollars, compared to 520 billion dollars in the case of the EFTA.[13] This larger increase in income was partly caused by the customs union itself: by better resource allocation due to increased international specialization, by the increasing returns to scale of a greater market, by more competition on the domestic market, and by additional incentives to invest. These growth effects were most important for France and Italy. Since Germany's export industry was strongly specialized in income-elastic goods (see section III), it particularly gained from import liberalization in France and Italy. But for Germany too, the EEC was most important on the import side, where the

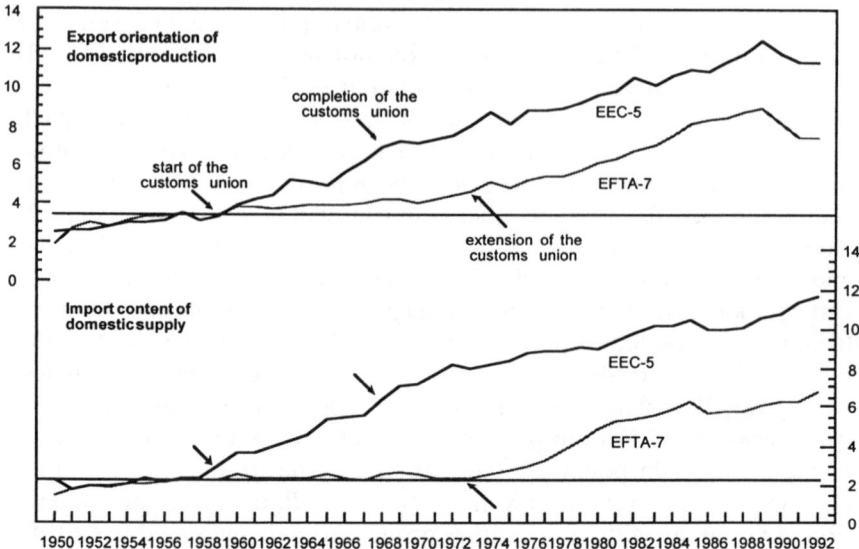

Fig. 2. Openness of West Germany with respect to EEC and EFTA, 1950–92[1] (export orientation of domestic production[2] and import content of domestic supply) For data sources, see fig. 1; calculations by the authors. *Note:* Due to measurement problems after the introduction of the Single Market, the data on Germany's trade with EU members are not reliable for 1993 and 1994. [a]Share of exports in domestic commodity production; [b]Share of imports in domestic commodity supply. 1990–93 without East Germany. For further details, see fig. 1.

share of the EEC members increased from 25.5 percent in 1957 to 42.8 percent in 1972, mainly due to rising intra-industry trade. Chemical products, non-electrical and electrical machinery, and transport equipment, Germany's initial specialization in the 1950s, became increasingly important for the export industries of France, Italy, and the Netherlands. From 1959 to 1965, those products were at the core of the internal market's growth dynamic.[14]

The EEC created an internal market where — as in the United States — substantial productivity gains could be obtained by a better division of labor, more competition, and mass production. Hence, the rapid increase in regional trade in industrial goods was a necessary condition for the EEC's process of catching up to the United States. However, at the end of the 1960s, the extent of interregional division of labor within the EEC remained far below that within the U.S. domestic market; the degree of specialization in industrial goods between the four main economic regions of the United States was four times higher than between the member states of the EEC—despite much larger distances in the United States.[15]

Recently, it has been claimed that the EEC was an inferior solution compared to a free trade zone for all of Western Europe, as was initially suggested by the British and other governments.[16] Instead of accelerating trade liberalization, the EEC is held responsible for a temporary economic division of Western Europe and a steadily increasing bureaucratization of Europe. But would *all* tariffs on industrial goods have been abolished by the end of the 1960s within the rather loose framework of a free trade zone? Two arguments indicate the contrary. First, the British free trade proposal originally had a political and not an economic intention. Britain wanted to prevent France from gaining political hegemony over continental Western Europe.[17] Second, Britain's commitment to free trade in Europe was not entirely credible because its economic interests were still deeply rooted in the colonial and postcolonial system of the Commonwealth, where 46 percent of all British exports went to (1953–59), compared with 24 percent to the continental European core. Both the geopolitical differences between Britain and France and its limited economic interests in the Continent do not make it very likely that tariffs for industrial goods would have been removed with a speed similar to that actually achieved within the EEC. More likely, trade liberalization in Western Europe would have been shifted to the GATT level, where progress was slow and more painful.[18] Third, the removal of non-tariff barriers (NTBs) would not have been achieved within a free trade zone, as a comparison between the EEC and the EFTA clearly demonstrates. The Ceccini Report estimated that the removal of the remaining internal NTBs to trade through the creation of a single market would boost the Community's GDP by about 6 percent.[19] If an effect as significant as this resulted from only the last step in eliminating the internal NTBs, after most of them had already been reduced before, it is safe to assume that the additional economic growth from the creation and deepening of the EEC resulted more from the elimination of the non-tariff than of the tariff barriers. Hence, Europe's regional integration had far more to offer than the GATT and the free trade zone alternative.

The success of the EEC/EC rested on the combination of reasonable economic goals, similar political interests, and a firm institutional framework. The combination of a community of political interests and an institutional integration did have a strong impact on domestic political decision making: it isolated trade liberalization from nationalistic considerations and from the pressures of domestic interest groups. The EEC's economic success was also a strong incentive for the other

Western European states eventually to join the Community, starting with the United Kingdom, Ireland, and Denmark in 1973, followed by Spain, Portugal, and Greece in the 1980s and Austria, Finland, and Sweden in 1995. The integration of the markets for capital, labor, and services, the harmonization of laws and regulations, and the coordination of monetary and fiscal policies have promoted the economic—and political—integration of Europe to an extent not possible under a free trade agreement. State borders as trade-restraining forces have increasingly lost importance. However, the Common Agricultural Policy is widely considered to be a failure, with high costs—that is, expensive food—for European consumers and lower export opportunities for non-European producers of agricultural goods.

The Breakdown of Communist Rule in Eastern Europe

The breakdown of Communist rule in Eastern Europe will probably be the most significant institutional change affecting Europe's regional trade structure for the decades ahead. The impact of the breakdown of the system of state trading was immediately and strongly felt in the transition economies where, for decades, foreign trade was politically determined and only partly influenced by factor endowments, geographical proximity, and the trading partners' market size. The transition to the market economy inaugurated the restructuring of trade, but the transformation crises prevented Eastern Europe from fully utilizing the new trading opportunities. Because of their small and initially declining GDP, the opening up of Eastern Europe has not had, up to now, a major economic impact on the West. However, if trade structures are corrected for the size of the trading partner, a substantial restructuring of regional trade patterns can also be observed in the West. Germany adjusted its exports to the East more so than any other OECD country.

The future impact of trade integration with the East on Western Europe mainly depends on the economic recovery of the Middle and Eastern European economies and their ability to catch up to the West, hence on the success of their transformation process. Since imports of the EU from Eastern Europe have already been liberalized to a substantial degree, eastern enlargement of the EU will not be a precondition for the further trade integration of Eastern Europe. At the present stage, any eastern enlargement of the EU in the foreseeable future is not realistic anyway, because it demands a redesign of the system of structural funds within the EU. Since the poorer member states in the south will be on the side of the losers, they have a strong incentive to preserve the present, carefully negotiated status quo. The gradual integration of at least the Visegrád states (Poland, Hungary, the Czech and Slovak

Republics) will largely depend on Germany's political influence and its willingness to increase its contributions to the EU budget.

A Gravity Model for Germany's External Trade

Another way to assess the impact of institutions on Germany's regional trade is to estimate a so-called gravity model of bilateral trade.[20] The underlying theory assumes that bilateral trade between countries is positively influenced by the size of their domestic products, by their incomes per capita, and by a common border. Geographical distance exerts a negative influence. Trade policy might promote or reduce bilateral trade. If two countries have a larger domestic product they tend to trade more because their purchasing power, hence their ability to trade, is larger. A similar income per head means similar demand structures, which enhances the potential for intra-industry trade. Distance is a major obstacle to trade because of transportation costs, which reduce the gains from international specialization and because entrepreneurs tend to show a limited awareness of the opportunities distant markets offer. The distance can be measured by the geographical distance between the

TABLE 4. Relative Export Integration of Leading OECD Countries with Eastern Europe, 1967–73 and 1992–94

	1967–73	1992–94	Percentage Change	Percent of Total Exports in 1994
Germany	0.4	2.2	450	7.8
Netherlands	0.2	0.9	350	3.4
Sweden	0.4	1.7	325	3.7
Italy	0.4	1.6	300	6.1
Denmark	0.3	1.2	300	4.3
U.S.	0.1	0.4	300	1.1
Austria	1.2	3.8	217	13.6
Belgium-Lux.	0.2	0.6	200	2.2
Norway	0.2	0.5	150	1.9
France	0.3	0.7	133	2.2
U.K.	0.3	0.6	100	2.1
Switzerland	0.5	0.7	40	2.8
Finland	1.5	1.5	0	4.4
Japan	0.2	0.2	0	0.5
Canada	0.1	0.1	0	0.2

Source: See tables 2 and 3.

central industrial agglomerations of two countries. A common border is also a useful indicator for proximity because of cross-border trade. Finally, discriminatory trade policy has a positive influence if two countries reduce tariffs, quantity controls, and other restrictions between them to a greater extent than with most other countries. Here, we use a dummy variable for membership in the EPU in the 1950s and the EEC/EC from the 1960s onward. Additionally, we have included a variable for the state trading countries of Eastern Europe and Asia.

$$x_{ij} = f(Y_i, Y_j, Y_i^P \times Y_j^P, D_{ij}, B_{ij}, \text{trade policy}_j)$$

where

x_{ij}	= Trade between country i and j
Y_i, Y_j	= Domestic product of country i or j
Y_i^P, Y_j^P	= GDP per capita of country i or j (U.S. = 1)
D_{ij}	= Distance between country i and j
B	= Dummy variable for a common border between country i and j
Trade policy$_j$	= Dummy variable for discriminatory trade policy of country j.

The gravity model is usually tested as a linear equation with logarithmized dependent and independent variables. This has the advantage that the coefficients can be interpreted as elasticities: if the independent variable increases by 1 percent, the dependent variable is expected to increase by the percentage equivalent to the value of the estimated coefficient. In the literature, the gravity model is frequently tested for a group of countries for a single year. Here, it is estimated for one country but for several years from the early 1950s to the early 1990s. This allows us to test for country-specific variables and to compare the coefficients over time. In this case, the variable "GDP of the exporting country" has to be excluded. Since the standard approach uses several hundred or even thousands of observations, the t-statistics for the country estimate are most likely to be lower.

The variables of the core gravity model can explain to a large extent Germany's geographical trade pattern. The GDP and, to a somewhat lesser extent, the GDP per head have a consistently strong impact on trade. The value and the significance of GDP per head increases over time, indicating the rising role of intra-industrial trade in regional trade orientation. The influence of distance also increases over time, measured by the coefficient and by the t-statistic. However, this is contrary to what one would expect in view of strongly declining transportation costs over the last decades. The variable common border is insignificant, probably because it is collinear with distance. The inclusion of the trade policy variables enhances the explanatory power of the gravity equation only slightly; the only exception is the variable for state trading countries, which is significant for every decade. The fact that the variables for the EPU and the EEC are insignificant points to a strong collinearity with GDP, GDP per head, and distance. An additional dummy variable for common language (Austria and Switzerland) is insignificant.

The gravity model explains more for the 1960s, 1970s, and 1980s than for the 1950s. One major reason might be that we have no dummies for the developing countries' trade policies, which were particularly restrictive and discriminatory in the 1950s, mainly due to colonial preferences. A somewhat new pattern of regional specialization appears to have emerged in the 1990s: the explanatory power of the overall model declines, particularly with respect to GDP per head. Plausible explanations would be the sharp recession in Western Europe, the reorientation of West Germany toward the East German market, and, probably most important, problems with measuring intra-EU trade accurately after the introduction of the Single Market.

Cross-sectional analysis tends to give the impression that market-driven integration was more important than attempts to enhance regional integration by building institutions. Time-series analysis, however, suggests that institutions did indeed play an important role in shaping Germany's regional trade, its structure and its dynamics. How do we reconcile this apparently contradictory result? Institutions did have a profound impact on the geographical structure and the dynamics of Germany's external trade insofar as they were intended to restore and deepen the trade structure of Western Europe as a natural trading bloc. In a world of initially mounting quantitative restrictions, high tariffs, inconvertible currencies, and a general shortage of U.S. dollars, the regional integration strategy was the only one politically feasible. Later on, the step-by-step liberalization of trade, foreign direct investment, and movement of labor between an ever increasing group of members of the European Community proved to be more successful than the sometimes painfully slow liberalization within the framework of the GATT.

III. From Early Maturity to Relative Decline?

In comparison to other industrial countries, Germany's commodity structure of exports shows a remarkable stability over time. For more than four decades, Germany's major export items have been machinery, transport equipment, and chemicals, despite increasing intra-industrial trade

TABLE 5. Institutions and Geographical Trade Structures: A Test of the Gravity Model for West Germany, 1950–94 (dependent variable: average value for bilateral exports and imports)

	1950–52	1960–62	1970–72	1980–82	1992–94[a]
GDP[a]	0.5	0.6	0.6	0.6	0.7	0.8	0.7	0.7
	(4.2)	(5.1)	(9.8)	(10.9)	(8.5)	(8.6)	(13.7)	(13.8)	(9.3)	(8.7)
GDP per head[b]	0.6	0.4	0.5	0.4	0.6	0.6	0.5	0.5	0.2	0.2
	(3.0)	(2.2)	(4.8)	(4.6)	(5.3)	(5.1)	(6.0)	(5.7)	(2.2)	(2.4)
Distance[c]	−0.1	−0.2	−0.2	−0.3	−0.4	−0.5	−0.6	−0.7	−0.6	−0.6
	(0.6)	(1.0)	(1.9)	(3.0)	(3.8)	(4.1)	(6.6)	(6.7)	(5.3)	(3.9)
Common border	1.0	0.6	0.8	0.2	0.5	−0.2	0.4	0.1	0.3	0.3
	(1.7)	(0.9)	(2.5)	(0.6)	(1.1)	(0.3)	(1.3)	(0.3)	(0.7)	(0.7)
EPU		0.4								
		(0.8)								
EEC/EC				0.7		0.9		0.04		−0.1
				(1.7)		(1.6)		(0.1)		(0.2)
State trading countries		−1.3		−0.8		−0.6		−0.7		0.4
		(2.4)		(3.3)		(1.9)		(2.4)		(0.9)

Constant	−1.8 (1.2)	−1.2 (0.7)	−1.1 (1.2)	−0.4 (0.5)	1.1 (1.0)	1.6 (1.4)	1.4 (1.6)	1.9 (2.1)	3.7 (3.2)	3.5 (2.6)
Number of countries[d]	71	71	74	74	76	76	76	76	78	78
$\bar{R}^2$	0.491	0.547	0.807	0.844	0.794	0.810	0.891	0.898	0.790	0.785

Source: Trade data: Statistisches Bundesamt, *Statistisches Jahrbuch*, various issues; IMF, *Direction of Trade Statistics* database. GDP at current prices and purchasing power parities and population: OECD, *National Accounts*; *Penn World Table 5.5*; missing data were obtained from A. Maddison, *Monitoring the World Economy 1820–1992*, OECD Development Center Studies (Paris: OECD, 1995), GDP at constant prices and purchasing power parities; all GDPs were normalized to USA = 1 and thereafter multiplied by the U.S. GDP in current U.S. dollars. Distance: calculated on the basis of the degrees of longitude and latitude of the respective capital city. Calculations and estimates by the authors.

Note: Estimated with ordinary least squares (OLS); all variables except dummies are expressed in natural logarithms; *t*-statistics in brackets.

[a]Germany
[b]Measured at purchasing power parities
[c]Estimated as the distance between Frankfurt and the country's capital city
[d]Some countries were excluded because of missing GDP data for the earlier years.

and competition from low-cost producers. Already in 1953, those industries contributed about 40 percent of Germany's total exports. The indices for revealed comparative advantage (RCA) show an extremely high specialization for those industries. This sectoral trade pattern was a legacy of the past. As early as the last decades before World War I, Germany became one of the foremost exporters of technologically advanced goods on the European and the world market.[21] During the interwar period, German export industry was able to strengthen this position. However, the economic difficulties of the 1920s and 1930s — the overall stagnation and the high instability of European and world trade — prevented Germany from fully exploiting this technological lead. The postwar period was entirely different: European and world trade expanded extremely rapidly due to import liberalization and the rapid growth of domestic products, which, in turn, was fueled by a historically unprecedented investment boom. In the wake of that boom, there was an extraordinarily strong increase in the demand for those goods in which Germany was already specialized.

During the following decades, the revealed comparative advantage in the "core export industries" strongly declined. This cannot be interpreted as a sign of declining competitive strength in these industries but of rising import penetration. This, in turn, was the result of rising intra-industry trade: that is, of increasing international specialization *within* industries. What has thus changed is the export structure of most other industrial countries: they caught up to Germany's initial pattern of specialization. But Germany maintained a comparative advantage in the core export industries, which still account for nearly 50 percent of Germany's total exports. This, in turn, indicates how advanced Germany's trade structure was after the war — much more advanced than what could be expected from the level of overall economic development then.[22]

In recent years there has been increasing concern that Germany has lost touch with the leading group of countries regarding technological innovation. German industry, it is conceded, remains strong in the technologies characteristic of the "second industrial revolution," but not with respect to the technologies of the "third industrial revolution," such as microelectronics, information technology, new materials, and biotechnology. Germany is seen as repeatedly losing out in the face of the Japanese and American challenge. The reason for this, it is claimed, is the path-dependence[23] of the German technological system: being successful in traditional technologies imposes high costs in switching over to key technologies of the future, not only because of heavy and risky investment in R&D but also because it means sacrificing the well-established position on traditional markets without an overwhelming

TABLE 6. West Germany's Trade Structure by Sectors, 1953-73 (goods and services)

	1953	1963	1973	1983	1993[a]
Export Structure (in percent of total exports)					
Agriculture	2.1	1.9	4.0	4.7	4.5
Mining	11.2	7.1	0.9	1.6	0.3
Chemicals	8.8	9.7	9.1	10.7	10.1
Other intermediate goods	21.4	18.7	13.6	10.7	9.0
Machinery	17.8	19.5	15.9	12.3	12.8
Electrical equipment	5.1	6.9	6.8	6.7	8.6
Transport equipment	7.9	13.8	13.8	15.0	15.6
Various finished goods	6.4	7.6	24.7	26.8	25.5
Services[b]	19.4	14.7	11.3	11.5	13.7
Total	100.0	100.0	100.0	100.0	100.0
"Core export industries"[c]	39.5	50.0	45.6	44.7	47.1
Revealed Comparative Advantage[d]					
Agriculture	−267	−229	−138	−83	−56
Mining	−115	−116	−207	−204	−254
Chemicals	140	97	63	48	43
Other intermediate goods	43	1	−9	−1	−8
Machinery	201	127	133	101	81
Electrical equipment	234	120	52	27	−4
Transport equipment	287	179	111	92	48
Various finished goods	131	51	−5	−5	−2
Services[b]	37	−38	−52	−33	−48
Total	0	0	0	0	0
"Core export industries"[c]	197	130	95	70	42

Source: UN, *International Trade Statistics Yearbook*, various issues; Statistisches Bundesamt, *Volkswirtschaftliche Gesamtrechnungen;* IMF, *Balance of Payments Statistics;* calculations by the authors.
[a]United Germany
[b]Excluding factor incomes
[c]Chemicals, machinery, electrical equipment, transport equipment
[d]Revealed comparative advantage (RCA) is a measure of international specialization, which normalizes the trade balance in each product category by the total trade balance. The measure employed here is normalized to 0, if the country exports the same amount in a commodity group as it imports. Formally: $\ln[x_i/m_i)/(_i\Sigma_{xi}/_i\Sigma m_i)] \times 100$, where x_i are the exports and m_i the imports of sector i.

pressure from new competitors. The relatively high returns from investing in and improving upon traditional products prevented German companies from gaining a competitive edge in new growth industries. One might even point to organizational inertia, such as the tradition of electromechanical and inorganic chemistry, risk aversion on behalf of management of the big corporations, and the lack of venture capital for start-up companies. Similar arguments have been put forward to explain the relative decline of the British manufacturing industry in the first half of this century.[24]

Before we further investigate this hypothesis, let us first analyze Germany's current pattern of international specialization in comparison to the other industrial countries. In order to analyze Germany's performance in high technologies, we have to choose a classification of industries according to their technology intensity. During the last years, various attempts have been made; the most widely used classification is that of the OECD, which groups industries into high-tech, medium-tech, and low-tech according to the share of R&D expenditure in gross production. If an industry invests heavily into R&D, it is said to produce technologically more advanced goods than other industries. Currently, the OECD classifies the product groups aerospace, computer and office equipment, communications equipment and semiconductors, electrical machinery, pharmaceuticals, and scientific instruments as high-tech.[25] The remainder of chemicals, machinery, and transportation equipment is classified as medium-tech. We use a refined classification that assigns electrical machinery without telecommunications and professional goods without professional equipment as medium-tech.

The RCAs for industrial goods show that Germany has a clear revealed comparative advantage in medium-tech industries and a clear revealed comparative disadvantage in low-tech and, to a lesser extent, in high-tech industries. The picture is different for the United States and Japan, which are strongly specialized in high-tech, and Japan also in medium-tech. France's specialization is rather equally distributed over those three industry groups; Italy is specialized in low-tech and the United Kingdom in high-tech, but not as strongly as the United States and Japan. This is perfectly in line with the concerns about Germany's weakness in leading-edge technologies. However, there might be a different possibility of interpretation. It might be the case that the negative assessment of Germany's technological performance is based on misleading empirical methods.

First, RCAs are traditionally calculated only for trade in the manufacturing sector. But economic theory tells us that *all* industries compete against each other for scarce factors of production. If one industry offers

TABLE 7. International Specialization and Domestic Production in Technology-Intensive Industries, 1992

	Germany[a]	U.S.	Japan	France	Italy	U.K.
RCA[b], manufacturing trade						
High-tech[c]	−25	35	47	2	−54	17
Medium-tech[d]	42	10	85	10	−8	15
Low-tech[e]	−38	−42	−114	−10	22	−24
Total manufacturing	0	0	0	0	0	0
RCA[b], total trade						
High-tech[c]	−7	25	105	0	−41	12
Medium-tech[d]	59	0	143	7	5	10
Low-tech[e]	−21	−52	−56	−13	35	−29
Total manufacturing	18	−10	58	−3	13	−5
Primary goods	−178	−43	−494	−50	−184	−36
Services[f]	−35	46	−81	18	−5	26
Total trade	0	0	0	0	0	0
Value added as percent of GDP[g]						
High-tech[c]	3.5	3.8	3.9	2.5	1.8	2.9
Medium-tech[d]	9.9	4.7	9.7	6.1	4.9	5.3
Low-tech[e]	14.5	8.6	14.3	12.1	14.4	11.0
Total manufacturing	27.9	17.0	27.9	20.7	21.1	19.2
Domestic demand as percent of total domestic expenditure[g,h]						
High-tech[c]	4.0	3.9	3.5	2.7	2.2	2.9
Medium-tech[d]	9.2	5.1	9.1	6.0	4.8	5.6
Low-tech[e]	16.8	9.7	15.8	12.8	13.7	12.4
Total manufacturing	28.9	17.7	26.8	21.0	20.7	19.8
Import penetration[g,i]						
High-tech[c]	46.4	23.4	8.6	40.3	43.0	59.5
Medium-tech[d]	27.9	21.1	3.8	41.1	30.0	38.5
Low-tech[e]	23.2	11.4	6.3	23.1	15.3	25.3
Total manufacturing	27.2	16.0	5.7	30.4	21.9	33.5

Source: OECD, *STAN Database, Industrial Structure Statistics, National Accounts Statistics;* IMF, *Balance of Payments Statistics;* international trade database of the German Institute for Economic Research (DIW); calculations by the authors.

[a]The data on industry value added, GDP, and total domestic expenditures refer to West Germany.

[b]$\ln[x_i/m_i)(\Sigma x_i/\Sigma m_i)] \cdot 100$, where x_i are the exports and m_i the imports of sector i; the measure is normalized to be 0, if the adjusted trade balance in that sector is 0.

[c]Drugs and medicines; office and computing machinery; radio, TV, and communication equipment; aircraft; professional equipment

[d]Chemicals without drugs and medicines; non-electrical machinery without office and computing machinery; electrical machinery without radio, TV, and communication equipment; railroad equipment; motor vehicles; professional goods without professional equipment

[e]All other manufacturing industries

[f]Excluding factor incomes

[g]Data for France, Italy, and U.K. refer to 1991.

[h]Sectorial value added plus net imports minus net exports as percent of the sum of private consumption, public consumption, and gross investment. Net imports and net exports were estimated using the share of value added in total production of the respective sector.

[i]Imports as percent of gross production minus exports plus imports

high rates of return for capital owners and workers, it will attract more investment and more and better-educated workers. In consequence, comparative advantage of all other industries will suffer. Hence, it is necessary to take into account RCAs for the total trade including primary goods and services without factor incomes. The results show that Germany has only slight revealed comparative disadvantages in high-tech products but strong disadvantages in services, whereas the United States has a much stronger comparative advantage in services than in high-tech products. Japan has an exceptional comparative advantage in high- and medium-tech products due to its extreme scarcity in natural resources and its language, which is a major cultural obstacle for exporting services. For France, Italy, and the United Kingdom, the RCAs for technology-intensive industries do not strongly change in 1992.

Second, Germany is generally more specialized in high-quality goods than most other industrial countries, regardless of whether those goods are classified as high-tech (precision instruments), medium-tech (machinery), or low-tech (clothing). For example, Germany's major export items have in nearly all product categories higher export unit values than other EC countries.[26] Germany's major export items are, therefore, among the most expensive in the respective product category. Since Germany is doing well in exporting those goods, they must have a higher quality. This is confirmed by the frequently made observation that many of Germany's major export industries produce tailor-made products for sophisticated customers who also expect extensive after-sales service. A higher product quality requires relatively more input of human capital and R&D. This is confirmed by the fact that Germany's wages in industry are generally higher than in most other countries and that major medium-tech industries such as chemicals and machinery invest relatively more in R&D in Germany than in other industrial countries. This pattern of specialization seems to have intensified during the last years. For example, the German machinery and electrical machinery industries have, on the one hand, lost substantial market shares to Japanese companies in mass-production businesses such as machine tools, office equipment, and consumer electronics but, on the other hand, gained market shares in customer-oriented businesses such as integrated printing streets and electrical power stations.[27] Internationally standardized classifications of industries according to their technology content are therefore most likely to underestimate Germany's technological strength.

Third, RCAs only tell a story about specialization in international trade, but not about the absolute size of the high-tech industries. If one talks about the technological performance of a country, the first question to be answered should be: What is the contribution of technology-intensive industries to value added of the entire economy? In Germany, the United States, and Japan, more than half of the industrial value added is generated in high- and medium-tech industries. In France, Italy, and the United Kingdom, low-tech industries have a greater weight. The contribution of high- and medium-tech industries to GDP is in Germany and Japan substantially larger than in the United States, France, Italy, and the United Kingdom. Even high-tech industries in Germany contribute nearly as much to value added of the entire economy as in the United States and in Japan.[28] Even more remarkable is the observation that in Germany, as in the United States, there is an above-average demand for high-tech products on the domestic market; in medium-tech products, Germany and Japan are the leading purchasers. It can be shown that domestic production of and domestic demand for technology-intensive goods are highly correlated. Countries that produce more technology as a percent of GDP also demand more technology as a percent of domestic expenditures, and vice versa.

We come to the conclusion that Germany is strong in high-tech as well as specialized in medium-tech. How do we explain this phenomenon? We have to consider four characteristics of the German economy: (i) it has an above-average share of manufacturing in GDP; (ii) within manufacturing, it is traditionally specialized in production and export of medium-tech products; (iii) it invests an above-average share of GDP in R&D; and (iv) it has open markets and is — according to its high level of economic development — a strong importer of high-tech products. Characteristics (i) to (iii) also hold for Japan, but not (iv); hence Japan has also a strong RCA in high-tech products. Only (iii) and (iv) are valid for the United States, which is expressed in a strong RCA in high-tech products but not in medium-tech. Germany's alleged weakness in high-tech products is therefore a corollary of its strength in medium-tech, and thus a relative and not an absolute disadvantage. A similar pattern emerges if one looks at patent statistics (patents per head and patent specialization). Hence, there is no convincing evidence that Germany's technological capabilities are fundamentally weaker than those of the United States and Japan. Consequently, we should refrain from drawing too-quick parallels between Britain's relative decline in the first part of the twentieth century and Germany's situation at the end of the twentieth century. Path-dependence might lead into structural conservatism, but it does not have to.

IV. Exchange Rates Regimes, Price Competitiveness, and Export Performance

For many decades, Germany's domestic economic actors — the central bank and the collective bargaining parties in particular — have shown a greater preference for price stability than those of most other industrial countries. What impact did this have on export expansion? In order to answer this question, it is necessary to distinguish between two international monetary regimes: the fixed exchange rate regime of Bretton Woods (1949–73); and the hybrid regime of increasingly fixed exchange rates within Western Europe and freely fluctuating exchange rates vis-à-vis the rest of the world economy (since 1973).

Under the Bretton Woods system of fixed exchange rates, the rate of inflation of a small open economy was, at least in theory, entirely determined by world inflation. All currencies were linked to the dollar, while only the dollar was linked to gold. Monetary policy in the United States, therefore, largely determined money supply and interest rates abroad. If domestic costs and prices increased less than those abroad, international competitiveness improved, causing the international demand for domestically produced tradable goods to rise, which, in turn, increased the demand for the local currency. In order to defend the exchange rate, the central bank had to supply more money. An increased supply of money fueled domestic inflation up to the point where the inflation differential to the other industrial countries was equalized. In the absence of controls on international capital transfers, monetary policy was even more limited. A restrictive monetary policy would push up the domestic interest rates, which would immediately cause an inflow of foreign capital searching for higher returns. Within a few days or even hours, the currency would come under strong pressure to appreciate. In order to defend the exchange rate, the central bank would be forced to buy up the in-flowing dollars — thus inflating the liquidity of the banks — and to increase the overall money supply, lowering interest rates again.

Under the post–Bretton Woods system of flexible exchange rates, every country could, at least in theory, pursue independent monetary and wage policies because any deviation of the domestic cost and price increases from that of other industrial countries would be cushioned by the exchange rate. Stability-oriented countries would experience a systematic appreciation of their currency, less stability-oriented countries a depreciation. However, liberalization of the international capital markets has made exchange rates a major object of speculation. In consequence, the currencies experienced, not only in the short run but also in the medium run, major deviations from their purchasing power parities, rendering entire industries uncompetitive at home while artificially boosting the competitiveness of industries abroad, and vice versa. In order to achieve more currency stability and deepen market integration, Germany, France, and other Western European countries decided in 1978 to tie their currencies to each other, eventually evolving into the European Monetary System (EMS) of quasi-fixed exchange rates between the major trading partners in Europe. This reestablished a fixed exchange rate system between a nucleus of major trading partners in continental Western Europe. The Bundesbank increasingly became the dominant actor of the system. The EMS helped to reduce the impact of speculative exchange rate fluctuations on Western Europe's economies.

Domestic Policies under Two Exchange Rate Regimes

What was empirically the relationship between wages, prices, and exchange rates under both monetary regimes? The picture is rather clear: under the Bretton Woods system, the domestic cost of Germany's tradable sector—measured by unit labor costs in manufacturing—largely followed those of the other industrial countries. Only during the "economic miracle" of the 1950s could Germany, albeit temporarily, improve its competitiveness. Under the post–Bretton Woods system, Germany could and did pursue an independent monetary policy; hence unit labor costs in national currency increased consistently more slowly than those of the major trading partners. Only the years 1987, 1992, and 1993 were an exception. This much lower cost increase overall was the driving force behind the substantial appreciation of the German mark vis-à-vis the U.S. dollar and most other currencies. As more and more countries decided to join the EMS, the member states had to adjust their inflation rate to the German one. The real exchange rate fluctuated substantially, but until the end of the 1980s it largely followed those of the other industrial countries. For the unit labor costs of the total economy, this even holds until 1993. This is precisely what open economy macroeconomics predicts.

Henceforth, attempts of monetary and wage policies to increase the *long-run* price competitiveness via lower wage increases and domestic inflation can be regarded as unsuccessful under both regimes, once currency convertibility was established. In the short run, however, there is an important difference. Under the fixed exchange rate system, a wage restraint and a lower rate of inflation meant an *improvement* in competitiveness. This, in turn, caused a surplus on the current account, which relieved monetary policy of the balance of payments constraint. Under the flexible exchange rate system, wage restraint and lower inflation

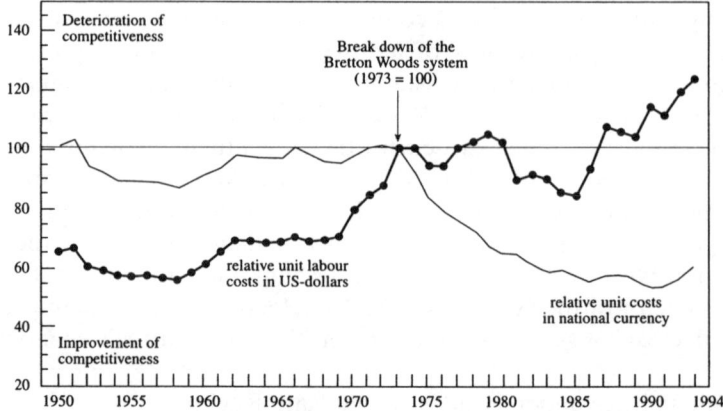

Fig. 3. Germany's domestic costs relative to the main competitors, 1950–93 (unit labor costs in manufacturing in national currencies and in U.S. dollars). (For data sources and comments, see Fig. 4.)

frequently gave rise to an overly optimistic assessment of a country's standing on the international capital markets, causing an overshooting of the currencies, which resulted in a short-run *deterioration* of international competitiveness.

Price Competitiveness and Export Performance

For the 1950s and 1960s, it is frequently claimed that the extraordinarily rapid growth of German export demand and the increasing surplus on the current account were to a substantial extent promoted, if not caused, by a favorable development of Germany's unit labor costs and export prices, compared to the other industrial countries.[29] After the currency crisis of 1950–51, a comparatively weak pressure on domestic costs created an ever increasing competitive edge of Germany's industry, resulting in a strongly increasing world market share. Although other factors such as the liberalization of world trade and the high income elasticity of German export products were also mentioned, there seems to be a consensus that the extraordinary increase of Germany's world market share and, indeed, much of the export-driven growth dynamic of West Germany have been caused to a substantial but not exactly quantified and quantifiable extent by favorable domestic cost increases.[30]

Unfortunately, the literature has yet failed to prove the point. It was merely shown that the rate of inflation in Germany, measured by the consumer price index or the GDP deflator, was lower than in a number

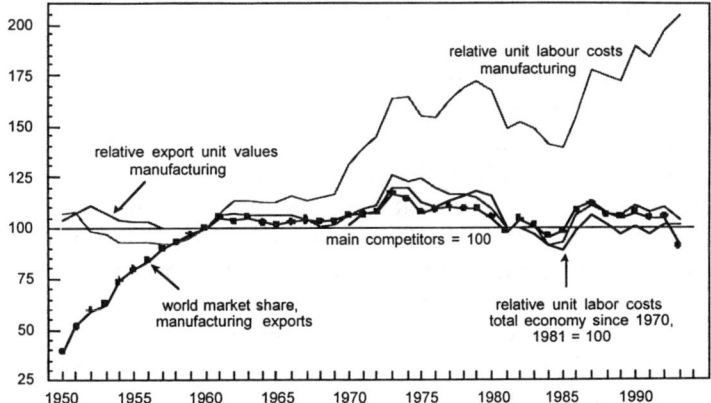

Fig. 4. Price competitiveness and export performance in manufacturing, 1950–93 (1960 = 100). (Data from Exports of industrial goods and export unit values: UN, *Yearbook of International Trade Statistics, Monthly Bulletin of Statistics,* various issues. Exchange rates: IMF *International Financial Statistics, Yearbook.* Unit Labor costs in national currency: United States Department of Labor, Bureau of Labor Statistics, *Comparative Growth in Manufacturing Productivity and Labor Unit Costs in Selected Industrialized Countries* (Washington, DC, 1977); *Monthly Labor Review,* various issues. Unit labor costs for the total economy: OECD, *Main Economic Indicators.* Calculations and estimates by the authors. *Note:* "World" trade in manufacturing refers to the exports of 13 leading OECD countries. The real effective exchange rate is calculated using Germany's export unit values and labor unit costs in national currency, multiplying them with Germany's nominal effective (i.e., trade share–weighted) exchange rate, and dividing them with a weighted average of the respective indices of the competitor countries. As weights, the share of the competitor countries in the manufacturing exports of their total group in each year was used.)

of other industrial countries, that the wage share declined in the 1950s, that public budgets had a structural surplus, and that exports increased faster than imports. It was not proven that German price competitiveness in international trade, measured by export prices or unit labor costs in manufacturing, improved in comparison to other industrial countries. Usually, the *real effective exchange rate* (REER) is used to measure this. The REER is a cost- or price-adjusted nominal exchange rate divided by a weighted average of the main export economies on the world market. For a long time, Junz and Rhomberg's work was the only study to test the relationship between the REER and export performance for the major industrial countries for the 1950s and early 1960s.[31] Their results for Germany were, however, inconclusive. Lindlar has reexamined the relationship between price competitiveness and export performance for all major industrial countries for 1950 to 1973; he finds that Italy's and Japan's increasing world market shares were positively correlated with increasing price competitiveness and that the declining world market shares of the United States and the United Kingdom were also positively correlated with a decreasing price competitiveness.[32]

The evidence for Germany looks different: from the early 1950s to the end of the 1960s, the REER, measured by export unit values and unit labor cost in manufacturing, remained stable in trend while Germany's world market share increased from 7.3 to 19 percent (see fig. 4). The REER on the basis of export unit values did not even fluctuate substantially in subperiods, whereas the REER on the basis of unit labor cost depreciated from 1951 to 1958 and appreciated substantially from 1959 to 1962. The latter was only in part due to the revaluation of the German mark in 1961. Overall, Germany was not able to permanently improve its competitiveness via restrictive monetary and wage policies.[33] And it is even doubtful whether the temporary improvement in competitiveness during the 1950s under the umbrella of the EPU clearing mechanism did have a strong impact on export performance: the strongest depreciation of the REER occurred from 1951 to 1954, that is, at a time when Germany, driven by a surge of price-inelastic demand for its traditional export goods, returned to its prewar position in the international division of labor.[34]

The reconstruction process in industry was driven by an extraordinarily strong improvement of productivity in the export-oriented part, which initially suffered from the biggest slump after military defeat. Because the wage increases in industry followed more the overall productivity growth, export-oriented manufacturing could capture an above-average improvement in competitiveness. Because the reconstruction was supported by strong export demand, it seems to be more likely that the causality ran from export growth to an improvement in competitiveness, and not the other way around.

But why could Germany keep its world market share stable from the early 1960s until recently despite the fact that the REER, as measured by unit labor costs in manufacturing, more than doubled? We suggest that relative unit labor costs in manufacturing is an unreliable indicator for Germany's price competitiveness in world trade, compared to export unit values, the consumer price index, or unit labor costs of the total economy. The latter indicators indicate an improvement in competitiveness from 1973 to 1984, but a return to long-run stability thereafter.[35] This is in line with the stability of Germany's world market share since the early 1960s. Overall, our analysis suggests a clear case for reconsidering conventional wisdom.

Institutions and Germany's Monetary Regime

Under the Bretton Woods system, international institutions shaped Germany's monetary regime. Under the post–Bretton Woods system, the opposite was true: domestic institutions shaped Germany's monetary regime and, by virtue of their increasing reputation as a safeguard for low inflation, became adopted in other European countries as more and more countries decided to join the EMS or otherwise to use the German mark as a nominal anchor. Under the Bretton Woods system, public preferences in the West were generally more growth- than stability-oriented. Germany was forced to follow the — albeit moderate — inflationary trend of the Western world economy. As the Bretton Woods system broke down, German economic policymakers could, for the first time in postwar history, pursue a monetary policy independent of that of the other industrial countries. Because Keynesian demand policies were increasingly considered to be unable to cope with rising inflation and unemployment in the West, economic policymakers and the general public in Germany's Western European neighboring countries became more and more convinced of putting price stability at the top of their priorities, thus adjusting their preferences to Germany. However, this strategy clearly had a price. The unwillingness of the Bundesbank to make sacrifices in their fight against domestic inflation that accelerated after unification has been one of the driving forces for the de facto dissolution of the Exchange Rate Mechanism (ERM) in 1992. This, in turn, has reinforced the search for monetary institutions within the European Union that would be independent of national considerations. It remains to be seen whether a single currency and a European central bank will serve this objective, while achieving the same degree of independence from politics that the Bundesbank has enjoyed.

Summary and Outlook

The essay has addressed the question of whether Germany's export expansion over the last four decades can be interpreted as an enduring success story. The answer is: yes, if the yardstick is not the exceptional *Wirtschaftswunder* years but the economic performance of other OECD countries since the 1970s. Exports still grow consistently faster than domestic product, and imports still follow, with the exception of some years after unification, with a lag. Germany has maintained strength in its traditional export industries instead of facing, like Britain, a massive deindustrialization. Germany is among the most open of the large OECD economies, which allows for large gains from international specialization.

Three factors have continued to shape Germany's external trade over the last 40 years.

Geography: Germany was and still is at the center of the European economic system. During the 1950s and 1960s, Germany took advantage of the extremely rapid recovery and eventual process of catching up of the neighboring economies in continental Western Europe. During the 1970s and 1980s, Germany was at the center of the deepening economic integration within Western Europe. Today, Germany has successfully adjusted to the emerging new markets in Eastern Europe, more so than almost any other OECD country. Indeed, the unification and the transition of Eastern Europe to the market economy as well as the greater trading potential due to lower transportation costs, fewer trade restrictions, and similar incomes per head have made Germany, more so than ever before, the center of the European economy as a natural trading bloc. Regional institutional arrangements—the OEEC, the EPU, and the EEC—made possible and facilitated the reintegration of Germany into the European economic space and its eventual return as the dominant economy.

Pattern of specialization: From the onset of the postwar boom, Germany was highly specialized in exports of machinery, transport equipment, and chemicals. This pattern of specialization was a legacy of the past. It became one of Germany's key assets during the 1950s and 1960s as the major trading partners experienced rapidly rising incomes and a historically unprecedented investment boom. Rising intra-industry trade lessened Germany's initial specialization, but its major export industries have managed to maintain a competitive edge in the high-quality market segments. Germany has also become a major supplier of the newly emerging high-technology products. Measured by their contribution to GDP, Germany's high-technology industries are nearly as strong as those of the United States and Japan. Hence, Germany's alleged weakness in key technologies of the future is the corollary to its still prevailing specialization in medium-tech products.

Monetary arrangements: Monetary and wage policies were, for most of the postwar era, more stability-oriented than abroad. A lower rate of inflation than abroad ("price stability") and a surplus on the current account ("external equilibrium") have been among the most important macroeconomic goals in Germany. However, under the Bretton

Woods system Germany was not able to isolate itself effectively from international inflation. German domestic costs increased largely in line with the major competitors; until 1967 the trend of the real effective exchange rate remained stable while the world market share nearly tripled. As the Bretton Woods system gradually disintegrated, the German mark experienced a substantial real appreciation. However, this was not accompanied by a loss of export markets. During the post–Bretton Woods era, German labor unit costs in national currency increased substantially more slowly than those of other industrial countries. But no enduring advantages could be obtained since the German mark appreciated in nominal terms. Germany's relatively high wage costs in manufacturing today are predominantly the outcome of a consistently appreciating German mark rather than of aggressive union wage policies.

Will Germany also be able to meet the challenges of the future in an increasingly globalized world economy? We have, as indicated above, good reason to believe so. But not everybody shares this view, at least not in Germany. The manufacturing industry is currently experiencing a massive structural change. The share of manufacturing in total employment declined in West Germany from 33.3 percent in 1991 to 28.5 percent in 1996; more than 1.5 million jobs, that is, more than one out of six, have been lost in manufacturing. It is widely feared that the upswing since 1994 continues to be characterized by jobless growth. These are facts not easy to ignore. But we believe that they do not indicate a fundamental "competitiveness problem," at least not in the western part of Germany. They are, rather, a sign of delayed structural change and a restrictive macroeconomic policy.

First, the western part of Germany is increasingly becoming a service economy. This process was delayed by the European export boom of the late 1980s and the unification boom of the early 1990s. The recession made apparent that West Germany's industrial capacities are oversized. Second, in order to counteract the surge of inflation emanating from the unification boom, the Bundesbank opted for a sharp contraction and slow relaxation. Indeed, German monetary policy was restrictive for nearly five years, longer than ever before in postwar history. In consequence, West Germany experienced its deepest postwar recession and its slowest recovery. The slump was magnified by the appreciation of the D-mark and by pro-cyclical budget consolidation. Budget consolidation was pro-cyclical because at first the government delayed public expenditure cuts and tax increases to finance the huge transfers to the East (7 percent of West Germany's GDP), and when the cuts started, not at least to fulfill the Maastricht criteria, Germany was in deep recession.

Presently, the German economy seems on the way toward higher growth, strongly supported by a depreciation of the D-mark but constrained by creeping domestic expenditures. While profitability is high, capacity utilization remains insufficient, and investors lack confidence. Given its rigid interpretation of the Maastricht convergence rules and its cautious monetary policy, Germany seems to have locked itself in an unemployment trap.

Of course, one could argue that the microeconomic supply side is the true constraint toward more growth and employment. In the public policy debate, frequent references have been made to the United States, where the unfettered forces of the market are said to have laid the foundations for a huge expansion of employment in recent years. Although it cannot be denied that it is indeed entrepreneurial activity that is at the heart of job creation in the market economy, one wonders how the "U.S. job machine" would have worked under macroeconomic policies prevailing in Germany since the early 1990s.

NOTES

We would especially like to thank Andrew Bernard, Rebecca Kaplan, Kathleen Thelen, and Ulrich Thießen for their comments on this essay. A shorter version of it has been published in the *European Review of Economic History* 1 (1997): 217–46.

1. A critical assessment of this debate can be found in Ludger Lindlar, "Does West Germany have a Competitiveness Problem?" *Economic Bulletin* 32 (November 1995): 33–40.

2. Frequently, the so-called Korean boom is seen as the starting point of West Germany's export-led growth. See, for example, Henry C. Wallich, *Mainsprings of the German Revival* (New Haven: Yale University Press, 1995); Klaus H. Hennings, "West Germany," in *The European Economy: Growth and Crisis,* ed. Andrea Boltho (Oxford: Oxford University Press, 1982), 480; Werner Abelshauser, *Wirtschaftsgeschichte der Bundesrepublik Deutschland: 1945–1980* (Frankfurt/M: Suhrkamp, 1983), 67–70; and Herbert Giersch et al., *The Fading Miracle: Four Decades of Market Economy in Germany* (Cambridge: Cambridge University Press, 1992), 70. However, both Peter Temin and Lindlar demonstrate that this interpretation is at odds with the actual course of events. See Temin, "The Korea-Boom in West Germany: Fact or Fiction?" *Economic History Review* 48 (1995): 737–53; and Lindlar, *Das Mißverstandene Wirtschaftswunder: Westdeutschland und die westeuropäische Nachkriegsprosperität* (Tübingen: J. C. B. Mohr, 1997), 244–46.

3. Lindlar, *Das Mißverstandene Wirtschaftswunder,* 153.

4. Between 1870 and 1913, German exports increased on average by 4.1 percent p.a. On this issue, see Angus Maddison, *Dynamic Forces in Capitalist Development: A Long-Run Comparative View* (Oxford: Oxford University Press, 1991), table F.2.

5. On this issue of methods, see Jens M. Haas and Karin Peschel, *Räumliche Strukturen im internationalen Handel: Eine Analyse der Außenhandelsverflechtung westeuropäischer und nordamerikanischer Länder—1900–1977* (München: V. Florentz, 1982), chap. 2; and Kym Anderson and Helge Nordheim, "History, Geography, and Regional Economic Integration," in *Regional Integration and the Global Trading System,* ed. Kym Anderson and Richard Blackhurst (New York: Harvester/Wheatsheaf, 1993), 21–26.

6. It is also necessary to adjust the world imports by the total imports of the exporting country, since a country cannot export to itself. A simple example illustrates the case: Assume just two countries exist in the world economy. Both are exporting the same amount of goods to each other. Without adjusting the world import share in the denominator, the relative export integration measure would be 1.0/0.5 = 2, although, apparently, each country has no alternative but to trade with the other. If the world import share is adjusted by the world imports of the exporting country, the measure becomes 1.0/1.0 = 1. If one country exports into a group of countries to which it belongs, the total imports of that group have to be adjusted by the total imports of the exporting country, too.

7. In interpreting the calculated figures, it is important to keep in mind that this measure is not scaled linear-symmetrically around 1; a low value of 0.2 is equivalent to a high value of 5.

8. For the opposite view, see Ludolf Herbst, *Option für den Westen: Vom Marshallplan bis zum deutschfranzösischen Vertrag* (München: dtv, 1989), 189; and Wilfried Loth, *Der Weg nach Europa: Geschichte der europäischen Integration: 1939–1957* (Göttingen: Vandenhoeck & Ruprecht, 1990), 136.

9. Douglas A. Irwin, "The GATT's Contribution to Economic Recovery in Postwar Western Europe," in *Europe's Postwar Prosperity,* ed. Barry Eichengreen (Cambridge: Cambridge University Press, 1995).

10. For its history, see Jacob J. Kaplan and Günther Schleiminger, *The European Payments Union: Financial Diplomacy in the 1950s* (Oxford: Oxford University Press, 1989), 128, 158. Barry Eichengreen provides an economic assessment in his *Reconstructing Europe's Trade and Payments: The European Payments Union* (Manchester: Manchester University Press, 1993).

11. See, for example, Robert Gilpin, *The Political Economy of International Relations* (Princeton: Princeton University Press, 1987), 133, 192: "Establishment of the Bretton Woods Systems did usher in an era of unprecedented growth in international trade. . . . As a consequence of numerous GATT negotiations in the early postwar period, the merchandise trade of industrial countries grew from 1950 through 1975 at an average of 8 percent a year."

12. In eight of the 12 leading Western European economies, between 60 and 76 percent of total exports went to Western Europe; in three, it was between

43 and 54 percent. The data, in this case, refer to the period 1953–59 and include Western Europe's periphery.

13. Measured in constant prices and purchasing power parities.

14. Bela Belassa, "Trade Creation and Trade Diversion in the European Common Market," *Economic Journal* 77 (1967): 1–21.

15. Gary C. Hufbauer and John G. Chilas, "Spezialisierung von Industrieländern: Umfang und Auswirkungen," in *Probleme der weltwirtschaftlichen Arbeitsteilung,* Schriften des Vereins für Sozialpolitik, vol. 78, ed. Herbert Giersch and Heinz-Dieter Haas (Berlin: Duncker & Humblot, 1974), 9, 32.

16. Giersch et al., *The Fading Miracle,* 116–24, 166–73.

17. Hanns Jürgen Küsters, "Zollunion oder Freihandelszone? Zur Kontroverse über die Handelspolitik Westeuropas in den fünfziger Jahren," in *Wirtschaftliche und politische Integration in Europa im 19. und 20. Jahrhundert,* Geschichte und Gesellschaft, Sonderheft 10, ed. Helmut Berding (Göttingen: Vandenhoeck & Ruprecht, 1984), 302–5.

18. Ibid., 302, 304.

19. Paolo Ceccini, *The European Challenge 1992: The Benefits of a Single Market* (Aldershot: Wildwood House, 1988).

20. Hans Linnemann, *An Econometric Study of International Trade Flows* (Amsterdam: North Holland, 1966); Jeffrey B. Bergstrand, "The Gravity Equation in International Trade: Some Micro-economic Foundations and Empirical Evidence," *Review of Economics and Statistics* 67 (1985): 474–81; and Carl B. Hamilton and L. Alan Winters, "Opening Up International Trade with Eastern Europe," *Economic Policy* 14 (1992): 77–116.

21. Lindlar, *Das Mißverstandene Wirtschaftswunder,* chap. 7.2.

22. For the general relationship between trade structure and development level, see Moshe Syrquin and Hollis B. Chenery, *Patterns of Development: 1950 to 1983,* World Bank Discussion Papers, no. 41 (Washington, D.C.: World Bank, 1989).

23. For the concept, see Paul David, "Clio and the Economics of QWERTY," *American Economic Review: Papers and Proceedings* 75 (1985): 332–37; and W. Brian Arthur, *Increasing Returns and Path Dependence in the Economy* (Ann Arbor: University of Michigan Press, 1994).

24. See B. Elfbaum and W. Lazonick, eds. *The Decline of the British Economy* (Oxford: Clarendon Press, 1986).

25. OECD, *Industrial Policy in OECD Countries: Annual Review, 1994* (Paris: OECD, 1994).

26. Dieter Schumacher et al., "The Technological Strength of the West German Economy: Better than Its Reputation," *Economic Bulletin* 32 (September 1995): 11.

27. For the machinery industry, see Henning Klodt and Jürgen Stehn, *Standort Deutschland: Strukturelle Herausforderung im neuen Europa,* Kieler Studien 265 (Tübingen: J. C. B. Mohr, 1995).

28. In Germany, telecommunication equipment accounts for nearly half of the value added of the high-tech industries.

29. On this issue, see Charles P. Kindleberger, *Europe's Postwar Growth: The Role of Labor Supply* (Cambridge: Harvard University Press, 1967); Hajo Riese, "Strukturwandel und unterbewertete Währung in der Bundesrepublik Deutschland: Bemerkungen zur theoretischen Position des Instituts für Weltwirtschaft Kiel," *Konjunkturpolitik* 24 (1978): 143–69; Hennings, "West Germany"; John Llewellyn and Stephen Potter, "Competitiveness and Current Account," in Boltho, *The European Economy,* 139; and Giersch et al., *The Fading Miracle,* 108–16, 176–84.

30. Giersch et al., *The Fading Miracle,* 68–71.

31. Helen B. Junz and Rudolf B. Rhomberg, "Prices and Export Performance of Industrial Countries: 1953–63," *IMF Staff Papers* 12 (1965): 224–71.

32. Lindlar, *Das Mißverstandene Wirtschaftswunder,* chap. 6.2.

33. One might argue that the German mark was already strongly undervalued after the currency realignment in 1949, and that it remained so until the end of the 1960s. However, it is difficult to explain how a country with a grossly undervalued exchange rate can run into a severe balance of payments crisis in the following years, as did Germany in 1950–51.

34. A. S. Milward, "The Marshall Plan and German Foreign Trade," in *The Marshall Plan and Germany: West German Development within the Framework of the European Recovery Program,* ed. C. S. Maier (New York: Berg, 1991); and Lindlar, *Das Mißverstandene Wirtschaftswunder,* chaps. 6.4, 8.2.

35. Deutsche Bundesbank, "Reale Wechselkurse als Indikatoren der internationalen Wettbewerbsfähigkeit," *Deutsche Bundesbank: Monatsbericht* (May 1994): 47–60.

The German Welfare State: Principles, Performance, Prospects

Claus Offe

I. Organizational Principles and the Main Institutional Components of the German Welfare State

The German welfare state can best be visualized as an institutional architecture that consists of four floors. This structure has been erected over the course of roughly one and a half centuries. Both the sequence in which the floors were built and their internal structure are markedly different from the experience of the other capitalist industrial societies in the West and the specific institutional patterns of their welfare states. Each of these institutional patterns—the German, the Anglo-Saxon liberal, the Scandinavian social democratic, the Mediterranean—can be "read" as the outgrowth of a set of values, ideas, concerns, and historical experiences that gave rise to specific welfare state configurations. In order to outline the German welfare state's distinctiveness (*Sonderweg*), let me condense and simplify a long and exceedingly complex story that has been investigated in recent years in a number of comparative studies by historians and political scientists.[1]

The oldest layer is protective regulation of the labor process itself. It dates back, in Prussia, to the temporal limitation of the working life (through the ban on child labor, accomplished in part through mandatory primary education) and the limitation of the workday. Further regulations applied to health and safety issues, to women, and to grievance procedures and surveillance and enforcement agencies (such as *Gewerbeaufsicht*). The overriding concern was to protect workers at work, and this concern was held to justify certain limitations imposed upon the freedom of contract. The construction of this floor is still going on, as illustrated by the postwar debates on work humanization and *Mit-*

bestimmung am Arbeitsplatz.[2] These issues dominated the industrial relations and labor law debates in Germany during the early 1970s.[3]

The second floor comprises all those measures and programs that are designed to protect workers (and gradually also their dependent family members and eventually survivors) outside of work through the specific German version of social security (*Sozialversicherung*). Compensation schemes for some of the standard work-related risks, including industrial accidents, illness, and the inability to work due to old age, were introduced by Bismarck's pioneering reforms of the 1880s. With the later invention of retirement,[4] the compensation for old age was generalized and began automatically after a worker passed a certain age limit.[5]

The trajectories that the development of these social security schemes followed are well known.[6] Wider and wider segments of the universe of the employed were included into the ranks of mandatory contributors to and beneficiaries of social security. These eventually came to include the self-employed but consistently excluded civil servants (*Beamte*). Further, more risks were covered, including survivors' pensions, health services, and eventually unemployment, and the monetary replacement rates were steeply increased in the history of these schemes.

More importantly, in the German version of social security the contractual relationship between worker and employer that is established through the labor contract is automatically enshrined into a status order. This order is imposed upon the contracting parties by a paternalist state that authoritatively imposes duties (to contribute) and rights (to benefits) upon those subjects that perform the economic role of a regular employee.[7] This arrangement is of a special legal quality: It is a status order not negotiated between the parties involved in it, but it applies, at the same time, only to gainfully employed workers. It also differs from an actuarial insurance contract, as rates and benefits are politically fixed and the state budget guarantees and in part subsidizes the social security budget. Nor does this status order originate from a democratic political process.[8] It is, rather, an imposition executed by an enlightened, farsighted, activist-paternalistic state executive that finds it expedient to endow certain categories of its subjects with protection and obligation. The order's roots are neither liberal nor socialist, but derive directly from Lorenz von Stein's ideas of "social monarchy"[9] and the perceived need to preserve its own authority by mediating autonomously and in collectively beneficial ways between the conflicting forces of a class-divided society. The complement of the status order of privilege and positive rights is the simultaneous ban from political life executed against social democracy through the *Sozialistengesetze* in force from 1878 to 1890.

The implicit moral theory or social philosophy that is built into this arrangement is evident. It can be summarized in three points. First, given the realities and contingencies of working-class life, the worker is both in need and deserving of collectivist protection. Second, the provision of such protection cannot be left to the spontaneous insight of either the individual worker or workers' associations and cooperatives, as neither of them can be trusted to be sufficiently farsighted and/or sufficiently loyal to the industrial order. Therefore, third, the state is called upon to provide for protection, which is also in its best interest because the protective arrangement will help to reconcile workers with the social order and thus quell social conflict. As social security represents and promotes the common good, it must be paid for (through contributions) by workers and employers alike.

Such were the ideas and concerns that gave rise to an amazingly robust social policy regime that turned out, in the course of a century, to be as flexible in its operation as it is constant and even rigid in its basic logic. The main components of this institutional logic are the following.[10]

- Insurance is mandatory for employers and employees. Being employed (within a full-time and lifelong "standard employment relationship" held by the typical male breadwinner) implies being insured. It also means the reverse: only those members of society (including their dependents) are insured who have "earned" this status through regular employment.
- The legal validity and fiscal viability of the arrangement is guaranteed by the state, which subsidizes the balance between contribution and claims but is not allowed to divert contributions to purposes other than those of the social security of the insured. The fund is thus seen as the collective quasi-property of the "community of the insured."
- The system, most significantly the pension insurance, implements a peculiar "vertical" concept of social equality: it is not the crosscutting norm of equality that narrows the gap between the well-to-do and the recipients of low income, but the "longitudinal" norm of equivalence, which is designed to minimize the gap between the present (wage-based) and the future (pension-based) level of income of one and the same person. The equality that is to be achieved is not equality among employees (which would involve, it is feared, undesirable incentive effects), but equality between the time-slices of the worker's life, which also involves constant

differentials between a recipient of social security benefits and other recipients as well as current earners of income. Two legislative reform measures (1957, 1989) have strengthened this equalizing effect that extends over the life course by establishing the norm that pensions not only increase in proportion with lifetime income of the pensioner, but also in proportion with the current real income of the population within standard employment. Moreover, payment of benefits is in no way tied to need—as little as need by itself provides access to the pension fund's resources. The pension claim is a right "earned" through employment.
- The social security funds (except for the accident insurance fund, which is employer-financed and hence exclusively employer-controlled) are a collective capital financed and "owned" to equal degrees (*Beitragsparität*) by the two corporate collectivities of employers and standard employees. The peculiar kind of property rights thus established stand in the way of its resources being mistaken for state revenues available for discretionary political purposes. Thus the collective owners can be reasonably certain that their "property" is not used for any purposes other than those of the "community of the insured" (*Versichertengemeinschaft*), a corporate collectivity that also enjoys the exclusive right to the joint collective management (*Selbstverwaltung*) of the funds within the framework of statutory regulations.
- The status group of the "community of the insured" defines a broad middle stratum of the population in gainful employment, often described as those in a "standard employment relationship" (*Normalarbeitsverhältnis*). At the upper end of this stratum, there is an income level beyond which fixed proportional contributions are no longer deducted, although recipients of incomes exceeding this threshold keep their membership status. At the lower end of the income scale, there is an income threshold, currently DM 610 per month, below which wage income is considered "insignificant" (*geringfügig*). This carries the double implication that low-wage owners, insofar as they do not contribute, lack any direct entitlement to social security benefits, and that those who do enjoy pension rights have their claims tied not to general average income, but to the average income of all "standard" workers who are actually covered by the insurance scheme. This makes the reference income according to which pensions are indexed higher than it would be in the case if it were tied to all earned income, including, that is, the income of recipients of "insignificant" incomes, who are exempt from mandatory contributions.

- Not only can no "outsider" (such as the state or the poor) dispose over the funds, but potentially divisive internal redistributive effects, that is, effects of redistribution between high and low income earners among the insured, are also kept within narrow limits. True, contributions are neither flat rate nor progressive (as in taxation), but strictly proportional across the entire range of the lower and the upper thresholds. This fact still leaves open the possibility, particularly in the health insurance system, that very high income earners pay into the fund more than they could statistically ever expect to claim as benefits, thus subsidizing all other participants. In order to forestall conceivable adverse reactions of those who might feel that their collectivist solidarity is being overtaxed, an upper limit of income (both in the pension and the health insurance funds) has been introduced beyond which further income is not liable to proportional contribution. The insured also have the opportunity to opt out of mandatory insurance and buy insurance in the private health insurance market. There is a component of redistribution built into the health, pension, and unemployment systems that, however, cuts across income categories as it pertains to family status and health status. Dependents of insured workers are also insured and thus can collect benefits (or cause an increase of the claim of the insured worker in the case of unemployment), thus leaving single workers (as well as workers with below-average medical needs) in a relatively disadvantageous position. This redistributive effect occurring between families and single persons is sometimes justified in terms of an "investment" that the latter are legitimately (and ultimately in their own collective interest) called upon to make as a contribution to the costs of raising the next generation of contributors, who will in turn generate the income from which the future pensions of present contributors will derive.
- Finally, by "taxing" employers and employees at equal rates and by granting both the joint right to self-government of the insurance funds, interclass cooperation is encouraged and a quasi-public role is assigned to the partners in wage bargaining, as the results of their bargaining will affect not just the active, but indirectly, via indexation, also the former workforce, presently retired.

The secret of the impressive robustness of a social security system thus constructed resides, I wish to submit, in two characteristics. First, it is rather reliably insulated from (class and party) politics, as collective ownership by all employers and employees of the social security funds is safely established. Social security funds are state-guaranteed and state-regulated, but by no means "state-owned" — hence they cannot be diverted to other purposes by the state, as can all forms of social assistance. Second, the moral demands placed upon participants are quite low. No participant in the system is called upon to overcome the natural reluctance to spend parts of his/her income in favor of others. What is more, the moral hazard of shortsightedness, for example, by living lavishly today at the expense of one's future, is minimized through mandatory contributions. Redistribution is mainly temporal, not social. To the extent it does occur between categories of persons and not just between stages of the life cycle, the benefits and burdens of redistribution are largely randomized and cannot be anticipated as to their incidence by social class or occupational category. After all, behind the veil of ignorance concerning future life events prevails the perception that "all of us" can fall victim to accidents, illness, unemployment, or the premature death of breadwinners. Before discussing some of the implications of these two features of the moral economy of social insurance, let me move up to the third floor of our building.

On the third floor, the issue is not health and safety of the worker at work nor the income security of the worker outside of work, but the determination of workers' income. The institutional provisions that we find here concern the regulation of the wage rate.[11] Collective wage bargaining between the collective actors of labor and capital was licensed, and the resulting wage rates were declared mandatory (*Allgemeinverbindlichkeitserklärung*), in Germany during and immediately after World War I. This innovation included the corollary provisions that (*a*) the state must keep out of direct wage determination (*Tarifautonomie*, enshrined in Article 9 of the *Grundgesetz*); and (*b*) the right to strike is limited to cases in which strikes are sponsored by unions and properly voted on by union members. Typical union statutes require a 75 percent majority for starting a strike and a 25 percent majority for ending a strike. The basis for determining the majority in each case is the number of card-carrying union members within the respective sector and region, not the number of employees.

As the system of industrial relations was developed and refined during the period after World War II, three institutional divides became ever more marked. First, the divide between trade unions and political parties widened, with unions becoming at least nominally nonpartisan (*Einheitsgewerkschaft*). Second, the divide between bargaining on the company and on the sectoral and regional level opened up. The former was given precedence over the latter and made both unions and employer's associations capable and willing to act "responsibly" by taking into account the lower marginal cases of income and profitability in their respective constituencies. Third, the divide between the organizational domains of unions ("one shop, one union," that is, the *Industrieverbandsprinzip*) became more marked, rendering inoperative virtually any interunion disputes and rivalries.

Finally, the top floor can be visualized as consisting of a set of macroeconomic policies, as well as contingent favorable economic effects and conditions, that have yielded consistently high levels of employment in the period 1955 to 1975.[12] It is debatable to what extent this favorable condition was induced by a context of a global economy that found itself on an unexpectedly long and steep trajectory of expansion, thus providing the German economy with the opportunities of export-led growth and employment; to what extent this condition was intentional and policy induced (monetary policies, but also policies aiming at infrastructure, technology, and human capital development); and to what extent it was a mere by-product of the working of the main components of the "social constitution" (*Sozialverfassung*) of the Federal Republic as I have just described them, as the inventory of floors two and three of the institutional edifice. The success story of a well-functioning system of full-employment welfare capitalism can to some extent be alternatively accounted for in terms of favorable opportunities, prudent policies, or a well-designed institutional order. While the first two of these explanatory perspectives are commonly invoked, the third is less so. Let me briefly elaborate what it might have contributed to the realities of the "golden age" of German postwar economic and labor market development.

Shortly before the eve of the social-liberal period in German postwar history (1969–82), the Social Democratic chancellor Helmut Schmidt stated (I suppose) half-seriously that while the other advanced economies are endowed with the conventional three factors of production, the *Modell Deutschland* economy is blessed with a fourth, namely, "social peace." Indicators such as number of workdays per thousand workers lost through strikes and the incidence of nonofficial strikes strongly support his point. But the institutional structures that govern social security and industrial relations have done more than just spare the Federal Republic from the conflicts, frictions, and inefficiencies that other advanced economies have suffered through during the same period. All three of the arrangements described so far have also helped to make labor a "precious" commodity. The high costs of employing labor, both wage cost and the costs of employment, helped to impose upon investors/employers the managerial priority to economize on labor, to introduce efficiency-enhancing technical innovations, to invest in the training and updating of workers' skills, and to cultivate cooperative labor-management relations so as to maximize the yield of labor. All of these incentives had the welcome aggregate side effect of allocating the costly workforce to the continuously modernized production of high-quality and internationally highly competitive products. Through the economic incentives originating from it, the *Sozialverfassung* itself was to play a critical role in making the German economy into a growth machine capable of generating full employment, at least for a period that now most definitely belongs to the past.[13]

There is a second incentive built into the institutional structure. It prompts state policies, particularly in the areas of economic, fiscal, trade, and monetary policy, to give high priority to considerations of full employment because the failure to achieve full employment generates, given the rather generous and state-guaranteed transfer incomes granted to the unemployed and the retired, painful repercussions upon the state budget. It is only if average unemployment is relatively low, or if high levels are of short duration, that legally guaranteed social wages are claimed by just a moderate number of recipients and that hence a sufficient number of people earn income and pay contributions in order to maintain a fiscal balance of social security. For if unemployment rises and lasts at high levels, the number of claimants grows and the number of contributors decreases (and probably also the rate of increase of their wages), thus posing serious problems, both electorally and fiscally, to governments of whatever political color. In order to avoid either of these contingencies, every government must give high priority to policies aiming at high levels of employment.

The pursuit of such policies has been facilitated through the unions' wage moderation, again partly an outcome of the institutional structure of German industrial relations. The institutional separation of the unions from political parties and of industry-level bargaining from company-level bargaining played a significant role in dampening the interclass redistributive ambitions of the unions. Such an *expansive Lohnpolitik* was advocated by the radical minority within German trade unionism. Instead, unions favored wage demands largely in line with productivity gains, that is, a *produktivitätsorientierte Lohnpolitik*.

II. Growth and Consolidation in the Post–World War II Era

The quartet of regulation, social security, collectivist income determination, and full employment played a decisive role in the political consolidation of the Federal Republic and its "social market economy." As early as the late 1950s, after the Communist Party had been outlawed as anticonstitutional, the Federal Republic had joined the Western military alliance, the Adenauer government had introduced an automated link between levels of pensions and levels of inflation as well as real income, and the Social Democrats had taken their famous Godesberg turn, the Federal Republic served as the model for Otto Kirchheimer of his "waning opposition" thesis.[14] The consensual, centripetal, and cooperative nature of German politics is nowhere more clearly evident than in the field of social and economic policy in the sixties. After all, this decade saw the consensual adoption of basic and comprehensive economic policy, labor market, and vocational training legislation (*Stabilitätsgesetz, Berufsbildungsgesetz, Arbeitsförderunggesetz*), together with the formation of Konzertierte Aktion and eventually the Große Koalition.[15]

This spirit of consensus applied (and mostly still applies) to the two major parties, where the right wing of the Social Democrats with its strong de facto base in the member unions of the German Federation of Unions (DGB) has almost always joined forces with the labor wing of the Christian Democrats (CDU-*Sozialausschüsse*). Conflicts, to the extent they occur at all, concern the margins of policies, not philosophies or institutional designs. This cooperation, aptly referred to as a "latent social policy grand coalition,"[16] is further corroborated by the trade union federation's (DGB) as well as most of its member unions' longstanding practice of having at least one CDU member on their respective boards. Furthermore, there has been, until very recently, a striking absence of conflict concerning the question of mutually demarcating, on the one hand, the *Länder*'s and federal government's proper sphere of action from, on the other, the proper sphere of the "social partners" and their collective bargaining practice of negotiating contracts that are valid for whole regions and whole sectors of industry. The former's sphere of action is legitimated through the principle of territorial representation, while the latter's sphere is based upon patterns of "societal corporatism." Its legitimation is based upon the principle of functional representation and Article 9 of the Basic Law (*Koalitionsfreiheit* and *Tarifautonomie*). Equally absent (until recently) is also the conflict between the realms of collectivist arrangements and the jurisdiction of contracting individuals, be they employees or employers. The remarkably stable division of jurisdictions is further highlighted by the viability of the dualist system of having employees' interests represented through two separate pillars. The first pillar consists of the statutory works councils (*Betriebsräte*), which are responsible for negotiating (mostly) personnel issues and working conditions on the shop and company levels. The second pillar consists of the voluntary trade unions, which enjoy the exclusive right to call and end strikes.

A pervasive feature of the structure just described is the top-down, or "statist," logic of the "social state" (*Sozialstaat*). All four of the components of the German welfare state have been initiated by governing political elites out of consideration for the apparent need for a state-sponsored, state-guaranteed status order of an industrial society. The formalized and codified social rights (*Verrechtlichung*) underpinning this order are not only summarily referred to in the constitution (Articles 20 and 28 GG) and enforced by the state, but declared inalienable premises governing contractual relations.[17] As a consequence, liberal contractual voluntarism is heavily constrained by an industrial status order imposed by the state. As a direct consequence of this logic, a multitude of representative collective actors and agencies that are endowed with state-assigned competencies and jurisdictions emerge on each of the successive floors, from the early factory inspectorates of *Gewerbeaufsicht* to *Sozialversicherungsträger* (social security funds), trade unions, works councils, labor courts, and the *Sachverständigenrat* (council of economic advisors).

As a general description of the German system of social, industrial, and labor relations as it evolved throughout the period 1949–89, it is striking to see, both relative to the Weimar experience and relative to the experience in Britain, France, and Italy, how stable, consolidated, and viable this configuration of collective agents has consistently turned out to be. The mark of such solidity — and of institutional stability more generally — is the result of three characteristics. I emphasize these three features because they serve as a yardstick by which we can assess the changes that are currently under way. The first feature is the practically unchallenged demarcation of the respective domains of collective actors. A dense and durable network of cooperative communication is the second feature. It is often based on career patterns, elite continuity, and informal interlocking relationships, and it spans domain boundaries between, for example, the various political parties and between parties and unions, unions and works councils, unions and employers' associations, unions and municipal governments, and social security funds and federal and state governments. This network also includes significant elements of the public electronic mass media, academic elites, and both major Christian churches. The third feature is the presence of representative collective actors within the various domains. They serve as two-way transmission belts in that they do not just transmit the demands of their constituency to others, but also serve to educate, discipline, and exert a formative influence upon their constituent members. This "hegemonic" role of collective actors contributes to the often subtle and imperceptible socializing or habituation effect of institutions and their representative agents that gradually lets them appear to those involved in them as almost natural, normal routines that rightly claim the agents' loyalty and that can be trusted and expected to last.

III. Unification, Integration, and Globalization: The Employment Crisis and Its Political Impact

I have used the architectural metaphor throughout this account so far, in spite of its mechanical and schematic connotations, in order to highlight problems of sequence, hierarchy,[18] and statics. While in traditional architecture the upper floors and the roof rest upon, and hence owe their stability to, the solidity of the lower parts of the building, the inspection of many modern (or rather postmodern) buildings teaches us that the reverse can also be true, as we see major and often quite massive parts of the structure literally hanging from the ceiling even as it is often not immediately evident what makes the ceiling capable of withstanding the potentially destructive forces of gravity. This metaphor of seemingly "inverse" architecture suggests an instructive "downward" reading of our piece of architecture. The lesson to be learned here is this: Unless the top is solidly in place, all the rest of the building is in danger. Unless the most recent component of the *Sozialstaat* building, namely, effective full employment, is stabilized, the institutional infrastructure (labor protection, social security, autonomous collective bargaining) will suffer from increased stress and strain.

The disturbing fact is that, by the mid-1990s (and by no means as a sudden and short-lived aberration from normal conditions, but as the peak of a long-term trend), unemployment has reached an unprecedented official rate of 12 percent, with the average duration of unemployment by case and the number of discouraged workers and hidden unemployment still on the rise. All parties agree that this condition constitutes the domestic policy problem number one. It has also become the object of competing theoretical interpretations and explanations. One way to account for the failure to achieve high levels of employment is in terms of "globalization" and the new "openness" of the economy. The crumbling of borders—and of the institutional regime that is viable only if protected by such borders—is evidently of greater consequence for an economy (such as the German one) that is dependent upon and "used to" the protective shell of a state-sponsored status order than it would be for a more liberal (though for that reason arguably also less efficient) version of capitalism. In this sense, the German economy was simply not "used" to an inflow of foreign labor and foreign goods (which increasingly turn out to be both price and quality competitive) as well as the net outflow of investment and jobs.

Mainly as a consequence of these two adverse flows, German registered unemployment was around 12 percent (or 4.3 million) in 1997, with extreme and increasing regional variation most badly affecting the east and the north, but also parts of the southwest (Saarland). Quite symptomatically, the term "full employment" (which used to be the battle cry of Christian and Social Democrats alike as late as the mid-seventies) has virtually disappeared from the scene of political discourse. Instead, politicians and unions have begun to call for "more employment," or, increasingly, "reversing the trend." Some economists go so far as to declare the only feasible option to be "slowing down" further increases in unemployment. It is no surprise that the politics of employment have changed so drastically. For none of the previous booms in the history of the Federal Republic has so consistently bypassed the labor market as the admittedly flat one that began in 1994. Econometric estimates suggest that the growth rate of GNP at which unemployment ceases to further increase is 2.5 percent, with a mere 400,000 jobs created with any 1 percent of growth beyond that figure.

To be sure, the present level of unemployment, unprecedented concerning both its level and its duration in the postwar history of Germany, does not only have to do with deficient demand for labor, but also with the growth of supply of persons seeking employment. Diminishing this "supply excess" was the aim of the working time policies initiated by IG Metall and other unions in the mid-eighties. The reasoning behind such initiatives as the 35-hour workweek was obvious: as the supply of jobseekers increases, the supply of hours per worker must be decreased more than proportionally in order to adjust it to a shrinking volume of demand for labor. A further supply-inflating factor is the increasing (though still comparatively moderate) female labor market participation, having to do in turn with fewer, smaller, and less durable families. Moreover, a well-known inversion of the supply curve of labor may begin to manifest itself. If wages and employment security are anticipated to decline further, labor supply (both in terms of persons per household and of hours per person) goes up—particularly as adequate social security (unemployment, old age) is contingent upon its having been "earned" through sizable stretches of employment.

It must be noted that the employment crisis has not just quantitative, but also qualitative repercussions. The key concept that captures these is that of "denormalization" of jobs, that is, the dramatic increase of low-paid, involuntary part-time, unprotected, contracted-out, workfare, and fixed-term forms of employment or pseudo-"self-employment." This denormalization also includes the rise of the illegal labor market, where neither taxes nor contributions are paid and the margin of competitiveness thus achieved is used to undermine the demand for "standard" forms of employment even further.

Policy responses to high and lasting levels of unemployment are, as far as the broad center of the political universe is concerned, as unoriginal as they are ineffective. Vocational training, working time policies, measures enhancing mobility and flexibility, reduction of wages, reduction of taxes, subsidization of innovative technologies, the use of "second" labor markets, and facilitating early or temporary retirement from employment are the standard ingredients proposed by most Social and Christian Democrats alike. The more these prescriptions fail to generate much of a visible impact, the more pronounced become advocates of radical solutions on the extremes of political Right and Left. The former seeks the state's protection of workers (i.e., keeping foreigners — and ideally also women — out of the domestic labor market, as well as foreign products out of the goods market); the latter seeks the state's protection of existing (and even the state-financed creation of new) jobs. Given the evident adverse repercussions of playing a Keynesian employment strategy in an open and export-dependent economy, the leftist alternative, however, has largely vanished from the debate. To be sure, some union officials still argue that the fact that some company has received government subsidies in the past creates a moral obligation (and preferably also a legal one that is to be instituted and somehow enforced) not to fire workers. Such a line of argumentation provides unwitting support, however, to the view held by orthodox market economists: whenever you concede subsidies, this concession will become self-augmenting, because recipient firms will disregard (or will be forced to ignore) considerations of efficiency and competitiveness.

The traditional social democratic Left, taking a top-down perspective on the welfare state edifice, is concerned with the following condition: employment must be maintained (and, in fact, significantly increased), in order to strengthen and defend all the other components of the welfare state structure (the role of unions, social security and its financial viability, the regulation and regulatory machinery of working conditions), which otherwise are in an acute danger of abolition or attrition. But also their liberal-conservative opponents have a point when they stress the bottom-up perspective: in order to restore tolerable levels of employment, much of the welfare state's institutional infrastructure, together with its costly rigidities, has to go. This view, of course, is based upon the implicit denial of the beneficial effects of that slightly mysterious "fourth" factor of production that Chancellor Schmidt had invoked some 20 years ago at a time that now seems to belong to a different age. To the contrary, the institutions that govern labor relations, industrial relations, and social security are widely seen as a definite liability that is to be shed off, rather than as an asset. It is not only due to the weakening of the electoral fortunes of the Social Democrats that the former of these two frames and policy perspectives has been noticeably weakened in recent years. Unburdening employers from some of the costs of social security and labor protection is an imperative that unions and Social Democrats no longer seriously resist. As there is virtually no policy proposal available that would plausibly claim to treat and manipulate employment as an independent variable, the purely defensive position has become defenseless. Its intellectual and political defeat has been epitomized by the position taken in the past by Gerhard Schröder. He has argued that in today's economic policy debate there is no longer the alternative between Social Democratic and liberal, but only the alternative between outdated and "modern" courses of economic policy.

The failure of the economy, public policies, and the features of the institutional setting of the German welfare state to generate a condition that was once called "full employment" is also widely addressed within the public debates in terms of a "fiscal crisis," which is seen to be both a cause and a consequence of this failure. But what is a fiscal crisis? Let me propose a slightly unorthodox definition: a fiscal crisis is a way of framing a situation of public finance that provides taxpayers with opportunities to frustrate government's moves to increase revenues in proportion with expenditures. Of these opportunities, the most significant is opting for investment abroad. If the holders of financial capital consider this move preferable and if they cannot be prevented from executing it, the condition of "fiscal crisis" ensues—with its two painful components being (a) diminishing revenues from current income and (b) a diminishing tax base from which future revenues can be extracted.

These were the terms in which the *Standortdebatte* (controversy concerning locational disadvantages for investment in Germany in the context of the European and global economies) was framed prior to the 1994 federal elections. The question was this: how can investors be induced to forgo those exit options that European integration, as well as global markets for financial investment, makes available to them? If that could be accomplished, the expected and hoped-for chain of consequences would be domestic investment, increasing levels of employment, and an increasing volume of revenues with even reduced tax rates.

To be sure, the most dramatic change of the German polity and its agenda has occurred with unification. In my view, it will be the task of generations of future historians to disentangle the paradox that the project, so consistently carried out by the West German governing elites, to keep West Germany intact as East Germany was incorporated (rather than to undertake a constitutional and institutional redesign of the foundations of the newly united nation, as originally provided for by Article 146 of the "provisional" Basic Law) has in its aggregate effect done more to debase and invalidate *Modell Deutschland* than its worst enemies could ever have hoped to accomplish. As everything was intended to stay as "we" knew it, everything changed beyond recognition—the Lampedusa principle stood on its head.

The motivation behind the strategic decision to pull the former GDR under the institutional roof of West German institutions, rather than to revise and innovate those institutions themselves, is easy to detect. This motivation unfolded within the cognitive frame of the reconstruction of the East German economy being a fast and easy process that would be served best by organizing it in accordance with the tested institutional patterns of the West German success story. This extension of West German institutions to the East, known as *Wirtschafts-, Sozial- und Währungsunion* (effective 1 July 1990), was also designed to protect West German institutions (e.g., the health sector) from being infected, as it were, by principles and practices that were embodied in the old regime of the GDR. As a consequence of this colonization approach, wages (as well as pensions!) in East Germany were allowed to rise far beyond productivity, with the direct further consequence of the massive collapse of East German firms and a resulting level of unemployment unheard of in any industrial society.[19] The reason for allowing this to happen was that the alternative, namely, the maintenance of significant interregional wage differentials between East and West would have created an "internal low-wage country" with the built-in incentives for labor to move west and capital to move east, neither of which was deemed economically or politically sustainable. But the alternative of wage equalization, vast deindustrialization, and record-level unemployment also had its price. This price came in the form of massive West-East subsidies and transfers, designed to close the productivity and employment gaps and to modernize the East German infrastructure. The total amount of these subsidies, to be transferred to the East for many years to come, is currently DM 170 billion per year, or an average of almost DM 30 per East German per day.

The distributional effects of this giant transfer machinery are still largely opaque. What is clear, however, is the fact that subsidized East German capital formation is largely in the hands of West German owners. This pattern invites the complaint that the unprecedented fiscal deficit is largely spent in highly regressive ways, namely, for the augmentation of the capital stock of West German companies and investors. Moreover, Western social security contributions (*Lohnnebenkosten*) to the unemployment and pension funds could be considerably lowered (supposedly with desired effects upon West German employment) if it were not for the fact that they need to be fixed at the present level (of 26 percent of gross wages) in order to support the East German unemployed, early retirees, and general pensions. Unsurprisingly, the key catchword in the politics of social security has become the phrase "versicherungsfremde Leistungen," suggesting that not the "community of the insured" (*Versichertengemeinschaft*), but the federal government should underwrite, out of general tax revenues and the public debt, the bill for the social costs of the particular course of unification that was adopted in 1990.

Still more disappointingly for the policymakers who have adopted this course, the vast fiscal efforts made and distributional pains and strains inflicted have not translated so far into political integration. To the contrary, a rather heterogeneous group of political forces has established itself under the roof of the postsocialist PDS as a regional protest party that with at least constant, if not growing, success claims the role of a political advocate for the interests of the people in the new *Länder*. Contrary to the model of settled collective actors involved in a dense network of institutionalized communication and negotiation I have introduced above, the conflict between the old and the new *Länder* is a macropolitical cleavage and conflict within the political economy that lacks a proper arena — a table at which it could be carried out and eventually reconciled. As neither party competition with coalition politics (from which PDS politicians are still categorically banned) nor the institutions of German federalism (within which the West German *Länder* control a comfortable statutory supermajority according to the Unity Treaty) provide such a forum, the most basic conflict currently unfolding within the German polity can at the same time be described as one of the least institutionally encapsulated ones.

IV. European Integration and the Vanishing of Institutional Rules

European integration is a process that facilitates and accelerates a process of economic internationalization while inhibiting (rather than promoting through spillover effects, as the functionalist reading of future history would have it) a parallel process of regulatory transnationalization or the "spontaneous" appearance of a transnational European governing capacity. This is so because Europe is not a federal state and is not on its way to becoming one. Transnational regulatory schemes, to the extent they have emerged, are still predominantly a matter of binational or multinational agreements that definitely involve a greater or smaller number of its 15 partners within a voluntaristic framework of "variable geometries." Europe is a group of nation-states (which are the only providers of democratic legitimacy and cultural identity) with an intergovernmental arrangement at the top. As long as and to the extent that unanimity is the decision rule at that top, the transaction costs for reaching binding agreements (and the opportunities for opportunistic defection on the part of individual states) remain prohibitive. The net result is a (declared or undeclared) politics of regulatory disengagement, particularly as the nongovernmental collective actors that play a significant role in regulatory policy-making within member states do not have a counterpart at the European level but are embedded in national regulatory regimes.

The congruence of the scopes of interdependency and regulation, which is what used to define a "national" economy, has ceased to exist. European economies could actually be described, as late as in the seventies, as "national" economies embedded in the framework of national welfare states and regulatory regimes. Today they are open internationalized economies. The competitive advantage of each of them calls for regulatory inaction, be it for the explicit commitment of governments to the neoliberal creed or be it for the sheer difficulty of replacing or complementing former national social policy regimes with transnational ones.[20] The European market has rendered both the maintenance of existing national patterns and regimes of state intervention and intergovernmental accords concerning new patterns of intervention more costly and hence less likely. The overall picture is well captured by what Streeck calls increasing "voluntarism." He writes: "National polities are increasingly finding themselves forced to . . . move away from hard obligations to soft incentives, from regulation to voluntarism, and from social-interventionist to liberal democracy."[21]

The virtually universal response to the new post-full-employment, postunification, and post-Maastricht situation has been — triumphant on the part of economic liberals, reluctant on that of unions and social democrats — to call for cutting the costs of employment (*Lohnnebenkosten*), as opposed to wage costs directly and across the board. This debate is euphemistically heralded as one concerning "remodeling" the welfare state (*Umbau des Sozialstaats*), with so far only a few bold and shrill voices from within the disintegrating liberal party (FDP) advocating the welfare state's outright if partial demolition (*Abbau*). Umbau aims at three objectives. The first objective is lowering the costs of mandatory social security, which (nominally) fall upon employers and employees in equal proportions, thereby lowering total costs of employment, while protecting jobs and creating new ones. The second objective entails expanding the low end of the wage scale.[22] The third objective is cutting tax-financed expenditures by cutting social assistance to the long-term unemployed (*Arbeitslosenhilfe,* financed out of the federal budget) and those entitled to general welfare (*Sozialhilfe,* paid for by local governments). In both cases, the lowering of expenditures is expected to translate into more jobs whether this comes through the lowering of taxes, the lowering of claims that the local and federal state has to make on credit markets, the redirection of budgets from consumption to investment, or the strengthening of the preparedness of those now deprived of some of their welfare entitlements to take up (or make any conceivable concession in order to stay in) jobs.

Also, very popular among policymakers (although rarely announced and declared as such) is a pattern of "negative" labor supply policy. As the overall demand for labor cannot be increased, the focus almost "naturally" shifts to diminishing supply. Supply-cutting measures such as early retirement, an at least passive discouragement of female labor market participation, and the dumping of surplus labor into the so-called secondary labor market (through tightly administered and exceedingly costly workfare measures, or *Arbeitsbeschaffungsmaßnahmen* [ABM]) have been the favored means of response to the plainly catastrophic East German employment situation. But the economic and fiscal dilemma inherent in such measures is also plain. They all increase the imbalance between the (diminishing) volume of social security contributions and the increasing number of claimants caused by these measures, thus burdening the employed labor force with still increased per capita costs of employment (*Lohnnebenkosten*).

Further proposed social policy innovations and adjustments make their appearance in the media virtually every second week. What would have been considered weird provocations a decade ago — reduced entry wages for younger workers; discontinuation of sick pay for the first six weeks of illness; wholesale deregulation of shopping hours in retail trade; a semiofficial statement by the antimonopoly commission, enthusiastically supported by the liberal business media, pointing out that trade unions are an aberrant phenomenon in a market economy; suggestions that employers' shares in the mandatory health insurance (GKV) should be paid to workers directly rather than into the health fund; a new and aggressive debate on welfare cheating—have presently become standard ingredients of the remodeling (Umbau) discourse.

Cuts—and proposed cuts—are not the only indicators of the destabilization of the entire political economy of the German welfare state. Proposals such as the ones just referred to are typically voiced by individuals or small factions within parties and other collective actors, not officially by representative actors themselves after extended periods of internal deliberation and exploratory contacts with relevant partners in politics and associations. German collective actors, once famous for their "corporatist" qualities—that is, their capacity to generate broad and inclusive representational monopolies and thus exercise external influence through the internal discipline they impose upon members—are presently suffering from symptoms of rampant disorganization. The decline of industrywide regional collective agreements (*Flächentarifverträge*) and the rise of company-level wage bargaining, but also evidently irreconcilable policy controversies within the system of employers' associations and subsequent waves of defection, are cases in point. Densities of membership are declining in trade unions, business interest associations, and political parties alike, both through the defection of former members and the increasing failure of potential members to join. Instead of relatively solid, disciplined, and durable "blocs" or camps, each of them held together by its own traditions, precedents, and informally enforced rules, the universe of political actors and strategies seems increasingly to consist of elite personnel engaged in personalistic rivalries carried out through opportunistic surprise moves, short-lived campaigns, and populist appeals. It is unlikely that this splintering of organized agency and the concomitant change of the style of politics and policymaking are well suited to the processing of issues of distribution, social rights, and security—issues that by their complex and sensitive nature and long-term effects presuppose stable arenas, reliable coalitions, trust-generating procedures, enforceable pacts, and, above all, strong collective actors. In this perspective, the recent resounding electoral defeats of German Social Democrats, as well as their almost obsessive preoccupation with issues of leadership personnel and the correlative neglect of substantive policy issues, appear to be symptoms of a more general "postmodernist" change of the form and content of German politics.

Together with the fragmentation of agents and arenas, there is a notable shift in the discourse concerning all four levels of the welfare state structure. Two consecutive shifts are discernible here. First, much of the discourse moves from rights-based arguments to functionalist arguments.[23] Second, while functionalist arguments in support of the welfare state (pointing to its effect of maintaining social peace, stabilizing demand, enhancing labor productivity, motivation, and mobility, and preventing the costs of ex-post-strategies) have always been popular, now the attention focuses on the welfare state's inefficiencies and the damages it inflicts upon competitiveness, productivity, and workers' (as well as investors') motivation.

As I have argued above, I consider it to be the criterion of the robustness, durability, and "consolidation" of a system of institutions if there is a generally recognized "map" with relatively uncontested demarcation rules separating spheres of competencies and responsibilities; if there is also a set of representative actors within each of the institutional spheres able to extract the material resources needed for its operation; and if across these demarcation lines and between representative actors there occurs a constant stream of communication that ranges from information, mutual observation, and negotiation to joint rule-making, and that is informed by largely shared cognitive frames, perceptions, and reference values. In the ideal case, agents would be contained within specified arenas that also provide them with clear instructions as to their substantive agenda and procedural mode of interaction. Stated in negative terms, border disputes, the emergence of new agents and issues, and violations of established routines of interaction would all be rare, adjustments slow and piecemeal, and "basic" alternatives absent from the practice of "normal politics." Employing these components of the ideal-typical condition of "consolidation" as a checklist to assess the present situation of the German welfare state, it is hard to avoid the conclusion that it is currently undergoing a rapid process of de-consolidation that is unprecedented in the experience of the last half-century.

NOTES

1. See P. Baldwin, *The Politics of Social Solidarity* (Cambridge: Cambridge University Press, 1990); G. Esping-Anderson, *The Three Worlds of Welfare Capitalism* (Princeton: Princeton University Press, 1990); and G. A. Ritter, *Der Sozialstaat — Entstehung und Entwicklung im internationalen Vergleich* (München: Oldenbourg, 1989).

2. For a recent German proposal on these issues, see Hildegard Matthies, *Arbeit 2000: Anforderung an eine Neugestaltung der Arbeitswelt-eine Studie der Hans-Böckler-Stiftung* (Reinbek bei Hamburg: Rowohlt, 1994). Incidentally, the development of the European Community's social policies seems to follow the same sequence. Both the Social Action program of 1972 and the introduction of the "social dimension" in the late 1980s were, to the extent they were more than of a declamatory and symbolic nature, concerned with issues of health and safety at work and with equal employment opportunities for women.

3. Needless to say, the building that I am going to describe here also has a basement. For before workers can be protected at work, they must be brought to work. The main project of social policy in the incipient industrial revolution in Germany, roughly in the period from 1790 to the late 1840s, was to terminate traditional communal forms of poor relief and charity with modern, state-sponsored approaches to the vast incidence of poverty. To that end, a new division had to be established in moral, economic, and legal-institutional terms that was previously unknown: the division between categories of people that were legitimately out of work (i.e., "deficient" persons such as children, women as mothers, and the handicapped) and those illegitimate nonworkers that were considered able but unwilling to work. The restrictive admission to the first of these categories corresponded to the punitive and disciplinary efforts directed at those deemed belonging to the second. See ALR 1794, II, 19 as quoted in E. Pankoke, *Die Arbeitsfrage* (Frankfurt: Suhrkamp Verlag, 1990). This division is the root of policies that provide aid (*Fürsorge, Sozialhilfe*) to the "deserving" needy, who have recognized reasons for not participating in the labor market.

4. See J. Ehmer, *Sozialgeschichte des Alters* (Frankfurt: Suhrkamp Verlag, 1990); and A. M. Guillemard, "France: Massive Exit through Unemployment Compensation," in *Time for Retirement*, eds. A. M. Guillemard et al. (Cambridge: Cambridge University Press, 1991).

5. The fourth standard risk of workers outside work, namely, the disemployment of able-bodied workers seeking employment, was to be covered only with a delay of some 40 years with the AVAVG of 1927. The fifth standard risk outside work, namely, the need to undergo long-term care, has only recently been covered by a social security system that became effective in 1995 (*soziale Pflegeversicherung*).

6. J. Alber, *Vom Armenhaus zum Wohlfahrtsstaat* (Frankfurt: Campus, 1982).

7. In this case *regular employee* means performing full-time paid labor in a firm or enterprise for the duration of one's working life.

8. See F. Nullmeier and F. W. Rüb, *Die Transformation der Sozialpolitik: 1889–1980* (Frankfurt: Campus, 1993), 75–83.

9. See E. W. Böckenförde, "Lorenz von Stein als Theoretiker der Bewegung von Staat und Gesellschaft zum Sozialstaat," in *Staat, Gesellschaft, Freiheit* (Frankfurt: Suhrkamp Verlag, 1976).

10. See C. Offe, "Akzeptanz und Legitimität strategischer Optionen in der Sozialpolitik," in *Sicherheit und Freiheit*, eds. C. Sachße and H. T. Engelhardt (Frankfurt: Suhrkamp Verlag, 1990), 182ff.

11. As both contributions and benefits are tied to wages, there is a backward linkage here between the third and the second floor: increments of retirement incomes do directly depend upon the rate of increase of wages of presently employed workers. There is also a backward linkage to the first level, as collective agreements, both those resulting from negotiations between works councils and management on the company level (*Betriebsvereinbarungen*) and those resulting from collective bargaining between unions and employers' associations

on the sector/region level (*Manteltarifverträge*), pertain also to issues of working conditions, hiring and firing practices, and working time regulations. Note, however, that among the three categories of items that workers are typically interested in — namely, working conditions, wages (including social wages), and employment security — only the first two can be determined through collective bargaining, while the third remains a residual variable, that is, one that neither social partners nor national governments can ever make binding commitments on (a fact that has obviously been neglected by the initiators of a widely acclaimed recent proposal by IG Metall to "contractualize" employment levels by fixing them at negotiated levels in exchange for unions' wage restraint).

12. Charles S. Maier, in comparing the experience of the Weimar welfare state with that of the second German republic, suggests the decisive role of full employment conditions or policies that I depict here as the fourth floor of the welfare state and that the politics of Weimar never allowed to be erected. Cf. his "The Two Postwar Eras and the Conditions of Stability," *American Historical Review* 86, no. 2 (1981): 327–67, especially 334 and 344.

13. See W. Streeck, "Neo-voluntarism: A New European Social Policy Regime?" *European Law Journal* 1, no. 1 (1995): 31–59.

14. Otto Kirchheimer, "Germany: The Vanishing Opposition," in *Political Opposition in Western Democracies,* ed. Robert Dahl (New Haven: Yale University Press, 1966).

15. The conflicts that did emerge at the time and that helped to unveil some of the dirty secrets on which the Federal Republic was founded were most symptomatically neither focused upon nor emerging from issues of class and industrial relations. In fact, the moment that the student movement tried to address these issues, it disintegrated.

16. Quoted from an interview with a leading official of the Federation of German Employers' Associations (BdA).

17. It is these rights that distinguish the German from the Japanese case, which in many other respects is similar to the German welfare state.

18. The German case, for instance, is a clear deviation from T. H. Marshall's British-based stage model in that the stage of "social rights" is an antecedent (and even an intended antidote) to, rather than a consequence of, the stage of democratic rights (including the right to associate in "combinations" for the pursuit of interests).

19. A realistic idea of the level of unemployment prevailing in the new *Länder* is not given by the official figures on registered unemployment (which is about 15 percent), but by the portion of the working-age population out of regular employment who seek employment. Although this latter figure is not to be found in any official statistics, it is estimated to be on the order of 35 to 40 percent.

20. See Streeck, "Neo-voluntarism."

21. Ibid., 58.

22. An interesting variant of this strategy has been proposed by Fritz Scharpf, who argues that drops in wages of the less skilled and therefore low-

wage echelons of the workforce need not necessarily correspond to a loss of income of those groups; alternatively, the loss can partly be compensated for by degressive tax-financed income subsidies (i.e., a variant of negative income taxes) paid directly to the worker.

23. A notable exception is the 1990 decision of the Constitutional Court concerning the exemption of families' subsistence income from taxation. The Court determined that the threshold of subsistence income beyond which taxation starts is unconstitutionally low and hence must be raised.

Norms, Ideology, and Institutions: (En)Gendered Retrenchment of *Modell Deutschland?*

Patricia Davis and Simon Reich

> *Solidarity is not only demanded when it is a question of making demands and fighting for them, as in wage restraint and job conflicts. There is also a solidarity of workers with the jobless . . . In the present situation in Germany, solidarity of workers in the west with workers in the east is also required.*
>
> Helmut Kohl (Financial Times, 1 May 1992)
>
> *The strikes thus far failed to impress the Italian workers at the Amico restaurant in the Charlottenburg district. They commented that, like almost everything else in Germany, the strikes, planned long in advance and carried out to the letter, were predictably dull.*
>
> Unnamed Correspondent (Financial Times, 30 April 1992)

In the Bundestag elections of 1976, the Social Democratic Party ran for office with the slogan "Model Germany" (*Modell Deutschland*). This label was then widely adopted by scholars outside Germany, spawning a series of books and articles debating the nature of the German political and social welfare system, the source of its apparent stability, and the relationship between Germany—this apparent new paragon—and its neighbors.[1] The German public, on the other hand, was not as convinced of the rectitude of this label as were these foreign scholars. Indeed, those scholars who seemed to accept the title uncritically failed to appreciate the irony that the original German proponents of that view, the SPD, actually lost ground to the CDU in that election of 1976.

Yet the label stuck, predicated on the assertion that, as Andrei Markovits wrote over a decade ago, Germans

> seemed to travel more, consume more, enjoy more extensive social services, benefit from longer vacations, and suffer from less inflation and unemployment than just about anybody else in the advanced industrial countries, with the possible exception of Austria and Switzerland. Complementing this economic bliss was a domestic stability that seemed to permeate all aspects of politics in an era when other countries suffered from social upheavals . . . The FRG conveyed this image of an island of stability, strength, prosperity, and confidence surrounded by a sea of nations plagued by insurmountable adversities.[2]

Continuing, he claimed that "the key concepts were expertise, competence, moderation, and predictability" — assets that the Italian waiters apparently regarded with disdain.

It is precisely these quintessential characteristics of *Modell Deutschland,* however, that critics claim will prevent the system from surviving the current pressures brought on by the process of economic globalization. Many scholars suggest that *Modell Deutschland* cannot sustain itself financially[3] or technologically[4] in the face of the increased economic competition wrought by deregulated markets and liberalized investment rules with resulting high unemployment.

Certainly, dating from the early postwar period, it was the Federal Republic of Germany (FRG) that was considered to be a nation most approximating the combination of neo-corporatist institutions and a cooperative "ideology of social partnership" among the larger of the advanced industrial states.[5] Advocates asserted that it was both these particular institutional structures and their dominant values that together explained the FRG's supposed economic vibrancy over the prior two decades, its resilience in the face of two oil crises, and its characteristically systematic response to the staggering costs of unification. Implicit in these adoring portraits of Germany is a normative belief in social justice and egalitarianism in the allocation and distribution of resources, in contrast to the United States, which generates a greater but less egalitarian distribution of resources. Notably, as Markovits suggests, "the more positive, uncritical, indeed glowing, judgments about Model Germany emanated more from abroad than within the model itself."[6] Moreover, consistent with this view, some Germans (perhaps reflecting a growing outspokenness) have suggested that this model might be "exportable" as a model. For example, the former minister of labor, Nor bert Blüm, once suggested that the German system also serve as a model for South Africa and Asia, proclaiming that "Our [Germany's] social system is an export article."[7]

Two questions are posed in this essay. The first concerns the sustainability of this model within Germany, particularly its egalitarian aspects, in the context of the structural dislocation wrought by a combination of liberalizing economic processes coupled with the enormous costs of unification; and, if it is to be sustained, in what form. If Germany's model system is indeed threatened with significant retrenchment, then this raises the larger issue of what the consequences might be for the character of the new Germany. If *Modell Deutschland* is indeed composed of institutional structures that, according to its advocates, explain the stability of the German state, then any sustained challenge (i.e., the combined effects of globalization and unification) to the major constituent parts of that system will potentially have significant implications for both economic and political relations among the major constituent actors within Germany.[8] By extension, changes in the character of *Modell Deutschland* raise questions about the disjuncture between its image and a more realistic appraisal of its features, and the appropriateness of its assignation as an "export article," with major implications for those nations adopting "the German model."

Second, we ask if Germany is indeed a model in empirical terms. For comparative data on the gender distribution of social well-being and prosperity indicate that Germany is anomalous; that the FRG demonstrates a gendered bias not only in comparison to egalitarian states like Sweden but also in comparison with countries far less noted for egalitarian instincts — such as the United States and the United Kingdom. Asserting that Germany is an anomaly in this regard, we attempt to address the question of why this might be the case.

In this essay we suggest three things: first, that *Modell Deutschland can* (and will) survive in a form recognizable to its advocates; second, the reason for this is due to institutional limits inherent in the *original* mandate that formed the foundation of the system; and third (and perhaps most importantly), not only is the discriminatory nature of current German institutions disposed toward the maldistribution of burdens but it in fact *predates* the Bonn Republic, and as such is rooted in a historical German ideology and political culture. Thus, we argue, *Modell Deutschland* will sustain itself, but will do so in a form that deliberately narrows the core of those benefiting from it. *Modell Deutschland*'s safety net will narrow. It will no longer serve to provide social support for all. In that sense, while the institutional architecture of *Modell Deutschland* will remain intact, its egalitarian features will come under increasing assault, extending a preexisting hierarchy among potential recipients. Germany's anomalous response, in gender terms, will thus help to preserve the system, although it portrays a historic, normative bias.

Crucial to our argument is the recognition that the system *from the beginning* was never designed to create economic and social equity along gender lines. Rather, Germany's ideological roots, predating both the Bonn and Berlin Republics, have emphasized discriminatory aspects not peculiar to social welfare but also extending to other aspects of economic policy (e.g., employment policies). These values, we argue, have influenced and continue to influence the institutional structure of German social policy.

As a means of supporting this argument, we initially examine some comparative data on social welfare before providing a preliminary evaluation of the German welfare and employment system, proposing that in the aggregate it only *professes* to reflect the values of egalitarianism and social justice in its allocation. In contrast, a reading of empirical data reveals that, in fact, this system generates policies predicated on different values; that the German social market economy is patriarchal and discriminatory in its distribution of resources. Gender acts as a determinant of "who gets what."

In sum, it may be that these discriminatory characteristics have always been present but were submerged in the context of the Cold War structure in which Germany thrived.[9] If that was formerly the case, however, the pressures wrought by unification, in tandem with globalization, have revealed and magnified these tendencies toward patriarchy and discrimination. Without the characteristics of equity and social justice ascribed to it by advocates of *Modell Deutschland,* Germany may still be a democracy, but it is one of a potentially differing character from that depicted by its advocates.[10]

In the end, we contend that while we believe that Germany *will* retain a democratic organizational structure — and thus clearly, definitionally, remain a capitalist, liberal democracy — its current tougher tones and sharper edges suggest that, at least symbolically, it increasingly echoes prior incarnations of "Deutschland" in the patriarchal values it embraces and the discriminatory policies it implements at home. It will not be the paragon of a social market economy epitomized by the stylized version of *Modell Deutschland.* The core institutional structures of the Federal Republic may therefore remain largely unaltered. But as the coffers of the Berlin Republic shrink, its leaders may increasingly evoke the patriarchal values they were able to submerge during periods of economic growth. This retrenchment is creating a more divisive Germany as reflected in the social policies of its government

Modell Deutschland Compared

How do we know that *Modell Deutschland* is any different than other industrialized nations undergoing the same alleged pressures of globalization? Is the situation of women in Germany any worse than in other market economies? A comparison with three other nations would suggest that women in Germany do indeed endure disproportionate inequalities. In the critical cases of the United States, Sweden, and the United Kingdom,[11] it would appear that in terms of female participation in both the public *and* private sectors of society, women in Germany lag behind their counterparts. In the public sector, women in Germany are disproportionately underrepresented in postsecondary educational institutions as well as in political offices, as table 1 illustrates. This disproportionality is also present in women's participation in the paid labor force, which, as we discuss later, is a crucial prerequisite for enjoying the benefits of Germany's social welfare system (see table 2).

Taken together, these measures place women in Germany in an unfavorable situation compared to men, a situation that in other countries is not as unfavorable. Germany's gendered system has a decidedly negative impact on women's employment, as table 3 indicates. In the end, then, because of this negative situation of women in Germany, they

TABLE 1

Females as Percentage of Full-Time Male University Enrollment, 1991

France	116
U.S.	111
Sweden	91
FRG	68

Women in Government, 1995 (percentage)

	Total	Ministerial Level
Sweden	33.3	47.8
U.S.	30.1	21.1
France	8.8	6.5
FRG	6.8	16.0

Source: Human Development Report, 1997 (New York: United Nations Development Program, 1997).

TABLE 2

Female Economic Activity Rate, 1995
(as percentage of male rates)

Sweden	90
U.S.	80
U.K.	73
FRG	69

Females as Percentage of Males in Labor Force

	1970	1992
Sweden	61	92
U.S.	59	82
U.K.	55	75
FRG	n.a.	70

Source: Human Development Report, 1997 (New York: United Nations Development Program, 1997).

TABLE 3

Females as Percentage of Male Unemployment, 1991–92

U.S.	91
Sweden	67
U.K.	40
FRG	169

Female Incidence of Long-Term Unemployment, 1995 (percentage)

	More than 6 mos.	More than 12 mos.
U.S.	16	8
Sweden	32	13
U.K.	51	32
FRG	68	51

Source: Human Development Report, 1997 (New York: United Nations Development Program, 1997).

lag behind women in the other societies in terms of overall prosperity and development, as table 4 illustrates.

Modell Deutschland as a Construct

In order to analyze the sustainability of *Modell Deutschland,* we first examine the notion of "social market economy" implicit in its system. More than merely an organizational definition, *Modell Deutschland* as a conception is both an economic *and* a political construct. Since the FRG's inception in 1949, its institutional foundations have been composed of two key elements that, over time, have become closely linked. The first cornerstone has been the unique match of a sophisticated and comprehensive social welfare system with a remarkably effective and durable (if not always robust) capitalist structure. The second is a restructured polity, consisting of citizens who profess an abiding allegiance to democratic values, of which equality is a key aspect. Crucial to the success of this "marriage" of capitalism and democracy in the FRG is an active yet limited state that is aggressively engaged in setting the social rules and norms governing both issues of employment as well as the institutionalization of social welfare.

TABLE 4

Earned Income Share (percentage to women)	
Sweden	45.0
U.S.	41.0
U.K.	35.0
FRG	34.8

Gender-Related Development Index Rank (industrialized countries)	
Sweden	3
U.S.	5
U.K.	13
FRG	16

Source: Human Development Report, 1997 (New York: United Nations Development Program, 1997).

The Three Pillars of German Social Welfare

This integral role of the state is formally anchored in Germany's constitution (*Grundgesetz*). Article 20, paragraph 1, states, "The Federal Republic of Germany is a democratic and social republic." This proclamation has been interpreted to mean that the state has the duty to protect its citizens from material need in case of sickness, accident, or unemployment and to safeguard the welfare of its citizens in retirement. The institutional component of this social welfare policy is itself a three-tiered support system, comprising three "principles" (as they are called in Germany): security, entitlement, and welfare. Each principle ascribes different rights to different groups in society. Although the German state does provide an extensive material safety net in the form of various social insurance programs, it does not address the issue of equal access. Thus, while the state does have the duty to protect its citizens, *how* it does so does not necessarily guarantee equality.

The security cornerstone consists of the so-called social security programs: health care, retirement pensions, worker's compensation, unemployment benefits, and, only recently, compensation for nursing home/hospice care for senior citizens. The entitlement cornerstone includes benefits for those who "serve" the state or have "suffered" for the good of the community. This group is chiefly composed of veterans, expellees, and (somewhat perplexingly because of their inclusion with the other "sufferers") civil servants (*Beamte*). The last cornerstone is the welfare structure: specifically, financial and/or material "social assistance." The crucial distinctions between these three sets involve contrasting roles for the state and the differing citizen access to their benefits. These differences are important because they provide insight into the discriminatory social ideology at work.

In terms of the first pillar, social security institutions, they are considered self-financing, private (i.e., nonpublic) programs. Its programs are therefore financed by contributions from the workers themselves. The philosophy behind this "private" construct is to establish solidarity for "self-help" among private citizens; to get members of society to aggregate resources in order to share the burdens and risks of potential catastrophes. Many social welfare benefits (e.g., unemployment, health care, pensions, etc.) are therefore merely *restitutional* benefits. Minimally, the role of the state is thus to provide whatever subsidies are necessary to cover expenditures not met by contributions. Yet the state actually plays a much larger role here in that it commands obligatory membership from its citizens. In other words, it is *not* the state guaranteeing these benefits but rather its authority to mandate others to do so.

In doing so, it is discriminatory because it validates the conviction that only those who contribute to the system are entitled to such restitutional benefits. As we shall discuss later, the discriminatory effect here is caused by the fact that women are encouraged to *not* participate in the paid labor force, thus leaving them ineligible for these benefits.

The second pillar, entitlement benefits (*Versorgung*), is even more restrictive. Its programs are intended to establish solidarity among the *civic* community in that it provides benefits for those who serve the state. Since these benefits are in compensation for service to the community, they are financed by the taxes of *all* citizens. Again, crucial here is the confirmation of the belief that only those who concretely contribute to the good of the state are thus *entitled* to benefits from the state at a shared cost.

The last cornerstone — welfare institutions — is the most recent and the least restrictive in terms of access. Social assistance is available to all who can demonstrate need, whatever the cause, although its benefits can be claimed only when it is proven by a potential claimant that the benefits of the other two institutions are insufficient. No contributions are required, and its programs are financed by federal taxes. Here the role of the state is intended to provide assistance to enable all of its citizens to lead a "dignified" life. Yet, as we shall argue, this most crucial pillar of the social market economy is also the institution *most* susceptible to curtailments and other reductions.

Evolving Critics of *Modell Deutschland*

The dominance of this model as an abiding (and benign?) image of Germany effectively went unchallenged from mainstream critics during the 1970s. Initially, it was predominantly Germans from the Left who criticized the German model, notably on *political* grounds. Above all, these critics claimed that the system impinged on civil liberties as well as on the political and economic rights of the working class through a strategy of co-optation.[12] It was over a decade before subsequent revisionist studies by Germans, most notably that by Fritz Scharpf, effectively questioned the *economic* efficacy of the model in the 1970s and 1980s, rather than merely criticizing its political desirability.[13] But these challenges to the presumption of its economic capabilities proved to be the "tip of the iceberg"; indeed, by the end of the 1980s some critics suggested that West Germany was a prime example of "Euro-sclerosis" rather than that of a locomotive engine of prosperity.[14]

In the economic context, then, this construct's legendary status among observers has, potentially, outlasted the actual achievements of the German economy, which has suffered from both cyclical and structural problems over the course of the last two decades.[15] But the legendary reputation of the German economy persists abroad in the 1990s despite evidence of its occasional failings — such as a shrinking GDP[16] — supported by the FRG's impressive capacity to generate enviable trade surpluses, to maintain the value of a hard currency and large international reserves, and to sustain low inflation rates while minimizing (relatively) and routinizing conflictual labor relations (remaining, as the Italian waiters suggested, "predictably dull") even under the most adverse of circumstances.

This issue of the continued viability of the model as an economic construct is, of course, of relevance to us since the system cannot continue if it is strained beyond recognition by issues of solvency. However, this dimension is only part of an issue. What is of equal significance is the question of the model's *political* desirability, if only because it highlights aspects of the character of the new Germany.[17] And, as we have implied, these two issues are intrinsically related.

Modell Deutschland in the Bonn Republic

Historically, Germany has always enjoyed a relatively extensive and sophisticated welfare system, a tradition sustained in the FRG, where it was considered a fundamental cornerstone of the state's objectives from its very inception.[18] As noted by one preeminent scholar, Claus Offe, the primary ideological foundation of the institutions of the German social welfare system since its inception is trust; in sum, its stabilizing capacity is predicated on the effectiveness of its institutions *in the past*.[19] Fundamental to this trust is the receipt of a service or payment to which an individual is entitled for specific reasons. For example, as originally conceived, since only industrial workers contributed to the social insurance funds, they were also the only ones to benefit from them on the basis of their contributions. This notion of restricted entitlement continues today. In essence, the primary purpose of the social security system is to "maintain the status" of those who have *already* achieved some prominence within the paid labor force. This approach contrasts, for example, with one designed to create opportunities for those who have never achieved status within the "public sphere" of paid employment, such as an affirmative action program.

When instituted in the 1880s, the initial design of social insurance was therefore meant to protect the aristocracy of industrial workers. Over time, its programs have incrementally been expanded to include more groups based on the same principle — restitution for those who are "inside" the system (i.e., employed in the labor force). Not devised to redress historical inequities, the system therefore has historically had a minimal effect upon social inequality in Germany. In particular, it does not seek to give a "head start" to the disadvantaged (e.g., women who have lesser training or work experience outside the home). Moreover, it is not organized as a universal insurance system, but one of "exclusive" (yet in most cases mandatory) membership. As such, then, it offers little to ameliorate the potential development of social conflict if the number of nonrecipients grows too large or disgruntled. In fact, this exclusivity permits officials to, when necessary, restrict the benefits of outsiders, while protecting the benefits of the insiders.

This is not to imply that there is no social "safety net" in Germany. During the Weimar Republic the German government introduced the third pillar of the social welfare system, namely, the principle of *Fürsorge*, as discussed above. The German state, however, has, critically, *not* contracted to aid those who "fall through the cracks." Rather, such aid is the beneficence of the state. As such, financial and material aid is a *privilege*, not a right. This means, in turn, that in times of economic adversity this "privilege" can more easily be curtailed, or even revoked by the state. Thus, while this system of social welfare has been extended, the initial philosophy still remains and provides a justification for discriminating between claimants: contribution to the state (whether in the form of labor or service) is the basis of *entitlement* of receipt from the state.

In institutional terms, the system of social security operates on a private, nonprofit basis with a clear government mandate. Yet it has always been the case that the government subsidizes the programs' generous benefits. Sustaining such a system for those that potentially qualify therefore requires maintaining a careful balance between contributions and expenses.

Logically, any structural change that threatens to disturb this fundamental balance on a permanent basis has to be redressed by either expanding revenues or constraining benefits; more taxes are required from a shrinking pool of employed or fewer resources are awarded to a growing pool of unemployed. If neither policy is pursued in the context of growing demand, the state risks a fiscal crisis. The question for government officials is therefore a reasonably stark one (although ostensibly open to compromise): How much should wage earners "sacrifice" in comparison to the unemployed? But, whatever the ultimate arrangement that results, the system always operates predicated on the assumption that only past contributors can legitimately seek restitution when faced with adversity (while financial aid recipients are dependent on the largess of the state).[20]

German conservatives consider this construct acceptable because it gives workers a "stake in the system." Socialists tend to see it as a way of institutionalizing class solidarity. Trade unionists support it because they fear that any reforms will hurt their members' interests. Finally, given the fact that the system is generally administered outside of the auspices of the central state, political liberals support it precisely because it militates against state intervention.[21] Welfare payments and services are developed and dispensed through a decentralized system.[22]

But, according to Offe, all of these justifications share a common attribute — they are based on a very narrow conception of what work is, and how it is carried out. Acquiring "full welfare citizenship" requires conforming to a "normal" work process — continuous employment on, minimally, a half-time basis. The social insurance system is thus a "core working-class fortress" that does not include "precarious labor" — low-skilled, low-paid, "flexible" labor. It is this group of "outsiders" (of which a disproportionate number are women, as noted below) that is particularly vulnerable. Since most employment opportunities for them are considered "fixed-term" or casual labor, and not "normal" labor as required for social insurance, they tend to fall between the cracks of the system. Moreover, the relevant actors in this system have little reason to change this situation. Granting full welfare citizenship rights to these disadvantaged workers would be costly to both employers and employees alike, since they would have to finance the added costs through their contributions. Indeed, the incentives of the system thereby *encourage* firms to use temporary or part-time labor, denying access to those who seek to establish the basis for subsequent social welfare restitution.[23]

For the past century, then, social welfare has been progressively expanded from a labor aristocracy outward to encompass more workers. Indeed, measured against its own prescribed goals, the system has been remarkably successful. Workers in Germany enjoy substantial benefits and protections, surely one crucial reason for the long periods of labor stability in the Bonn Republic. However, we suggest that these accomplishments have never been extended beyond the ethnic German male — in short, women (and foreign workers) have been left behind. Thus, while many outside of Germany may envy the achievements of the German system, what they do not see are its discriminatory aspects. Moreover, on the verge of a new century, that discriminatory dynamic has become even more apparent, evident in the retreat of the social welfare system under pressure as privileged welfare has shrunk and only entitled benefits have remained intact. In the section that follows we examine this tendency in the context of the role of women, deferring a discussion of the treatment of foreigners for another occasion.

Private Patriarchy: Gendered Norms and Ideology

"Gender roles are constituted by society. There are no tasks beyond the biologically given roles of childbirth and breast-feeding that require a woman rather than a man."[24] Gender roles in Germany clearly delineate a gendered division of labor—women are seen by society as embodying the primary role of caregiver, a role that is largely supported by legal codes and legislation. In fact, whether gender equality should prevail in German society is rather unclear given its ambiguous laws regarding that issue. Article 3, paragraph 2 of the Basic Law anchors the ideal of equal gender rights. Yet at the same time the Basic Law also explicitly incorporates many patriarchal laws from Wilhelmine, Weimar, *and* Nazi Germany, particularly as reflected in the German social welfare system.[25] These are most deeply rooted in the norms and rules governing labor, paid and "unpaid" (i.e., familial). Indeed, the German model relies on an explicitly "gendered" division of labor: men are assumed to be the employed "breadwinners" while women are to be responsible for the private household. Moreover, the socially implicit understanding of women's role, and thus their welfare citizenship rights, is that of carrying out reproductive labor, that is, the nonpaid labor of childbearing and caretaking. These distinctions are most evident in three basic sets of codified norms: those regarding "family rights," "motherhood protection," and female employment.

Historically, German norms have always placed a strong emphasis on women's duties as housewives and mothers, as reflected in laws regarding "family rights."[26] The original Family and Marriage Code of the Bonn Republic "enshrined" a woman's domestic role in law and even gave husbands some control over their wives' rights to work. In fact, the code explicitly stated that it was a wife's duty to take care of the household, a task from which she could be freed only in consultation with her husband.[27] It was not until 1977 that this law was reformed, at which time gender-neutral language was introduced. The household division of labor was not to be gender-specific, and partners are to agree on tasks of housekeeping. Yet according to Eva Kolinsky, German courts continue to interpret the law as it was before 1977, that is, explicitly assigning women housekeeping responsibilities. Subsequent judgments and legal commentaries, for example, have specified that young children need a full-time person to care for them, usually the mother. Furthermore, Kolinsky claims that in divorce cases, the power of courts to grant maintenance payments appears to have been used as an instrument to perpetuate traditional role patterns for women.[28]

Consistent with this historic view, the government itself ensured that the interpretation of the 1977 reforms would not precipitate the demise of social norms. Elaborating on the amended rule that each partner has to take due regard of the family when accepting employment, court officials nonetheless stated:

> The rule does not suggest a schematically equal treatment of man and woman. The wife has . . . to take particular regard of the needs of the family, for example when children have to be cared for and brought up.[29]

The second example of codified norms institutionalizing patriarchy concerns the laws governing "motherhood protection" — the employment of pregnant women and mothers. Germany has very explicit regulations regarding the workforce "protection" it affords pregnant women and mothers of newborns. Article 6 of the constitution states that every mother has a claim to the protection and assistance of the community (not the state). Fulfilling its role of establishing norms and procedures for the private "social insurance" sector, the German state mandated private health insurance firms to guarantee women extensive services. Furthermore, employed mothers are guaranteed up to four months' maternity leave. This legislation is clearly nondiscriminatory in nature since it allows female choice, providing guarantees that enable women to pursue both parental and employment roles.

Where the legislation, such as the Act on the Protection of Working Mothers, becomes discriminatory is in the context of actual work regulation. Pregnant women are prohibited from working during the last six weeks of their pregnancy and from beginning work again until at least eight weeks after delivery (12 weeks for multiple births or premature births). Pregnant women and nursing mothers are prohibited from working night shifts and weekends. Moreover, expectant or working mothers are also forbidden to engage in labor considered physically demanding or associated with high risk for illness.[30]

Many hail these laws as "progressive" because they guarantee the labor rights of working mothers.[31] But they are, contends Hevener, simultaneously implicitly biased against women as a codification of "implied incompetence":

> The view of women that such documents [e.g., motherhood protection] project is analogous to that of children. Since women, like children, are considered unable to make intelligent, informed, and rational decisions about their own lives, they are subjected to the paternal power of the State.[32]

They are not designed to facilitate choice, but rather mandate that all mothers are equally "disabled" during and after pregnancy.³³

The third type of codified discriminatory norm concerns the employment of women in general. Due chiefly to the efforts of the SPD, the same basic prohibitions or "protections" for working mothers have been universally applied to women. All women, for example, are forbidden to work in any position that requires physically demanding labor. Thus, regardless of whether a woman wants to (or is able to) bear children, she has been subjected to the same restrictions. These types of "protections" reemphasize the traditional social definition of a woman as wife and mother. Hence,

> [t]he focus of legislative attention is not on her actual activity but rather remains on her domestic role, and it is the perceived characteristics of this role that the law allegedly seeks to protect. Thus, when the sphere of her actual work involvement is viewed as being outside the normal domain of women, her presence may be seen as necessitating protection if her primary role [as mother and caregiver] is to be preserved.³⁴

But even if women should in Germany follow the "traditional" role that is expected of them, that is, as primary, nonpaid childbearers and/or caregivers, they still face certain barriers in qualifying for compensatory social welfare benefits. In particular, these norms have two directly negative consequences for these women when they reach "retirement age."

The first negative consequence is in terms of Germany's social security benefits: since housewives do not pay into the social security system (e.g., pension programs, disability plans, etc.), they are not entitled to its benefits, most notably when they reach retirement age. Instead, they are expected to rely on a husband who had a full-time, "normal" work experience. Offe sees deeper consequences here:

> As such, the social security system contains a 'hidden curriculum' which declares labor and employment to be much more than a legal and economic category, namely a form of respectable and even dignified existence. Implicit in this curriculum is the gender division of labor in which the male breadwinner spends his economically active life in full-time employment and thus acquires the employment record necessary for full pension and other security rights, while his wife does not spend her life in (full-time) employment and hence does not earn any independent social security entitlements. The male breadwinner's wife relies on the legal rights and claims

that she derives, directly or indirectly, from her institutional status within the family.[35]

Second, those women who remain at home and fulfill societal expectations are not considered to be "serving the state." They are therefore not entitled to any of the benefits of the second category (i.e., entitlements for state service), although there is one ironic example where the state considers nonworking women to have "supported" the state: the so-called *Trummerfrauen* (rubble women), who literally removed the rubble after the devastation of World War II. These women did receive some special consideration when *Kindererziehungsleistung* (special retirement benefits for child care performed by a working parent who interrupted their employment to do so) laws were passed in 1987.[36]

There is, however, one option for nonworking women to be eligible for state entitlements: by bearing children and caring for them at home. The federal *Erziehungsgesetz* (child-rearing legislation), introduced in 1985, includes a provision for *Erziehungsgeld* (or "child-rearing benefits"). According to the legislation, one parent, independent of previous employment status, is entitled to receive financial compensation for up to two years after the birth of a child. Eligibility for this benefit, however, means the relevant parent must stay at home to take care of the child and forgo full-time employment. While perhaps progressive, it gives little incentive for wage-earning men to take advantage of this opportunity because the payments are a mere DM 600 per month. Indeed, available data point to the limited effect of this provision as an incentive to men — at its inception in 1986, only 1.44 percent of the parents receiving child-rearing benefits were male; by 1991 this figure had only increased to 1.48 percent.[37]

These examples illustrate, then, how socially and legally constructed gendered norms concerning "burden sharing" work to the disadvantage of women — prescribing acceptable behavior while proscribing unacceptable, and thus reducing choice. Women desiring participation in both reproductive and productive labor face obstacles constructed by social norms and legal restrictions. Female entitlements are correspondingly constrained.

Public Patriarchy: Institutionalized Marginalization

The discriminatory effects based on cultural socialization have been no more apparent, however, than in the material employment of women, as they continue to be socialized to believe that it is still their primary duty to assume the role of child-rearing even though they also work outside the home.[38] A more institutionalized form of discrimination befalls these women who wish to combine motherhood and profession in seeking a way out of the social welfare dilemma. Thus, even when women go into paid employment, much of the subordinate role of women is carried over in the form of "public patriarchy"—lower pay, status, and power in the workplace.

Women in Germany face numerous obstacles in their pursuit of full welfare citizenship, some more explicit than others. Since German schools are only in session for half-days, and the restrictive store-opening hours in Germany only allow very limited evening and weekend shopping, it is virtually impossible to both work and be a primary provider of parental responsibilities on a full-time basis without excessive amounts of assistance. As a result, part-time work has become the domain of women—nearly 33 percent of all employed women work only part-time. Even more revealing is the fact that nearly 90 percent of all part-time employees are women.[39] Moreover, the demand for jobs exceeds the number of available positions, so women have become part of the "silent reserve" of the structurally unemployed: women who are not registered as unemployed and do not appear in the statistics but are looking for part-time work. Ultimately, even if women prefer part-time work, the consequences are less than desirable:

> part-time working has not enhanced anything but the quick-and-ready opportunity to earn some money. On the ambitious level of employing women in line with their qualifications and potential, and rewarding them with job security, promotion chances and substantive opportunities of equal employment, part-time working has been a hindrance rather than an asset in the search for equality. It has consolidated the gender gap in the labor market, and the position of women at the less favoured end as far as status, prospects, and pay are concerned.[40]

Yet even for that two-thirds majority of women who do manage to work full-time, it is clear that they also face gender discrimination, most evidently in terms of pay. Consistent with this view, data reveal a significant earnings gap between western German male and female workers and that this gap is actually widening, as reflected in table 5. Between 1980 and 1993 the gap between male and female average gross monthly income therefore grew from DM 900 to DM 1,400. The situation is even more distressing for female white-collar employees. As with overall employment trends, the earnings gap among white-collar workers is increasing: in 1980 the gap was over DM 1,400, and by 1993 the gap had grown to DM 2,300. Moreover, female white-collar workers were still earning less in 1993 than male workers in 1980. The German Economics Institute attributes this difference primarily to the fact that women still very rarely advance to high managerial positions. They thereby dispute the traditional interpretation of these skewed results and claim it is due less to the high proportion of female part-time workers and more to the fact that women are heavily represented in low-paid, unskilled jobs. Comparative data support this assertion, as demonstrated by the fact that in Germany the number of women in administrative and managerial positions is by far the lowest.

Finally, the dilemma for women striving for full welfare citizenship is most devastating for single working mothers, women who conflict with German norms in two regards: bearing children with no husband and working after doing so. A growing category of women in Germany, the number of female-headed households has nearly doubled in absolute numbers, from 1.9 million in 1980 to 3.2 million in 1993, while the number of male-headed households has remained nearly constant at 11.3 million.

TABLE 5. Average Gross Monthly Income of All Employed Persons (by Gender) (DM)

	1980	1993
Male	2,811	4,625
Female	1,930	3,221

Source: Deutsches Institut für Wirtschaftsforschung, "Zur Einkommenslage der westdeutschen Arbeitsnehmerinnen," *Wochenbericht,* no. 31 (21 September 1994).

TABLE 6. Average Gross Monthly Income of White-Collar Employees by Gender (DM)

	1980	1993
Male	3,691	5,987
Female	2,249	3,670

Source: Deutsches Institut für Wirtschaftsforschung, "Zur Einkommenslage der westdeutschen Arbeitsnehmerinnen," *Wochenbericht,* no. 31 (21 September 1994).

Yet disposable income in households headed by single mothers lags fully *two-thirds* behind similar households headed by men. Moreover, as the following data illustrate, female-headed households had *less* disposable income in 1993 than male-headed ones had already in 1980, some 13 years earlier.

In the end, we argue that the result for women is that they are caught in a paradox that is virtually inescapable. Achieving full welfare citizenship becomes impossible without making personal trade-offs, as table 9 illustrates. For example, women who have no children and who do not engage in paid labor have no rights to entitlement or compensation. Essentially, they must depend on a gainfully employed husband for

TABLE 7. Percentage of Female Administrators and Managers (1990)

U.S.	42
Sweden	39
U.K.	33
FRG	19

Source: Human Development Report, 1997 (New York: United Nations Development Program, 1997).

TABLE 8. Average Monthly Disposable Income for Single-Headed Housholds by Gender (DM)

	1980	1993
Male	3,553	5,535
Female	2,245	3,482

Source: Human Development Report, 1997 (New York: United Nations Development Program, 1997).

TABLE 9. Trade-Offs That German Women Face

	Entitlements	No Entitlements
Compensation	Working mothers	Working women (no children)
No Compensation	Stay-at-home mothers	Women with no children and no paid employment

such rights (or fall below poverty levels). Such women are eligible for a small entitlement should they bear children (*Kindergeld*) and remain at home to care for them (*Erziehungsgeld*). At the same time, women who work and do not bear children only receive compensatory rights and no entitlements. It is only the working mother who is eligible for both compensatory benefits and entitlements. Yet, as discussed above, it is precisely this category of women who face the most significant discrimination in terms of paid employment.

This paradox places German women in a difficult situation, one that seems less burdensome for women in other societies. For example, comparative data reveal that it is apparently easier to combine motherhood with participation in the paid labor force. It would seem, in other words, that German women are "voting" with their wombs and opting for no children.

Sustaining *Modell Deutschland:* A Gendered, Shrinking Core

Peter Katzenstein may well be correct in asserting that the process of policy change in the Federal Republic is an incremental one.[41] But this

TABLE 10

Fertility Index in 1994 (1970 = 100)	
Sweden	102
U.S.	92
U.K.	78
FRG	64

Female Share of Adult Labor Force (percentage)		
	1970	1991
Sweden	36	48
U.S.	37	45
U.K.	36	43
FRG	39	41

Source: Human Development Report, 1997 (New York: United Nations Development Program, 1997).

Note: The only countries with larger drops in fertility rates were the Catholic countries of Spain, Ireland, Italy, and Portugal, as well as Greece.

assertion says nothing about the *direction* of policy change: in fact, dating from the 1973 oil crisis, successive German governments of the Left and the Right have incrementally pursued bipartisan policies that (minimally) reduced benefits to those who were eligible and above all (systematically) reduced access by tightening eligibility requirements for those seeking social welfare citizenship.[42]

According to Offe, such policies were the product of a conscious strategy shared by both the SPD and the CDU — to protect the organized heart of Germany's workforce — to the detriment of the weaker members of the labor force who could be easily isolated and discriminated against. To support this contention, he identifies a series of government policies implemented after 1975 that were designed to adapt to a new period of austerity. These measures actually created what Germans have come to refer to as the "two-thirds" society (*Zweidrittelgesellschaft*). According to this definition, the larger group enjoys all the benefits associated with the extensive German welfare system, while one-third remains unprotected by labor regulation and welfare.[43] Evidence of such tendencies is reflected in legislation introduced in the Bonn Republic that was passed with the agreement of both major parties, dating from the Budget Structure Act and the restrictive regulations on employment insurance of 1975, to the Fiscal Consolidation Laws of 1977 and 1978, and ultimately to the Old Age Pension Reform Act of 1989. This bipartisan consensus, Offe contends, enabled both sides to cut the benefits and increase the burdens of groups in society in proportion to their political clout: "Under these tactics of careful, gradual, and largely consensual management of potential conflict, a polarized politicization of social policy issues could not emerge."[44] In other words, cuts were introduced in small doses and were spread around highly diverse categories, avoiding those groups who were best able to offer an effective counter-response.[45] As Offe states:

> The policies of social policy adaptation and consolidation adopted by federal governments since 1975 show a rather clear pattern of selective protection and discriminatory exclusion which, apart from its substantive redistributive effects, has also played the role of a 'hidden curriculum' by projecting images and symbolic demarcations as to which social categories 'deserve' to enjoy undiminished benefits and levels of security and other social categories that can justly (as well as safely, in terms of their potential for resistance and conflict) be deprived of some of their status rights . . . The overall pattern is clear enough. The underlying strategy is to remove cuts and austerity measures from institutional locations where they can

easily become the focal point of collective action to locations where they remain largely imperceptible to the wider public, and difficult to interpret as a collective condition and experience on the basis of which organized action might become possible. It is as if the maxim had been followed to make it more difficult to pinpoint the winners, losers and those responsible for the transaction.[46]

Over time the form of these measures varied. For example, the 1975 economic crisis touched off a public campaign of defamation of the "unemployed" by accusing them of refusing work in order to profit from generous unemployment benefits. This shift in public perception enabled the first major modification in unemployment laws as officials tightened up the categories of "reasonable employment," which meant that should an unemployed worker refuse such a "reasonable employment," his/her unemployment benefits could be rightfully curtailed.

The distinction between the protected and unprotected became exacerbated with the simultaneous, related growth of a major structural unemployment problem in Germany in the 1970s and 1980s. For the first time, it became apparent that the labor market exhibited deep structural disparities. Certain groups were disproportionately affected by long-term unemployment; thus, despite the improving job market, they were unable to secure new positions. In particular, unemployed women became a special "problem group" in that they regularly constituted more than one-half of the unemployed. Especially problematic was the fact that they had relatively lower job skills than men and that large numbers sought part-time work in order to combine employment with family duties.[47]

Women were disproportionately affected by the policy cutbacks that followed. For example, the rules were again tightened up in terms of eligibility; a longer period of employee contributions prior to unemployment was demanded in order to become eligible for benefits. For women who had a more difficult time finding employment due, usually, to lack of desirable job skills and for women who had taken time off to raise children, this new regulation was particularly problematic. And given that women were disproportionately represented among the long-term unemployed, they were many times hit hardest by these restrictions.

Many of these women were among the long-term unemployed because of their less-qualified skills or because they had taken time out of the labor force to raise children. They were, therefore, most in need of retraining programs. Yet it was precisely the retraining programs and assistance for unemployed part-time workers that were first sacrificed in the 1983 budget cuts by the Federal Agency for Labor (Bundesanstalt für Arbeit). Ironically, even after the agency achieved a budget *surplus* one year later, it did not move to restore these programs to their former funding level but instead chose to lower the contributions required of employed workers, that is, shield the insiders from increased burdens.[48]

These measures were tolerable, as Offe contends, because empowered Germans (i.e., the employed) had elected to reject a collectivist, solidaristic response in favor of a zero-sum approach. Indeed, they were encouraged to do so by a corresponding structure that made every increase in benefits to the unemployed or underemployed contingent upon greater contributions by the employed, but not the employers.[49]

This new trade-off may best be illustrated by examining the relative share of each major contributor financing the social budget (i.e., employers, federal government, and private households) (e.g., employee contributions to social insurance funds, governmental subsidies, and personal income tax) for financing the total social budget. For workers, this share increased substantially in the period from 1965–90, while at the same time the share of employer contributions only increased marginally. Moreover, the contribution made by the federal government dropped dramatically. These workers continue to be disproportionately burdened with financing the social security programs. As a result, unions, in the interest of their working members, have chosen not to defend the universal and inclusive nature of social security. Overall, the net effect of these developments, claims Offe more generally, has instead contributed to the rise in these disparities between the haves and the have-nots.[50] Moreover, despite growing trade surpluses (which averaged DM 100 billion between 1984 and 1988) and impressively low levels of inflation, no political leadership in the zero-sum game of the German social welfare system emerged that was willing to grant full welfare citizenship rights to those not enfranchised by Germany's social security system.

Consistent with our broader argument, according to Fritz Scharpf, it was women who were among those who disproportionately suffered during this period, while middle-aged, male workers remained untouched by

TABLE 11. Sources of Finance of the Social Budget (percentage of total expenditure)

	1965	1990
Employers	29	31
Private households	20	29
Federal	29	20
Others	22	20

Source: Eric Owen Smith, *The German Economy* (London: Routledge, 1994), 203.

these events.[51] This evidence corroborates our argument that the emerging, distinct, discriminatory system represents a retrenchment to the ingrained values of German society: it is perfectly acceptable to protect male workers at the expense of women, since their "natural" (in reality, socially constructed) role in the division of labor is in the field of reproductive labor. The core insider groups of the social insurance system — skilled male workers — were thus shielded from any cuts in their benefits wrought by the pressures of declining economic growth.

Not only, then, have women suffered disproportionately under these changing economic conditions, but certain forms of institutionalized discrimination have also increased. We therefore suggest that the policies and practices of the federal government, labor unions, and business enterprises have discriminated against women as "outsiders," due to the gendered norms regarding women's roles and responsibilities in society. Table 12 illustrates how the situation of women corresponds to policies and practices in the Federal Republic. Consistent with the gendered norms and ideologies discussed earlier, box 1 of table 12 suggests that working mothers face a series of problems relating to insufficient day care and restricted store hours. Mothers outside of the paid labor force face major disincentives to reentry. "Potential mothers" experience the glass ceiling effect noted in box 4 and the limitations to becoming more viable as a high-skilled employee noted in box 3.

Five forms of evidence support these claims.[52] The first concerns governmental measures relating to child care provisions in the 1980s. Although the number and availability of child care opportunities in-

TABLE 12. Corresponding Policies and Practices Regarding Women

Situation of Women	In the Workforce	Not in the Workforce
With Children	Insufficient day care; restricted store hours; school half-days (1)	Paid family leave (biased toward female participation); lack of "flex-time" or part-time employment (2)
Without Children	"Glass ceiling"; no quotas or affirmative action programs (4)	Overrepresented number trained in sunset industries; cutbacks in vocational training to reenter labor force (3)

creased in the 1980s, these new facilities were *not* designed to free women for full-time employment, primarily because they provided only half-day child care. Moreover, little was done to create child care facilities for children under the age of three.[53] Thus, the primary concern of many German mothers wishing to return to full-time employment (infant care and daylong child care) was not alleviated by the government. In the end, then, these measures only enabled more part-time (low-skilled) employment for working mothers.

Second, the 1985 Employment Protection Act, ostensibly designed to provide protective legislation for part-time work, only increased the attractiveness of part-time employment. In a progressive manner, the legislation does give regular part-time employees (more than 15 hours per week)[54] the same employment rights and benefits as full-time workers, if only in pro rata terms. Yet an analysis of this legislation suggests that these reform measures have merely locked women into "dead-end" part-time positions instead of facilitating full-time employment, for example, by means of introducing "flexible time" or job-sharing.

A third piece of evidence is the federal *Erziehungsgesetz* of 1985. Introduced as a replacement for the previous maternity leave policy (*Mutterschaftsurlaub*), it was meant to make child-rearing a gender-neutral task within the family. This family leave legislation was designed ostensibly to enable *either* parent to take up to three years of unpaid family leave from their place of employment.[55] Yet in the case of double-income families, this policy requires that one income be surrendered during the period of unpaid leave. In a context where, of the two partners, the male member of the household is overwhelmingly likely to be paid significantly more, it is likely that the lower-paid parent takes the leave of absence. Indeed, as the data show, it has been and continues to be women who interrupt their career advancement. However, this result need not have been inevitable. Evidence that prevailing German forces deliberately chose to perpetuate a gender-biased phenomenon is provided by the fact that the SPD Bundestag fraction introduced legislation designed to combat this problem. In their proposal, family leave time was to be extended in those cases where *fathers* also participated in the official child-rearing (a similar provision is included in the Swedish family leave policy). Yet this legislation never received the needed parliamentary support.

Comparisons with France and the United Kingdom reveal that German working mothers are more limited in their formal labor participation. In 1987, far fewer women with children in Germany were employed outside the home than in the United Kingdom and France. Moreover, the age of the children seemed to play little role in the percentage of outside employment.

These figures add credence to Lane's thesis that "the state has made it financially worthwhile for women to stay at home with their children." At the same time they also suggest that the ploy to provide "incentives" for women to remain "outsiders," thus freeing resources for "insiders," has succeeded.

Fourth, proactive governmental support for women as wage or salaried labor in the form of affirmative action programs has not been forthcoming, even though women seeking full-time employment have been one of the groups hardest hit since the mid-1980s. Instead, most action has seemingly protected male employment. For example, European Community directives on equal opportunity legislation were initially strongly opposed in Bonn on the grounds of "deregulation of the labor market" imperatives. In the end, despite subsequent pressure, the measures were only halfheartedly implemented.[56] Even the pathbreaking decision of the European Court of Justice to uphold the constitutionality of a law in North Rhine–Westphalia giving preference to equally qualified women in cases of promotion has not been formally embraced by the German federal government. When the SPD-led opposition called on the German government to go one step further and put forward an affirmative action plan that would include quota provisions, the official reply was curt and negative. According to Claudia Nolte, Federal Minister for Women, the government does want to end discrimination. "But most women, according to Nolte, oppose quotas."[57]

Finally, the modification of vocational education and training benefits in the 1980s tended to benefit men more than women. Little effort was made to provide incentives (or, indeed, implement affirmative actions) in terms of training girls for "jobs with a future." In fact, women (and foreign workers) are disproportionately employed and/or trained in the "sunset" industries.[58] Additionally, when benefits for vocational education and training were cut in the 1987 reform, women were again the primary losers, since it was mostly retraining programs that took the bulk of budget cuts. Since women had benefited more from these pro-

TABLE 13. Labor Participation by Mothers in 1987 (in percentage, by age of child[ren])

	Less than 2 yrs.	3–5 yrs.	6–13 yrs.
FRG	37	42	52
U.K.	40	55	72
France	60	67	70

Source: Lane, "Gender and the Labor Market," 279, 282.

grams because they were situated in those careers that offered little prospect for advancement, they again proved to suffer an undue burden. Finally, even though female employment tends to be concentrated in the service sector, women in Germany have *not* benefited from the shift from manufacturing to service industry, as elsewhere, because Germany's service sector remains small in comparison to other industrial nations.

Modell Deutschland in the Aftermath of Unification

We therefore argue that Erhard's epithet "social market economy" is an ill-fitting term for describing the Bonn Republic of the 1970s and 1980s. It is no more appropriate for the Berlin Republic of the 1990s. Instead, heightened tensions have been generated by a new emphasis in Germany on decoupling these two terms by systematically stressing the market economy aspects at a cost to the social.[59] But just how have the shortcomings of social welfarism in Germany been exacerbated in postunified Germany? And in particular, how have gendered norms permitted a systematic discrimination against women as a means of coping with these new stresses?

For the Kohl government, the ultimate answer to the crucial issue of who should pay for the staggering costs of unification became everybody *but* those in Germany who initially formulated the policies and those fully enfranchised and embedded citizens (largely male workers and businessmen in the west) who supported those policies; in other words, everybody but the Kohl government's electoral base. Principally included among those targeted to pay at home were marginalized workers (mostly female) considered dispensable and not politically threatening.[60]

Overall, the number of marginalized workers in Germany has grown, creating an enlarged gap between the "haves" and the "have-nots." This tendency is part of an accelerated trend in the aftermath of unification, that of fragmenting German society into smaller constituent units. Such a trend makes the comment of Helmut Kohl quoted at the outset of this essay at the very least laughable, at most outrageous, because CDU policy under his leadership sustained a series of policies designed to decouple the "haves" from the "have-nots," to fragment national solidarity — and thus to institute policies that "divide and rule." Those "haves" who are in the pool thus still enjoy unrivaled benefits. But access to that pool is becoming harder to achieve. It is increasingly composed of white, middle-aged and middle-class males — and their dependents. It increasingly curtails the prospective membership of other groups in society.

We therefore argue that, while the benefits available to those Germans who qualify remain relatively generous, even in the face of these recent cuts, there is an intentional, secular trend toward shrinking the proportion of people eligible to receive such benefits.[61] Thus, while the debate is in terms of how much individuals receive, it is also about who is eligible to receive them. The terms of "welfare citizenship" appear to be immutably changing in Germany. The cherished welfare aspects of the social market economy that have been assailed take two forms. First and foremost, the restitutional aspects of welfare (in particular, unemployment assistance and social assistance) have retrenched as legislative reforms have curtailed benefits,[62] reducing both the variety and amount of available resources to recipients. Advocates of such reforms suggest that this retrenchment is necessary as a result of dealing with the apparently unforeseen costs of unification — including periodic claims of unofficial unemployment levels of 30 percent in the five new *Länder*[63] and the legacy of waves of immigrants (who flooded into Germany in the early 1990s seeking employment) and asylum seekers in (especially) western Germany — above and beyond the pressures of globalization.

Defenders of such retrenchment like to point out that even if the German welfare system is currently under attack, its system of benefits still far outdistances its European neighbors.[64] Generous family leave legislation, for example, is the envy of any British, French, Italian, or indeed American parent. Only the Swedes can match the relative expanse of German welfare benefits among the countries of northern and southern Europe, although they, too, passed laws in the early 1990s designed to cut the range and cost of welfare programs.[65] So a limited cut in relatively generous welfare benefits alone would hardly constitute a major indictment and justify the claim that the character of the system itself is changing. But a second, and perhaps more notable, trend than simply the constriction of these benefits has taken place in Germany in the 1990s. This second trend is toward introducing increasingly severe constraints on who has access to the pool of welfare resources in the Federal Republic. It is not just the amount of benefits but the membership pool itself that is changing, as our early comparative figures indicated. Although its seeds clearly predate unification, this shift from universal to selective coverage symbolizes a change in the character of the post-1989 German state.[66]

Indeed, Germany is a country that, through its many incarnations, has repeatedly distinguished between "insiders" and "outsiders" in many different realms.[67] Such behavior extends into the realm of gender relations and more traditional aspects of economic policy.[68]

Chancellor Kohl persistently stated that Germany needs a new "social consensus" for confronting today's social and economic challenges.[69] But it will be of little surprise when we suggest that many of the trends that we have identified in regard to cuts in the social welfare provisions have been sustained, indeed accentuated, since 1989. The fact that social welfare benefits have been cut, in the context of a Europe-wide recession, can presumably be defended. Some welfare moderation in such a generous system in the context of a fiscal crisis is explicable.

What is more puzzling is the way in which the burden of costs has been distributed. There has been no solidarity between the employed and the unemployed in carrying the load, as Helmut Kohl suggested would be a responsible form of behavior. Kohl's government was the major agent in further dividing a labor aristocracy from the rest of the German workforce.

Consistent with the theme of this essay, we suggest that women, above all, have borne a disproportionate burden in the aftermath of unification. We present evidence illustrating how "insiders" (male workers, both employed and unemployed) have been protected at the expense of "outsiders" (female workers) in three areas. These involve women as long-term unemployed workers; those already engaged in paid (often marginalized) labor; and finally (and most blatantly), the treatment of female workers in the former East Germany.

Long-Term Unemployed Women

One of the most formidable labor problems Germany faces is long-term unemployment (those persons unemployed for one year or longer). Nearly one-half of all unemployed fall under this category. Within this category women are overrepresented, marginally so in the case of west Germany and much more so in the case of former East Germany (see table 14). While women composed 42.8 percent of the paid labor force by the late 1990s, fully 44.8 percent of the long-term unemployed (unemployed for more than one year) are women. For women in the former GDR the numbers are even more alarming: they make up 77 percent of long-term unemployed in eastern Germany. Of these long-term unemployed women, 22 percent were previously employed as part-time workers. As a consequence, their unemployment assistance benefits are proportionately lower than those received by long-term unemployed men (of whom only 0.5 percent were part-time employees). Moreover, these women also receive less aid in retraining and qualification advancement programs. Exacerbating this problem is the fact that there are a very limited number of qualified part-time jobs.[70]

The unwillingness of the current government to collectivize benefits can be seen in its treatment of these long-term unemployed women. While the Kohl government has been struggling to reduce the number of long-term unemployed overall, it consciously chose *not* to mandate that long-term unemployed women be given special treatment in its program to combat long-term unemployment. In 1989 the federal government established an elaborate program to reduce long-term unemployment by "encouraging" employers to hire this category of unemployed. The incentives for employers to cooperate are wage subsidies that range up to 80 percent. The program has been called a success by its creators, and in 1995 the Bundestag extended its funding through 1999 (for a total of DM 3 billion).

Yet six years after the program's start, officials realized that women were not benefiting proportionately from its measures. In recognition of this problem, policy officials considered establishing some type of quota system for these women proportionate to their share of unemployment. In the end, though, this "affirmative action" policy was not mandated. Formal quotas were rejected, ostensibly on the basis that they would infringe on the procedures of the liberal market economy. Moreover, some officials claimed quotas are irrelevant, since it is ultimately employers, and not the governmental employment offices, who decide to utilize the employment instruments the government provides.[71] Instead, mere "guideposts" were established for employment offices and potential employers.

As a result, of the long-term unemployed in 1991 who were able to secure a position through this program (west Germany only), only 34 percent were women (compared to 28 percent in 1989). Although the share of women benefiting from this employment program rose to 50 percent by 1994, this ratio is distorted since it includes east Germany as well, where more than 70 percent of those securing jobs were women. Yet it must be noted that the unemployment rate for women in east

TABLE 14. Structural Dimensions of German Unemployment (end of September 1994)

Area	Category	Total Numbers	Men	Women
West Germany	Short-term unemployed	1,655,000	56.6%	43.4%
	Long-term unemployed	798,000	55.2%	44.8%
East Germany	Short-term unemployed	680,000	38.4%	61.1%
	Long-term unemployed	361,000	23.0%	77.0%

Source: Gerhard Gröbner, "Mit verstärkter Kraft: Langzeitarbeitslosen Programm," *Bundesarbeitsblatt*, no. 4, 1995, p. 7.

Germany is substantially higher (77 percent versus 23 percent of men in the mid-1990s). Even this official report concedes that women are still underrepresented in the employment program.

Beyond these disadvantages for women, this program also illustrates the eroding solidarity among employed and long-term unemployed workers overall. At the 1995 "Chancellor Roundtable" (an annual event designed to facilitate "friendly dialogue" between officials from the chancellor's office, employer associations, and labor unions — the core of Germany's neo-corporatist system), labor union representatives enthusiastically agreed to support the extension of this program, ostensibly as a means of also maintaining the international competitiveness of German industry. Yet the *Süddeutsche Zeitung,* a leading source of liberal criticism in Germany, chided the agreement as being nothing more than a "consensus over wage nonsense" (*Konsens über tarifpolitischen Nonsens*).

Newspaper officials (and SPD representatives) claim that the agreement is, instead, a weak accord that does not attempt to deal comprehensively with long-term unemployment. The agreement seems more geared toward satisfying the material needs of the ruling coalition, employers, and employees, and has little concern for the unemployed. The unions will not have to accept wage reductions, while employers get wage subsidies of 80 percent without any actual obligation to create new positions (i.e., the subsidies can be used for currently available positions). Finally, funds for the special program will come primarily from the Federal Agency for Labor (Bundesanstalt für Arbeit) as well as through "redistribution" in the budget of the Ministry of Labor (Bundesarbeitsministerium). The federal budget will not increase in size. Ironically, therefore, the money designed to ostensibly help the long-term unemployed will come out of the same pot meant to help all unemployed, a mere shifting of resources rather than an addition.[72]

Another sign of the disintegrating solidarity among workers is the recent announcement by the head of Germany's largest and most powerful union, IG Metall, that as part of the "Partnership for Work" program (Bündnis für Arbeit), the union would agree to allow long-term unemployed to reenter the labor force at reduced wages. Such a step would go well beyond the traditional union bargaining practice, creating the possibility for employers to push wages *down* for those most in need. Among the concessions demanded from employers were that they hire 30,000 of the nearly one million long-term unemployed. Such a demand may appear to demonstrate solidarity. But, as a quid pro quo, the union is demanding that work layoffs be prohibited for the next three years and that 300,000 new jobs be created. The job security for union members would thereby be secured in exchange for making cheap labor available. The union therefore appears to be more concerned about its own immediate core membership than the future of the long-term unemployed.[73]

Women as Employed Workers

A second crucial situation where women are exposed to discriminatory practices and norms is within the context of the paid labor market. One of the most sensitive issues for working mothers has been the lack of adequate and affordable day care. Dating from the mid-1970s, discussion of revamping day care, seen as part of the FRG's constitutional duty to protect life, has simultaneously accompanied the abortion debate. In fact, the same section of the 1990 unification treaty that regulated the issue of abortion in the former GDR also laid the basis for a nationwide overhaul of the child care system in the expanded FRG. According to the treaty, the federal states were mandated to provide day care by 1996. There is an overall shortage of an estimated 600,000 day care places and 40,000 professional day care staff.[74]

Yet several states sought to postpone implementation of the requirement for day care provisions until 1999, on financial grounds. The shortage, however, is primarily in *western* Germany (some day care centers have actually closed in the eastern states, where the decreasing birthrate means that there are still more day care spots than children to fill them). It is therefore not the eastern states that are not fulfilling their obligations, but the wealthier states of western Germany. Indeed, as of 1 August 1996, only five of Germany's *Länder* had fulfilled their legal obligation to provide sufficient day care space. Ironically, four of these five *Länder* are in eastern Germany. Only one western *Land* (Rheinland-Pfalz) has created sufficient capacity.[75]

Beyond the federal and state governments' lack of support for working mothers, labor and management have also been willing to accept the pattern of discrimination between the haves and the have-nots. Within the context of the competitiveness debate in Germany (*Standortdebatte*), labor and management have reached compromises that seem to employ a familiar pattern of gender discrimination. These practices are most evident in the efforts to move the German economy away from "clean competition" to "lean production"; away from the concept of thwarting low-wage competition toward the notion of "greater flexibility" in labor regulations. This shift confounds critics, because it confirms the belief that the German model can be maintained this way, albeit for an ever smaller and privileged core.

A 1994 agreement between Adam Opel AG and its workers provides a telling example of the redefinition of "social welfare citizenship." In an attempt to lower labor costs, labor and management agreed to allow certain jobs to be contracted out to "supplier firms." The wages and benefits of these contract workers would no longer be covered by plantwide agreements. Since the majority of these jobs fell within the service category (e.g., cleaning, food preparation, etc.), and the majority of those jobs are traditionally filled by women, female employees bore an overwhelming proportion of the burdens for this decision as it shifted from unionized to non-unionized female employment.[76]

Another illustration of organized labor's willingness to allow effective gender discrimination is a recent court case that ruled that differing pay rates for men and women at the same job are permissible. In this case, four women filed the suit, with the support of their labor union, claiming that they were not receiving "equal pay for equal work." The unfavorable ruling was explained by the court on the grounds that although the job being performed was the same, the men had been hired under a different job description, thus justifying different wage scales. According to the women's lawyer, however, the case was lost because the union had incorrectly filed suit; in fact the union should have pressed the issue of gender-specific job descriptions. The union therefore implicitly accepted the notion that jobs could be defined in gender-specific terms, with the slightest distinction being used to justify pay discrimination.[77] In another case, a December 1997 ruling by the Federal Social Court deemed it legal to pay employees in typically female professions less than coworkers in classically male professions, thereby rejecting a complaint filed by a female social worker.

Within the context of German unification, however, even the new Berlin Republic has admitted to the anachronistic nature of these norms. These restrictive job classifications for women were *not* extended to women in east Germany. Women in eastern Germany are free to work evenings, weekends, and in physically demanding positions. This exception was justified by the claim that the west German code needed revamping. But to date no changes have been made in these restrictions on west German women. It is therefore permissible to discriminate against female workers in west Germany, under the guise of "female protection," while women in east Germany are ostensibly not in need of such protection.

Women in East Germany

Finally, we argue the most visible area where white males appear to have secured their social welfare rights has been in the process of integrating the former East Germany into the unified German economy. The women of the former GDR have been one of the hardest-hit groups.[78] During the 45 years of communist rule, women made remarkable gains in terms of overcoming the primary disadvantages of a patriarchal society. Support structures for women in the GDR included institutional features such as nursery schools and kindergartens for more than 80 percent of the children below school age, and publicly run service houses attached to firms, at which, for example, laundry could be dropped off in the morning, to be picked up at the end of day. Labor law regulations were equally generous. These included obligatory affirmative action programs; paid reductions in normal working hours for women with more than one child; and provisions that entitled women to a second chance to obtain formal vocational or professional credentials.[79]

Women in the former GDR have borne the overwhelming costs of unification in terms of lost employment. Data from March 1995 reveal that, of the more than one million unemployed in eastern Germany, fully 62.4 percent were women.[80] Nearly 20 percent of all women were unemployed in March 1995 (versus 23 percent in March 1994); at the same time only 11 percent of males were unemployed (compared to the March 1994 figure of 13 percent).[81]

Women have notably been affected by these job losses differently than men, especially when distinguished by sectors of employment. Women are overrepresented in sectors that reduced employment and production most sharply. Yet decisions regarding these reductions were often *not* based on the grounds of efficiency (or non-efficiency), since such inefficient core industries as steel and shipbuilding did *not* reduce employment at as rapid a rate. Rather, according to Maier, the restructuring process in these equally inefficient sectors was "slowed down by state and trade-union intervention, whereas in female-dominated industries exposure to the market had an immediate effect." Furthermore, citing a German Institute for Economics study, Maier explains how other cutbacks have disproportionately affected women:

> The social departments of enterprises were closed down as the firms were now seen as exclusively economic organizations, thus reducing employment opportunities for nurses, teachers, cooks, etc. and destroying the social infrastructure used by the women employed in these firms. Women occupying typical male jobs in the industrial production sphere, such as foremen, were dismissed more often than their male counterparts and women in intermediate managerial positions tended to lose these positions, if not their jobs.[82]

Such decisions have therefore been politicized, rather than left to market factors, forcing women to bear a disproportionate share of the burden.

In the end, we argue that the Kohl government therefore achieved the opposite of that specified by the rhetoric noted in the opening quotation of this chapter. Terms such as "solidarity pact" portray an image of a Germany in which the sacrifices are collectivized and the benefits are either diffused or, if apportioned, then based on need. The reality is that the costs that have been isolated to the "one-third" of society, and the benefits, rather than being apportioned on a "needs" basis, have been seized on a power basis. According to *The Economist*, the CDU, in the aftermath of unification, was supposed to contain a strong left wing, "considered its 'social conscience,' " and to be boosted by the arrival of east Germans who were supposed to be "much keener on bolstering the welfare state than . . . deregulating markets."[83] But this has not been reflected in the party's subsequent policies. The result, Claus Offe contends, has been the creation of a new, economically disenfranchised German underclass.

Conclusion

Germany's combination of a market economy and an extensive social welfare system is widely admired. Proponents note the retrenchment of the welfare system, but often correctly insist that its relative scope and domain far exceed those found in the other major countries of western and northern Europe. What they fail to note is that retrenchment is not equitably distributed among the German populace. In stark contrast, the burden of retrenchment has been imposed disproportionately on women.

The basis for this maldistribution is the distinction between entitlement and privilege in Germany, a distinction that has generated policies for which the institutions of the German social welfare system have proven remarkably malleable. Predicated on an enduring ideological structure whose cornerstone is discrimination, these institutions have proven remarkably adept at shifting the costs of retrenchment away from a protected core group of white males and toward women as "outsiders."

We should find nothing surprising in this phenomenon. Predating the formation of the Bonn Republic, the German state has consistently demonstrated a proclivity toward distinction — particularly on the basis of gender. But the fact that such tendencies have been reinforced by measures supported by the major political parties of the Bonn and Berlin Republics is of concern. These include the 1986 child care reforms;

the 1988 legislation concerning retraining and vocational education; the dissolution of the GDR's extensive day care system after unification; or, more recently, the preferential employment of men over women in the traditionally female-dominated service sector. The sustained tendency toward "gendered norms" is also evident in the willingness of trade unions to adopt measures that do not necessarily protect the employment rights of women. That the state has sustained such gendered norms can be seen in its ambivalent behavior regarding help-wanted advertisements. The Second Equal Rights Act went into effect in September 1994 with a provision forbidding employers to write job ads in such a way that it is directed solely toward men or toward women. Yet a subsequent study confirms that an overwhelming number of firms continue to do so (41 percent of a survey of 13,000 job advertisements). For upper management positions, discriminatory advertising was even more common and had a stronger trend on the increase: only 29.3 percent of such ads used neutral language, down from 53.4 percent in a similar sample the year before.[84]

In the end, many would argue that these changes in attitudes can be reconciled with the claim that Germany remains a capitalist democracy. A free press and elections, and the primacies of market economics meet the minimal qualifications demanded. Germany appears in no danger of sacrificing these attributes. But the evidence presented here supports the contention that the FRG is apparently losing its social component in the epithet "social market economy." Without this cornerstone of *Modell Deutschland,* Germany will perhaps, at best, cast off the *Sonderweg* label and become an ordinary country in this regard.

Should our analysis and the trajectory it portends prove correct, the net effect may be a future Germany that is less than exemplary; it certainly will not be a model of domestic policy in at least this dimension of social welfare. We recognize that, in aggregate terms, the German welfare system remains among the most "progressively" organized and coherent in Europe, as is reflected in the employment system in Germany. It is well organized, with clear rules of governance that protect employees, and co-opts large sections of the labor force. But Heinrich Winkler's comment that this corporatist construct is "the human face of fascism" — if overstated — nevertheless bears examination. For below the impressive collective figures lies a reality that contradicts elements of this progressive image. For Germany to be progressive, someone must pay the bill. And, as in much of German history, the living wages of the dominant political and economic actors are now subsidized by those groups marginal to the central economic and political processes. The core of Germany's impressive *Modell* remains white men. They have been the last ones forced to pay the bill in Germany for the cost of unification and globalization—at least in the realm of social welfare and employment.

As in the past, gender is one of the factors determinative of the allocation of costs—and benefits—albeit in a far milder form than in some of Germany's darker days. While the German state may be fragmented, it is not completely "tamed." It retains a hierarchical and discriminatory streak, one fostered by political parties that often appeal to cynical electoral need; but it is also a state whose consensual ideological proclivities condone such "structural discrimination" and whose institutional structures implement appropriately consistent policies—whether by the state or through employer or trade union organizations.

This approach is a manifestation of a common enough theme in contemporary politics—the revolt of the white male in the face of rising costs and shrinking pies. In Germany, however, this discriminatory edge is submerged under the guise of an apparent social consensus. This consensus, nevertheless, is a view shared only among the politically and economically enfranchised, as the deaf talk to the deaf—and the mute pay the price.

NOTES

The authors wish to thank Beverly Crawford, Andrei Markovits, and two anonymous reviewers for their comments.

1. For examples of works that took up this theme, with varying responses, see Wilfrid L. Kohl and Giorgio Basevi, eds., *West Germany: A European and Global Power* (Lexington, MA: Lexington Books, 1980); Andrei S. Markovits, ed., *The Political Economy of West Germany: Modell Deutschland* (New York: Praeger, 1982); and William E. Patterson and Gordon Smith, eds., *The West German Model: Perspectives on a Stable State* (London: Frank Cass, 1981).

2. Andrei Markovits, "Introduction: Model Germany—A Cursory Overview of a Complex Construct," in Markovits, *The Political Economy of West Germany,* 2.

3. See Howard K. Rosen, "The Competitiveness Issue: Can Germany Compete?" (presentation delivered at the Nineteenth Annual Conference of the German Studies Association, Chicago, IL, 22 September 1995); and American Institute for Contemporary German Studies, "Competitiveness: Defining the Terms, Shaping the Policies: A German-American Dialogue," AICGS Seminar Paper No. 1 (Washington, DC, May 1995).

4. Wolfgang Streeck, "German Capitalism: Does It Exist? Can It Survive?" in *Modern Capitalism or Modern Capitalisms?* ed. Colin Crouch and Wolfgang Streeck (London: Francis Pinter, 1995).

5. Peter J. Katzenstein, *Small States in World Markets: Industrial Policy in Europe* (Ithaca: Cornell University Press, 1984), 200–201.
6. Markovits, "Model Germany."
7. *Wirtschaftswoche*, no. 17, 20 April 1995, 19.
8. In this essay we will define major constituent actors according to both economic and sociological characteristics. Thus, our primary concern—as will become apparent—is definition by gender.
9. This, of course, does not address the possibility that such issues were purposely suppressed from debate in the political agenda in favor of the axiom of Cold War engagement. The *Berufsverbot* laws, for example, denied left-wing "radicals" positions in the German bureaucracy—a wide categorization that extended to multiple job classifications such as railway workers and schoolteachers. For details, see Gerald Braunthal, *Political Loyalty and Public Service in West Germany: The 1972 Decree against Radicals and Its Consequences* (Amherst, MA: University of Massachusetts Press, 1990).
10. For example, from an early date, political leaders in the FRG always maintained that social policy was a key ingredient to achieving the overall aims of the Bonn Republic. See Hans Zacher, cited in Peter J. Katzenstein, *Policy and Politics in West Germany: The Growth of a Semisovereign State* (Philadelphia: Temple University Press, 1987), 168.
11. We choose these countries as representative of Esping-Andersen's "three worlds of welfare capitalism"—the United States as a liberal regime, Sweden as a social democratic regime, and Germany, of course, as a conservative-corporatist regime. See Gosta Esping-Andersen, *The Three Worlds of Welfare Capitalism* (Princeton: Princeton University Press, 1990).
12. This issue is discussed in Markovits, "Model Germany," 6.
13. Fritz W. Scharpf, *Crisis and Choice in European Social Democracy* (Ithaca: Cornell University Press, 1991), especially 41–55.
14. See, for example, Simon Bulmer, ed., *The Changing Agenda of West German Public Policy* (Aldershot, England: Dartmouth Publishing, 1989); and Lowell Turner, *Democracy at Work: Changing World Markets and the Future of Labor Unions* (Ithaca: Cornell University Press, 1991).
15. See in particular Stephen J. Silvia, " 'Holding the Shop Together': Old and New Challenges to the German System of Industrial Relations in the Mid 1990s," *Berliner Arbeitshefte und Berichte zur sozialwissenschaftlichen Forschung*, no. 83 (Berlin, July 1993); and Crouch and Streeck, *Modern Capitalism or Modern Capitalisms?*
16. For example, see Ferdinand Protzman, "Rosy View of German Economy," *New York Times,* 11 August 1993.
17. Moreover, both issues highlight aspects of change and continuity—a sustained theme of historians, political scientists, and sociologists who study Germany. See, for examples, Gordon A. Craig, *Germany 1866–1945* (Oxford: Oxford University Press, 1978); Ralf Dahrendorf, *Society and Democracy in Germany* (New York: Norton, 1979); Geoff Eley, *From Unification to Nazism: Reinterpreting the German Past* (Boston: Allen & Unwin, 1986); Fritz Fischer,

Germany's Aims in the First World War (New York: Norton, 1967); Alexander Gerschenkron, *Economic Backwardness in Historical Perspective* (Cambridge, MA: Belknap Press of Harvard University, 1962); Simon Reich, *The Fruits of Fascism: Postwar Prosperity in Historical Perspective* (Ithaca: Cornell University Press, 1990); and Hans-Ulrich Wehler, *The German Empire, 1871–1918* (Dover, NH: Berg Publishers, 1985).

18. See the election campaign slogan adopted by the CDU in 1949 ("Düsseldorfer Leitsätze: Sozialmarktwirtschaft") and subsequent policies implemented by the Adenauer and Erhard governments. The origins and policies are discussed in Werner Abelhauser, *Die Langen Fünfziger Jahre* (Düsseldorf: Schwann, 1987).

19. Claus Offe, "Smooth Consolidation in the West German Welfare State: Structural Change, Fiscal Policies, and Populist Politics," in *Labor Parties in Postindustrial Societies*, ed. Frances Fox Piven (London: Polity Press, 1991), 125.

20. This distinction is clearly illustrated when one observes the legal channels available should a German citizen choose to challenge a decision regarding her or his social welfare benefits. In the case of social security benefits (health insurance, retirement benefits, disability or unemployment compensation) or entitlements (e.g., veteran benefits), there is a *Sozialgericht* (or a type of court system similar to public administration boards in the United States). For appeals involving these two areas of the social welfare system, the legal process is very explicitly defined. On the other hand, those who wish to challenge a decision regarding financial and/or material aid (welfare) face a labyrinth of bureaucratic routes that must be pursued. Indeed, in the government publication describing this process, the authors themselves note that although there are legal channels, for such a course of action a citizen must "have much time, since this process is long, very long, if s/he is to make it through all appeal stages" (*Soziale Marktwirtschaft im Schaubild*, ed. Helmut Reuther [Bonn: Transcontact Verlaggesellschaft, 1994], 56).

21. Offe, "Smooth Consolidation," 127–28, 130.

22. For details on the institutional structure of the German welfare system, see Katzenstein, *Policy and Politics*, 175–80.

23. Offe, "Smooth Consolidation," 131.

24. "Flexibility through Feminisation?" 107.

25. See in particular Robert Moeller, *Protecting Motherhood: Women and the Family in the Politics of Postwar West Germany* (Berkeley: University of California Press, 1993).

26. For a complete account of Germany's "mommy politics," see Moeller, *Protecting Motherhood;* and Myra Marx Ferree, "The Rise and Fall of 'Mommy Politics': Feminism and Unification in (East) Germany," *Feminist Studies* 19 (spring 1993): 89–115.

27. See paragraphs 1356 and 1360a of the Family and Marriage Code.

28. Eva Kolinsky, *Women in West Germany: Life, Work, and Politics* (Oxford: Berg Publishers, 1989), 54–55.

29. *Bundestagsdrucksache 7/650*, p. 98, cited in Kolinsky, *Women in West Germany*, 53.

30. "Protection for Working Mothers," *Social Security in Germany*, 1997, <http://www.bma.de/soziales/englisch/chaptr05.htm#e11> (July 1, 1997).

31. It is a great irony that while many consider these laws socially progressive, the fact is that these motherhood protection laws stem from legislation passed in 1938.

32. Natalie Kaufman Hevener, *International Law and the Status of Women* (Boulder: Westview Press, 1983), 5.

33. Kolinsky, *Women in West Germany*, 6–7. Here it is notable that in the official document published by the German government to explain its social welfare system, the page describing "motherhood protection laws" is juxtaposed against the laws protecting youth in the labor force, creating the impression that women and children are equally in need of protection. Moreover, these are the only two employment laws also considered "protection" laws (*Schutz*), the rest being defined as "regulations." See *Soziale Marktwirtschaft im Schaubild*, 1994, 50–51.

34. This discussion of the patriarchal treatment of women as codified in "protective conventions" is based on Hevener, *International Law*.

35. Offe, "Smooth Consolidation," 126–27.

36. Johannes Frerich and Martin Frey, *Sozialpolitik der Bundesrepublik Deutschland bis zur Erstellung der deutschen Einheit* (Munich: R. Oldenbourg Verlag, 1993), 33. Although these women had *not* contributed to the pension program, apparently their "service" was deemed significant enough to provide them some restitution upon their "retirement"; the average amount was DM 28.80 per month. A total of 433,697 mothers benefited from this special entitlement.

37. Ibid., 332.

38. The continuing prevalence of this cultural norm can be observed in the fact that the opinion polls in Germany show that both men *and* women still widely endorse such a traditional role for women. See Kolinsky's discussion of what she calls the "gender gap of everyday activities." Kolinsky, *Women in West Germany*, 92–95. Another study finds that Germany lags far behind the United Kingdom and Denmark in the number of households favoring an egalitarian type of partnership between male and female partners within the home. Indeed, in Germany those preferring the "traditional" type exceeded those preferring the egalitarian type, as reported in "Tomorrow's Second Sex," *Economist*, 28 September 1996, 25.

39. Kolinsky, *Women in West Germany*, 174.

40. Offe, "Smooth Consolidation," 178.

41. This comment is made in relation to social welfare policy in Katzenstein, *Policy and Politics*, 175.

42. Frerich and Frey, *Sozialpolitik der Bundesrepublik*.

43. Offe, "Smooth Consolidation," 135.

44. Ibid., 140–41.

45. Ibid., 137.

46. Ibid., 128–29.

47. Frerich and Frey, *Sozialpolitik der Bundesrepublik*, 176–77.
48. Ibid., 178–80.
49. Offe, "Smooth Consolidation," 141, 144.
50. Ibid., 135.
51. Scharpf, *Crisis and Choice*, 50–51.
52. The following discussion relies on Christel Lane, "Gender and the Labor Market in Europe: Britain, Germany, and France Compared," *Sociological Review* (1993): 272–301.
53. Indeed, the prevailing ideology of the German state is that provision of child care for three- to five-year-olds is regarded as a public responsibility, but for educational reasons rather than as support for working mothers. By 1986 governmental kindergartens provided places for 12.6 percent of two-year-olds; 38.7 percent of three-year-olds; and 72.3 percent of four-year-olds. Yet, as noted above, these schools last only until one o'clock and do not provide lunch. Only 4 percent of school-age children were in after-school care centers. Lane, "Gender and the Labor Market," 298.
54. Employees working less than 15 hours per week are exempt from the mandatory contributions to unemployment, worker's compensation, and pension programs. They are also excluded from most collective bargaining agreements and fringe benefits.
55. Although unpaid, health care benefits would continue without contribution from the parent on leave; the three years would also count as years of employment in terms of pension benefits after retirement.
56. Lane, "Gender and the Labor Market," 280.
57. *This Week in Germany*, 14 November 1997, 2.
58. Frerich and Frey, *Sozialpolitik der Bundesrepublik*, 178–82; Friederike Maier, "The Labor Market for Women and Employment Perspectives in the Aftermath of German Unification," *Cambridge Journal of Economics* 17 (1993): 267–80.
59. We note that Germany is not alone in this process. A similar one unfolded, for example, in Great Britain after the election of Margaret Thatcher. But two aspects make this change in Germany more dramatic. The first is that the German state epitomized the combination of social democracy and capitalism in a way that Britain did not. The second is that while Britain has certainly experienced its share of urban problems, it has not reflected the substantial racial violence seen in Germany since 1991.
60. Later it became apparent that asylum seekers in Germany, too, would pay the price in the form of restricted rights and benefits, as well as foreign governments and their citizens by contending with the effects abroad of high German interest rates.
61. See Offe, "Smooth Consolidation."
62. Two crucial proposals have been brought forth. One systematically reduces the pay base of long-term unemployment assistance by 5 percent every three years of unemployment. The reasoning here is that the longer one is unemployed, the less likely the recipient is to find a position at the higher pay

scale. Second, increases in the amount of social assistance (welfare payments) are to be linked to net increases in wages, not to increases in the cost of living. Moreover, such welfare benefits are to be reduced 25 percent should the recipient refuse "reasonable work," no matter the pay scale. *Der Spiegel,* "Rutsche nach unten," no. 30 (1995): 30–31.

63. This figure is repeatedly cited, but see, for example, "Germany's Absent Vater," *Economist,* 12 September 1992, 14.

64. For a discussion of this issue and some supporting data comparing social welfare benefits across Europe, see Roger Cohen, "Europe's Recession Prompts New Look at Welfare Costs," *New York Times,* 9 August 1993, A1.

65. Sweden, for example, has introduced measures raising the first year of pension eligibility from 65 to 66, and has eliminated sick pay for the first day of work missed. Ibid.

66. A recent announcement by the governing coalition illustrates this trend. One proposal is to cut federal support for social assistance (welfare) recipients who are able to work by 25 percent if they refuse "reasonable" work. Ostensibly, there are 400,000 to 500,000 welfare recipients who fall into this category. The discriminatory context of this policy is revealed in the alleged targets. As one report recently suggested, "Those in question are particularly expected to accept employment which thus far has been *refused by Germans* [emphasis by authors] . . . [for example,] garbage pickup, help at inns and during harvest as possible areas of employment." See *German News Service,* English edition, Bonn, 9 May 1995.

67. See Wehler, *The German Empire.*

68. One of the lesser known, recurrent features of the twentieth-century German state has, for example, been its willingness to discriminate among firms that have received favorable treatment and those that have not, based on their source of national origin or their willingness to be co-opted by the state. The source, practice, and effect of such behavior on the structure and achievements of the German economy are addressed in Reich, *The Fruits of Fascism.*

69. See, for example, *Süddeutsche Zeitung,* 25 January 1995.

70. Bundesanstalt für Arbeit, "Längerfristig Arbeitslose," *Arbeitsmarkt in Zahlen,* September 1994.

71. Gerhard Gröbner, "Mit verstärkter Kraft: Langzeitarbeitslosen Programm," *Bundesarbeitsblatt,* no. 4 (1995): 12.

72. *Süddeutsche Zeitung,* 27 January 1995.

73. "Metalworkers Union Proposes 'Alliance for Work' to Revive Germany's Sluggish Labor Market," *This Week in Germany,* 3 November 1995.

74. *This Week in Germany,* 17 February 1995.

75. Data from the Deutscher Familienverband, internet, 27 July 1996.

76. David Herman, Managing Director of Adam Opel, remarks made at the American Institute for Contemporary German Studies Conference, "Competitiveness: Defining the Terms, Shaping the Policies: A German-American Dialogue," Washington, DC, 15–16 December 1994.

77. This court ruling demonstrates the fact that the constitutional norm of

equal rights has not been readily translated into working life and the collective bargaining agreements that govern it. As Kolinsky points out, the *Grundgesetz* itself is contradictory. While Article 3 guarantees equal rights, Article 9 guarantees the autonomy of the two sides of industry and their right to agree amongst themselves on the conditions of work and pay. Kolinsky claims that the trade unions and employer associations have interpreted this as the freedom to set women's and men's pay and working conditions at different levels. Kolinsky, *Women in West Germany,* 54.

78. Interestingly enough, the largest "winners" in the east after unification have been pensioners. Indeed, retirees in eastern Germany have weathered the vicissitudes of unification much better than their compatriots. According to a spokesperson for the Bundesversicherungsanstalt, pension amounts in the east have more than doubled since unification in 1990, while the cost of living has risen by only 44 percent. That retirees there overwhelmingly vote CDU, then, should not come as a surprise.

79. There is a vast literature studying the impact of German unification on east German women. For example, see Hedwig Rudolph, Eileen Appelbaum, and Friederike Maier, "After German Unity: A Cloudier Outlook for Women," *Challenge* (November/December 1990): 33–40; Gertrude Schaffner Goldberg, "Women on the Verge: Winners and Losers in German Unification," *Social Policy* (fall 1991): 35–44; Myra Marx Ferree and Brigitte Young, "Three Steps Back for Women: German Unification, Gender, and University 'Reform,' " *PS: Political Science and Politics* (June 1993): 199–205; and Marilyn Rueschemeyer, "Women in the Politics of Eastern Germany," in *Women in the Politics of Postcommunist Eastern Europe,* ed. M. Rueschemeyer et al. (Armonk, N.Y.: M. E. Sharpe, 1994): 87–116.

80. The following account is based on Maier, "The Labor Market for Women."

81. Bundesanstalt für Arbeit, Nürnberg, "Die Arbeitsmarkt im März 1995 Bundesrepublik Deutschland," *Presse Informationen,* no. 24/95. Note that critics suggest that these official figures grossly underestimate unemployment levels.

82. Maier, "The Labor Market for Women." 284.

83. Both quotes come from "Germany's Subdued Celebration," *Economist,* 29 September 1990, 53–54.

84. "Promoting Upward Mobility for Women in the Corporate World: A Matter of Language," *This Week in Germany,* 22 September 1995.

The Question of Nationhood:
The Evolution of National Identity
in the Federal Republic

The End of Longing? (Notes toward a History of Postwar German National Longing)

Charles S. Maier

> "What did we mean by longing?" he asked, and he answered his own question: We longed for something unattainable or absent, which was not, however, the same as irrevocably gone. To long, he said softly, was to turn back the hands of time and bring the object of our longing into our present. To cross boundaries in order to take possession or to be taken into possession: that was another sense of longing. But above all, he saw in longing those forms of expectation and yearning which determined every wish-dream. Anything that no longer found a place in our longing was dead and gone, he asserted, and in this sense he wished to speak of Egenlund and of the [Heimat]museum established there as a place where longing had become an active force. "Why are we here?" he asked, and again he answered his own question: "To celebrate something created out of longing." . . . Throughout history people had always been deprived of their native lands. There had been no epoch without its exiles, its refugees, its banished peoples. People had always been forced from home,to wander in foreign lands, and they survived only if they had ceased to see the past as their only truth . . . "I know your lovely land," he said again: "now it is a neighboring country. We are not indifferent to it; but the true task that lies before us is this: to transform our longing for the old homeland into new neighborliness."
>
> Siegfried Lenz, Heimatmuseum

I

Siegfried Lenz's protagonist of the mid-1970s builds and destroys a museum to the 600-year German presence in Masuria. In the mid-1990s Germany is no longer longing. At least not on the national political level: the united Federal Republic renounced its aspirations to Masuria in 1990 (as did its two component states in 1950 and 1970), and the two postwar German Republics have — in what must be construed as a miracle of recent history — overcome their separation. They need not long for each other; they need not pretend to long for each other; they need not even pretend to have longed for each other. Do their inhabitants long on the unofficial level? Christian von Krockow, Marion Dönhoff, and the many publishers of Germany's longing industry produce evocative photo albums of East Prussian wide horizons, horse farms, capacious family seats — sacrificed, it is correctly recognized, by military hybris and genocidal brutality, nonetheless a punishment that fell on "innocent" families, those who cultivated and hunted, supported village churches, recorded immemorial customs, spoke German. Coffee table longing? Children of Sudeten Germans mobilize their lobbyists, descend on CSU headquarters, see an opening for a windfall in President Havel's impolitic discomfort at Czech ethnic cleansing. Class action longing? In any case, no longer national longing. But transformation of longing into new neighborliness? Not quite yet. And perhaps longing can reappear.

So much of German national feeling has involved longing; so much has traditionally been expressed in terms of longing or yearning — that is, hankering after a wholeness that no longer or does not yet exist — that it may be fruitful to investigate the history of longing. Of course, national longing was not the only hankering after completion: there was the Protestant northerner longing for the sunny pagan warmth of Italy, the repressed homosexual longing after the nubile Tadzio; or the post-adolescent yearning for male bonding and demanding friendship of the mountain hike or the duel or the assault on Langemarck; the youthful heterosexual longing for the flirtatious and beckoning village Gretchen; the poet yearning for a fantasy of Greek perfection and "noble tranquility"; the Jewish bourgeois aspirant longing to be credentialed as German by the community of his suspicious neighbors whose language he could often write so much more skillfully. So much longing — at least by males (women are represented as enduring or suffering or redeeming, but rarely longing outside of private relations) — so nurtured, so frequently confessed.

This essay, though, tries to focus on public rather than on private longing. By public longing I mean primarily national longing, but for a time in the former GDR socialist longing played a role as well. Obviously public longing may incorporate or express private yearnings, but this essay will examine it on its own terms. Psychohistory can be intriguing, but I will take sublimation and displacement as givens. Public longing itself can have several dimensions: in the German case it has involved both yearning for national incorporation of places beyond German state borders, and a hankering for some mystical enhancement of political authority or political community inside the borders that exist. Territorial longing and communal purification — usually they have gone hand in hand, but they are separable longings. Sometimes they are treated as utopias, but to analyze utopias is to narrow the phenomenon that I think important. The utopianism that preoccupied, say, Norman Cohn involves creation of coherent world views that posit a devious and clever, indeed devilishly clever, adversary. Public longings may underlie utopias, but some are less articulated and less paranoid.

Certainly the inhabitants of other regions experience longing. It is part of the human condition. Yearning, however, does not become the mode of national consciousness. *Sehnsucht,* then, as *Sonderweg?* Of course, a ready answer exists to the obvious initial question: why is national or public yearning so important in Germany? Germany, so the historian is tempted to respond, did not have a national framework early on, as did the French or the British; so the latter did not have to long. But the Czechs did not have a national framework. Did they yearn? No, the peoples of the Habsburgs aspired or conspired, but did not really yearn. Their status was subjection, not fragmentation. *Fragmented peoples* introduce longing into their projects (Zionism before 1948; German nationalism). But *subject peoples* submit, migrate, worship, revolt, or plot. For the "non-historical" nations of the Austro-Hungarian monarchy, the Empire was either a prison to be destroyed or, if they bought into the Habsburg project, the surrogate for their vulnerability. The earlier Empire, the one whose wispy remains were finally left to blow away between 1803 and 1806, might remain an object of yearning for former free knights or celebrants of Grossdeutsch dreams. But it was too obviously a hopeless artifact to serve as magnet for revivalistic longing.

Longing, even revivalistic longing, is *not* the same as nostalgia, although the two are related, and what I have termed above coffee table longing may be little more than nostalgia. Nostalgia is to longing as kitsch is to art; it is a sort of stereotyped yearning, and it is never meant to be overcome. Nostalgia must be oriented around memory; it involves the cultivation of a melancholy that can never be assuaged because it accepts that the past is irrevocably lost, whereas longing often has a future orientation: it can be gratified. Nostalgia bathes in memory, so to speak, but never attempts to swim upstream against its current. Which does not mean that it cannot be connected with violence. In the case of German history, nostalgia may have played a role in facilitating that compartmentalized violence that in the Third Reich involved the murder of victims in remote sites while the organizers pet dogs or consumed pastries at home. Certainly it would be interesting to write a history of German nostalgia, or the nostalgia of any society. Some of the phenomena studied would be the same as in a history of longing—cultivation of *Heimat,* the wearing of *Trachten,* the endless reproduction of calendar prints of eighteenth-century city views, the dubious claims of older Germans that they miss Prussian *Pflicht* and selflessness. But nostalgia retains a bounded, finite quality. Indeed, nostalgia is often the longing for what was bounded—family or province or childhood experience—precisely because it was bounded. (Some of this nostalgia is redolent today among former GDR citizens who miss their republic.) Longing is harder to contain, less oriented toward the mental evocation of particularity, and more open-ended. It also does not content itself with evocation, but seeks satisfaction through political action. Although nostalgia can be exploited for political ends, in itself it remains less politically exigent.

II

The editors of this volume have asked us to weigh the respective influences of political culture and political institutions on recent German historical outcomes. Their question implies that political culture is deep—and potentially troublesome. Well-designed institutions, taken in part from earlier German experience, borrowed in part from abroad after 1945 (so the question elaborates), may have helped stabilize a postwar democratic Germany; old "cultural" legacies might be resurfacing in hostility to foreigners or skinhead violence. Now, I cannot survey the well-developed literature on political culture. For the purposes of this essay, I would assert that culture and institutions are not readily separable. Is it not just as useful to think of political culture as the sediment deposited by old institutions; that is, cannot a generation or two of democratic praxis, even if brought about by institutional mechanisms, create the subsequent generation's political culture? To offer an answer to the organizers' question (so I can go on to what for me is the more interesting issue of what behavior postwar *circumstance* fostered), I am uneasy with assigning critical roles to either institutions or political culture. To my mind, the democratic achievement of the Bonn Republic has depended as much on its placement within the noncommunist coalition of the West (e.g., NATO, the European Community, etc.) as on any indigenous elements or even on structures that frame West German national life as such. This is not to say that the Federal Republic did not become democratic, but that it might not have become democratic outside the supporting web of other democracies. And the same holds for other countries now embarked on democracy, such as Spain since the mid-1970s, or Argentina, or postwar Japan. Global context as well as institutions or culture has proven crucial.

Still, to focus on longing is to scrutinize a behavior or trait that is arguably particularly German. The culture has been redolent with longing. It remains saturated with discourses in which longing often lurks under the surface: namely, discourses of identity, of historicization, of life worlds and rationality. German public longing can claim specificity as a formative discursive element of German national political culture. But to repeat, political culture is the product of enduring institutions — but not just political institutions. International comparison suggests that the organization of religion has probably exerted a crucial impact on the role of public longing. Even when an ethnic nation-state had not yet been organized or liberated and reconstructed, the existence of a vital and undivided national church could take the edge off public yearning. That is, off longing as the hankering after some transpolitical community. Did the Irish yearn? They too were a subject people; consequently they could nurture grievances and find a negative focus for their communal longings. Did Poles long or yearn? I am not familiar enough with their nineteenth-century history to answer, but my impression is that they cherished memories and later burnished aspirations: cultivating memories is not quite the same as longing; it is a more bounded political emotion. In any case Irish and Poles (perhaps, too, Slovaks and the indigenous peasant strata of Lithuania and Latvia) had a single national Church as a continuing and indeed revitalized vessel for their communal identity; they did not have to long for a missing transcendental component of loyalty. Energetic bishops help demystify the objects of political longing.

German confessionalism brought about somewhat different results. Catholics in Bavaria, Lutherans in Brandenburg, had regional churches that might buttress the same non-transcendental accepted hierarchies of the countryside as did, say, the Anglican vicarages of Somerset or Oxfordshire. The confessional churches were not suitable for national longing. When the German intelligentsia evoked the Catholic Church — say, from Novalis to the aging and mendacious Carl Schmitt — they depicted it as a proxy, not for Germanness, but for "Europe" as some vanished transnational spirituality. Once again, longing — now to return, not just to before 1806, but 1517 — yearning pure and simple, velleity without will. German Lutherans yearned less; they saw their church as a constituent of the Kleindeutsch country they were in fact constructing. The more Protestantism mattered, the less longing had to be involved because the Protestant Church was one representation of the feasible nation-state.

Perhaps, finally, outside Germany Russian Slavophiles longed—for some unfractured pre-modernity of religious and village community. Orthodoxy, of course, did not stand in opposition to the Russian state, as did Catholicism during the epoch of European nation-state construction. Orthodoxy was compatible with the spirituality of empire; its alignment with Tsardom allowed considerable scope for transcendental national longings, and German and Russian yearners often recognized some spiritual kinship. This was tough on Poland, but then longing, as the Lenz novel recognized, has its zero-sum elements. In general, German or Russian longings were hard on the neighbors. The national aspirations bound up with longing have been by nature demanding at home and abroad. They have tended to envisage a political community that overcomes internal divisions and simultaneously calls into question the frontiers of the community whose harmony is so ardently sought. The more longing, the more longed for. The point is that until 1989, postwar German history had to be a process of learning how not to long. Perhaps, however, that has been changing.

III

"People had always been forced from home . . . and they survived only if they had ceased to see the past as their only truth . . . the true task that lies before us is this: to transform our longing . . ."

By this standard, each of the two postwar German states had to be built upon a subtle transformation of longing. Unified Germany was not to be forsworn, but not to be achieved by force. Germany might beckon as memory, as cultural community, but no longer existed in fact. It was not, say, Masuria—somewhere, but elsewhere—but it was a nation in the subjunctive. What is the difference between a country that has not yet existed but beckons for the future (unified Germany before 1870) and a country that used to exist but exists no longer (Germany, 1945–90)? The first animates intellectuals and politicians, the second produces more universal senses of disorientation. Few of us seem vexed by the state of our earlier non-being before birth, but many of us are bothered by the prospect of non-being after death. Germans, of course, were not the only people who have had to transform longing. Decimated Indian tribes expelled from their forests or prairies; Africans transported into slavery; Confederate slaveholders whose "peculiar institution" and would-be nation collapsed in 1865; European colonizers compelled to exit Algeria or Indonesia. The losers must work through their longing. Victors, too, must transform their longing if they wish to found a state:

Jews in Israel after 1948 and perhaps Palestinians in the 1990s. How, though, did the Germans transform their longing?

Two German national constructions as well as the Oder-Neisse Line changed the parameters of longing. Longing, so Lenz writes, claimed those uprooted from their ancestral homelands in the East. It cathected to territories now Polish. But for citizens of the Federal Republic and the German Democratic Republic, there was also yearning for some earlier national whole. The yearning was officially inscribed in the Basic Law by the West Germans who declared their state the legitimate bearer of German statehood. At the same time, there had to be some form of coming to terms with incompleteness after 1945, a public transformation of longing.

What were the phases and milestones of this transformation? I wish to propose a stage theory of longing for both postwar Germanys and for two sorts of public longing: national and socialist. The particular turning points can certainly be debated; conflicting doctrines and loyalties usually exist simultaneously within any society. Nonetheless, we can establish, I believe, a rough chronology of longing. Longing remained politically significant for about a decade after the founding of the two German states. Sometime during the 1960s and 1970s, the majority of inhabitants of both German states left longing behind. They accepted the loss of the territories provisionally "under Polish administration"; in the East German case by treaty in 1950. And they accepted the seeming permanence of a divided statehood. Not without bitterness and sadness, but irrevocably nonetheless.

East Germans learned repeatedly between 17 June 1953 and 13 August 1961 that longings came at a price. De-Stalinization and "Tauwetter" might briefly seem to sanction a more tolerant socialism and perhaps even the resumption of intellectual ties with West German intellectuals. But the Hungarian uprising ended any toleration for these wistful currents, as the SED regime imprisoned Wolfgang Harich and others thought to be too close to the heterodox Georgi Lukács (who himself had to do public penance). Five years later the closing of the Berlin frontier put even greater coercive power into the hands of the Ulbricht regime. As the GDR Army Band sang:

Im Sommer 61, am 13. August (Tirili),
Da schlossen wir die Grenze,
und Keiner hats gewußt (Tätärätä).
Klappe zu, Affe tot.
Endlich lacht das Morgenrot (dädädä).
Wiederholung (Tsching Bum!)[1]

Not much scope for longing in that atmosphere! Despite this vulgar bravura, those whom I spoke with in the winter of 1964 had not renounced their longing to travel. The memory of united Germany still hovered on both sides of the Harz. So, too, for intellectuals in the 1960s, who might combine national and socialist yearnings in a wistful utopian agenda. Might the regime's control over the frontier not allow it to tolerate a less repressive climate? In late May 1963 Roger Garaudy came from Paris to a portentous conference on Franz Kafka and discerned the first swallows of a new spring, only to be lectured by one of the local cultural commissars, Alfred Kurella, that one should not confuse the swallows with the bats: "Good and evil, light and darkness should remain cleanly separated: there exists not the slightest reason to obscure the border between decadence and realism."[2] Intellectuals and dogmatists contended on and off in the late 1960s: Stefan Heym, Stephan Hermlin, the young Wolf Bierman faced Ulbricht and Hager; others tried to tack between these fronts. Anna Seghers, not, we know, the most courageous writer, still argued that despite the existence of two German states, the best writers in both of them shared a common culture and commitment. This was a debatable proposition at best; nonetheless, vague longing to reestablish a German cultural community still persisted. East German writers also yearned to produce a literature that dealt with the persistence of loneliness in a socialist society. Instead Ulbricht instructed them in 1967 that cultural sciences and arts should become "specialists in anticipation" and look ahead into socialism. After the suppression of the Czech reform efforts in 1968, the leeway for intellectuals narrowed further: "no concessions to the decadence of late capitalism," Ulbricht told the ninth plenum of the Central Committee two months after his troops helped enforce socialist orthodoxy in Czechoslovakia. A year later it was the turn of Christa Wolf to be hectored by the watchdogs of the Writers' Union: "Think about your roots, think about our continuity, if you want to serve the German working class, its party, and the success of socialism."[3] By the late 1960s and 1970s, the regime had no more patience with downbeat literature; its Communist Catos condemned complexity of all kinds; they chastised those intellectuals who could not celebrate the positive achievements of existing socialism, and they insisted that German socialism was creating a new authentic national entity. The few who revealed their continuing longing for a less repressive socialism or a more encompassing German identity faced the loss of their writers' privileges, orchestrated denunciations from their colleagues, perhaps prison or expulsion from their small Republic.

Erich Honecker's doctrine of a socialist German nation and its corollary — "real existing socialism" — meant that longing was clearly off-limits. Instead, braggadocio was in. As Honecker warned ominously in February 1981, "If today certain people in the West hammer out great German slogans then we say 'Be careful. Socialism will hammer at your door one day, and when the day comes in which the working classes of the Federal Republic start the socialist transformation of the FRG, then the question of the unification of both German states will be posed in a new way. Then there can be no doubt how we shall decide."[4] Even as he called for a "coalition of reason" four years later, Honecker insisted "It should certainly be clear in 1985 that history has cast its judgment and that a revision of this judgment cannot be managed by anyone. And that in this judgment, the German Reich disappeared forever in the flames of the Second World War and that on German soil two sovereign states have arisen, independent from each other, the GDR and the FRG. They embody the different social orders of socialism and capitalism, belong to different alliance systems, Warsaw Pact and NATO . . ."[5]

The triumph of the two-nation theory? Some ambiguity attended the new promulgated concepts. If ideologues and even poets insisted that "Two nations lie where Germany stood," the East Germans were clearly seeking to reappropriate a patrimony that they shared with the West: the 500th anniversary of Luther's birth or the 700th anniversary of Berlin. "Preußen ist wieder chic," wrote Hans-Ulrich Wehler, and it was probably truer in the East than the West. So the very insistence on the existence of two Germanys actually refocused civic attention on the common German history they both shared. Even more disabling for Honecker's reinvention of tradition was the fact that at the very moment the GDR was endeavoring to emphasize its national credentials, Gorbachev's new team of foreign policy advisers was having doubts about the robustness of the state their now tiresome ally was vaunting. Even the Soviets understood that the longing had not disappeared. Brezhnev and Gromyko, so Gorbachev has admitted, were clearly wrong "to let themselves be led by the leading politicians of the GDR" to accept the thesis in the early 1970s that "Two German nations had arisen, the German question had been solved, and there was no purpose in raising it once again."[6] Nonetheless, if socialist institutions did not establish a new nationality, 40 years of East German statehood did produce a public identity—if hardly an imagined community, at least a constrained one. It was characterized by its sense of *Geborgenheit,* of shelteredness and boundedness, the comfortable provincialism of "our republic" that attracted intellectuals and non-intellectuals alike. "Freedom, unity, and socialism," confided one aging woman pilot who had a job as a guard in the Dresden military history museum, "meant progress, love for the German fatherland, and a content life with my little white miniature poodle."[7] One came to terms with finitude. To cite the poet Sarah Kirsch, who left for the West in 1977:

> Thinly settled the land.
> Despite vast fields and machines
> the villages lie sleepy
> in boxwood gardens; thrown stones
> rarely hit the cats. . . .
> If one doesn't read a paper
> The world is in order.[8]

It was the final irony that precisely this sense of boundedness, of constrained community, would provide the source of post-1989 longing or at least nostalgia (to recall the distinction made above). The SED had condemned longing; the PDS would do its best to exploit it. Longing not for Germany, nor really for socialism, but for the predictability of a state that had itself found longing too subversive to sanction.

IV

For West Germans the end of longing followed from several major developments: the development, first, of Ostpolitik, then the preoccupation with prosperity, and finally the European project of the 1980s. Ostpolitik required a renunciation of many yearnings, or at least their indefinite postponement, for it recognized that the FRG had to make its peace with the status quo in order to make the lot of those in the East more decent and bearable. From another perspective, however, Ostpolitik changed the nature of longing, rather than suspending it. It focused yearning on transformation, not on unification; on change, not recovery. This was a significant difference. "The effort to project a historical homeland as a form of national identity, despite the reality of a divided Germany, into the idea of German reunification (in peace and freedom) lost significance in the 1970s and 1980s."[9] Ostpolitik was not the only force for the adjournment of reunification. Public energies poured into economic activity (as they had in the reconstruction decade as well). Harold James has correctly emphasized how strong a component of German identity is formed by economic activity.[10] In the 1960s and 1970s that economic component centered increasingly around consumption as well as production: West Germans envisaged themselves, at least in their advertising, as catching up in their enjoyment of life: smoking, drinking, vacationing, refurnishing, opening up to a liberated sexuality, bringing, in short, the perceived glitz of New York or Los Angeles to

Munich or Cologne. In this respect, too, longing was certainly sublimated, if not satiated. Finally, the European project did really provide a new matrix for identity (as well as mere interest), especially among younger Germans who studied and vacationed abroad. Wroclaw was forgotten, Leipzig unfamiliar, Tuscany was virtually native ground.

Nonetheless, the history of national longing did not end in the West with Ostpolitik or consumerism any more than it ended in the GDR with the declaration of a socialist nation. I do not mean by this merely that the drive for unity, now made possible in 1989–90, encompassed the old longing. What signaled the reemergence of national longing, in fact, was not the drama of unification, but the reevaluation of German identity *within West German borders*. By 1985, that is, with the advent of a decade of anniversary commemorations of Allied victories, German longing reappeared, not to revise borders, but to reevaluate history. Political longing implies a particular historical narrative. *Sinnstiftung* is the historians' contribution to *Sehnsucht*. The *Historikerstreit* gave us an insight into the narrative of longing, and while the extreme claims that Hitler carried out the Final Solution as a response to, and in imitation of, Stalinist terror did not prevail, neither did the "revisionists" abandon their exculpatory arguments. Indeed, older tonalities that seemed to have disappeared in the early days of the Federal Republic could be heard again: "The mention of the name 'Auschwitz' has the function of bringing every free movement of thought to an immediate halt. . . . The postwar era is over, at the latest since the fall of the Berlin Wall on the ninth of November 1989. One has to take both [fascism and socialism] seriously as efforts to deal with fundamental problems in the continuum individual–community/society, including the problems that liberalism sought to solve through repression, which is an extremely dangerous procedure. . . . We need therefore a new view of the history of the twentieth century. The optic of the victors of 1945 no longer suffices."[11] Reading this, one wonders whether longing will make a comeback — justified in terms of transcending the Western victors' view of 20 July or 8 May, in terms of rejecting supposed taboos, or of overcoming "PC," or even of accommodating ecological imperatives. (There is still space in the political spectrum for Ökofaschismus or at least Eco-populism.) If there is to be comeback for longing, what difference will unification have made?

V

Unification must change the terms of longing. Consider the transformation of the long-nurtured longing that moved intellectuals in Vienna or

Prague and was expressed as the idea of Mitteleuropa, or Central Europe. Forget the Austro-German imperial project of 1916–17; the idea of "Central Europe" in the 1980s encoded the longing for a political potential among the elites of the former Habsburg domains who felt suffocated by Communism, or in Gyorgy Konrad's formulation, by the Soviet-American condominium expressed in Yalta. Leave aside the problematic equivalence that this reading of Yalta established; "Central Europe" served as a way to rally East Central Europe against the Soviets. It had many attractive exponents: Timothy Garton Ash and Jacques Rupnik, among others. But with the end of Communism, and the allure of Brussels, Central Europe sells today at a discount.[12] Today, with unification, the terms of German national longing will also change. Perhaps the longing for ceded provinces beyond the eastern frontier so solemnly accepted in 1990 will someday play a role again. Is it illegitimate to be sad about the areas that for six centuries were settled by Germans? Is it forever to be excluded that Pomerania be German? More to the point, are we certain that Germans will forever exclude it? After all, the recuperation of Kaliningrad as Kantstadt no longer seems so unthinkable. Of course such longing seems remote. But the politics of longing is never settled once and for all. Longing, after all, is not just an innate feeling. It is a constructed sentiment: nurtured by history, myth, remembrance, demagogy, sadness, too.

More relevant perhaps for the near term, longing involves not just the extent of the polity, but its internal arrangements. I think that longing is going to play a larger role in politics in the next 20 to 50 years than it has — and not only in Germany. *But what shall the Germans long for?* Just the musical sense of life that can keep at bay the universal anxieties that rack us all, as Tilman Krause suggests? "German inwardness," so he proposes, "does not necessarily stand in opposition to the cultural connection with the West. It only puts another accent on it. Its main interest is the subjective sensitivity to the cosmos. If we trust it, it doesn't have to lead at all to the German *Sonderweg*. . . . Rootedness in the imaginary . . . the inclination to the absolute and a longing for metaphysical anchoring in existence, the unsuitability for commerce or for letting the ego serve the laws of the world of consumption; a feeling for life that both remains exalted and melancholically inclines to self-doubt and strives for profundity; finally the insufficiency of social and communicative conventions (in the sense of 'social clamor' that remain superficial) — this somewhat pre-civilized underlying attitude the world owes, according to Thomas Mann, to something 'nationally completely unique and incomparable,' that even the German crimes of this century cannot discredit completely."[13] *Auch nach Auschwitz am deutschen Wesen soll die Welt genesen*? Still, if it's Winterreise or Wotan, German longing may have its place. This author too remains a sucker for the Ring.

But the heralds of German public longing are not so easily confined. "The late-modern has nothing to say on the theme of Heimat," writes another contributor to the same longing (if hardly longed-for) collection, "since its entire culture is alien to Heimat, rootless and bereft of origins, enlightened, intellectualistic, cynical. . . . the Romantics' utopia is a utopia of fulfillment, while the modern utopia of de-placement, which we learned about through the ideology of humanity, is a utopia of emptying out. . . . Heimat can never be created, but only rediscovered. . . . German Heimat has the special property that it was characterized by an intimate connubium with nature, and hence the word remained untranslatable. Only in Germany could the idea be grasped that Hölderlin expressed in *Hyperion,* that there is a Heimat of Nature. . . . From the universality of their spirit the Germans have the unique property of feeling responsible for all needs of the world."[14] Ah, planetary longing. But a bit dotty, and more geocentric than geopolitical. Only the Jews are as "open to the world" as the Germans, concedes the author: an apparently friendly comparison that makes the possibilities of longing seem less menacing, although he notes that only Germans and Russians share an intense *Heimweh.* And not all longing is tender: "Morgenthau Plan, division, and allied popular education were internalized by German intellectuals as National Masochism," writes another contributor to the same collection, who laments that a German editor can enjoy the appearance of a Polish pizza parlor in the former East Prussia: "The beginning of something. . . . A world in which all differences have faded. Until at the end all borders are wiped out and all that remains of history is that multicultural null-identity—*Verfassungspatriotismus*—that at best can serve as historical underpinning for a Berlin-Kreuzberg ward festival."[15]

To answer the question in my title: No end of longing! And finally it behooves us to ask not only what the Germans will long for but what shall we long for? All electorates, I believe, are going to long for communities that are more and more difficult to achieve, that is, communities of cohesive and ultimately ethnic territoriality. That is what Ross Perot or Franz Haider or the Québecois or the Brooklyn settlers in Samaria long for. That is what the German writers of *Die selbstbewußte Nation* long for. But there are in fact many Germans who have given up this yearning, have settled on more cosmopolitan orientations, or workaday professional aspirations. If they remain responsible, perhaps Germany, with its earlier history of overcoming longing, with its history of settling on economic relations as a proxy for some transcendental nationhood, will be able to show us how to live without being overwhelmed by longing.

NOTES

1. Tilo Köhler, *Unser die Straße — Unser der Sieg: Die Stalinallee* (Berlin-Kreuzberg: Transit, 1993), 61.
2. Cited in Manfred Jäger, *Kultur und Politik in der DDR, 1945–1990* (Cologne: Edition Deutschland Archiv, 1995), 113–14.
3. Ibid., 136–38.
4. Excerpt from a speech to an SED conference in East Berlin, 6 February 1981, in Hermann Weber, ed., *DDR, Dokumente zur Geschichte der Deutschen Demokratischen Republik, 1945–1985* (Munich: DTV, 1987), 380–81.
5. "Coalition of Reason," 23 March 1985, cited in Weber, *DDR, Dokumente*, 399.
6. Michail Gorbatschow, *Erinnerungen* (Berlin: Siedler Verlag, 1995), 701.
7. Stefan Moses, "Farewell and Beginning: East German Portraits, 1989–1990," photographic exhibit organized by the German Historical Museum in Berlin.
8. Cited in Hermann Glaser, *Die Kulturgeschichte der Bundesrepublik Deutschland*, vol. 3, *Zwischen Protest und Anpassung, 1968–1989* (Frankfurt/Main: Fischer Taschenbuch Verlag, 1990).
9. Glaser, *Kulturgeschichte*, 338. "Der Versuch, trotz des faktisch geteilten Deutschland geschichtliche Heimat in form nationaler Identität auf die idee einer deutschen Wiedervereinigung (in Frieden und Freiheit) zu projizieren, verlor in den siebziger und achtziger Jahren an Bedeutung." Although I provocatively cite an obviously pre-unification judgment, I should express my admiration for this brilliant history.
10. Harold James, *A German Identity, 1770–1990* (New York: Routledge, 1989).
11. Reinhard Maurer, "Schuld und Wohlstand: Über die westlich-deutsch Generallinie," in *Die selbstbewusste Nation,* eds. Heimo Schwilk and Ulrich Schacht (Berlin-Frankfurt/M: Ullstein, 1995), 77, 83.
12. See Timothy Garton Ash, "Does Central Europe Exist?" in *The Uses of Adversity: Essays on the Fate of Central Europe* (New York: Random House, 1989), 179–213; Jacques Rupnik, "Central Europe or Mitteleuropa?" *Daedalus* 119 (winter 1990): 249–78; Gyorgy Konrad, *Antipolitics,* trans. Richard Allen (New York: Harcourt, Brace, 1984); Karl Schlögel, *Die mitte liegt Ostwärts: Die Deutschen, der verlorene Osten und Mitteleuropa* (Berlin: Corso bei Siedler, 1986); and Charles S. Maier, "Whose Mitteleuropa? Central Europe between Memory and Obsolescence," in *Austria in the New Europe: Contemporary Austrian Studies,* vol. 1, ed. Günter Bischof and Anton Pelinka (New Brunswick: Transaction, 1993), 8–18.
13. Tilman Krause, "Innerlichkeit und Weltferne: Über die deutsche Sehnsucht nach Metaphysik," in Schwilk and Schacht, *Die selbstbewusste Nation,* 140.
14. Gerd Bergfleth, "Erde und Heimat: Über das Ende der Ära des Unheils," ibid., 106, 109, 116. The author envisages a new religion of the earth: a *Weltwende* that will even restore a pre-Copernican geocentrism.

15. Klaus Rainer Röhl, "Morgenthau und Antifa: Über den Selbsthaß der Deutschen," ibid., 97–98. (I have translated *historisches Unterfutter* as "historical underpinning"; but given the two meanings of *Futter* as "lining" and "feed," "historical junk food" would also fit the tone.)

The Late Flowering and Early Fading of German Nationalism

Ernst Haas

During the 1980s German historians were debating whether German history is an aberration from the West's, whether Germans had trod a *Sonderweg* because they had jettisoned liberalism and the Enlightenment for the murder and repression of the Nazis. In the 1990s some German commentators harped on another aspect of German uniqueness: Germany's unquestioned lack of constitutional and territorial continuity (its present borders date from 1991), and the concomitant fact that Germans disagree with one another as to what it means "to be German." During the nineteenth century, other German historians held that German history was uniquely different from the West's because Germans had to fashion a common state that never included all Germans long after a "German nation" had come into existence.

This chapter is devoted to the proposition that the history of the formation of the German nation-state is not unique; nor is the racist-integral nationalist interlude. Both events have occurred elsewhere. All such episodes are instances of the multifaceted character of nationalism and of the difficulties of achieving a happily rationalized society after contending nationalist ideologies have begun to fight one another. Germany did not finally achieve rationalization until the 1950s. Mere approximations to integration were attained by quasi-authoritarian means in the Wilhelmine era and by totalitarian measures under the Nazis.

I hold that the rationalization of a polity is manifested by the acceptance of a consensual national myth in a modern or almost modernized society and economy. I also hold that successful rationalization may be upset and disrupted and that a rerationalized polity may be patched together by adaptive steps, or firmly cemented by acts of social learning. Rationalization, derationalization, and rerationalization may be understood as having elective affinities with variable combinations of these features: the sequence of steps that led to the nation-state, the extent of social mobilization at the inception of the process, the degree of prior cultural homogeneity of people being integrated, and the gulf between the elite and the folk cultures.

Germany, along with many other countries, represents the combination of these factors I label Type C, which suggests that the victory of a liberal-nationalist rationalization formula is in doubt. In Germany such a formula was struggling for acceptance before 1949 without ever succeeding. Social mobilization was almost complete when Bismarck began the process of fashioning a German nation-state, always a factor that complicates the victory of liberalism over competing syncretist formulas that inspire various articulate segments of the public. Weimar and Wilhelm II sought to fashion a patchwork of liberal and syncretist institutions; one fell victim to World War I, the other to the Great Depression, a fact used by contemporary German historians to justify their *Sonderweg* argument. Only the elites of the post-1949 Federal Republic (FRG) exhibit true social learning. As they succeeded in rationalizing modern Germany under liberal auspices, they also seem to be running up against the limits of their nation-state's ability to satisfy all the demands of the German people. Hence continued rationalization is seen by many as depending on the successful integration of the FRG into a united Europe. But others see a secure future in a renewal of German national hegemony over Mitteleuropa. Different people learned different lessons from the failures, crimes, and tragedies of German nation-statehood. Which is the final, the true lesson? Which mode of reasoning is consistent with theories of progress and reasoning linked to liberalism?

A Brittle Polity Comes into Being

French Invasion Triggers German Nationalism

Nationalist sentiment among the numerous German literate elite during the eighteenth century lagged far behind similar attitudes in Britain and France, a condition due to the peculiarly apolitical situation in which the German bourgeoisie was placed. The well-educated and numerous German *Bürgertum* of the eighteenth century was certainly mobilized; however, while by no means assimilated as equals into the ruling nobility and autocracy, it did not seek equality and the right to participate in political life. The reigning ideology of *Bildung* taught people to seek a moral life based on education and hard work, but it discouraged them from engaging in public affairs. Since there were 2,000 political jurisdictions in the pre-Napoleonic German polity, each practicing cameralism, there was ample opportunity for well-educated commoners to find administrative careers. Prussia, the most developed bureaucratic autocracy, employed many non-Prussians in that capacity because most of the native nobility, the Junker, disdained education and entrepreneurship until well into the nineteenth century. The socially mobilized middle class of eighteenth-century Germany was composed overwhelmingly of state-employed members of the free professions, not of merchants and manufacturers or agricultural entrepreneurs. Such professionals still accounted for almost 90 percent of the elected delegates to the revolutionary parliament of 1848. Unlike their counterparts in Britain and America, they lacked many opportunities for civic participation. "Obedience is the first duty of citizenship," said a Prussian minister of the interior.

German *Bürger* remained indifferent to the idea of a German nation until after 1810. The courts aped French institutions while the bourgeoisie admired Britain's. The major writers of the period considered themselves cosmopolitan adherents of the French Enlightenment, not Germans. Only the excesses of the French Revolution caused many of them to reconsider their position and, like Fichte and Hegel, take seriously the possibility of a syncretist German nationalism anchored in the Prussian state.[1] The triggering event was the military humiliation of Prussia by France in 1806, followed by France's truncating and occupying Prussia. This trauma gave rise to the period known as reform and liberation, the end of cameralism and of serfdom, and the admission of commoners into an army now based on universal military service. *Bildung* was now reinterpreted to include patriotic service to a "fatherland." The mobilized bourgeoisie was officially assimilated into a state that made itself into a mouthpiece of "the people" for the first time, even though the sole purpose of this pseudo-populism was the expulsion of the French. It was unclear then and later whether the proper focus for this populist German identity was to be the existing state (as tended to be true in Prussia and German Austria) or an as yet nonexistent all-German state. While Prussia and Austria made no constitutional changes after the defeat of Napoleon, some of the southern German states did enlarge the ability of the *Bürgertum* to participate in politics. In general, the French shock was followed by nonadaptive policies that safeguarded the aristocratic order while also strengthening the administrative power of the rulers.

The Failure of Liberals to Fashion a German State

The so-called liberal revolution of 1848 was in fact not so liberal; it also failed because the King of Prussia was compelled by the Emperor of Austria to forgo the crown that the Frankfurt Assembly had offered him, thus dooming the birth of an all-German state. Before being forced to decline, he had expressed his reluctance to accept the crown of Germany because it was offered by popularly elected delegates and not by his fellow rulers. In any event, the offer was made only by those delegates who favored a German state that excluded Austria; the Assembly had been divided on the question of whether Austria was or was not German.[2]

Following this debacle, the liberals were reduced to working at the level of the 39 German states. All along, a syncretist nationalist movement existed alongside the Liberals. The Syncretists generally wished to retain vestiges of the system of estates and guilds in their opposition to free market industrialism. They were unabashed monarchists and admirers of pre-modern Germanic folkways. Student organizations and Protestant clergy were prominent among them. Some Catholics felt ambivalence over the national question, identifying with the Catholic ruling dynasties of their states rather than with an all-German polity that was going to be ruled by Protestants. Nonliberal ideologies were represented among the parliamentary delegates in 1848; they tended to favor the confederal "great German" (or pro-Austrian) constitution for the new state, whereas the Liberals tended to advocate the more centralized "small German" (or pro-Prussian) solution.

The Liberals' commitment to constitutional freedoms was tested during the 1860s in Prussia and shown to be hollow by Bismarck. They had fought him tenaciously in 1862 when he disregarded the constitution, but they capitulated when their economic demands were met. Successive Prussian governments had brought about the economic unification of Germany by 1867 by means of the gradual creation of a customs union north of the Main River and the abolition of all internal tolls and fees on trade. After 1867 German Liberals were agitating primarily for the completion of German economic unity in the form of the standardization of weights and measures and of money, of company law, a common postal system, credit regulations, and patent rules. By the end of the 1870s they were asking for a protective tariff for the Reich and for more aggressive government assistance in foreign trade. Upon gaining all of these goals, success seemed to sap their interest in also pursuing a liberal political agenda.

Bismarck Fails to Fully Rationalize Germany

German unification in 1870, in form, came about as a confederal compact among the rulers of the German states, who proclaimed the King of Prussia as their Kaiser. In doing so, however, they also accepted a proto-liberal confederal constitution drafted by Bismarck, used after the war of 1866 to integrate the northern German states with Prussia. This constitution was endorsed by the chastened all-German Liberal Party. The Liberals also hailed the acts of Prussian conquest that created the North German Confederation that, in turn, became the German Reich when the south German states joined. But its confederal character and monarchical sheen pleased the reformist and traditional syncretists as well.

Unification happened against a backdrop of almost-completed social mobilization in a setting in which there was no conflict between elite and folk cultural values. This meant, of course, that there was a large, literate, and aroused public to contest the content of the all-German nationalism that was to endow the new state.

By 1871 only 4.8 percent of Germany's population lived in cities with a population of over 100,000, while almost 64 percent still lived in towns of 2,000 people and less. But only 43 percent still made their living from agriculture, 98 percent were literate (though this included a fair number of functional illiterates and people who knew little or no German), and 20 percent of the population was able to vote (as opposed to 27 percent in France and 9 percent in Britain).[3] By that time the rate of industrialization, urbanization, and modernization in Germany was a good deal faster than in Britain and France. Just under 5 percent of the labor force was in government service by 1895, almost twice as many people as in Britain and France. The Germans spent 34 percent of the federal budget on defense in 1872, almost 11 percent on science and education, and 9.6 percent on public health and social welfare. But still there was no national myth even after the creation of the Reich.

But Bismarck sought to create one. His government used the schoolroom and the churches, as well as the academic community and the army, to create the symbols, tradition, and values to buttress a national self-consciousness focused on the Reich. These efforts were only partly successful. Poles in the east resisted German-language schools; Catholic Bavarians objected to the attempt to introduce Hohenzollern-oriented patriotism into theirs. The peasantry elsewhere objected to compulsory extended school attendance laws and reforms of the curriculum that seemed to threaten patriarchal family life, indeed to any kind of secularization. Catholic and social-democratic subcultures with their own organizations retained their existence alongside those of the new state that sought to extend downward the reformist-syncretist nationalism that characterized its elites.

The most painful evidence of the lack of a nationalist consensus was the so-called *Kulturkampf*, Bismarck's and the Liberals' effort during most of the 1870s to strip Prussia's Catholic population of its subculture by means of state-sponsored discrimination against Catholics and their institutions. In the east this also took the form of enforced Germanization of Poles, and the settlement of Germans in these lands to create family farms at the expense of both German and Polish-owned large estates. The *Kulturkampf* "amounted to a centralist drive for the primacy of the citizen-state relation in the organization of public life, with radical implications for other traditional ideas of social order and the Prusso-centric version of federalism.... For liberals the *Kulturkampf* meant exactly what the term said, a struggle to unlock the potential for social progress, freeing the dynamics of German society from the dead hand of archaic social institutions."[4]

The *Kulturkampf* represented an effort on the part of the National Liberal party to enforce its notion of a modern secular German citizen against groups that remained hostile to this conception of solidarity and identity. In that it ran counter to the Conservatives' more traditional preferences; Bismarck supported the Liberals only because he considered Catholic institutions as rivals to those of the Prussian state and therefore subversive of the loyalty to be expected of a subject of the Hohenzollern rulers. In any event, they lost the battle against the Catholics and against Social Democrats, whom they branded enemies of the nation. But as they proceeded to make the new Germany safe for industrial capitalism, they never managed to make friends of those who remained attached to a pre-modern view of politics, the many reformist and traditional Syncretists, particularly in the parts of Prussia that were conquered in 1866. But even in Prussia a traditional-syncretist form of nationalism flourished. It insisted on the Christian foundation of the fatherland and on rulership based on divine grace rather than on popular consent, and it objected to the free market capitalism of the Liberals and the government.

Traditional notions of German identity were represented by the patriotic historians, notably by Heinrich von Treitschke, their dean. He recast the telling of German history—and this became official curricular policy—so as to make the founding of the Reich the natural and only possible culmination of all previous events, and the Hohenzollern dynasty the agent of Providence and of destiny. The German *Volk* is an organic body with a will of its own. One motto of the new state, as if to cover over the brittleness of its ideological underpinnings, was "one *Volk,* one Reich, one God." Yet that people could not agree on a national holiday or national anthem!

The fragmentation of German society was extreme. Conservative nobles saw themselves as the sole authentic carriers of German nationality, just as Liberals insisted that they alone deserved being called the German nation. Artisans spoke of themselves as the historically true

Germans, and salaried employees, in identifying with the National Liberals, were insisting on their special status in order to avoid any possibility of confusion with the despised manual workers.

As table 1 shows, modernization, urbanization, and industrialization progressed rapidly during the 1880s and 1890s. This entailed the rapid increase in the working-class population and the drive to organize trade unions. It also implied the growing appeal of the Social Democratic Party, which espoused a Marxist-revolutionary ideology, though the unions were far less revolutionary than the intellectuals who led the party. The Social Democrats were the chief advocates of universal male suffrage in Prussia (it already existed for Reich elections) and of rigorous respect for civil liberties. They were feared by the bureaucracy and the National Liberal Party. Hence, upon failing to vanquish the Catholics, Bismarck began a decade-long persecution of the Social Democrats and of their trade unions as potential subversives.

But he also sought to preempt their appeal. The German government that persecuted Socialists and trade unionists and presided over the West's most thorough industrialization process also invented the compulsory state-operated, state-subsidized social security system. This was no coincidence. Before the great innovations enacted in the 1880s, German

TABLE 1. Public Expenditures of All German Governmental Entities by Major Function as Percentage of Total Expenditure

Year	Defense	Housing	Education, Science	Public Health	Social Security[a]	Economy/ Environment
1872	34.0	0.2	10.8	3.0	5.8	1.1
1881	25.6	0.3	17.6	3.9	3.8	1.6
1891	26.3	0.5	17.4	4.1	3.6	1.7
1900	25.2	0.7	18.1	4.5	3.9	2.0
1913	26.6	0.7	19.5	5.0	5.2	2.4
1925	4.4	7.8	16.2	5.2	21.6	2.1
1932	4.9	2.3	15.0	3.3	33.7	3.2
1935	24.8	2.0	10.7	2.5	18.7	4.0
1948	24.7	5.9	11.2	5.0	21.2	4.7
1955	11.9	7.9	9.8	3.7	26.8	5.6
1960	12.9	7.4	10.5	3.9	24.4	7.0
1970	10.1	2.2	15.1	5.2	20.6	7.3
1975	9.1	2.2	17.3	6.0	24.0	4.3

Source: Peter Flora, *State Economy and Society in Western Europe, 1815–1975*, (Chicago: St. James Press, 1983), 1:391.

[a]Figures do not cover all social insurance benefits, only federal and *Land* subsidies to social insurance institutions.

employers and local governments had provided poor relief and paternalistic services for workers (such as housing and child care), but coverage was spotty and entitlements uncertain. Academic social reformers had advocated a more consistent policy of state-supported and regulated social services since the 1870s in order to mitigate the impact of drastic industrialization and urbanization, to avoid the marginalization of the working class. Christian conservatives held that the state had an obligation to do these things, to moderate the workings of an individualistic capitalism of which they disapproved. Liberals, while far from enthusiastic about measures that would interfere with free markets, acknowledged that pure and untrammeled individualism should not be a German trait, and they acquiesced in compulsory health and disability insurance and to pensions to which they, as employers, had to make financial contributions. Bismarck and the bureaucrats with whom he drafted the legislation, moreover, were very concerned with presenting the new Reich as a Christian state, a state with a social conscience, because only thus did he consider it possible to link the worker to the state and make him truly German rather than a rootless proletarian. The bureaucracy wanted to remove incentives for workers to join trade unions, to keep wages, hours, and working conditions from becoming subjects of large-scale bargaining. Therefore, along with the insurance entitlements came corporatist tripartite commissions to administer insurance funds and adjudicate claims, conceived deliberately as substitutes for unions and parliamentary "agitation."

Superficially, however, the polity seemed rationalized after 1870. Catholics and workers, though discriminated against, did not threaten to rebel. Neither did the oppressed Poles. There was little industrial unrest.[5] The principle of succession for the Kaiser was never in doubt. People paid their taxes, draft evasion was minimal. The war against France had been universally popular, as was the annexation of Alsace-Lorraine. Bismarck's foreign policy was entirely peaceful thereafter. Nobody challenged it even when, after 1880, he acceded to the imperialist requests of the Liberals by becoming interested in the acquisition of a colonial empire in Africa and the Pacific.

Failure of Superficial Rationalization

Between 1890 and 1917 Germany almost became a rationalized nation-state as institutional and symbolic devices began to bring about a rapprochement among the contending claimants to rival notions of German identity and purpose. Superior economic performance certainly helped as well, as did a deliberate policy of making industrialization more bearable for the working class. But defeat in World War I laid bare the brittleness and superficiality of the compromises. We now discuss the reasons for the brittleness: Germans could never agree whether a primordial ethnicity or loyalty to the state defines their collective identity; the adoption of social imperialism and the practice of selective upward mobility did not suffice to mute class conflict; ethnic minorities were not sufficiently assimilated; the "democratizing" reforms of Wilhelm II were all rhetorical.

The mirage of successful rationalization, of pseudo-rationalization, between 1890 and 1918 illustrates the limitations of social adaptation, as opposed to social learning. True learning occurs when key elites systematically examine their failures to integrate their society, when they seek to understand why the values they sought to impose failed to catch on. True social learning occurs when key elites realize that institutions fail to represent and affirm desired values. True social learning, therefore, involves the reasoned search for new values and for new institutions more likely to integrate the views of a squabbling people. That search is based on knowledge, on analysis, on reasoning, not merely on instrumental compromises among rival positions and groups. The adjustments attempted in Germany, however, mostly lacked the quality of reasoned search. They were instrumental adjustments, temporary deals among antagonists, adaptations of the moment that only lasted a moment.

People or State as Definer of Identity

One could be a German because of one's descent from German stock — the primordial tie of *Blut und Boden*. In German history this position is known as *völkisch* (ethnic). One could also be German by virtue of being a loyal subject of the sovereign — the state and its constitution define citizenship — which meant a popular-parliamentary view should prevail. Or one could seek a formula that somehow combined both positions. If so, one had to offer a conception that simultaneously dealt with the cultural roots of identity and the constitutional role of the Kaiser.

If Bismarck's first allies, the National Liberals, had remained united as the mainstay of the new Reich, the formula would have stressed the unitary-parliamentary, secular, and populist aspects. A "liberal" Kaiser was seen by them as a quasi-plebiscitary patriot-ruler of a united Germany cast as an enlarged Prussia. Some called this a "National Monarchy." But the Liberals fragmented in 1880, and Bismarck played down the unitary and parliamentary aspect in favor of a confederal formula that camouflaged Prussian hegemony, though he accepted the populist emphasis. Catholic traditional syncretists preferred a Kaiser who symbolized the continuation of the medieval-corporatist-Christian ideas, explicitly designed to oppose the Prussian-patriotic view; other traditionalists saw in Wilhelm I the linear successor to the Reich's founder, Charlemagne; both wanted to counter the parliamentary-populist emphasis of the Liberals.

Wilhelm II saw things differently. He sought to legitimate his rule by stressing continuity with the medieval Reich, with the Prussian-dynastic view, and with a quasi-Bonapartist populism that allowed him to rule "his people" directly, without chancellor, parliament, or parties. He attempted a kind of democratic authoritarianism that also raised the issue of Germany's civilizing world mission. A syncretist *Nationalmonarchie* became a distinct formula for some German conservatives after 1910. As Friedrich Meinecke said of the Kaiser in 1913: "We are not satisfied with the knowledge that our nation is a great spiritual *Gesamtpersönlichkeit*, we also demand a leader for it for whom we would walk through fire."[6]

In the first decade of the twentieth century many commentators linked this symbolism to the introduction of a "democracy" that stressed the citizens' loyalty and devotion to the dynasty as representing the people, not history. The dynasty represented continuity and stability, whereas the parties and parliament evoked the image of confusion and strife. A superficial rationalization was the result. As even Catholics came to accept the Protestant dynasty, Liberals hoped to exploit the populist notion of *Sozialmonarchie* in favor of perfecting parliamentary institutions and instituting new social reforms.

Yet the syncretist parts of this program remained more pronounced than the liberal. The romantic-conservative German youth movements endorsed this pseudo-democratic view of rulership. Love of country was to be a searing personal experience, linked to strengthening Germany against its foreign enemies, to antisemitism, to the protection of Germans living outside the Reich. The Kaiser became the symbol of these views, in opposition to parliamentary and bureaucratic institutions, to political parties and interest groups. The target of such groups as Wandervogel, the Pan-German League, and the German School League was the Marxist-derived class basis of social and political identity advocated by the Social Democrats and their trade unions. Being German was supposed to mean being part of an organic whole; ethnicity was the ultimate definer of identity. A People (*Volk*) was more important than the state, though the unity of people and state was seen as a desirable situation. Modern secular values were suspect, though not all were rejected, not even all aspects of industrialism. We are confronting a powerful reformist-syncretist nationalism in these reorganizations.

Permanently Excluded or Successfully Assimilated?

The *völkisch* assertion of Germanness was expressed primarily in policies directed toward the Germanization of Poles, Danes, and the small group of French-speaking Lorrainers. The Jewish minority was eager to assimilate. The anti-Polish effort was the most sustained and extensive. Until 1886, Prussia was content to have loyal subjects in its eastern provinces, irrespective of their ethnic identity. Thereafter things changed. Poles migrated to the Ruhr in large numbers to become miners and to East Prussia to seek work on landed estates. The *Kulturkampf* was interpreted by Liberals and Protestants as demonstrating the persistence of institutions hostile to the new German state not only because of Catholic identification with Rome but also because so many Catholics were Poles. (In 1910, 10 percent of the Prussian population was still Polish.) In 1886 the Prussian government began a systematic policy of settling German peasants in the eastern provinces and of alienating the necessary farmland from the big Polish landowners. Nationalists had urged such policy to create the economic infrastructure for a policy of gradually eliminating Polish culture. Social Darwinist arguments as well as geopolitical ones were marshaled in defense of policies that made the German language compulsory in all schools, and that urged the creation of a German citizenry with a single culture. After the turn of the century such policies were intensified under the pressure of new associations of German settlers in the eastern provinces, supported by the bureaucracy in Berlin. The speaking of Polish at public meetings was prohibited. While the events of 1919 demonstrated the failure of many of the Germanizing policies in the frontier regions, they were ultimately successful in other parts of Germany where Poles had settled.

On the other hand, German workers became patriotic citizens *even though* the Social Democrats and the trade unions also grew very rapidly; but unions became less revolutionary as they increased in numbers and in power. This was true even though Social Democrats were systematically excluded from the civil service even if they scored well on the entrance examinations; neither were they accepted as officers in the armed services. (Jews and Catholics were equally subject to discrimination in employment in higher civil service and army positions, even though the Reich authorities leaned over backward to provide proportional representation in the federal civil service for candidates from all the *Länder* even at the expense of discriminating against better qualified Prussian candidates.) Other institutions too tended toward rationalizing the polity because of their appeal to the middle class. Many could vicariously identify with the nobility because they were given reserve officer's commissions in the army. Student organizations (*Burschenschaften*), in aping aristocratic manners, permitted university students to identify similarly. Many other ways of giving official recognition to middle-class people and organizations gave Germans a status that bound them to the state.

Wilhelm II as Would-Be Reformist Syncretist

The accession of Wilhelm II to the throne in 1890 marked the beginning of a deliberate government policy of inclusion, evidenced most importantly by the repeal of the antisocialist laws, a higher tariff, acceptance of Catholics, and intensified imperialism in Africa and China. The government aimed at the creation of a unified Right to face a restless working class that was to be won over to the nation. As in Britain and France, the ideology of social imperialism was invoked to woo the working class as new colonies and a battle fleet were acquired. The inclusionary course embraced modernity, industry, and science (and was therefore acceptable to the Liberals provided that civil liberties were also protected); it was also opposed by traditional-syncretists, who were ill at ease with modernity. Artisans, small businessmen, some professionals, and German migrants to the eastern lands were especially bothered, and thus they flocked to the patriotic and imperialistic associations described above. These became mass organizations using modern means of mobilizing people, though devoted to fighting modern values. The Right sought to protect itself against downward social mobility as it saw other segments of the middle class join the upper classes in a marked rise in social status and wealth.

Those who benefited from the pace of modernization accepted the Reich, and those who felt themselves harmed by it attempted to save the Reich from its own modernizing success. Both trends embraced nationalism, albeit different strands, and both accepted imperialism as right and good. Liberal nationalists as well as traditional Syncretists gloried in the global spread of German might and culture, though for different reasons. But it was the successful industrialists and their allies who increasingly defined the content of German nationalism; they gave the Right its program, not the landed nobility that held the visible reins of power. Yet the ideological rapprochement among the various rightist elements never resulted in an organizationally unified conservative party professing a single strand of nationalism.

Derationalization, the War, and the Revolution of 1918

Before as well as during World War I, Germans did their military service and paid their taxes; after 1914 they died for the fatherland in very large numbers. That bloodbath was also the high point of what seemed to be a great patriotic coming-together under the legitimating aura of a popularly based imperialism in which even some Social Democrats seemed to glory. The development of the German party and electoral system before 1914 explains the surprising moratorium on ideological confrontation that was to last until 1917.

Federal (but not *Land*-level) electoral participation — a good indicator of legitimacy — rose steadily between 1900 and 1910, as did the numbers and membership of interest groups. The intensity of political party activity, as measured by the number of local branches and their meetings, also rose sharply. Socialists, Poles, and Catholics all voted in record numbers despite efforts to intimidate them. On the other hand, where, as in Prussian elections, voters saw the system as hopelessly rigged against them while favoring the upper classes, they stayed away from the polls in droves.

The 1907 Reichstag elections were interpreted as a plebiscite endorsing Germany's *Weltpolitik,* its policy of assertiveness to secure "its place in the sun": colonies, trade, naval might, as well as recognition of its premier position in central Europe. All parties, including the Catholic Center and the Progressive Liberals (but not the Social Democrats), affirmed the justness of imperialism. The Center became part of the governing coalition. The Social Democrats saw the handwriting on the wall; a major segment of the party affirmed its patriotic commitment, muted its opposition to imperial expansion, and supported Germany's role in the war in the summer of 1914. However, the rift between an emotionally patriotic Right and a "me-too" patriotic Left only grew:

> This multiplicity of nationalist conceptions . . . made nationalist appeals as much a source of conflict as unity. Despite its own elevated sense of classless cultural solidarity, nationalist ideology could never escape the conditions of German society before the First World War.[7]

The size and importance of the colonial empire that Germany had managed to acquire was far from impressive, a condition that fueled the demand for more colonies. The Pan-German League continued to articulate these demands, as did the other patriotic associations. But it also stressed, along with the Conservative Party and Friedrich Naumann's Liberals, the need for consolidating a German Mitteleuropa, to advocate expansion toward Russia. A strong foreign policy was also equated with a strong culture, a strong national character, all needed in the Social Darwinist–defined struggle for survival among peoples and nations. Social imperialism was a favorite theme of many across the political spectrum. In response to the question "what is national?" a leader of the Pan-German League replied:

> Everything that relates to the preservation, promotion, future, and greatness of our people and Reich is national; that means that national questions of the first order are: the army, the navy, colonies, Germanization of the Prussian eastern provinces and North Schleswig, de-Latinization (*Entwelschung*) of Alsace-Lorraine, honorable representation of the German Empire, protection of Germans, preservation of the citizenship and civil rights of Germans abroad, cultivation of the German language and German schools abroad combating the treacherous (*vaterlandslose*) [sic] Social Democrats.[8]

It is still a matter of historical debate whether Germany's entry into World War I was motivated by imperialism or was due to miscalculation about British and French responses to the Russian and Austrian behavior in the Balkans. In any event, imperialist appetite soon developed after the outbreak of war. Those who see German imperialism as the glue that sustained the society can point to the plans to create Polish and Baltic client states in the east, annex parts of French Lorraine, seize more of Africa, and create an independent Ukraine. Continental annexationism became more popular and important than overseas imperialism. *Völkisch* notions of cultural-racial solidarity came into their own after 1914.

The war years also marked the high point of interclass cooperation and government planning. The Allied blockade of Germany meant that after 1916 it became necessary to organize the entire German industrial and manpower apparatus into one giant planned war economy, run by Walter Rathenau and General Erich Ludendorff. Trade unions, even socialist ones, and trade associations were given administrative and decisional tasks as they were organized to implement decisions of the bureaucracy that they had helped to make. Strikes were avoided until nearly the end of the war, prices were controlled, raw materials allocated, and trade organized by these means. The very difference between government and the private sector was obscured by these corporatist arrangements, even though some employer associations at first balked at joining socialist worker representatives in common bodies of governance. Some industrialists even saw in the war economy "an opportunity to create a German Gemeinwirtschaft under which German capitalism would be organized in the spirit of Prussian discipline and self-sacrifice and under which corporate groups would administer a planned economy in the service of the national welfare."[9]

The revolution that ended Germany's role in the war shattered such dreams. In any case the agricultural sector was never included in the corporatist scheme of the *Burgfrieden*. Germans did not learn to live with industrialism, with ideological conflict, and with inequality after 1890. But the beginnings of the welfare state, the possibility of electoral coalitions, and the halfhearted revolutionary spirit of most workers might have become steps toward learning to live in harmony — if the lost war had not poisoned the national well. But it is also true that social insurance, like the war economy corporatism, like social imperialism, was inspired by the ideology of a harmonious society ruled by a benevolent state and its bureaucracy, realizing its historical destiny, *not* by consensual knowledge about how such a state of affairs might be designed. Action based on ideological conviction and on instrumental motives is not action justified by rational knowledge.

Racist Nationalism Rerationalizes Germany

Why Weimar Lacked Legitimacy

Until engulfed by the Great Depression in 1931, postrevolutionary Germany looked like a temporarily stricken industrial giant who was recovering speedily. There was considerably less industrial strife in Germany than in France and Britain, though unemployment rose to one-third of the labor force in 1933. In 1925, 8.5 percent of the labor force worked for the government, a considerably higher percentage than in France and Britain. The state spent only 4 percent of its budget on defense in the 1920s (because of the one-sided disarmament obligations of the Treaty of Versailles), but 6.8 percent went on housing, 13.6 percent on science and education, and a whopping 33.6 percent on social security, even though taxes in Germany were somewhat lower than in Britain and France during the 1920s (14.8 percent of GDP in 1925). Taxes rose to 22.7 percent of GDP by 1937, reflecting the massive rearmament and public works programs launched by the Nazis in their successful effort to spend their way out of the depression.

Yet Weimar Germany was far from happy (see table 2). The halfhearted revolution that overthrew the monarchy was carried out by Social Democrats and supported even more halfheartedly by the Catholic Center and the Democratic Party. During the 14 years of the Weimar Republic, 22 cabinets attempted to rule, an average of a little less than eight months per government. Nine elections to the Reichstag were held during this period. The highest vote garnered by any party in any election was the 44.2 percent obtained by the Nazis in 1933. The three parties who refused to accept the liberal Weimar constitution as legitimate earned together 64 percent of the vote in 1933; 27.6 percent in 1928, when things appeared to be going well for democracy; and 34.9 percent in 1920, a year of considerable unrest. Because they aroused so much critical opposition (as well as praise), the striking scientific, artistic, literary, and aesthetic achievements of the Weimar years contributed to the political and economic turbulence rather than counteracting it.

Germany's population was almost completely socially mobilized, highly urbanized, and dependent very heavily on an industrial economy. In terms of its problem-solving capacity, the government seemed to be doing well until it lost a terrible war. However, the tensions that the Wilhelmine elite had been unable to resolve now reappeared with a vengeance. The immediate years following the revolution were beset with communist conspiracies and strikes; these were repressed with some gusto by the rump armed forces, who were somewhat slower to put down the rightist putsch launched by militant veterans' organizations and the fledgling Nazis. Two monarchist parties were less violent, but no less opposed to the postrevolutionary regime and its trade unionist and bourgeois leadership. Unemployment was a problem even before the

TABLE 2. Germany: Extent of Rationalization

	1880	1910	1930	1940	1970	1990
1. Political succession	yes	yes	yes	no	yes	yes
2. National myth in education	some	yes	no	yes	yes	yes
3. Religious institutions	no	yes	yes	some	yes	yes
4. Civil religion	no	some	some	yes	yes	some
5. Cultural uniformity	no	some	yes	yes	some	no
6. Language	yes	yes	yes	yes	yes	some
7. Income distribution	some	some	yes	yes	yes	yes
8. Workers' organizations	no	some	yes	yes	yes	yes
9. Farmers' organizations	yes	yes	yes	yes	yes	yes
10. Payment of taxes	yes	yes	yes	yes	yes	yes
11. Conscription	yes	yes	n.a.	yes	yes	some
12. Fighting wars	yes	yes	n.a.	yes	n.a.	n.a.
13. Administrative cohesion	some	some	yes	no	some	yes
14. Foreign policy	yes	yes	no	yes	some	yes
15. Peaceful change	some	yes	no	yes	some	yes
16. Legitimacy	some	yes	no	yes	yes	yes
Total (%)	59	84	68	84	83	83

Great Depression because general unemployment insurance was not created until 1927, proving totally inadequate after 1931. The noncommunist workers, tenant farmers, and middle class supported the Republic, partly because it promised to protect society from Bolshevism and from harsh peace terms. The spotty success of the republican coalition in foreign and domestic policy induced many middle-class voters to turn to the conservative parties, thus further weakening the Weimar coalition and giving solace to integral nationalists. Farmers who owned their own land opposed the Republic because of low agricultural prices. The German People's Party (right-wing liberal), led by Gustav Stresemann, became the middle-class vehicle for a dignified foreign policy, of rejoining the liberal West while also obtaining less humiliating peace terms; but Stresemann also acted as a member of the anti-Weimar Right; his party would not join a government that included the Social Democrats. Nor were the Catholics united, as a separate Bavarian Catholic party arose over its disagreement with the Center's increasing reliance on initiatives from Berlin, where it formed the pivot of almost all Weimar cabinets. On the Right, the Nazis and the Conservatives competed for the same electorate, while from extreme Left the strong Communist Party attacked everyone (except the Nazis after 1933).

The Weimar constitution was not consistently secular. It sought to please all organized religious interests by offering state salaries for the clergy (though all religions were recognized as official) and religious instruction in public schools, thus undoing the anticlericalism of the Democrats and the Social Democrats. The religious establishments were tax supported despite a rhetorical endorsement of the separation of the churches from the state. Tax-supported denominational schools were tolerated as well. Weimar Germany's civil religion was riddled with contradictions.

Industrial and economic relations in Weimar began with the corporatist war economy system fully intact and endorsed by the unions and by industry in 1919 as the *Zentralarbeitsgemeinschaft*. The system collapsed in 1924 because the deeply divided parliament was unable to adopt legislation to make it permanent, thus reintroducing a sharper class conflict as economic conditions deteriorated. Its downfall also symbolized industry's willingness to seek allies on the Right rather than work with the trade unions. While industrial corporatism lasted, it gave major benefits to the workers and successfully circumvented antilabor proclivities in the bureaucracy and in the Reichstag. After its demise the employers renounced many of the concessions earlier made to the unions. Ironically, these developments would later be seized upon by the Nazis in their attacks on capitalism and "plutocracy," even though the Nazis also accepted campaign contributions from industrialists!

The Right despised Weimar. In an excess of devotion to liberal principles of interest representation, the drafters of the constitution introduced a system of proportional representation that guaranteed almost all shades of organized opinion a few deputies, thus of course contributing further to government instability and making impossible the formation of stable coalitions anchored in a few large parties. The Right was electorally rewarded for campaigning on the claim that Germany had not lost the war in the field of battle, but as a result of a stab in the back by the Marxist parties (who had indeed been instrumental in organizing the mutinies in the fall of 1918 that broke out after the defeat in France). Syncretist and integral nationalists took solace in this face-saving fable. They blamed the antinationalist "treason" on the members of the Weimar coalition. For the Right, the very democratic features of the constitution were insults to German identity, to the continuity of German history as symbolized by strong, heroic leaders unconstrained by legalistic provisions.

The liberals were further weakened by their acceptance of the peace treaty with its major losses of territory, and with the galling placement of Germans under Polish, French, and Belgian rule. Equally galling was the forced acknowledgment of responsibility for having initiated the war (the famous "war guilt" clause of the Treaty of Versailles), and the admission of having committed war crimes. Because of its rigidity on church and school issues, the Center, unlike its Christian Democratic successors in 1948, never managed to expand its electorate beyond the Catholic core, many of whose members later were to vote for the Nazis. The Conservatives, unlike their pre-1918 predecessors, became a mass-based party with supporters in all parts of Germany.

Versailles and the Great Depression Trigger
Racist Integralism

Where, then, did the Nazis recruit their supporters? The party entered electoral politics at the federal level in 1924 and garnered 6.6 percent of the vote, apparently from lower-middle-class people especially badly hurt by the hyperinflation just concluded, taking votes from both center and Right. The core clientele, it appears, consisted of small retail merchants, pensioners, artisans, and farmers who blamed large-scale corporate capitalism for their economic plight but who rejected class-struggle explanations and solutions in favor of formulas stressing German organic unity. After 1930, the appeal of the Nazis spread to middle-class voters of all types as all liberal parties became the main losers in all depression-era elections. In rural areas, moreover, the Nazis gained at the expense of the right-wing conservatives. The Nazis became a party with equally strong foundations in traditional rural society as well as in industrial-urban settings in which Socialist and Communist power had eroded. "The NSDAP, after 1930, was well on the way to becoming the long sought-after party of middle-class integration."[10]

Yet the Nazis did very poorly in the last pre-depression elections, in 1928. It seems likely that the Weimar coalition might yet have survived if it had been able to master the depression instead of being swamped by it. Liberals and Social Democrats paid no attention to Keynesian demand-enhancement prescriptions in their macroeconomic policies, though Keynes's work was well known to German economists and appreciated by some. Things were complicated by the post-Versailles reparations issue, which had the effect of linking economic with overall foreign policy matters. Thus, the democratic parties wanted to make an effort to pay reparations and keep Germany within the rules of the still-liberal international economic system, while also stressing civil liberties in domestic life. Parties to the right of the coalition, however, linked their preference for authoritarian governance with rejection of any obligation to carry out the reparations clauses of the Versailles treaty. Nor was the Right committed to German participation in a liberal world economy. Heavy industry turned protectionist and hostile to the continued payment of reparations, even after they were rescheduled in 1929, and joined others in demanding a revision in Germany's favor of the territorial settlement of 1919. In short, the deterioration of the economy went hand in hand with ever shriller challenges to terms of the Versailles treaty. Integral visions of German identity and German "needs" successfully challenged more liberal ones.

It was the Nazis who benefited from this vipers' nest of passions, conflicting interests, and failed policies. They found an ideology able to cross the lines of tension and hatred in Weimar Germany to become a myth, albeit for only a dozen years. They catered to the fears of those who felt cheated and threatened by the large-scale impersonalism of corporate capitalist life, by the compassionless tyranny of instrumental rationality and bureaucratic efficiency, by Weber's Iron Cage. They gave solace to those who wanted to defy Britain and France, the "plutocratic capitalist" oppressors of the German people's heroic nature. They promised to save Germany from Jewish-Marxist materialism. The Nazis undertook to give Germans the self-respect of which Versailles had robbed them. To fulfill the promise, of course, Germany was given a revolutionary-totalitarian national myth, not the comfortable small-town *Gemütlichkeit* of the traditional syncretism of which pre-1933 Nazi propaganda reeked.

The Nazi Racist Integral Myth

When Adolf Hitler became German chancellor, his party was clearly the most successful in attracting support from all classes and regions of Germany, from Protestants overwhelmingly but from a good many Catholics as well. The Nazis had made a special appeal to elderly people on fixed incomes despite their youth-dominated self-image and propaganda. By 1932 they had also acquired a large constituency among university students, farmers, and civil servants. They had made inroads into the upper middle class, and even among blue-collar workers not organized by the large industrial unions.

This electoral appeal contained many opportunist arguments that effectively camouflaged the truly revolutionary ideology that constituted the core of Nazi beliefs. The Nazis despised the German upper classes, bourgeois as well as noble, as tainted by cosmopolitanism and capitalism. The leadership of the party came largely from the lower middle class, from marginal professionals, from World War I veterans who had been unable to adjust to civilian life, not people likely to inspire confidence in the upper middle class–dominated German bureaucracy and industrial circles. The Nazis appealed to all who were, or felt themselves to be, in trouble and who blamed "the system" for their difficulties. It appealed to people unable or unwilling to analyze their difficulties with the help of unemotional and analytic cognitive tools, who preferred the "salvational" means promised by a charismatic leader who demanded full surrender and loyalty from his followers. Nazism was a true political religion not only in its ritual and symbols but also in its psychological appeal. Since the faults of "the system" included not only the capitalism practiced by oligopolistic firms but also the bureaucracy of soulless efficiency, Nazi followers expected that Nazi functionaries would take the place of the old civil servants. While this did not quite happen, Hitler got the support of industry and of large-scale agriculture for Nazi macroeconomic policies in exchange for his promise to destroy the trade unions and to create instead Nazi-controlled unions that would lack the power to influence wages. That promise was kept: trade unionists found themselves in Dachau along with Jews, freemasons, Marxists, journalists, and members of the Reichstag.

Despite their successful destruction of the old trade unions, as well as of all other voluntary organizations of Weimar "civil society," the Nazis also sought a comprehensive inclusion of the working class in the national community. All *Volksgenossen* were equals. All former trade unionists belonged to the compulsory Labor Front, which, along with several other party organizations, became responsible for the disbursements of social security, leisure time, and vacation benefits. The Hitler Youth took the place of the youth organizations that had been associated with the former political parties. Robert Ley, the head of the Labor Front, noted that "nothing is more dangerous to a state than homeless men. In such circumstances, even a bowling club or a skate club assumes a state-maintaining function."[11] He was right; the working class was indeed successfully integrated into the state, albeit by totalitarian devices.

The Nazis espoused an egalitarian sense of community based on racial purity alone, not status or wealth. They remained ambivalent toward Christianity, that "slave religion," denying it any role in defining German values, or — more accurately — Aryan values. Politically engaged clerics were persecuted along with all enemies of the *Volk*. The central importance of antisemitism in Nazi ideology was directly linked to Nazi opposition to capitalism and socialism because Jews were held to be the leaders of both. Moreover, they, along with Slavs, were said to threaten the purity, and therefore the survival, of the Aryan race because of the threat of miscegenation. The survival and the revival of the Aryan race, in the form of the German nation, were one and the same thing; they demanded the conquest of living space for the *Volk* and the creation of a new European order under German direction. Racial thinking was used to justify not only genocide but also eugenics legislation, euthanasia, and rules governing procreation among the racially most pure and for relations between Germans and non-Aryans.

All non-Aryans were removed from public life after 1933. Capitalism was to be purged and made accountable to the people. The red menace was to be curbed for good. The military glory of Germany was to be restored. The Nazi Party was the embodiment of the emotional commitment of the individual to the collectivity — one of the favorite Nazi slogans was *Gemeinnutz geht vor Eigennutz* — and the main instrument of collective action. The rule of the party was to be total. Everything it demanded was licit and everything of which it disapproved illicit. Integralism in ideology and commitment included also integralism in leadership: all governance was totally hierarchical and flowed from the will of the leader, a charismatic person imbued with superhuman powers, who in turn delegated some authority to lower-level leaders.

The leadership principle was the sole constitutional norm of Nazi governance and the preservation of racial purity the core theme of Nazi integral nationalism. In fact, the Nazi Party never achieved the monopoly of totalitarian control that it sought because of the survival of pre-totalitarian institutions on which the conduct of the war depended: the bureaucracy, the armed forces, and the large corporations. Nazi institutions came into being alongside the older ones, to compete with them. Thus, the Nazis created a party-led army (the SS) alongside the Wehrmacht and party police (the Gestapo) alongside the regular police. They also created their own civil administration, whose competencies were not clearly differentiated from those of the regular civil service. And they set up a system of party-controlled industrial enterprises, eventually staffed with slave labor, of which today's Volkswagen automobile is a survivor. Government made generous use of terror against any putative domestic enemy of the new order.

Racist Ideology in Action

The Nazis aimed at a total remaking of European society, a true continental revolution, though their preoccupation with the war that was being lost made implementation of most of these plans impossible. Still, as one Nazi writer argued, "a new organically structured Europe was coming into being, led by a Reich aware of its heavy responsibility. The peoples of Europe formed a community of destiny, within which each nation had the living space and freedom necessary for the unfolding of its own unique strength and tradition."[12]

That freedom turned out to be defined strictly by Nazi racial thinking. Aryans would rule; the Scandinavian and Dutch peoples were part of the master race along with Germans; Britons were potential allies whom Hitler sought to woo until 1941. Part-Aryan cultures (Czechs, Balts, French) were to be allowed some autonomy as helpers to the master race.

Nazi administration reflected these ideas. Bohemia and Moravia were annexed to the Reich but not treated as colonial territory; a similar fate was planned for the Baltic countries. The conquered "Aryan" western and northern countries were ruled by local Nazi allies, though their Jews were slated for extermination (as elsewhere) and many people were taken to Germany as slave labor. Slovakia and Croatia were made "independent" fascist states allied with Greater Germany; Italy, Hungary, and Romania already had fascist governments allied with the master race.

The Nazis regarded Slavic eastern Europe as agricultural lands to be stripped of their native population and given over to German colonization. Those Poles, Ukrainians, and Russians who survived the systematic killing of all educated and skilled people were to be confined to menial tasks in the service of German peasants who were to be moved to the East. As it happened, the parts of Poland and the Soviet Union incorporated into the Greater German Reich proved most unattractive to potential German settlers, and military defeats kept the genocide of Poles and Ukrainians from being carried to its planned completion. Jews and Gypsies were not equally fortunate.

It still seems incredible that this regime, apparently, rerationalized Germany into a coherent nation-state. The economy began to perform very well; Germans accepted the reintroduction of militarism and of conscription with seeming enthusiasm; Nazi racial policies aroused no opposition; terror and police-state methods were not experienced by most Germans, while informing on friends, neighbors, and even parents was accepted as patriotic. Germans fought tenaciously in six years of unprecedentedly violent war, despite suffering enormous casualties. Only one ineffective effort was made to overthrow the Nazi regime, the failed assassination plot of July 1944. We cannot tell, of course, whether the Greater German Reich would really have remained rationalized for even a fraction of the thousand years Hitler prophesied if Germany had not been defeated in 1945. Nor can we be wholly certain of the role of repression in giving us a false impression. As matters stand, the Nazis successfully combined "a messianic and apocalyptic vision of history *within* the political, bureaucratic, and technological system of a highly developed industrial society. What took place within Nazi Germany were interactions between totally heterogeneous phenomena: messianic fanaticism *and* bureaucratic structure, pathological ideology *and* routinized administrative decrees, archaic modes of thinking *and* a highly complex modern society."[13] Integral racist nationalism *is* able to reunite such fissiparous strands, to provide murderous bonds of identity as its acolytes seek to transcend a past they see as tainted. Fortunately, we were spared a test of its staying power.

Liberal Nationalism Rationalizes the German Federal Republic

The defeat in 1945 destroyed the German state and shattered its society and economy. Physically, German cities were in ruins as a result of Allied bombing, which killed 300,000 and wounded 780,000 civilians and eliminated 20 percent of residential units; 12,350,000 refugees streamed into the western occupation zones from territories east of the Oder-Neisse Line, escaping from the Soviet armies. There was no German government until 1949; the country was cut up into four separate occupation zones, each ruled by a foreign military government. Heavy American aid was required to reignite the economy as the Soviet occupation forces stripped away, in the form of reparations, much of the industrial plant still intact. There was little food and less fuel. Inter-Allied commissions made the key decisions for German industry.

The evolution of the Federal Republic started from this low point. By 1970 over 30 percent of the population lived in cities over 100,000 inhabitants, and only 18.7 percent remained in villages; 7.5 percent of the labor force was still active in agriculture. The service sector now accounted for over 43 percent of the labor force; 10.6 percent worked for government at all levels. Sixty-seven percent of the population was enfranchised in 1960, 99 percent was literate. In 1950, government still spent 13.5 percent of total public expenditures on defense, though social security took 45.7 percent! Education and science took 7.3 percent, while 4.9 percent was devoted to government-subsidized reconstruction of the housing stock. By 1960, 20 percent of the GDP was devoted to government social programs. The fledgling Federal Republic was on its way to continuing the German welfare-state tradition with a vengeance. It is especially noteworthy that during the travail of economic reconstruction between 1945 and 1950, German administrators and their American overlords were determined to avoid the economic errors of the Weimar governments, especially hyperinflation.

How Liberal Nationalism Became the Civil Religion

The Federal Republic (FRG) that emerged from the ruins is a much more successfully rationalized state than were Wilhelmine and Nazi Germany, not to mention Weimar. Prussia was dissolved as the hegemonic entity; Catholics ceased being an inner-directed minority, as confessional differences lost much of their earlier salience; the nobility and its base in the armed forces disappeared. Perhaps most importantly, the terrible moral burden of the criminal Nazi past made any pretension to an assertive foreign policy quite unthinkable before 1989, the miracle year of modern international politics.

Before we can explain how political parties that barely tolerated one another under Weimar learned to practice diffuse reciprocity, we must identify the new actors on the political scene. The western Allied occupation authorities actively encouraged the forming of parties dedicated to liberal democracy at the local level, with the result that three major parties had emerged by 1949. They, in turn, negotiated the Basic Law of West Germany—which became the all-German constitution in 1990—under strict supervision of the occupation authorities, who decreed that the constitution could not be as centralized as Weimar's had been, but not as decentralized as Bismarck's. The Basic Law was declared to be "provisional," valid only until the Soviet-occupied eastern zone, later the German Democratic Republic (GDR), would be allowed to rejoin West Germany. The FRG declared itself the sole authentic successor state to former German states, thus stigmatizing the GDR, which was under the totalitarian control of the communist-run Socialist Unity Party (SED), as illegitimate.

No explanation of how and why the FRG is fully rationalized under the auspices of liberal nationalism is credible until we come to the end of this chapter. In this section the institutional elements of the liberal national myth are presented: new political parties who trust one another, a flowering of pluralism and of participatory social movements, the democratization of public education and of the military, the commitment to peaceful change, and the maintenance of civil liberties.

The new political parties encouraged by the occupation authorities remembered the strife of Weimar only too well: they were determined not to reenact it. The only party to emerge from the Nazi era relatively unscathed was the Social Democratic Party (SPD). The SPD at first remained Marxist, committed to a democratic but anticapitalist workers' state, opposed to NATO and European integration as inconsistent with the goal of German reunification. It won no federal elections with this stance. In 1959, the SPD officially abandoned the class struggle and its proletarian orientation, opposition to the Western alliance, and anticlericalism. Instead it embraced the principles of the "social market economy" and European economic integration in its search for a broader electoral constituency. It also became virulently anticommunist and a staunch defender of the civil libertarian content of the Basic Law. The Free Democrats (FDP) were torn during the 1950s between a pro–free enterprise wing dominated by northern industrialists and a small enterprise/welfare state–oriented southern section. Marginalization at the hands of the dominant Christian Democrats (CDU) forced the FDP toward the left. It remained a defender of the social market economy and of Germany's pro-Western bias, and it functions as a small possible coalition partner for both major parties.

The CDU originated as the former Catholic Center's bid to become a force devoted to basing policy on Christian values; it opened its doors to Protestants and has since lost its confessional coloration altogether. At first torn between conservatives devoted to free enterprise and Christian socialists who sought state control over large corporations, the CDU became a center-right party; it invented the idea of the social market economy, an economy owned and managed by private business, including very large corporations, but constrained by the practices of corporatist decision making (which gave the trade unions a special role of importance) and made tolerable to workers by an extensive system of social security and social entitlements. The CDU is otherwise nonideological, devoid of a special program, a catch-all party. It made itself the architect of all of German postwar foreign policy with the exception of the SPD's *Ostpolitik* of the 1970s. Its catch-all character provided a big incentive for the other two parties to downplay their ideological commitments and to become partners in a tolerant consensus that went unchallenged until the advent of the Greens.

No liberal national myth would have arisen if the Western Allied authorities had not carried through a program of denazification and reeducation. High-level Nazis were systematically purged from public life, and many were jailed. Communists, accused of being hostile to the practice of electoral democracy, were actively discriminated against in public employment in the West, as were noncommunists in the GDR. The Allied authorities, together with reform-minded Germans, at first planned major changes of the educational systems, which were largely shelved under the pressure of Cold War thinking. There are major curricular differences among educational systems run by the various *Länder*. In general, however, textbooks were systematically rewritten to remove glorification of the German past and to tone down German nationalism. When a non-aggressive national anthem had to be chosen, Konrad Adenauer substituted the pacific third stanza of the *Deutschlandlied* for the objectionable first. The flag of the 1848 democratic unity movement (also the flag of the Weimar Republic) became the new national colors. Social studies were deemphasized in primary and secondary schools, though the inculcation of democratic civic values became an important task for the schools. The secondary school system was made more accessible to working-class and lower-middle-class children; no tracking was to take place until a student's sixteenth year. Social mobility was also to be encouraged by the construction of large numbers of new universities, some of which, after 1968, fell under the control of radical antidemocratic groups for some years. Nevertheless, it appears to be true that the system of secondary and higher education is still disproportionately geared to the aspirations of the middle class, whose children benefit far more from the secondary schools than do working-class children in terms of success at universities. While the teaching of contemporary history is neglected in secondary schools, both German states took care to use history texts to vilify each other, to inculcate students with the belief that the "other" Germany lacks legitimacy. The children of immigrants must attend school, where they are treated as Germans, though some of the *Länder* offer some work in lower grades in the immigrant's language until the student is deemed ready for instruction in German alone. Most bilingual education is paid for by the country of the immigrant's origin or by private immigrant-aid associations. On the whole, the FRG is not eager to make special services available to immigrants. To the extent that any values are taught in school, the ideals are liberal and cosmopolitan.

The FRG's armed forces were explicitly designed to avoid the practices associated with former German armies, navies, and air forces. Recruitment relies on conscription; however, generous exceptions from service are provided in the form of conscientious objection and alternative public service. Draft evasion has been heavy at times, though it declined as the period of services was shortened and as the Bundeswehr seeks an increasingly professional basis.

Civilian control over the armed forces is absolute and unquestioned. Soldiers are citizens in uniform. The legislature decides on the deployment of forces outside Germany. The first such deployment took place in 1995, following an authorization by the Federal Constitutional Court. The democratic attitude of the armed forces is fostered by a principle labeled "self-guidance," which is used in the indoctrination of all troops. Each soldier, far from being the obedient automaton of earlier German armies, is a "co-responsible citizen" who expresses in personal conduct the liberal German values he or she is to defend. The German soldier need not obey orders that violate the rules of German democracy; he or she enjoys all civil rights. Military legitimacy derives uniquely from the mission to defend the democratic order.

This remarkable act of social learning did not go unchallenged. Self-guidance did not find acceptance without bitter resistance from the center-right. It was widely criticized by the Left as inadequate during the 1980s. There continues to be disagreement over the extent to which the Bundeswehr ought to feature, in the names of units, uniforms, and ceremonial, the tradition of its predecessor armed forces. The architects of the Bundeswehr wanted to minimize such traditions; but the CDU tends to favor their retention and continues to agitate for the restoration of symbols that had been removed. Similarly, while the SPD and Greens want Bundeswehr personnel to be conscious of the crimes of the Wehrmacht and the Nazis, right-wing opinion wishes troops to identify proudly with their predecessors irrespective of possible political taint.

Civil liberties are widely respected despite the travail of post-1945 nation-formation. The police, like the Bundeswehr, were subjected to legal-democratic control as a result of the occupation. In general, German criminal jurisprudence allows for few convictions and even fewer incarcerations. Violent crime was minimal until the 1990s. Thus, when in the late 1960s and during much of the 1970s a wave of left-wing terrorism struck German society, this policy of forbearance was severely tried. The outbreak of right-wing violence in the 1990s was seen by many Germans as being fueled by an overly restrained police response.

Between 1970 and 1979 there were 649 acts of political violence, including 31 assassinations and 163 hostage-takings. Between 1980 and 1985 there were over 1,600 violent acts, now committed by both the Left and Right. The government responded by creating a federal criminal police and enhancing surveillance techniques, much to the lament of civil libertarians in the parties of the Left. Nevertheless, German democracy survived unscathed despite the administrative recentralization of *Land* police forces and the stepped-up interpolice cooperation among European countries.

Despite the presence of many refugees from formerly German areas, now Polish, Russian, and Czech, who wanted to go back to their homes rather than assimilate into the culture of the FRG, most people had accepted the finality of the Oder-Neisse border by the 1960s. When given the choice between the continuation of prosperity in the context of the alliance with the West or efforts to bring about reunification, almost everyone opted for the status quo. West Germans overwhelmingly identified as *West* Germans by 1970, not as the Germans who inhabited the Germany of 1938. Citizens of the GDR were taught that they were the true Germans, the Germans of the new socialist person, the heirs of what was always superior in German culture.

By 1970, the erstwhile refugees had been successfully absorbed into FRG society. Differences between Protestants and Catholics were so lacking in salience that, by 1974, 69 percent of all marriages were cross-confessional. Not only the CDU but the chief trade unions were now interconfessional in membership. All churches receive state recognition and state subsidies paid for by the income tax, though separate confessional school systems are in decline. Churches are prominent in political advocacy even though they make little effort to impose their spiritual values on a population that, on the whole, is growing indifferent to all organized religion. In Bavaria alone is there a tendency to make Catholicism the state religion.

Legitimacy and Participatory Pluralism

In the mid-1970s, 80 percent of respondents said they prefer the FRG to any other historical German state. Konrad Adenauer is voted by over 50 percent every year as having done the most for Germany because he restored German dignity, independence, and friendship with France, while Bismarck was mentioned by only 10 percent. In 1983, only 56 percent of respondents claimed that they felt proud to be German. German history is no longer taught systematically in public schools; when, in 1986, the government proposed the creation of two new museums of German history, many objected because they could not agree on which modern events to memorialize. In the mid-1970s only 22 percent of Germans thought they had more in common with other Germans of a different social class, as contrasted with Frenchmen of the same class. Reunification was actually opposed by 14 percent of West Germans in 1989. Eighty-two percent pronounced themselves satisfied with their lives in 1973, while 88 percent felt this way in 1990. In 1973, only 44 percent were satisfied with the workings of German democracy, but in 1990 81 percent expressed satisfaction. In 1970, 70 percent were content with incremental reforms in German society; in 1990 the number was only 55 percent, while 39 percent wanted to curtail freedoms in order to control subversives.

Transitions among governments have been unruffled by controversy. Thanks to the rule that no party receiving less than 5 percent of the national vote may receive legislative representation, no right-wing extremist party has seats in the Bundestag, though such parties sometimes win 10 percent in local elections. The strongly negative reaction to the appearance of violence-prone extraparliamentary political groups bespeaks general respect for electoral and party practices. No call for a strong leader to save the nation has been heard. Voters turn out in large numbers. People continue to pay their taxes and do their national service without going out of their way to sanctify the state they serve. The economic policies and practices that went along with these sentiments surely helped to produce this widespread sentiment of legitimacy.

> While the increase in support for the present system and the decline in positive feelings for past regimes have been the result of both generational changes and the performance of the Bonn system, the important point . . . is that all major social . . . , economic, and political groups ranked high in their support for political competition, freedom of political expression, sense of representation, and the parliament. Support, at least for the liberal Republic established in 1949, has by the 1970s become diffuse, not significantly related to any particular group or policy of the government. These principles and processes have become accepted norms for the conduct of politics in the Federal Republic.[14]

Though most institutions are legitimate and most differences over policies no longer elicit passionate conflict, one major new controversy came to the fore as a result of the government's full-scale endorsement of nuclear energy as the way to achieve energy autonomy: *the quality and future of technology and of technological innovation.* Grassroots movements challenged unquestioned adjustment to unbroken technological innovation. The Green Party's emergence in the 1980s is the expression of this disaffection with modernity. Belief in science and progress remains strong, but the previously unchallenged faith that science will solve all problems is gone. The fear of environmental degradation and the desire to foster a wiser use of natural resources pit a "postmaterialist" younger generation against the older people. New extraparty movements challenge the sanctity of the institutions and policies blamed for environmental crises: capitalism, bigness, materialism, arms racing, the Cold War, the unconstrained pursuit of private group rather than of the general interest. Though skepticism toward science has not meant the rejection of telematic and information technologies, or the wholesale condemnation of innovation, many West Germans have indeed rejected a policy of "progress at any price." The ruling parties, however, still believe that technological innovation remains the guarantee of prosperity. The Greens, moreover, pose a much more basic challenge to the German consensus, a challenge that extends to foreign and defense matters.

Social mobilization, apparently, does not stop when all citizens have become literate, most of them vote regularly, the huge majority are aware of events around them, many travel, and all know they are part of a world they experience regularly on television. Social mobilization continues because people who were normally inactive politically are now aroused to action and self-assertion. These newly mobilized were the rebelling students of 1968 who became the Green and extreme left-wing parties of the 1970s and 1980s. They express a syndrome of poorly integrated passions including radical ecological sentiments, pacifism, antinuclear commitments, condemnations of the Cold War and of nuclear deterrence, neutralism, feminism, radical Marxism, and opposition to further technological change. The substantive connections among these themes are weak. In Germany at least, supporters of this syndrome tend to shun the older parties in favor of the Greens, though the left wing of the SPD is strongly sympathetic to some of these causes, to the contempt for bureaucracy and the distrust of the state.

The German Greens made the transformation of capitalism and the abolition of militarism the core demands derived from their analysis of ecological crisis. They question the moral validity of most German institutions and denied, at first, the very legitimacy of the Bonn Republic. Electoral successes, of course, made most Greens more accepting of existing institutions, particularly as they attained almost 10 percent of the popular vote in some *Länder*. They reject military preparations in favor of tactics of nonviolent resistance. While some Greens are clearly integralists and proto-totalitarians (though not nationalists), others subscribe to a cosmopolitanism in which it is hard to discern a specifically German identity. Were European liberalism to falter, it is quite possible that the Greens would offer the forum in which a new German "nationalism" might take shape, stressing participatory democracy and non-bureaucratic administration, anchored in small groups of the committed. The German Greens so committed would show "the way" to the rest of the world. In the meantime, the Greens fight the foreign policy consensus and the materialist complacency of the majority of Germans.

The postmaterialist trend was an unintended consequence of the reforms in higher education undertaken in the 1960s. These had resulted in a huge increase in the number of young people attending universities, in upward mobility, in expectations of a rewarding professional career. However, the economic crises of the 1970s led to disappointment because a considerable amount of intellectual underemployment and unemployment developed, fueling feelings of alienation from "the system." During the 1980s, admission to universities and to some disciplines was made more difficult as state subsidies to students were reduced.

But the blooming of hundreds of new voluntary movements is far from guaranteeing effective legislation and administration. Prior to the increasing prominence of postindustrial issues, most controversies in the FRG were discussed by corporatist bodies before they were submitted to orderly legislative debate. The new issues on the agenda make this practice more difficult because the clashing opinions jump class and party lines, unlike the older economic differences. Postindustrial issues greatly complicate democratic-corporatist decision making.[15]

By the time reunification came about, citizens of the FRG were smugly self-satisfied, with the exception of the minority of postmaterialists. They had largely forgotten the sentiments and symbols of all pre-FRG all-German formulas of identity. Legitimacy was rooted in a shallow sense of national self, in a weak commitment to the liberal collectivity. Moreover, that legitimacy seemed to have its roots in the corporatist social market economy.

Democracy, Legitimacy, and the Social Market Economy

By 1966, the FRG's economy had developed from the basket case it had been in 1945 to the world's third largest; Konrad Adenauer and Ludwig Erhard had brought about the "German economic miracle" by means of the social market economy, which expressed the balance between the liberal and the social democratic impulses in postwar Germany. Labor—protected by social insurance, formal recognition of its organization rights, political freedom and . . . workers' comanagement [of industry]—was willing to accept the linkage of wage gains to productivity. Germany entered a period of labor peace. . . . German capitalists could thus count on a steady supply of highly skilled, hardworking labor. Government policies encouraged growth and support. Erhard's tax laws encouraged the reinvestment of profits and gave substantial benefits for investment in capital equipment, while tight monetary policy kept inflation very low, which helped provide the necessary stability for foreign trade.[16]

The state created the parameters for and behaviors by the private sector from which prosperity emerged, stressing the prevention of inflation and providing a very generous system of social entitlements. Active management of investment and production was left to the private sector, albeit a private sector that functioned according to corporatist principles of consultation. The social market economy was far from being the unregulated free-enterprise utopia of classical liberals, though Keynesian demand management was rejected at first. Efforts for a more comprehensive form of planning were not made until 1967, when medium-term investment plans for the entire economy were worked out in Bonn, which were then enforced jointly by the federal and *Land* governments by means of an agreed fiscal policy. This form of planning, under SPD leadership, led to a short period of Keynesian demand management in the early 1970s. German methods of economic steering, though they differed from practices elsewhere in the industrialized world, nevertheless proved very effective in legitimating the liberal values that inspired them.

The successful integration of Germans into their FRG is in no small measure due to the economic success of their nation. Conversely, the lack of legitimacy of the GDR had a great deal to do with the economic failures of that regime. By 1990 the German economy was the largest and the most export-prone of the European economies. Its labor force was thoroughly unionized, but the number of industrial disputes remained among the lowest in Europe. In 1979, 10 percent of the labor force consisted of foreign immigrants, and in 1976, 17 percent of all live births occurred in the families of guest workers. In the mid-seventies, the FRG only devoted 6.4 percent of its public expenditures to defense, but an overwhelming 46.4 percent to social security, 12.2 percent to education and science. As a result of the pivotal position given the D-mark under the rules of the European Monetary System that came into being in 1978, the FRG became Western Europe's central banker in fact though not in law.

Institutionalized interest group participation in the making of policy—societal corporatism, as distinguished from the state-directed variety—is a central liberal value in much of Europe.[17] In Germany, it flowered because economic thinking was dominated by export-oriented industrialists allied with democratic trade unions rather than the coalition familiar from earlier eras of German history, heavy industry and large-scale agriculture catering to a protected home market. German-style corporatism is expressed in a variety of institutions. German corporatism differs from other European models because the state does not occupy a directing position at all times. Legal frameworks made by the state, nevertheless, shape the institutions of corporatist governance of the economy. Worker codetermination is practiced on the shop floor as well as in corporate boardrooms. Consequently, labor leaders, having access to the firms' books, are well informed about the ability of the firm to pay wages and benefits while remaining profitable. This, in turn, strongly influences the pattern of collective bargaining, which takes place at the level of industrial sectors, not of firms (as in the United States) or the entire economy (as in Sweden). Finally, corporatist institutions include a very large number of advisory councils to government departments that are staffed by experts representing the major organized interests.

There are limits to participatory democracy as acted out in corporatist institutions, even though industrial peace, the smooth functioning of corporatist-run social insurance funds, and overall prosperity are associated with it. Major investment decisions are made by large banks. The state is willing and able to ignore its advisory committees when the bureaucracy and the ruling parties feel strong enough to do so; they sidestepped the consultative bodies of the health insurance funds when they imposed a law limiting the earnings of pharmaceutical firms and physicians. The state subsidizes industrial research and the social insurance funds; it has sharply reduced its contributions in the 1990s. Perhaps most important, the Bundesbank, after all, controls the value of money with its bias against inflation, thereby imposing sharp limits on the range of meaningful collective agreements. The bank, after 1973, adopted a consistent monetarist stance and thus reinforced the supply-side emphasis given to the social market economy by the Schmidt and Kohl governments. Nevertheless, Helmut Schmidt felt compelled to retain some demand-stimulation measures as well because of his commitment to the Group of Seven to act as a "locomotive" for the ailing Western economies.

Despite severe shocks in the 1970s and early 1980s, the corporatist social market economy continues to perform well. Keynesian ideas of macroeconomic steering never really won out in German thought, though they inspired policy in Bonn between 1966 and 1973 because the SPD was ideologically predisposed toward demand management. Yet even the Social Democrats subscribed to the lesson learned during Weimar: never let inflation get the better of you. The Schmidt and Kohl governments therefore reverted to an upgraded social market economy with its emphasis on supply-side forces, self-regulated competition, and reliance on exports. More important, German economic analysts, after the first oil shock of the 1970s, persuaded the government of the need for an industrial policy in the form of public assistance to certain key sectors of the manufacturing branches. Even before this decision was made, however, the Keynesians had prevailed to the extent of persuading the *Länder* governments to plan together with Bonn the kind of economy that could adjust continuously to technological change while maintaining full employment, a step that called for more government intervention than the social market economists preferred. But toward the end of the 1970s the government once more adopted deflationary measures in preference to subsidizing firms in trouble. Committed to wage restraint, the main trade unions prefer to counter declining employment opportunities due to technological innovation by reducing the workweek to 35 hours, a decision approved by the government.

Sectorally focused industrial policy was the key measure adopted. The impetus was the perceived need for developing energy sources alternative to oil, and because of the high cost of R&D, encouraging superfirms that could act as national champions. Public funds for research designed to lead to such guided innovations, to include environmentally sound technologies and technologies to humanize the workplace, were voted in 1978. Justified by SPD economists and bureaucrats as *Strukturpolitik,* these measures were fully endorsed by the trade unions. It was taken for granted that in an economy in which full employment was thought to be dependent on high export capacity, it was also considered imperative that Germany remain internationally competitive, which in turn called for unceasing technological innovation. The unions, locked into the collective decision-making process by the prevailing corporatist institutions and practices, practiced wage restraint and concentrated instead on safeguarding existing entitlements, strengthening their control over state-financed training and retraining programs and improving conditions on the shop floor. Industry did not oppose *Strukturpolitik,* cautioning, however, that it should not lead to state control over investments or to export cartels. These restrained measures, in which none of the parties seeks to score a full victory, have been especially visible in the troubled steel industry, in which modernization turned out to be less painful than elsewhere because of the substantive consensus on what needed to be done and the procedures for satisfying all the parties (except unskilled and foreign workers). Corporatism protects the most skilled workers disproportionately. Yet it assured relatively smooth adjustments to an economy as much exposed to the winds of change as any.[18]

Germans also learned how to cope with challenges to their welfare state. In their determination after 1945 not to slide again into the intense internal conflicts of the Weimar period, Germans learned to appreciate the virtues of solidarity and burden-sharing. The principles of equity that undergird the social insurance system illustrate this lesson learned. The generous system of pensions was indexed to changes in the cost of living. Richer *Länder* agreed to transfers of tax revenues to subsidize the poorer ones. Unemployment insurance sought to guarantee that joblessness — unacceptable in principle — be made dignified. The myriad private health and occupational accident insurance funds were subsidized by Bonn.

This system was threatened by serious cost overruns as well as by hard economic times by 1975. Severe cutbacks were made in funds for education, housing, and health care. Additional cutbacks came between 1988 and 1992: in reimbursable health costs, old-age pensions, and occupational accident insurance. Yet consumers, when confronted with the statistics of early depletion and cost overruns, expressed a preference for curtailment of benefits over increases in their contributions to the funds. Solidarity and burden-sharing, it seems, are principles that work in good as well as in hard times.[19]

The political legitimacy of Germany's democracy, undoubtedly Whiggishly liberal but not markedly nationalistic, quite clearly derives from the successes of the social market economy and its corporatist mode of governance. Germans feel they "never had it better"; they experience a sense of pride in their achievements. Polls show that voters express their approval of the parties in response to the size of their pocketbooks. Yet the social market economy functions on the basis of publicly regulated competition; it is not rooted in wholly free markets. Says Wolfgang Streeck:

> The German state is neither *laissez-faire* nor *etatiste,* and is best described as an *enabling* state. Its capacity for direct intervention in the economy is curtailed by vertically and horizontally fragmented sovereignty, and by robust constitutional limitations on discretionary government action.[20]

It has learned, since being reconstituted by the United States, Britain, and France, to help groups organize themselves, and therefore avoid the extremes of pure market-driven incentives and authoritative central allocation of values.

The Pro-Western Foreign Policy Consensus

Germany could have been reunified in 1952 if Stalin's offer to end the division in return for the neutralization and demilitarization of the united country had been accepted. Rejection of the offer was a foregone conclusion because it was not for Konrad Adenauer to accept, but for Washington. The FRG was not to be fully sovereign until 1955; until then most Allied control powers remained in force. Washington, together with its major European allies, had by then decided on the rearmament of Germany and on its inclusion in whatever Western military union was to emerge. The CDU government had decided that the future security and welfare of Germany was wholly dependent on a close alliance with the West; such an alliance was seen as an absolute prerequisite to eventual reunification.

Between 1952 and 1956, the FRG joined NATO and became a founding member of the supranational institutions from which the European Economic Community (EC) emerged in 1957. The removal of Allied controls was explicitly premised on the enmeshment of the newly sovereign FRG in the webs of regional economic and military integration. This evolution speeded up after the rapid communization of the GDR following the abortive revolt of 1953. The division of Germany seemed to become irreversible after NATO, in effect, tolerated the building of the Berlin Wall in 1961, constructed by the GDR to prevent the continuation of the heavy flow of its citizens toward the West. Everyone understood that the return of the FRG to international respectability was allowed only because the exercise of sovereignty was also curtailed by membership in intergovernmental and supranational organization. Everyone thought that close German association with the West effectively precluded reunification; Moscow was hardly going to agree to augment NATO's power by ceding the GDR to it, at least not before 1989.

The CDU's foreign policy was thought by the government to have a direct relationship to the strengthening of democracy in the FRG. Adenauer and his group sought close association with their occupiers in part because they wanted Western protection against any lingering German hankering after integral nationalism. When forced by events to choose between a Western guarantee for German security and welfare on the one hand and reunification on the other, the CDU and FDP did not hesitate to choose the former, much to the chagrin of the SPD, which favored neutrality, demilitarization, and aloofness toward European integration until 1959. Conversion to the CDU and FDP position, the formation of a foreign policy consensus of deemphasizing reunification, came only after the SPD decided to shed its Marxist patina. While jettisoning an all-German policy in fact, Bonn nevertheless kept up the pretense of speaking for all of Germany. It did so by refusing to recognize the GDR or have any dealings with it, and by breaking relations with any government that recognized Pankow. The GDR in 1967 created a specific East German citizenship, whereas the FRG stuck to Adenauer's policy of considering anyone born within the 1937 borders of the Reich as a (West) German national, including refugees from the GDR.

The SDP's approach, made definitive by Willy Brandt and Helmut Schmidt after 1969, confirmed the atrophy of unification efforts and also sought to mitigate its consequences. Technical and cultural exchanges with Pankow were authorized and the policy of absolute non-recognition abandoned. The policy of paying the GDR for releasing people to the West, begun by the CDU, was intensified, along with financial subsidies and symbolic gestures.[21] Brandt, apparently, wished to keep alive the consciousness of an all-German nationality even as he recognized the GDR as a sovereign state and accepted the existing borders as final. He initiated a series of personal meetings with his GDR opposite number and announced the doctrine of "one German nation, two German states." Brandt thus denied the existence of two rival German nation-states while also admitting the lack of a single one. Nevertheless, his formula suggested the potentiality that a single nation-state might reemerge, a position that ran counter to the popular attitudes that had formed by then. In 1972, the CDU unsuccessfully challenged as unconstitutional the treaty whereby the two Germanys recognized each other formally; the party opposed the agreement to defend its claim that the FRG alone was the German nation-state.

We cannot be sure whether these SPD-inspired measures, continued by the CDU government in the 1980s, helped to bring about the East German vote to merge with the FRG. We can be reasonably certain that the SPD-inspired *Ostpolitik,* launched in 1972 but also continued by the CDU in the 1980s, helped to bring about the relaxation of Cold War tensions in Europe. Institutionalized as the Helsinki Process, a series of military and cultural measures were initiated by the NATO and Warsaw Pact states after 1975 to increase contacts across the Iron Curtain, improve the observation of human rights in the East, advance the control over conventional arms, and relax military tensions. This policy was the cornerstone of German foreign policy; it recognized the finality of postwar political borders — unless changed by popular vote — and forswore the use of violence in interstate disputes.

Moreover, there were voices on the left of the SPD who demanded more: a nearly neutralized FRG and GDR, mediating between the antagonistic Cold War blocs, pioneering a postindustrial decentralized society, devoted to principles of ecology and humane industrial life. When the United States, with German approval, insisted on deploying a new generation of intermediate-range nuclear missiles in Germany in the early 1980s, a massive popular opposition movement sought to block the deployment. Though the movement did not succeed, the Kohl government sidestepped NATO policy by continuing its active policy of détente with the GDR as well as the symbolic recognition of its existence.

Nobody expected the GDR to collapse in the wake of Soviet withdrawal, an equally unanticipated event. West Germans did *not* learn to conciliate communists in order to earn reunification. *Ostpolitik* had not prevented the further integration of the FRG into the dense network of the Western economic, military, and legal web. *Ostpolitik* contained no effective challenge to the deepening of German enmeshment into the institutions and practices of Western cooperation; German nationalism was no longer assertive enough to challenge the perceived benefits of interdependence. Membership in the EU has meant the FRG's loss of control over its tariff and its agricultural sector; it has compelled the government to subsidize the prices French and Italian farmers receive for their products. The Bundesbank has become the lender of last resort for the other EU central banks. German consumers pay more for their food because of the EU control over agriculture. Environmental regulations are subjected to rules made by the EU; economic policies were regularly reviewed and criticized by the OECD. Because German leaders considered themselves more dependent on French support than on British, they backed de Gaulle in blocking British membership in the EC, but they backed the United States in France's quarrel with Washington over European defense. Any temptation to profess a more highly focused German nationalism than the weak sense of identity that actually prevailed in the FRG was held in check by these regional commitments and responsibilities.

Germans learned to put a sober and considered choice concerning issues of material welfare and security ahead of passionate belief, spirited advocacy, and unbending commitment. They learned to substitute instrumental for consummatory reason in permitting themselves to be tied to Western collective choices instead of insisting on the single-minded pursuit of national unity. When asked in 1969 what freedoms they would be willing to give up in exchange for reunification, only 3 percent were willing to forgo the freedoms of speech, free elections, and multiparty competition, while 10 percent were willing to sacrifice freedom of assembly. In 1951, 80 percent of the adult population opposed the finality of the postwar territorial status quo, but in 1972 that number had shrunk to 18 percent. The days of heroic foreign policy feats were over; the foreign policy of the sword yielded to that of the briefcase.

The GDR as a Failed Nation-State[22]

The communist government of the GDR, before and after *Ostpolitik*, tried very hard to make the former Soviet occupation zone into a socialist nation-state. For many years observers were deceived into believing that the leaders were succeeding, despite the heavy flights of East Germans toward the West. It took the massive popular demonstrations of 1989 and their demands for democracy to expose the lack of appeal that the communist nationalist ideology had evoked. As if sensing its isolation from popular feelings, the Socialist Unity Party (SED) had changed the content of the ideology a number of times, though none of the changes had the effect of establishing a separate GDR identity that could have prevented the effortless annexation of the state by the FRG in 1990.

Before 1971, the SED's Walter Ulbricht claimed that the GDR alone could exercise moral leadership over Germans because it was free from the Nazi and imperialist taint of its rival. The SED spoke of the inevitable reunification under socialism after the inevitable defeat of Western imperialism. Until then, however, reunification must be sacrificed to building a socialist nation-state in the GDR. The FRG's *Ostpolitik* was greeted by Pankow with the launching of a policy of *Abgrenzung,* of drawing a cognitive line between the two states in order to emphasize the separate identity of the East German nation. The ideology stressed historical ties between Germany and the Slavic world. References to the all-German past were removed from the constitution; use of the adjective "German" was curtailed. The identity of Eastern Germans, the SED said, lay in their class origins and their socialist mission, not their culture, which, admittedly, did not distinguish them from West Germans.

During the 1980s the SED went out of its way to claim older German symbols and personalities for its own. The leadership argued that such persons as Martin Luther, Frederick the Great, and Otto von Bismarck were "progressives" in the overall trajectory of German history and therefore were legitimate definers of solidarity for later socialist

Germans. The SED did this in the face of FRG efforts to use the same personalities and symbols in its continuing claim to be the sole legitimate successor to earlier German states. These themes were advanced without resurrecting the argument for reunification after the demise of "imperialism." The cultural unity of all Germans was now emphasized!

Why undertake these ideological gyrations? The SED leaders, thanks to the extensive opinion polling of the secret police apparatus, knew that there was no real GDR nationalism at the level of the populace. What little there was had declined during the 1980s, notably among young people. This caused them to redouble efforts to create such a sentiment. When border crossings, visits, and economic contact multiplied during the 1970s and 1980s, the model of the successful capitalist German neighbor in which personal freedom had flourished had to be countered. So did the rehabilitation as authentic German heroes of the old Prussian and Saxon personalities. The countering had to take the form of cultural symbols that stressed Germanness rather than the new socialist personality, which was quite obviously worse off than its capitalist cousin. A feeble attempt at maintaining *Abgrenzung* just the same was still made in the form of the claim that the GDR represents the most progressive portion of German history. While this claim, as we learned in 1989, carried no weight with those who clamored for reunification, it did not fall on entirely deaf ears. Neues Forum and the Evangelical Church organizations, the most active proponents of democratization in 1989, rejected reunification in favor of a drastically reformed but still separate, anticapitalist, and anti-NATO East German state, only to be repudiated in the elections that followed Erich Honecker's resignation. The ideological ingenuity of the SED was never able to overcome the example of a successful, if very attenuated, German liberal national myth next door, a myth whose adherents could display their achievements quite effortlessly on the television that almost all East Germans watched.

Unified Germany, Europe, and the World

Germany and the Unification of Europe

After a short period of delirium about the new unity of the Germanys, it became clear that nothing like a reborn German nationalism, a hankering after a restored historical identity, a new search for hegemony in central Europe, was in the making. East Germans grumbled about the economic and personal hardship incurred by giving up socialist bureaucracy for markets and competition, dictatorship for democracy. West Germans grumbled about the laziness and inefficiency of their ethnic siblings and about the costs of updating and cleaning up East German industry. The Kohl government felt it necessary to reaffirm its loyalty to European integration in no uncertain terms, to symbolize its leadership in that process by joining France in demanding that the EU become the military and foreign policy forum of Western Europe as it completes the economic and monetary union. In short, it seems as if the reunified Germany is not really a rationalized nation-state any longer, but a state already committed to achieving a new rationalization in a larger European structure. What would account for the shift away from nation-statehood, if indeed it is occurring?

The conviction that Germany's wealth and economic security are inseparable from the ability to export remains unshaken. Therefore, industry and the trade unions share the bureaucracy's implacable commitment to free trade and the free movement of capital, globally as well as on the European continent. Since, however, German influence over global economic policy encounters that of Japan—with which it often clashes—as well as the United States, with which it is not always in complete agreement, free movement of all factors of production within Europe offers a more attainable objective. German industrialists have been enthusiastic promoters of interfirm cooperation under the direction of the EU Commission for research and development efforts in the fields of computers, telecommunications, electronics, and new materials, as well as advocates of the creation of completely free internal markets for the EU Fifteen. German trade unions, similarly motivated and committed, because of codetermination procedures, to industry programs, have also identified with European integration without necessarily being committed to European federalist ideologies or persuaded by their French and Benelux colleagues. They must seek to compensate at the level of the EU for the loss, after 1992, of economic power they formerly enjoyed by virtue of German law alone. Economic and institutional commitments have induced all major German economic actors to anchor their fortune in a united Europe rather than a sovereign Germany. They have so far been even willing to subsidize the farmers of some other EC countries in exchange for having a nearby market for manufactured goods that accounts for over 20 percent of GNP.

It is generally recognized in Germany that the creation of a single economic sovereignty in the EU cannot be restricted to economics. The three governing parties favor the creation of federal or confederal EU institutions, collective decision making that allows for parliamentary participation and denies a veto power to individual governments. In addition, the SPD backs the unions in calling for a very strong EC charter of social rights, the condition that would allow the unions to

Europeanize German-style codetermination and corporatist decision making. When it comes to defense policy, however, matters get more divisive. The CDU is willing to have the EU evolve into a defense community and to use German troops for multilateral peacekeeping while a slow process of multilateral arms control continues. The SPD, however, wishes to accelerate disarmament, and it opposes using German troops outside Europe. The SPD agrees with the CDU in upgrading a unified European deterrent force in preference to complete reliance on the American presence.

The Greens, of course, oppose all of this. They lack interest in Europe as a focus of German identity, hesitating between a global vision of humanity and a special vision of a utopian Germany that would become the light of the world. They clearly reject any upgrading of the EU into a military entity because they cling to their belief in nonviolent resistance as the only legitimate form of self-defense. For the majority, however, the unwillingness to mount a purely national defense against an enemy who is less and less real acts as an additional incentive to seek security in a larger European union, whose need for high-technology arms would fit nicely into Germany's economic calculations in any case.

German popular identification with European integration is permissive, not wildly committed. In 1990, 80 percent favored European unification; 62 percent thought the EU was a good thing; 53 percent thought Germany had benefited from membership; 48 percent said they would regret the disintegration of the Community while an equally large number professed to be indifferent. When asked which policy areas should be handled jointly by the European countries under EU auspices, the results show a clear decrease in interest (see table 3). One poll asked whether people would sacrifice membership in NATO and/or the EU for reunification; West Germans answered as follows: 11 percent would forgo NATO and the EU, 15 percent NATO but not the EU, and 5 percent the EU but not NATO. But before unification only 28 percent wanted to give the EU a mandate for defense policy, while 66 percent were in favor of a strong European social charter. These attitudes are sufficiently stable and general, if shallow, to allow far more solidly committed policy elites to pursue active integrationist measures.

Elite support for European integration has been unswerving, though based on both instrumental motives and socially learned behavior. Since unification the instrumental side of the support has probably grown in importance. German elites advocate the expansion of the EU by giving the Brussels organs additional powers, especially over monetary policy, *and* by expanding the membership to include newly democratic eastern Europe. But they hedge their support by insisting that the Bundesbank continue its high-interest policy and extend it to the projected European monetary union, and that German subsidization of the EU budget be curtailed.

On the other hand, German elites have clearly learned that most major policy problems are not amenable to national solutions, that the national political playing field does not permit the construction of political bargains that will adequately deal simultaneously with economic, environmental, and military security. Perhaps equally important, they have learned that they can play a more important and autonomous role in foreign policy after reunification only if they "sanitize" their initiatives by packaging them as European multilateralism. Only thus can they reassure their foreign allies as well as Germans still reluctant to play an active global role.

TABLE 3. Preference for EC/EU rather than National Decision Making in Germany, 1991–94

"Some people believe that certain areas of policy should be decided by the [NATIONAL] government, while other areas of policy should be decided jointly within the European Community/European Union. Which of the following areas of policy do you think should be decided by the [NATIONAL] government, and which should be decided jointly within the European Community/European Union?"

	I	II	III	IV	V	VI	VII	VIII	IX	X	XI
1991	—	—	—	78	54	73	69	54	—	37	43
1992	66	47	—	72	47	70	75	57	54	37	54
1993	72[a]	52	71	77	50	66	72	63	55	41	55
1994	54	42	—	71	45	64	68	62	46	32	50

Source: For 1991: *Eurobarometer,* no. 35 (June 1991), table 19, p. A21; for 1992: *Eurobarometer,* no. 38 (Dec. 1992), table 27, pp. A32–33; for 1993: *Eurobarometer,* no. 39 (June 1993), table 24, pp. A26–7, except "immigration," "unemployment," and "poverty" from table 27, p. A29; for 1994: *Eurobarometer,* no. 41 (July 1994), table 22, pp. A34–35.

Note: I to XI refer to the following policy areas: I, "immigration policy"; II, "dealing with unemployment"; III, "fight against poverty"; IV, "protection of the environment"; V, "currency"; VI, "scientific and tech[nological] research"; VII, "foreign policy towards non-EC/EU countries"; VIII, "defense"; IX, "industrial policy"; X, "education"; and XI, "rates of Value Added Tax."

[a]This figure represents the percentage of respondents who answered "for" on the following question: "Irrespective of other details of the Maastricht Treaty, what is your opinion on each of the following proposals? Please tell me for each proposal, whether you are for it or against it . . . The governments of EC Member States should work towards common rules in matters of political asylum, refugees and immigration."

Liberal Germany Faces the World: Uncertainties

The liberal consensus in Germany was clearly shaken by the travail of reunification. Violence against non-Western immigrants reached alarming levels, especially in east Germany. There is a revival of right-wing extremism that stresses Nazi racial themes. This expression of an integral nationalism is thematically inchoate because it is found largely among lower-class unemployed youth, again disproportionately from deindustrializing areas of east Germany. After the government made special aid programs available, anti–immigrant violence subsided. The racist-integralist party, the Republikaner, is more ideologically circumspect and remains electorally marginal, perhaps because of the institutional barrier posed by the 5 percent rule.

Disaffection from liberal nationalism is expressed more effectively in the vote for the former GDR Communist Party, now reborn as the PDS. In the federal election of 1994 it gathered 4.4 percent of the national vote, but nearly 20 percent of the ex-GDR vote. Its supporters feel that life under the old regime was not so bad after all, that they miss its policies of guaranteed employment and cheap housing. Disproportionately they distrust democratic institutions, especially parliamentarism. They are recruited from the ranks of students, former officeholders, former supporters of Neues Forum, pacifists, and workers who lost out as a result of the introduction of markets.

We do not know whether this form of alienation from liberalism is going to flourish in the future. We do know, however, that pro-European cosmopolitanism — and its concomitant, the weakening of liberalism focused on national identity — is being questioned in postreunification Germany, though it has not been displaced. Its continued hold on policy, however, will surely depend on the particular conception of German identity that will eventually triumph, a point we take up later. At the present, the cosmopolitan consensus is challenged by left-wing pacifism and by a conservative "revival of German national interest" school of thought.

Even before 1990, *the pacifist left wing of the SPD and the Greens considered any use of military force, especially nuclear weapons, incompatible with German identity.* These groups were not afraid of possible Soviet aggression, considering the Soviets to be a status quo power fearful of a nuclear Western alliance. This group spearheaded the pacifist opposition to the deployment of nuclear weapons on German soil and sought to downplay any military role for the FRG, any overly close involvement with Western Europe that meant the practical abandonment of additional ties with the GDR. The Greens, however, are not only pacifists who favor the FRG's leaving NATO and disbanding the Bundeswehr, but also active neutralists. They favored the demilitarization and neutralization of both the Germanys before 1989 in order to remove the military argument against unification. The very appeal of the Greens' argument, of course, had the effect of drawing voters who previously had identified with the pacifist wing of the SPD. The Greens' neutralism and advocacy of unilateral disarmament were a direct result of their concern for the environment; they argue, not unreasonably, that Germany's ecology is more vulnerable to a European nuclear war than anyone else's, that humane ends cannot be attained by using inhumane means. For them, not the unity of the wealthy capitalist states ought to be the main goal of German foreign policy, but service to the poor Third and Fourth World countries.

Conservatives are concerned that there is no adequately articulated German national interest because of the a priori commitment to multilateral institutions as forums for thinking about German foreign and defense policy. They complain that there is no German strategic thinking. They wish to emulate the American practice of defense analysis carried out by civilian defense intellectuals. They regret that one of Helmut Kohl's advisers could argue that "the *Staatsräson* of a united Germany is its integration in Europe."[23] German defense officials anticipate that there will be more ethnic conflict in southeast Europe. They worry that Germany might have to start worrying about retaining access to strategic raw materials and, as in the Gulf War, rely too much on allies whose interests might not exactly match Germany's. Some think that the CDU/SPD policy has been entirely too Eurocentric.

Though the core framework of the conservative defense thinkers remains participation in multilateral institutions, they worry about the possibility that the allies lack a consensus for a common decision or will take too long to arrive at one. Germany, therefore, ought to be able to make its own military moves autonomously. Toward that end, the Defense Ministry now favors small, mobile, rapid deployment forces that may operate as part of a NATO or a United Nations force, or they may not. In short, critics of the past policy of self-abnegation foresee a German diplomatic and military role similar to the one played by Britain and France in the context of multilateral forums.

Mainstream thinking in the SPD favors multilateralism above all. The party supports rapid progress toward full European federation. Its hesitating support for German military participation outside the traditional NATO area is contingent on German immersion in multilateral forces. Mainstream thinking in the CDU is only marginally less committed to European federation and somewhat more willing to mount German military might even if not all foreign countries approve.

The essence of the mainstream view was articulated by Hans-Dietrich Genscher, for two decades foreign minister, a major architect of the Maastricht treaties and of German reunification. But that view is now being questioned even in the CDU and FDP as insufficiently mindful of Germany's true national interests. Genscher considered power politics obsolete, the use of military force a thing of the integral nationalist past. Liberal Germany's special role was to demonstrate to the world what can be accomplished with diplomatic skill and economic prowess alone. But the exercise of this role demanded that Germany assert herself more than she had before reunification, but assert herself *only* in the context of multilateral enmeshment. Once such a role is asserted successfully, Germany would be obligated to contribute more heavily than in the past to collective operations. Checkbook diplomacy would not suffice.

The commitment to multilateralism still dominates as the primary rule of German engagement in the world. If that painfully learned lesson continues to prevail, German liberal nationalism will continue to blend into an anational cosmopolitanism, opposed only by the alienated but impotent fringes on left and right. Cosmopolitanism, whether focused on Europe or on the world as a whole, is the attitude of the elites. The mass public tolerates cosmopolitanism without strongly identifying with it. But it might come to oppose cosmopolitanism if that stance comes to be identified with economic or strategic failure, with personal and emotional suffering. Hence, the still competing conceptions of the most desirable form of German identity are likely to dictate who will feel comfortable with a squishy cosmopolitanism and who will opt for an assertive national self.

Mastering the Past or Fashioning a Usable Past?

In 1986, before anyone took seriously the possibility of a peaceful reunification of the two German states, there erupted among German intellectuals the "Historians' Fight." It was triggered by the argument, supported by then Chancellor Kohl and many in the CDU, that the FRG ought to be seen as a fully developed nation-state with its own national character, which had nothing to be ashamed of and ought to take its place among the nations as a proud and self-confident member. Crucial in this argument, of course, was the contention that the crimes of Nazism were exaggerated and ought not be allowed to burden the present generation of West Germans. Modern German identity ought to be "normalized" by the recognition that Nazism was no worse than Stalinist communism, against which it was a legitimate defense. The German people, to survive as a distinct people, must be given a "usable past."

Left-wing opponents of the "conservative" historians countered that normalization implied going back on the moral benefits of liberal cosmopolitanism. Making up a "usable past" is to master the past by papering it over. The Left wanted no new self-righteous nationalism in Germany, even if its ideas were derived from the west European Enlightenment and even if Nazism was to be seen as an aberration (as Kohl repeatedly suggested). In short, the essence of postwar German learning to be civilized implies the recognition that Germany remains tainted by the Nazi legacy. A usable past is an unacceptably nationalistic one. To master the past means to live forever with the knowledge of a great crime.

The argument remains unresolved, though several planned symbolic acts endorsing the conservative view of the matter were not carried out. What is the evidence offered by German public opinion as to which view is the more popular? If the conservatives are tapping a hitherto hidden vein of opinion, unified Germany may move in the direction of a strong, reborn sense of national identity, though probably still liberal. It would then provide support for the reassertion of a distinct national interest in Germany's relations with its neighbors and with the world. If not, the legacy of Hans-Dietrich Genscher will continue to prevail in foreign policy, and the anational cosmopolitanism of most German elites will still dominate public life.

Many in the CDU favor the redefinition of a German identity that buries the memory of the Nazi interlude altogether because, they say, it should not burden generations of Germans innocent of any part in it. Other measures also suggest support for this view. German law governing the acquisition of citizenship strongly favors the *jus sanguinis:* descent, irrespective of domicile, determines citizenship. Naturalization is very difficult. Recent changes in the law allowing the German-born children of immigrants to become German citizens were regarded with some suspicion by the Right. The formerly generous right to asylum was sharply curtailed. Foreigners residing in Germany should not be allowed to vote in local elections. On the other hand, ethnic Germans who had lived in eastern Europe and the Balkans for centuries were greeted as citizens when they emigrated to Germany in large numbers during the 1980s.

Upgrading the position of the military in German life is seen as a direct support for the rebirth of national identity. Germans killed in World War II are to be honored, as are surviving veterans, because Germany ought to be seen as much a victim of the war as its perpetrator.

The Bundeswehr ought to be more visible, more honored, frequently on display. Kohl lobbied hard to have German units included in the events celebrating the fiftieth anniversary of the Normandy landings and of the end of the European war. Active participation of German forces in multilateral "out of NATO area" operations is part of this assertion of identity. Half of Germans surveyed support such a policy, but half consider it a violation of human rights. In 1993, a poll of young people revealed that 91 percent would have *no* sympathy for violent riots over the issue of granting asylum to foreigners.[24]

Yet the evidence suggesting the persistence of an anational mood is there as well. East Germans tend to oppose any kind of adventurous foreign or defense policy; moreover, they remain very confused and conflicted about their own history after being told that the Nazi and Marxist versions were false. In 1992, when asked "Are you proud to be German?" 69 percent of west Germans answered in the affirmative, but 71 percent of east Germans said yes. In 1993, of a sample of Germans aged between 14 and 27, 47 percent of west Germans professed themselves proud of being German, whereas 68 percent thought so in the east. In 1991 only 47 percent in the west and 45 percent in the east reported that they feel close to the country (the average for the EU being 53 percent). Among the young, only 3 percent of west Germans and 17 percent in the east said they could not imagine having a foreign friend.

It even seems as if east and west do not consider themselves part of the same nation. In 1990 almost 60 percent of east Germans felt that the two Germanys share the same culture, but only 33 percent of west Germans felt that way! By 1992, only 35 percent of east Germans felt they were more all-German than East German. A year later, only 22 percent of west Germans and 11 percent of easterners felt "together as Germans"; huge majorities in each section of the country thought they were divided by large opposing interests. Indeed they were: 65 percent of west Germans were not eager to pay for upgrading living standards in the east; 59 percent were unwilling to curtail their own living standards to raise that of the east. Western contempt for the perceived laziness, helplessness, and lack of skills of easterners is pervasive.

Upgrading Germany's military role continues to arouse a great deal of opposition. The Greens espoused an extreme position on this point: they want to get rid of the German state altogether by splitting Germany into self-governing regions. European peace in general is to be sought by radical decentralization of state power. Most people, according to opinion surveys, continue to think of Germany as a nonmilitary country even if they want Germany to take a more active world role. Most people see such a role as being best played by fostering arms control and humanitarian and development aid in the Third World. Many Germans see world peace and global prosperity not in terms of national, but rather as universal rights, the rights of the world community. Such a commitment, then, leads easily away from thinking in terms of unique national interests — as Genscher had urged — to the recognition that there are few solutions Germans can contrive alone to solve even German problems.

Learning to Transcend the Nation-State?

When West Germans were queried in 1989 about what characteristics all Germans share, 91 percent mentioned language, the most obvious and least emotionally charged response, and 68 percent mentioned history; national identity and way of life elicited a positive response from 38 percent and 22 percent respectively. Yet 55 percent say they never think of themselves as Europeans in addition to being German. These sentiments do not bespeak a strong sense of either national or European identity. The continued insistence on safeguarding a hard-won prosperity and technological leadership suggests an underlying sense of fear that catastrophe might still be in store for Germany. The reluctance to give up NATO and the insistence on finding a new unity among all Europeans suggest a lingering sense of physical insecurity as well. Have Germans learned a collective lesson, as compared to 1870, 1919, or 1933?

Germans have learned two lessons, almost at the same time, about their national identity: to trust each other and to trust their neighbors. The crimes and catastrophes of the Nazi era taught them the costs of integral nationalism; their dependence on American help in regaining economic security linked to active resocialization gave support to the attractiveness of liberal nationalism. The need to repudiate wholly a criminal past delegitimated integralism and lingering syncretist sentiments, while defeat in 1918 had not delegitimated the monarchy. A polity successfully reorganized under the auspices of liberal nationalism, albeit partly imposed, then prospered and regained its dignity in close cooperation with the former victims of Nazi imperialism, thus further legitimating liberal nationalism as practiced in Western Europe. Thus Germans learned, at one and the same time, to trust each other within a single national myth *and* to rely on their neighbors by engaging in a process of successful collective decision making.

The same paradox that characterized the recent history of France also appears in the German case: just as a previously deeply divided polity achieves integration under a commonly accepted set of rules and principles, just as it is rationalized under liberal auspices, its citizens find it necessary to safeguard their newly found coherence and prosperity by transferring power to regional institutions. Safeguarding successful national integration when achieved under conditions of high industrialism and democracy requires augmentation with a new focus in a larger identity. Confidence in one's power to solve all problems within the confines of a sovereign nation is questioned when one lives with rapid and unpredictable technological change, when one fears technology while hoping for unending progress, when great prosperity is mixed with apprehension that all might end in unemployment and inflation. We have no reason to think a European regional identity is emerging in the minds of Germans, but we have ample reason to conclude that Germany is no longer the focus of many expectations, no longer the core of most people's unthinking loyalty. To seek a more effective forum for satisfying one's perceived needs is to learn.

NOTES

I gratefully acknowledge the research assistance and acute criticism of Michael Gorges and Karen Adelberger. Peter Katzenstein and John Leslie read the manuscript and saved me from making many mistakes.

1. German intellectuals, in general, despised Prussian absolutism prior to 1806. The Enlightenment triggered an interest in patriotism (which was identified with individual liberty) and natural rights but only very rarely a specifically German sense of political identity. Among the exceptions was Klopstock, who revived and popularized the "Hermann der Cherusker" myth of German primordialism. On the other hand, Herder's primordial arguments about language and national genius were not used by him to justify German nationhood, though they were so used by Fichte a little later.

2. All-German liberalism, before 1867, was represented by the Nationalverein, the Prussian component of which was the Progressive Party. The Nationalverein always stood for the federal parliamentary constitution opposed by Bismarck. It also stood for keeping the working class and its unions out of politics, and for an assertive German foreign policy. The Nationalverein never gained much strength south of the Main. The confused character of German national symbolism is described by George L. Mosse, *The Nationalization of the Masses* (New York: Howard Fertig, 1975).

3. All statistics dealing with social mobilization and public expenditures in this chapter come from Wolfgang Zapf and Peter Flora, "Differences in Paths of Development," in S. N. Eisenstadt and Stein Rokkan, eds., *Building States and Nations* (Beverly Hills: Sage, 1973), 1:190, 193–94; and from Peter Flora, ed., *State, Economy, and Society in Western Europe, 1815–1975* (Chicago: St. James Press, 1983).

4. Geoffrey Eley, *From Unification to Nazism* (Boston: Allen & Unwin, 1986), 69.

5. The Social Democrats, as the repressive legislation went into effect, polled just over 300,000 votes in the Reichstag elections of 1881; in 1890, just before the legislation was repealed, they polled 1,427,000 and, with 19.7 percent of the vote, became the largest party in parliament. Before 1890 the unions were weak, but thereafter they became a major interest group and drew away from the Social Democratic Party. The Socialists' Erfurt Program (1891), though orthodox-Marxist in content and committed to the complete overthrow of bourgeois society, nevertheless opted for parliamentary-electoral tactics to achieve this aim.

6. Elisabeth Fehrenbach, *Wandlungen des deutschen Kaisergedankens, 1871–1918* (Munich-Vienna: R. Oldenbourg), 91. Efforts were made to represent this view of the monarchy in the school curriculum, in the creation of a monumental architecture, and in singling out Richard Wagner's music as emblematic of German culture. The Kaiser's special military role was also an important rationalizing symbol. Wilhelm II was referred to as Oberster Kriegsherr and as the special patron of the Imperial Navy being created in the decade preceding World War I.

7. Eley, *From Unification,* 76.

8. Roger Chickering, *We Men Who Feel Most German* (Boston: Allen & Unwin, 1984), 79.

9. Gerald Feldman, "German Interest Group Alliances in War and Inflation," in Suzanne Berger, ed., *Organizing Interests in Western Europe* (New York: Cambridge University Press, 1981), 164.

10. Thomas Childers, *The Nazi Voter* (Chapel Hill: University of North Carolina Press, 1983), 178.

11. Cited in Gregory Luebbert, *Liberalism, Fascism, and Social Democracy* (New York: Oxford University Press, 1991), 275.

12. Quoted in Robert E. Herzstein, *When Nazi Dreams Come True* (London: Sphere Books, 1982), 36.

13. Henry L. Mason, "Implementing the Final Solution: The Ordinary Regulating of the Extraordinary," *World Politics* (July 1988): 549, paraphrasing Saul Friedländer. Emphasis in original.

14. David P. Conradt, *The German Polity* (New York: Longman, 1989), 54–55.

15. Policy-making for civilian nuclear energy illustrates the complication. In 1973 the FRG committed itself to an ambitious program of reactor construction with the full support of all relevant trade unions and industry associations as well as of the CDU/CSU; the SPD and FDP were internally divided, though their leaders pushed the program. The tremendous public opposition sparked the formation of the Greens and of antinuclear groups, but it was all in vain until the Chernobyl disaster reignited the opposition. Thereafter the SPD wanted to stop the program, and the CDU/CSU split over the issue, leading to enormous uncertainties as *Land* and federal governments repeatedly clashed over the issuing of operating licenses, after many billions had been spent on the equipment. As of 1995, none of the facilities planned in 1973 had come on line.

16. Peter A. Gourevitch, *Politics in Hard Times* (Ithaca: Cornell University Press, 1986), 171.

17. I use the term *corporatism* more loosely than most to denote a mode of democratic governance in which many important decisions are made only after extensive formal consultations among interest groups represented in organs established by law. Many commentators favor more restricted definitions. Some want to confine the term to voluntary decision making in the industrial economy, to collective bargaining in which the state plays a pivotal role. Others take this restricted definition but limit it further to situations in which the bargaining takes place between the state and the national peak associations of labor and industry, which leads to binding decisions for the entire economy. This is sometimes called "strong corporatism," as formerly practiced in Sweden and Austria. Somewhat weaker versions prevailed in Norway, Denmark, and Switzerland. Germany's pattern, for the purist, is very weak corporatism. See Kathleen Thelen, "Beyond Corporatism," *Comparative Politics* (October 1994): 107–24.

18. Some commentators dispute that the social market economy performed well in the 1980s and after. They argue that it was unable to provide for full employment for these reasons. Fiscal and monetary policies (the latter not under the control of the government) were not synchronized. The unions felt that they were cheated because their wage restraint was not matched by low profits. Unemployment increased despite the commitment to shorten the workweek. The Bundesbank was unable to banish all inflationary pressures. Moreover, administrative cohesiveness was undermined by the fact that the necessary close coordination between federal and *Land* policies was often lacking because of long delays in decision making. See Fritz Scharpf, *Crisis and Choice in European Social Democracies* (Ithaca: Cornell University Press, 1987).

19. Not all commentators agree with this evaluation. Wolfgang Streeck fears that the strain of unification may undermine the ability of the system to perform well. He also fears that increasing globalization of production may undermine the social insurance and codetermination systems. See Wolfgang Streeck, "German Capitalism: Does It Exist? Can It Survive?" in Colin Crouch and Wolfgang Streeck, eds., *Modern Capitalism or Modern Capitalisms?* (London: Francis Pinter, 1995), 14–15. Claus Offe thinks that the shrinking actuarial base of the insurance funds threatens the future of all social insurance. The core of the German system of social insurance is groups of insured workers; the shrinking industrial workforce results in a much larger pool of uninsured people.

20. Streeck, "German Capitalism," 6.

21. Between 1963 and 1989—the effective end of communist rule in the GDR—nearly 34,000 political prisoners were "bought free," more than 2,000 children reunited with their parents in the West, and more than 250,000 family reunifications arranged by the Bonn government. A total of DM 3.5 billion was paid to Pankow for these purposes. A single "freedom purchase," after 1977, cost DM 95,847. In addition, DM 2.4 billion was invested by the Bonn government in the GDR. Almost 1 billion in commercial credit was also provided. See

Timothy Garton Ash, *In Europe's Name* (New York: Random House, 1993), 146, 658–59, 154–55, 514.

22. This section is heavily indebted to the work of Susan Siena.

23. Quoted in Hans-Peter Schwarz, "Germany's National and European Interests," *Daedalus* (spring 1994): 84.

24. All public opinion figures in this section come from one of these sources: Elisabeth Noelle-Neumann and Renate Köcher, eds., *Allensbacher Jahrbuch der Demoskopie, 1984–1992,* vol. 9 (Munich: K. G. Sauer, 1993); Heinrich August Winkler, "Rebuilding of a Nation," *Daedalus* (winter 1994): 107–27; *Eurobarometer,* no. 36 (December 1991), table 63.

The Federal Republic as a Nation-State

Peter Krüger

During the deliberations of the West German Parliamentary Council (1 September 1948 to 23 May 1949), an unusual though fascinating process took place. There was initial uncertainty about what the delegates were called upon to do, whether they were to work out a makeshift organization of government in West Germany, or whether they should try to achieve more and to be responsive to the challenge and chance of a new constitutional start after the breakdown of the first German republic, after the Germans had gambled away their first republic and risked their existence in the disaster of National Socialism. Urged by the military governors of the three western zones to prepare a constitution and a West German state within the orbit of these zones and in accordance with the principles of democracy, human and civil rights, and federalism and, moreover, to make it such that it might be extended to Germany as a whole, the minister presidents of the German *Länder* had decided to restrict the task of the Parliamentary Council to the elaboration of a provisional order.[1] They were anxious not to be accused of having deepened the rift in Germany. However, in spite of their different political starting points, interests, and personal views, and in the course of their hard, even arduous work on the details of a new order, the delegates ended up by creating a comprehensive and consistent constitution, a framework for democracy and nation-building in conformity with Western patterns.

In a situation that demanded fundamental decisions, the Parliamentary Council (*Parlamentarischer Rat*) and its achievements became the focus of all constitutional thinking and political preconditions preceding the foundation of the Federal Republic, as well as the pivot of all later efforts to develop and complete a German nation-state based on the principles of liberty, representative democracy, pluralism, and national self-determination, which was interpreted as political self-determination and the participation of all citizens in major political processes from the local to the federal level. What I would like to show here is the predominance of this Western political concept of a liberal nation-state as a framework for an open society in West Germany and that, in this sense, the Federal Republic was a nation-state from its origins and did not adhere to the traditional German concept of a nation-state based on language, culture, ethnicity, or even race.[2] Moreover, the guidelines of this book, the approach whereby postwar German transformation is to be explained in terms of the influence of institutions, culture, and international constraints, will here be linked to the exceptional situation of Germany and the particular driving forces in her development after 1945, since these greatly influenced an unusual course of reconstruction and change. Therefore, the Parliamentary Council requires attention as a turning point in the history of the German nation and nation-state, as does the *Grundgesetz* as a new framework and pivot of a modern national order and community. The Federal Republic as a nation-state started its career in 1949 and not in 1989.

I. Representative Democracy and Liberty before Nation

It is well known that the Allied powers, and in particular the government of the United States, vigorously pursued the democratization and decentralization of a "highly centralized dictatorship," the demolition of the coercive system of an extreme nationalism.[3] The threatening national power of Germany and its presumptuous ideology of German national and racial superiority had to be broken. In spring 1945, the U.S. administration and military government took the lead and provided guidelines, undisputed in principle by the British and French authorities notwithstanding their temporary disagreement about German affairs: democracy, decentralization, and individual freedom from the bottom up. Therefore, "federalism and local self-government should be encouraged to the maximum in order to destroy the military potential of Germany and promote democracy,"[4] although it was obvious that some central organization was needed. However, it was to become decidedly federal in character, and the constituent units of the envisaged federation were to be states. This principle, already employed as a guideline for the new *Länder* constitutions,[5] became one of the cardinal points in the directives handed over to the German minister presidents on 1 July 1948, when they were requested to prepare a constitution as the basis of a West German state. The other essentials were a democratic structure and guarantees of individual rights and liberties, the backbone of political liberty, freedom of opinion, and political opposition. The institution to achieve this was representative democracy as opposed to direct, basic, or democracy by council, overstrained for propagandistic reasons and determined to conceal dictatorship in the later GDR.[6] Yet even the suggestion that the creation of a federal form of government would ultimately be the most appropriate means of restoring German unity could not allay the justified fears of the German minister presidents that they would be forced to relinquish their claim to the reconstruction of a German nation-state. Therefore, from the first decisions and steps toward building a West German state, the fate of the German nation and nation-state loomed large, both in the subsequent negotiations and in the deliberations of the Parliamentary Council, albeit at times only as a kind of unspoken assumption. Basically, this complicated process was an act of determined delimitation from the Soviet zone, or GDR, from the Eastern bloc and system, a delimitation of principal importance for nation-building in the structural East-West conflict.

However strongly considerations of national unity influenced the political debate in West Germany, the starting point of postwar politics in the western zones of occupation was democratization on the level of local, municipal, and regional agencies and their autonomy as well as the removal of all traces of National Socialism. The reconstruction of national forms of government was explicitly postponed. This meant that the classical symbiosis of democratic foundation and nation-building was broken up under exceptional and extraordinary circumstances: the occupation of Germany by the Allied armies, the demolition of all government authority, the efforts to purge Germany of all traces of National Socialism (as well as of exaggerated nationalism in general) down to the local level and then to reestablish democratic administrative and political structures from below. This all was accentuated by the growing alienation between the Soviet Union and her former Western allies in the early stages of the Cold War, resulting in the partition of Germany and Europe. This absolutely unusual situation rendered possible a process that started with democracy and added the nation-state later. In this case, it is difficult to assess whether democracy, mainly determined by democratic, individual self-determination and political participation and requiring a delimitable area and political community, can be achieved at all or in the long run without nation-building. For the next step, the foundation of the Federal Republic, followed quite fast and was at the same time not unequivocal because of the inevitable formation of a West German constituent state only. But the rapid progress from the foundation of democracy in West Germany to a West German state may, after all, provide some evidence of the indispensable nation-state if the complicated development is explained carefully. In any case, Karl Dietrich Bracher's much quoted characterization of the Federal Republic as a postnational democracy[7] may well be reversed: in the beginning she represented the strange phenomenon of a pre-national democracy resulting from a pronounced contrast with an essential part of Germany's traditional political culture: ethnic and cultural nationalism. Imperative for this about-face was the terrible experience of the National Socialist era as well as the desire to make a new start with new institutions in the double sense of the word: a new set of norms and rules as well as a new organizational framework for German society. Moreover, there was pressure from outside, with limited options allowed the Germans by the occupying powers. Paramount among these factors were the efforts to achieve a new institutional start, yet the other factors provided the indispensable basis and framework. The most salutary effects, however, resulted from the unique chance to develop new institutions within a protected sphere, an oasis in a turbulent era. The Western occupying powers provided guidelines but renounced interference, or restricted it to a minimum, in the process of constitution-making both in the *Länder* and in the Parliamentary Council.[8] They allowed West Germany to proceed step by step starting with democratization at the lowest, the local, level instead of starting with insoluble central issues and thus running the risk of being distracted by a reemerging quarrel about national issues: protection of a more thorough domestic development as well as protection and security against any danger from abroad.

II. The Parliamentary Council as a National Constituent Assembly

Security, dependence on the decision of the Western powers — though this dependence had always been mutual, in an asymmetrical sense, given the requirement of a constructive cooperation of the Germans — and, in addition, the Marshall Plan as the only real prospects of future economic recovery and political restoration on equal terms: all these fundamental conditions and endeavors could only be successfully integrated into a coherent policy — of this the political majority in West Germany was convinced — by consolidating West Germany through the establishment, for the time being, of a West German state and by integrating it into some West European and transatlantic system. To be sure, this concept was developed only gradually, and it was highly disputed because of the danger of deepening the rift between East and West Germany and because of the lack of freedom of decision in Germany. This was the well-known struggle over priorities faced with the Cold

War: consolidation of the western part of Germany within a Western network or concentration on the reconstruction of Germany as a whole and making this the prerequisite for any further decision. The complicated endeavors and processes of coming to terms with this difficult situation have been thoroughly investigated.[9] The formative power of these debates for the foundation of a West German society, polity, and self-image was tremendous. When West Germany's crucial hour came in the guise of the Frankfurt documents of 1 July 1948, requesting the construction of a West German state, the compromise over an inconclusive debate in the western zones was to work out a provisional organization of West German government and administration as a kind of emergency measure. There was general agreement, strongly advocated by the Social Democrats, that the statute to be elaborated should by no means be a constitution, and the delegates assembled to prepare such an organizational statute should by no means be a national constituent assembly.[10] But exactly this was the outcome. The Parliamentary Council proved to be a national constituent assembly, and what it produced was a fully fledged constitution and the foundation of a Western-type nation-state.

This dramatic change did not occur suddenly or smoothly. It ensued from protracted debates among the delegates in the key committees of the Parliamentary Council, debates that originated in an intensive grappling with the manifold and complicated concrete problems of building a new order.[11] It was essential not only to find appropriate and coherent solutions in order to enable a modernizing society to find its way, but, although in keeping with tradition, especially of the first German republic, to eliminate the failures and mistakes of past constitutions and abortive sociocultural values, to deal indirectly but convincingly with National Socialism in concentrating all efforts on restoring human dignity, rights, and liberties as the core of the future constitutional order, and to reconcile it with the German tradition of law, which could not be altered completely.

The deliberations of the Parliamentary Council at large provide ample opportunities to study this deep change, but concentrating on the central committee and the committee on principal questions is especially illuminating.[12] Three substantial features of the *Grundgesetz* were emphasized during the debates: (1) its character as a fully valid constitution; (2) its cardinal point in guaranteeing self-determination, human and civil rights, adaptable political institutions, and the sovereignty of the people as a new political basis of the German nation; and finally, (3) the foundation of a Western-type liberal nation-state.

1. Whereas Carlo Schmid (SPD), a leading advocate of the concept of a provisional order, tried to apply a kind of delaying policy (without

being able to maintain it fully in view of the intellectual challenge and opportunity of framing a new order), another leading delegate, Theodor Heuss, proclaimed at the beginning of the second reading of the *Grundgesetz:* "We have to create a state order (*Staatsordnung*) for Germany, even though, for the time being, only for the western part."[13] Quite telling was the elaboration of the preamble; the majority of the committee on principal questions soon adopted the view that the German people, "by virtue of its constituent power,"[14] was participating in the Parliamentary Council. This was a classical formulation of democratic nation-building, even if such power was restricted to those who were able to express their free will. The mandatory regulation to complete German unity, strengthened by the Federal Constitutional Court (*Bundesverfassungsgericht*) in 1973,[15] was, therefore, by no means an isolated issue, a clause that might be eliminated from the *Grundgesetz*. It belonged to the essentials, the fundamental principles of the *Grundgesetz* as a whole — not simply because of the weight of reunification but because of the sovereignty of the people, the basis of the constitution. As long as part of this people had no chance to express its will, this clause could not be abandoned. A further important feature of a constitution is the comprehensive treatment of foreign relations power (*auswärtige Gewalt*). Here, again, was one of those cardinal points that evoked protest from Carlo Schmid, whose concept of a limited organizational statute was dismantled piece by piece.[16] And the most important factor within a new and durable constitutional order was the creation of a Federal Constitutional Court with impressive and, later on, even extended competences, another break with German tradition.[17] The influence of this Court on the development of the Federal Republic as a nation-state was outstanding. The prohibition of any alterations to the essential parts of the *Grundgesetz* (Article 79 plus Article 19 [2]) excluded any idea of a provisional order, as did the following clause: The *Grundgesetz* "shall be put into force for other parts of Germany on their accession" (Article 23 [2] in its original version),[18] notwithstanding the final and optional clause (Article 146), opening the possibility of a totally new constitution-making process if desired by the whole German people. A total revision of the *Grundgesetz* was unlawful in all other cases.

2. In pronounced contrast to the denial that there was a virtual constitution, the claim to represent Germany, to work for a national constitution, and to reject the idea of any provisional nature prevailed. Soon the Frankfurt documents were seen as merely having launched the constitution-making process. At all events, the right and the legitimation of the Parliamentary Council to frame a new order in free decisions and in pursuit of the right of self-determination of the whole German nation

were stressed, thus confirming the thesis that the German state had never ceased to exist.[19] Of particular interest are some subtle remarks of Ludwig Bergsträsser (SPD) on the importance of the sovereignty of the people in reestablishing a German nation-state and warding off the dominant and traditional claim of the several German states and their executives to be responsible for its amalgamation. He refuted the idea that the *Länder* restored the national community—they only set it working again, and the German people acted as a self-determinant body in and through the *Länder* (a fact sometimes overlooked today).[20] Even the parties gained full acceptance as national parties, as an integral part of the national political community, only after 1948, when they overcame a traditional aversion to parties as being antinational, particularistic, and addicted to the representation of narrow group interests.

Schmid himself—and the Social Democrats, particularly their chairman, Kurt Schumacher[21]—substantiated the call for German political integration and independence as a prerequisite of the national constituent power by stressing the difference between exaggerated nationalism and democratic nationalism: democracy depended on the will of the people to maintain self-preservation and self-esteem, and democracy was seen as "the political form in which the people expresses" this will. Self-esteem was the basis of democracy, and the people should be informed of the fact that this was no traditional nationalism that might return and that it could only be headed off successfully by this democratic national consciousness.[22] After the *Grundgesetz* had been promulgated, Schumacher and his party were the first to acknowledge the Federal Republic as the new basis of German unity, a national unity that could only be achieved through warranting democracy, individual freedom, political liberty, and social justice. The Federal Republic was now the only legitimate trustee of the whole German nation.[23] This was a remarkably clear characterization of the concept of the liberal, democratic nation-state.

3. The perspective of a modern democratic and pluralistic German nation-state that would overcome traditional ethnic and integral nationalism was already motivating leading delegates of the Parliamentary Council. Heuss confirmed Schmid's remarks on the importance of the democratic self-esteem of a people and put this idea more precisely in insisting several times on "the great task of our generation, to cure the Germans of shabby nationalism," contrasting such nationalism with the kind of self-confident national community that ensues from the rights, liberties, individual self-determination, and political participation of a civil society— though he (and others) did not couch it in these terms. In discussing what later became Article 20 of the *Grundgesetz,* that is, the fundamental

political structure of Germany as a democratic and social Federal Republic in a comprehensive sense, Heuss stressed the fact that framing this article was an effort to change and to raise the notion of "Germany" from its ethnic and cultural sense to its meaning in public and constitutional law. Others linked this debate with that on the preamble; the notion of a Federal Republic of Germany in a comprehensive sense — and not only valid for West Germany — had soon been generally accepted, and everybody knew how deep a change was at stake. The debate was continued in order to clarify whether "Germany" was an ethnic or a political notion. And the clear-cut answer was that "Germany" was clearly not being used in an ethnic, cultural, or geographic sense but in the legal, constitutional, and political sense. Here Schmid confirmed this, saying that it should have the same connotations as "La France," and he deepened this distinction when he reminded the committee of the fact that this was something new. "Germany" had never been used in this sense before. Now, for the first time, a German constituent assembly defined "Germany" as sharply outlined — and limited — politically, legally, historically, and spatially.[24] Although the two latter delimitations were perhaps somewhat questionable, this was indeed a fundamental change, from the rather mystical and therefore unlimited character of the *Deutsches Reich* and the ethnic as well as cultural definition of what is German to a declaration of a modern, constitutionally and politically defined and limited "Germany." Therefore, the delegates reinforced the point that the *Grundgesetz* should be valid for Germany as a whole, organized as a democratic, social, and federal republic. A couple of days later, Heuss completed this argument by characterizing the *Grundgesetz* as a result of the constituent power of the German people and something that created a new legal order and constitutional state for Germany.[25]

In the history of the postwar transformation of Germany the constitution-making process and the founding of the Federal Republic marked a decisive epoch. This is obvious in all aspects of German political and social life, and nobody would deny it. However, it is particularly important for the beginning of a new chapter in the history of the German nation-state. The opportunity, since 1945, to achieve a fundamental change in the German conception of nation, state, and government had not been wasted, whatever weaknesses revealed themselves in this new start. Hence the national quality of the Federal Republic was obvious: the substance and the prerequisites of a Western-type nation-state — democratic, pluralistic, and guaranteeing rights and the liberty of the individual — were already inherent in the foundation of the Federal Republic and in the *Grundgesetz,* both of which are based on general participation and acceptance.

A complex concurrence of outstanding developments, influences, concepts, and initiatives was responsible for this outcome: the end of World War II, the German catastrophe, the divisive repercussions of the occupation, and the Cold War. Paramount, however, was a determined institutional strategy in West Germany to lay down and to consolidate in a constitution a new system of government as well as of political norms, rules, public functions, and authorities and their competences. Nevertheless, international and external constraints from 1945 on formed the preconditions of these West German efforts. There were the demands and the control of democratization as well as the consciousness-raising influence of the Western occupying powers, which had a considerable impact on the process of political change and of establishing new institutions as well as providing guidelines of political behavior; the initiative to found the Federal Republic and the albeit rather ineffectual attempts to supervise the process came from the Western powers as well. As to the influence of cultural legacies and political tradition, they were obvious in many details of the reconstruction of political life and a constitutional order between 1945 and 1949 but definitely not in the question of nationhood (although there is no doubt that relics of traditional German nationalism have remained alive until today, even in the *Grundgesetz,* as Article 116 shows). The vital importance of establishing new institutions during the constitution-making process of the Parliamentary Council in this regard was that the *Grundgesetz* created a framework for a modern German nation-state in pronounced contrast to, and averting a reappearance of, past forms of German cultural and ethnic nationalism. However, in order to avoid misunderstandings, it may be necessary to emphasize the fact that the emergence of a considered, non-ethnic notion of nationalism in the Parliamentary Council did not at all mean the disappearance of traditional thinking about the nation in ethnic terms. Nevertheless, those who still preferred such thinking were a shrinking minority, and the political power of traditional German nationalism was broken — a fundamental change.

It should be added, however, that there was yet another deep impact on the national foundation of the Federal Republic. This was the Holocaust. It was an impact that depended on the increasing yet painstaking realization of a thoroughly democratic German society (and that subtle dependence would explain, in part, the long period required to fully comprehend it). This does not only mean the often emphasized anti–National Socialist consensus as a political basis of the Federal Republic but also a new national consciousness that must include the remembrance and acceptance of the disasters of German history, above all the horrors of National Socialism, as well as, deeply linked to this memory, a thorough, considered, and at the same time pragmatic democratization based on adequate constitutional and institutional guarantees and on the inviolable dignity of man: the nation-state as the framework for democracy, an individual as well as collective sense of responsibility for human rights, and the basis of good government as well as international intertwinement, resulting in a multilateral style in international politics — and in domestic politics as well — embedded in a community of states with shared values.

III. A Nation-State to Be Acknowledged

During the first decades after 1945, though gradually decreasing, the national feeling of the older generation was dominant.[26] Partly still influenced by traditional German nationalism, partly in the desire to form a strong German democracy in the reunited fatherland, the dwindling hopes of an early reunification, or at least the strong desire to keep it on the agenda as a political priority, contributed much to looking on the Federal Republic in its early years as a provisional entity. In fact, Adenauer's priority was to integrate the Federal Republic into the West and to postpone reunification, although the reassurance — and hope — that integration into a strong Western community superior to the Eastern bloc would provide the only way to German unity in freedom helped to reconcile the majority of Germans to the status quo.[27] This tendency was strongly supported by the unimaginable economic upswing. Often perceived in connection with it, the new political and social order proved successful. Both developments contributed substantially to the acceptance of the Federal Republic. The crisis from the Soviet Berlin ultimatum in 1958 to the raising of the Berlin Wall in 1961,[28] therefore, only strengthened West German solidarity, while the rift between East and West Germany had deepened. The consolidation of a new German nation-state in the West was under way,[29] even though many Germans did not realize it or shrank from admitting as much.

The German impetus and efforts to promote democracy are due honor, but, in fact, there was little choice in view of the stern democratizing intentions of the Western powers. In any case, this part of democratization yielded fruit, particularly amongst the younger generation — even more than many of the older generation were able to stomach. National Socialism had completely discredited nationalism; it was banned after 1945. The vast majority of Germans developed an aversion against displaying national attitudes or emotions, except perhaps at extraordinary moments such as the address hailing the German soccer team that had won the world championship in 1954 with the "German flag in their hearts," certainly an important moment in the recovery of national pride, but a diction and a feeling that were becoming outmoded or being replaced by a growing self-confidence about personal success as well as West German reconstruction, efficiency, and productivity. This change was deepened considerably and gained new momentum and quality by the succession of generations.

The younger generation, one that grew up in the Federal Republic, launched the students' revolt and other forms of protest against their parents' generation and its insufficient, inadequate way of dealing with the existential problems of man and society in the past—particularly the National Socialist past—and in the present. Nationalism counted less than ever in the Federal Republic, and a new kind of internationalism or cosmopolitanism was spreading in defense and support of so-called progressive movements, struggles, and revolutions all over the world. Hence the succession of generations was combined with a marked and continuing change of values, especially between the mid-1960s and the mid-1970s—and not only in West Germany. The younger generations became the beneficiaries of the Federal Republic's democratization, constitutional standards, tolerance, personal, social, and international security, and well-being. The result was a shift from traditional values and duties toward values that concentrated on individual self-determination and self-realization. Moreover, this shift increased the potential for, as well as the possibility and legitimacy of, political dissent and protest considerably. This, in turn, initiated new political priorities—such as environmental protection—and new dynamics of democratization and participation.[30]

The repercussions of this development on the Federal Republic as a nation-state were indirect but crucial. What was at stake was the very substance of the national intentions as discussed in the Parliamentary Council and concentrated within the *Grundgesetz,* the only pledge of the nation's future, the basis of a new order. Here lie the origin and the core of constitutional patriotism.[31] The crucial question since the 1960s was whether the *Grundgesetz* and, above all, the new institution that had been established to guarantee the *Grundgesetz* itself as well as a political development and a living constitution in conformity with its principles, the Federal Constitutional Court, would be strong enough to maintain their position as the regulative center of German society and eventually of national loyalty in a period of sometimes bitter political and social controversies and conflicts evoked by new social forces and value systems. Constitutional patriotism is more deeply rooted than many people are aware in the terrible experience of lawlessness before 1945 and in the elaboration of the *Grundgesetz* with its concomitant national hopes of a new start. In all conflicts the Federal Constitutional Court gained an unprecedented reputation and became a trusted guardian of constitutional rights even to those dissenting minorities that questioned majority decisions and were fighting for a different republic. This gave the constitution, as the core of any future national development, an impressive legitimation and substantially enhanced the authority of the *Grundgesetz,* thus paving the way for a deepened embodiment in German society of both, the *Grundgesetz* and constitutional patriotism. The more the Federal Republic, despite far-reaching controversies, mistakes, and missed opportunities, was able to prevent deep cleavages and proved capable of integrating even protesting groups, extraparliamentary opposition, alternative movements, etc. (except those on the fringe of society that used violent means to achieve their goals), the more it succeeded in becoming a really modern, pluralistic nation-state by means of its institutions. This presupposes a spirit capable of reforms, tolerance, and of coping with change.

To achieve this, even some lasting and characteristic political traditions in Germany proved helpful, above all a special way of solving problems: the initiation of negotiations among all relevant groups and the introduction of processes of bargaining in order to integrate even conflicting forces and interests (although the reverse of the medal is the traditional German ideal of the congruence of the national and the social community still alive today and, backed by the precedence of the welfare state, another force making the Federal Republic a nation-state). Derived from domestic policy, this procedure was applied to foreign policy too in the Federal Republic (there was already a certain — though weak — tradition from the Weimar Republic). This multilateral political style proved to be quite modern in increasingly intertwined international systems and particularly appropriate for combining politics of détente and compromise from the sixties with those exercised from the origins of the Federal Republic in the complicated field of Western integration. West Germany acquired a certain image in international politics due to a specific national approach toward foreign policy characterized by cautious and circumspect procedures in pursuing national goals, as far as possible, indirectly within a framework of intertwined states, systems, and international organizations in a continuous effort to influence the rules and practice of their intercourse. This attitude allowed for a new form of national identification, supported by an extended influence of domestic policy and public opinion just because of international restraints and narrowed options, which ensued from the unusual origins and the very existence of the Federal Republic within the framework of Western integration, a situation that supported the retreat from an arcane sphere of "free hand" power politics and formed a distinct style of foreign policy, so important for a growing national identity. Under these circumstances and the pressure of a new start, it was easier for the Federal Republic than for other countries to adopt new methods, attitudes, and forms to exert power that respond to the challenge of growing intertwinement, interdependence, and the rise of numerous international organizations as well as transnational, nongovernmental actors in international politics. This development favored—at least in the Western world—indirect ways of bringing to bear national influence, particularly by having a voice in setting the rules and the agenda of international systems, regimes, and integrated areas (in addition, this new situation seems to provide at least part of an answer to the question of why the Federal Republic has restrained its exercise of power).

This process is underscored by some additional aspects of foreign— decidedly multilateral—policy. Here, again, history provides evidence that the nation-state had undergone deep changes. It was no longer isolating itself from international intertwinement but proved capable of initiating integrative measures, above all within the European Community. In striving to participate in Western integration, the Federal Republic, immediately after its foundation, grew into this new task of the nation-state. On the other hand, promoting European integration and other international organizations and unions required a functioning nation-state, capable of safeguarding national interests in a framework of integration and international organization based on the cooperation of nation-states.[32] In this environment only the firmly established modern nation-state is able to provide the national consensus necessary to advance integration, as well as national interests, to renounce sovereign rights, and to allow for transnational loyalty. Therefore, even in this special variety of internationalism, there was a hidden impetus for the Federal Republic to assume the function of a nation-state.

German *Ostpolitik* is the most prominent case in point of the national repercussions of international politics. The policy of détente with the Eastern bloc and the arrangements with the Soviet Union, Poland, the GDR, and Czechoslovakia, above all on the most difficult and delicate border issues,[33] was an important step toward an eased development and self-understanding of the Federal Republic as a nation-state. The modus vivendi and the clarification of the relations with these countries relieved foreign as well as domestic politics and were part of a comprehensive and conclusive program of reform. Dead ends and immobility of foreign policy as a consequence of wrong priorities in the question of reunification could be avoided. Accepting the Oder-Neisse Line and improving the relations with the GDR offered at least a chance for a more efficient and realistic approach to dealing with the division of

Germany by giving the federal government more freedom of action in order to change conditions in East Germany in accordance with the principles of the *Grundgesetz*. Restricting in this way the reunification issue to the relationship with the GDR and meeting the responsibility of the Federal Republic for the Germans in the eastern part of the country could, moreover, mark a more favorable starting position, should there be a chance to reunite Germany. Above all, however, these ramifications of *Ostpolitik* were an additional impulse for the Federal Republic to acknowledge its position as a nation-state in its own right.

Since the nation-state has changed considerably since World War II and has demonstrated its vitality as well as its capability to adapt to new conditions, particularly to the chances and exigencies of supranational organization and to new ways of advancing national goals by selective integration, it has become imperative to fend off all tendencies of immobilization, to maintain and to expand an open society, and thus to keep the nation-state on the track of continuous reform and improved adaptability to change. This depends on national institutions that are based on a liberal and democratic constitution, able to preserve and to develop a free country. Moreover, the history of Western Europe after 1950 shows that the nation-state is not only losing traditional competences, but it is strengthening its influence on the supranational level and gaining new competences in the process of integration. That means that vague escapes into some kind of Europeanness, cosmopolitanism, or universalist pluralism are counterproductive because they destroy their very basis. For the time being, only the nation-state, which might disappear one day but cannot be discussed away, is able to provide the basis of legitimate and accepted action in the vast field of international cooperation and integration. To rely on freely floating, cross-cutting networks for different functions in an ever more pluralistic, internationalized society that will replace the states may prove a dangerous illusion, not least in view of a political vacuum that might be filled by uncontrolled, incalculable forces.

IV. Conclusion: Nation-State and National Unity

German reunification only became possible because it was not pursued as an aim with high priority and with, for other countries, necessarily alarming claims that would most probably have resulted in early and severe restrictions on a troublesome Federal Republic. Equally important was the often underestimated fact that the Federal Republic always maintained its legal position regarding reunification as well as the obligations of the three Western powers. It was realistic not to renounce legal claims without need — in contrast to the views of those who wanted to do just this from a misunderstood sense of détente and neglecting the fundamental importance that a free decision of all Germans on their national future had for the Federal Republic and its concept of a free, democratic, and national constitution. This included from the beginning the right of East Germans to deny reunification, especially if reunification had not taken place in 1990 and the differences between both parts of Germany had become too great. Both solutions, however, reunification or its denial, could not impede or prevent the development of the Federal Republic as a nation-state, since it did not depend on them. Although West Germans—understandably—needed some time to live up to their new nation-state, all the ingredients of a Western-type nation-state were at hand, in particular an impressive democratic constitution, the success of the new state, the rapidly growing acceptance it gained, and—most importantly—the development of a political community, well-balanced in its legitimacy and independent of any additional justification. East Germans could and should join them, and the responsibility for their free decision (and the improvement of their situation) remained.

Nevertheless, nearly all commentators dealing with the difficulties of a German nation-state after 1945 hesitate to follow the concept of a Western-type nation-state to its logical conclusion and tend to confuse it with remnants of the ethnic nation—especially when speaking of the German nation to be preserved or even of a cultural nation that has no clear substance at all and may become a dangerous loophole allowing a return to the concept of the ethnic nation. If a nation is based on the constituent power of the people and on their consent to the constitution this is sufficient, even if in the beginning there are others who would like to join this new nation-state but are prevented from doing so (such as Saarland) or suppressed (such as East Germany). Conditions may be changed, but they cannot alter the decision of those who are free to express their will. It should be stressed, because it is often neglected, that the modern nation-state had changed considerably and that, in the case of the Federal Republic, it is unjustified to speak of some kind of "postnational democracy" until 1989 and of a nation-state thereafter. It was the same nation-state, only extended by the accession of the former GDR.

NOTES

1. For negotiations and considerations in preparation of the Parliamentary Council, see *Der Parlamentarische Rat, 1948–1949: Akten und Protokolle*, vol. 1, *Vorgeschichte* (Boppard: Boldt, 1975).

2. Peter Krüger, ed., *Ethnicity and Nationalism* (Marburg: Hitzeroth,

1993), 9–20; see also Peter Krüger, ed., *Deutschland, deutscher Staat, deutsche Nation* (Marburg: Hitzeroth, 1993), 9–24, 41–69.

3. "Decentralization of the Political Structure of Germany: Preliminary Report by the Special Advisory Committee for Decentralization, US Group, CC, 23 March 1945," *Vierteljahrshefte für Zeitgeschichte* 24 (1976): 316.

4. Ibid., 320; see *Foreign Relations of the United States*, 1945, 3:416.

5. See Peter Krüger, "Staatsgründung unter fürsorglicher Obhut: Die hessische Verfassung vom 29. Oktober 1946 im Kontext amerikanischer Verfassungs- und Politikberatung für die Militärregierung," in *Staat, Gesellschaft, Wissenschaft: Beiträge zur modernen hessischen Geschichte*, ed. Werner Speitkamp (Marburg: Elwert, 1994), 100–101; idem, "Zwei Epochen: Erfolg und Mißerfolg amerikanischer Einwirkung auf den Verfassungswandel in Deutschland nach dem Ersten und Zweiten Weltkrieg," in *Wandel und Kontinuum*, ed. Helmut Bernsmeier and Hans-Peter Ziegler (Frankfurt a. M.: Lang, 1992), 311–22. For a general discussion, see Hans-Peter Schwarz, *Vom Reich zur Bundesrepublik: Deutschland im Widerstreit der außenpolitischen Konzeptionen in den Jahren der Besatzungsherrschaft, 1945–1949*, 2d ed. (Stuttgart: Klett-Cotta, 1980). For organizational details, see *OMGUS Handbuch: Die amerikanische Militärregierung in Deutschland*, ed. Christoph Weisz (München: Oldenbourg, 1994).

6. *Der Parlamentarische Rat*, 1:30–36.

7. Karl Dietrich Bracher, Wolfgang Jäger, and Werner Link, *Republik im Wandel, 1969–1974* (Stuttgart-Mannheim: DVA, Brockhaus, 1986), 406.

8. See Erich J. C. Hahn, "U.S. Policy on a West German Constitution, 1947–1949," in *American Policy and the Reconstruction of West Germany, 1945–1955*, ed. Jeffrey M. Diefendorf, Axel Frohn, and Hermann-Josef Rupieper (Washington, D.C.: German Historical Institute, 1993), 21–44; and also my article "Einflüsse der Verfassung der USA auf die deutsche Verfassungsentwicklung," *Zeitschrift für Neuere Rechtsgeschichte* 18 (1996): 226–47.

9. See Ludolf Herbst, Werner Bührer, and Hannes Sowade, eds., *Vom Marshallplan zur EWG: Die Eingliederung der Bundesrepublik in die westliche Welt* (München: Oldenbourg, 1990).

10. See Wolfgang Benz, ed., *Bewegt von der Hoffnung aller Deutschen: Zur Geschichte des Grundgesetzes: Entwürfe und Diskussionen, 1941–1949* (München: dtv, 1979); see also n. 1 above.

11. On the work of the Parliamentary Council, see Erhard H. M. Lange, *Die Würde des Menschen ist unantastbar: Der Parlamentarische Rat und das Grundgesetz* (Heidelberg: Decker & Müller, 1993).

12. *Parlamentarischer Rat: Verhandlungen des Hauptausschusses, Bonn 1948/49* (Bonn: Parlamentarischer Rat, [1949]), cited hereafter as *HA*. See also *Verhandlungen des Parlamentarischen Rats: Parlamentarischer Rat, Ausschuß für Grundsatzfragen: Stenographischer Bericht*, 1948–49, cited hereafter as *GA*. I quote from the original manuscript and give session number and page, e.g.: *GA*, 7, p. 32. These deliberations have also been published as *Der Parlamentarische Rat 1948–49: Akten und Protokolle*, 5 vols. (Boppard: Harold Boldt Verlag, 1993).

13. *HA,* p. 315 (15 December 1948).
14. Preamble of the *Grundgesetz,* translated in Albert P. Blaustein and Gisbert H. Flanz, eds., *Constitutions of the Countries of the World: Federal Republic of Germany* (Dobbs Ferry, N.Y.: Oceana Publications, 1985).
15. *Der Grundlagenvertrag vor dem Bundesverfassungsgericht: Dokumentation zum Urteil vom 31 Juli 1973* (Karlsruhe-Heidelberg: Müller, 1975).
16. *GA,* 7, pp. 18–22 (6 October 1948); Art. 32, 73(1), 87(1).
17. *HA,* p. 269 (8 December 1948), p. 461 (13 January 1949); Art. 92–95.
18. When, on 30 December 1956, in accordance with this clause the *Grundgesetz* was extended to the Saarland, this set a precedent; see *Bundesgesetzblatt,* 1956, pt. I, 1011.
19. *GA,* 21, pp. 15, 27 (16 November 1948); *HA,* p. 308 (10 December 1948).
20. *GA,* 21, pp. 18–21 (16 November 1948).
21. See *Kurt Schumacher: Reden—Schriften—Korrespondenzen, 1945–1952,* ed. Willi Albrecht (Berlin-Bonn: Dietz, 1985), 473, 670, 740–41; and Heinrich August Winkler, "Das Deutsche Reich muß als Ganzes erhalten bleiben: Kurt Schumacher und die nationale Frage," *Frankfurter Allgemeine,* 31 October 1995, 15.
22. *HA,* p. 374 (7 January 1949); *GA,* 8, p. 30 (7 October 1948).
23. See Schumacher, *Reden-Shriften-Korrespondenzen,* and Winkler, "Das Deutsche Reich."
24. *GA,* 8, p. 30 (7 October 1948); 20, pp. 3, 14 (10 November 1948).
25. *GA,* 21, pp. 40–41 (16 November 1948); *HA,* p. 308 (10 December 1948).
26. *Jahrbuch der öffentlichen Meinung,* vols. 1 (1947–55), 2 (1956–57), 3 (1958–64), ed. Elisabeth Noelle-Neumann (Bonn: Verlag für Demoskopie, 1947–1974). For a general discussion, see Elisabeth Noelle-Neumann, *Demoskopische Geschichtsstunde: Vom Wartesaal der Geschichte zur deutschen Einheit* (Zürich: Edition Interfrom, 1991); and also Werner Weidenfeld and Karl-Rudolf Korte, *Die Deutschen—Profil einer Nation* (Stuttgart: Klett-Cotta, 1991).
27. See Henning Köhler, *Adenauer: Eine politische Biographie* (Frankfurt a. M.–Berlin: Propyläen, 1994), 450–73, 553–697.
28. *Dokumente zur Deutschlandpolitik,* ser. 4, vol. 1/1.2 (10 November 1958–9 May 1959); vol. 7/1.2 (12 August–31 December 1961), comp. by Ernst Deuerlein and Hannelore Nathan (Frankfurt A. M. Metzner, 1971).
29. Concerning the character of the FRG as a nation-state, I would agree with K. Jaspers, W. Besson, M. R. Lepsius, H. and W. J. Mommsen, L. Niethammer, K. Sontheimer, and others who were sharply criticized on a methodologically insufficient basis in the compendium-like books of Tilman Mayer, *Prinzip Nation* (Opladen: Leske & Budrich, 1986), 210; and Jens Hacker, *Deutsche Irrtümer* (Berlin–Frankfurt a. M.: Ullstein, 1992), 379. But my approach is different, and I cannot agree with the thesis of a "bi-nationalization" of the FRG and the GDR. Comprehensive and penetrating, though an advocate of the "postnational democracy" and of 1989 as the starting point of a new German

nation-state, is Heinrich August Winkler, "Nationalismus, Nationalstaat und nationale Frage in Deutschland seit 1945," in *Nationalismus—Nationalitäten—Supranationalität,* ed. H. A. Winkler and Hartmut Kaelble (Stuttgart: Klett-Cotta, 1993), 12–33. See also H. A. Winkler, *Streitfragen der deutschen Geschichte: Essays zum 19. und 20. Jahrhundert* (München: Beck, 1997).

30. See Helmut Klages et al., *Werte und Wandel: Ergebnisse und Methoden einer Forschungstradition* (Frankfurt a. M.: Campus, 1992); also Wilfried von Bredow and Rudolf H. Brocke, *Krise und Protest: Ursprünge und Elemente der Friedensbewegungen in Westeuropa* (Opladen: Westdeutscher Verlag, 1987).

31. This notion became prominent after it was used by Jürgen Habermas in the "Historikerstreit." See the documentation *Historikerstreit: Dokumentation der kontroverse um die Einzigartigkeit der nationalsozialistischen Judenvernichtung,* ed. Rudolf Augstein et al. (München: Piper, 1987), 75. Habermas obviously borrowed it from Dolf Sternberger, *Verfassungspatriotismus* (Frankfurt a. M.: Insel, 1990).

32. See Alan Milward, *The European Rescue of the Nation-State,* 2d ed. (London: Routledge, 1994); and also my *Wege und Widersprüche der europäischen Integration im 20. Jahrhundert,* Schriften des Historischen Kollegs, Vorträge 45 (München: Oldenbourg, 1995).

33. Ingo von Münch, ed., *Ostverträge,* 3 vols. (Berlin–New York: de Gruyter, 1971–73).

Immigration and Nationhood in the Federal Republic of Germany

Christhard Hoffmann

There is hardly an area in the political life of the Federal Republic that arouses more disbelief and uneasiness in Western observers than immigration policy and the official treatment of "foreigners." "How can a country that is so proud of its modernity," asked a French journalist in 1991, "continue to live with this relic called the blood law? With a law that privileges the descendants of Swabian peasants who emigrated two hundred years ago to the steppes of central Russia, and rejects the children of Turkish immigrants in Kreuzberg, who know no horizon other than the Kottbusser Tor or the Kurfürstendamm?"[1] And after the brutal wave of attacks by German youths against asylum-seekers and Turks in 1992–93, an American commentator expressed the wish that Germany would finally seize the opportunity to institute fundamental structural changes, beginning with citizenship law, and transform itself into a multicultural society, "from exclusively white and Christian to brown, yellow and black, Muslim and Jewish."[2] In the last few years, increasing criticism has been voiced within Germany itself against national self-understanding in ethnic terms, and against the "anachronism" of *jus sanguinis* (blood law) as a legal reality.[3] Although thoroughgoing reform of German citizenship law has been promised by the government for years, as of yet very few changes have been instituted. How is it possible that the *Reichs- und Staatsangehörigkeitsgesetz,* which is based on the principle of ethnic homogeneity, has remained in effect in the same essential form since its inception in 1913? Is this simply a matter of an "outdated costume," as is often asserted in the current discussion,[4] which can easily be shed because it has long since been outgrown? Or is it rather evidence of a powerful continuity in national self-understanding, one that still defines "Germanness" in terms of common descent, language, and culture, and excludes everything else as "un-German"?

In this chapter, I suggest that both statements contain an element of truth. There has indeed been a powerful continuity of the ethnically homogeneous self-understanding in the Federal Republic. But it would be misleading to conclude from this continuity that neither the politics of immigration nor German self-definition have changed at all since 1945, or even since the late nineteenth century, as it is sometimes argued. In what follows, I illustrate the interplay between continuity and change by examining three points: (1) the historical reasons for maintaining *jus sanguinis* in 1949; (2) the legal and social status of foreign workers in West Germany; and (3) the public debate about immigration and national identity. Finally, I will briefly discuss the impact of unification on the issue of immigration and nationhood.

The Continuity of *Jus Sanguinis*

In the current political debate in Germany, it has been claimed that the definition of citizenship as a community of descent runs counter to the principles of democracy and human rights, which are explicit anchors of the German federal constitution. The institutional survival of *jus sanguinis* is seen as the prime reason that German citizens and non-German immigrants have such difficulties peacefully coexisting.

One might with justification protest that the early-nineteenth-century transformation of the legal definition of citizenship away from one of territorial inhabitance (*jus soli*) to one of blood or descent (*jus sanguinis*), which occurred in many German states, was not the expression of ethnic nationalism, but rather served to consolidate the newly formed German territorial states by creating a new definition of "belonging."[5] Moreover, one might argue that the principle of descent is theoretically neutral with regard to the question of the ethnic composition of a state: it treats Germans of Polish, Vietnamese, or Turkish origin equally, as long as they have first attained citizenship. But this is precisely the decisive point: in practice, the principle of descent largely prevents immigrants of non-German origin from attaining citizenship in the first place. It thus ensures the ethnic status quo. For this reason the law has been a medium of *Volkstumspolitik* during periods of immigration. Although Germany was largely a nation of emigration prior to 1890, in the 1880s Germany was forced to respond to the mass westward migration of Jews from the tsarist and Austro-Hungarian empires.[6] Then, in the 1890s, the shortage of manpower that was experienced first in the agrarian sector and then in the industrial centers led to the importation of foreign labor. The result was a surge in the alien population from 270,000 in 1871 to more than 1.2 million by 1910. However, the

Eastern European Jewish businessmen or the Polish foreign workers in the German *Kaiserreich* were never perceived as immigrants or as potential Germans. Rather, they were viewed as a reserve army of cheap labor who were deemed acceptable only if their presence in some way contributed to the interests of the state or the economy. Official measures taken by the various German states aimed at admitting foreigners to German territory, but simultaneously excluding them from the body politic. This administrative practice of the individual states was made into law with the *Reichs- und Staatsangehörigkeitsgesetz* of 1913. It withheld the legal right to naturalization from the foreigners and their children who worked and lived in the German *Kaiserreich,* while making it possible for Germans who settled permanently outside the *Reich* to maintain their German citizenship for an unlimited period of time.[7]

In theory, foreigners who fulfilled certain formal requirements (legal capacity, clean police record, proof of income and domicile) could apply to be naturalized. However, in actual practice, immigration authorities in the *Kaiserreich* systematically discriminated against particular groups, especially Eastern European Jews and Poles, who were considered "undesired elements."[8] The extraordinarily broad latitude granted to the immigration authorities allowed them a high degree of selectivity with regard to the applicants' national, religious, and social background. The decisive principle was usually "usefulness"; ethnic criteria were important, but not exclusively so. In fact, a tradition of official state neutrality in ethnic-national questions — which had begun when Prussia was forced to deal with its sizable minority population after 1815 — remained in force, though with ever declining influence. In this sense, the citizenship law of 1913 and naturalization practice in the *Kaiserreich* differ fundamentally from the 1935 *Reichsbürgergesetz* and Nazi naturalization practice.[9] The former defined citizenship in racial terms, and the latter required even after 1939 that the returning *Volksdeutsche* (emigrants mainly from Eastern Europe and Russia) undergo "racial testing." Skull shape, "Nordic" or "phaelic" appearance, and cultural avowal of *Deutschtum* ("Germanness") were the most important criteria for inclusion in Nazi Germany. Four categories of citizenship were created according to these criteria. The supposed percentage of "German blood" present in a person determined the level of his category and his corresponding rights.[10]

An understanding of past tradition is important in order to be able to evaluate questions of continuity and discontinuity regarding national self-understanding in the *Kaiserreich* and the Federal Republic. If it seems incomprehensible today that an ethnonational — and not a purely political — definition of citizenship was adopted in the Basic Law, it is necessary to remember the function such a definition had in 1945. Retaining the principle of descent offered the only opportunity for the Federal Republic to maintain the idea of a single German nation despite the division of Germany and the foreign administration of the eastern territories. Thus Article 116 of the Basic Law states that "in the eyes of the constitution, everyone is a German who holds German citizenship or who, as a refugee or expellee of German *Volkszugehörigkeit,* or as a spouse or descendant of such a person, has been admitted to the territory of the German Empire as it existed on December 31, 1937."[11] As the legal successor of the German *Reich,* the Federal Republic felt itself obliged to offer permanent asylum to all the *Volksdeutschen* who had been expelled or persecuted. The admission of over eight million expellees, evacuees, and refugees by 1950 was thus understood as an act of solidarity and an attempt to deal justly with the consequences of the war, not as a political measure designed to reinforce *Deutschtum.* While *völkisch*-style thinking may have still been widespread among politicians, bureaucrats, and certain segments of the population directly after the war, this was not the crucial factor in the decision to preserve *jus sanguinis.* More important was the Federal Republic's claim to speak and act "for all Germans" following the collapse of the Third Reich. This, of course, included those living in the Soviet occupation zone and in Eastern Europe, where, the young Federal Republic argued, free political participation was obstructed. Such a claim was possible only if citizenship rights were defined not in terms of territorial inhabitance, but of descent.[12] Maintaining *jus sanguinis* thus became a political objective of the highest order as long as Germany was divided. Citizenship based on the principle of descent formed the legal basis for the "unity of the nation." In my view, the extraordinarily long life of this legal institution is due primarily to its function in this capacity.

The definition of a German as a member of a "community of descent" (*Abstammungsgemeinschaft*) in Article 116 of the Basic Law had considerable consequences for the political self-understanding of the republic. It meant that the citizens of the FRG, the concrete *Staatsvolk,* formed only a part of the entire German people and were obligated, when making political decisions, to consider the interests of its potential citizens, the *Statusdeutschen,* living outside the territory of the Federal Republic. However fictitiously this construction might have been used in actual politics, it could nevertheless always be interpreted as limiting the sovereignty of the West German citizenry, at least in questions of national identity. Conservative politicians have thus argued that the FRG had no right to transform itself into a multiethnic state by promoting the immigration of non-Germans, since the Germans in the GDR were not able to participate in making such a fundamental decision.[13] It is important to note that the politicians responsible for retaining the principle of descent in 1949 were not concerned with preserving German "national identity" vis-à-vis non-German immigrants. Indeed, in 1949 it seemed beyond belief that a physically and economically destroyed Germany could ever attract foreign laborers. Nevertheless, the decision to retain the institution of *jus sanguinis* was a fateful one, greatly affecting the "immigration question" during the ensuing decades.

Maintaining an ethnic definition of the "German people" through the Basic Law had considerable consequences on the politics of immigration in the Federal Republic. Although the Basic Law assigns general responsibility for immigration to the federation, there has, so far, been no single, comprehensive immigration law. This is no coincidence. It stems from the fact that the Federal Republic classifies those entering Germany into several distinct legal categories that cannot be subsumed under one general concept of "immigrant." There are essentially three groups. First are the *Statusdeutsche* recognized by the Basic Law. These include those ethnic Germans who come from the GDR, the former German "eastern provinces," or Communist-controlled Eastern European countries. Since they have the automatic right to claim German citizenship, their entry into the FRG is not considered to be immigration, but rather resettlement, or return.[14] In the second category are the foreign workers from non–European Union countries and their families whose presence was solicited by the Federal Republic in terms of bilateral agreements with countries of origin between 1955 and 1973. As the official designation of "guest worker" indicates, they were initially considered to be only temporary residents of Germany, who would eventually return to their countries of origin.[15] The third group is formed by asylum-seekers who entered the Federal Republic under Article 16 of the Basic Law, which guarantees asylum to the politically persecuted. This article was instituted as a consequence of the terrible experiences endured by many emigrants who were forced to flee Germany after 1933. It guarantees the individual the right to asylum regardless of his or her political beliefs.[16] Since it was conceived as a type of emergency help for the politically persecuted, the right to asylum has little to do with the issue of immigration itself. It grants permission to reside in Germany for an unlimited period of time only to those who have been officially recognized as legitimate asylum-seekers.

As late as the 1980s, this system of categorization could hypothetically result in a situation in which three young Poles from the same village would each be conferred a wholly distinct legal status that resulted in correspondingly different living conditions.[17] The first might be recognized as a German citizen upon entry because his German grandmother had married a Pole after the war. On his first day in the Federal Republic, he would be granted not only all the rights of citizenship, but also access to an extensive network of social services, including unemployment and welfare benefits, as well as special help to get him situated in his new country. The second, entering as a tourist, might have worked legally or illegally in Germany during the summertime, returning to Poland after three months in order to do the same the next year. The third might have come seeking asylum. He would then be barred from any gainful employment and be placed in a residence for asylum-seekers until his case was decided (often taking up to two years). Supposing his petition for political asylum was denied, he might have nonetheless been granted permission to remain as a refugee for a limited time, during which he would only be allowed to accept a job if there were no German citizens available to fill it.

This hypothetical example illustrates why the Federal Republic never developed an understanding of itself as a country of immigration. The legal categorization of immigrants into "Germans" and "foreigners" prevented a consideration of the common situation in which *all* immigrants find themselves. Thus by 1990, the 15 million "Germans" who had been accepted and integrated into the Federal Republic were never understood as "immigrants," although from a social and cultural perspective this was certainly the case, especially during the later years. The question of inclusion was answered automatically by the principle of descent. The status and situation of the foreign workers, on the other hand, was for a long time not recognized, or ignored against better judgment, because in their case permanent exclusion was predetermined. The logic of *jus sanguinis* has thus ensured that the self-understanding of the Federal Republic would remain as a "nonimmigrant country."

The Legal and Social Status of Migrant Workers

Starting with the 1955 German-Italian Agreement on Worker Recruitment, West Germany recruited foreign labor from Mediterranean countries in order to compensate for labor shortages in the growing economy. These so-called guest workers became especially important after the Berlin Wall halted the stream of refugees entering from East Germany in 1961. As we have already noted, the term indicates that their stay in Germany was originally intended to be only temporary. Working and residence permits were first issued only for one year, so that the length of stay and the overall extent of foreign labor could be flexibly regulated according to the needs of the economy. Although the original principle of worker rotation proved impractical in the long run, the assumption that foreign workers would eventually return to their countries of origin remained an essential element of "guest work." An extension of the working and residence permits was only possible if the "interests of the Federal Republic were not damaged."[18] Some German courts interpreted the intention of foreign workers to remain in Germany indefinitely to be in violation of their recruitment agreements and to be just cause for their deportation. In addition, foreign workers were subject to the strict control of the labor and alien affairs agencies, in which traditional legal instruments, such as the 1938 Alien Police Order and the 1933 Alien Employee Order, were adopted in largely unchanged form in the 1965 Alien Law. It granted a broad interpretive latitude to the respective agencies regarding issuing working and residence permits and cemented the "exceptional" status of foreigners, a status that afforded little legal protection. The "guest workers" were viewed as a mobile reserve army for the German labor market, as a "buffer" within the economy that could simply be sent back home in case of high unemployment. According to Knut Dohse, the Alien Law of 1965 "conceived . . . the relation between the state and aliens . . . not as a legal relationship which submits administrative action to the legal limitations of a constitutional state, but rather as a relationship of opportunity which makes possible relatively unrestrained administrative practice oriented not to the legal positions of the aliens, but to unstable and changing political goals."[19] Under these conditions, the predicament of the "guest worker" in the Federal Republic differed little from that of the foreign migrant laborer in the *Kaiserreich*.

A partial amelioration of this situation was initiated not from the political, but from the legal realm. Relying on the principle of the constitutional and social state, courts granted foreign workers who had repeatedly renewed their residence permits the right of *Vertrauensschutz*. This meant that it became legally very difficult, and eventually impossible, to deny these workers further residence, political and economic motivations notwithstanding. The Federal Constitutional Court upheld this decision in 1978, ruling that the political understanding of the republic as a nonimmigrant country must yield to the constitutional principle of *Vertrauensschutz*.[20] The right of residence was "secured" on this basis for long-term residents, given that they fulfilled certain conditions (proof of domicile and permanent employment, clean police record, and elementary knowledge of German). After five years of short-term residence, they were entitled to claim indefinite residence; after eight years, to claim the full "right of residence" (*Aufenthaltsberechtigung*), which ensured almost complete protection against expulsion. A parallel development occurred with regard to the resettlement of family members. Government agencies had been especially restrictive in granting residence permits to spouses and children following the 1973 cessation of recruitment and again in the context of the policy of "delimitation" during the early 1980s. The courts lifted many of these restrictions by appealing to the protection of marriage and family that is guaranteed in the Basic Law.[21]

The provisions in the Basic Law regarding universal human rights thus provided a counterbalance both to the exclusivist regulations regarding citizenship and aliens' rights as well as to the restrictive practices of governmental agencies. The treatment of foreign workers merely as a disposable labor force entirely dependent on the state of the market was thus substantially curbed. In addition to this, other forms of integration emerged that had the effect of including foreign workers in the West German social welfare system.[22] The unions had insisted on equal pay for "guest workers" in order to prevent the type of instrumentalization of foreign labor that took place during the *Kaiserreich*. This meant that, from the outset, foreign workers were ensured the same salary and social benefits as their German colleagues. The inclusion of the "guest workers" in the Federal Republic's social security system aroused no protest at first, since it was expected that the young workers would mainly be paying into the system and would be returning to their countries of origin before needing to draw large-scale benefits. In addition, their official status in the social security system as full equals was in part negated by stipulations in the Alien Law, since unemployment or accepting welfare was considered grounds for expulsion.[23] Here, too, the federal courts upheld the rights of foreigners to receive social welfare benefits and forestalled the practice of individual states of expelling aliens because they were unemployed or receiving welfare payments.[24]

Though the legal security of foreign workers was improved in this way, their right to political participation remained blocked. Since the Basic Law distinguished between "human rights" and so-called German rights—valid only for German citizens—the right to vote, among other things, was withheld from "guest workers." The Federal Constitutional Court ruled in 1990 that the laws adopted by certain federal states that allowed long-term foreign residents to vote in communal elections are not compatible with the Basic Law in Germany. Two courses of action have been discussed as a solution to this problem. Either the restrictions on naturalization can be eased and dual nationality permitted, since many foreigners are hesitant to relinquish their old citizenship—in the case of Turks, for example, this would mean giving up all inheritance claims in Turkey—or a new law regarding permanent residence can be introduced, which would allow immigrants who want to become long-term residents (but not citizens) to do so, with a guaranteed legal status that confers certain basic rights and obligations of citizenship.[25] Though all the political parties in Parliament now agree that the present laws governing citizenship must be reformed in order to correspond to the current reality of immigration, there are still substantial differences of opinion regarding both the extent and the details of reform.

Public Discussion of National Identity and Immigration

Unlike during the *Kaiserreich,* when the importation of Polish seasonal labor in the 1890s unleashed vehement protest from nationalist circles who feared for the ethnic homogeneity of the *Reich,* the introduction of foreign workers in the 1950s did not generate a "national" debate.[26] There were a number of reasons for this. Nobody could foresee in the 1950s that the recruitment of foreign labor would become a question of immigration. The number of foreign workers entering Germany was comparatively small, and at first mainly seasonal. The international agreements did not provide for long-term residency. Furthermore, immediate past experience had taught that the importation of foreign labor during economic booms was a "normal" and only temporary market-induced measure. A critical assessment of the exploitative foreign labor practices of the Third Reich did not take place in the 1950s. In order to demonstrate a "new beginning," the pejorative designation *Fremdarbeiter* was simply exchanged for the more benign-sounding *Gastarbeiter.* On those few occasions when the recruitment of "guest workers" was mentioned in the context of the "national question," it was done so in positive terms, as fostering "international understanding" and "European integration." As Minister of Labor Theodor Blank stressed in 1964, the employment of foreigners ensured that "the merging together of Europe and the rapprochement between persons of highly diverse backgrounds and cultures in a spirit of friendship" would become a reality.[27]

There was also no "national" debate over immigration when the economic downturn of the 1970s resulted in a cessation of "guest-worker" recruitment and a worsening of the social climate with respect to foreigners. Although there were a few figures during this time who tried to paint an ethnic face on growing social ills and who warned about an ostensible "foreign takeover" of Germany, the goal guiding both the public discussion and the policies of the Social Democratic government in Bonn was that of social stability, not ethnic homogeneity. In order to ensure domestic peace in the face of increasing unemployment, employment opportunities for foreigners were to be curtailed by ceasing recruitment and promoting native German labor. "Guest workers" would be encouraged to return to their countries of origin. On the other hand, the goal of social stability encouraged certain positive measures regarding the integration of foreigners, that is, for unemployed youth. But, as always, "integration" as such was imagined only in a temporary time frame. The self-understanding of the Federal Republic at this time was expressed largely in terms of its social achievements. Immigration policy was framed in terms of securing living standards and social stability.[28] These terms can be clearly seen in a 1982 "Success Report" from the Ministry of Labor: "Since the cessation of recruitment in 1973, the number of employed foreigners in the Federal Republic has decreased by over 600,000. This development has noticeably relieved the German labor market and has contributed to the fact that the Federal Republic has been spared grave social and economic conflicts."[29]

Only in the early 1980s *did* a public debate about national identity and immigration emerge. It had the effect of greatly polarizing the Federal Republic. The future-oriented ideas about social reform that guided discussion in the 1970s were largely abandoned in the wake of economic stagnation and long-term unemployment. Historical continuity appeared more important. If "emancipation" had been the leading intellectual concept of the 1960s and 1970s, by the 1980s "identity" had replaced it. This had considerable consequences for the perception of the "immigration question."

By the end of the 1970s, it was clear that against its will, the Federal Republic had become a de facto country of immigration. Heinz Kühn, the first Federal Commissioner of Immigration Affairs (*Ausländerbeauftragter*), ascertained in a 1979 memorandum that the situation of having so many foreigners and their families living in the FRG was "a development that is no longer reversible . . . The majority of those in question are no longer 'guest workers' but immigrants for whom a return to their original countries is no longer a consideration for many different reasons."[30] Along with this came the realization that measures based purely on the labor market could no longer regulate the movement of foreigners into the Federal Republic. Although the number of foreign workers had declined since the cessation of recruitment, the number of total foreigners actually grew because of the increased resettlement of family members, a high birthrate, and a rapidly expanding group of asylum-seekers. By 1980, the total number of foreigners living in the FRG had exceeded that of 1972 by one million.[31] This led to higher social tension in the larger cities and resulted in the first overt attacks against foreigners.[32]

In this atmosphere, the voices seeking to end immigration based on ethnic arguments grew louder and more numerous. The most radical of these was the "Heidelberg Manifesto." Initiated in 1981 by a group of professors, it had unmistakable racist undertones. The manifesto decried the "infiltration of the German *Volk* by the immigration of millions of foreigners" and called for the "preservation of the German *Volk* and its cultural identity on the foundation of our Christian and Western heritage." They defined *Volk* as an unchangeable biological phenomenon:

> *Völker* are (biologically and cybernetically) living systems of a high order, each with its own systemic characteristics that are transmitted genetically and through tradition. For this reason, the integration of large masses of non-German foreigners is impossible for the simultaneous preservation of our *Volk* and leads to the well-known ethnic catastrophes of multicultural societies. Each *Volk*, including the German *Volk*, has a natural right to preserve its identity and uniqueness in its own environment.[33]

This represents an extremist position that was heavily criticized at the time and gained little influence outside the radical right spectrum. However, the more moderate but very influential arguments of prominent CDU/CSU politicians were based on a similar fear of being overrun by foreigners (*Überfremdung*) and a desire for cultural homogeneity. On the one hand, they appealed to the principle of reunification in the Basic Law and derived from this a proviso of sovereignty for the Federal Republic in national questions: "The role of the Federal Republic as a nationally united state and part of a divided nation does not permit the introduction of an irreversible development toward a multiethnic state (*Vielvölkerstaat*)."[34] On the other hand, they argued in populist style that certain groups could not be successfully integrated because of their alleged "alien" culture. CDU Bundestag member Alfred Dregger, for example, distinguished between four categories of foreigners. The first two groups, those with foreign citizenship but either of German background or from the "European sphere of culture," are easy to "integrate and then to assimilate." By contrast, Turks or those from Asian or African countries are "not only not assimilable, but can be integrated only with difficulty."[35] Dregger argued that in order to assure cultural homogeneity and avoid ethnic conflict in Germany, the immigration of culturally "alien" groups must be as limited as possible. According to the logic of this argument, there were only two alternatives in the long run for culturally "alien" foreigners like the Turks: either complete assimilation and naturalization, or a return to their country of origin. The idea of cultural pluralism was rejected, since national identity continued to be defined in terms of a *Volk* unified by a common language, history, and culture.[36] The boundaries of "culture" were broadened, however, to include all of "Christian" Europe, sometimes also described in vague terms as "Western civilization." The effect was to exclude people of other cultural backgrounds, especially Muslims, Africans, and Asians.

The concept of a "multicultural society" was introduced in the early 1980s as an explicit rejection of the conservative insistence that Germany was not a country of immigration, but a state composed of a single ethnic group. It was promulgated mainly through the newly formed Green Party and a segment of the Social Democrats, though individual CDU and FDP politicians as well as churches and labor unions also employed the term. This wide spectrum lent the concept of multiculturalism differing accents:[37] first, as a simple description of the fact that Germany had long had ethnic and cultural minorities living within its boundaries, and that it was now time to recognize this reality explicitly; second, as a programmatic guiding light for a future society of cultural pluralism, openness, and tolerance, and a rejection of the nationalist, xenophobic, and racist elements of the German past; and third, as a pedagogical concept that postulates the equal value of all cultures and rejects the adaptation of immigrant culture to that of the native majority. Unclear and vague as the various notions of a multicultural future sometimes were, they shared a fundamental critique of the contradictory policies and unfair practices of the German authorities vis-à-vis the foreigners living in their midst. This critique became more pronounced when the CDU-led government announced a "turn," or change, in immigration policy. Bonn declared the voluntary repatriation of foreign workers and a change in asylum law to be top priorities in their new program. Taking the opportunity to engage in electoral politics, the CDU initiated a campaign to "dam the tide of asylum-seekers" and declared themselves opposed to "phony asylum-seekers and being overrun by foreigners (*Überfremdung*)."[38] In rejecting this populist propaganda, which had sought to extract political gain from growing xenophobia, groups such as the Greens engaged in what they believed was "resistance" in the antifascist tradition. In their view, Turks and asylum-seekers had become the modern Jews. The unswerving moralistic tone of their position added to the emotional charge of the debate. On the one hand, this made reaching a pragmatic solution based on compromise more difficult. But on the other hand, it mobilized broad public support for the rights of foreigners and asylum-seekers for the first time.

The political dispute intensified in the mid-1980s, when the number of *Volksdeutsche* entering Germany rose sharply due to the liberalization under way in the Soviet Union. The Federal Republic, which until then had supported a "ship-is-full" campaign with respect to foreign immigration, now asked the population to stand in solidarity with the entering ethnic German immigrants. Thus, while the government was giving foreign workers money to return to their countries of origin, it was simultaneously paying for ethnic Germans to emigrate to Germany and then generously assisting them once they arrived. This policy was severely criticized by members of the opposition parties as *Deutschtümelei,* a regression back to the ethnically oriented politics of *Volkstum.* But because it was written into the Basic Law, the government had no alternative but to admit all ethnic Germans who desired "repatriation." The public increasingly felt that the immediate inclusion of these immigrants alongside the simultaneous exclusion of "foreigners" who were born and raised in the Federal Republic was an anachronistic and unfair policy. The large-scale immigration of *Aussiedler* in the mid-1980s thus directed the focus of public discussion to the persistence of *jus sanguinis,* now increasingly criticized as an outdated relic.[39]

The confrontation between conservatives of the "we-are-not-a-country-of-immigration" stamp and the mainly leftist supporters of a "multicultural society" had little to do with the concrete problems faced by foreigners in the Federal Republic. CDU/CSU politicians knew that Germany had become irreversibly a country of immigration, even when they asserted the opposite. And even the Green fundamentalists were not naive enough to believe that their calls for a politics of totally "open borders" and the "right to stay for all" could ever be concretely realized.[40] The debate was about symbolic, not practical, politics. It was about garnering votes, hegemony in public discourse, and the self-understanding of the Federal Republic.[41] For this reason, the immigration debate must be viewed in the context of another central debate of this era, that of "rearmament versus pacifism" or " 'normalcy' versus memory (of the Nazi past)." Both debates were conducted along the same lines of conflict and largely by the same figures. The consequence of the debate about identity for immigration politics was rather negative. The polarization of viewpoints and intensity of emotion obstructed the search for pragmatic solutions and further postponed long-overdue decisions: "With regard to the issue of migration, the . . . 1980s were a lost decade."[42]

It is true, however, that large segments of the population underwent a cultural shift away from suspicion and toward acceptance of immigration. This was shown clearly in 1988, when the draft of a new Alien Law prepared by the Ministry of the Interior met with solid public opposition from an extraordinarily united front comprising churches, welfare organizations, labor unions, employer organizations, the media, and opposing political parties. The draft was quickly withdrawn.[43] But due to the balance of political power in Bonn, an institutionalization of this new self-understanding did not occur. The new "Alien Law" that took effect in January 1991 exhibited some of the same fundamental contradictions as the old one. On the one hand, it secured the legal status of long-term residents for the first time and eased the naturalization of children born to foreigners living in the Federal Republic. But on the other hand, it retained the supervisory capacity and broad discretionary latitude granted to the immigration authorities. It was not possible to construct a consistent policy on this basis.[44]

The Situation after Unification

The unresolved problems of immigration and the integration of foreigners represent a heavy burden that the old Federal Republic brought into the new unified Germany. The social and cultural trauma of the "unification crisis" and the new immigration situation following the opening of borders in Eastern Europe added even more weight to the burden. Nevertheless, there are indications that, paradoxically, a consensus on these issues can be reached more easily now, after unification, than while Germany was still divided. In what follows, I will outline in five points the often conflicting developments that have taken place since the opening of the Wall.

1. The opening of international borders following the end of the Cold War led to a dramatic increase of immigration into the Federal Republic. In 1990 alone, 400,000 ethnic Germans entered the FRG from the Eastern bloc, claiming their right to citizenship. At the same time, the number of asylum-seekers rose from 370,000 in 1990 to 430,000 in 1992. In 1992, the number of immigrants who entered the Federal Republic rose to 788,000, higher than in either Australia or Canada. Expressed as a percentage of total population, the Federal Republic had the highest net immigration rate in the industrialized world.[45] This tremendous influx could not be managed through existing legal and administrative structures. In order to limit the increasing immigration of German descendants from the ex–Soviet Union, the right to immediate naturalization was substantially restricted in the *Aussiedleraufnahmegesetz* of 1990 and the revised version of the *Bundesvertriebenengesetz* of 1992. While the principle of naturalization for immigrants of German descent was kept intact, immediate entry was granted only to those who were threatened by persecution or discrimination in their countries of residence. Moreover, the *Aussiedler* eligible for repatriation were restricted to those born before 1 January 1993.

The asylum compromise reached by the CDU, FDP, and SPD and

signed into law on 1 July 1993 prevented asylum-seekers who had entered Germany through a "secure third country" from requesting asylum. Although this reduced the number of asylum-seekers by about one-half, this number was still much higher than expected.

The long-standing, bitter debate[46] that had been conducted on such rhetorically charged terms helped create the impression in many German citizens that politics was unable to address the issue. Thus the grounds had been prepared for the waves of violence against asylum-seekers that spread throughout the reunited Germany beginning in 1991.[47] The attacks on asylum-seekers by German youths in Hoyerswerda (1991) and Rostock (1992) and the murders of Turkish families in Mölln (1992) and Solingen (1993) eventually gave rise to outspoken and widespread condemnation. Mass demonstrations, huge candlelight vigils, and media campaigns against xenophobia combined with rapid police action and prosecution to isolate and punish the perpetrators. The number of xenophobic acts of violence has since decreased, but with 860 attacks in 1994 (1,608 in 1993), it remains alarmingly high.[48]

2. There is a tendency on the part of former West Germans to blame the increase in hostility toward foreigners on the supposedly reactionary East. It is argued that since Eastern Germans had no "multicultural" experience with foreigners, they reacted with particular violence when confronted with a reality they found undesirable. There is no evidence whatsoever to support this generalization. On the contrary, opinion polls convincingly demonstrate that Westerners are more apt than Easterners to have an outlook that is hostile toward foreigners.[49] Yet there are certain peculiarities that deserve explanation. Directly after the Wall fell, for example, citizens of the GDR were particularly ill-disposed toward Turks, although there were no Turks living in East Germany at the time. Turks were apparently seen as competitors for limited job openings and social welfare benefits. The relatively secure economic and social position of these "foreigners" in West Germany was thought to be inappropriate given the high level of unemployment and general insecurity among (East) "Germans." Granted the potential for serious dissatisfaction in the East that is so easily transformable into hostility toward foreigners, it is rather remarkable that it found no expression in organized political terms. Unlike in the West, the Republikaner found virtually no support in the East. Social frustrations were directed against the capitalist West, not against foreigners. The PDS, not the Republikaner, profited from this. After the wave of violence in 1992, opinion polls show that support for politics based on anti-foreigner rhetoric retreated substantially both in the East and the West.[50]

3. The unification of the two German states was celebrated by adherents of *Volk* ideology as the confirmation and triumph of their viewpoint. The exclamations by the East German demonstrators "We are one *Volk*" seemed to indicate that a strong unified national consciousness had survived 45 years of artificial division. The persistence of *jus sanguinis* in the FRG along with the official goal of achieving a single, united German people was interpreted as having finally paid off. Unification could thus be understood not as a political act of constituting the German citizenry on the basis of a new constitution, but rather as a quasi-natural, organic process of "growing together."

However, the revival of an ethnic German nationalism, so feared by observers, has not yet occurred, nor does it seem likely that it will. Why? The experience of the last five years has made East and West Germans painfully aware that the idea of a preexisting harmony based on national homogeneity is an illusion. Differences in circumstances, perspectives, life-experiences, and identities continue to exist. Although the experience of mutual difference may initially have been interpreted as a transitional phase, the underlying ideals of "inner unity" or "the" national identity are now widely rejected as being fundamentally misconceived. Paradoxically, the experience of living together in a unified Germany has led not to a revival of the idea of ethnic homogeneity, but rather to a greater acceptance of difference and the ideal of pluralism. Whereas the "imagined community" was homogeneous, the "real community" is diverse.

4. With the unification of the two German states, the German *Volk*, or nation, has become once again identical with the *Staatsvolk*, the "people," or citizenry. The term "German" can now be used exclusively to describe the citizens, and only the citizens, of the Federal Republic of Germany. The justification for retaining *jus sanguinis* or an ethnic definition of the nation in Article 116 of the Basic Law therefore no longer holds.

It remains, however, an open question whether the new legal and political situation after unification will lead to a revision of Article 116 of the Basic Law. Advocates of a change argue that in order to achieve a measure of clarity in the two-decades-old debate about immigration, the ethnic understanding of *Volk* must be stricken from the Basic Law and replaced by a political definition of citizenship. Only when "being German" no longer signifies belonging to a closed community of descent will the doors of the Federal Republic be truly open for immigrants of other ethnic backgrounds. Of course, such a change would require rejecting the idea of ethnic homogeneity and would, therefore, be difficult to enact given the opposition of the conservative wing of the CDU and CSU. As recently as 1993, CDU chairman Wolfgang Schäuble could explain in an interview, "We—the old states of the old Europe—are classic nation-states. We create our identity not by committing to an idea, but by belonging to a particular nation (*Volk*)."[51]

Nevertheless, it seems that the willingness to compromise in order to reform German citizenship law is greater today than ever before. The shock of xenophobic violence has led to a political realignment. Conservative CDU/CSU politicians are much more restrained now than in the early 1980s when discussing issues concerning foreigners. They must reckon with the opposition not only of a more sensitized public, but also of the more moderate wing within their own party. On the other side, leading politicians in the Greens have realized that liberal immigration policies cannot be enacted against the will of the majority of German citizens. Thus for the first time in 15 years there seems to be a way out of the political deadlock.[52] A change in citizenship law is also supported by broad segments of the population. Recent opinion polls show that a majority of Germans agree that long-term residents should be naturalized. Responding to the question "Who should be a German citizen?" 38 percent answered "those born in Germany"; 44 percent answered "those who have been living in Germany for a long time." Only 14 percent wanted to base citizenship on German descent.[53] After years of such slow progress the latest proposal of Gerhard Schröder's red-green coalition to alter German citizenship is a sign that the pace of reform is increasing.

In contrast to this, government politics had until recently been moving at a snail's pace. In their coalition talks of November 1994, the CDU/CSU and the FDP reached an agreement about introducing a so-called child citizenship law for foreigners. According to the proposal, children of foreign parents who have each been living in Germany more than 10 years, and at least one of whom was born in Germany, would be entitled to acquire German "child citizenship," in addition to retaining the citizenship of their parents. At the age of 19, these "child-Germans" would decide which citizenship they want to keep. This proposal met with vehement criticism in the public realm.[54] It was described as a phony solution that offered less for the naturalization and integration of foreigners than the existing order.

5. The history of immigration policy and the official treatment of foreigners in the Federal Republic show clearly that the legal and institutional tradition of national self-definition as a community of descent has obstructed the development of a rational and consistent immigration policy and hindered the integration of foreigners in German social and

political life. A rejection of the principle of descent and a regulation of immigration issues through a new, comprehensive immigration law, one may conclude, are necessary steps if the Federal Republic is to resolve the contradictions inherent in the present situation and thereby open a clear view to the future for immigrants and natives alike. However, it would be insufficient to examine this issue solely in the context of German history. As the French and British cases indicate, even in European countries with a more liberal tradition of national self definition, ethnic conflict and social unrest are becoming increasingly widespread. Indeed, at the end of the twentieth century we face an atmosphere of re-ethnicization and increased cultural division.[55] The potential clash of competing value systems in contemporary Europe is played out perhaps most vividly between Muslim immigrants and the Western majority societies. The measure of success in the new German nation-state lies, therefore, not only in whether *jus sanguinis* can be effectively overcome, but also in whether the Western-Christian majority and the growing Muslim minority can find common ground for peaceful coexistence.

NOTES

Translated from the German by Steven Bileca. I am also grateful to Anthony Dirk Moses (Berkeley) for comments and help.

1. Luc Rosenzweig, *Die Zeit,* 5 July 1991, 5.
2. Jeffrey M. Peck, "Comment," in Jürgen Fijalkowski, *Aggressive Nationalism, Immigration Pressure, and Asylum Policy Disputes in Contemporary Germany,* Occasional Paper No. 9 (Washington, D.C.: German Historical Institute, 1993), 32.
3. See Lutz Hoffmann, *Die unvollendete Republik: Zwischen Einwanderungsland und deutschem Nationalstaat* (Köln: PapyRossa, 1990); Dieter Oberndörfer, *Die offene Republik: Zur Zukunft Deutschlands und Europas* (Freiburg: Herder, 1991); and Daniel Cohn-Bendit and Thomas Schmid, *Heimat Babylon: Das Wagnis der multikulturellen Demokratie* (Hamburg: Hoffmann & Campe, 1993).
4. See, for example, the debate in the German Bundestag on 9 February 1995, in *Deutscher Bundestag, 13. Wahlperiode, Stenographischer Bericht,* 9 February 1995, 1217–38.
5. See Rogers Brubaker, *Citizenship and Nationhood in France and Germany* (Cambridge: Harvard University Press, 1992), 53ff.; and Albrecht Funk, "Wer ist Deutscher, wer ist Deutsche? Unentwegter Versuch, einem amerikanischen Publikum die Geheimnisse der deutschen Staatsbürgerschaft zu erklären," *Leviathan* 23 (1995): 307–20.

6. See Klaus J. Bade, ed., *Auswanderer, Wanderarbeiter, Gastarbeiter: Bevölkerung, Arbeitsmarkt und Wanderung in Deutschland seit der Mitte des 19. Jahrhunderts*, 2 vols. (Ostfildern: Scripta Mercaturae Verlag, 1984), 429ff.; and Ulrich Herbert, *A History of Foreign Labor in Germany, 1880–1980: Seasonal Workers/Forced Laborers/Guest Workers* (Ann Arbor: University of Michigan Press, 1990), 9ff.

7. See Brubaker, *Citizenship and Nationhood*, 114ff.

8. Jack Wertheimer, *Unwelcome Strangers: East European Jews in Imperial Germany* (New York: Oxford University Press, 1987).

9. See Brubaker, *Citizenship and Nationhood*, 165–68.

10. See J. Noakes and G. Pridham, eds., *Nazism, 1919–1945: A History in Documents and Eyewitness Accounts*, vol. 2 (New York: Schocken Books, 1988), 942ff.

11. Quoted in Brubaker, *Citizenship and Nationhood*, 169.

12. See Funk, "Wer ist Deutscher, wer ist Deutsche?" 311.

13. See Hoffmann, *Die unvollendete Republik*, 175.

14. See Hubert Heinelt and Anne Lohmann, *Immigranten im Wohlfahrtsstaat am Beispiel der Rechtspositionen und Lebensverhältnisse von Aussiedlern* (Opladen: Leske & Budrich, 1992).

15. See Zentrum für Türkeistudien, ed., *Ausländer in der Bundesrepublik Deutschland: Ein Handbuch* (Opladen: Leske & Budrich, 1994); Detlev Bischoff and Werner Teubner, *Zwischen Einbürgerung und Rückkehr: Ausländerpolitik und Ausländerrecht der Bundesrepublik Deutschland*, 3d ed. (Berlin: Hitit, 1992); Cord Pagenstecher, *Ausländerpolitik und Immigrantenidentität: Zur Geschichte der "Gastarbeit" in der Bundesrepublik* (Berlin: Betz, 1994); Karl-Heinz Meier-Braun, *Integration und Rückkehr? Zur Ausländerpolitik des Bundes und der Länder, insbesondere Baden-Württembergs* (Mainz: Grunewald, 1988).

16. See Hans-Peter Schneider, "Das Asylrecht zwischen Generosität und Xenophobie: Zur Entstehung des Artikels 16 Absatz 2 Grundgesetz im Parlamentarischen Rat," *Jahrbuch für Antisemitismusforschung* 1 (1992): 217–36; and Ursula Münch, *Asylpolitik in der Bundesrepublik Deutschland: Entwicklung und Alternativen*, 2d ed.(Opladen: Leske & Budrich, 1993).

17. See Klaus J. Bade, *Ausländer, Aussiedler, Asyl in der Bundesrepublik Deutschland* (Bonn: Bundeszentrale für politische Bildung, 1992), 10.

18. Alien Law, paragraph 2, quoted in Herbert, *History of Foreign Labor*, 214.

19. Knut Dohse, *Ausländische Arbeiter und bürgerlicher Staat: Genese und Funktion von staatlicher Ausländerpolitik und Ausländerrecht: Vom Kaiserreich bis zur Bundesrepublik Deutschland* (Königstein/Ts.: Hain, 1981), 250.

20. See Bischoff and Teubner, *Zwischen Einbürgerung und Rückkehr*, 47.

21. See Pagenstecher, *Ausländerpolitik und Immigrantenidentität*, 49f.

22. For the general problem of integration without citizenship, see Yasemin Nuhoglu Soysal, *Limits of Citizenship: Migrants and Postnational Membership in Europe* (Chicago and London: Chicago University Press, 1994); and Rogers Brubaker, "Membership without Citizenship: The Economic and Social Rights

of Noncitizens," in Rogers Brubaker, ed., *Immigration and the Politics of Citizenship in Europe and North America* (Lanham, Md.: University Press of America, 1989), 67–80.

23. See Pagenstecher, *Ausländerpolitik und Immigrantenidentität*, 34.

24. Funk, "Wer ist Deutscher, wer ist Deutsche?" 313.

25. See Bischoff and Teubner, *Zwischen Einbürgerung und Rückkehr*, 169–79.

26. See Herbert, *History of Foreign Labor*, 214; and Pagenstecher, *Ausländerpolitik und Immigrantenidentität*, 35–37.

27. Herbert, *History of Foreign Labor*, 213.

28. Pagenstecher, *Ausländerpolitik und Immigrantenidentität*, 62.

29. Quoted in Pagenstecher, *Ausländerpolitik und Immigrantenidentität*, 62.

30. Cited in Bischoff and Teubner, *Zwischen Einbürgerung und Rückkehr*, 97.

31. Herbert, *History of Foreign Labor*, 235.

32. See *Der Spiegel*, no. 38 (15 September 1980): 19–26; and Werner Bergmann, "Xenophobia and Antisemitism after the Unification of Germany," *Patterns of Prejudice* 28 (1994): 67–80, at 67.

33. Die Zeit, 5 February 1982, 13.

34. Cited in Pagenstecher, *Ausländerpolitik und Immigrantenidentität*, 55.

35. *Verhandlungen des Deutschen Bundestages, 9. Wahlperiode: Stenographische Berichte*, vol. 120, 2 February 1982, 4892f.

36. See Laura M. Murray, "Einwanderungsland Bundesrepublik Deutschland? Explaining the Evolving Positions of German Political Parties on Citizenship Policy," *German Politics and Society*, no. 33 (fall 1994): 23–56, at 28ff.

37. See Bade, *Ausländer, Aussiedler, Asyl*, 145–62; and Michael Klöcker and Udo Tworuschka, eds., *Miteinander—was sonst? Multikulturelle Gesellschaft im Brennpunkt* (Köln and Wien: Böhlau, 1990).

38. Bade, *Ausländer, Aussiedler, Asyl*, 24.

39. See *Der Spiegel*, no 45 (7 November 1988): 118–26.

40. See the interview with Daniel Cohn-Bendit, *Der Spiegel*, no. 22 (29 May 1989): 98–103.

41. See Thomas Faist, "How to Define a Foreigner? The Symbolic Politics of Immigration in German Partisan Discourse, 1978–1992," *West European Politics* 17 (1994): 50–71.

42. Klaus J. Bade, *Das Manifest der 60: Deutschland und der Einwanderung* (Munich: C. H. Beck ,1994), 13.

43. See Meier-Braun, *Integration*, 71; and Bade, *Ausländer, Aussiedler, Asyl*, 18.

44. See Bade, *Ausländer, Aussiedler, Asyl*, 19f.

45. See Funk, "Wer ist Deutscher, wer ist Deutsche?" 315.

46. See Heribert Prantl, "Hysterie und Hilflosigkeit: Chronik der Asyldebatte seit der deutschen Einheit," in Bernhard Blanke, ed., *Zuwanderung und Asyl in der Konkurrenzgesellschaft* (Opladen: Leske & Budrich, 1993), 301–37.

47. See Klaus J. Bade, "Einheimische und Fremde im vereinigten Deutsch-

land," in Alexander Demandt, ed., *Mit Fremden leben: Eine Kulturgeschichte von der Antike bis zur Gegenwart* (Munich: C. H. Beck, 1995), 220–34; and Rainer Erb, "Rechtsextremistische Gruppengewalt in den neuen Bundesländern," in Wolfgang Benz, ed., *Rechtsextremismus in Deutschland* (Frankfurt/M.: Fischer Taschenbuchverlag, 1994), 110–36.

48. See Bundesminister des Inneren, *Verfassungsschutzbericht 1994* (Bonn, 1995).

49. See Uwe Markus, "Zur Dimension der Ausländerfeindlichkeit in Ostdeutschland," *Jahrbuch für Antisemitismusforschung* 1 (1992): 160–65; Horst Becker, "Einstellungen zu Ausländern in der Bevölkerung der Bundesrepublik Deutschland 1992," in Blanke, *Zuwanderung und Asyl,* 141–49; and Werner Bergmann, "Antisemitism and Xenophobia in the East German Länder," *German Politics* 3 (1994): 265–76.

50. See Bergmann, "Antisemitism and Xenophobia," 73.

51. *Der Spiegel* 47, no. 11 (15 March 1993): 53.

52. On the party positions on citizenship policy, see Murray, "Einwanderungsland."

53. *Der Spiegel,* no. 47 (21 November 1994), 17.

54. See, for example, *FAZ,* 25 November 1994, 14; *Die Zeit,* 25 November 1994, 12; and *Der Spiegel,* no. 47 (21 November 1994), 22.

55. In the current German debate, the problems of ethnicization are used as an argument against changing the citizenship law. See, for example, Josef Schmid, "Eine Mischung aus Güte und Überheblichkeit: Die Weltfremdheit der deutschen Einwanderungsdebatte und die Gefahren fortschreitender Ethnifizierung," *FAZ* 8 (November 1995): 11.

Two Discourses of Citizenship in Germany: The Differences between Public Debate and Administrative Practice

Jost Halfmann

I. Introduction

During the current debate on citizenship, Germany has been portrayed as the only major European country that adheres to an exclusive *jus sanguinis* principle in defining citizenship.[1] The *jus sanguinis* principle implies that only children born to a German parent can become German citizens. In the view of its critics, this principle appears to be thoroughly inadequate for dealing with what James Hollifield calls the "migration crisis in Western Europe."[2] Over the last two decades, Germany has attracted more immigrants than any other European country: between 1989 and 1992 about one million people migrated annually to Germany, primarily asylum seekers, refugees from the civil war in former Yugoslavia, and *Aussiedler,* the so-called ethnic Germans from Eastern Europe and the former Soviet Union. Since the outbreak of civil war in Yugoslavia, more than 600,000 refugees have sought protection in Western Europe, more than half of that number (350,000) in Germany. Germany hosts the largest foreign population in Europe; in 1996 it amounted to about 7.3 million, which equates to roughly 9 percent of the total population.[3] The German government has been chided for not making sufficient efforts to facilitate the procedures for naturalizing foreign residents, especially for those who have been living in Germany for many years or for their children who were born and brought up in Germany.[4] Germany has also been criticized for failing to devise a clear immigration policy and for refusing to consider itself an immigration country.

The *Einbürgerungsrichtlinien* (administrative guidelines on naturalization) of 1977 state that "the Federal Republic is not a country of immigration (and) does not strive to increase the number of its citizens through naturalization."[5]

The criticism leveled against the immigration policy of a state is usually based on moral considerations referring to universal human rights. Migrants can claim protection under these rights no matter on which side of the borders of a nation-state they may be at a certain moment. There is an inherent problem with this kind of reasoning. Apart from the fact that it does not help explain the behavior of states, it overlooks one important implication of the parallel evolution of human rights standards and of nation-states. From the vantage point of the twentieth century, there seems to be a contradiction between the all-inclusiveness of human rights and the exclusiveness of nation-states. All modern democratic states pledge allegiance to human rights, but at the same time they reserve certain rights (such as the voting right) to nationals only. Human rights take humanity or world society as the context of inclusion and claim that every human being has a right to be included. The question is: inclusion in what? The French Revolution had "solved" the puzzle by declaring that every human being has a right to be a member of a nation-state. The human right to membership in one nation-state implies that one cannot be a member of another state. Obviously, there is a discrepancy between the universalism of human rights and the particularism of nation-states' rights that coexist in most democratic constitutions.[6] In terms of a theory of societal evolution, the spread of nation-states over the globe has led to a politically segmented world society. By establishing and policing borders, nation-states create differential zones of inclusion and exclusion.

While humanity is not an entity that can offer membership, nation-states can. The first form of membership in nation-states results from inclusion in the political system: citizenship. For states, citizenship means legal and administrative control over a population within a territory enclosed by borders. Citizenship is membership in a state that, as a rule, is permanent, exclusive, and direct.[7] Citizenship is permanent in the sense that states cannot revoke membership acquired by birth; it is exclusive in the sense that membership is possible only in one state;[8] and it is direct in the sense that no other loyalties (such as personal or political ones) can interfere in the citizen-state relationship. For citizens, citizenship as membership in a state carries with it certain rights (the right to vote, to be elected to office, etc.) and obligations (such as military service). The idea of rights and duties being associated with citizenship has formed the basis for concepts of the nation-state as a community of citizens, or: a nation.

A second important form of inclusion—inclusion in social systems such as education, health, or economy—is mediated through a host of state (-supervised) organizations, comprised under the heading of the welfare state system.[9] Historically, a major problem for emerging nation-states was the allocation of a population to a territory over which a state could exercise authority. From the beginning, nation-state building in Europe had to deal with migration, especially migration of the poor. The collapse of familial and local forms of authority during the formative period of European nation-state building in the seventeenth and eighteenth centuries created a large flow of migrant poor people. Such migration posed a particularly difficult problem for the emerging territorial states because control of a state over a territory meant first and foremost control over the resident population. Since membership in a state required residence in a state-controlled territory, the allocation of the poor to one or another state became a major problem in domestic and international politics of the emerging modern state.[10] State-building not only meant to exercise effective control over a certain territory, but also to transfer the responsibility for the poor (as well as for all other residents on the territory) from the communes to the state.[11] This double task had two implications: criteria for membership in a nation-state had to be created, and measures and organizations for supporting and maintaining the inclusion of the residents in social systems such as the educational or the market-economy system had to be devised. The first process led to the creation of the institution of citizenship with its two pure forms of *jus soli* and *jus sanguinis*. The second process—the emergence of the welfare state—has expanded in Europe into a comprehensive practice of state-mediated integration into society. States pursue a policy of mediating the inclusion into social systems such as the economic system (through labor-market policies or unemployment agencies), the health system (through health insurance programs), or the educational system (through providing school facilities, regulating the curricula, etc.).

While access to the provisions of the nation-state is dependent on citizenship status, access to the welfare state system is contingent on residence. (This is, however, less a direct consequence of the attempts of the early modern state to provide welfare on the basis of residence[12] than a late result of judicial decisions concerning the equal treatment of all legal residents in a country).[13] Migration poses a problem for nation-states in three respects: first, because it puts the state capacity of controlling access to the territory to a test; second, because it puts the capacity of the state to mediate inclusion into society to a test; and third, because it puts to a test the capacity for including newcomers into the political system of a nation-state. The solution to the first problem is not only sought in the policing of the borders, but also in international agreements on a "migration regime."[14] Solving the second problem is basically contingent on the state's capacity to mobilize sufficient legal and financial resources to extend its mediating role for inclusion into society. This raises several questions, among them whether migrants generate sufficient taxable income to finance welfare expenditures.[15] The third problem touches on the capacities of a society to develop a sufficiently abstract concept of national community to accommodate newcomers. Here it certainly makes a difference whether a country has a tradition of immigration (such as the United States) or of emigration (such as Germany). It is, however, not of major importance for any of the three problems whether citizenship is attributed on the basis of *jus soli* or *jus sanguinis*. Whether a nation-state adheres to a more or less liberal immigration policy depends wholly on the regulations of granting access to the territory, to the provisions of mediating inclusion, and to naturalization opportunities.

Migration can be described as the transition from the status of (forced or voluntary) exclusion from the social and political systems of one nation-state to the status of inclusion in the social and political systems of another nation-state. Modern nation-states view migration as a threat to their capacity of exerting effective legal and administrative control over their territories and citizenry.[16] Germany, like any other developed modern state, has become attractive for migrants because of its comprehensive welfare state system that mediates inclusion into society. Having been for most of its history a country of emigration, Germany has a tradition of a restrictive naturalization policy. In recent decades, however, it has eased access to its territory and to its welfare state system, and in some cases to its political system as well.

In this article I will discuss the issues of citizenship and immigration in terms of the tension-ridden relation between public discourses on the one hand and legal and administrative practices on the other. I will look into two specific problems that have dominated the public attention in immigration and citizenship matters over the last decades: the asylum problem and the ethnocultural definition of German citizenship. The two topics affect the relation between the public and the legal-administrative realms in very different ways. To compensate for the Nazi persecution of minorities, the asylum clause in the Basic Law grants an individual right of residence to asylum seekers. From the point of view of the administration, this politically induced provision constitutes a severe restriction on the state's capacity to control access to the German nation-state. While for the federal administration the asylum problem is one of maintaining or regaining control over the borders, for the public the controversy concerns the moral question of whether and how much support Germany owes refugees in the light of its past.

The *jus sanguinis* element in the definition of German citizenship has produced a different control problem for the administrative and legal system. Postwar legal decisions and administrative practice allowed aliens almost the same entitlements as German citizens. Hence it was the consequences of legal and administrative decisions that prompted the public debate over the question of how much solidarity Germans owe legal foreign residents.

I will look into these two cases—the asylum and the *jus sanguinis* problem—first from the perspective of the political debates that centered around these issues, and second from the perspective of the legal and administrative system. The article will be divided into three sections: in the first section I will present a brief overview of the public debate on asylum and immigration during the last two decades (II); the second section will be devoted to the recent legal and administrative measures regarding the "migration crisis" (III); and the final section will deal with the question of how these developments affect the process of social and political adjustment to continuous immigration in Germany (IV).

II. The Public Debate on Citizenship and Immigration in Germany

Any comparison of the political interests and views of the public with those of the state has to start from the peculiarity of the European tradition of modern nation-state building. The major departure from the medieval estate polity, inaugurated by the French Revolution, consisted in constituting what Reinhard Bendix calls the plebiscitarian relationship between the state and the populace. By removing all traditional corporate (*ständische*) allegiances, the state established a direct relationship between itself and the populace and considered itself the only legitimate source of the general welfare.[17] This idea of the modern state was not only pursued by republican polities in the French revolutionary tradition but also by enlightened absolutism such as the Prussian kingdom.

This definition of the state as independent of society, but dependent on the principles of the constitution, resonates in the modern German concept of the *Rechtsstaat,* which regards the state as the main champion of liberty and welfare.[18] Based on this understanding of statehood, the Basic Law of the Federal Republic defines the democratic German *Rechtsstaat* as an entity that pursues the common interest of the whole nation and that acts independently of the interests emerging in society. Within this tradition the *state* is defined as consisting of the legislative, executive, and administrative bodies and the legal system. The state distinguishes itself from the *public,* in which the people expresses its political will in a variety of ways: through the media, political parties, interest organizations, or social movements. Jürgen Habermas conceives of the public as a "network of opinions"[19] that is stabilized by a "civil-societal infrastructure" of professional and trade associations, public interest groups, and religious organizations.[20] Rather than exerting power, the public generates influence (in the Parsonian sense).[21] Conflicts and debates over political issues such as citizenship and immigration exhibit (and process at the same time) the underlying tension between the interests of the state and those of the public in which the plebiscitarian competes with the statist element of German democracy. Political parties mediate this rivalry of principles by transferring the political will of the people into the legislative and executive bodies and by providing the administrative bodies with implementable political decisions. The controversies over the issues of citizenship and immigration establish the context within which the interest of the state in providing the general welfare is challenged by the political expressions of the public. Political parties, by striving for governmental power within a system of "competitive democracy," have established themselves as the main mediators between the interests of the state and the public.[22] Public debates and administrative practices each have their own discursive logics; but their interaction, mediated through the political parties in power, affects policies in significant ways, as the cases of *jus sanguinis* and "asylum" will show.

Asylum

Article 16 of the Basic Law guarantees asylum in Germany to anyone who is a victim of political persecution. This clause constitutes an individual right for refugees granted by the German state. By introducing this clause into the Basic Law on humanitarian grounds, Germany not only presented itself as a champion of human rights beyond the protection offered by the Geneva Convention on Refugees, it also set the stage for future public debate on this clause should refugees indeed take this offer seriously. As long as applications remained at a modest level, the asylum clause reaped moral dividends for the German state without much cost. When, after the collapse of the Soviet empire, asylum applications suddenly surged, a public debate over the moral and financial costs of this clause immediately emerged. The number of asylum applicants had grown substantially from 1991 to 1992.[23] Violent attacks against the homes of immigrants in 1992 and 1993, causing several deaths, aggravated the political climate in Germany. Right-wing splinter groups demanded the ousting of all foreigners from Germany. The majority of the media expressed their deep shock, and spontaneous solidarity demonstrations sprang up (such as the *Lichterketten* candlelight vigils).[24] These actions impressed the populace as ensuing public opinion polls showed a decrease in radical right-wing attitudes and in support for the extremist right.[25]

The underlying theme of the public debates on the asylum issue in the 1990s was whether and to what degree the Germans owed support to refugees from foreign countries. Another implicit theme of that debate was whether the asylum seekers were sufficiently aware of the hospitality that Germany was offering them. Conservative politicians and intellectuals expressed their doubts about the practicality of an asylum paragraph that reflected a political situation of half a century earlier. In particular, representatives of the conservative parties in power were concerned that their electorate would fall for the propaganda of the extremist right that demanded an immediate end to what they termed *Asylmißbrauch* (the abuse of the asylum right). Conservative politicians played on the popular fears that immigration via asylum might increase beyond control and weigh further on tight welfare budgets. Opposition forces such as the Social Democrats and independent left-liberal groups tended to point out that Germany has a continuing moral obligation to protect those who are persecuted on political grounds. While conservatives would not dare to question a special moral obligation of the Germans, they tried to appeal to popular suspicions that many applicants seek asylum for economic rather than political reasons. Conservatives questioned the motives of asylum seekers by coining the notion of *Wirtschaftsflüchtlinge* (economic refugees)[26] Although the "asylum" issue played a certain role in the 1994 elections, the appeals of right-wing extremists to reject asylum immigration unconditionally have not found widespread support in the population.[27]

Jus Sanguinis and Immigration

Among the larger European states, Germany has defended most energetically the *jus sanguinis* principle in attributing citizenship by birth.[28] Since the 1980s, the public debate on citizenship in Germany has been very much dominated by the shadow of the Nazi past. The underlying belief of all actors in this debate is that Germany has to account for a crisis-ridden history of nation-building and that the xenophobic and genocidal politics of the Nazi regime might have an impact on current references to German ethnicity.

Proposing or defending the idea that Germans have a national tradition of their own and that the alien and immigration policy should be aware of this history was prone, therefore, to either being denounced as the continuation of a *völkisch* or "racist" concept of German ethnicity, as the radical left purported; or to being used as a provocative and taboo-breaking motto of national reaffirmation against overcrowding the country with aliens, as the extremist right claimed. It comes as no surprise that the *jus sanguinis* basis of German citizenship was placed at the center of political debate on immigration and citizenship. This becomes evident in the attention the coincidence of two very different events received. The sudden rise of xenophobic and racist incidents in the early 1990s[29] coincided with the unification of the two postwar German states. Some observers chose a shortcut interpretation of the connection between these two developments: to them the rise of xenophobic violence at the time of unification indicated the possible reemergence of an aggressive, nationalistic German state.[30]

The political debate in Germany reflected these fears, while at the same time using them in partisan politics. Immigration and citizenship issues had already played a role in the political debates of the seventies. During the mid-seventies, shortly after the *Anwerbestopp* (the end of the government-sponsored drive for recruiting foreign workers), the Christian Democrats in the state of Baden-Württemberg proposed hiring future foreign workers only on the basis of "rotating" them back into their countries of origin. This was meant to prevent these workers from settling in Germany. In 1979 the ruling Christian Socialist Union of Bavaria started a political campaign to appeal to right-wing voters that exaggerated the problems of the cultural integration of Turkish immigrants. These early attempts at using immigration issues as a topic for partisan politics culminated in the "Heidelberg Manifesto" of 1981, in which a group of German university professors proclaimed that further immigration threatened the purity of German ethnicity.[31] A public opinion poll conducted by the Allensbach Institute in the mid-eighties showed that the politicization of these issues had an effect on the public: while up to that moment foreign immigrants were generally considered an overall gain for the economy, the public now seemed to be divided between "tolerance" and "worry" with regard to foreign immigrants.[32]

Before the coalition of Christian Democrats and Free Democrats won the parliamentary elections of 1983, Helmut Kohl had demanded that the number of foreign *Mitbürger* (co-citizens!) should be reduced considerably. However, apart from a less than moderately successful government program of offering foreign workers financial inducements to return home, none of these radical programmatic goals was put into practice under the liberal-conservative government. In 1983 and 1984 the immigration problem was removed from the public agenda by the controversy over the NATO decision to install new medium-range missiles in Germany. In the mid-eighties, however, the immigration theme reappeared in public discourse with the founding of the extremist right-wing party the Republikaner, whose explicit anti-foreigners polemics gained surprising support in local and state elections.[33] Extremist right-wing parties won seats in the parliaments of states such as Bremen, Baden-Württemberg, and Schleswig-Holstein. The public attention to the successes of the Republikaner lasted, however, only until the unification of the Federal Republic with the German Democratic Republic in 1990.

After unification the debate on immigration and citizenship was resumed with full force and with occasional violent xenophobic acts. In the meantime, the political positions taken by the various political groups had become more clearly recognizable.

Jürgen Fijalkowski distinguishes between four different attitudes toward migration and citizenship: nation-state conservatism, liberal multiculturalism, regressive ethnonationalism, and strict egalitarianism.[34] Nation-state conservatism, a position held within the conservative parts of the Christian Democratic and Christian Socialist parties, views immigrants as a threat to societal solidarity in Germany. Liberal multiculturalism, a belief espoused by the more progressive factions of the Social Democratic Party as well as by church circles, portrays immigration as a means of furthering supranational communities (such as the European Community). These groups reject the exclusionary character of the modern nation-state.[35] Regressive ethnonationalism (as expressed in the Heidelberg Manifesto of 1981, but also in the programs of right-wing parties such as the Deutsche Volksunion and the Republikaner) fears that immigrants undermine German culture and ethnicity. Strict egalitarianism vis-à-vis aliens is demanded by grassroots movements from the left. The Green Party has adopted some of their positions, as the resolution "With Courage toward a Multicultural Society. Against Right-Wing Extremism and Xenophobia" of 1989 indicates.[36]

The idea of multiculturalism is very much at the center of the left-liberal views of immigration and citizenship. Multiculturalism as an ideology that embraces ethnic diversity departs explicitly from the ethnocultural tradition of German nationhood and adopts central concepts of the North American and Australian idea of nationhood. Such a concept of nationhood is neither oriented at assimilation (as in the French tradition) nor at separation (as in the German tradition) but at the coexistence of ethnic groups that is supported by legislation (such as minority protection or antidiscrimination laws) and governmental programs (such as stipulating hiring quotas and educational assistance programs).[37]

If one leaves aside extremist positions of the left and right, there are basically two views of citizenship and immigration that have had an impact on legislation and administrative practice. While the conservatives wish to integrate and (in a mild form) even assimilate the resident foreign population, the more progressive spectrum supports the idea of multiculturalism and an explicit immigration policy. In a way, one might say that the conservatives lean toward adapting elements of the French model and that the opposition opts for elements of the North American model. The political debate is, however, dictated by the rules of competitive party democracy. The latent agenda of partisan politics is to win over and (if possible) lock in a supportive segment of the electorate. This forces the parties to pursue a double strategy: to appeal to voters at the respective left or right fringes of the potential electorate and at the same time to demarcate themselves from their convictions. Because of Germany's Nazi past, the semantics of any political debate on citizenship and immigration are shaped by allusions to the alleged continuity or discontinuity with past immigration and citizenship policies. As a consequence, these debates tend to be often fierce and unfair, but they also produce unintended echoes among those segments of the population that the parties wish to win over and contain at the same time.

III. Legal and Administrative Practice in Immigration and Citizenship Matters

The legal and administrative practice in Germany is quite different from the political discourse in public. In the legal and administrative discourse the allegiance of the state to the values of the Basic Law and to the preservation of state authority over what it considers its proper realms (such as defense, taxing, or access to its territory) is the primary motive of action. The interest of the state in preserving the integrity of the political and social order of the Federal Republic leads to specific forms of reasoning with respect to how immigration affects citizenship.

The two types of reasoning constitute a marked difference between the discourse of the legal and administrative system and the political debate in public. There are basically two strategic orientations of the legal and administrative system, based on two pillars of constitutional reasoning at the outset of the Federal Republic of Germany. One of the most forceful trends of legal and administrative action in the postwar period in Germany is the extension of the principle of equal access to the welfare state system by all legal residents in Germany.[38] This implied, however, that, based on the same "integrationist" principle, fundamental changes of immigration and citizenship policy occurred in the course of German postwar history. While the German state pursued a very exclusionary policy toward non-German immigrants until the late 1970s, it slowly reversed its position toward a more integrationist stance once it acknowledged that a large part of the foreign population intended to stay in Germany.[39] Today, the alien policy is geared toward furthering the social inclusion of long-term foreign residents while at the same time preventing new immigration. This strategy of generalizing the equality principle on the basis of residence has, however, underscored the discrepancy between social and political inclusion, between membership based on citizenship and on residence.

The other general strategy of the administrative and legal system, which goes back to Article 116 in the Basic Law is directed at providing all ethnic Germans with the opportunity to express their political will freely. This guarantee extended to the citizens of the former GDR as well as to the ethnic Germans in Eastern Europe and in the former Soviet Union. Over time and against its original intent, this clause has led to the elaboration of basic elements of an immigration legislation and of the building up of a central administration for managing immigration matters.

With the simultaneous evolution of the nation-state and welfare state, two types of membership have evolved in Germany: first, membership in the nation-state (citizenship), which is based either on acquisition by birth (in the German case, via *jus sanguinis*) or on naturalization; and second, membership in the welfare state system, which is based on legal residence in Germany. There are two developments that best highlight the different course that administrative and legal practice has taken as compared to the political debate in public. One change concerns the consequences of immigration for the principle of membership based on residence and the other the consequences of departing from a *jus sanguinis* rule of membership acquisition in recent developments of naturalization policy. Each of these two developments has created a specific problem for the continuity of legal and administrative practice. The fact that new foreign and ethnic German immigrants are more dependent on welfare state provisions than long-term German and foreign residents has created substantial financial problems for the welfare state system. In the long term, the options are either to impede access to legal residence status for newcomers or to reduce and reorganize the welfare state system itself or to do both. The fact that more than 75 percent of the aliens in Germany possess a secure legal residence status has deepened the doubts about the validity of the current citizenship policy: the options are either to ease further the naturalization procedures or to depart from the exclusiveness of the *jus sanguinis* principle or to do both. Obviously, the decisions taken in one problem area will have repercussions for the other.

Immigration

Currently, there are two avenues for immigrating to Germany: one can either apply for asylum (by claiming protection under Article 16 of the Basic Law) or for recognition of the *Aussiedler* status as ethnic German from the former German settlements in Eastern Europe (by claiming access under Article 116 of the Basic Law).

Immigration under Article 16 (Basic Law): The asylum clause in the Basic Law grants asylum to all foreigners who apply for asylum on the grounds of political persecution in their country of origin. Since this article of the Basic Law grants an individual right vis-à-vis the German state, it restricts the capacity of the German state to control entry to the state territory. It comes as no surprise that from the perspective of the administrative apparatus, the increasing numbers of asylum seekers since the late eighties were perceived as an "asylum crisis." By 1994, 1.7 million refugees with a legal status according to the Geneva Convention on Refugees of 1951 were staying in Germany.[40] In 1992 almost 430,000 persons applied for asylum in Germany.[41] As a response to this crisis, the asylum article in the Basic Law was revised in 1993. This revision was intended to reduce the number of applicants and to speed up the processing of applications without denying the asylum seekers the individual right to asylum. Asylum applicants coming from "safe" countries of origin[42] or having come through safe *Drittstaaten* (states that could have granted asylum)[43] are not acknowledged as legal asylum seekers. Despite this revision, about 130,000 asylum seekers still managed to file applications in 1994 (as compared to 320,000 in 1993).

The interest of the state in protecting the functioning of the welfare system was the reason for removing asylum seekers from the entitlements of the *Bundessozialhilfegesetz* (Federal Social Security Act). The provisions for asylum seekers are regulated in the newly issued *Asylbewerberleistungsgesetz* (Asylum Seekers' Benefits Act), which specifies the entitlement for asylum seekers until their application procedure is completed.[44]

Immigration under Article 116 (Basic Law): The *Aussiedler* (resettlers) constitute a large share of the total numbers of immigrants. The *Bundesvertriebenen- und Flüchtlingsgesetz* (Federal Refugees Act) of

1953 defines *Aussiedler* as German citizens or persons of "German stock" who were residents of the former eastern provinces of the German Reich or of German settlements in Eastern Europe and the former Soviet Union prior to 8 May 1945.[45] Article 116 of the Basic Law considers these migrants to be Germans who will be granted citizenship upon entry in the Federal Republic of Germany.[46] *Aussiedler* were eligible for unemployment compensation, financial aid for educational programs, housing, low-interest loans, and preferential entry into the pension fund.[47] After the disintegration of the Soviet bloc, *Aussiedler* migration met fewer obstacles from the "originating" states. Between 1989 and 1992 about 1.2 million *Aussiedler* took up residence in Germany; in those four years alone more *Aussiedler* migrated to Germany than in the 20 years before. In 1990 a new law — the *Aussiedleraufnahmegesetz* (Resettlers' Admittance Act) — was issued that rules that *Aussiedler* have to apply for immigration in their country of origin, that this application has to be written in German, and that the applicants have to prove their German ethnicity. In addition, the *Aussiedler* status has been limited to persons born before 1 January 1993 (the so-called *Spätaussiedler,* late resettlers).

The *Aussiedleraufnahmegesetz,* in conjunction with changes in the *Bundesvertriebenengesetz* (Federal Refugees Act) of 1992, permits the establishment of quotas for *Aussiedler* who will be accepted annually to the territory of the Federal Republic. The number of *Aussiedler* together with the expected number of asylum seekers may not surpass 220,000 persons per year. The process of *Aussiedler* immigration is processed and overseen by the *Bundesverwaltungsamt* (Federal Administration Office). From the perspective of legal and administrative attempts at (re)gaining control over migratory cross-border movements, these legal and administrative procedures provide the Federal Republic with all necessary instruments of an immigration policy. This fact is underscored by Article 73 of the Basic Law, which attributes the legal competence for immigration to the federal government.[48]

Naturalization

Resulting from a policy of hiring foreign workers in the 1960s, a large foreign population has settled in Germany since then. By the end of 1994 almost seven million aliens lived in Germany, 65 percent of them being workers and their families from the former *Anwerberstaaten* (countries such as Italy, Spain, Portugal, or Turkey where workers were recruited). Naturalization rates have remained low despite the fact that in the meantime more than half of the foreign worker migrants have lived for 10 years or more in Germany and fulfill the requirements of the *Reichs- und Staatsangehörigkeitsgesetz* (RuStAG) (Reich and State Citizenship Act). In the past, naturalization was granted at the discretion of the alien administration; the RuStAG requires that naturalized aliens have to give up their former citizenship. As a consequence, between 1977 and 1986 only about 140,000 persons were naturalized. The *jus sanguinis* principle in the citizenship legislation has prevented the children of these aliens from acquiring a right to German citizenship by birth. In contrast to Germany, France as a country with a tradition of attributing citizenship via *jus soli* and of attempting to assimilate immigrants used to provide second-generation immigrants automatically with French citizenship at the age of 18. Since the reform of 1993 the citizenship legislation has started to deviate in significant respects from its *jus soli* basis. The revised law demands a *manifestation de volonté,* a formal declaration from the children of foreign parents to become French citizens.[49]

The asylum and the *jus sanguinis* issues have irritated the state in two very different ways. The asylum article of the Basic Law is alien to those administrative interests that are oriented toward safeguarding the state's control over its borders. As this article granted individuals the right to access German territory without prior proof of the legitimacy of their intention, the administrative system developed a vital interest in revoking the privilege that these groups of individuals enjoyed. As a result, the barriers against free access to the territory have been raised for asylum seekers. The German state has built up substantial obstacles for asylum seekers to reach German territory, where they can exert their right to stay until their case is decided. However, the political debates over the right to asylum have confirmed the constitutional fiat that none of the first 20 articles of the Basic Law should be abolished. The individual right to asylum has been preserved, but the state has improved its capacity to control the access of foreigners to its territory. The final shape of the revised Article 16 was very much influenced by the majority party in the government, the Christian Democrats, who, due to their nation-state conservatism, value societal solidarity of the politically and socially included members of the nation more highly than human rights universalism.

The *jus sanguinis* provision of Article 116 has caused a different control problem for the state. While it was meant to provide all Germans, including those living outside of the Federal Republic's territory, with equal citizenship and welfare opportunities, it strained not only the budgetary and administrative but also the integrative capacities of Germany. The sudden increase in immigration of ethnic Germans exceeded the logistic and financial resources of the cities and communities that had to carry most of the burdens of accommodating ethnic Germans from abroad. Similarly to the revised asylum policy, access for *Aussiedler* to Germany has become more difficult. *Aussiedler* now have to prove in their countries of residence that they meet the provisions of Article 116 of the Basic Law before they will be admitted to German territory. Even though the German state has raised the entry barriers for ethnic Germans and has shifted to a policy of encouraging ethnic Germans to stay in their countries of residence, the number of ethnic Germans filing their applications for migration to Germany has not substantially dropped in recent years.

The challenges of large-scale immigration both of ethnic Germans and asylum seekers had another unintended effect for the German state. It led to the design of an immigration policy and the buildup of an immigration administration without, however, explicitly acknowledging this fact. Immigration is dealt with either under the heading of the *Ausländergesetz* (and executed by the aliens' administration) or of the asylum legislation (and executed by the Bundesamt für die Anerkennung ausländischer Flüchtlinge, Federal Office for the Recognition of Foreign Refugees) or of the *Bundesvertriebenengesetz*.

IV. Conclusion

Public debates on issues such as asylum or *jus sanguinis* indicate critical developments that have moral as well as legal and administrative implications. At the outset, these debates are mere irritants to the established practice of the administrative system. Viewed from the opposite angle, public debates lead the way for a change of legal and administrative practices in the wake of crises of state control over matters of national interest. Public debates counteract the inertia inherent in the administrative and legal system. From the perspective of the interest of the nation-state in safeguarding societal integration, the turbulent debates on immigration and citizenship created the context and mobilized the means for readjusting policies and administrative and legal practice concerning these issues.

Despite radical right-wing violence, these debates take place against the background of a general devalorization of nationalist semantics.[50] Contrary to the reasoning in Harold James's book on "German identity,"[51] which suggests that anxiety over German identity springs up each time when economic depression looms large, the development of German immigration and citizenship policies point in a different direction. The stability or instability of the politics of inclusion and exclusion is less dependent on the ups and downs of collective concepts of German identity than on the degree to which the legal and administrative system can uphold a continuous practice of safeguarding the institutions and practices of the German nation-state and welfare state.

The tensions between the public and the administrative sphere are highlighted by the different ways in which the legal and administrative system on the one hand and the public on the other deal with the irritations caused by unexpected political developments. The first issue, the asylum right, became a problem only after a sudden surge in asylum applications since the late eighties. The loss of state control through the asylum paragraph devised at the outset of the Federal Republic of Germany became visible only after the emergence of an "asylum crisis." The administrative and legal attempts at regaining control of asylum immigration were curtailed by the repercussions of the public debate. The ever fragile moral standing of Germany was at stake not only because of the attempts at restricting asylum immigration, but also by the violent results of this debate itself.[52]

During most of the history of the Federal Republic, the second issue — the ethnocultural grounding of German citizenship — was hidden in the tradition of the *jus sanguinis* principle, which worked well for a nation-state without substantial immigration. Under the pressure of the current migration crisis, which dates back to decisions made in the early 1960s, the German nation-state is faced with the problem of adjusting the system of inclusion without putting its institutional and organizational stability at risk. Germany has developed into a state with two different concepts of membership: citizenship and residence. Citizenship creates membership in the nation-state and residence membership in the welfare state system. The *jus sanguinis* principle, which was once designed to preserve citizenship for Germans in the context of "incomplete" nationhood, has caused unintended consequences: an erosion of the exclusiveness of the membership principle based on citizenship. This loss of control poses a different political problem for the German state than that of the "asylum crisis." After many of the worker immigrants of the sixties had settled down in Germany, it became clear that citizenship was no longer the only form of membership in German society and that the state could no longer exert control over its territory by simply regulating access to German citizenship. Since membership in German society based on legal residence has become an option for a substantial part of the population, *jus sanguinis* threatens to pit a majority of the population (the citizens of Germany) against a minority of the population (the legal foreign residents of Germany) and thus to create disunity rather than unity within the realm of the German state's authority.

While the asylum clause of the Basic Law indeed explicitly signified a break with the politics of the National Socialist regime, a departure from the ethnocultural notion of citizenship in Germany is yet to come. Once the last ethnic German has migrated to Germany and immigration of non-Germans will prevail in the future, Article 116 of the Basic Law will completely lose its rationale. The changes that continuous immigration will eventually bring about for the design and extent of the welfare state system will, however, have a greater impact on the future stability of the German nation-state than the shedding of its ethnocultural tradition. The German welfare state system, which was once designed to further the integration of the population of a nonimmigration country, has perhaps contributed more to the establishment of stable German nationhood than democratic parliamentary rule. Thus, Germany will face difficult decisions in adapting the welfare state system to the new realities of having become an immigration country.

NOTES

1. Rogers Brubaker, *Citizenship and Nationhood in France and Germany* (Cambridge: Harvard University Press, 1992).

2. James E. Hollifield, "The Migration Crisis in Western Europe," in *Migration—Ethnizität—Konflikt: Systemfragen und Fallstudien,* Schriften des Institut für Migrationsforschung und Interkulturelle Studien, vol. 1, ed. K. J. Bade (Osnabrück: Universitätsverlag Rasch, 1996).

3. As measured by the size of population, however, Switzerland has a considerably larger share of foreigners than Germany

4. Klaus J. Bade, ed., *Das Manifest der 60. Deutschland und die Einwanderung* (München: Beck, 1994), 52–55.

5. This translation is taken from Brubaker, *Citizenship and Nationhood,* 147. For a more recent statement, see also Manfred Kanther, "Deutschland ist kein Einwanderungsland: Eine gesetzliche Regelung ist überflüssig," *Frankfurter Allgemeine Zeitung,* 13 November 1996, 11.

6. Dieter Oberndörfer, "Vom Nationalstaat zur offenen Republik," *Aus Politik und Zeitgeschichte* B 9/92 (1992): 21–28.

7. Rolf Grawert, *Staat und Staatsangehörigkeit: Verfassungsgeschichtliche Untersuchung zur Entstehung der Staatsangehörigkeit* (Berlin: Duncker & Humblot, 1973).

8. This principle refers to the state's interest in the loyalty of the citizen, in their willingness to "feel a common destiny." See Raymond Aron, "Is Multicultural Citizenship Possible?" *Social Research* 41 (1974): 655. This becomes particularly obvious in one of the central requirements for naturalization in most states: attachment to the institutional and legal order. For Germany, see Grawert, *Staat und Staatsangehörigkeit,* 196. States, however, function without

such strong commitment of their citizens, as Australia's practice of multiple citizenships shows.

9. For the distinction between political and social inclusion, see Michael Bommes and Jost Halfmann, "Migration und Inklusion: Spannungen zwischen Nationalstaat und Wohlfahrtsstaat," *Kölner Zeitschrift für Soziologie und Sozialpsychologie* 46 (1994): 406–24.

10. Grawert, *Staat und Staatsangehörigkeit*, 133–45.

11. Michael Bommes, "Migration und Ethnizität im nationalen Sozialstaat," *Zeitschrift für Soziologie* 45 (1994): 364–77.

12. Abram de Swaan, *In Care of the State: Health Care, Education, and Welfare in Europe and the USA in the Modern Era* (New York: Oxford University Press, 1988), 17.

13. Michael Bommes, "Migration, Nationalstaat und Wohlfahrtsstaat — Kommunale Probleme in föderalen Systemen," in Bade, *Migration — Ethnizität — Konflikt*, 213–48.

14. For the most recent development of a migration regime within the context of the EC, see Bernhard Santel, "Loss of Control: The Build-Up of a European Migration and Asylum Regime," in *Migration and European Integration: The Dynamics of Inclusion and Exclusion,* ed. R. Miles and D. Thränhardt (London: Pinter, 1995), 75–91.

15. Arne Gieseck, Ulrich Heilemann, and Hans Dietrich von Loeffelholz, *Economic Implications of Migration into the Federal Republic of Germany, 1988-1992* (Essen: Rheinisch-Westfälisches Institut für Wirtschaftsforschung, 1993).

16. Regarding the relation between modern nation-states and the problem of control, see Anthony Giddens, *The Nation-State and Violence* (Berkeley: University of California Press, 1985).

17. Reinhard Bendix, *Nation-Building and Citizenship: Studies of Our Changing Social Order* (New York: Wiley, 1964), 84.

18. Donald P. Kommers, "Building Democracy: Judicial Review and the German Rechtsstaat," paper presented at the conference "The Post-War Transformation of Germany: Democracy, Prosperity, and Nationhood," Center for German and European Studies, University of California at Berkeley, 30 November–2 December 1995.

19. Jürgen Habermas, *Faktizität und Geltung: Beiträge zur Diskurstheorie des Rechts und des demokratischen Rechtsstaats* (Frankfurt: Suhrkamp, 1992), 436.

20. Ibid., 431.

21. One need not share Habermas's view that the legitimacy of the law and the state rests on a functioning public to acknowledge the effects of the "network of opinions" on the factual outcome of decision-making processes in the state.

22. For the notion of "competitive democracy," see Ernst Fraenkel, *Deutschland und die westlichen Demokratien* (Stuttgart: Kohlhammer, 1964), 62–68; for the concept of the public as an actor in the polity, see Jürgen Habermas, *Strukturwandel der Öffentlichkeit* (Neuwied: Luchterhand, 1962), and idem, *Faktizität und Geltung,* 399–467; for the role of parties in the German political

system, see Kurt Sontheimer, *Grundzüge des politischen Systems der Bundesrepublik* (München: Piper, 1972), 88.

23. Thomas Faist, "How to Define a Foreigner? The Symbolic Politics of Immigration in German Partisan Discourse, 1978-1992," *West European Politics* 17 (1994): 50-71.

24. Peter Merkl, "The German Response to the Challenge of Extremist Parties, 1949-1994," paper presented at the conference "The Post-War Transformation of Germany: Democracy, Prosperity, and Nationhood," Center for German and European Studies, University of California at Berkeley, 30 November-2 December 1995.

25. Dietrich Thränhardt, "Die Ursprünge von Rassismus und Fremdenfeindlichkeit in der Konkurrenzdemokratie," *Leviathan*, no. 3 (1993): 336-57.

26. For a more detailed discussion, see Faist, "How to Define a Foreigner?" 64-65.

27. A study conducted by the Institut für Demoskopie at Allensbach claimed that since 1982 anti-foreign sentiments had substantially lost ground in the German population. See Renate Köcher, "Die Ausländerfeindlichkeit in Deutschland ist gering," *Frankfurter Allgemeine Zeitung*, 18 August 1993.

28. Mathias Bös, "Ethnisierung des Rechts? Staatsbürgerschaft in Deutschland, Frankreich, Grossbritannien und den USA," *Kölner Zeitschrift für Soziologie und Sozialpsychologie* 45 (1993): 619-43.

29. Which, however, did not reach the levels of xenophobic violence in England during the same period; see Thränhardt, "Die Ursprünge," 338.

30. For a very dramatic view, see L. Bellak, "Why I Fear the Germans," *New York Times*, 25 April 1990, A29. For a more cautious analysis, see Daniel Bell, "Germany: The Enduring Fear: A New Nationalism or a New Europe," *Dissent*, Fall 1990, 461-67.

31. Klaus Burghardt et al., " 'Heidelberger Manifest': Historisch-kritische Ausgabe," *Kulturrevolution*, 1983, 6ff; Bernhard Santel and Dietrich Thränhardt, "Ausländer," in *Handwörterbuch des politischen Systems der Bundesrepublik Deutschland*, ed. U. Andersen and W. Woyke (Bonn: Bundeszentrale für politische Bildung, 1992), 9-13.

32. Thränhardt, "Die Ursprünge," 342; Manfred Steger and Peter F. Wagner, "Political Asylum, Immigration, and Citizenship in the Federal Republic of Germany," *New Political Science*, 24/25 (1993): 64.

33. For an overview of the program and the electoral successes of the Republikaner, see Thomas Saalfeld, "The Politics of National-Populism: Ideology and Policies of the German Republikaner Party," *German Politics* 2 (1993): 177-99; and Jost Halfmann, "Moderne Gesellschaft und die Konstruktion einer nationalen Solidargemeinschaft: Zur Bedeutung eines neuen Nationalismus in der Bundesrepublik Deutschland," in *Die Kontinentwerdung Europas*, ed. H. Timmermann (Berlin: Duncker & Humblot, 1995), 581-603.

34. Jürgen Fijalkowski, "Nationale Identität versus multikulturelle Gesellschaft: Entwicklungen der Problemlage und Alternativen der Orientierung in der politischen Kultur der Bundesrepublik in den 80er Jahren," in *Die Bundes-*

republik in den achtziger Jahren, ed. W. Süß (Opladen: Leske & Budrich, 1991), 235–50.

35. Very outspoken in this respect is the Komitee für Grundrechte und Demokratie, a small organization of left-liberal intellectuals and university professors, which rejects the concept of an immigration law on the grounds that it makes explicit the exclusionary character of modern nation-states. See Komitee für Grundrechte und Demokratie, *Deutsche Bürger, Europäische Bürger, Weltbürger—Ortsbestimmung menschenrechtlich-demokratischer Politik in der Bundesrepublik inmitten einer mobilen Welt: Eine Denkschrift* (Sensbachtal, 1994).

36. Die Grünen, *Argumente: Die multikulturelle Gesellschaft* (Bonn, 1990).

37. Christian Joppke, "Multiculturalism and Immigration: A Comparison of the United States, Germany, and Great Britain," *Theory and Society* 25 (1996): 449–500. Proponents of the concept of multiculturalism in Germany are Daniel Cohn-Bendit and Thomas Schmid, *Heimat Babylon: Das Wagnis der multikulturellen Demokratie* (Hamburg: Hoffmann & Campe, 1992).

38. Kay Hailbronner, "Der Ausländer in der deutschen Sozialordnung," *Vierteljahresschrift für Sozialrecht,* no. 2 (1992): 77–98.

39. For a history of the exclusionist stance of the German state toward foreigners, see Knut Dohse, *Ausländische Arbeiter und bürgerlicher Staat: Genese und Funktion von staatlicher Ausländerpolitik: Vom Kaiserreich bis zur Bundesrepublik* (Königstein, Ts.: Anton Hain, 1981).

40. CDU/CSU-Fraktion, *Ausländer/Asylbewerber,* 60.

41. Ursula Münch, *Asylpolitik in der Bundesrepublik Deutschland: Entwicklung und Alternativen* (Opladen: Leske & Budrich, 1993).

42. States that do not engage in political persecution of individuals on the grounds of race, religion, nationality, or political beliefs.

43. This clause reflected the coming in effect of the Schengen Agreement in March 1995, which allows free movement within the territory of the signatory states. That would have allowed multiple application attempts for asylum seekers once they reached the territory of one of the Schengen states.

44. Bommes, "Migration, Nationalstaat und Wohlfahrtsstaat."

45. Klaus J. Bade, *Ausländer, Aussiedler, Asyl: Eine Bestandsaufnahme* (München: Beck, 1994), 285.

46. Silke Delfs, "Heimatvertriebene, Aussiedler, Spätaussiedler: Rechtliche und politische Aspekte der Aufnahme von Deutschstämmigen aus Osteuropa in der Bundesrepublik Deutschland," *Aus Politik und Zeitgeschichte* B 48/93 (1993): 3–11. For a more detailed account of the historical origin of the *Aussiedler* article in the Basic Law, see Jost Halfmann, "Immigration and Citizenship in Germany: Contemporary Dilemmas," *Political Studies* 45 (1997): 260–74.

47. Michael Bommes and Ulrich Rotthoff, *Europäische Migrationsbewegungen im kommunalen Kontext* (Osnabrück: Institut für Migrationsforschung und Interkulturelle Studien, 1994).

48. Michael Wollenschläger, "Nationalstaat, Ethnizität und Einwanderungsgesetzgebung in Deutschland," in Bade, *Migration—Ethnizität—Konflikt.*

49. Willy Zimmer, *Die Reformen des Ausländerrechts, des Asyl- und Staatsangehörigkeitsrechts in Frankreich und Deutschland,* Speyerer Forschungsberichte No. 163 (Speyer: Forschungsinstitut für Öffentliche Verwaltung, 1996); Catherine Withol de Wenden, *French Immigration Policy* (typescript, Paris, 1997).

50. Bommes, "Migration und Ethnizität."

51. Harold James, *A German Identity, 1770–1990* (New York: Routledge, 1989).

52. Ignaz Bubis, the chairman of the Zentralrat der Juden in Deutschland (Central Council of Jews in Germany), once remarked that it is telling that it is the German foreign minister who presents the official government views on the firebomb attacks on the homes of Turkish families and asylum seekers.

Germany's Place in the World

The Enduring Transformation of Postwar German Foreign Policy

Thomas Banchoff

The postreunification debate about the normalization of German foreign policy has obscured the enduring nature of its postwar transformation. In the years after reunification, the leaders of the Federal Republic slowly adopted a less reticent approach to military policy instruments, one more like that of their U.S., British, and French counterparts. This change, most obvious in German participation in peacekeeping operations in the Balkans, has deflected attention from a striking element of continuity across the 1990 divide: the new Germany, like the old, remained firmly bound to the West, strongly committed to the Atlantic Alliance and the European Community. The postwar transformation of the German role in Europe — the break with the nationally oriented *Schaukelpolitik* of the past — outlasted the revolutionary changes unleashed by the collapse of bipolarity and reunification.

What accounts for the postwar transformation of German foreign policy and its persistence in the post–Cold War context? International institutions appear to offer an explanation at once parsimonious and persuasive. The Federal Republic, founded in 1949 under the tutelage of the Western powers, did not secure its external sovereignty until six years later. One can argue that ultimate allied responsibility for Bonn's international status made Konrad Adenauer's policy of Western integration, which culminated in NATO membership in 1955, a foregone conclusion. Similarly, it is possible to argue that reunification within Western institutions, the North Atlantic Treaty Organization (NATO) and the European Community (EC), bound the new Germany firmly to the West. Chancellor Helmut Kohl's continued strong pro-Western orientation, in this interpretation, was a rational response to institutional constraints.

This chapter takes issue with these parsimonious institutional explanations. It argues that while institutional constraints prevented a return to aggressive nationalist policies, first after the war, and then after the Cold War, they cannot explain the Federal Republic's strong Western orientation in both periods. The institutional context of the early 1950s did not make Adenauer's Western integration inevitable; and that of the early 1990s did not dictate Kohl's subsequent focus on solidarity with the West. In both cases, particular foreign policy ideas, informed by reflection on historical experience and its lessons and anchored on a firm political foundation, shaped responses to ambiguous institutional constraints and patterned the direction of German foreign policy. The adoption and persistence of a strong Western orientation cannot be reduced to international forces. It also emerged out of *German* reflection on the past and its lessons.

This argument is set out in three sections. A first section outlines straightforward institutional explanations for the postwar and post–Cold War cases. A second section criticizes those explanations and argues that in the German cases and others, three kinds of ambiguity can intervene between institutions and action to create a significant range of policy choice. A third section brings in foreign policy ideas, and historical memory in particular. It examines the views of the past and its lessons that underpinned the policy orientations and informed the policy choices of both Adenauer and Kohl. The conclusion argues that changing views of the past—together with shifts in the international constellation—may influence future changes in the direction of German foreign policy.

The Case for Institutions

The recent surge of interest in institutions in political science, sociology, and economics has given rise to a number of incompatible definitions and typologies. There is considerable definitional discord surrounding the relationship between formal rules and informal norms and practices; between those rules, norms, and practices and the economic, cultural, and political environments within which they are embedded; and between institutions and the individuals and groups who interact with them. Contrasting approaches to institutions, within and across disciplines and subfields of inquiry, have plagued efforts at theory-building. They have not, however, prevented institutional analysis from illuminating a wide array of empirical phenomena.[1]

Douglass North's definition of institutions as sets of rules and norms that constrain choice has proved among the most useful and influential.[2] In the foreign policy context, North's definition has the further advantage of mirroring leading conceptualizations in international relations theory—although here, too, there is nothing like definitional consensus.[3] Institutions such as NATO and the EC can be conceptualized as bundles of rules and norms — consultation, cooperation, multilateralism, shared sovereignty, etc. — that constrain the choices facing national leaders. Institutions, so conceived, cannot explain everything about foreign policy: particular policy decisions emerge out of a complex set of factors. But they can sometimes explain overall patterns of foreign policy within a given international environment.

The case of the Federal Republic would appear to lend itself well to a straightforward institutional analysis. Over the course of the postwar period, no other West European state was enmeshed in as thick a web of international institutions. From the allied occupation regime of the 1940s, to membership in NATO and the EC in the 1950s, to the Eastern Treaties of the 1970s and the Two-Plus-Four reunification settlement of 1990, German leaders found themselves embedded in a dense institutional constellation. There are strong a priori reasons to expect institutional arguments about the trajectory of postwar and post–Cold War foreign policy to be persuasive.

Western Integration, 1949–55

The case for the force of institutions during the postwar period appears the stronger of the two. Unconditional surrender in 1945 left Germany occupied and divided. The United States, Britain, and France combined their zones of occupation to form the FRG in 1949 — the same year the Soviet Union created the German Democratic Republic (GDR) in its zone. The Western powers sought to establish viable democratic institutions. But they were also determined to shape the contours of German foreign policy. The German constitution, or Basic Law, drafted under the watchful eye of the occupying forces, proscribed any revival of militarist expansionism. It banned preparations for aggressive war and ruled out a German military role outside of a multilateral context.[4]

Although the founding of the Federal Republic put an end to the occupation regime, it did not mark the formal refounding of German foreign policy. Working through their respective High Commissioners, the Western allies continued to exercise the FRG's external sovereignty. They only permitted the formation of a German foreign ministry in 1951. And they only granted German sovereignty in May 1955, when the Federal Republic was integrated into NATO. Given this lack of sovereignty, Adenauer's foreign policy consisted mainly in his dealings with the allies. Initiatives such as his 1950 decision to join the Council of Europe were subject to allied approval.

Institutional logic, in and of itself, cannot explain the transition from restrictions on sovereignty in 1949 to membership in the Atlantic Alliance, the cornerstone of Western integration, six years later. One can argue, however, that the norms and rules governing German ties with the allies interacted with changes in the international environment to drive the transformation. In this interpretation, the outbreak of the Korean War in June 1950 represented the decisive environmental change. The perception of an acute Soviet threat in Europe led allied leaders, previously wary of the prospect of German rearmament, to back FRG participation in Western military institutions. When the European Defense Community collapsed in 1954, they pushed to make the Federal Republic a sovereign member of NATO.

The argument here, then, is that the combination of a particular institutional constellation and changes in the East-West environment drove the postwar transformation of German foreign policy. In founding the Federal Republic, the Western powers maintained institutional controls over its foreign policy. With the outbreak of the Korean War, U.S., British, and French leaders — at different speeds and with different levels of enthusiasm — began to press for German integration within the Western military institutions. Adenauer followed the allied lead, agreeing to membership in NATO in exchange for the granting of German sovereignty. Firmly bound to the West, the Federal Republic could not return to the aggressive nationalism or *Schaukelpolitik* of the past. A decade after war's end, the German role in Europe had been transformed.

Western Solidarity, 1989-95

The case of post-Cold War foreign policy also appears to lend itself to a parsimonious institutional explanation. In late 1989 and early 1990, the revolutions in Eastern Europe and the collapse of the GDR created pressure for rapid reunification. At the same time, the strength of the Federal Republic's ties with the West created pressure for its continued membership in core Western institutions. George Bush, the allied leader most supportive of rapid reunification, was outspoken in his insistence on continued NATO membership without any new conditions. François Mitterrand, less supportive at the outset, combined insistence on NATO membership with a determination to secure continued German commitment to the European integration process. In his negotiations with Mikhail Gorbachev, long vehemently opposed to the new Germany's membership in the Atlantic Alliance, Kohl did not waver in his support for Western integration. When Gorbachev finally abandoned his opposition, the Two-Plus-Four talks were completed, paving the way for reunification in October 1990.[5]

Reunification, like the founding of the Federal Republic four decades earlier, reduced but did not eliminate institutional constraints on

German foreign policy. The FRG gained its full sovereignty: the Four-Power regime in Berlin, the former Reich capital, was dismantled. And with the incorporation of the GDR into the FRG, a united Germany again emerged as the most powerful state in the heart of Europe. At the same time, however, the existing European institutional architecture constrained the new Germany in important respects. It is true that the FRG found itself well-positioned to fill the power vacuum left by the collapse of the Warsaw Pact and the breakup of the Soviet Union. But continued participation in key Western institutions—NATO and the EC—precluded a break with multilateralism and a return to an independent Ostpolitik.

The fact that reunification took place within this institutional framework cannot, in itself, explain Kohl's continued strong Western orientation during the years that followed. One can argue, though, that as in the early 1950s, environmental changes combined with the norms linking Germany with its allies to generate a commitment to solidarity with the West. In this interpretation, NATO and the EC remained the most important guarantors of vital German material interests. In military terms, the Federal Republic was still ultimately dependent on the United States and its nuclear deterrent for its military security. And in economic terms, the EC remained the most important outlet for Germany's export-driven economy. From this angle, German insistence on continued transatlantic solidarity made sense. So too did Kohl's strong support for the goals of European political and monetary union set down in the Maastricht Treaty of February 1992.

A straightforward institutional argument suggests that the circumstances of reunification and the course of events in Europe in the years that followed created momentum for a continued strong German Western orientation. The new Germany, while fully sovereign, remained embedded in NATO and the EC. And its concrete interests in security and prosperity created pressure for continued solidarity with the United States, France, and Britain. It is true that Germany, more than its allies, faced pressing policy challenges in the former Soviet bloc. But its commitment to multilateralism and its limited resources ruled out a relative shift of attention eastward. For these reasons, one can argue, Kohl made solidarity with the West his overriding foreign policy priority. The postwar transformation of the German role in Europe persisted across the 1990 divide.

Institutions, Ambiguity, and Policy Alternatives

These institutional arguments have the advantage of parsimony. They begin with a given institutional constellation and show how, at two crucial junctures, it interacted with its environment to shape the direction of German foreign policy. They have the major drawback, however, of obscuring the range of choices open to German leaders. In general, three sources of ambiguity can unsettle the constraints posed by international institutions and enlarge the freedom of action facing national leaders. Ambiguity often characterizes the relationship among different institutions that constitute the overall institutional constellation; the relationship between the norms and rules embedded in particular institutions and specific policy contexts; and the relationship between those institutions and the military, economic, and political environments in which they are situated. Ambiguity at each of these three levels — the institutional constellation, particular institutions, and the broader environment — can generate more freedom of action for state leaders than a straightforward institutional account would suggest.

The Ambiguity of the Institutional Constellation

At the level of the overall institutional constellation, leaders are often confronted with an ambiguous set of cross-cutting constraints. They find themselves at the intersection of diverse military alliances, political accords, and economic agreements, each embodying particular rules and norms. Sometimes those institutions and constraints are self-reinforcing and frame choices in clear-cut ways. More often than not, conflicting rules and norms create an ambiguous context for policy. In privileging some institutions over others — granting them greater salience in their policy calculations — leaders simplify reality and narrow policy choices. An outside observer's effort to construct an institutional explanation follows a similar logic. He or she must break a particular institution out of a broader web of institutions in order to isolate its effects on action. Unless this is done carefully — unless the observer is attentive to the ambiguity of the context facing national leaders — the full range of foreign policy choice can be obscured.

The straightforward institutional arguments in both German cases exemplify this problem. In the early 1950s, for example, restrictions on German sovereignty were only one part of the institutional context of FRG foreign policy. The institutional framework set up at the Potsdam Conference — Four-Power responsibility for questions relating to Berlin and Germany as a whole — was also salient. Through 1955, the United States, the Soviet Union, Britain, and France all professed support for the goal of German unity, although their particular prescriptions clashed in practice. The juxtaposition of both institutional frameworks — Western strictures on sovereignty and the Four-Power regime—generated conflicting norms and rules, fostered ambiguity, and created room for German choices. Allied leaders, while committed to Western integration, were aware of its negative implications for German unity, and wary of simply imposing it on their German counterparts. German leaders, situated at the intersection of Western and Four-Power institutions, possessed greater freedom of action than a sole focus on the former would indicate. As Thomas Schwartz has recently argued, U.S. leaders in the early 1950s "insisted that German leaders make a choice between pressing for negotiations for reunification and following the path of European integration and tight association with the United States."[6]

The postreunification case also reveals the existence of choice within an ambiguous institutional constellation. In the years after 1990, German links with the West through NATO and the EC existed alongside institutional links with the East. A series of bilateral Eastern Treaties, reworked in the wake of reunification, framed German ties with the states of Central and Eastern Europe. And the CSCE (Conference on Security and Cooperation in Europe) continued to represent a fragile but not insignificant framework for German foreign policy. Together, both sets of institutions, East and West, embodied sometimes conflicting constraints and generated a significant range of German choice. In this constellation, the German choice between East and West was not a stark either-or, but rather how best to combine ties with the West and engagement in the East. In several policy contexts, including the issue of deepening versus widening of the EC, this came down to a choice of priorities: whether to stress solidarity with the West or more assertively pursue German interests in the East within a multilateral framework, risking frictions with the allies in the process.[7]

The Ambiguity of Particular Institutions

The argument that the overall institutional constellation tends to be ambiguous is open to the objection that certain institutions are, by their very nature, more salient than others. Institutions that contribute to security and prosperity, for example, often figure most prominently in the calculations of national leaders. However, even where ambiguity disappears at the level of the overall constellation, it often reappears at the level of particular institutions. The rules and norms embedded in salient institutions often constitute ambiguous prescriptions for action. Their openness to diverse interpretations can give national leaders greater leeway than straightforward institutional logic implies. In such instances, an observer who imposes a particular interpretation from without — who draws an unambiguous link between institution and action — is likely to miss a significant element of choice.

The two German cases illustrate the relevance of ambiguity at the level of particular institutions. In the early 1950s, allied High Commissioners tended to interpret limitations on German sovereignty as restrictions on German autonomy. They periodically expressed the view that Bonn was bound to follow the lead of Washington, London, and Paris on important international issues (assuming these could agree among themselves). Adenauer rejected this interpretation. While his allegiance to the West was never in doubt, he often proved an uncomfortable interlocutor, pressing his view of German interests in interactions with his allied counterparts.[8] Adenauer's approach to institutional constraints represented one of several conceivable alternatives. He could have chosen to embrace the allies' more restrictive interpretation of sovereignty restrictions. Or he could have insisted even more strongly on greater German sovereignty and equality. Institutional constraints in 1949–55, then, were compatible with different foreign policies, that is, different patterns of interaction with the allies.

German foreign policy in the early 1990s also illustrates ambiguity at the level of particular institutions. In the postreunification context, NATO and the EC did not preclude a more forceful articulation of German interests, particularly toward the East. The norm of multilateralism certainly ruled out a return to a fully independent Ostpolitik. And the norm of shared sovereignty ruled out a nationalist foreign policy orientation. But neither norm explicitly bound the Federal Republic to make solidarity with the West its top priority or to forswear a more active Ostpolitik within a Western institutional framework. Kohl, for his part, tended toward a more restrictive interpretation of multilateralism. He argued that Ostpolitik should only go as far as unity with the West would allow. But in one important instance he interpreted multilateralism more loosely. During the second half of 1991, he pressed Britain and France to join Germany in recognizing Croatia and Slovenia, straining ties with both.[9]

In both the postwar and post–Cold War cases, then, the salience of particular institutions did not eliminate the existence of a significant range of choice. Limits on sovereignty did not deflect Adenauer's freedom of action on the key issue of relative priorities — whether to press for rapid Western integration or the pursuit of Four-Power talks. And the norm of multilateralism did not resolve the question of priorities that faced Kohl — whether to deepen European integration or press more assertively, within multilateral forums, for the integration of Central and East European countries into Western institutions. Adenauer, Kohl, and their governments could have chosen different foreign policy trajectories than they did.

The Ambiguity of the Institutional Environment

In these cases and others, it is possible to buttress institutional arguments by bringing in the broader international environment. In some policy contexts, the mix of military, economic, and political forces makes some interpretations of rules and norms more compelling than others. This is not true, however, when the environments within which institutions are situated are themselves ambiguous and open to interpretation. Overall military, political, and economic trends can be shot through with contradictions. Rarely can national leaders automatically situate institutional norms and rules within particular environments and draw clear policy conclusions. An outside observer inattentive to ambiguity at the level of the environment — to the multiple ways in which broader forces can be seen to intersect with particular norms and rules — is likely to underestimate the range of choices compatible with a given institutional context.

In the German cases, bringing in the international environment does not resolve institutional ambiguities. The argument that the Cold War increased institutional pressures for Western integration obscures the ambiguity of East-West relations in the early 1950s. The outbreak of the Korean War did see the height of East-West hostility. On the other hand, the period 1952–55 saw a revival of Four-Power diplomacy on Germany and first hints of détente in Europe. Each of these trends had potentially contradictory effects. The intensification of the Cold War not only increased German dependence on the allies. It also underscored the importance of a German military contribution for Western strategy, increasing German weight within the Western camp. First hints of détente and the revival of Four-Power diplomacy not only raised the specter of a German settlement at FRG expense. They also created a potential opening for Germans to press the reunification issue. The existence of these ambiguities undermines the argument that restrictions on sovereignty combined with the Cold War to bring about Western integration.

In the postreunification case, too, there is no simple way to link institutions and the environment in a persuasive explanatory strategy. The argument that military and economic trends combined with norms and rules embedded in NATO and the EC to generate Kohl's strong Western orientation neglects another salient component of the international environment: the uncertain situation in the former Soviet bloc. It is true that the FRG remained dependent on the West for its security and prosperity. But there were also good military and economic reasons to make Ostpolitik a greater priority than it was. The German stake in East and Central Europe was greater than that of its allies: the Federal Republic had more to lose through instability and more to gain through stability in the region. Overall trends in Europe did not unambiguously favor a continued emphasis on unity with the West or the alternative of greater initiative in the East.

In both cases, then, the international environment did not rule out particular foreign policy alternatives. Institutions and the constellations of interests within which they were embedded framed German choices. But they did not dictate them. They left German leaders with reasonable alternatives. Amid the ambiguity of the early 1950s, with its mix of Cold War and first traces of détente, the option for Western integration over efforts to spur Four-Power talks was not clearly superior. And during the early 1990s, when changes in the West coincided with new policy challenges in the East, there was no compelling reason to make deeper Western integration a priority over a more active multilateral policy toward the East. In both cases, institutions allowed for significant foreign policy choices.

Bringing in Historical Memory

When confronted with ambiguity generated by international institutions, national leaders reduce complexity and narrow choices in different ways. Socialization into particular norms and values, altered or reinforced by personal experience, creates frameworks for coping with ambiguity. Scholarly work on learning and foreign policy ideas has explored such psychological mechanisms.[10] Another fast-growing body of literature charts the effects of domestic political constraints on the direction of foreign policy. National leaders act within the international and domestic arenas; their policy choices in the former are often shaped by their political positions in the latter.[11] The links between historical memory and foreign policy choice, particularly important in the context of the Federal Republic, have been the object of less scholarly attention.[12]

Historical memory is defined here as reflection on national historical experience and its relevance for the present.[13] National memories are not necessarily collective memories: they can differ in substantive ways from one individual to the next. But they do revolve around a collective subject, the nation-state, and its historical experience. So defined, historical memory has many repositories—in public attitudes and rituals, for example, and in cultural and scholarly production. Here, the views of the past articulated by the political elite, and by national leaders and the major rivals for office in particular, are crucial. Within the broader context of political discourse, those views have the greatest actual and potential impact on the course of foreign policy. Elite perspectives are, of course, embedded within broader societal and cultural environments. Within the confines of this chapter, however, the origins of memories are less important than their content and capacity to reduce ambiguity and pattern choice.

Dimensions of Memory: Narrative, Evaluative, Prescriptive

The historical memories articulated by national leaders have three related dimensions.[14] The first and most obvious is narrative. In their public statements, leaders often intersperse discussion of present and future issues with references to the past. They typically select disparate elements from national experience and juxtapose them in a meaningful way. Narratives—or narrative elements—often relate seminal events such as a nation-state's founding, its revolutions, wars, and depressions. They can privilege events in the recent or distant past, in internal politics or external relations. Authoritative foreign policy statements by Adenauer and Kohl, for example, tend to emphasize particular elements of the German past: the legacy of Franco-German rivalry; the crisis of the Weimar Republic and the rise of Hitler; the catastrophe of World War II and the Holocaust; the stability and prosperity of the postwar years; and finally, for Kohl, the success of reunification.

This enumeration of examples from the German context points to a second, evaluative dimension of historical memory. In rendering the past, national leaders simultaneously pass judgment on it. Episodes tend to be construed as either positive (for example, postwar stability) or negative (for example, prewar crisis). And this evaluation is closely linked with a third, prescriptive dimension of historical memory: views of the past are often simultaneously lessons for the present. Leaders will depict current or future political and policy initiatives as a continuation of previous successes or as a break with previous failures. Adenauer, for example, portrayed his policy of solidarity with the West as a break with the disastrous nationalist politics of the past. In Kohl's view, Western integration, which made reunification possible, was to remain the cornerstone of German foreign policy.

The three dimensions of national historical memory—the narrative, evaluative, and prescriptive—are often closely intertwined. Leaders refer to the past from a particular critical perspective with an interest in a particular political or policy context. While linked, however, each of these dimensions enjoys some autonomy. The narration of the past does not impose particular perspectives or policy prescriptions. The same events can lend themselves to different interpretations and policy implications. At the same time, leaders cannot simply construct narratives to fit the policy and political imperatives of the present. The existence of a hard core of national experience — and a widely shared set of evaluations of certain aspects of that experience — limits the effective prescriptive uses of the past. The next two sections spell out links between historical memory and policy in the German case in more detail.

Western Integration, 1949–55

The institutional constellation left German leaders in the early 1950s with significant alternatives: whether to press for rapid integration within Western institutions or prod the allies to explore the possibility of a Four-Power settlement with the Soviet Union. To what extent did historical memory inform Adenauer's option for rapid integration into the West? Adenauer invoked a number of values in making the case for such integration: anticommunism and liberal democracy, for example. But his views of history and its consequences also figured prominently in the orientation of his foreign policy. The German catastrophe, he argued, made it necessary that Germans make winning the trust of the Western allies their top priority. "We Germans should not forget what happened between 1933 and 1945," he warned just weeks after taking office. "In the negotiations we will have to conduct with the allies in order to progressively win our sovereignty, the psychological aspect plays a very big role."[15]

Adenauer's support for rapprochement with France and European integration — two cornerstones of his foreign policy — was also rooted in his view of the past and its lessons. As he put it in his first government declaration as chancellor in September 1949, "The Franco-German rivalry that dominated European politics for hundreds of years and has caused so many wars and so much destruction and bloodshed must be abolished once and for all."[16] Two years later, in making the case for the European Coal and Steel Community and the European Defense Community, he argued that "the catastrophe brought the German people to the realization that an exaggerated nationalism had more than once destroyed peace. From this there emerged the recognition that our existence, along with that of all other European peoples, can only be maintained within a community that transcends national borders."[17] In both these cases, relations with France and support for European integration, three dimensions of historical memory were enjoined: an invocation and evaluation of the past linked with a policy prescription.

Adenauer's policy priorities—and the view of the past and its implications that underpinned them—were not an object of consensus in the early 1950s. Kurt Schumacher, SPD leader and his main rival for the chancellorship, supported looser Western ties and more active efforts to pursue reunification. He did not reject an alliance with the United States, Britain, and France or progress toward European unity. But he insisted that reunification should be the FRG's top priority, and that an end to allied controls should precede negotiations on association with the West. While Adenauer invoked the past in support of his patient, incremental approach to the allies, Schumacher articulated his stance with a different narrative. In light of the interwar precedent, he argued, continued Western efforts to discriminate against the Germans on economic and security matters would prove counterproductive. He openly admonished the allies not to repeat the disaster of the Versailles Treaty, which had sparked a nationalist reaction in Germany that helped Hitler to power. Like Adenauer, Schumacher censured the nationalist *Schaukelpolitik* of the interwar years. But he also argued that the failure of Weimar democrats to articulate national concerns effectively had left them to militant nationalists, with terrible consequences for democracy and peace.[18] For Schumacher and the SPD, his narrative construal of the past had policy implications: Germans should assertively press their national demands.

Historical memory was not the only force driving the reorientation of German foreign policy in the early 1950s. International constraints clearly narrowed the choices facing German leaders. And only by prevailing against Schumacher and the SPD at the level of electoral politics was Adenauer in a position to implement his priorities. Moreover, a variety of different foreign policy ideas besides views of the past— including norms, values, and perceptions—shaped the decisions that Adenauer made. At the same time, however, foreign policy ideas—and the domestic political clash around them—were profoundly influenced by views of German history and its consequences. This is not surprising, given the tumultuous historical background against which Adenauer acted. Perhaps because the transformation of German foreign policy subsequently proved so durable, the nature of the German choices that shaped it, and the views of history that informed those choices, have received relatively little scholarly attention.

Western Solidarity, 1989–95

What about the persistence of a strong Western orientation in the wake of reunification? Here, too, German leaders faced a significant degree of choice: whether to continue to make solidarity with the West a top priority, or to press actively for a multilateral Ostpolitik, perhaps creating friction with the Western allies in the process. How did historical memory shape Kohl's option for the first alternative?[19] Like Adenauer, he argued that the historical sensibilities of the Western powers made attentiveness to their concerns paramount. At a February 1994 party conference, for example, he cited François Mitterrand to the effect that once the Germans resolved problems linked with reunification, "they will be more powerful than ever before." Kohl's comment: "Our neighbors are all asking the question: 'What is going on with the Germans? What do you stand for?' "[20] Against the backdrop of these fears, he argued that the postwar experience should serve as a model for the post–Cold War period. As he put it in a November 1994 government declaration, "We will adhere to the proven course of German foreign policy, most of all to the solid integration of Germany in the Atlantic Alliance and the European Union."[21]

Kohl's support for European integration was informed not only by positive, but also by negative lessons from the past. Here, as with Adenauer, the prewar experience loomed large. In his first government declaration as chancellor of a united Germany, Kohl insisted that "old rivalries and nationalism cannot be allowed to revive."[22] Three years later, speaking before a CDU party conference, he invoked the interwar experience explicitly. Kohl reminded his listeners: "There was once a time, when Aristide Briand and Gustav Stresemann won the Nobel Peace Prize, in which almost everyone in Europe and Germany thought there would never again be war between Germans and French. Eight years later Hitler came, and six years after that, World War II." Kohl added, "history does not repeat itself," but insisted that an abandonment of European unification would lead Germans again into isolation and disaster.[23]

In contrast to the 1950s, these foreign policy priorities — and the views of history that informed them — were not sharply contested among the major parties. Rudolph Scharping, SPD chairman from 1993 to 1995, did not articulate foreign policy priorities or historical memories sharply different than Kohl's. He, too, pressed for deeper European integration and continued security cooperation with the United States and NATO — though somewhat less enthusiastically. Scharping and other SPD leaders did draw somewhat different conclusions than Kohl from the legacy of the militarist past. On the one hand, Social Democrats posited a clearer link between the memory of German war of aggression in the East and the importance of an active Ostpolitik. On the other hand they argued more ardently that the legacy of German militarism required a reticent approach to the use of German armed forces. In positing a connection between the German past and the necessity of both engagement in the East and an active "peace policy," Scharping took up themes previously articulated by Willy Brandt and Helmut Schmidt.[24] In the process, however, he never portrayed an active Ostpolitik as an alternative to Western integration. Had the SPD held the reins of government in the early 1990s, it might have placed greater relative emphasis on ties with the East. But a shared commitment to strong Western ties, reinforced by a shared view of history and its lessons, underpinned a far-reaching foreign policy consensus.

Like Adenauer's option for Western integration, Kohl's insistence on a strong Western orientation was informed by a particular view of the past and its lessons. The post-1990 institutional constellation framed German choices: it ruled out a break with the West and a turn to the East. At the same time, however, it would have allowed for a more assertive Ostpolitik within a multilateral framework — indeed, the recognition of Croatia and Slovenia provides an example of such an approach. Kohl's emphasis on Western solidarity in the years after 1991 was in part a reaction to the criticism that episode had evoked. But his sensitivity to that criticism, and his reluctance to strain ties with his Western allies on issues such as the pace and scope of EU expansion eastward, only make full sense against the backdrop of his view of the past and its consequences for the present. Kohl's historical perspective and its prescriptive implications — together with his command of German domestic politics in the years after reunification — contributed to the enduring transformation of postwar German foreign policy under new circumstances.

Conclusion

The transformation of the German role in Europe after World War II and the founding of the Federal Republic, and the persistence of that role after the Cold War and reunification, appear amenable to a straightforward institutional analysis. Upon closer inspection, however, the institutional constellations at both junctures were compatible with different foreign policy trajectories. The absence of German sovereignty through 1955 precluded a return to the aggressive foreign policies of the past. It did not, however, make Western integration inevitable. German leaders in the early 1950s were in a position to make the pursuit of reunification within a Four-Power framework a priority over closer association with the West. Four decades later, reunification within NATO and the EC precluded a purely national foreign policy or a unilateral Ostpolitik. But German leaders were in a position to press interests in the East more actively than they did — within a multilateral Western framework.

In both cases, historical memory served as an important guide for choice amid constraints. The views of the past and its lessons articulated by Adenauer and Kohl informed particular foreign policy paths. Adenauer articulated a historical narrative that linked nationalism with war and called for policies of reconciliation and integration with the West. In his support for a continued strong Western orientation after reunification, Kohl articulated the same themes. But he also invoked a particular interpretation of postwar German history, drawing a link between solidarity with the West and four decades of peace and prosperity. In both cases, the combination of strong domestic political positions and strongly held views of the past and its lessons helped to shape choices among present foreign policy alternatives.

The argument that the enduring transformation of German foreign policy emerged out of the interaction of institutions and historical memory suggests possible sources of future changes. In years to come, significant shifts in international institutions could reshape the German role in Europe. A prolonged crisis in the Atlantic Alliance or the European integration process, for example, could conceivably lead German leaders to embrace a more national foreign policy orientation and a more independent Ostpolitik. So, too, could unforeseen developments in the former Soviet bloc, such as an outbreak of nationalist violence or a crisis of Russian democracy. If German leaders are not able to address policy problems in the East in cooperation with the Western allies, they could conceivably move to do so alone. In this connection, former foreign minister Hans-Dietrich Genscher noted that Germans "would not like to monopolize relations with Russia and the other states of Central and Eastern Europe." He added that they had therefore "asked our partners not to leave us alone in this policy, because it is one we have to conduct."[25]

Even in the absence of dramatic developments at the international level, changing interpretation of past experience and its implications could ultimately serve as a catalyst for a new foreign policy direction. Here, the legacy of the New Ostpolitik could grow in importance: a future SPD chancellor might point to Brandt's opening to the East during the 1970s as a positive precedent for a shift in German attention eastward. And he or she might also, like Brandt, invoke Hitler's murderous war in the East in support of greater German positive engagement in the region.[26] There are some signs of the continued relevance of this particular historical legacy. Upon assuming the SPD leadership in 1995, for example, Oskar Lafontaine argued that "after the détente policy of Willy Brandt," Germans had a "special responsibility to forge a new security architecture in Europe that includes East European states and Russia."[27] Through the mid-1990s, however, SPD leaders continued to make Western integration — an enduring break with the catastrophic nationalist policies of the past — the foundation of their thinking about foreign policy.

A more dramatic future foreign policy shift could emerge out of a reassessment not of the implications of the German catastrophe for the present, but of its very relevance. It is conceivable that future German leaders will dispute what successive postwar leaders have asserted: that the pre-1945 experience, and Nazism in particular, should serve as a backdrop for the pursuit of German economic and security interests. Those who call for the "normalization" of German foreign policy sometimes appear to suggest such a break with past practice — not simply a less reticent approach to military policy instruments, but also a greater willingness to calculate and pursue national interests in a straightforward way, that is, unburdened by history. While this possibility has been expressed in academic circles, it does not appear to have taken hold within the political elite.[28] Given the ongoing salience of the past in German and European politics, it is probably unlikely to do so in the near future.

NOTES

1. For a discussion of this literature, see James G. March and Johan P. Olsen, *Rediscovering Institutions: The Organization of Politics* (New York: Free Press, 1991); and Sven Steinmo, Kathleen Thelen, and Frank Longstreth, eds., *Structuring Politics: Historical Institutionalism in Comparative Analysis* (Cambridge: Cambridge University Press, 1992).

2. See Douglass C. North, *Structure and Change in Economic History* (New York: Norton, 1981).

3. See, for example, Robert O. Keohane, *International Institutions and State Power* (Boulder: Westview Press, 1989); and the exchange on institutions in *International Security* 20, no. 1 (Summer 1995): 39–93. For a critique of positivist approaches, see Friedrich Kratochwil and John Gerard Ruggie, "International Organization: A State of the Art on an Art of the State," *International Organization* 40, no. 4 (autumn 1986): 753–75.

4. See Articles 26 and 24, respectively, in *Grundgesetz* (Munich: Deutscher Taschenbuch Verlag, 1980). For an English translation, see *Documents on Germany, 1944–1985* (Washington, D.C.: U.S. Government Printing Office, 1985), 226–27.

5. On the diplomacy of reunification, see the account of Kohl's top foreign policy advisor, Horst Teltschik, *329 Tage: Innenansichten der Einigung* (Berlin: Siedler, 1991); and Stephen F. Szabo, *The Diplomacy of German Unification* (New York: St. Martin's Press, 1992).

6. Thomas Alan Schwartz, *America's Germany: John J. McCloy and the Federal Republic of Germany* (Cambridge: Harvard University Press, 1991), 268.

7. In late 1994, for example, Kohl did not make widening the centerpiece of the German presidency of the European Union, partly in response to French concerns about an eastward shift in the EU center of gravity. See Deutsche-Presse Agentur, 6 December 1994.

8. On Adenauer's interaction with the High Commission, see Hans-Peter Schwarz, *Adenauer: Der Aufstieg, 1876–1952* (Stuttgart: Deutsche Verlags-Anstalt, 1986), 671–90.

9. Beverly Crawford, "Germany's Unilateral Recognition of Croatia and Slovenia: A Case of Defection from Multilateral Cooperation," *World Politics* 48, no. 4 (July 1996): 482–521.

10. For a discussion of the learning literature, see Jack S. Levy, "Learning and Foreign Policy: Sweeping a Conceptual Minefield," *International Organization* 48, no. 2 (spring 1994): 279–312. On foreign policy ideas, see Judith Goldstein and Robert O. Keohane, eds, *Ideas and Foreign Policy* (Ithaca: Cornell University Press, 1993).

11. For recent work on the interaction of international and domestic forces in shaping foreign policy, see Peter B. Evans, Harold K. Jacobson, and Robert D. Putnam, eds., *Double-Edged Diplomacy: International Bargaining and Domestic Politics* (Berkeley: University of California Press, 1993).

12. For related work that centers on the role of historical analogies, see Richard Neustadt and Ernest May, *Thinking in Time: The Uses of History for Decision-Makers* (New York: Free Press, 1986); and Yuen Foong Khong, *Analogies at War: Korea, Munich, Dien Bien Phu, and the Vietnam Decisions of 1965* (Princeton: Princeton University Press, 1992).

13. On historical memory and German foreign policy, see also Andrei S. Markovits and Simon Reich, *The German Predicament: Memory and Power in the New Europe* (Ithaca: Cornell University Press, 1997). For a bibliography of work on historical memory, see Iwona Irwin-Zarecka, *Frames of Remembrance: The Dynamics of Collective Memory* (New Brunswick: Transaction Publishers, 1994), 193–205.

14. This section draws on Thomas Banchoff, "Historical Memory and German Foreign Policy: The Cases of Adenauer and Brandt," *German Politics and Society* 14, no. 2 (summer 1996): 37–39.

15. "Adenauer to Bundestag, 24 November 1949," in Hans-Peter Schwarz, *Konrad Adenauer: Reden 1917–1967: Eine Auswahl* (Stuttgart: Deutsche Verlags-Anstalt, 1975), 256.

16. "Adenauer address of 20 September 1949," ibid., 168.

17. "Adenauer address in London, 6 December 1951," ibid., 235.

18. See, for example, Schumacher's addresses before SPD party conferences on 9 May 1946 and 22 May 1950, in Willy Albrecht, ed., *Kurt Schumacher, Reden—Schriften—Korrespondenzen, 1945–52* (Berlin: Dietz, 1985), 397, 750. On Schumacher's foreign policy, see Peter Merseburger, *Der Schwierige Deutscher: Kurt Schumacher* (Stuttgart: Deutsche Verlags-Anstalt, 1995).

19. For a more detailed discussion of historical themes in Kohl's foreign policy discourse, see Thomas Banchoff, "German Policy towards the European

Union: The Effects of Historical Memory," *German Politics* 6, no. 1 (April 1997): 60–76.

20. Kohl's speech at CDU party conference of 20–23 February 1994, "Wir setzen auf den Sieg" (Bonn: CDU-Bundesgeschäftstelle, 1994), 21.

21. "Declaration of 23 November 1994," *Bulletin des Presse- und Informationsamtes der Bundesregierung,* 24 November 1994, 987.

22. "Declaration of January 30, 1991," ibid., 31 January 1991, 73.

23. Kohl, "Wir setzen auf den Sieg," 23.

24. See, for example, Scharping's 22 July 1994 address, in *Verhandlungen des deutschen Bundestags: Stenographischer Bericht,* ser. 12, 21174.

25. Author's interview with Genscher, 24 August 1992.

26. During the 1994 campaign, Rudolf Scharping called for a "new 'Ostpolitik' " while in Washington, D.C. "Address of 12 March 1994" (typescript, Friedrich-Ebert Foundation).

27. Lafontaine address of November 1995, *Presseservice der SPD: Parteitag Mannheim. 14.–17. November 1995,* 8.

28. See, for example, Hans-Peter Schwarz, *Die Zentralmacht Europas* (Berlin: Siedler, 1994).

Germany's Place in the World

Wolfgang Krieger

Both inside and outside Germany there is a great deal of uncertainty about Germany's place in the world of tomorrow. Some observers focus on the increased size of the economy. Others find a "new assertiveness" in Germany's dealings with its allies. Around Europe there is a concern about the European Union's ability to keep Germany firmly tied down in a larger framework of integration.[1] For various reasons people seem to think that such fears are somehow justified even if they are more speculative than based on sound reasoning.

Are such fears really justified? How are we to think about Germany's place in the world, particularly in the fast-changing European environment?

From a wide range of such writings it appears that two postwar developments may have not been sufficiently appreciated by many analysts, media commentators, and policymakers. The first has to do with the peculiar nature of the European integration process; the second concerns the fundamental discontinuities of postwar German foreign policy, which are hard to understand from the much more traditional notions that govern the foreign policies of most other nation-states, including Germany's main co-players—France, Britain, the United States, and Russia. In other words, the question concerning Germany's place cannot be answered without reference to the wider context of European developments and without taking into account the spoken or unspoken assumptions from which such debates set out. To complicate matters further, our analysis not only has to deal with two entirely novel factors, European integration and a nontraditional German foreign policy, but also with a gradual evolutionary process that was only partly understood even by the political decision makers at the time.

The New Foreign Policy

Back in the early 1950s, the first West German government under Chancellor Konrad Adenauer started to define and to implement on a very modest scale what eventually amounted to an entirely new German foreign policy. This was done against considerable domestic opposition and on the understanding, shared by virtually all Germans, that the ultimate objective could only be a reunified and internationally equal Germany. At that stage foreign observers watched with much goodwill but not always with great conviction how the new German leadership strove to dissociate itself from old Wilhelmine dreams of German grandeur and from the perverse racial imperialism of the Hitler regime. As this process of creating a new set of foreign and defense policies got under way, West Germany's example began to delegitimize what practically all other European states still considered the natural right of a nation-state. German leaders proclaimed the end of the European nation-states and thus the end of the era in which nation-states defined their foreign relations according to their national interests. Bonn's policymakers proclaimed European integration to be an objective in its own right and thus a full-scale replacement of the old system of nation-states.

Such ideas had been discussed all around western Europe even before 1945, but when it came to taking any practical steps, most governments were skeptical or even hostile. Britain's was the most obvious case of such early Euro-skepticism. While Winston Churchill's famous Zurich speech of 1946 is habitually quoted as an example of the new enthusiasm for "Europe," his own government followed in the footsteps of the 1945–51 Labour cabinets in rejecting all integration policies, including membership in the European Coal and Steel Community and the proposed treaty for a European Defense Community (EDC). Instead, Britain focused on rebuilding its war-shattered empire and sought a close linkage with the United States in the celebrated "special relationship."

The French reacted differently, hoping to use the notion of integration as a control system for Germany. French industry was eager to have access to German coal and iron products and to influence German price levels. At the same time France itself was careful not to become entangled in the process. This is why the French parliament rejected the EDC in mid-1954 and why General Charles de Gaulle remained highly skeptical of the entire integration process.[2] But there remained a fundamental contradiction that in many ways has not been resolved even today. How could German sovereignty be "integrated" without reducing French sovereignty by the same token?

In many ways France's rationale for integration was shared by the other participants. Back in the early postwar years, most political leaders in Europe saw European integration not as a utopian program for complete political change but as a means of reconstructing and strengthening their nation-states by pursuing three objectives.

- The first objective was to build a strong bloc vis-à-vis what they considered the Soviet military, political, and even technological and economic threat.
- The second objective was to have a structure into which Germany could be tied and that would assure that Germany would not become an expansionist neighbor or a Soviet satellite or a question left entirely to the discretion of the two superpowers.
- Third, there was always something of a Gaullist agenda in the sense that "Europe" should not suffer the fate of Latin America and become a backyard of American power — economically, culturally, or otherwise.

Because of its peculiar international status, Germany could not pursue those goals in the way others pursued them. As a result two conflicting concepts of nation-state sovereignty and of European integration developed. One assumed that the nation-state would largely be consumed by European integration, while the other saw integration as a means for propping up the nation-state only where it could no longer bear the weight of international challenges and threats.

It is against this background that three related questions must be addressed.

- First, why did and why do German leaders today dissociate themselves from the notion of German national interests, favoring instead a strongly integrationist course that voluntarily subjects large areas of German sovereignty to the European Union?
- Second, could it be that Germany's integrationist policies are actually a particularly intriguing way of pursuing its national interests rather than a way of voluntarily downsizing German sovereignty in the interest of a more powerful European Union, as is claimed in public?
- And third, what is the likely effect of these German policies internationally but also for the German body politic?

These questions lead us back to the radical post-1949 change in German foreign and defense policies, but also to the way in which political scientists, historians, and others have viewed the relationship between modern German history and the Federal Republic.

During the first two or three postwar decades, most scholars were guided by a deep concern that the old legacies of Kaiser Wilhelm and Adolf Hitler might have gone into hibernation, ready at any time to wake up and show their ugly faces again. This seemed only logical if one believed, as many did at least to a degree, that much of modern German history had been a preparatory stage for the Third Reich. Much ink was spilled on the notion of a German *Sonderweg,* which allegedly set apart Germany's history from the progressive, liberal-capitalist paths of the countries of western Europe. In this vein any right-wing activities in the Federal Republic could appear as typically German manifestations of illiberalism, whereas similar political movements or outbursts elsewhere would be regarded as mere aberrations or accidents.

However, as the postwar era wore on, it became more and more difficult to see the obviousness of such interpretations. If the 12 years between 1933 and 1945 had indeed been the logical, virtually inevitable outcome of German history, how was one to explain the Federal Republic's record of political stability, democracy, and international friendliness? In particular, how was one to explain the fact that many of the domestic institutions and political practices of the Federal Republic had survived from Germany's pre-1933 history while Nazi beliefs and mentalities by and large had not?

Since the 1970s there have been few scholars who sought to address in historical terms the question of the Federal Republic's unexpected stability. The bulk of the textbook literature even today does not seem much concerned with these inconsistencies. Most authors continue to divide modern German history along neat "turning points" (1871, 1918, 1933, 1945). In this way they tend to obscure the *longue durée* of political institutions and traditions that would link present-day Germany to its progressive, enlightened, modern, or liberal ancestry. To be sure, much of the research on the post-1648 "Holy Roman Empire," on "enlightened absolutism" in the second half of the eighteenth century, and on nineteenth-century political reforms indirectly suggests the need for rewriting twentieth-century German history, but in a direct and detailed way this has barely been attempted so far.

Among the points to reconsider are the fundamental continuity between the *Grundgesetz* (constitution) of 1949, the 1919 Weimar constitution from which it is largely derived, and the long tradition of German constitutionalism, particularly in the formerly sovereign states that made up the German Federation until 1866. Much of today's legal framework—for example, the criminal, the civil, and the business codes—

dates from the era of Bismarck and Wilhelm II, which in turn built on a long tradition of modern lawmaking. Today's political parties bear the stamp or even the name of their Weimar or Wilhelmine ancestors. The same is essentially true of the institutions of German economic life. A great number of private and state-owned companies, employers' organizations, and labor unions and much of the German labor law, business law, and welfare legislation predate the Federal Republic, as do the much-praised systems of apprenticeship and of co-determination at the workplace.

It is this continuity of domestic political and social institutions that makes one appreciate how different German foreign and security policies have been—first in the old West Germany and now in the united Germany. Beyond the obvious and complete break with Nazi racism and expansionism, it was neither entirely logical nor firmly required by the Allied powers that Germany should renounce those institutions and practices that other European nation-states revived and resumed after 1945. Therefore a good deal of those changes must have been due to a fundamental reordering of priorities on the part of the German foreign policymakers.

The case of the German defense forces, the Bundeswehr, provides a good deal of insight into why and how West German policy took an integrationist turn. Nowhere was the Federal Republic's break with traditional notions of national sovereignty more radical, and nowhere would it have been more difficult to continue in the old ways. In contrast with all larger defense forces in NATO, the Bundeswehr has never been a military force under national command. But the differences between the Bundeswehr and the other armed forces in Western Europe are not only organizational or institutional. They concern fundamental issues of war and peace that are only in part expressed by the ongoing German debates over German participation in United Nations peacekeeping and peace-enforcing missions. Although a gradual change toward such participation is under way and although Germany's participation in certain UN and NATO missions in the former Yugoslavia has helped to resolve some residual constitutional issues, one should not overlook that the issue of "just wars" still separates Germany from practically all its political and military allies. What might be called the "lesson of 1944," derived from the Allied landing operation in Normandy— that is, the idea that democracy, liberty, and justice can and sometimes must be brought to people by massive military force—is still alien to the postwar Germans. Therefore a German participation in a Gulf War–type coalition is still hard to imagine.

In contrast with Germany, other Western European armies fought numerous colonial and postcolonial wars after 1945, none of which took place under the NATO umbrella and at least some of which could not be said to have been in harmony with the United Nations charter. While most states still believe in their right to fight wars according to their own definitions of their national interests, Germany does not share this belief and in all probability will not in the foreseeable future.

The Two-Plus-Four Treaty of 1990 is further evidence of this peculiar German view of national security. In that treaty Germany accepted certain limits on its force levels that are practically unique in Europe because they are set down by an international treaty that is not primarily about arms control. Despite a reference to the CFE (Conventional Forces in Europe) conventional arms reduction treaty, the envisaged German force levels were not made contingent on force reductions in other states. Thus Article 3 of the Two-Plus-Four Treaty contains a unilateral German undertaking that merely "assumes" that other European states will also reduce their forces in due course. Taken together with the unqualified renunciation of weapons of mass destruction (atomic, biological, and chemical (ABC) weapons) in the same treaty article, Germany takes a leap of faith that is based on nothing more than unexplained optimism and that goes way beyond what other states have accepted in the Non-Proliferation Treaty and in parallel agreements on chemical and biological weapons. The old German fear of "singularization," that is, of having to accept a lesser status in national security and therefore a lesser overall international status, was somehow overcome (without any public debate!) as Germany agreed to a striking limitation of its right to self-defense.[3]

In the case of Germany's military security, it can of course be argued, though not to everyone's intellectual satisfaction, that the country's geographical position makes the idea of national defense an absurd one anyhow. Therefore it may be sensible to swallow one's pride (in terms of international status) and to buy all the international goodwill one can by any means possible. But when it comes to the planned currency union under the 1992 Maastricht treaty, it is much harder to claim that realistic alternatives to a massive surrender of sovereignty did not exist. For this reason Germany's signature to the currency union is a truly striking example of national self-limitation.

Both the genesis of the Maastricht treaty and the political struggle for ratification in the European Union member countries clearly indicate that the intention on the part of France and of certain other co-signers has been quite definitely to clip the wings of German economic power. Since this is clearly understood in Bonn — no matter how often it is denied by official spokespersons — it is all the more surprising that there is a near-uniform consensus in the Bundestag, both among the ruling coalition and the opposition parties, to implement this treaty on schedule or as close to schedule as possible. The bickering over additional strict criteria for the stability of the "Euro" is little more than window dressing for the purpose of domestic appeasement.

It is certainly hard to think of another example where the political leadership of a large, economically successful and powerful country went to its smaller neighbors and begged them to take away the chief instrument of economic policy-making, and thus of national power, on which much of the body politic and its social fabric so critically hinge. This may be good political strategy for Europe as a whole, but it cannot come as a complete surprise that people outside Germany ask themselves if there might not in fact be a sinister purpose behind so much unexpected idealism. Many found it hard to believe that it was an act of unselfishness when Helmut Kohl, his government, and its parliamentary opponents accepted the idea that Bonn would surrender in Maastricht a big chunk of sovereignty to compensate for the increase in power gained by German unification.

One way in which political leaders perceive and calculate the policies as well as the intentions of other leaders is by mirror-imaging. In the case of German unification, policymakers around Europe must have asked themselves how *they* would have reacted if their territory and population had increased by what used to be the German Democratic Republic. Therefore it must have been hard for them to understand the calmness, hesitation, and in part even reluctance with which the West Germans responded to unification or to appreciate the lack of any sense of triumph as Soviet military forces withdrew from German soil on 31 August 1994.

Many observers and policymakers were left with the distinct impression that Germany, that is, the German government—all public softpedaling to the contrary—was quite capable of defining its national interests and of pursuing them forcefully. Indeed, the German leadership was seen to act against the will of Germany's European partners. Enough documentary evidence exists to indicate that many key policymakers in France and Britain were deeply shocked by the process of German unification.

Most likely, the aftereffects of the "unification shock" will remain a psychological factor for a long time to come. Foreign policymakers will look at Germany from a perspective of the events in 1989–90, when German national interests allowed no time for the institutional rituals by which Brussels politics live. Above all it was the close collaboration between Moscow and Washington that gave rise to the worst fears concerning Europe's future. Britain and France took it as a personal insult that the two superpowers settled the German question between themselves and with the Kohl government, leaving the rest of Europe little choice but to agree.[4] In Paris and London those events are still considered a policy disaster that holds some obvious lessons for the future.

European Integration

Why was the early Bonn leadership so eager to embark on European integration? And how did Bonn's integration policies square with the quest for national unification, that most obvious of German national interests since 1945?

With the benefit of hindsight, the first question seems relatively easy. The dangers of a Soviet-manipulated Germany were all too obvious. In 1947 and 1948, when the Western publics became fully aware of the expansionist nature of Moscow's policy in Europe, even the reluctant French understood the need to prevent Soviet influence from reaching the Rhine. By the fall of 1950 the Cold War had intensified. After the first Soviet nuclear test in August 1949, the victory of the Chinese communists in October 1949, and the outbreak of the Korean War in June 1950, the original Potsdam Conference objective of a united, politically weak, and nonaligned Germany seemed unacceptable.

At that point a window of opportunity opened for Germany, at least for western Germany. As Adenauer saw it, the Federal Republic could be freed at least partly from its "Potsdam shackles," in which four-power diplomacy was at liberty to "solve" the German question any way it saw fit. In return Germany would substantially contribute to the security of Western Europe. Adenauer's hope was that a Federal Republic that was integrated into the West both militarily and economically would become too valuable an asset simply to negotiate away.

But his political calculations went way beyond Cold War security concerns. Better than most, Adenauer understood that in the long term neither the Soviet threat nor American pressure would suffice to make Britain and France accept a rapid economic recovery of the Federal Republic. In 1948–49 France had agreed to a west German state only under strong American pressure. At some later point France might again doubt that a prosperous Germany was in its own best interest. Paris might eventually seek to undo what had begun with the American effort to include western Germany in the Marshall Plan. The Marshall Plan itself was a program of limited duration, and Washington's lasting interest in European affairs could not be taken for granted. Even though the British were less outspoken in this respect, their urge to secure commercial advantages over Germany was an important *leitmotiv* both in the press and, as we now know, in London's secret government files.

In pursuing his policy of integration, Adenauer faced a number of serious domestic obstacles. One was to find enough electoral support. It was by no means clear how strong German nationalism still was. Clearly Kurt Schumacher, Adenauer's parliamentary opponent, believed that German postwar democracy could only succeed if such national sentiments were taken into account and if the Social Democratic Party (SPD) did not leave it to others to articulate such sentiments. There was an obvious lesson of the first federal elections of August 1949, in which neither the old SPD nor the new CDU/CSU drew overwhelming support but received merely 29.2 and 31 percent respectively.[5] Some 40 percent of the voters favored a variety of other political parties, most of which had a fairly nationalist outlook.[6] In other words, the domestic support for the political bargain that the Adenauer government had struck with the Western Allies was by no means assured in the initial stages.

Without the "economic miracle," without a fast and thorough economic recovery, the Federal Republic might well have been more reluctant to accept European integration, particularly in the 1950s, when both in matters of defense and of economic policy the idea of controlling Germany dominated all but the most innocent idealists. Therefore it was only wise not to abandon the call for a reunited, independent, and internationally equal Germany. Yet for the Western powers this part of the "German question" held a different lesson. They would not repeat the mistake of 1919 and see their interests hurt because of yet another group of well-intentioned but inherently weak democratic German politicians. This is why they demanded direct controls of the German economy plus physical guarantees against national German military forces.

In this situation it was Adenauer's mission to make the Germans realize that they could not hope to get rid of the Allied shackles quickly. The best Germany could expect was a set of looser, more comfortable shackles. As it happened, Adenauer was lucky and could take credit for the unexpectedly rapid economic recovery, which in itself did more than anything else to vindicate the politics of economic and military integration. Had economic recovery faltered, Adenauer would probably have been viewed as a well-meaning "fulfillment" politician reminiscent of his Weimar predecessors.

To make this argument is not to deny that in the 1950s there were a great number of genuine Euro-enthusiasts, particularly among the younger generation, for whom integration was a way of building a better Europe, a Europe without nation-states or at least without inherently antagonistic nation-states. Most of them, however, had an agenda that went well beyond international relations. One of their goals was to form a strong, domestic movement against communism. Another, less frequently noted goal was to do away with traditional, pre-modern, antidemocratic elites who had led and defined the old nation-states and whose politics had been based on traditional beliefs in social hierarchy and class distinctions. In that sense the movement for European integration had a social revolutionary character. And in a way this is still the case. In Britain, for example, most present-day supporters of European integration happen to be highly critical of their country's pre-modern political and social structures. In Italy the EU is seen as a remedy against the politics of the corrupt old elites.

Equally important, the European movement built on post-1918 Europe's democratic, antifeudalistic, and antibourgeois enthusiasm, which had been so tragically misused by the fascists and the National Socialists before and during World War II. With fascism and National Socialism utterly discredited, the European movement could now serve as a platform on which some of those post-1918 sentiments were revived and on which a new domestic consensus could be built, not just in the Federal Republic but in all those European states that had been torn up by the war and that were lucky enough to be west of the Iron Curtain.[7]

Leaving aside the actual agenda of uniting Europe — whatever it was in each national or personal perspective — it is easy to see why so many leaders in Western Europe would find it an attractive platform on which to reconstruct their countries' political, economic, and social lives. Among other things, it would convey a sense of social modernization. And it would deflect public attention from the inadequacies with which the politics of national reconstruction could be expected to battle for a very long time.

In the German case there were additional benefits. First, the idealism of European integration gave a more acceptable face to the inevitable surrender of German sovereignty. Second, it served to identify those Germans who were willing to respect the new rules of the post-1945 era and who were able to work within the new European institutions and frameworks. By the same token, the politics of integration excluded those who could not make themselves acceptable under the new circumstances. In other words, Europeanism served as a selection mechanism among German elites, a screening process that banned stubborn nationalists from public decision making.

Nowhere was this more obvious than in the Bundeswehr, which could only serve its purpose if it was wholly acceptable to the NATO partners. Full integration into NATO was the only way in which the Federal Republic could contribute to its own military security and the only way in which it could influence NATO policies. Therefore each and every senior officer had to be acceptable in a NATO context. This is why the screening process for personnel was much stricter in the upper echelons of the Bundeswehr than in almost any other German institution.[8]

This is not to say that former Nazis were only excluded to appease the Allied powers. Despite certain failures, it cannot be said that there was a reluctance to confront the Nazi past. However imperfect denazification had been, its unsatisfactory results cannot be wholly attributed to a lack of will on the part of the new political leadership. In a population that had at certain stages given majority support to the Nazis — never in free elections but no doubt by general sympathy — one could not hope to win democratic support solely by relying on people of formal anti-Nazi credentials. A flexible approach was necessary that would allow certain lesser ex-Nazis to prove themselves under the new circumstances. As a result, a new elite was formed for which the ability to work with "the victor powers," in this case the Western industrial democracies, served as an important selection mechanism.[9]

While Europeanism had an important function in consensus-building and elite restructuring throughout Western Europe, there was at least one substantial difference between the Federal Republic and the rest. The other Europeans could use the institutions of international economic cooperation to help restore their nation-states, as Alan Milward has convincingly argued.[10] The leaders in Bonn had no such authority. Quite explicitly, the Germans were not allowed to define their country's borders or its foreign policy allegiance. Nor did they have the right to negotiate a German peace treaty. Until 1990 all those powers lay exclusively in the hands of the four Allies, symbolized, lest it be forgotten, by their troops on German soil and by the special status of Berlin.[11]

The Survival of National Sovereignty

If European integration served several very diverse purposes, so did the politics of nation-state sovereignty. Compared to the novelty of international integration, nation-state sovereignty was of course a well-established political principle. It lay at the heart of the United Nations charter and was thus a key principle of international relations. It received strong support from the new postcolonial nations, who became increasingly powerful within the UN. Even the Soviet Union stuck religiously to the notion of sovereignty and made the related principle of noninterference the linchpin of its declaratory foreign policy, even though it proclaimed the Brezhnev Doctrine to explain the invasion of Czechoslovakia in 1968.

For these and other reasons, it cannot come as a surprise that a certain amount of traditional nation-state thinking survived in the Federal Republic as well.[12] The policy of national reunification was of course its most central expression. The voluntary acceptance of a reduced German sovereignty both in the West European institutions of integration and in NATO was as firmly linked to that national goal as it was to the Soviet threat. When both linkages disappeared in 1989–90, it was only logical that the German public needed to be given a new set of reasons if European integration was to be taken substantially beyond the existing levels and if Germany's newly won status of sovereignty was to be massively reduced. This was and still is the essence of the problem that Bonn faces with respect to the Euro.

In addition, a number of events showed that sovereignty, which in the German case was only the promise of eventual sovereignty, was not the same for everyone. To demonstrate the significance of this point, France rejected the European Defense Community in 1954, developed a national nuclear military force, and, in 1966, withdrew from the military structures of NATO. Each step was ample evidence that the international status of France would always be substantially above what Germany could hope to achieve. When Britain finally joined the EEC in 1973 and became a difficult member under the premiership of Margaret Thatcher in the 1980s, the example was not lost on the Germans either. If Britain "wanted her money back" and got it, the Germans could not follow suit with a comparably hard-nosed policy, even though there were (and still are today) some very real financial imbalances in Bonn's financial contributions to Brussels. In other words, each time the sovereignty issue was brought up in ways that could not be emulated by Bonn, the integrationists' claim of the disappearance of the nation-state suffered a severe setback.

In the face of such assertiveness on the part of France and Britain, one wonders why the German public did not become even more critical of Bonn's integrationist policies. This question is difficult to answer with any precision. Perhaps the extraordinary and unexpected boom of the German economy was regarded as a justification of the high costs of membership in the European club. No doubt the extraordinary success of German export industries and its critical dependence on nearby export markets played a very big role. Another reason is found in the great extent to which the security of the Federal Republic depended on the goodwill of the Western partners.

Nevertheless, there remains a need to explain how, in the very special West German case, traditional foreign policy goals could coexist with integrationist ones. Bonn's official answer was that the 1954 Paris treaties included a pledge on the part of the three Western Allied powers to support the idea of German unification. Therefore any further integration steps would both strengthen the Western camp and make unification more likely because a European peace settlement would be impossible without a prior or concurrent settlement of the German question. Integration seemed to be the way to keep the German question from becoming an isolated issue in a grand European settlement.

Privately, Adenauer and others were deeply worried about the prospect of such a settlement, justifiably so, as many of the now available British and American records show. The fear was that the Americans might wish to reduce their military burden in Europe and that the British showed little interest in the fine points of continental European affairs, which made them particularly dangerous from a German perspective. Right after Stalin's death in 1953, the American and British governments entered into competition over who was better qualified to talk to the new Soviet leaders about a final European peace settlement. Prime Minister Winston Churchill told his cabinet that a meeting of the great powers should be limited to the Big Three and "could take up the discussion at the point at which it had been left off at the end of the Potsdam conference in 1945." In a speech in the House of Commons on 11 May 1953, he offered a security package to the new Soviet leadership that included a neutral united Germany and a Poland that "will remain a friendly power and a buffer, though not, I trust, a puppet state."[13] While the United States did not consent to that particular proposal, it too was looking for compromise solutions.

A few years later, during the 1958–62 Berlin crisis, Adenauer was so disappointed with Washington's policy that he concluded an even closer alliance with France, the 1963 Franco-German treaty. French president Charles de Gaulle hoped to disrupt the close German-American relationship and to isolate Britain even further from Europe. At that moment, under American diplomatic pressure, a majority of the Bundestag pulled back and attached a disclaimer to the treaty ratification act. But it was that same fear of a superpower deal at Germany's expense that brought about Bonn's Ostpolitik only a few years later.

In the 1980s Chancellor Helmut Kohl continued and even intensified Ostpolitik. By then, however, the issue of German unity had moved far down the international agenda. Mutual nuclear deterrence between the superpowers was now considered to be fairly stable (though never completely assured). European security had come to be defined in terms of "stability," that is, as a dogma of status quo policy. Along the way, European integration gradually acquired a different meaning for Germany. What had been an insurance policy against an unfavorable European settlement was now considered a new destiny for Germany, or at least for West Germany. Promoting German exports took priority. So did the need to reconcile the smaller West European neighbors to the leading role of the German economy.

Even at that time West German politicians, both from the SPD and the CDU/CSU, never tired of assuring the world that German unification, unlikely as it had become, could only occur as part of the integration process.[14] However, in 1989-90, things happened in a very different manner. Unification was essentially granted by the Soviet Union and could not be influenced much by the West European powers, of whom only Britain and France — as World War II victors — were even involved in the relevant negotiations. But the key promoter on the Western side was outside Europe altogether. It was the United States under President George Bush who gave unrestrained support to Bonn, while Brussels played no role at all and Paris and London were desperately looking for ways to slow down or even undermine the process. Now many around Europe feared that a united Germany might soon lose its Euro-enthusiasm, particularly after one of the key reasons for Bonn's integrationist policies, the existence of an expansionist Soviet Union, had disappeared. Germany's controversial diplomatic recognition of Slovenia and Croatia in late 1991 was seen by many as evidence of a "new assertiveness" on the part of the Federal Republic.[15]

In actual fact the ruling elites of the Federal Republic had become too much wedded to the process of European unification to look for alternatives. Indeed, the younger generation of politicians had largely lost the habit of thinking in terms of nation-state policies and interests. After 1990 they worried lest the old or new anti-German sentiments that had been voiced during the unification process might further fuel nationalism around Europe and hurt German exports. The signing of the 1992 Maastricht treaty, including the surrender of the Deutschmark, was seen as a crucial step toward fulfilling a promise that Chancellor Kohl had made as part of his unification diplomacy. Far from abandoning European integration, Germany would intensify its integration policy and participate in a "great leap forward." Thus a substantial part of Germany's regained sovereignty would be surrendered to the European Union.

While the overall consequences of the Maastricht treaty are still impossible to assess, it seems surprising that the prospective abolition of the Deutschmark was accepted with so little fuss in Germany. Opinion polls have clearly indicated a disapproval rate of 70 percent or more, yet politically nothing has so far followed from such sentiments. Neither the federal election of 1994 nor any of the subsequent regional elections seem to have been influenced by the Deutschmark issue. How is this to be explained?

A definitive answer is impossible to give at this stage. It seems likely that the intense political confusion that surrounded and followed unification — think of the Gulf War, the dissolution of the Soviet Union, and the war in Yugoslavia — made it nearly impossible to have an intense political debate on Maastricht. Indeed, such a debate was avoided, even suppressed, by the major political parties. They followed the logic of Kohl's linkage argument and voted for the treaty in the Bundestag by a vast majority.

Apart from sharing Kohl's view that an integrationist answer had to be given to the questions surrounding the issue of a larger Germany, most members of the Bundestag also shared the fear that an assertive debate on German national sovereignty would only encourage certain right-wing groups who were already causing a great deal of trouble in connection with the fast-growing immigration problems. The fall of the Iron Curtain and the war in Yugoslavia had brought many hundreds of thousands of refugees and asylum-seekers to Germany, for which the country was totally unprepared. Racist outbursts and confused calls for law and order gave Germany a bad name internationally. Luckily, the right-wing parties remained marginal in Germany and never made it into the Bundestag, while in France, Holland, Belgium, and Italy they have drawn some 10–15 percent of the votes in recent elections.

Under those circumstances a number of anti-Maastricht initiatives also failed to get off the ground. Thus Germany continues to be different from other EU members in that it lacks any major political movement or political party that opposes European integration. Such movements have been highly effective in a number of countries. Norway is the most obvious example. (Switzerland needs to be mentioned.) And the case of the British Conservative Party is well enough known, too.

Most of them cannot be labeled as right-wing or illiberal, but in Germany they might well be pressed into that particular corner. A "healthy nationalism" is perhaps still only acceptable outside Germany. But is it realistic, in the long run, to expect the German political spectrum to differ so fundamentally from what is common and accepted elsewhere? Perhaps not. The implementation of the single European currency could yet lead to stronger anti–integrationist manifestations.

If the established German politicians are reluctant to disagree on the fundamentals of European integration, they are even less eager to discuss any scenarios of a potential Russian threat in the future. This issue is carefully kept out of sight with regard to NATO and EU enlargement. (Indeed, those two issues are hardly controversial in Germany.)

One prefers not to think about what would happen if Russia's reform process were to fail on a massive scale. Raising the issue would only beg uncomfortable questions about the weaknesses of Germany's defense policies, to which no answer seems available. Given the vast numbers of nuclear weapons that still exist in Russia, Germany quietly relies on the American nuclear umbrella, while Britain and France openly guard against such a security threat by keeping and modernizing their nuclear arsenals. The 1995–96 series of six French nuclear tests left Chancellor Kohl embarrassed and speechless.

Conclusion

What is the overall conclusion we can draw from looking at various aspects of post-1945 German foreign policy? What might Germany's place in the world be in the foreseeable future?

First, the change in the balance of power is likely to remain an asymmetrical one. The Federal Republic gained in territory and population. After the costly conversion of the ex-GDR economy, Germany will probably have a much larger productive capacity. Due to the Soviet military withdrawal and the fall of Soviet communism, Germany became the dominant power in central Europe, both in terms of access to markets and as a prime sponsor of NATO and EU enlargement. Whether Kohl's suggested trade-off, the surrender of the Deutschmark, will actually result in a net loss of power is therefore far from clear. More likely, a common EU currency will throw the member states into intense political battles over economic and tax policies, which in turn will either force the Germans to give up their strict monetarism or, more likely, will make them pressure the "softer" members of the Euro club to tighten the screws on their citizens. The resulting resentment toward Berlin is not difficult to imagine.

Second, a return or a readjustment to traditional nation-state foreign policies, comparable to France's and Britain's, seems highly improbable. Overwhelming domestic as well as external reasons are likely to keep Germany on a course that Adenauer initiated long ago. But this is not to say that Germany will always be a docile or trouble-free partner to its allies and neighbors. Much political dynamite can be expected to emerge from the gradual implementation of the currency union and the subsequent efforts to bring about a common European economic and fiscal policy. A substantial anti-integrationist movement may well arise in Germany.

Third, on balance the development of the EU is more likely than Germany to be the source of difficult future problems. Although global pressures of economic and technological competition will assure a certain degree of cohesion, a good deal of trouble can be expected to arise from the structural deficits of the EU. One solution might be to indicate clear limits to the extent to which the EU can infringe on the sovereignty of the member countries.[16] In this way it may also be possible to curb its propensity for regulatory intervention and bureaucratic growth. It is well to remember that most EU policies were constructed in an age when governmental intervention in economic life was still considered "modern politics," that is, when most railroads, airlines, telephones, and postal services and many banks, insurance companies, and coal mines were owned by national governments. The EU's agricultural policy is an obvious example of such equally costly and outdated EU institutional policies.

Apart from C. N. Parkinson's laws and apart from the vested interests of EU grant recipients, there are several obstacles of the "grand strategy" type. The smaller states appreciate a powerful EU apparatus as an instrument for restraining the larger members. Across the EU, societal institutions and interest groups, such as the labor unions and the environmental organizations, expect the EU to protect them against the adverse forces of market capitalism. For these and other reasons, any power shifts within the EU's structure are often feared to benefit German power, which under the current arrangements is underrepresented institutionally and overcharged in terms of the EU's budgeting. Thus Germany finds itself in a dilemma. If it talks about national interests, including more equitable EU membership terms, it is in danger of being called "assertive." If it puts its weight behind the integrationist camp, as Chancellor Helmut Kohl did, resentments toward "Brussels" tend to get directed against Bonn/Berlin.

It is perhaps the denial of German national interests, so frequently proclaimed by politicians in Bonn, that makes Germany's policies within the European Union so suspicious. After all, such interests are obvious enough when it comes to political reality. For example, over the last few years Germany drove a tough bargain to get additional stability guarantees for the Euro, and at the 1997 EU summit in Amsterdam Chancellor Kohl gave a clear signal that Bonn would henceforth take a tougher line on transferring additional sovereignty to the EU.

To restate the problem of the relationship between Germany and the EU: there are two conflicting proposals on the table. One is to intensify European integration as a protective mechanism against any future German fantasies of grandeur. The other is to restrict EU authority because a more tightly knit Europe, achieved at the expense of the nation-states, might provide the Germans with a more powerful instrument with which to force their interests on the smaller European states.

Both arguments were prominent during the 1992 Danish and French referendum campaigns on the Maastricht treaty. Supporters as well as opponents of the treaty claimed to have a better recipe for defending Danish and French interests against a larger, more assertive Germany.

In Germany the debates on Maastricht have run along somewhat different lines. Although substantial sections of German business people and bankers, of the press and academic community, particularly economists and legal scholars, have spoken out against Maastricht, it is important to note that most of them are not against European integration as such but are merely concerned that the new Euro-money may be prone to inflation and dangerously exposed to political compromises in Brussels. Thus Germany does not show a division of opinion on "Europe" at the elite level that would be comparable to the situation in Norway, Switzerland, Britain, Denmark, and perhaps even in France.

From these three concluding points it follows that a thorough reform of the EU will not only be necessary to accommodate new east European members, as is often argued. It will also be needed to prevent unproductive and quite possibly harmful conflicts in which Germany might increasingly become entangled. In other words, a further "deepening" of EU integration is only likely to have been a wise answer to the new post-1990 Germany and to post-Soviet Europe if the EU becomes less of an interventionist superstate. The old Euro-logic, the old policies and decision-making rules and rituals, will need to be thoroughly changed if the European Union is to be rescued from its present malaise. A leaner, less intrusive EU may be the answer to the challenge of keeping the new Germany and its neighbors happy about each other. Such reforms are above all needed to meet the infinitely larger challenges of EU expansion and of fiercely increasing global competition.

NOTES

1. The most thorough study on the subject was sponsored by the Deutsche Gesellschaft für Auswärtige Politik in Bonn. Karl Kaiser et al., eds., *Deutschlands neue Außenpolitik,* 4 vols. to date (München: Oldenbourg, 1994–98).

2. For an excellent new analysis, see Georges-Henri Soutou, *L'alliance incertaine: Les rapports politico-stratégiques franco-allemands, 1954–1996* (Paris: Fayard, 1996).

3. For the wider context, see Wolfgang Krieger, *The Germans and the Nuclear Question* (Washington, DC: German Historical Institute, 1995).

4. See Margaret Thatcher, *The Downing Street Years* (London: HarperCollins, 1993); for the circle around French president Mitterrand, see Jacques Attali, *Verbatim,* vol. 3, *Chronique des années 1988–1991* (Paris: Fayard, 1995).

5. It must be noted that former Nazis were excluded from voting until the 1953 federal elections.

6. For this reason the 1949 federal election has been dubbed "the last Weimar election."

7. For a comparative analysis of this process, see Tony Judt, "The Past Is Another Country: Myth and Memory in Postwar Europe," *Daedalus* 121, no. 4 (1992): 83–118.

8. By contrast, it was particularly deficient in the legal profession and in the domestic higher civil service.

9. Such outside pressure is obviously missing in today's eastern European reform states.

10. Alan Milward, *The European Rescue of the Nation State* (Berkeley: University of California Press, 1992).

11. The key documents were the 1954 Paris and London treaties for ending the occupation regime and for West German membership both in NATO and in the newly defined Western European Union (WEU). For the years before, the Occupation Statute of 1949 and various associated documents defined the authority of the Bonn government. These treaties and documents completely rule out of order the much-debated question, "Should Adenauer have accepted Stalin's reunification offer of 1952?"

12. Among those concepts was the allegiance to the ethnic Germans still living in Eastern Europe. Even today ethnic Germans from the successor states to the Soviet Union have privileged access to immigration permits and citizenship papers.

13. On the wider issue, see Wolfgang Krieger, "Churchill and the Defense of the West, 1951–55," in *Winston Churchill: Studies in Statesmanship,* ed. R. A. C. Parker (London: Brassey's, 1995).

14. The best study remains Timothy Garton Ash, *In Europe's Name: Germany and the Divided Continent* (London: Cape, 1993).

15. As I have argued elsewhere, there is little substance to this claim. See Wolfgang Krieger, "Toward a Gaullist Germany? Some Lessons from the Yugoslav Crisis," *World Policy Journal,* Spring 1994.

16. This point is made in more detail in Wolfgang Krieger, "Die deutsche Integrationspolitik im postsowjetischen Europa," *Europa-Archiv,* September 1992. For a different German viewpoint, see Christian Deubner, *Deutsche Europapolitik: Von Maastricht nach Kerneuropa?* (Baden-Baden: Nomos, 1995).

The Contemporary Power of Memory: The Dilemmas for German Foreign Policy

Andrei S. Markovits and Simon Reich

In trying to determine whether the new Germany is different from all others since 1871—let alone the many previous ones—we are reminded of what Chou En-lai reportedly said when asked what he thought of the French Revolution: "It's too soon to tell."

We cannot yet assess the outcome of such monumental changes. Our endeavor here is much more modest. We attempt to think about a potential framework for understanding how these changes will influence German thinking about foreign policy—through the lens of collective memory. While German collective memory is by no means uncontested in its formulation, we will argue that a predominant collective memory does exist in Germany that influences the framework of policy formulation. In that respect, collective memory links history to policy debates, forming a challenge to structural arguments that suggest that policies are largely the product of power relations. For realists, as they are termed in political science, interest is closely linked to power as measured by the classical adage in which "A has power over B to the extent that he can get B to do something that B would not otherwise do."[1] In contrast, both masses and elites, we argue, are affected by historical interpretation—as seen through the lenses of collective memory. Perhaps the clearest case of such a country is to be found in Germany—the substantive focus of this article.

Until 1989, at least, Germany represented an unusual case for thinking about foreign policy in the context of power relations. By virtue of its division and by having its two parts constitute the front lines of the two antagonists of the Cold War, Germany—even more than Japan—was not "normal" in power terms. It was institutionally tied to, and structurally constrained by, the framework of the Cold War. The Bonn Republic constituted an ideal-typical manifestation of neoliberalism, with its emphasis on institutional analysis and the primacy of structural interests, a view that we find helpful but flawed. The Bonn Republic was also impeded in its options and movements by key collective memories, most notably those of the Holocaust.

Varied international commitments (EU, NATO) did not completely "tame German power" but offered it a new framework of articulation, a new institutional context wherein Germany actively pursued a policy of creating a political union in which Germany was to receive pride of place. Since 1989 the institutions have largely remained the same: on that important level, there are very few changes between the Bonn and Berlin Republics.

Still, changes there are. Germany has become potentially more powerful. Shifts in values and priorities are detectable. Discussions of hitherto taboo topics, and the rethinking of hitherto unacceptable options, reflect such changes. But will that signal a momentous change in the thrust of German foreign policy? Or, rather, will the shifts be less significant than varied institutional changes might indicate in a country that continues to be tied in — as well as down — by its collective memory? In sum, will German foreign policy be debated within the same parameters of the last half-century or will Germany behave like a more "normal" country?

In addressing this question, we will first differentiate between history and collective memory, and show how it is mainly the latter — in its multiplicity, its murkiness, its malleability — that emerges as such a formidable force in the formation of German foreign policy. We will subsequently attempt to draw a map of the multiplicity of collective memories that currently compete in Germany's lively pluralist polity, relating key formative junctures and conceptual clusters that currently define German public discourse — and thus foreign policy as well. Indeed, we will highlight competing generations of collective memories that, again in contrast to history, are far from linear, cumulative, progressive, or even synthetic in a Hegelian sense. Rather, we will emphasize that they are circular, repetitious, and profoundly unpredictable.

I. Collective Memory and the Study of German Foreign Policy

At the core of realist theory lie assumptions about the dominance of self-interest defined as power, about states as the appropriate unit of analysis and as unitary actors in a hierarchically ordered domestic system in which policy is (for all practical purposes) perfectly implemented. Moreover, force acts as the dominant form of power.² For realists, Bonn's Federal Republic was an aberrant case—with its dissection and abrogation of sovereignty—in that it lay outside the rubric of "normal" nations. What made Germany "abnormal" was the structure of its external relations, caught in a spider's web whose four founding corners were beyond the sovereign authority of the German government: *Osthandel* and *Ostpolitik* vis-à-vis the East; the EU and NATO vis-à-vis the West. These structures absolved German politicians of so much responsibility in that they dissipated German sovereignty over military and economic security for decision making. Germany was thus not a "normal" country in terms of power relations.

But if we concur that the Bonn Republic is not yet "normal," it can be argued that the advent and features of the Berlin Republic provide evidence that Germany now has started on the road (once again) toward normalcy. This tendency was reflected in the debate and subsequent decision to expand the parameters of German troop deployment. It was also recognized by Klaus Kinkel, who said, "Making Germany a partner capable of assuming a full range of duties . . . is a priority task aimed at providing for the future. Our citizens understand that the time when we were in an exceptional situation is over . . . We no longer need to demonstrate our ability for normality both at home and abroad if we do not want to sustain severe political damage."[3]

But while becoming increasingly sovereign, our analysis suggests, Germany's leaders are no more interested in even the mildest form of military aggrandizement than they were in the Bonn Republic, and its neighbors (both mass and elite) show no greater sense of fear of German domination than before.[4]

If Germany is becoming more normal, then German leaders should increasingly behave in a manner consistent with realist assumptions. But our analysis suggests that this is not the case. The definition of security, for Germans, is inconsistent with even the weakest form of the realists' argument. Furthermore, the historical context adds weight to the problem that Germany presents to realists (although it should be critically noted that, in the search for greater parsimony and generalizability, many realists have discarded historical analysis in favor of increasing theoretical abstraction).[5] As the dominant economy located in the heart of Europe, Germany—at least in part—has exhibited a historical orientation toward the ideologies of *Weltpolitik* and of *Lebensraum* that has often best approximated the realist tradition (which justified German expansion as a means of securing national survival through its establishment among the "great powers," by which it could use deterrence to "command the peace").[6] Among the major powers of Europe, Germany has therefore perhaps most closely approximated in historical terms the behavior of a country consistent with the realist paradigm — a power seeker whose behavior is dictated by self-interest, often defined as territorial expansion, military aggrandizement, and economic domination.[7] Should German behavior revert to this style and substance, it will provide important confirmation of the theories generated by the realist paradigm.[8]

Yet Germany also represents an important opposing test case for those interested in the influence of the psychological and cultural features of collective memory and how contrasting collective memories contest with each other to form the ideological contours that may influence a country's foreign policy. For in no other contemporary "great power" (except perhaps Japan) are history, identity, and foreign policy so intertwined.[9] The historical orientation of Germany's ideology and foreign policy is consistent with the rudiments of realism, yet its modern ideology and foreign policy are in severe conflict with those rudiments.

While the clusters of collective memories characterized in the second section of this essay competed in the Bonn Republic, a dominant, consensual view emerged among Germans that was comfortable with an "ideology of smallness"; one happy to define Germany as a *Handelsstaat* driven by the normative idea that Germany is presently not, nor should it ever seek to become, a "great power" whose actions deeply influence the fortunes of others.[10] Thus, as we chronicle in our work, both Germany's citizenry and its contemporary governments look to abstain from assuming a role of international governance — through limited forms and scope of engagement — and with it the responsibilities that Germany must exercise.[11] Germany thus exercises power — through structural means such as the huge size of its economy and the setting of agendas, consistent with a second and third "face of power" — but does not seek aggrandizement of its military security (in a realist sense, as represented by the "first" face of power), as realist theory would predict.[12]

Germany stands on the threshold, minimally, of assuming the position of a great power internationally and that of a dominant one regionally. Will it accept and, indeed, aspire to that role? Alternatively, will it reject that course of action in favor of that of what we have elsewhere characterized as a "hegesy" — a country structurally capable of assuming a dominant position, but one that rejects such an option by virtue of an ideological orientation that makes it reluctant to engage in expansionist patterns of behavior consistent with realist expectations?[13]

If the new Berlin Republic is to reject the "realist option" and maintain the course set for itself under the Bonn Republic as a "small country," it will do much to repudiate the basic thrust of the realist paradigm. A sustained rejection of the vision of Germany as a "power holder" by national decision makers will do much to reinforce the view that the dominant German ideology has an increasingly important position in explaining German foreign policy—and, correspondingly, not analysis focusing on the importance of power—even in the more "normal" Berlin Republic. As Stanley Hoffmann, in reflecting on the German question, concludes:

> It would take an extraordinary amount of mischief to turn the new German state into a modern version of the dangerous and unsettling Germany of the past. Neither Germany's partners, nor even its adversaries in the East, are in any way eager to antagonize or provoke it; and German elites have no desire to return to that past.[14]

We therefore stress nonrational, ideological factors. Why is this important? Because our critique informs about the limits and the substance of German aspirations in Europe—not to build a power base exercised through institutions or through cruder forms of influence peddling, but through a certain form of genuinely felt reluctance, hesitation, and reserve. Germany's aim is not to seek power, but often to forgo opportunities that it has clearly had because of the limits imposed on its freedom to maneuver in the realm of foreign policy by dint of a particular salience of an exceptional collective memory.

Terms such as *ideology, norms,* and *culture* are often used interchangeably. But from where do ideologies come? The answer is often historical experience, with Japanese techno-nationalism as a prime example (see, for example, the prominent work of Richard Samuels in *Rich Nation, Strong Army*).[15] But saying that history shapes ideology is both true and meaningless, in the sense that it underspecifies the relationship between them. A possible instrument for better understanding the relationship between the two is to think about the concept of "collective memory"; how ideological frameworks are contested and subsequently constructed. Such a concept is important as a sociological foundation for the building blocks for understanding why countries do what they do.

Germany is a country where collective understanding has been so contested in the twentieth century, yet where a majority of the population has reached some consensus about Germany's role in the world. And it is an important case because Germany's conception of its foreign policy is so important to how Germany acts, and, in turn, Germany's actions are absolutely central to European development. Collective memory is one of the key ingredients of contemporary ideology; contemporary ideology, in turn, informs German foreign policy; and what Germany does is important to Europe. Thus, Germany's collective memory and its "memory map" are significant factors in the future construction of what Mikhail Gorbachev called the "common European home."

Alternative structural approaches that focus on states as largely unitary actors cannot integrate the notion that choices are nonrational and thus based on an alternative criterion of decision making (and therefore are likely to be suboptimal). By focusing primarily on ideology, we offer an alternative explanation for behavior that seeks to explain patterns that are inconsistent with rational explanations. Key among these is to shed some light on the puzzle of why the Germans sometimes chose not to exercise power when they might have gained, in a tangible sense, from doing so. We seek to explain, for example, that bad consequences — European Monetary Union, Croatia — were not the product of German intent. Rational arguments can often only account for intended consequences by inferring them from outcomes.

We seek to unearth the compelling linkage between history, ideas, domestic politics, and foreign policy. Collective memory, we argue, might be a means toward achieving such a linkage. Indeed, the larger body of work to which this essay is related attempts to locate the form, roots, and influence of this ideology on the future of German foreign policy. It suggests that among the Bonn Republic's accomplishments were a resistance to military engagement or expansionist foreign policy, and, correspondingly, a greater acceptance and trust of Germany among its traditional adversaries. Ironically, these developments have created a greater potential "space" for German decision makers to exploit, should the thrust of their policies shift decisively toward a realist orientation. Yet evidence suggests that such a shift is less likely to happen than ever, creating a problem that either realism will have to address, or ignore to its detriment. The clusters of collective memories among Germany and its regional partners have been transformed into the way that both conduct foreign policy. Will Germany's foreign policy of the Bonn Republic be sustained in the Berlin Republic, or will it revert to the impulses of earlier, darker periods in German history, to which realist theory still points? The initial indications are that some incremental changes may be in process. Where will they take Germany? Returning to Chou's adage, it is too soon to tell.

What it is not too soon to tell is a fascinating intra-German debate on Germany's collective memory. Begun in the latter phases of the old Bundesrepublik (notably with Bitburg and the historians' debate of the mid-to late 1980s), it received a completely new political quality after the momentous events of 1989–90. We believe that the nature — as well as the very existence — of this debate affects Germany's foreign policy. It is therefore to a more detailed discussion of collective memory that we now turn.

II. History and Collective Memory—Key Players in the Construction of Foreign Policy

In what has arguably remained one of the most influential works on collective memory, Maurice Halbwachs differentiates astutely between history and historical memory on the one hand; and collective memory on the other.[16] A brief characterization of each yields the following features: History, according to Halbwachs, is an externalized and objectified process anchored in the task of preserving the past. It is factual, impartial, unitary, and universalistic in its endeavor to preserve the past in a cognitively accountable manner. History records events of the past. It is about knowing and understanding it.

In notable contrast, collective memory is not a repository of objective facts, a record of events, but a locus of tradition. If history is universalistic, collective memory is particularistic. If history is timeless, collective memory is time-bound. Above all, collective memory is always plural. Each group — just like each epoch — has its collective memory. As such, it is quite erroneous to use the concept of "collective memory" in the singular. "Collective memories" would be a more appropriate description of this phenomenon. While, according to Halbwachs, one could in fact speak of one history, one could never do the same in connection with collective memory. If history is about cognition and knowledge, collective memory is about experience and feeling. If history is a matter of the past, collective memory is most definitely a phenomenon of the present. Indeed, one could interpret collective memory to be — among others — a contemporary experiencing and constant reinterpretation of the historic past. Collective memory is thus always present. It is in constant flux, subject to mood swings and relatively sudden changes. Many different memories can — and do — coexist in every society, sometimes in harmony with each other, at other times in competition. They overlap freely, and obvious contradictions among them do not diminish their potency and experienced reality. Collective memory is akin to the Sorelian notion of "myth": only tangentially related to "empirical truth," it plays a key role in the symbolic discourse of politics, in the legitimation of political structures and action, and in the justification of collective behavior. Collective memory is a key ingredient of the symbolic language of politics, which, as Murray Edelman's classic has taught us, is arguably one of the most—if not *the* most—important ingredients of modern politics.[17]

On a panel of the American Historical Association's 1995 meeting in Chicago appropriately called "Collective Memory and Historical Analysis: A History of Ambiguities," three fine papers offered the following useful insights for our own work on collective memory as a major ingredient of modern politics.[18]

1. There exists a clear relationship between collective memory and modernity. By being closely tied to two of the most essential pillars of modern politics—the individual and nationalism—collective memory in politics is either an artifact of modernity or—at the very least—it is heavily fostered by it. At a minimum, modern means are absolutely necessary to politicize, mobilize, revive, sustain, subdue, and perhaps even "delete" collective memory.

2. Collective memory has much more to do with the present than it does with the past. Indeed, one would not be remiss to say that collective memory constitutes the past's instrumentalization for present and contemporary purposes. As such, collective memory is clearly a functionalized phenomenon. It is, in fact, utilitarian for the here and now. Collective memory is the selective use of the past to legitimate present conditions of power.

3. This functionalization occurs both structurally as well as through an active process of instrumentalization on the part of actual people. While the purposes of the latter are manifold, one definite factor entails the use of collective memory for purposes of legitimation of power and rule. Crudely put, it would not be wrong to say that the ruling collective memories in any given society at any given time are the collective memories of the ruling class. (One could easily substitute the Paretian, Moscaian, and Michelsian concepts of elites or the Weberian notion of power holders of all sorts if one is uncomfortable with the narrow Marxian notion of the "ruling class.") The point here is that collective memory has much to do with contemporary power that harnesses the past for its own present purposes.

4. Collective memory has a very skewed and orthogonal relationship to history, but a relationship nonetheless exists. It is, therefore, useful to point out that many of the alleged "primordial" hatreds that have fueled the vengeful and lethal collective memories of certain peoples in the Balkans are far from primordial and ancient. Indeed, they are of recent

historical origin. Moreover, their current acerbity has much more to do with contemporary power relations and struggles than with the actual history of the alleged conflicts. Thus, it is certainly accurate to argue that the recent genocidal tragedy in the former Yugoslavia is a consequence of elite politics, particularly the megalomaniacal and mutually reinforcing behavior on the part of Slobodan Milošević and Franjo Tudjman. The destructive dimensions of these collective memories were clearly fanned from above.[19] Still, collective memories are not random. They are historically anchored if not necessarily accurate. Thus, Hungarians do not invoke the Swiss in their collective memory of victimhood and frustration; Romanians do not talk about the Swedes, Serbs hold few grudges against Norwegians, and Poles are far less anti-Turkish than Greeks. In other words, collective memory as myth is in fact anchored in some real-life events—that is, in real history—of any collective. Hatreds have to be contextualized in memory that has to be based, at least to some extent, in some sort of believability. Thus, collective memory is deeply influenced—though not exclusively determined—by geography and time. While it is obvious that the argument that focuses on the "primordial hatreds" between Serbs and Croats is seriously flawed in explaining the recent crisis, it is evident that this crisis would not exist had the relations between these two groups been harmonious or even indifferent. In other words, the activation of collective memory as a political force—its mobilization into the political arena—occurs at the behest of elites and the political class. It is thus subject to manipulation "from above." The repository of collective memory, however, remains in the domain of "the people." Without this the elites would have nothing to manipulate.

The following rule of thumb applies: The greater the temporal and spatial distance to any event, the less likely will be its appearance and acuteness as an ingredient of collective memory. To be sure, Serbs still rally around the collective memory of the Battle of Kosovo Polye, in which their armies were defeated by the Ottoman Turks in 1389; Jews bemoan the destruction of the Second Temple in Jerusalem at the hands of Titus and his legions in 70 C.E.; and William III's (Prince of Orange's) victory over the Catholic armies at the Battle of the Boyne in 1690 still leads to annual tensions and disturbances between Catholics and Protestants in Ulster.

Serbs, Jews, and the Catholics of Ireland are all good cases in point. It is, of course, not the events proper that rile the respective collective memories of these communities; instead, it is the constant use of these icons, their contemporary and repeated enactment on an annual basis over centuries, that render them so real. Their reality is reinforced by their symbolic representation of much more recent — and genuinely experienced — hardships: Jasenovac in the case of the Serbs; centuries of persecution and antisemitism in the case of the Jews; discrimination and subjugation in the case of the Irish Catholics. Collective memory is enlivened and history is skewed for a very contemporary purpose. Regardless of how many thousands of times the citizens of Quebec stare at their province's license plates adorned with the unmistakable "Je me souviens," none of them actually remember the defeat of General Montcalm and the French army at the hands of the British led by General Wolfe at the battle on the Plains of Abraham in early September 1759. It is not history that is invoked on the Quebecois license plates but collective memory, which in the case of the French-speaking citizens of La Belle Province speaks to a sense of centuries of subjugation — thus, victimization — at the hands of the victorious English and the subsequent domination of British culture and politics in Quebec until Charles de Gaulle's epoch-setting "Vive le Québec libre" speech on the balcony of Montreal's city hall in June of 1967. Without the contemporary trigger of 1967, the symbolic meaning of 1759 would be far less acute than it has become in Quebecois politics of the last three decades. Put bluntly, history in a Halbwachsian sense remains confined to libraries and the domain of scholarship. Collective memory finds its way onto the license plates of millions of cars.

Actually experienced collective memory does not reach further back than barely one century or the life span of human beings who experienced these events either as active participants or even as simple contemporaries. (The German word *Zeitzeuge,* time witness, delineates this concept superbly.) With the physical disappearance of *Zeitzeugen,* collective memory enters the realm of ideology and myth. Thus, collective memories are among the building blocks, the foundations, of ideologies. These ideologies, more directly, are the guiding instruments of foreign policies (in a positivist sense). Collective memory is what links ideology to historical interpretation. Collective memory is profoundly tied to generations, a point to which we will return below. Spatially, too, proximity has played a crucial role, at least until the era of colonialism and the arrival of modern transportation and communication in the age of industrialization. To be sure, Britain and France continue to play certain roles in the collective memories of their former colonies, as does the United States in places such as the Philippines and, most notably, Vietnam. Feedback effects exist in all cases, since, being creations and results of social processes, collective memories arise through interdependence. Thus, Algeria, Dien Bien Phu, and everything that they symbolize continue to play a role in some key collective memories in France, just as "the Vietnam experience" is far from a closed chapter in the political fabric of the United States. Thus, Vietnam continues to be part of American collective memory, not only of American history.

5. Collective memory is a key ingredient of what Emile Durkheim, Maurice Halbwachs's post-Bergsonian idol, labeled "conscience collective."[20] Comprising both collective conscience and collective consciousness, "conscience collective" is a difficult-to-describe social bond among a group of people whose shared experiences and contemporary interpretations of the past form a crucial foundation of their community.

6. For reasons that seem somewhat obscure to us, collective memory on a national level loves to dwell on negative experiences. In particular, the notion of victim, victimhood, and victimization plays a crucial role in the collective memory of virtually every country. Stronger in some than in others, differing in its intensity according to time and space, every country seems to have had at least one trauma in its past that continues to haunt its collective memory. "Coming to terms with the past" is thus not only confined to Germany. It is a ubiquitous phenomenon. Clearly, one of the driving forces of the salience of victimhood and victimization in collective memory is the desire for justice. There seems to be an overwhelming human need and wish to "right wrongs." This contributes the "positive" side of the salience of victimhood and victimization. The "negative" aspect manifests itself in the human trait of *ressentiment* that Friedrich Nietzsche characterizes so poignantly in his *On the Genealogy of Morals*.[21] Both "positive" and "negative" aspects are constantly present in a nation's collective memory. It is only their articulation and manifestation that vary both synchronically and diachronically. It is interesting that the collective memories of "shame cultures" exhibit a similar prevalence of victimization and victimhood as do those of "guilt cultures."[22] The expression and articulation of each might be different in the respective cultures, more extrovert in the former, more introvert in the latter. But in both, victimization and victimhood offer a powerful filtering of the past that affects each culture's assessment of its present and future.

Like generals who always fight the last war, countries seem to fight their last trauma, the last event in which they were somehow wronged by somebody and victimized by something. What is interesting in this is that *regardless* of who the actual perpetrators, instigators, or activists were in the event, collective memory eventually succeeds in always clustering around the axis of victimization and victimhood. Collective memory in the United States sees Americans as the victims of the Vietnam War even though the argument can certainly be made with considerable legitimacy that it was the United States that destroyed Vietnam rather than the other way around. On all counts — the POWs/MIAs, the 58,000 dead and many more wounded, and, of course, the absence of a final victory — the power of the "Vietnam experience" lies precisely in the fact that Americans regard themselves as (at least partial) victims of this awful war.

As we have argued elsewhere, most Europeans continue to share considerable reservations about German power precisely because in their collective memories they see themselves as having been victimized by Germany in the course of this century.[23] As Tony Judt shows in a brilliantly argued paper, this notion of having been victimized by the Germans became an absolutely indispensable staple of the collective memories of most postwar European peoples, even those, significant in number, who had in fact benefited from Germany's power and presence during the Nazi era.[24] Thus arose the collective myth of a resistance against the Nazis, which, according to Judt, was essential in legitimating a feel-good Europe of the postwar era in which victimization by the Germans developed into an essential pillar of the "foundation myth." This is not to argue that the Nazis did not victimize millions of Europeans. It is merely to show that even those whom they did not in fact victimize developed a myth of victimization in their collective memory that — on the whole — served them well in the legitimation of their postwar policies. Be it Austria's legendary cover-up that led to the Austrians' being declared as Nazi Germany's first victims (and thus to that country's official exoneration via the Moscow Declaration of 1943), or France's 50-year-old myth of being a nation of resistance fighters against the Nazi regime, every country derived considerable postwar mileage from having been victimized by the Germans.[25] Among this number are included, of course, the Germans. They, too, were "victims" of the Nazis. Lest victimization remain solely confined to that era of German history, the Germans could — and did — construct further instances of recent victimization for the multiplicity of their collective memory: the forced displacement of millions of Germans from Eastern Europe and the Soviet Union immediately following the war; the occupation of Germany by the three Western powers and most notably the Soviet Union; and Germany's subsequent division. In short, there are very few countries (perhaps some very small and very rich ones such as San Marino, Monaco, Liechtenstein, but certainly not Kuwait) in whose collective memories some sort of slight, plight, or wrong does not play a significant myth-making and legitimating role. Why human collectives dwell so persistently on bad things is not immediately clear to us—that they do, however, is clear.

Even less clear, though much more remediable, is the virtual absence of the study of collective memory in the formulation, conceptualization, and implementation of foreign policy. Indeed, the study of collective memory is virtually unknown to the discipline of political science. In a nicely compiled annotated bibliography of major scholarly works of the past decade on collective memory, Iwona Irwin-Zarecka's list of 55 English-language entries and 10 French-language titles does not include a single political scientist.[26] The group comprises an eclectic array of historians, sociologists, anthropologists, and students of literature and culture, as well as journalists. The topic of collective memory for political scientists seems to have remained outside of their interest in good part because of its perceived "mushiness." In a discipline in which measurement is increasingly reified as explanation, where numbers and calculations are the only valid expressions of conceptual rigor, collective memory will hardly be viewed as an analytic category worthy of serious study.[27] This is not surprising, though all the more lamentable, since we believe that collective memory is a crucial ingredient in every country's policy-making atmosphere, arena, and process. Perhaps it is nowhere more important than in the realm of foreign policy. To be sure, there are some notable exceptions to this valid generalization about the lack of studies of collective memory and politics. Thus, for example, in a powerfully argued paper on the role of ideas in the construction of German foreign policy, Thomas Banchoff offers a very convincing argument for the primacy of ideas and memories in the formulation and implementation of foreign policy in the Bundesrepublik of the past 40 years. Focusing his paper on the Federal Republic's integration into the West in the early 1950s and Willy Brandt's *Ostpolitik* of the late 1960s and early 1970s, Banchoff makes a powerful case as to how, at both of these crucial junctures of the Federal Republic's postwar political identity, Adenauer's and Brandt's *ideas* mattered immensely. These ideas, in turn, were contextualized in the larger frameworks of particular collective memories.[28]

Moreover, in a fascinating dissertation on foreign policy decision making after wars, Gideon Rose examines five different schools in the international politics literature in terms of their particular approach to an understanding of this issue.[29] Rose delineates the following five categories: realist theory; domestic values theory; domestic politics theory; lessons of history theory; and bureaucratic politics theory. It is under Rose's fourth category that we read the following useful analogy to our concern with collective memory as a factor in foreign policymaking: "1)

Foreign policy decision makers evaluate situations and formulate policies partly through the use of historical analogies. 2) These analogies consist of sequences of events, actions, and consequences. 3) The most striking analogies will be those from the previous war. 4) A nation's behavior during the endgame of a particular war, therefore, will be based on the lessons its key policy makers draw from the endgame of the previous war."[30] And barely a page further, we read the following interesting point apropos our analysis of the primacy of victimization and victimhood in collective memory: "Past failures may leave deeper impressions than past successes."[31] These failures may in fact leave the most lasting psychological imprints on decision makers as well as their successors. And then, quoting extensively from a work of Robert Art, Rose asserts that "the best explanation for a nation's foreign policy is to understand, not its people's hopes, but rather its fears . . . We are all creatures of history in the sense that we try, even if we fail, not to repeat the mistakes of the past . . . Whether anything can in fact be learned from the past . . . is irrelevant . . . In learning from the past, people are motivated by the negatives, not the positives. They are concerned first and foremost with what to avoid, not with what to achieve. They are out to minimize losses not to maximize gains. If this is the manner in which decision makers and their public calculate, then both are guided by the failures of the past, by their sense of what did not work and by their judgements of why not."[32] Rose uses Yuen Foong Khong's fine work about America's decision to enter the war in Vietnam to buttress his own exposé of the lessons-of-history theory of international relations.[33]

On a national level, collective memory is the view of the past articulated by national leaders and the political class. It is collective memory in two senses, First, it is memory about a collectivity, the nation-state, about its domestic developments and foreign involvements. Second, it is, in an extended sense, memory of a collectivity. National leaders, representatives of the polity as a whole, articulate memories in the name of the nation-state. The citizens of a particular state — and members of the political elite — will rarely agree on a given account of the past. But the memories articulated by national leaders can be considered collective memories in much the same way that their external actions constitute a single, national foreign policy.

As Thomas Banchoff notes in his discussion of collective memory in this volume, the collective memories articulated by leaders have three related dimensions: narrative, evaluative, and prescriptive. The narrative dimension is the most obvious. According to Banchoff, leaders tend to select "disparate elements from national experience and juxtapose them in a meaningful way." Narratives relate seminal events such as a nation-state's founding, its revolutions, wars, and economic depressions. They can privilege events in the recent or distant past, in internal politics or external relations. The evaluative dimension is embedded within the narrative itself. In rendering the past, national leaders simultaneously assess it, through the use of literal and figurative qualifiers and the selection and juxtaposition of events. Finally, there is the prescriptive dimension: historical memory not only renders and evaluates the past; it also serves to prescribe action for the present and future. The evocation of the past in its narrative and evaluative dimensions often serves to construe current actions as continuous with previous successes or discontinuous with previous failures.

The memories articulated by national leaders are not simply the result of individual reflection on the past and its implications for the present. They also have broader national and international sources. At the national level, leaders draw on memories articulated by political, social, and cultural elites. Those memories are embedded in the authoritative texts, rituals, and commemorations of key institutions: government bureaucracies, political parties, interest groups, the media, and academia. At the international level, national elites increasingly interact with their counterparts in other states. As a result, collective memories embedded in national institutions can be influenced by participation in international networks.

Leaders, then, draw on memories articulated within and around multiple institutional sites. Individual experience remains important. During their early socialization and later political careers, leaders experience and interpret world events. Their reflection on those events, and on those in the more distant past, shapes the memories that they articulate as leaders. Still, their views of the past are never unmediated. They emerge out of interaction with national elites and institutions and, as their careers advance, out of increasing international contacts.

Political constraints, too, shape the collective memories that national leaders articulate. Leaders are politicians as well as problem solvers. Their efforts to win and maintain office can shape their articulation of historical memories. Because leaders depend on the support of a shifting coalition of parties and societal groups, they are likely to espouse views of the national past that resonate within them.

The collective memories articulated by national leaders, then, are shaped by broader international and national forces. They emerge out of the interaction of leaders with institutions at both levels. Drawn mainly from recent experience, they reflect, to some extent, particular constellations of policy and political constraints. Ultimately, however, there are two senses in which reflection at the individual level remains important.

First, there is a moment of autonomous choice in the articulation of particular memories at the intersection of different forces. The memories articulated by leaders cannot be reduced to broader international and national pressures. And second, those memories, once articulated, can have significant effects on policy, which, in turn, shapes new events that eventually will be the source for new collective memories.

The effects of collective memory can be grouped in three main categories: the orientation, legitimation, and communication of foreign policy. At the individual level, memories of the past can serve to orient national leaders confronted with international ambiguity. At the national level, those memories can serve to legitimate policy choices in the domestic political sphere. And at the international level, they can serve to communicate policies to other governments.

At the individual level, historical memory can serve to reduce complexity and narrow choices. When confronted with ambiguous international constraints, with major policy problems that do not lend themselves to obvious or routine solutions, leaders often draw on historical analogies. Such analogies, the juxtaposition of past and present narratives, provide a way to gauge the options of the relevant actors, the relative desirability of possible outcomes, and the preferable policy option. National leaders do often seek to employ alternative decision-making strategies: the maximization of material benefits or adherence to established practices. But the greater the ambiguity of the policy context, the greater the difficulty of calculating costs and benefits and relying on set rules and norms. Collective memory thus grows more salient.[34]

In concluding the second section of our essay, we can thus assert with a fair degree of accuracy that in the formulation, conceptualization, and implementation of virtually every country's foreign policy, that country's collective memories will play a significant role. This does not necessarily mean that the country's eventual course of action will be diametrically opposed to its earlier missteps and mistakes; nor does it mean that it will be a replica of earlier policies. It is merely to say that collective memory and its constant construction and reconstruction constitute a key ingredient in every country's political behavior vis-à-vis its internal as well as external environment. One cannot understand recent American foreign policy and its search for a new world order without recognizing the significance of the Vietnam syndrome, Munich, and the collective memory of the Cold War. The French are confined by an amalgam of postcolonial blues mixed with a goodly portion of imperial projection: Algeria and Dien Bien Phu on the one hand, and a showing-it-to-the-Americans panache on the other. Britain's foreign policy predicament is somewhat similar, though much less concerned with exhibiting the imperial grandeur combined with a fine dosage of anti-Americanism that is evident in the French case. However, its collective memory of splendid isolation from the troubles and vagaries of continental Europe remains a potent force well beyond the confines of cranky "Euroskeptics" on the Tory back benches. Israel's foreign policy remains deeply anchored in the collective memory of the Holocaust;[35] Japan's in the country's World War II experience; and Russia's in a competing web of admiration for, as well as fear of, the West, coupled with the powerful presence of the Great Patriotic War and the Cold War. We now turn to the third section of our essay to delineate, very briefly, Germany's postwar memory map as a context for the country's projection abroad.

III. Germany's Postwar Memory Map: The Creation of New Memory Alignments

As we have seen in section II of this essay, virtually all societies and countries have certain problems in reconciling events and experiences of the past with the political realities and exigencies of the present. The plausible argument can certainly be made that few, if any, societies have had to face this task with the same qualitative enormity as has Germany since 1989. After all, Germany is the only country in Europe, perhaps in the world, that in the course of this century has experienced all of the following political regimes: an authoritarian monarchy; a centrifugal and failed liberal democracy; arguably the most murderous, predatory, and revolutionary manifestation of fascism in the guise of National Socialism; a division of the country for nearly half a century that witnessed the institutionalization of a stability-oriented and prosperous liberal democracy in the western part and the imposition of a politically brutal and economically incompetent Stalinist-type communist regime in the eastern section; and lastly the unification of the two under the unquestioned hegemony of the western variant, leading to an immensely successful continuity of the pre-1989 success story on the one hand, yet also exhibiting new strains as a consequence of this unification on the other. It would not be a mistake to envision Germany as a microcosm of the political developments (as well as tragedies) of the twentieth century. All major facets of this development—fascism, communism, liberal democracy—are at the core of German politics of the past 70 years. In no other country is this the case. Thus, in no other European country does the memory map exhibit the qualitative complexity and controversial diversity that it does in Germany. Coupled with Germany's importance and power in Europe, this memory map is therefore of more than mere academic interest to Germans and Europeans.

We distinguish the following memory clusters and "generations" in the current German polity for purposes of descriptive brevity and analytic clarity. As will be evident, not all memories cluster around negative experiences; not all feature victimization and victimhood. Particularly those memories and values that we attribute to the Bundesrepublik are quite positive in nature, at least for the time being. This offers an excellent case in point for the argument that the construction, activation, and maintenance of collective memories depend on the existence of institutions. We argue emphatically that the institutions of the Bundesrepublik had the power to transform society and thus create values that have entered the realm of collective memory in the current German polity. We would certainly maintain that institutions are constitutive of social practices and ultimate cultural norms and values. The Bundesrepublik is correctly construed as one of the prime examples of the maxim that "getting the institutions right" is essential to the future trajectory of social and cultural transformation. As we stated above, dominant classes create dominant memories. The same pertains to institutions. Indeed, institutions can be seen as the "fine tuners" of an array of values and memories on behalf of—if clearly not at the behest of—dominant classes. In our opinion, complementarity between classes and institutions is an important point for the following reason: a concentration on institutions alone could yield a formal interpretation of power that might miss crucial subtleties and historical continuities. Thus, for many, the Bundesrepublik represents a completely new beginning by virtue of the institutional novelties and innovations that undoubtedly characterized the so-called *Stunde Null* (Zero Hour).[36] This, of course, is not incorrect, though it is incomplete. An analysis of classes, that is, of social actors, lends agency its due, which it is denied by "simple" institutionalism. We need agency to contextualize institutions (and, of course, the other way around). The construction of collective memory is a consequence of both.

As to the most critical "memory moment" or "memory junctures" of recent German history, we would like to designate the following five events: 1945, which featured the defeat (*not*, as is often mentioned, the collapse) of the Third Reich, with the former clearly connoting an external process whereas the latter falsely implies an internal one; 1949, which saw the foundation of the two republics; 1968, which witnessed the most powerful generational challenge with the most lasting legacy anywhere in the advanced capitalist world; 1985, which marked the events at Bitburg, the first concerted attempt to revive a dormant and partially illegitimate collective memory; and 1989, the system-shattering events that resulted in the collapse of the Berlin Wall and led to unification of Germany in October of 1990. To be sure, none of these junctures alter the content of the already-existent memory map. They merely create new memory alignments, new coalitions, new configurations. These events "coincide" with the memory clusters themselves, which can be characterized as follows:

1. The Weimar cluster. For reasons that are evident, there developed a strong collective memory in Germany that focused on avoiding the mistakes of the Weimar Republic that, in turn, helped Hitler attain power. Be it in the Federal Republic's industrial relations system and the realm of its unions, its *Einheitsgewerkschaft* and *Industriegewerkschaft*, for example; or in management's moderation in its approach to seeing labor as its junior partner in running the economy, not as its deadly rival, the memory of Weimar still informs the Federal Republic's public discourse. This memory is nowhere more pronounced than in the German people's sensitivity toward inflation and the immense legitimacy that the Bundesbank thus enjoys as Germany's most reliable institution, empowered to confront the dangers of inflation in its infancy and to fight inflation with all possible means. The Bundesbank's role as "inflation slayer" has consistently rendered this otherwise soulless institution one of the most highly regarded, virtually untouchable, perhaps even beloved symbols of the Federal Republic. Unlike in the Weimar period, when the German people were severely victimized by inflation, the Bundesbank will now see to it that nothing of the sort will happen again. Weimar as collective memory continues to be alive and well mainly as a huge warning system; a larger-than-life caveat for Germans to remember that unbridled social conflict, poor economic performance, and irresponsible political posturing could once again render the Germans victims of terrible troubles. Bonn derived immense (and conscious) legitimacy by not being Weimar. Whatever the Berlin Republic will become, it is fair to say that most Germans do not want it to be anything close to its Weimar predecessor. As such, the Weimar Republic as collective memory serves as a warning for many Germans about how things could once again become if caution is not properly exercised.

2. The Nazi cluster. To be sure, this collective memory is so overwhelming and so ubiquitous that there exists virtually no aspect of German public life that is not in some manner affected by its continued presence. It would be foolish to attempt even a vague summary of this collective memory in such a brief space, especially since we are of the firm opinion that this collective memory "crowds out" any and all others in the way Germans are viewed by the world and themselves; how they construct their public choices both at home and abroad; and the manner in which they implement their choices once they have been made. We would like to distinguish four interrelated facets that compose this immensely complex and continuously current cluster.

a. Germans as victims of National Socialism. Let us not forget that both East and West Germans derived an immense amount of legitimation by portraying themselves (though not each other, of course) as victims of National Socialism. East German victimization at the hands of "fascism" reached such mythic dimensions in the East Germans' "conscience collective" that it was not uncommon to hear East German schoolchildren sing the praises of Germany's "progressive forces" who, together with the Red Army, "liberated" Germany from fascism.[37] If the East Germans were victimized by capitalism, of which National Socialism was merely a particularly heinous, though structurally congruent, manifestation, then the West Germans viewed National Socialism as an evil machination by a handful of ruthless men who somehow succeeded in bamboozling the German nation to follow them on a path of adventure and conquest, ending in Germany's eventual destruction and political emasculation. The collective memory of Germans as victims of National Socialism has remained a consistently potent one in the political discourse of all German republics since the end of World War II. If anything, this facet of the Nazi cluster has received additional support through events such as Bitburg, the fiftieth anniversary celebrations of D-day in June 1994, and the subsequent worldwide testimonials commemorating the end of World War II from May until August 1995.

b. Germans as perpetrators of National Socialism. Public opinion polls corroborate the presence of this collective memory loudly and clearly: with the passage of time, more Germans came to view National Socialism as a criminal regime in which Germans participated with at least tacit complicity, if not outright enthusiasm. While in the 1950s there developed what Theodor Adorno so aptly termed an atmosphere of "cold and empty forgetting" regarding the Germans' participation in the Nazi regime's crimes and brutalities, things began to change, albeit very gradually. Change was initiated by the Auschwitz trial in 1963, continued with the two parliamentary debates concerning the expiration of the statutes of limitation for genocide in the late 1960s and late 1970s, was supported by the airing of the television series "Holocaust" in 1979, and culminated in Richard von Weizsäcker's legendary speech to the Bundestag and the Germans on 8 May 1985 (commemorating the fortieth anniversary of the end of World War II). As a result, there developed a solid, if not overwhelming, popular view that the Germans had something to do with National Socialism's crimes; that they were not only the machinations of an evil but determined coterie of thugs, or of capitalist rule, but a combination of historic circumstances and a confluence of developments in which the German people assumed the role of active participant instead of passive bystander or, worse, innocent victim. If the first interpretation focuses on Germans as victims of National Socialism, this collective memory identifies with National Socialism's victims both domestically and abroad. The people for whom this collective memory remains salient are the "good guys": they are the ones who join *Aktion Sühnezeichen* and perform their national service amongst peoples where the Germans under Nazi rule behaved with special cruelty; they take field trips to Auschwitz, visit Israeli kibbutzim, enjoy the sound of klezmer music, learn Yiddish, fight racism, and come to the aid of persecuted foreigners. In short, they are the thousands of Germans who exist in every metropolis, city, town, and even village and who continue to speak out against anything they feel might once again resemble the harbingers of National Socialism. In many ways, the active presence of this collective memory embodies perhaps the most forceful articulation that a nightmare similar to the one of National Socialism remains unthinkable in contemporary Germany and that of the immediate future.

c. Germans indifferent to National Socialism. In contrast to the just-mentioned collective memories about National Socialism, there also exists the collective memory of amnesia. Even though oxymoronic and patently contradictory, it could be categorized as an actively sought "non-memory," or a collective effort to forget the past. This amnesia does not deny the Nazi regime's atrocities or the Germans' involvement in them. It merely prefers to remain silent and "let bygones be bygones." This interpretation could be called the collective memory of the *Schlussstrich*.

d. Germans approving of National Socialism. Though clearly the smallest of the four facets discussed in this ubiquitous cluster of collective memory, it cannot be dismissed as completely insignificant. It appears in various guises, ranging from the widely held view that National Socialism was basically a fine idea that was merely poorly implemented, to the many varieties of "Holocaust denials" that have enjoyed a growing popularity among many Germans. The efforts of revisionist historians in the 1980s represented an attempt to legitimate this response.[38]

Adding political potency to each of these four facets of the "Nazi cluster" is the fact that their prevalence closely follows the political allegiances and sympathies of the German population and is far from random. Thus, facet *b* is much more prevalent among adherents of social democracy and various other manifestations of Germany's political left than anywhere else in German society. Conversely, the collective memories of Germans as victims of Nazism, of amnesia concerning Nazism, and the approval of Nazism have always been more at home on the right side of the German political spectrum. As with all collective memories, these, too, have consistently furnished important ammunition for battles of contemporary politics, such as those concerning the admission and treatment of immigrants.

3. *The Bundesrepublik cluster.* In this area we also distinguish several facets that are each worthy of a brief sketch. It is obvious that in the context as temporally immediate as is that of the Federal Republic, collective memory blurs with values and norms. People's memories and experiences are simply too close to allow an analytically meaningful distinction. However, even though the Bundesrepublik represents the present, its inhabitants have formed certain opinions about it, share certain values with it, and express feelings toward it, which are in part shaped by memories of it. Thus, the Bundesrepublik, too, has developed its myths and collective memories that shape the political climate of the country.

a. The Bundesrepublik as an economic success: the saving and investment story. Beginning with the so-called reconstruction period of the late 1940s and early 1950s, there developed the collective memory of the hard-working Germans, the *Trümmerfrauen,* who with their bare hands and nothing to sustain them were able to scrimp and save, eventually beginning the Federal Republic's successful economic recovery. This collective memory features the "economic miracle" and takes pride that no adversity, regardless of its magnitude, could stop the Germans from once again picking themselves up, like a "phoenix from the ashes," to become the economic envy of the world. This collective memory features the German as hard worker, as ascetic, as profoundly apolitical, as private. It focuses on the areas of saving, frugality, and investment. One could easily label it the collective memory of hard work and deprivation, a sort of collective memory of the Protestant ethic.

b. The Bundesrepublik as an economic success: the consumption story. By the late 1950s, there developed a sort of *Wohlstandsideologie,* a memory of abundance and comfort based on an unprecedented level of public and private consumption. The Bundesrepublik became identified with the good life and the "cure": six weeks of paid vacation; the shops in the downtown pedestrian zones of even the smallest German towns filled with exotic fruits, state-of-the-art electronic gadgetry, and the latest in international fashion; Germans traveling the world in record numbers (Germans have consistently been the "world champions" in international tourism as measured by per capita travel on the part of the population); the obligatory second car; nice small house or equivalent condominium in a squeaky-clean neighborhood; no material wants unfulfilled. This item furnishes the collective memory of the Federal Republic as secure provider of material abundance, as procurer of the "good life."

c. *The Bundesrepublik as Germany's most successful democracy.* As Seymour Martin Lipset demonstrates so effectively in his classic *Political Man,* economic success, particularly when brought to bear with consistency and dependability on a troubled country with a weak polity, possesses a great potential for democratizing a formerly undemocratic political culture and legitimating what had previously been a barely legitimate political order.[39] The Bundesrepublik is a perfect case in point. Hardly accepted by the population in the late 1940s and much of the 1950s, the Bundesrepublik was a rump Germany, which—to add insult to injury—was occupied by the victorious (and much disliked) Allied powers. These Allied powers, particularly the Americans, did gain substantial affection by saving West Berlin during the dark days of the Berlin blockade in the late 1940s. Furthermore, the German population also developed a certain tolerance for them simply for not being Russians and other Soviets. The Bundesrepublik, however, was hardly loved in the beginning. With the exception of a few members of the (largely Catholic and West German) political elite, the citizens of the Federal Republic tolerated but far from embraced this new political construct. They had little choice in the matter, so they made do with something that, whatever it was, was certainly *not* "that thing over there"—the much despised and feared eastern zone, dominated by the hated Soviets and their communist rule. Thus developed one of the Bundesrepublik's most powerful Western pillars: its opposition to anything Soviet, and its deeply ingrained anticommunism. Due to this non-Soviet construct's economic success, the West Germans gradually began to appreciate and welcome its political institutions and its constitutional arrangements. In a classic case of the economy preceding—and, in part, defining—politics, the Federal Republic's profound political legitimacy was built almost exclusively on the success of its economic power.

Verfassungspatriotismus, which by the 1970s had developed into a genuine political reality well beyond the narrow world of intellectuals such as Jürgen Habermas, had its origins not in the still elusive German bourgeois revolution, nor in the particular affect that the citizens of the Federal Republic conveyed toward the Basic Law, but, therefore, in the Bundesrepublik's economic performance. Perhaps of greater importance than the Federal Republic's "economic miracle" has been its unheralded and unnamed "political miracle," meaning that in the course of the Federal Republic's nearly 50-year existence, its institutions of liberal democracy, constitutionalism, and *Rechtsstaatlichkeit* have become completely acceptable to a large majority of Germans. It is only through this lengthy process of successful democratization propelled by a powerful economy that Germans are now beginning to develop a genuine—and proud—collective memory of the Bundesrepublik.

The affect expressed by Germans vis-à-vis the Bundesrepublik continues to remain tainted by the immense shadows of the collective memories of the Nazi cluster—and thus cannot express itself with similarly unbridled emotions as those of the French toward France, of the Americans toward the United States, and of the Italians toward Italy. But there exists a strong republican consciousness in Germany that is proud of the Federal Republic not because of its economic prowess but because of its deep anchoring in the good liberal values of the West: republicanism, constitutionalism, parliamentarism; free speech; and an independent judiciary, to name but a few key uniting items. This collective memory welcomes Germany as a thoroughly Westernized society whose values convey the triumph of Western liberalism over all previous German arrangements of illiberalism, to use the most broadly gauged common denominator. Whereas flag-waving still remains largely confined to the fans accompanying the very successful German national soccer team, pride in the Deutsche mark has become a quasi substitute for many Germans as a legitimate expression of their affect for the Bundesrepublik. Thus "D-mark waving" is an unusual but telling manifestation of the collective memory that is proud of the Bundesrepublik's economic prowess as well as its full integration into the world of Western political values.

d. The Bundesrepublik as a powerful player. A related collective memory and source of identity to this "democratic" perspective is also linked to the Bundesrepublik's Western ties. But in contrast to the prior one, which accords pride of place to Western values such as liberalism, constitutionalism, and due process, this collective memory, though obviously related, is rooted in the West as a community of power. This collective memory's major pillars are based on the Bundesrepublik's being an integral, indeed leading and indispensable, member of the North Atlantic Treaty Alliance. The memory focuses on the struggles of the Cold War in which the Bundesrepublik developed into the bulwark and the front line of the West's determined defense against the alleged attempts of the Soviets and the communists to conquer all of Europe, if not the whole world. The major carriers of this memory are the Federal Republic's Atlanticists—institutions such as the venerable *Atlantikbrücke* and those few (and diminishing) policymakers who are still indebted to the United States for the helping hand it offered in rebuilding the western part of Germany and protecting it, as well as the divided Berlin, from the Soviet menace. If the former group of Westernizers' collective memory rejoices in the Bundesrepublik's Westernization in terms of its values of permissiveness, tolerance, and constitutionalism, then this group's identity centers around the Federal Republic as an integral player of a common security alliance and a powerful defense community. If the former group is represented by Jürgen Habermas, the latter is best personified by Michael Stürmer. To the former, the West constitutes the core values espoused by the French and American Revolutions. To the latter, the West means NATO.

e. The Bundesrepublik as the heart of Europe. Without a doubt, one of the key pillars of the Bundesrepublik has been its activism and centrality in all matters concerning the construction of a new economic and political Europe. Beginning with the grand old Catholic men such as Konrad Adenauer, Charles de Gaulle, Robert Schuman, Jean Monnet, and Alcide de Gasperi, whose views had been formed by the collective memories of World War I, the interwar period (the Weimar experience), and, of course, World War II, the Bundesrepublik's enthusiastic engagement on behalf of a new and integrated Europe was obviously a major attempt to eradicate any remnants of German history, structures, and values that perhaps once again might lead to something resembling the scourge of National Socialism. "Europe" for Germans developed into a surrogate identity, replacing German nationalism, at least on a temporary basis. While it was unacceptable, given the continued power of the collective memory of the Nazi cluster among all of Germany's neighbors as well as within Germany itself, to express German nationalist sentiments, it was more than commendable to develop into an enthusiastic European. Thus, Germany, more than any of the other large European countries, always pursued an inclusionary strategy in Europe. The Bundesrepublik always advocated an extension of the European Community. While obviously driven by economic interests and those of political power, this largesse was also a consequence of deeply felt ideas that any inclusionary politics would diminish possible conflicts that — given Europe's history — could end in terrible wars.

At the very core of the Bundesrepublik's European identity and strategy lay its special relationship with France. This, too, was propelled by collective memories between the two countries, which — certainly since the French Revolution — had been predominantly negative. Fraught with symbolism at every turn (Mitterrand and Kohl holding hands at Verdun in 1984; the exclusion of the Germans at D-day festivities in 1984 and 1994; the inclusion of German troops on the Champs-Elysées in the special ceremonies celebrating V-E Day in May 1995), reconciliation with France has developed into one of the most consensually anchored, virtually sacrosanct, and politically unchallenged tenets of the Bundesrepublik's collective identity.

f. The Bundesrepublik as Western Europe's gate to the East. With the Western option becoming a fait accompli by the late 1950s and assuming the position of a dogma and a veritable declaration of faith, the East remained all but an anathema to the collective identity of the Bundesrepublik. It served as deterrent, as everything that the West could have become had it not been for the prudent leadership of the Federal Republic and its unwavering preference for the Bundesrepublik's anchoring in the West. Much of this changed in the course of the mid- to late 1960s. The acceptance of the East—culminating in the *Ostpolitik* and *Osthandel* of Willy Brandt and the social-liberal coalition—established in a curious way the natural order of things for Germany, that is, its bridging function between Western and Eastern Europe. It was this new collective memory that began to distance a large, though distinct minority of West Germans from the previously ironclad collective memory of Westernism, which defined much of the Federal Republic's dominant discourse during the postwar era. Coupled with an increasing criticism of and distancing from the United States on the part of a growing number of the Bundesrepublik's political class, Germany's affinities with Eastern and Central Europe developed into a viable political identity in the increasingly motley memory map of the Federal Republic's public debate.

Though far less pronounced than in the "Nazi cluster," the "Bundesrepublik cluster," too, features variants of victimization. Thus, for example, one frequently encounters the argument that the Bundesrepublik's Westernization was, in fact, performed against the will of the Germans; or that—given the natural order of things—the Germans would not have opted for such a course had they been totally free to choose. Even the collective memory of economic success emphasizes the role of victims in the form of the so-called two-thirds society, meaning that the success, though impressive, was partial in that it only favored two-thirds of the population, who enriched themselves to the direct detriment of the lower one-third, the forgotten Germans, the losers of *Modell Deutschland*.[40]

4. The GDR cluster. Nowhere is the centrality of victimization more pronounced than in a completely new collective memory that has entered the political discourse of the post-1989 Berlin Republic with a vengeance: that of the former GDR. Here, two key dimensions of victimization define competing political identities that vie for public recognition, sometimes with an acerbity only encountered around the collective memories associated with the Nazi cluster. The first pertains to the victimization of thousands — perhaps even millions — of former East Germans at the hands of a brutal regime that never enjoyed the support of its subjugated population. In almost complete contrast to this collective memory — and to the surprise of many — there developed a second, and much more politically potent, collective memory featuring the self-perceived victimization of virtually all East Germans at the hands of the allegedly imperialist, callous, and rapacious West Germans. Thus, there developed a "GDR nostalgia," a powerful collective memory that accords the GDR (posthumously) a legitimacy, even an affect, by millions of former East Germans that the regime did not even come close to attaining during its 40-year existence.

What renders matters so interesting in contemporary Germany is that we are witnessing a veritable memory war, pitting all four memory clusters delineated in this section against each other in a fascinating, unregulated competition. This phenomenon is accompanied by a corresponding amalgam of newly constituted, peculiar, and precarious coalitions featuring the strangest of bedfellows. The timing and eventual content of this outcome is anybody's guess. At this specific moment we can only observe the deconstruction and demythologization of existing collective memories; we are still very far from seeing the establishment of the Berlin Republic's permanent memory map in which one cluster of memories will eventually enjoy something of a hegemonic position until a new challenger emerges. Currently, we are witnessing the disturbing delegitimation of the GDR's collective memory on the part of many Germans by equating the horrors of this regime with those committed by the Nazis. The equation of Nazi Germany with the German Democratic Republic has many facets and enjoys much support among conservative and right-wing Germans who — in one of the most cynical moves of recent German history — want to punish the East German perpetrators of crimes lest they, too, are completely absolved of their heinous acts as were thousands of top Nazi officials in the course of the Bundesrepublik's successful establishment in the late 1940s and early 1950s.

This memory clash was clearly visible during the elaborate festivities and massive publication campaigns surrounding the German commemoration of the fiftieth anniversary of V-E Day in early May 1995. In Chancellor Kohl's official statement alone, one could easily detect a memory clash among what we termed the Nazi cluster, the Bundesrepublik cluster, and even the GDR cluster. More important than these intercluster tensions, one could also discern crucial intracluster discrepancies, such as, for example, Kohl's mention of the victims of National Socialism while at the same time also characterizing the Germans as victims of the war, especially at the hands of communism and the expulsions from the eastern part of the Continent. Kohl's speech all but equated these two victimizations, thereby creating a clear memory clash between two very different constituencies of the Federal Republic. Largely as a consequence of the Bundesrepublik's inordinate success, V-E Day had become for many Germans a day of liberation from Nazi dictatorship. This new collective memory of V-E Day on the part of many Germans was in stark contrast to the historical reality of V-E Day 1945, when most Germans viewed this day as a day of shame, of defeat, of occupation by two hated enemies — one of which, however, was much preferable to the other by virtue of its soldiers' dispensing chewing gum, cigarettes, and chocolate instead of seeking revenge.[41] It took the collective memory of the Bundesrepublik to arrive at two very interesting developments in the collective memory of many contemporary Germans: first, being able to admit readily and freely that National Socialism constituted a political regime that, with very minor exceptions, enjoyed the total backing and unequivocal support of the vast majority of Germans well beyond Nazi activists and even regular party members; and second, that 50 years of hindsight buttressed by the collective identity of a successful Bundesrepublik developed a collective memory in the Germans that was nothing short of an obvious distortion of history. It is therein that one can genuinely gauge the Federal Republic's immense success in creating a new way of thinking *and* feeling in Germany.

IV. The Context of Europe

Collective memory is not a means of explaining the behavior of countries per se. Collective memories are intergenerational, and they compete against each other, the winner (often by no means unscathed by the battle) emerging as the predominant national interpretation of history. Collective memories are thus impressionistic, vague, often incoherent and heavily normative. They often reflect the consensus of the majority, not necessarily that of the whole population. But they play a crucial role in that they link history to ideology, the former being objective and descriptive, the latter subjective and the foundation for prescription. For ideology, as we argue elsewhere, is more consistent and coherent than collective memory, but collective memories form the foundation for ideology, and the latter can play an important role as a determinant of foreign policy.

Explanations that use the concept of collective memory to construct ideology may in fact be more conditional than structural approaches such as neorealism or liberalism. But the former type has the potential virtue of being able to explain nonrational policies, and it may be clearer in forming a linkage between history, ideology, and foreign policy.

In no country are collective memories more contested or influential in guiding foreign policy than in Germany. And, in the battle between the various generational clusters, the Bundesrepublik cluster has consolidated into an "ideology of reticence," one where Germans seek to integrate their country into broader decision-making structures but where they recoil at the conscious unilateral exercise of power. Although this approach is largely benign in intent, it is fraught with anxiety — perhaps more among Germans than even among their European neighbors. For such a reluctance fails to recognize the enormous economic (and, increasingly, political) structural power that Germany exercises.

One thing seems certain: whether Germany is to become a "large Switzerland," as many on the left-liberal spectrum of the country's political class surely hope; whether it regains and flexes its political prowess, conforming to realist theory and the wishes of its conservative constituents; or whether it attains a public character somewhere between these two (unlikely) extremes, Germany's every move will occur in the context of a new Europe. There can be no doubt that, beginning in the mid-1980s and exponentially increased by the events of 1989–90, Europe has become a fundamentally different construct from that which formed the context of the Bonn Republic's actions. On many levels — notably pertaining to the economy — Europe has experienced a rapid centripetal transformation in which Germany is accorded obvious pride of place. But on the levels that form the central concern of this essay — that of collective memory and foreign policy — no such centripetality appears even vaguely on the horizon. If anything, new forces of centrifugality have emerged that derive much of their potency from using collective memories that were assumed to have been safely dormant, if not totally moribund. Precisely because there is no such thing as a collective European memory buttressed by European symbols and legitimated by European rituals; precisely because this level of politics continues to be dominated by the traditional nation-states and various *sub*national (rather than *supra*national) entities, the reality of a European foreign policy remains ephemeral. To be sure, the EU has common positions on global trade, on relations with the Middle East combatants, on human rights, and on an array of issues that are far away and relatively abstract. But as long as this discourse remains a matter of the head and the intellect rather than that of the heart and commonly shared emotional experiences, Europe as such will remain a technocratic construct, devoid of common collective memories as well as an effective and meaningful foreign policy. One of the paradoxes, perhaps even the tragedies, in the current developments of a genuinely unified Europe is that no single country is in the position of being the leader of this enormous task. Germany has some of the necessary prerequisites, but by being "merely" a hegesy, it lacks the cultural power to fulfil this role of leadership. Add to this the prominence of victimhood in the construction of all collective memories, and Germany's burdened past further disqualifies it from being the sorely needed leader. As long as collective memories in Europe remain primarily national and local rather than European, the changes of the last decade will prove to be monumental though far from harmonious.

NOTES

1. Robert A. Dahl, "The Concept of Power," *Behavioral Science* 2 (1957). This formulation, subsequently characterized as the "first face of power," lies in sharp contrast to the second face of power characterized by theorists such as Peter Bachrach and Morton S. Baratz in *Power and Poverty: Theory and Practice* (New York: Oxford University Press, 1970) and an additional third face formulated by Steven Lukes in *Power: A Radical View* (New York: Macmillan, 1974). It is these formulations of power, reflected in the capacity to set agendas and to define the ways in which decision makers think about problems, that we argue are more reflective of German power than the first face employed as an explanatory tool by realism.

2. For a discussion of the inner core of realist assumptions, see Joseph Grieco, *Cooperation among Nations: Europe, America, and Non-Tariff Barriers to Trade* (Ithaca: Cornell University Press, 1990), 3–4. For a discussion about the relative merits of realism and neoliberalism based on such tests, see pp. 14, 19.

3. From *Responsibility, Realism: Providing for the Future German Foreign Policy in a World Undergoing a Process of Restructuring,* Statements and Speeches, XVI, 5 (New York: German Information Center, 1993).

4. See Andrei S. Markovits and Simon Reich, "Should Europe Fear the Germans?" *German Politics and Society,* no. 23 (summer 1991).

5. Although this propensity toward increasing abstraction was evident in some of the early postwar work of Hans Morgenthau, *Politics among Nations: The Struggle for Power and Peace* (New York: Knopf, 1973), it has become increasingly evident since then, with perhaps the most notable example of the last decades being found in the work of Kenneth Waltz, *Theory of International Relations* (Reading, MA: Addison-Wesley, 1979).

6. Alexander Gerschenkron, *Economic Backwardness in Historical Perspective* (Cambridge, MA: Belknap Press of Harvard University Press, 1962), 23.

7. See, for example, Albert O. Hirschmann, *National Power and the Structure of Foreign Trade* (Berkeley: University of California Press, 1945).

8. Waltz, *Theory of International Relations.*

9. There are substantial differences between Germany's and Japan's dealing with their respective past involvements in World War II. Whereas Auschwitz has not permitted the Germans to claim the role of victim (though the bombing of Dresden in February 1945 has certainly been invoked for that purpose, especially by the German right), Japan has had Hiroshima as an important element that categorized Japan as a victim. The "Hiroshima effect" has allowed the Japanese to belittle, even deny, their own war crimes in Asia (particularly in China). To this day, it is virtually impossible for any Japanese politician to apologize for Japan's war crimes in direct language without couching such an apology in relativistic obfuscations. Hiroshima made the creation of a Japanese equivalent to Richard von Weizsäcker superfluous. There also exists an institutional difference between Germany and Japan in that the latter was permitted greater continuity with its prewar existence by the decision of the United States to leave the Emperor as head of state. To conclude: in contemporary Germany, Auschwitz is recognized by a majority of Germans as a German crime against humanity. In contrast, Hiroshima is seen by a majority in Japan as humanity's crime against the Japanese. Auschwitz bears with it a burden of guilt and responsibility, while Hiroshima confers a halo of righteousness. For a fine discussion of this comparison between Germany and Japan, see Ian Buruma, *The Wages of Guilt: Memories of War in Germany and Japan* (New York: Farrar Straus Giroux, 1994), and Steven D. Wrage, "Germany and Japan Handle History Very Differently," *International Herald Tribune,* 17 August 1995.

10. For a domestic perspective on Germany's changing context, and the relationship between the domestic politics of the *Handelsstaat* and foreign policy, see Christian Hacke, "Deutschland und die neue Weltordnung: Zwischen innenpolitischer Überforderung und außenpolitischen Krisen," *Aus Politik und Zeitgeschichte* 46, no. 6 (November 1992): 3–16.

11. For journalistic accounts of such attitudes, see "Today's Germans: Peaceable, Fearful—and Green," *Financial Times,* 4 January 1991; and "Germans Favor a Low Profile in World Affairs," *Financial Times,* 4 January 1994.

12. For a second face, see Bachrach and Baratz, *Power and Poverty;* and an additional third face formulated by Lukes in *Power.*

13. See Markovits and Reich, *Memory, Identity, and Reluctant Power.* We did not coin the term "hegesy," though we have appropriated and interpreted it independently for our own purposes. The earliest formulation we have found was offered by Nicos Kotzias, "Die Rolle der Bundesrepublik Deutschland in der neuen Architekture Europas," in Caroline Thomas and Klaus-Peter Weiner, eds., *Auf dem Weg zur Hegemonialmacht? Die deutsche Aussenpolitik nach der Vereinigung* (Cologne: PapyRossa Verlag, 1993), 111–29.

14. This quotation forms part of the conclusion of an alternative critique of the realist position that focuses more on the nature of Germany's external relations in arguing against German expansionism. See Stanley Hoffmann, "Reflections on the German Question," in *The European Sisyphus: Essays on Europe, 1964–1994* (Boulder: Westview Press, 1995), 257–65. The quote is from p. 264.

15. Richard Samuels, *Rich Nation, Strong Army: National Security and the*

Technological Transformation of Japan (Ithaca: Cornell University Press, 1994), 33–78.

16. Maurice Halbwachs, *The Collective Memory,* translated from the French by Francis J. Ditter Jr., and Vida Yazdi Ditter (New York: Harper & Row, 1980).

17. Murray Edelman, *The Symbolic Uses of Politics* (Urbana: University of Illinois Press, 1964).

18. Alon Confino, "Collective Memory: A Useful Analytical Tool or a New Historical Catch-Word?"; Susan Crane, "Loss vs. Preservation: The Difference between Historical Memory and Collective Memory"; and Elliot Neaman, "Gravediggers of Memory: Young Conservatives and the Nazi Past in Post-Unified Germany."

19. The literature on the Yugoslav tragedy is vast. On the role of collective memory as a continued major factor in the destruction of the former Yugoslavia and relationship among the various peoples of this region, see Laura Silber and Allan Little, *Yugoslavia: Death of a Nation* (New York: TV Books/Penguin USA, 1995). On the role of collective memory as a crucial arena of contestation, see Chris Hedges, "After the Peace, the War against Memory," *New York Times,* 14 January 1996.

20. Emile Durkheim, *The Division of Labor in Society* (New York: Free Press, 1952).

21. Friedrich Nietzsche, *On the Genealogy of Morals,* trans. Carol Diethe, ed. Keith Ansell-Pearson (Cambridge: Cambridge University Press, 1994), especially 52–54.

22. On the distinction between shame cultures and guilt cultures, see Ruth Benedict, *The Chrysanthemum and the Sword: Patterns of Japanese Culture* (Cambridge, MA: Riverside Press, 1946), 222–24.

23. Andrei S. Markovits and Simon Reich, "Germany's Image in Thirteen European Publics," paper presented to the annual meeting of the American Political Science Association, Chicago, IL, September 1992. See also Andrei S. Markovits and Simon Reich, "Germany's Image in the New Europe: The Controversy Continues," in Peter H. Merkl, ed., *The Federal Republic of Germany at Forty-Five: Union without Unity* (New York: New York University Press, 1995), 33–43.

24. Tony Judt, "The Past Is Another Country: Myth and Memory in Postwar Europe," *Daedalus* 121, no. 4 (fall 1992): 83–118.

25. For the Austrian case, see Robert E. Clute, *The International Status of Austria, 1938–1955* (The Hague: Martinus Nijhoff, 1962). Not until the Waldheim affair of the middle 1980s was Austria's official status as National Socialism's first foreign victim publicly debated in postwar Austria. On the Waldheim affair and its ramifications for Austrian politics, see Richard Mitten, *The Waldheim Phenomenon in Austria: The Politics of Anti-Semitic Prejudice* (Boulder: Westview Press, 1992). For the French case, see the brilliant book by Henri Rousso, *The Vichy Syndrome: History and Memory in France since 1944,* trans. Arthur Goldhammer, foreword by Stanley Hoffmann (Cambridge, MA: Harvard University Press, 1991). That this issue continues to preoccupy France and

still possesses great contemporary relevance is best demonstrated by the fact that President Jacques Chirac was the first French president since the war who publicly apologized to the real victims of Nazi terror in France for the complicitous behavior on the part of many French people, without whose active participation on their behalf the Nazi occupiers would not have been as successful in carrying out their deadly policies. The fact that Chirac chose this very topic to differentiate himself from his predecessor, François Mitterrand, is further evidence for the continued salience of this collective memory in contemporary French politics.

26. Iwona Irwin-Zarecka, *Frames of Remembrance: The Dynamics of Collective Memory* (New Brunswick, NJ: Transaction Publishers, 1994), 193–205. Among political scientists, the nearest example that might qualify for inclusion is Benedict Anderson's superb work, *Imagined Communities: Reflections on the Origin and Spread of Nationalism* (London: Verso, 1983).

27. For a fine critique of the social sciences, particularly political science, concerning their failure to study collective memory, see Herbert Hirsch, *Genocide and the Politics of Memory: Studying Death to Preserve Life* (Chapel Hill: University of North Carolina Press, 1995), especially chap. 7, appropriately entitled "Trivializing Human Memory: Social Science Methods and Genocide Scholarship," 73–82.

28. Thomas Banchoff, "Historical Memory and German Choices: The Cases of Adenauer and Brandt," paper presented at the seminar "Historical Memory and German Foreign Policy," held at the American Institute for Contemporary German Studies, Washington, DC, 6 February 1996.

29. Gideon Rose, "Victory and Substitutes: Foreign Policy Decision-Making at the Ends of Wars" (Ph.D. diss., Harvard University, Cambridge, MA, October 1994).

30. Ibid., 61.

31. Ibid., 62.

32. Robert Art, as quoted in ibid., 62, 63.

33. Yuen Foong Khong, *Analogies at War: Korea, Munich, Dien Bien Phu, and the Vietnam Decision of 1965* (Princeton: Princeton University Press, 1994). Khong's argument is that the United States decided to launch the war against Vietnam in order to avoid the mistakes of Munich, Korea, and Dien Bien Phu.

34. We owe the preceding section entirely to Thomas Banchoff's insights as articulated in a correspondence with Andrei Markovits dated 11 January 1996.

35. For a fine discussion of this point, see Yael Zerubavel, *Recovered Roots: Collective Memory and the Making of Israeli National Tradition* (Chicago: University of Chicago Press, 1995).

36. The classic statement of this view is to be found in Mancur Olson, *The Rise and Decline of Nations: Economic Growth, Stagflation, and Social Rigidities* (New Haven: Yale University Press, 1982), especially 75–77.

37. It is telling, of course, that neither the East Germans nor the West German left used the term "national socialism" very often, preferring the much more generic expression "fascism" instead. "Fascism" does delineate an internationally specific and readily recognizable form of political repressive rule. What

it decidedly fails to do is give the particular case its home-grown flavor. By labeling the Nazis' rule "fascism" instead of "national socialism," the East German regime as well as the West German left tried to universalize a political rule whose German particularism was in many ways much more telling of its true nature than its universal characteristics. To be sure, the Nazis' rule had much in common with fascism in Italy, Spain, and Portugal. But the differences vis-à-vis other fascisms were at least as pronounced and important as the similarities, if not in fact much more so.

38. The conservative position is presented in Rudolph Augstein et al., *Historikerstreit: Die Dokumentation der Kontroverse um die Einzigartigkeit der nationalsozialistischen Judenvernichtung* (Munich: Piper, 1987). For a summary of the debate, see Norbert Kampe, "Normalizing the Holocaust? The Recent Historians' Debate in the Federal Republic of Germany," *Holocaust and Genocide Studies* 2 (1987): 61–90. A comprehensive critique was offered by Charles Maier in *The Unmasterable Past: History, Holocaust, and the German National Identity* (Cambridge, MA: Harvard University Press, 1988).

39. Seymour Martin Lipset, *Political Man* (Baltimore: Johns Hopkins University Press, 1986).

40. On *Modell Deutschland,* see Andrei S. Markovits, ed., *The Political Economy of West Germany: Modell Deutschland* (New York: Praeger, 1982).

41. Norman Naimark, *The Russians in Germany: A History of the Soviet Zone of Occupation, 1945–49* (Cambridge, MA: Belknap Press of Harvard University Press, 1995).

The Burdens of Memory: The Impact of History on German National Security Policy

Thomas U. Berger

In few countries do memories of the past color the contemporary debate on defense and national security as much as in Germany. Despite over half a century of democratic government and cooperative relations with its Western neighbors, ghosts from Germany's militarist and authoritarian past continue to haunt the way both the outside world sees the new united Germany and the way Germans see themselves. The Federal Republic's dialogue with the Soviet Union stirs fears of a new Rapallo pact. Germany's campaign first to extend diplomatic recognition to Croatia and Slovenia, and then to expand NATO and the EU to include the nations of Eastern Europe raises suspicions on the part of many observers that Germany once again is trying to carve out a sphere of power and influence in Mitteleuropa. And above it all, like a dark specter, lurks the fear that Germany may succumb once again to the temptations of hypernationalism, with World War II and Auschwitz as the ultimate symbol of what that nationalism can lead to.[1]

Such fears can hardly be viewed as surprising. After having initiated two world wars in which over 60 million people were killed and having committed the most systematic, cold-blooded acts of genocidal evil in human history, it is little wonder that the outside world remains sensitive to German actions. And after themselves undergoing two catastrophic defeats, experiencing national partition, and enduring international opprobrium for decades, it can also come as no surprise that most ordinary Germans desperately want to avoid any repetition of the past.

German leaders feel constrained to demonstrate to domestic and foreign audiences that they have drawn the appropriate lessons from history. After having been driven by a mad lust for power — the *Daemonie der Macht,* as Friedrich Meinecke called it—during the first half of this century, Germany today strives to remain a "civilian power," a nation dedicated to the enhancement of its economic prosperity and social stability while shying away from the use of force.[2] The official discourse on defense and national security is designed to reassure domestic and foreign audiences about the Federal Republic's intentions, stressing its sense of responsibility to its allies, its commitment to an open and stable international order, and its most fervent desire to avoid conflict all around.

Skeptics, however, question whether the past really informs German state behavior as much as one might think from listening to German rhetoric. They point out that Germany has benefited considerably from its foreign policy posture in the postwar period. Insulated in a cocoon of multilateral institutions—NATO, the European Community, the Western European Union, and the Conference on Security and Cooperation in Europe (CSCE)—Germany has been able to concentrate its energies on economic development and a broad social agenda while other countries, above all the United States, bore the brunt of providing for its security. Arguably, any alternative course of action—such as seeking a position of armed or lightly armed neutrality between the two superpowers—would have involved unacceptable costs and risks. In fact, skeptics maintain, the Federal Republic has pursued the optimal strategy for realizing its national interests. German reunification and its reemergence as the most powerful nation in Western Europe are ultimate proof that this strategy has paid off.

Since the end of the Cold War, however, Germany's latitude for independent maneuver has expanded considerably. No longer a divided nation on the front lines of the East-West conflict, with hundreds of thousands of foreign troops on its soil and threatened by the greatest array of weapons of mass destruction ever assembled, Germany today is a powerful nation of over 80 million, larger and richer by a wide margin than any of its immediate neighbors, and is faced with a new and complex security environment. As a result of these structural changes in the international environment, many observers predict that Germany inevitably will break with its postwar pacifist or antimilitary traditions and begin to behave in a more assertive manner, whether independently or, as is perhaps more likely, within the existing framework of multilateral institutions.[3]

A number of post–Cold War developments could be cited in support of such a view. The forceful German diplomacy during the unification process—in particular Kohl's 10-point proposal of 28 November 1989—came as an unpleasant surprise to many of Germany's neighbors.[4] Likewise, Germany's insistence on EU recognition of Croatia and

Slovenia over the objections of its other allies has been viewed as the harbinger of a new, national assertiveness. Finally, its decision to reverse its decades-old ban on Bundeswehr participation in "out-of-area" military missions—those beyond the territorial confines of the NATO alliance—has been widely viewed as a harbinger of a weakening of the post-1945 German taboo against the use of military force. In short, after decades of sitting on the sidelines of world politics, there are signs that Germany is beginning to act like a "normal" great power.[5]

This essay will argue against such a view. On the contrary, it will present the case that a careful analysis of recent German policies and the German domestic internal debate surrounding national security reveals far greater continuity than discontinuity with the patterns of behavior established by the Federal Republic during the Cold War. Instead of taking advantage of the changed international environment to become more assertive in international affairs, whether within or outside the existing framework of multilateral institutions, German policymakers have made every effort to further strengthen and expand those institutions. Rather than to seek greater autonomy or enhanced power, the Federal Republic's foreign policy has been designed to further embed it in the existing network of institutions and further constrain national power.

The primary reason for this remarkable continuity in the face of massive change in the international system is the continuing impact of historical memory on the way German decision-making elites as well as the general German public view the world and Germany's place in it. The German obsession with their recent past serves as the basis of a peculiar culture of antimilitarism—a general distaste for the use of force as an instrument of foreign policy and a strong preference for multilateralization. This culture of antimilitarism first emerged in the wake of Germany's catastrophic defeat in World War II and subsequently became firmly ensconced in the German national psyche over the course of the Cold War. As a result, when at the end of the Cold War the international security environment was transformed and reunification had been achieved, German policymakers acted to preserve the essential features of its established antimilitaristic approach to defense and national security. In short, rather than shifting their beliefs and behavior to meet changes in its security environment, German policymakers endeavored—not without some success—to mold that environment to fit their ideals.

Although German foreign policy-making will continue to adapt itself to changes in the international system, the lessons of the past will remain a powerful influence for some time to come. They are now embedded in the German educational system, its political discourse, and its popular culture in ways that make them independent of any particular individual or group of individuals, and they are being transmitted to new generations of Germans with no direct experience of the war or its aftermath. This newly established political-military culture will make it highly unlikely that the Federal Republic will adopt the more activist approach to defense and national security policy that many foreign policy analysts and international relations theorists predict, even with the departure of Helmut Kohl from power.

In the following sections, this essay will first briefly examine the dominant Neorealist and Neoliberal approaches to international relations in explaining German behavior since the Cold War and will then offer a brief sketch of an alternative "constructivist" model of foreign policy formation. It will then proceed to outline the basic features of Germany's post-1945 political-military culture and its emergence. To test the continuing relevance of the newly established political-military culture in the post–Cold War era, the essay will subsequently undertake a brief survey of German national security policy-making and the debates surrounding it since 1989. The essay will conclude with some speculations on the general directions in which German defense and national security policy is likely to develop in the future.

International Relations Theory and German Foreign Policy

At the core of much of the recent confusion over the future direction of German foreign policy is the general tendency of contemporary international relations theory—which has an impact, it should be added, that reaches beyond the cloistered halls of the academy—to assume that the structure of the international system largely determines how states act, regardless of the institutional and cultural features of the state in question. Both Neorealism and Neoliberal institutionalism maintain that all states, regardless of their internal characteristics, respond to the exigencies posed by their external environment. While the vagaries of individual leaders, domestic politics, and other such factors may for a time, at least, lead to departures from the norm, over time external pressures will force states to pursue interests that are determined by their position in the international environment.

Normalization, however, can mean different things, depending on the analyst's understanding of the international system. For Neorealists it means a return to a foreign policy guided by a sensitivity to power, and in particular military power.[6] For Neoliberals normalization means further German integration into NATO and the European Union, but also an increased willingness to more actively pursue its interests within the confines of such multinational frameworks. From a Neoliberal perspective, when all is said and done, the Federal Republic should be no more constrained from the use of force in achieving its ends than states such as Britain or France are.[7]

Realist scholars agree that German foreign policy is likely to become more like that of other major Western powers. However, since they place little faith in the power of international institutions or in the capacity of the democratic political system to mitigate conflict in the international system, normalization implies that Germany will rely increasingly on the use of force as an instrument of foreign policy while concomitantly becoming less likely to accept the restraints placed on it by international institutions. In the absence of a new common security threat, Realists expect that the alliance structures that had bound the Western nations together during the Cold War will begin to unravel. In their scenario Germany will be forced to expand its sphere of influence in order to assure stability at its borders, and perhaps even to acquire its own nuclear deterrent capabilities.[8]

Despite dramatically differing predictions, both Neoliberals and Realists share the view that foreign policy is driven by rational calculations of objective national interests as determined by international structures rather than by subjectively held values and beliefs. The two merely differ with regard to which structures are important, with Realists placing greater reliance on the distribution of capabilities—especially military capabilities—and Neoliberals stressing the power of international institutions.[9] When these systemic structures change, state behavior should change as well, regardless of the lessons of history and the values a country professes to espouse.

More recently, however, there has emerged a third school of thought in international relations alongside the dominant Neorealist and Neoliberal paradigms, the so-called constructivist approach, which focuses on how the systemic forces stressed by Realists and Neoliberal institutionalists are mediated and shaped by collectively held societal beliefs and values. The mere existence of a particular military balance of power or a set of international institutions does not automatically determine how states respond to them. The way states perceive and interpret such systemic structures is of decisive importance. Or, as Alexander Wendt rather neatly put it in the title of an article, "Anarchy is what states make of it."[10]

Recently a growing number of analysts of German foreign policy have been drawn to the constructivist approach to analyzing interstate behavior, partly because constructivism seems to offer a possible solution for the continuity in German behavior despite the far-reaching changes the international system has undergone.[11] But constructivism is also attractive to the student of modern-day Germany precisely because the past seems so palpable in the contemporary discourse. In this sense, contemporary Germany represents an important test case for constructivist theory in international relations; if such ideological factors play an important role anywhere, then surely they do so in the German case.

There are, however, a wide range of different approaches that can be fit under the rubric of "constructivism." There are also a number of serious methodological difficulties involved in applying the analysis of socially held beliefs and values to the study of foreign policy. Before proceeding to the analytical analysis, it is therefore necessary that a bit of time is spent spelling out what is meant by constructivism and laying out how some of these methodological problems can be addressed.

A Constructivist Model of Foreign Policy Formation

The central insights of constructivism derive from sociological theory.[12] Despite considerable differences, scholars make use of Max Weber's epistemologically based insistence that social scientists must analyze individual actions in terms of their intentionality, that is, in terms of the subjective meanings actors attach to them.[13] This dictum applies to the mundane activities of ordinary people on the microlevel of society, just as it applies to macrolevel activities of institutions and states. Social meanings are seen to be the product of interactions between groups and individuals, and they serve as the basis for collective action. For example, without a common understanding of what it means to be a soldier—what are the duties and obligations of a soldier, who can or must become a soldier, and so forth—it is impossible to create an army. New constructions of meaning typically occur in situations of flux when old meanings no longer apply or have been proven invalid. Once meanings thus constructed have solidified and become widely accepted within a given group, they tend to take on a dynamic of their own. In the words of the French sociologist Emile Durkheim, they become "social facts" and must be treated as real.[14] The sum total of meanings constructed in this way, when integrated with each other in terms of what Weber has called an "elective affinity," may now be called culture. In other words, the concept of culture lies at the core of any constructivist approach.[15]

The central task of the political scientist working within the constructivist paradigm is to investigate the intersubjective webs of meaning their research subjects attribute to particular aspects of social and political life and to explore how these webs of meaning are anchored and reproduced in the political institutions of a given society.[16] In this, constructivism differs from the dominant paradigms in the study of foreign policy formation, which share a view of foreign policy as being made by rational state or bureaucratic actors seeking to maximize their interests within the constraints imposed by the international and domestic political systems. Constructivism "problematizes" fundamental categories — such as identity and interests — that other approaches treat as givens and places the analysis of how these properties emerge and become institutionalized in wider society at the center of their empirical investigation. In other words, constructivists pay special attention to the role of values, social norms, and cognition, which are usually treated as epiphenomena by other approaches.

This is not to say that constructivists deny the important role instrumental rationality plays in political culture. Nor do they claim that culture is a static entity. Rather, they see an interplay between ideational and material factors and appreciate that culture can and does change in dynamic fashion in interaction with forces external to it, simultaneously influencing and being influenced by them. In other words, culture is perceived not merely as the subjective reflection of objective reality, but values and memories subjectively constructed actively influence and shape that objective reality as well. While some beliefs change relatively easily — such as those relating to consumption and taste — theories of culture postulate that core sets of beliefs change only very slowly and incrementally, and then only under great duress. This core endows culture with a degree of continuity and prevents it from being merely an ephemeral variable with no causal power of its own.

Political theorists interested in questions of epistemology will, of course, recognize that this view of culture and its evolution bears close resemblance to Imre Lakatos's description of how theories evolve in the natural sciences, and it will not be difficult for them to translate what has been said here into Lakatosean and even Kuhnean terms.[17]

Change, when it does occur, is politically mediated. It is important to appreciate that no political culture is monolithic. Within any given polity there exist a number of subcultures — each motivated by distinctive experiences and interests — that seek to establish their understandings as binding for the rest of society. This is true especially in pluralistic political systems, where no single group finds it easy to impose its views on the rest. To pursue their agenda, political actors are compelled to enter into debates and negotiations with other groups, making compromises and concessions along the way. Compromises once reached, however, have to be legitimated both internally within the group and externally to the rest of society. Such legitimations often involve a reinterpretation of past events, current conditions, and future goals. In this way, politics is not only a question of who gets what, but of who persuades whom as part of an ongoing negotiation over the nature of reality.

At first such compromises are precarious. Political actors are keenly aware of their arbitrary and artificial nature, and many may hope to reverse them at the earliest possible opportunity. Once agreed upon, however, these negotiated realities, once institutionalized in the political system, cannot be easily changed even if there is a shift in the balance of power among the different political actors. Decision-making rules, such as the requirement of a two-thirds majority to revise the constitution, may create high barriers to the reversal of agreed-upon policies, while the credibility of leaders may be damaged by a constant shifting of positions. Over time, the legitimations offered on behalf of these compromises — particularly if they are perceived as successful — are reified. Subsequent generations of decision makers come to take for granted these legitimations and the beliefs and values on which they are based. What originally may have been an ad hoc response to historical necessity becomes conventional wisdom. In this way legitimations enter into the political culture of the nation and can have a lasting impact on state behavior long after the circumstances that gave birth to them have passed.

The study of the political-military culture of an entire nation requires detailed, multilayered research strategy and involves three central empirical tasks. First, it is necessary to investigate the original set of historical experiences that define how a given society views the military, national security, and the use of force, paying careful attention to how different groups in the society interpreted these events. Second, one needs to examine the political processes by which actual security policy was made and how particular decisions were subsequently legitimated. In this context it is important to define the essential features of both the political-military culture and the security policies associated with it at a particular point in time. Third, it is necessary to examine the evolution of both political-military culture and defense policies over time, monitoring how they evolved in response to historical events and pressures. Particular attention must be paid to the degree of consistency between behavior and expressed beliefs over time. If culture (in this case political-military culture) changes without any corresponding shift in behavior, there are grounds to question the posited relationship between the two. Likewise, if behavior changes without shifts in the expressed beliefs associated with earlier policies, then again we have reason to doubt that the two factors influence one another. In other words, expressed cultural beliefs and values should develop in tandem with behavior — in this case defense and national security policy. When there is a disjuncture between the two — between the existing norms and values and the kinds of new policies that political actors are attempting to implement — an appropriate degree of tension should be observable in the political system. Following such a research strategy allows the analyst to uncover both the webs of meaning and the shared understandings underlying foreign policy behavior and to test whether historical memory has the kind of long-term impact a constructivist approach posits.

The Origins of Germany's Culture of Antimilitarism

Germany's defeat in World War II and its subsequent occupation by the Allied powers came as a tremendous shock to its old political-military culture and led to a fundamental reevaluation of both the military as an institution and the German view of its role in the international system.[18] The sheer magnitude of Germany's material losses — six and a half million dead and its partition into two — together with the totality of its military defeat, shattered the myth of German martial prowess and prevented the reemergence of a *Dolchstoß Legende* of the sort that had emerged after 1918. More importantly, World War II had been not only a military, but also a moral defeat. The efforts of the Allies to prosecute war criminals and to purge the German political system of those guilty of committing atrocities were deeply flawed and met with only partial success. Nonetheless, for the most part German intellectual and political elites accepted the Allied view that their country bore responsibility for starting the war and had been guilty of horrendous crimes against humanity.

Although most Germans preferred for many years to forget about the past and concentrate on the task of reconstruction, the acceptance of moral responsibility had a number of very real, long-term consequences. For one, it became very difficult for any politician with a known Nazi past to pursue a political career, and, conversely, a record as an opponent of the Hitler regime became a valuable political asset.[19] For another, even after the American occupation had ended, the German state continued to pursue and prosecute former war criminals. In this way the issue of war guilt was kept alive until a new generation revived it — with a vengeance — in the 1960s.[20]

In this context, the contrast with the other major Axis power defeated in World War II, Japan, is instructive. Unlike in Germany, many figures closely associated with the wartime regime soon reemerged to assume positions of authority. For instance, Kishi Nobosuke, former munitions minister in the Tojo government and signatory of the declaration of war against the United States, returned from jail to become prime minister in 1958. In the German context such a rehabilitation would have been unthinkable. It would have been as if Albert Speer had sauntered out of Spandau prison to become chancellor of the Federal Republic. As soon as the American occupation had ended in Japan, virtually all of those who had been imprisoned for war crimes were released quietly, and the issue of Japanese responsibility for wartime atrocities virtually disappeared from the domestic political agenda.[21]

The stigma of the Nazi regime extended to the armed forces. German forces had been responsible for extending the murderous Hitler regime across all of Europe, and many of its soldiers had been directly involved in the most horrible of crimes. After the war the German war machine was dismantled, and many military men had been brought to trial at Nuremberg and other war crimes tribunals. Likewise, the use of force in the service of the national interest had been fundamentally discredited. From the point of view of many ordinary Germans, they had been asked to march off to war twice in a space of 40 years in the name of national honor and the interest of the state, and twice their efforts had been rewarded with defeat, death, and humiliation. Small wonder, then, that there existed little enthusiasm at the prospect of rearmament. The new antimilitary ethos found its institutionalized expression in the new Basic Law's injunction against waging aggressive war (Article 87a of the *Grundgesetz*) as well as in provisions guaranteeing the right of conscientious objection.[22]

The issue of national security, however, would not disappear. With the intensification of the Cold War, the German government was soon compelled to consider the possibility of rearmament. Almost immediately, the topic became a central point of contention in West German politics. In the ensuing political debates, two broad coalitions of political forces emerged, each with very different views of the German past and with sharply different agendas for the future. These two groups can be viewed as proponents of distinct political-military subcultures, one on the Left and the other on the Right. On the Right there was the conservative Adenauer government, backed by the West German business community, the Catholic Church, and the Christian Democrats' political allies, including the Free Democrats (who relied heavily on veterans' organizations during this period) and the German expellee organizations.[23]

Adenauer and other conservatives attributed the demise of prewar German democracy to its ambiguous spiritual and strategic position between East and West. To prevent a recurrence of past mistakes, the conservatives advocated that Germany commit itself as closely as possible — economically, politically, and militarily — with the Western allies. Rearmament and military alignment were part of the price that

Germany would have to pay for that integration. Both, however, had to be legitimated not merely in terms of West Germany's security needs, but in spiritual terms that firmly anchored the country's new identity in a greater West European civilization (*Christliches freies Abendland*) and would help redeem the nation. Reunification was temporarily abandoned as a goal, though in the long run Adenauer maintained that a united front by the West would force the Soviet Union to allow reunification on far more acceptable terms than they were prepared to offer during the 1940s and 1950s. It was no accident that his position also served the interests of conservative constituencies in business and the Catholic Church.

On the other side of the debate stood the German Left, centered in the Social Democratic Party and supported by the powerful trade union movement, much of the German intelligentsia, and elements within the German Evangelical Church. Unlike the conservatives, the Left placed greater stress on the domestic origins of Nazism and argued that farreaching reforms of Germany's economic and political institutions were needed to prevent its reemergence. Even though they rejected the Stalinist model that had been imposed on Eastern Europe, they feared that integration with the West would hinder reform efforts. Instead, many on the Left hoped to find a "third way" between East and West, a political model that would be at once egalitarian and democratic. In terms of foreign policy, such a Germany would adopt a neutral position between the Eastern and Western blocs, aligning with neither side and defending itself with a purely defensive territorial militia that would pose no offensive threat to Germany's neighbors.[24] As was the case with the Right, concrete interests helped support this Left position, as it was widely believed that the SPD would enjoy a decisive electoral advantage in a reunited Germany.

Space does not permit a recounting of the ensuing political battle, which has been detailed in many other sources.[25] Suffice it to say that although the Left enjoyed significant popular support for its positions, it was unable to translate neutralist, blatantly antimilitary sentiments into electoral victories. Instead, the Adenauer government—aided by rapid German economic recovery and inept Soviet diplomacy—was able to hold onto control of the Bundestag and achieve its main policy objectives of alignment with the West and limited rearmament.

To win public support and at least limited cooperation from the Social Democrats, Adenauer was compelled to compromise with the Left on a number of issues. In the area of civil-military relations, the new Bundeswehr, under the rubric of "internal guidance" (*innere Führung*), adopted a unique program of democratizing the armed forces and integrating them into society.[26] The federal government was also constrained to promise pursuit of arms control talks with the Soviet Union while, at the same time, it agreed to the deployment of NATO theater nuclear weapons on German soil.[27] In both instances, these compromises were justified to the public as reflections of the Federal Republic's commitment to peace and democracy. These compromises were to have long-lasting effects on German defense policy that were largely unanticipated at the time. The Christian Democrats and the Right accepted these policies in large part for purely instrumental purposes. In the process they accepted publicly the principles on which those policies were based. In other words, reality had been negotiated.

The basic security stance that emerged by the end of the 1950s became the template for German national security policy for the rest of the Cold War period and beyond. In the area of alignment policy, Germany would seek to integrate itself ever further into the Western alliance, gaining in the process growing influence on Western strategic planning and reaping considerable benefits in terms of trade and political recognition. At the same time, Germany would pursue what could be called a "dual-track" approach to military security, seeking to engage the Soviet Union in dialogue whenever it acted to strengthen its deterrent potential. This pattern was repeated in the 1960s and 1970s with the Harmel Report and the dual-track decision to deploy new theater nuclear forces while at the same time pursing arms control talks. The present German position on the Partnership for Peace initiative can be seen as a further extension of this pattern.

Militarily, West Germany created a substantial, conventional military force geared toward territorial defense and capable of rapid expansion in the event of hostilities through the mobilization of large reserves permitted by a universal conscription system. The Bundeswehr was placed under a stringent system of bureaucratic controls, and efforts were made to integrate it into German society in order to prevent the armed forces from becoming once again a "state within the state" or acting as the propagator of militarist values in society (*Schule der Nation*).

These policies were closely linked with Germany's broader national identity as a peaceful, democratic Western nation. This identity and its associated defense policies were still strongly contested in the late fifties. The hope for reunification acted as a powerful lure that undermined the legitimacy of Germany's new defense and security policies. A 1956 survey, for instance, showed that 38 percent rated reunification as the most important issue in their minds, followed by the economy (28 percent) and peace (16 percent).[28] Throughout the decade, support for some form of neutralism generally outweighed popular backing for rearmament and alignment with the West.[29] Had the Soviets been more adept at exploiting these sentiments, and Adenauer less resolute in his pursuit of integration with the West, a rather different set of outcomes would have been conceivable at the time.

Development and Consolidation during the Cold War

Over the course of the next three decades, issues of defense and national security remained highly controversial in the Federal Republic. During the late 1960s and again in the early 1980s, issues of alignment and national security seized center stage in German politics, first over relations with Eastern Europe, and subsequently over the issue of the deployment of a new generation of theater nuclear weapons on German soil. In both cases, on the surface it appeared that there had occurred a fundamental shift in German policies, sparking concern both domestically and abroad that the Federal Republic was embarked on a dramatic new course. Yet in the final analysis West Germany's active security policy changed relatively little, while underneath the political Sturm und Drang elite and public opinion consolidated in favor of the moderate multilateralist approach that had emerged from the political debates of the 1950s.

During the 1960s and early 1970s, the emergence of U.S.-led policies of détente and an evident willingness to tolerate long-term German partition undermined the Christian Democrats' policies toward Eastern Europe. At the same time, a new generation of Germans entered the political scene, a generation accustomed to material prosperity and raised in a far more liberal social and political environment than their parents had been. Demands for increased contacts with Eastern Europe were combined with calls for further democratization of German political institutions and an emotional new debate over Germany's Nazi past, culminating in the coming to power of Willy Brandt and the SPD.

Brandt's brand of Ostpolitik marked a dramatic break with the policies of previous governments. It turned Germany from being one of the chief obstacles for détente in the 1950s and 1960s into one of its chief promoters in the 1970s and 1980s. Nonetheless, Germany's fundamental commitment to the policy of alignment and integration with the West remained unshaken. Arguably, Ostpolitik removed a major source of stress on the German domestic political consensus in support of the alliance, and public support for NATO and the European Community shot up after 1972. In this sense, Ostpolitik helped the West Germans to come to terms with the fact of national partition.

The demise of détente in the late 1970s and the reintensification of the Cold War posed a new challenge to the German consensus on defense and, once again, led to considerable domestic political turmoil. The federal government's decision to deploy cruise and Pershing II missiles in order to counter Soviet deployments of SS-20s triggered extraordinarily virulent protests and contributed greatly to the fall of Helmut Schmidt's Social Democratic government. Likewise, during the early 1980s the conservative Kohl government's support for the Reagan administration's tougher military policies toward the Soviet Union — especially the Strategic Defense Initiative (SDI) — attracted widespread criticism.[30]

Yet despite the controversy generated by the rekindled defense debate of the early 1980s, German defense policy in fact changed very little. The Pershing IIs were deployed in numbers that did not provide a serious first-strike capability vis-à-vis the Soviets and, as usual, were accompanied by new offers of arms control talks and other diplomatic gestures designed to reduce Soviet perceptions of threat.[31] Similarly, the Kohl government's support of SDI and more offensively oriented American military doctrines was motivated more by a desire to demonstrate alliance solidarity than by a genuine switch in German strategic thinking.[32] German defense spending as a percentage of GNP actually declined during this period, from 3.3 percent in 1980 to 3.1 percent in 1986.[33]

Over the course of the Cold War, both public and elite support for the basic patterns of German defense and national security consolidated, as reflected by public opinion data as well as elite pronouncements. Popular support for the military alliance with the United States grew, and approval of the policy of integrating with Western Europe increased even more markedly. Although in 1965 a large majority of West Germans (69 percent) still said that given a choice they would opt for reunification over integration with Europe, by 1973 the balance had shifted dramatically, with 65 percent preferring European integration over German reunification.[34] At the same time, popular support for Ostpolitik and détente remained strong. Public support for Ostpolitik continued to increase even as superpower relations deteriorated in the late 1970s and early 1980s. In January of 1980, even after the Soviet invasion of Afghanistan, the vast majority of West Germans supported the further promotion of détente — 74 percent versus 17 percent.[35]

Elite opinion as well showed signs of moving toward a consolidation of views in support of the basic, low-profile approach to national security that had been established during the Adenauer period. The first important step in this direction came in the late 1950s when, after their historic party congress at Bad Godesberg, the Social Democrats shifted decisively toward acceptance of NATO and of integration with the West.[36]

Even in the late 1980s, after the SPD partially reversed itself on national security in response to pressures from the Greens and a new, more radical generation within the party, they refrained from calling for withdrawal from NATO. Indeed, whereas in the 1950s the SPD had bitterly opposed NATO and integration with Western Europe, in the 1980s it came out in favor of greater European integration in the hope that a united Europe could provide a counterweight to the United States and preserve détente.[37] For its part, the CDU/CSU came to accept Ostpolitik and détente in the 1980s, conducting its own mini-détente with the German Democratic Republic even at the height of the U.S.-Soviet confrontation of the early to mid-1980s.[38]

This is not to deny that there continued to be sharp and real differences between the Left and the Right grounded in very different understandings of German history and very different visions for Germany's future. These differences reemerged in a highly visible fashion during the mid-1980s, first in the guise of a polemical debate among historians over how to evaluate Nazism, before spilling over into the political arena.[39] These bitter debates between the Left and Right, however, masked the fact that on many issues of substance — for instance, integration with the West and Ostpolitik — a great deal of convergence had taken place.

In sum, during the Cold War there was a remarkable continuity in both German national security policy and in elite and public attitudes regarding defense issues, despite considerable shifts both in Germany's international environment and in Germany's relative power. To be sure, these shifts led to some changes in both policies and attitudes. Yet they were accompanied by considerable domestic political friction — much as the proposed model of incremental cultural change would suggest. Moreover, if viewed from a long-term perspective, the net effect of the three decades between 1959 and 1989 was a consolidation of Germany's new political-military culture and a strengthening of its overall antimilitarism.

After the Cold War: Change or Continuity?

The end of the Cold War and the fall of the Berlin Wall in 1989 heralded the most dramatic shift in Germany's strategic situation since 1945. Suddenly and quite unexpectedly, the partition of the country had ended, and the Soviet military threat that had hung over the country like the proverbial sword of Damocles all but disappeared. While the residual threat of reactionary takeover in the Russian Republic remained, even in the worst-case scenario Russian forces would be both weaker and would soon be further removed from German borders than at any time during the Cold War.

Despite these auspicious developments, the German government of Chancellor Kohl reacted almost with a sense of panic to the new international environment. Instead of seeking to exploit this opportunity to create a new and more independent Germany — either as a classic great power or as a lightly armed neutral nation — the Kohl government embarked on a course of action that over the course of the next year and a half reconfirmed virtually every one of the main features of post–World War II West German national security policy, be it in the area of alliance politics, military doctrine, or civil-military relations.

Rather than leaving or weakening NATO and the European Community, Kohl worked to strengthen and deepen the complex web of international institutions that had anchored West Germany for the past 40 years and to extend it to cover the newly unified German state. Frequently quoting Thomas Mann's famous dictum that what was needed was to Europeanize Germany rather than Germanize Europe, West German leaders insisted that German unification made an acceleration of the European integration process necessary.[40] Following the extraordinary EC summit of April 1990, Kohl and Mitterrand set in motion the diplomatic process leading to the signing of the December Treaty of Maastricht. Under the terms of the Maastricht treaty, the European Community was given broad new powers, and the member nations committed themselves, albeit in vague terms, to the "eventual framing of a common defense policy, which might in time lead to a common defense." At the same time, the European leaders agreed to revive the Western European Union (WEU) and turn it into the military arm of the European Community, while simultaneously enjoining it to work together with NATO.

To reach this agreement, Germany was compelled to make concessions on a wide range of issues. The most important of these concessions was its offer to sacrifice the German mark — the most potent symbol of postwar West German national economic prowess — in order to create a common European currency. In so doing, Chancellor Kohl provoked powerful domestic political resistance — from the Bundesbank and from the FDP, as well as from segments of the media. Nonetheless, he forged ahead in the conviction that failure to strengthen the EC might trigger a disintegration of the postwar order in Europe, once again leaving Germany isolated and vulnerable in the center of the continent.[41]

Kohl also insisted that Germany remain in NATO, despite various indications that the Soviet Union might refuse to allow unification to take place if Germany were to do so. Arguing against Foreign Minister Genscher and others, Kohl maintained that residual security threats in Europe required the ongoing presence of the Western alliance.[42] At the same time, in keeping with the by now well established German dual-track approach of combining reassurance with deterrence, Kohl convinced Gorbachev to permit a united Germany to remain in NATO by offering various incentives and forms of reassurance, including massive sums of foreign aid and new restrictions placed on the size and composition of the German armed forces.[43]

Germany also agreed to a deepening of its military integration into NATO. At the London NATO summit in July 1990, new emphasis was placed on the creation of multinational units, especially among NATO's combat-ready rapid reaction forces. While a number of factors motivated this policy move, the desire to further contain German military power was key.[44] At the London summit Germany pushed a redefinition of NATO's military doctrine designed to further reassure the Soviet Union by placing new stress on political cooperation with Eastern Europe and defining the alliance's primary mission as political rather than military in nature.[45]

Finally, the German government reaffirmed its commitment to *innere Führung* and the universal male conscription system, even though many commentators suggested that the system was a Cold War anachronism and that Germany no longer needed a large standing conventional army and ready military reserves. Public opinion surveys at the time indicated that a majority of Germans would welcome the abolition of the highly unpopular military service, while the number of those who applied for conscientious objector status soared. Despite these pressures, the German political elite preferred to continue some form of national service, including a strong military component, as a means of integrating the armed forces into civilian society and as a way of instilling an ethic of national service in the broader population.[46]

Despite the alacrity of its diplomacy, events soon proved that the Federal Republic was unprepared for the new strategic environment in which it found itself. In particular, the German government was taken by surprise by the Gulf War and the powerful pressures placed upon it by the Americans and its allies to become directly involved militarily as well as financially.[47]

Early on in the crisis, Chancellor Kohl and his defense minister, Volker Rühe, advocated sending some forces to the Middle East, albeit if only in a logistics capacity, on the grounds that it was vital that Germany demonstrate its solidarity with its allies. They soon ran into a powerful barrage of criticism as Germany was rocked by the largest peace demonstrations that it had seen in a decade.[48] Public opinion data showed that while many Germans (41 percent) thought that the German forces could be permitted to participate in UN-led peacekeeping missions, only 17 percent supported allowing the Bundeswehr to engage in military missions under a UN command like British and French forces in the Gulf.[49] At the same time, the number of conscientious objectors skyrocketed.[50] Faced with such formidable opposition, the best that the Kohl government could manage was to provide substantial financial assistance to the allied war effort and make a token show of support by sending fighter squadrons to its NATO ally, Turkey. Even these forces, however, could only be used in the unlikely event that Turkey was attacked, and steps were taken to downgrade their immediate operational availability.[51]

In the aftermath of the Gulf crisis, Kohl and his advisors were convinced that Germany needed to participate in military operations outside of the NATO area.[52] For the next three years, the Christian Democrat–led government waged a protracted political campaign paving the way for precisely such a contingency. The key element in this process was to provide for a gradual expansion of the kind of missions the Bundeswehr could engage in, beginning with the provision of humanitarian aid under UN auspices in Somalia and culminating in July of 1995 with making German air combat forces available for use in the former Yugoslavia.

In short, the Gulf War served as a catalyzing event, forcing Germany to reach beyond its standard repertoire of policy responses and take on the kind of broader international security role that it had avoided for over 40 years. Yet before we leap to the conclusion that the Realists are right after all in that Germany has become a "normal nation," there are two important points to be made.

First, the new German policy on overseas dispatch is broadly consistent with the multilateralism that has been such a pronounced feature of the German approach to national security policy, and German participation in such missions is justified in the domestic political debate largely in terms of fulfilling Germany's international obligations and supporting the cause of peace. Nowhere in the mainstream German political debate are there to be found the highly skeptical views of the value of collective security arrangements that are commonplace in other Western nations, such as Britain, France, and — above all others — the United States.

Second, domestic political resistance to this change in policy was very real and powerful, crippling German policy responses to the Gulf crisis and undermining German alliance policy in Bosnia and elsewhere for over three years.[53] Under different circumstances, such a delay could have had serious international political repercussions. For instance, if the United States had suffered much more serious casualties as a result of its military involvement in the Gulf or the former Yugoslavia while German forces were perceived to have sat on the sidelines, there well might have been an upsurge of American isolationist sentiment that would have undermined the international security arrangements upon which the Federal Republic has come to depend. From either the Realist or Neoliberal point of view, Germany's inability to respond effectively to the Gulf crisis represents a puzzling failure to realize and act on the national interest.

Since the Gulf War, the Federal Republic has continued to pursue its traditional moderate, multilateralist policies, and German public and elite opinion continues to reflect a pronounced resistance to assuming a great power military stance. According to survey data in 1993, a large majority of Germans indicated by a margin of 58 percent to 37 percent that they would prefer that Bundeswehr forces be restricted to nonmilitary missions.[54] While initially public support for military service and the NATO alliance dipped in the afterglow of the fall of the Wall, both have recovered to levels close to those of the early 1980s, with 55 percent of those surveyed saying that Germany still needed conscription (*Wehrpflicht*) and 69 percent supporting the NATO alliance. Even in East Germany, where after reunification support for the armed forces and the alliance had been much lower than in the rest of the country, East German views on national security issues have become virtually identical to those of their Western brethren.[55]

Likewise, strong elements among the German intellectual and political elites remain strongly opposed to any expansion of Germany's security role abroad, despite much publicized reports of conflicts within the peace research community between "pacifists" and "bellicists."[56] The Social Democrats and the Greens strenuously opposed the decision to send German combat forces to Yugoslavia, warning darkly of an "escalation dynamic" that takes events out of the control of decision makers and accusing members of the CDU/CSU of following in the footsteps of their conservative predecessors who twice in the first half of the twentieth century had plunged Germany into war.[57] Commentary from the liberal and left-wing press was similarly sharp and bitter.[58]

Since the bitter debate over the out-of-area deployment of the Bundeswehr, the SPD has apparently returned to a more moderate, pro-alliance stance on national security, one that arguably differs more in nuance and accent than in substance from the official positions of the government.[59] The SPD, however, contains many different groups, many of whom are less willing to compromise on the party's traditional antimilitary and anti-alliance ideals and are more inclined to entertain collective security alternatives to NATO than the party leadership at times may be. Moreover, the Social Democrats must remain sensitive to their position vis-à-vis the Greens/Bündnis 90 and the PDS, whether as electoral competitors or possible coalition partners. And while under Joschka Fischer the Greens have moved toward greater pragmatism on national security matters, a substantial wing of that party remains true to the Greens' peace movement roots.[60]

Of course it remains perfectly conceivable, even likely, that pragmatic forces among the left parties will be able to hammer out a moderate, pro-alliance set of policies in order to attract centrist voters and possibly set up a coalition with the Free Democrats. Nonetheless, much like the Atlanticist consensus within the SPD after the reintensification of the Cold War in the 1980s, such a compromise could prove fragile if tested by external events.

Meanwhile, on the right wing of the political spectrum there is little sign of a decisive move toward a more openly nationalistic foreign policy course. Despite a much publicized upsurge of nationalist rhetoric in some segments of the conservative intelligentsia, there is little evidence that such views are spreading, or even that they are any more influential than they were during the 1970s and 1980s.[61] Public support for a more nationalist foreign policy remains weak — although there is considerable trepidation over the possible demise of the Deutsche mark — and electoral support for the far-right parties remains marginal at around 2 percent.

So great is the inertia on security matters that there has been little change even in the area of civil-military relations. Despite continued attacks from the Left on military service, and despite the fact that France has abolished compulsory military service, the policy-making establishment continues to insist on the preservation of the *Wehrpflicht*, arguing that it is necessary both as a means of integrating the armed forces into society and to fulfill German alliance commitments.[62]

Conclusions

As we have seen, German defense and national security policy has evolved much along the lines that the constructivist model of defense policy formation presented earlier suggested that it would. Actual state behavior has developed more or less in tandem with the expressed views regarding security issues. When Germany's latitude to shape its own environment increased, as it did in 1989–91, German elites acted quickly to try to preserve the core values of Germany's new political-military culture — multilateralism, a nonthreatening force posture, and a model of civilian control based on democratizing and integrating the armed forces into society. When domestic and international forces pushed the Federal Republic to change its policies in ways that ran counter to the established patterns of behavior, considerable domestic political friction was generated, imposing severe domestic political costs on German decision makers.

In the future, German defense and national security policy is bound to continue to evolve in response to developments in the international and domestic political scenes. Yet, barring a major shock of much greater magnitude than anything that the Federal Republic has experienced since 1945, it appears likely that change will continue to come in an incremental fashion and that German policymakers will seek to adhere as closely as possible to the low-key, low-profile approach to national security policy that has been characteristic of the Federal Republic since its inception.

The two most likely candidates for such a shock would be either a stark failure of the extended deterrence system or a gradual dissolution of the Federal Republic's alliance structures despite its own best efforts. Even were such scenarios to materialize, however, much as in the aftermath of World War II, the German response would not follow the clear, rational lines that structuralist approaches to international relations would predict. In all likelihood there would emerge a multiplicity of different political actors, each offering different interpretations of recent events and proposing drastically different solutions. The ultimate outcome of the ensuing political battle would be contingent upon various factors — including such Realist and Neoliberal factors as the balance of power and the kinds of opportunities for communication and cooperation afforded by international institutional structures.

Barring such an event, however, the present German culture of antimilitarism and the particular understanding of history that undergirds it are unlikely to change significantly. To be sure, that particular view of history will be constantly challenged by internal critics, as it has for much of the Federal Republic's 50-year history, and new generations of Germans will undoubtedly feel somewhat less guilt than their parents did. And external events will present new problems and opportunities to the existing set of foreign and defense policies, forcing German leaders to make adjustments. Yet, much as some Germans would like to, it seems unlikely that Germany will be able to escape the burdens of its memories for some time to come.

NOTES

An earlier version of this essay appeared in *German Politics* 6, no. 1 (April 1997): 39–59, under the title "The Past in the Present: The Impact of Historical Memory on German Foreign Policy."

1. For a recent example, see Jacob Heilbrun, "Germany's New Right," *Foreign Affairs* 75, no. 6 (November/December 1996).
2. On the concept of "civilian power," see Hans Maul, "Germany and Japan: The New Civilian Powers," *Foreign Affairs* 65, no. 1 (winter 1990–91). See also Hans Peter Schwarz, *Die Gezähmten Deutschen: Von der Machtbesessenheit zur Machtvergessenheit* (Stuttgart: Deutsche Verlags-Anstalt, 1986).
3. For an interesting review of the kinds of scenarios that Germany might choose to pursue, see Timothy Garton Ash, "Germany's Choice," *Foreign Affairs* 73, no. 4 (July/August 1994).
4. On diplomatic maneuverings leading up to reunification, and in particular the strongly negative European reaction to German unilateral statements during the process, see Philip Zelikow and Condoleeza Rice, *Germany Unified and Europe Transformed* (Cambridge, MA: Harvard University Press, 1995), 118–25, 137–38.
5. Stephen Kanzer, "Germany Is a Challenge for Post-Soviet Europe," *New York Times,* 27 December 1991; Beverly Crawford, *German Foreign Policy after the Cold War: The Decision to Recognize Croatia,* University of California Public Relations and Institutions Research Group, Working Paper No. 2 (Berkeley, CA, August 1993).
6. There is considerable disagreement among Realists, however, as to what kind of policy Realist decision makers are likely to pursue. For instance, some Realists maintain that most states are likely to maximize their power whenever they can; others argue that instead most states seek to maximize their security and may eschew the short-term pursuit of power. In short, while Realists share many common assumptions about the international system, the theory as such is underdetermining.
7. Jeffrey J. Anderson and John B. Goodman, "Mars or Minerva: A United Germany in a Post–Cold War Europe," in *After the Cold War: International Institutions and State Strategies in Europe, 1989–1991,* ed. Robert O. Keohane, Joseph Nye, and Stanley Hoffman (Cambridge, MA: Harvard University Press, 1993), especially 60–62.
8. John Mearsheimer, "Back to the Future," *International Security* 15, no. 1 (summer 1990); Christopher Layne, "The Unipolar Illusion: Why New Great Powers Will Rise," *International Security* 17, no. 4 (spring 1993), especially 41–45; Kenneth Waltz, "The Emerging Structure of International Politics," *International Security* 18, no. 2 (fall 1993). For a more moderate version, see Philip H. Gordon, "The Normalization of German Foreign Policy," *Orbis,* spring 1994.
9. For the most authoritative formulation of the Neorealist view, see Kenneth N. Waltz, *The Theory of International Politics* (New York: McGraw-Hill,

1979). For Neoliberalism, see Robert O. Keohane, *After Hegemony: Cooperation and Discord in the World Political Economy* (Princeton: Princeton University Press, 1984). For a more extended discussion of the commonalities of the Neorealist and Neoliberal understandings of international relations, see Ronald L. Jepperson, Alexander Wendt, and Peter J. Katzenstein, "Norms, Identity, and Culture in National Security," in *The Culture of National Security,* ed. Peter Katzenstein (New York: Columbia University Press, 1996), 37–52.

10. Alexander Wendt, "Anarchy Is What States Make of It: The Social Construction of Power Politics," *International Organization* 6, no. 2 (spring 1992).

11. See, for instance, Thomas Banchoff, "German Policy towards the European Union: The Effects of Historical Memory," *German Politics* 6, no. 1 (April 1997); Gunther Hellmann, "The Sirens of Power and German Foreign Policy: Who Is Listening?" *German Politics* 6, no. 2 (August 1997); Andrei S. Markovits and Simon Reich, *The German Predicament: Memory and Power in the New Europe (*Ithaca: Cornell University Press, 1997); Thomas Berger, "The Past in the Present," and Berger, *Cultures of Antimilitarism: National Security in Germany and Japan* (Baltimore: Johns Hopkins University Press, 1998).

12. Wendt, "Anarchy Is What States Make of It," 396–97.

13. Max Weber, *Gesammelte Aufsätze zur Wissenschaftslehre* (Tübingen: J. C. B. Mohr, 1956), 427ff.; Max Weber, "Soziologische Grundbegriffe," in *Wirtschaft und Gesellschaft: Grundriß der Verstehenden Soziologie,* vol. 1 (Tübingen: J. C. B. Mohr, 1956), 1ff.

14. Emile Durkheim, *The Rules of the Sociological Method* (London: Collier-Macmillan, 1964), 14. The term *social construction of reality* comes from Peter L. Berger and Thomas Luckmann, *The Social Construction of Reality* (New York: Doubleday-Anchor, 1966).

15. A variety of other terms can be safely substituted for "culture" as broadly defined here, including "discourse," "mentalité," or "habitus." For a general discussion of the general features of all cultural theories of action, see Harry Eckstein, "A Culturalist Theory of Political Change," in *Regarding Politics: Essays on Political Theory, Stability, and Change,* ed. Harry Eckstein (Berkeley and Los Angeles: University of California Press, 1992), 267–71.

16. There has been a strong tendency in political science to see institutions through rational actor lenses—as sets of rules either imposed or mutually agreed upon by actors seeking to solve collective action problems—and focus solely on formal legal institutions. For a useful overview, see the introduction to Kathleen Thelen, Sven Steinmo, and Frank Longstreth, *The Structure of Politics* (New York: Cambridge University Press, 1992).

17. See Imre Lakatos, "Falsification and the Methodology of Scientific Research Programmes," in *Criticism and the Growth of Knowledge,* ed. Imre Lakatos and Alan Musgraves (New York: Cambridge University Press, 1970); and Thomas Kuhn, *The Structure of Scientific Revolutions,* 2d ed. (Chicago: University of Chicago Press, 1970).

18. On Germany's old political-military culture, see Gerhard Ritter, *The Sword and the Scepter: The Problem of Militarism in Germany,* trans. Heinz

Norden, 4 vols. (Coral Gables: University of Miami Press, 1973); Volker R. Berghahn, *Militarism: The History of an International Debate, 1861–1979* (Cambridge and New York: Berg Publishers, 1981), especially chap. 3; and Geoff Eley, *Reshaping the German Right* (Ann Arbor: University of Michigan Press, 1980).

19. The most prominent exception was one of Adenauer's top aides, Hans Globke. It should be pointed out, however, that Globke was a highly controversial figure and was never elected to office.

20. Adalbert Rückerl, *NS-Verbrechen vor Gericht* (Heidelberg: C. F. Müller, 1982).

21. For a more extended comparison of German and Japanese political-military cultures, see Thomas Berger, *Cultures of Antimilitarism: National Security in Germany and Japan* (Baltimore, MD: Johns Hopkins University Press, 1998). For a general comparison of German and Japanese attitudes toward the war, see Ian Buruma, *The Wages of Guilt* (New York: Farrar, Straus & Giroux, 1994).

22. Gerhard Wettig, *Entmilitarisierung und Wiederbewaffnung in Deutschland, 1943–1955* (Munich: Oldenbourg, 1967), 238–43; Paul B. Stares, *The Restrictions on the Forces of the Federal Republic of Germany* (Washington, DC: Brookings Institution, 1991).

23. The Free Democrats during this period were considerably to the right of the CDU on defense issues. See Dietrich Wagner, *Die FDP und Wiederbewaffnung* (Boppard am Rhein: Harald Boldt, 1978).

24. For an overview of the debate among intellectuals, see Bob Burns and Wilfred van der Will, *Protest and Democracy in West Germany* (New York: St. Martin's Press, 1988).

25. Mark Cioc, *Pax Atomica: the nuclear defense debate in West Germany during the Adenauer era* (New York: Columbia University Press, 1988); Klaus von Schubert, *Wiederbewaffnung und West Integration* (Stuttgart: Deutsche Verlags-Anstalt, 1970); Ernst Nolte, *Deutschland und der Kalte Krieg*, 2d ed. (Stuttgart: Klett-Cotta, 1985); Rolf Steininger, *Die Wiederbewaffnung Deutschlands* (Erlangen-Wien-Bonn: Straube, 1989).

26. Donald Abenheim, *Reforging the Iron Cross* (Princeton, NJ: Princeton University Press, 1988); Wolf Graf Baudissin, *Soldat für den Frieden: Entwürfe für eine zeitgemässe Bundeswehr* (Munich: R. Piper, 1969); Ulrich Simon, *Die Integration der Bundeswehr in die Gesellschaft* (Heidelberg/Hamburg: R. v. Decker's Verlag G. Schenk, 1980).

27. Cioc, *Pax Atomica;* David Schwartz, *NATO's Nuclear Dilemmas* (Washington, DC: Brookings Institution, 1983), 70–72; Helga Haftendorn, *Sicherheit und Entspannung* (Baden-Baden: Nomos Verlag, 1986), 162ff.

28. Elizabeth Noelle-Neumann, "Die Verklärung Adenauer und die öffentliche Meinung, 1949–1976," in *Konrad Adenauer und seine Zeit, Persönlichkeit und Politik des ersten Bundeskanzlers,* ed. Dieter Blumenwitz et al. (Stuttgart: Deutsche Verlags-Anstalt, 1976), 531. See also Berthold Meyer, *Der Bürger und seine Sicherheit* (New York: Campus, 1983), 234–47; and Hans Jacobsen, "Zur

Rolle der öffentlichen Meinung," in Militärgeschichtliches Forschungsamt, ed., *Aspekte der deutschen Wiederbewaffnung bis 1955* (Boppard: Harald Boldt Verlag, 1975), 65–67.

29. Meyer, *Der Bürger und seine Sicherheit,* 216, table 3.2.1.

30. Jeffrey Herf, *War by Other Means: Soviet Power, West German Resistance, and the Battle over the Euromissiles* (New York: Free Press, 1991); Thomas Risse-Kappen, *Sicherheitspolitik in der Krise* (Frankfurt am Main: Campus Verlag, 1986).

31. Haftendorn, *Sicherheit und Entspannung,* 250–51.

32. For German views of conventional military doctrine during this period, see Reimar Scherz, "Land- und Luftstreitkräfte in Europa," in *Konventionelles Rüstung im Ost-West-Vergleich,* ed. Erhard Fordran and Hans Joachim Schmidt (Baden-Baden: Nomos Verlagsgesellschaft, 1986); and Klaus Naumann, "The Forces and the Future," in *The Bundeswehr and Western Security,* ed. Stephen S. Szabo (London: Macmillan, 1990), especially 174ff.

33. See Simon Duke, *The Burdensharing Debate: A Reassessment* (New York: St. Martin's Press, 1993), 116.

34. Institut für Demoskopie, Allensbach, *Jahrbuch 1976,* 83; Hans Rattinger, "The Federal Republic of Germany: Much Ado about (Almost) Nothing," in *The Public and Atlantic Defense,* ed. Hans Rattinger and Gregory Flynn (Totowa, NJ: Rowman & Allanhead, 1985); Meyer, *Der Bürger und seine Sicherheit,* especially 217.

35. Meyer, *Der Bürger und seine Sicherheit,* 255, table 6.7.8.

36. Lothar Wilkes, *Die Sicherheitspolitik der SPD, 1956–1966: Zwischen Wiedervereinigung und Westorientierung* (Meissenheim: Anton Hain, 1975); Gordon D. Drummond, *The German Social Democrats in Opposition, 1949–1960* (Norman: University of Oklahoma Press, 1982).

37. Berthold Meyer, *Die Parteien der BRD und die sicherheitspolitische Zusammenarbeit in Europa,* Hessische Stiftung für Friedens-und Konfliktforschung, Bericht 2 (Frankfurt/Main, 1987), chap. 3.

38. Clay Clemens, *Reluctant Realists* (Durham, NC: Duke University Press, 1989).

39. Charles S. Maier, *The Unmasterable Past: History, Holocaust, and German National Identity* (Cambridge, MA: Harvard University Press, 1988); Hans Jürgen Wehler, *Entsorgung der deutschen Vergangenheit? Ein polemischer Essay zum 'Historikerstreit'* (Munich: C. H. Beck'sche Verlagsbuchverhandlung, 1988).

40. Hans-Dieter Genscher, *Die Zeit,* 30 August 1991, 5–6; Horst Teltschik, "Was die anderen von den Deutschen erwarten," *Die Zeit,* 3 May 1991, 6.

41. Peter Rudolf, "Doomed to Lead? German Foreign Policy in a New Europe" (unpublished manuscript, Cambridge, MA, February 1992), 2–3; Harald Müller, "German Foreign Policy after Unification," in *The New Germany and the New Europe,* ed. Paul B. Stares (Washington, DC: Brookings Institution, 1992).

42. Horst Teltschik, *329 Tage Innenansichten der Einigung* (Berlin: Siedler, 1991), 138–41, 163, 168–69, 185–87.

43. Ibid., 313–45; Karl Kaiser, "Germany's Reunification," *Foreign Affairs* 70 (winter 1991).

44. Otfried Nassauer, "Die NATO—Aufbruch zu neuen Ufern?" in *Siegermacht NATO,* ed. Erich Schmidt-Eenboom and Jo Angerer (Berg am See: Verlagsgesellschaft Berg, 1993), 75–84; Thomas-Durrell Young, *The New European Security Calculus: Implications for the U.S. Army* (U.S. Army War College, Strategic Studies Institute, Carlisle Barracks, 1 March 1991).

45. Catherine Kelleher, "The New Germany," in Paul B. Stares, ed., *The New Germany and the New Europe* (Washington DC: The Brookings Institution, 1992), 24–25.

46. Hans-Adolf Jacobsen and Hans-Jürgen Rautenberg, eds., *Bundeswehr und Europäische Sicherheitsordnung* (Bonn: Bouvier, 1991), 50–51, 55–59; Jürgen Kuhlmann and Ekkehard Lippert, "Wehrpflicht Ade? Argumente für und wider die Wehrpflicht in Friedenszeiten," in *Die Zukunft der Streitkräfte angesichts Weltweiter Abrüstungsbemühungen,* ed. G. Kladrack and P. Klein (Baden-Baden: Nomos Verlagsgesellschaft, 1992).

47. For examples of foreign criticism, see Michael Lind, "Surrealpolitik," *New York Times,* 28 March 1991; "Germany's Ostrich Politik," editorial in *New York Times,* 26 January 1991; Alan Sked, "Cheap Excuses: Germany and the Gulf Crisis," *National Interest,* no. 24 (summer 1991); and Jeffrey Garten, *A Cold Peace: America, Japan, Germany, and the Struggle for Supremacy (*New York: Time Books, 1992), 162–67.

48. New York Times, 10 September 1990, A1.

49. *Der Spiegel,* 11 March 1991, 36.

50. Der Spiegel, 4 February 1991, 98–99; 11 February 1991, 18–26.

51. Der Spiegel, 4 February 1991, 18–22; interview with Genscher in the same issue, p. 22.

52. Thomas Kielinger, "The Gulf War and Consequences from a German Point of View," *Außenpolitik* 42, no. 3 (1991); interview with Wolfgang Schäuble in *Der Spiegel,* 25 January 1993, 20.

53. On the constitutional crisis provoked by German out-of-area actions, see *Der Spiegel,* 5, 12, 19 April 1993; *Frankfurter Allgemeine Zeitung,* 25 March 1993, 1; and *Frankfurter Zeitung,* 8 April 1993, 1.

54. EMNID data, cited in *Der Spiegel,* 26 April 1993, 21.

55. Renate Köcher, "Unerwartete Wende," *Frankfurter Allgemeine Zeitung,* 14 June 1995, 5.

56. See, for example, *Frankfurter Allgemeine Zeitung,* 2, 16 July 1993; 2 June 1995.

57. Frankfurter Rundschau, 1 July 1995, 5.

58. See, for instance, Rudolf Augstein, "Bleibt draußen!" *Der Spiegel,* 19 June 1995, 38.

59. Rudolf Scharping, "Deutsche Außenpolitik muß berechenbar sein," *Internationale Politik* 50, no. 8 (1995); Karsten Voigt, "Plädoyer für eine Zivile NATO," *Internationale Politik* 50, no. 12 (1995): 15–20.

60. Most recently the tensions within the party have taken the form of a

much publicized dispute between Fischer and Jürgen Tritten. See interview with Tritten in *Der Spiegel,* 20 October 1997, 34–35, in which Tritten states that alliances led to both World Wars I and II and argues that any new security structure in Europe must include the Soviet Union. For a more general overview of the dispute, see *Der Spiegel,* 27 October 1997, 25–26.

61. Heilbrunn, "Germany's New Right," 80–98; and the response to Heilbrunn's article by Josef Joffe et al., "Mr. Heilbrunn's Planet," *Foreign Affairs* 76, no. 2 (March/April 1997): 152–61. For examples of neo-nationalist views on foreign policy, see Heimo Schwilk and Ulrich Schact, eds., *Die selbstbewußte Nation* (Berlin: Siedler, 1995); and Rainer Zitelmann et al., eds., *Westbindung: Chancen und Risiken für Deutschland* (Frankfurt a. M.: Propylaen 1993).

62. On the failure of anti-*Wehrpflicht* forces in the FDP to budge the party, see *Frankfurter Allgemeine Zeitung,* 18 November 1997. For an overview of the issue, see Bernhard Fleckenstein, "Warum wir die Wehrpflicht (noch) brauchen," *Aus Politik und Zeitgeschichte* B29–1997 (11 July 1997).

Conclusion

From the Bonn to the Berlin Republic and Beyond: Critical Junctures and the Future of the Federal Republic

John S. Brady and Sarah Elise Wiliarty

Exploring the sources of continuity and change in German politics and society has consistently occupied the social scientists who study the Federal Republic.[1] In their analyses of the first 50 years of the Federal Republic, the contributors to this volume not only document the relative significance of continuity and change in the postwar development of Germany, they also highlight certain key periods in postwar German history in which the Federal Republic's political actors departed from past political practices in a significant manner. The immediate postwar interval and the late 1960s are two of the most prominent examples of such critical junctures in the Federal Republic's history.[2] As the numerous examples provided by the authors indicate, in both of these periods the Federal Republic's political leaders and citizenry had the opportunity to influence both the institutional makeup and cultural traditions of German society and thereby establish distinct political and cultural legacies that powerfully affected the Federal Republic's subsequent development.

Arguably, the Federal Republic finds itself in the midst of another period of intense political and social change. The beginnings of this present period can be traced to the end of the seventies and the beginning of the eighties. Writing in 1981, the authors of the influential volume *Germany Transformed* noted that the Federal Republic, like other Western societies, stood on the threshold of the postindustrial era. Factors such as an increase in affluence, greater educational opportunities, and developments in mass communication and transportation in combination with a rise in geographic, structural, and social mobility had produced in

503

Germany and the rest of the West "a fundamental transformation in the nature of . . . politics."[3] In the course of the 1980s, the increasing degree of economic competition associated with globalization also exerted pressure on the German polity to make changes in its political and economic institutions. Likewise, at the end of the decade and the beginning of the 1990s, the unification of Germany and the collapse of the Eastern bloc have placed the necessity of change on the Federal Republic's political agenda with renewed urgency. Examining the continuities between the old Federal Republic and the new unified Germany, Jürgen Kocka has argued that "unified Germany will not and cannot be merely an enlarged version of the Federal Republic. Change, it seems, will extend much farther than the architects of unification intended."[4]

If this is the case, it raises the question of what type of change is needed and desirable in the new Federal Republic. Writing on this theme, Peter Kielmansegg has noted that in facing the necessity for change, the citizens of the unified Germany are confronted with a dual task. They must, on the one hand, found a new republic capable of integrating two diverse populations, while, at the same time, preserving those aspects of the old Federal Republic that facilitated Germany's liberal, democratic development in the postwar period.[5] In confronting this dual task, what must the Germans and their political leaders accomplish, especially in the areas of building democracy, ensuring prosperity, and answering the question of nationhood?

While the contributors to this volume have concentrated primarily on Germany's past, they nonetheless offer insights on this question and direct our attention to what we might expect in the development of the Federal Republic's institutions and political culture. Based on the evidence they present, we argue that in the institutional realm, the challenge of the present period in the Federal Republic's development lies in making German institutions more inclusive and open to reform. The party system is a case in point. Facing the antiparty mood of the German citizenry, German political parties, as Michaela Richter points out, need to open themselves to the participatory, citizen culture that has developed in the course of the postwar period. In contrast to the institutional realm, the challenge in the cultural realm is the critical expansion of German political culture. As we note below, the contributors to this volume argue that Germany has successfully broken with many of the problematic cultural traditions of its past to forge a liberal, democratic political culture. Yet at times echoes of these past traditions are still heard in German politics. This state of affairs demands that German political actors maintain a critical vigilance in the cultural realm in order to avoid the potential harm done by the revival of these traditions. What is more, in certain key areas, for example in the definition of membership in the German nation, the key categories of German political culture need to be expanded to include those individuals and groups who have traditionally been located outside of this culture's borders. In what follows we explore in more detail both the possible developments in German politics suggested by the authors in this volume and the areas of possible institutional and cultural development in the Federal Republic of the future.

The Question of Democracy

The democratization of the Federal Republic in the postwar period is a major success story. In the years following World War II, the people of West Germany and their political leaders successfully developed the institutions and political culture to support a liberal democratic society. Yet this fact has not stopped some observers from worrying that the more powerful and independent Germany that has emerged in the wake of unification will relapse into a version of its imperialist and nationalist past. While such a development is rejected by the authors in this volume, they make clear that German democracy, while likely to remain stable, must confront a number of tasks in solidifying its institutional and cultural supports. These include determining the future role of the PDS in the party system, coming to terms with the role played by the Federal Constitutional Court in the Federal Republic's future political development, and, finally, establishing the future relevance of militant democracy.

For the contributors analyzing the question of democracy in this volume, the emergence and growing strength of the PDS represent the best evidence that the unification of the two Germanys is far from complete. Originally expected to disappear after the first all-German election of 1990, the PDS now appears to be here to stay, at least for the medium term. This presence of the PDS has presented practical challenges for the Federal Republic's other major political parties. Particularly in the eastern Landtage, the party has won enough votes to make coalition-building very difficult. The virtual absence of the FDP and the Greens from the East has forced the CDU and the SPD to form several grand coalitions, with the PDS as the only opposition.

Both Peter Merkl and Michaela Richter analyze the potential effects of the continuing presence of the PDS on the German electoral landscape for German party politics. For Richter, the continuing popularity of the PDS is a sign of the general renewal of antiparty sentiments in the Federal Republic. These antiparty sentiments, bundled together into a "discourse of disaffection," are based on the twin beliefs that, on the one hand, parties as vote-maximizing machines are closed to the concerns of ordinary citizens and, on the other, that they are unwilling to confront such pressing issues as the environment, employment, housing, and peace. As part of this antiparty trend in German politics, the PDS, emerging from the 1994 elections as the third-largest party in the five new *Länder,* has become the party of choice for those East Germans unhappy with the unification policies of the Bonn government. Merkl is more negative in his assessment of the PDS. Like Richter, he notes that the PDS has become the repository for the political resentments of East Germans unsatisfied with the unification process. Going beyond Richter's analysis, he also wonders to what extent the PDS, in its criticism of the unification process and related issues, actually strengthens the alienation between East and West, an alienation some commentators have called the "wall in the minds of East and West Germans."

Merkl and Richter's exclusive focus on the negative implications of the political success of the PDS causes them to neglect the possible positive contributions to be made by the party, for example, in both the political socialization and integration of eastern Germans and in the broadening of the country's political discourse. Yet, they certainly are correct to highlight the significance of the PDS for the continuing development of the Federal Republic's party system. In Richter's opinion, confronting the political challenge of the PDS involves a constructive opening of the party system to the legitimate criticisms of how parties function in German politics. She argues that the main parties, having aided the emergence of a more mature and self-confident citizenry, must now provide the mechanisms for involving the citizenry in resolving the increasingly complex issues facing united Germany. Thus, while she may read the PDS through a negative lens, Richter does not go so far as to call for forcing it out of the electoral arena. Indeed, such a strategy could have profound negative effects for German party politics. Isolating the PDS or, for example, denying it the state funding that other parties receive for electoral campaigns could only serve to make the party less accountable and undermine its ability to make a critical contribution to the continuing evolution of German democracy.

As the authors who analyze the party system in this volume note, the political parties have played an instrumental role in the growth of German democracy. An equally important institution in this regard is the Federal Constitutional Court (FCC). In his detailed analysis of the Court and judicial review, Donald Kommers demonstrates how the creation of a culture of constitutional interpretation in the Federal Republic has supported the construction of Germany's liberal democracy. Interestingly enough, the Court has aided this construction by limiting at key points the actual reach of Germany's democracy; in this respect, the FCC has been both liberating and restrictive in its guidance. Thus in its rulings on political parties and the party system, the FCC has celebrated the concept of popular sovereignty, even as it has insisted on a limited view of the German people in its decisions on citizenship and local voting rights for resident foreigners. As Kommers suggests, this restrictive role played by the Court may have been appropriate at the beginning of the republic. However, as German civil society and its political culture have developed, the restrictive guidance may no longer be quite so essential and may even stand in the way of needed political change, especially on citizenship issues.

The final challenge for German democracy lies in the unclarified status of militant democracy. As a set of constitutional provisions and political practices that support an extremely vigilant stance against political extremism, militant democracy played a particularly significant role in German politics during the 1960s and 1970s. Although the militant protection of German democracy at times involved the infringement of individual civil rights, German politicians justified this infringement with reference to the high value of the democracy thereby protected. As Merkl points out, militant democracy is a matter of maintaining a balancing act between the two extremes of negligence in the face of extremism and overzealous enforcement, which actually damages the very democracy it is trying to protect. In this regard, both Gregg Kvistad and Merkl feel that the potential exists for the abuse of militant democracy. Although in the postwar period Merkl feels that the Federal Republic has generally balanced successfully between the extremes of negligence and zealous enforcement, it has occasionally protected too severely against left-wing extremism, while being too lenient vis-à-vis right-wing extremism.

Looking to the violence surrounding the asylum issue, Merkl reminds us that new extremist challenges are still a real possibility in the Federal Republic. The latest scandals regarding the toleration of right-wing extremism in the Bundeswehr are further evidence in support of Merkl's argument. This is the case even as the legal provisions of militant democracy are undergoing change. The *Radikalenerlaß* (Radicals Decree), once a central instrument in the state's effort to combat extremism, has suffered what Kvistad calls an "incremental death" over the course of the late 1980s and early 1990s. What shape will the practices of militant democracy take in the future? Given the proven ability of German civil society to mobilize against extremism, are heavy-handed provisions such as the Radicals Decree even necessary in today's Federal Republic? These are some of the central questions to be answered as the practice of militant democracy takes shape in the future.

Initially, the study of German democracy in the postwar period concerned itself with whether democracy was even possible in a country burdened with the legacies of authoritarianism and nationalism.[6] Subsequent political developments in the Federal Republic have made such an approach obsolete. Indeed, as the contributors to this volume demonstrate, the German polity possesses solid institutional and cultural foundations of a democratic political order. These include an active citizenry, a liberal, constitutional political culture, and effective institutions and organizations of interest intermediation. Of course, as in any other democracy, there is room for improvement in Germany. Hopefully, the Berlin Republic can avoid some of the negative political consequences of the antiparty tendencies in German political culture highlighted by Richter. Thus, even as scholars underline the successes of Germany's democratic development, they also face the task of critically assessing ways in which the citizens of the Federal Republic can expand on their democratic heritage. The contributors collected here provide key elements of such an assessment.

Preserving Prosperity

Germany's *Wirtschaftswunder* in the early postwar period led to some great expectations about the country's economic performance. When the country's prosperity continued through the difficult 1970s, politicians and academics alike began to trumpet its success and consider the exportability of *Modell Deutschland*. Even with increasing unemployment in the 1980s, Germany fared better than most of its neighbors and did so with fewer serious economic adjustments than France or Great Britain experienced. In the late 1980s and early 1990s, as even the Swedish and Japanese economies experienced recession and adjustment, Germany seemed poised to handle even the pressures of unification. Then, in 1992, the recession arrived in Germany. The toll of unification appeared to be too high for the Germans to pay after all, particularly when the rest of the world was less able to purchase German exports.

The future of the German political economy is a point of serious contention. No one expects a return to the economic boom of the *Wirtschaftswunder* years. Germany is equally unlikely to lose its competitiveness so completely as to become internationally irrelevant. But what will happen to the German economy? Will it recover relatively easily from its latest woes, as it has so often in the past? Or has it finally met its match in increased capital mobility and trade — which make the German strategy of well-paid, highly skilled workers producing high end products untenable?

The authors in this volume present radically differing visions of Germany's economic future. They disagree about both the source and the extent of the country's economic difficulties. One point of consensus that does emerge from these contributions, however, is that unification is not the primary source of Germany's economic difficulties, although it has exacerbated the problems and certainly made them more visible. The incorporation of eastern Germany provided added strain to an economy that was already experiencing difficulties, although in 1990 they had not yet become terribly salient.

While the authors also agree on the importance of Germany's persistent high unemployment, they have different interpretations of this difficulty. For Claus Offe, Germany's full employment policy of the past represents a critical element in the country's institutional infrastructure. The abandonment of that policy by the German government and the increased unemployment caused by directly transferring West German institutions to the East created a population of unemployed people too large to be sustained. The loss of full employment represents the removal from the welfare state of the institution that kept the balance between winners (those with jobs) and losers (those temporarily without jobs). As the number of losers grows too large for the winners to pay for, the entire system — including the apprenticeship program, the social partnership between unions and employer organizations, health insurance, and unemployment insurance — can be called into question.

The German welfare state has functioned so well in the past partially because it has been isolated from party politics. In Offe's view, this period is now over; the welfare state has become an object of contention among the parties. The CDU is attempting to scale back benefits in an effort to liberalize the economy and create jobs; the SPD, on the other hand, seeks primarily to defend the status quo, claiming that welfare benefits are needed more than ever when economic times are tough. Ironically, efforts to liberalize the German economy with the purpose of increasing employment will likely destroy *Modell Deutschland* if the institutions that allowed Germany's focus on the high-end export market are removed.

Like Offe, Carl Ludwig Holtfrerich and Ludger Lindlar see Germany's high unemployment as problematic, but unlike him they do not view it as threatening Germany's economic framework more generally. Noting the country's continued success in exports as well as its strength in both high-and medium-technology products, their main fear is that the Bundesbank's tight monetary policy — in their view a prime contributor to Germany's unemployment — will hurt the country's competitiveness by allowing the mark to appreciate to the extent that German exports become too costly. While they acknowledge that some of Germany's unemployment is due to delayed adjustment in the switch from a manufacturing-oriented economy to one more focused on services, they believe a change in Bundesbank policy would solve the country's most pressing economic problems.[7]

Although Holtfrerich and Lindlar are not as explicit in their argumentation as Offe is, in fact their argument also relies on the idea that Germany's economic strength is based on its institutions (although they probably would not consider the full employment policy to be one of these institutions). The apprenticeship program, the ability of unions and employer organizations to negotiate wage agreements, and the publicly supported research and development organizations have all contributed to Germany's economic strength. While the independent Bundesbank's clampdown on inflation is usually also considered a part of this economic strength, in their view the Bundesbank is taking this policy too far. In contrast with Offe's analysis, Holtfrerich and Lindlar do not see the German institutional framework as endangered. One element of that framework, the Bundesbank, is simply currently misguided. If the Bundesbank can be convinced to change its policy, then the economy will likely recover and the unemployment problem will abate.

Like Lindlar and Holtfrerich, Patricia Davis and Simon Reich do not see the institutional framework of Germany's social market economy to be in danger of collapse. Noting the resilience of the social market economy in their analysis of the Federal Republic's social welfare system, they expect it to adjust to the current difficulties and survive into the future. This adjustment will be aided by the institutional safety valve that allows the costs of adjusting the social welfare system to changing economic and political circumstances to be shifted to those parts of the population least able to protest politically, women and immigrants. They argue that this institutional bias has been present throughout the postwar period, but that it becomes most visible in hard economic times, such as Germany is currently experiencing.

As Davis and Reich point out, the roots of this bias are to be found in the cultural definitions of work and gender that support the social welfare system. These cultural norms, defining what constitutes proper work and what roles women should ideally play in society, are problematic insofar as they discriminate against women as a group and serve to exclude them in certain cases from the full acquisition of welfare citizenship. Davis and Reich's focus on the problem of such discriminatory cultural norms underscores the continuing necessity of critical assessment of specific cultural traditions and their effect on political practices in the Federal Republic. As the retrenchment of the German welfare system continues, it will be interesting to see to what extent the attempt to work against such discrimination will be a part of the political agenda.

The conflict over Germany's political economy is just beginning. Commentators still disagree about both the cause and the extent of the problem. The debate boils down to whether Germany's economic arrangement is still suitable for today's increasingly competitive international environment. Although the analysts in this volume use different language to talk about the problem, the issues and questions they confront are often the same. Are Germany's economic problems due to "temporary" (although perhaps fairly long-standing) bad policy decisions, or is something more seriously amiss? Have changes in the international economy forced Germany to either change or to make do with much less prosperity than its population is accustomed to? Furthermore, will the set of actors that has steered the German political economy in the past remain the same, or will new actors arrive while old actors depart? Kathleen Thelen has pointed out the dramatic decrease in membership in both unions and employer organizations,[8] which raises the additional question, if these critical actors depart, will new ones take their places? Perhaps most importantly, if change in the country's basic economic framework is necessary, how much change is possible before some piece of the highly integrated economic system breaks down and brings the whole system down with it? What will be the impact not only of the end of the full employment policy, but of new changes in welfare benefits, or of potential changes in the apprenticeship system? The essays here begin to address some of these questions, but there is much work to be done to resolve the current debate.

The Politics of Nationhood

In his essay in this volume on public longing and national sentiment in modern German politics, Charles Maier notes:

> In the German case it [public longing] has involved both yearning for national incorporation of places beyond German state borders, and a hankering for some mystical enhancement of political authority or political community inside the borders that exist.

If this is the case, what does the future hold for the question of German nationhood? The evidence presented in this volume suggests that a return to the nationalist excesses of Germany's past will not occur, as some exaggerated pessimistic commentaries would submit. Indeed, the postwar development of the Federal Republic has been characterized by impressive movement away from the politics of nationalism both in the domestic and foreign policy arenas. Domestically, the politicians and citizens of the Federal Republic have succeeded in forging a national identity anchored in liberal democratic tenets and institutions. Internationally, the Bonn Republic did not formulate its foreign and defense policies according to the dictates of national interest but instead took the lead in pursuing the integration of Europe. These shifts in the politics of nationhood have continued even through the tumultuous period of unification and the creation of the Berlin Republic. Thomas Banchoff argues in his study of postwar foreign policy that Germany's break with the nationally oriented *Schaukelpolitik* of the past and the transformation of its role in Europe have outlasted the revolutionary changes unleashed by the collapse of bipolarity and reunification. Of course, the significant progress that the Bonn and Berlin Republics have made has not led, as our authors are quick to point out, to the end of the national question. There will be no end to longing, Maier maintains, and national sentiments and interests will continue to play a role in German politics and society. Thus the central question for the future is not whether the issue of nationhood will occupy German political actors, but rather how this central issue will manifest itself in the public life and policy-making of the Federal Republic.

For our thinking about the future of the Federal Republic, one of the important insights that can be gleaned from the contributions to this volume is the uneven and incomplete manner in which the question of nationhood has developed in the postwar period. This is especially true in the case of immigration and asylum. The pressing task of integrating close to seven million immigrants from a diverse collection of countries and ethnic groups has brought the issue of nationhood to the center of German political debate. In the multicultural present of the Federal Republic, what constitutes membership in the German nation? While this question has been raised in the course of the political conflict surrounding immigration and the reform of Article 116 of the Basic Law, no clear answer has been given, as the analyses of Jost Halfmann and Christhard Hoffmann demonstrate. What's more, the nature of the changes that have occurred within the institutional realm and the policy-making arena has been decidedly different from those taking place in civil society.

The pace of change in immigration and asylum policy has been slow and by no means without contradictions. This is especially the case with regard to the policies regulating social and political membership. Reviewing the administrative and legal practice surrounding the extension of social rights to immigrants, Halfmann notes that the German state pursued an exclusionary policy vis-à-vis non-German immigrants until the late 1970s. Once, however, state authorities recognized that a large portion of the foreign population intended to stay, they adopted a more integrationist stance, with the result that today state policy is geared toward furthering the inclusion of long-term foreign residents into the social welfare system while at the same time preventing new immigration. This expansion of social membership has not been matched by a similar redefinition of German citizenship, thus creating a discrepancy between membership in the social system and political society. One of the primary institutional barriers impeding the political integration of foreigners into the Federal Republic is Article 116 of the Basic Law. Based on the principle of ethnic homogeneity, it defines citizenship in terms of descent, thus excluding immigrants and even their children born on German soil from political membership. The new Foreigners Law, which took effect in 1991, did introduce some changes in naturalization policy, including easing the naturalization of children born to foreigners living in the Federal Republic. Yet the law retained both the supervisory capacity and discretionary latitude given to the immigration authorities.

In contrast to the legal and administrative practice in immigration matters, which is dominated by the desire to preserve state authority, the public debate over immigration has revolved around moral concerns for human rights and the future of German national identity. In the 1980s, the debate pitted national conservatives who employed ethnic and populist arguments calling for the end of immigration and asylum against left liberals who argued for the introduction of a postnational, multicultural society as the most just way to integrate Germany's newest members into society. Increasingly acrimonious, these debates were often far removed from the everyday concerns of immigrants. In the case of asylum, the polarization of views, as Christhard Hoffmann notes, helped give to many German citizens the idea that politics was unable to address the issue. In Hoffmann's opinion, this paved the way for the waves of violence against asylum seekers that spread throughout the reunited Germany starting in 1991.

Yet the results of these debates were not completely negative. As Halfmann points out, they did help to counteract the inertia of the administrative and legal system. Indeed, civil society is an important source of change in the immigration debate, and the progress made on the issues in this arena has outstripped that made in the policy realm. During the 1980s there was a shift in public attitudes away from suspicion and toward acceptance of immigrants. What's more, new political alliances consisting of traditional organizations such as churches and trade unions and newer groupings such as the various multicultural initiatives have coalesced around the issues of citizenship and asylum. Through their lobbying efforts and activities in the German public sphere, these new alliances have been able to influence policy, forcing, for example, the government to withdraw its 1988 draft of the new Foreigners Law. Finally, the shock of the postunification violence against immigrants and asylum seekers has led to a political realignment and a softening of the terms of public debate. The question that remains open is whether these changes in civil society and public attitudes can facilitate a fundamental change in federal policy.

In comparison to the immigration and asylum issues, there is a more decisive break with past national traditions in the foreign and security policy realms. In the course of the postwar period, the policymakers in the Federal Republic gave German foreign policy a strong Western orientation, joined NATO, and took the lead in creating the institutions of the European Union. Moreover, the norms of shared sovereignty and multilateralism became the guiding principles of the Federal Republic's foreign policy. All of the authors in this volume agree about the significance of these changes, although they disagree as to the role that national interests continued to play in German foreign policy in the postwar period.

Wolfgang Krieger interprets Germany's creation of new foreign and defense policies and the institutions to support them as the end of the nation-state era in German foreign policy. For Ernst Haas, the Federal Republic is no longer a rationalized nation-state, but rather a state that is already dedicated to achieving a new rationalization in a larger European structure. In Haas's view, this fundamental change does not come about at the beginning of the postwar period, as Krieger suggests, but is only now starting after the successful completion of German unification. For his part, Thomas Banchoff suggests that German leaders had room within the institutions of NATO and the EC to articulate a foreign policy oriented to national concerns, although their institutional commitments and responsibilities precluded any return to the aggressive and nationalist foreign policy of the past. Looking to the future, the contributors to this volume do not forecast any radical departure from the trends that have dominated up to this point, not least because powerful social groups such as business, trade unions, and the bureaucracy solidly support the cosmopolitan and European orientation of German foreign policy.

This does not mean that national interests will no longer play a role in German foreign policy, that there will be a lack of conflict over foreign policy, or that further progress along the path to full European integration will necessarily be politically harmonious. In examining the possible sources of opposition to European integration and the cosmopolitan foreign policy consensus, the authors suggest the importance of public attitudes vis-à-vis European integration. The Federal Republic remains unique among the members of the EU because of the absence of any strong anti-Europe political party, and the analyses presented here, especially those of Haas and Krieger, do not forecast much change in this situation. The major parties in Germany have been strong supporters of European integration, while opposition to the EU has been relegated to the politically impotent pacifist wing of the Greens and the national conservative wing of the German right. Party support of the EU has remained solid, but the German public's support of European integration and cosmopolitanism has been "permissive, not wildly committed," and Haas and Krieger feel that if European integration becomes identified with economic or strategic failure, it could be the catalyst for an anti-European political movement in the Federal Republic.

One other possible source of change in the foreign policy arena is contemporary conflicts over the interpretation of Germany's national past. As Andrei Markovits and Simon Reich detail, current public debate in Germany over the proper interpretation of Germany's national past is marked by competition among conflicting "collective memories" offering different perspectives on the question of nationhood and German history. The outcome of this competition is not yet clear. But insofar as conceptions of collective memory have the power to shape the actions of political actors and policymakers, a point made most explicitly by Banchoff and Thomas Berger in this volume, the outcome of the collective memory debates will certainly have important consequences for the future development of German policy.

Banchoff and Berger are not alone in isolating the importance of collective memory for the future development of German politics. To varying degrees, all of the authors who analyze the nationhood question point out the significance collective memory has had for the politics of the Federal Republic. In so doing, they provide a key insight into the interrelationship between institutional and policy development and the evolution of cultural factors such as collective memory. The analyses also help to correct a deficit in foreign policy research and in political science generally, namely, the relative lack of attention paid to the role that interpretations of the past play in influencing political outcomes. At the same time, they leave a number of questions open that future research will have to confront. The primary question concerns the sources of collective memory. Who defines the content of collective memories? In this regard Markovits and Reich note that collective memories come to play a role in politics for structural reasons and because they are instrumentalized by social groups fighting for power. If this is the case, are there certain groups with greater opportunity to define and utilize conceptions of collective memory?

Second, there is the question of the relationship between institutions and collective memory read broadly, as an element of a nation-state's political culture. The authors in this volume tend to draw a fairly sharp distinction between institutions and memory. Yet cannot institutions help to generate collective memory, and are not their histories part of the collective memory of a polity? If collective memory is to be a useful analytical concept in the future, such issues will have to be clarified. The conflict surrounding the various interpretations of German collective memory represents a possible catalyst for change in German politics and raises the question, What will be the primary sources of change in the Federal Republic's future politics of nationhood? The contributors to this volume have delineated some possible answers, including changes in the international system, the evolution of domestic political and economic institutions, and political movements in civil society. What is needed in the future is research that identifies the other possible sources of change in how Germans define their national identity and how the various causal variables interact.

The assessment of the critical junctures in a society's political and social development involves determining the lasting legacies of these periods of change. The authors in this volume have contributed to our understanding of the past critical junctures in the Federal Republic's history. Using often innovative approaches, they have identified the legacies of the past critical junctures. What is more, the authors have provided the tools to help us understand the present period in German politics. On the one hand, they have identified the issues that characterize the present critical juncture and what is at stake in their resolution. On the other hand, they have also provided insights into the role that culture and institutions play in effecting political outcomes.

Social scientists often treat institutions and culture as two possible — separate — explanations for political outcomes; either culture was responsible for an outcome or institutions were. Taken together, the contributions to this volume suggest that this approach may not be the most fruitful one. Instead, we may be better able to further our understanding of politics and political change by examining how culture and institutions interact in the process of political change. The sections in this volume on democracy and the political economy suggest two different types of such interaction. The democracy section supports the view that while institutions shape culture, they do not completely determine the path of its development. Indeed, culture may "outgrow" the institutions initially important as catalysts for cultural change. The section on German political economy provides an example of how institutions and culture may mutually reinforce a particular political outcome. The institutions that have shaped Germany's political economy have facilitated growth by allowing market forces to work within a framework that controls and guides competition. These institutions have been supported by an economic culture that favors coordinated rather than purely profit-driven solutions to economic problems. The further assessment of the interaction of institutions and culture will remain a central activity both in the study of the Federal Republic and in the social sciences generally. Certainly, this exciting period in German politics will continue to yield more insights into the political impact of culture and institutions.

NOTES

1. Jutta A. Helm, "The Study of Germany in Comparative Political Science," in *From Bundesrepublik to Deutschland: German Politics after Unification*, ed. M. G. Huelshoff, A. Markovits, and S. Reich (Ann Arbor: University of Michigan Press, 1993), 9–30.

2. This analysis of critical junctures draws upon Ruth Berrins Collier and David Collier, *Shaping the Political Arena: Critical Junctures, the Labor Movement, and Regime Dynamics in Latin America* (Princeton: Princeton University Press, 1991), chap. 1.

3. Kendall L. Baker, Russell J. Dalton, and Kai Hildebrandt, *Germany Transformed: Political Culture and the New Politics* (Cambridge: Harvard University Press, 1981), 1–2. For a subsequent analysis of this issue, see Hans-Georg Betz, *Postmodern Politics in Germany: The Politics of Resentment* (New York: St. Martin's Press, 1991).

4. Jürgen Kocka, "Crisis of Unification: How Germany Changes," *Daedalus* 123, no. 1 (winter 1994): 189.

5. Peter G. Kielmansegg, "How New Is the New Federal Republic?" Occasional Paper Series (Berkeley: Center for German and European Studies, March 1995), 14.

6. Helm, "The Study of Germany," 11.

7. The current exchange rate is actually quite favorable for German exports to the United States, but this has less to do with any German policy and more to do with the strength of the dollar. The Bundesbank has by no means abandoned its tight monetary policy. However, the more favorable exchange rate has certainly not solved Germany's economic problems. Unemployment remains high,

suggesting that Germany's economic woes have a more complex cause than the wrong monetary policy.

8. Kathleen Thelen, "Beyond Corporatism: Toward a New Framework for the Study of Labor in Advanced Capitalism," *Comparative Politics* 27, no. 1 (October 1994): 107–24.

Contributors

Thomas Banchoff	Professor of Government, Georgetown University
Thomas U. Berger	Professor of Political Science, Johns Hopkins University
John S. Brady	Doctoral Candidate, Department of Political Science, University of California Berkeley
Beverly Crawford	Acting Director of the Center for German and European Studies, University of California Berkeley
Patricia Davis	Professor of Political Science, University of Notre Dame
Ernst Haas	Professor of Political Science, University of California Berkeley
Jost Halfmann	Professor of Sociology, Dresden Technical University
Christhard Hoffmann	Professor of History, University of Bergen, Norway
Carl-Ludwig Holtfrerich	Professor, John F. Kennedy Institute, Free University of Berlin
Donald P. Kommers	Joseph and Elizabeth Robbie Professor of Government and International Studies and Professor of Law, University of Notre Dame
Wolfgang Krieger	Professor of Modern History, Philipps University Marburg
Peter Krüger	Professor of Modern and Contemporary History, Philipps University Marburg
Gregg O. Kvistad	Professor and Chair, Political Science, University of Denver

Ludger Lindlar	Professor of Economics, University of Gronigen, Netherlands
Charles S. Maier	Professor of History, Center for German and European Studies at Harvard University
Andrei S. Markovits	Professor of Politics, University of California, Santa Cruz
Peter H. Merkl	Professor emeritus of Political Science, University of California Santa Barbara
Claus Offe	Professor of Political Science, Humboldt University Berlin
Simon Reich	Professor of Political Science, University of Pittsburgh
Michaela Richter	Professor of Political Science, College of Staten Island, CUNY, New York
Sarah Elise Wiliarty	Doctoral Candidate, Department of Political Science, University of California Berkeley

Index

Abgrenzungsbeschluss, 81
abortion policy, 104–9, 256
Adenauer, Konrad. *See also* Christian
  Democratic Union (CDU) and Christian Socialist Union (CSU)
  and historical memory, 412–13
  integration of radical right, 41, 45
  as a promoter of political parties, 128–31
  and sovereignty, 408, 427–28
  and Western integration, 8, 43, 401, 412–13, 427
affirmative action, 234, 250, 254, 258
anti-foreigner violence, 4, 53–54, 274, 313, 329, 357, 366, 371, 383, 385
antimilitarism, 414–15, 474–76, 481–85, 487, 490–91. *See also* Bundeswehr; political culture, political-military culture
anti-radicals decree, 9, 47, 51, 71–72, 82–85, 507
armed forces. *See* Bundeswehr
arms control, 484, 486
asylum, 49, 53, 109–11, 361–62, 370–71, 383–84, 389, 512–13. *See also* immigration
Atlantic Alliance, 403–4, 414
Ausserparliamentarische Opposition (APO). *See* extraparliamentary opposition
Aussiedler. See ethnic Germans

Baden-Württemberg, 52, 385
Bahr, Egon, 80
Baring, Arnulf, 80
Basic Law, 7, 8, 37–40, 104–11, 133, 349–50, 359–60, 461
  and above-parties ideology, 63
  and Bundeswehr, 403
  and continuity with earlier constitutions, 423–24
  contradictions in, 98
  and nationhood, 18
  and *Rechtsstaat,* 96
  and unification, 344
Bavaria, 52, 290, 313, 385
Bavarian Party, 40
Berlin, 36, 49, 77, 112, 139, 279
Bismarck, 289–93
Blüm, Norbert, 226–27
Brandt, Willy, 46, 47, 78–81, 83, 134–35, 485–87
Bremen, 42, 52, 81
Bretton Woods, 14, 164, 171, 174, 190–92, 195
Brezhnev, Leonid, 81
Britain, 421, 429
  and collective memory, 454–55
  and European Community, 431–32
Bund der Heimatlosen und Entrechteten (BHE), 40–41
Bundesbank, 14, 488, 509–10
  fighting inflation, 12, 190, 195, 318, 457
Bundeswehr, 403, 414–15, 424, 429–30, 441–42, 482. *See also* antimilitarism
  democratization of, 312, 483–84, 489
  out-of-area participation, 401, 424, 441, 475, 490–91
  scandals, 507
Bush, George, 404, 433

Catholic Center Party, 38, 40, 302–3
childcare, 248–49, 256, 258
child-rearing benefits, 240, 244, 249, 252
Christian Democratic Union (CDU)
  and Christian Socialist Union (CSU), 37, 40, 43, 138, 310–11. *See also* Adenauer

521

522   Index

Christian Democratic Union (*continued*)
  and abortion policy, 105–6
  and anticommunism, 80–81
  and anti-radicals decree, 47, 84
  cooperation with SPD, 210
  criticism of, 137–44
  and European Community, 326–28
  foreign policy, 321, 482–83, 487, 490–91
  and immigration policy, 367–69, 373, 384–85, 386, 391
  integration of right-wing parties, 8, 36, 41, 43, 45, 53
  and unemployment, 213–14
Christian Socialist Union (CSU), 272, 385
Churchill, Winston, 421, 432
citizen initiatives, 139, 145, 315
citizenship, 111–13, 294, 322, 332, 379, 384–87, 391–94, 513. *See also* immigration
  child citizenship, 373
  reform of law, 357, 359–60, 372–73
civil servants, 70–71, 73–75, 83, 85, 101, 203, 232. *See also* civil service
civil service, 89, 126, 305. *See also* civil servants
  institutional role of, 8, 64, 67, 69
  in the nineteenth century, 288, 296
  and political parties, 64–66, 129–30, 141, 296
civil society, 79, 95, 143, 345, 383
  destroyed by Nazis, 305–6
  and political parties, 129, 141, 146
  as threat to democracy, 64, 71, 74–78, 101, 125
class, 65, 203, 233, 456
Cohn, Norman, 273
collective bargaining. *See* industrial relations; unions
collective memory, 25–26, 439–40, 443–44, 446–49, 451–55, 515–16. *See also* historical memory
  and Federal Republic, 460–64
  and German Democratic Republic, 464–65
  and institutions, 456, 516
  and Nazi regime, 457–60
  and victimization, 449–52, 458, 464–66
  and Weimar Republic, 457
Common Agricultural Policy, 178

Communist Party of Germany, 38, 40, 42, 47, 49, 80–81
  banning of, 40, 42, 73, 76, 210
  re-emergence of, 46, 76
Conference on Security and Cooperation in Europe (CSCE), 407
consensual politics, 210
constitutional patriotism, 349–50, 461–62
Constitutional Protection Service, 45, 48, 54, 85
constructive vote of no-confidence, 7, 39, 50
constructivism, 26, 477–81, 492–93
corporatism, 210, 220, 226, 299, 302–3, 318–20
critical junctures, 406, 456, 503, 516
culture. *See* political culture
currency reform, 164
currency union, 166, 216, 425

de Gaulle, Charles, 421, 432, 448
denazification (and reeducation), 36–37, 41, 68–69, 130, 311, 430, 481
Deutsche Gewerkschaftbund (DGB). *See* German Federation of Unions
Deutsche Kommunistische Partei (DKP). *See* Communist Party of Germany
Deutsche Volksunion (DVU). *See* German People's Union
Dregger, Alfred, 367
Dutschke, Rudi, 76, 82

East-West relations, 46–48, 79–81, 173, 178–79, 348, 409, 416, 486. *See also* foreign policy
  influence on nation-building, 341–42, 351–52
Economic Cooperation Administration (ECA), 173
economic miracle, 40, 43, 76, 191, 428, 460
Economic Reconstruction Union (WAV), 40
education, 290, 311–12, 316
egalitarianism, 226
electoral system, 7, 40, 45, 65, 98, 298, 303
Emergency Laws (*Notstandsgesetze*), 46, 47, 76. *See also* extremism; radical right; terrorism
employers' associations, 207–8, 299

entitlement benefits, 232–33, 239
Erhard, Ludwig, 44, 76, 251
Erziehung benefits. *See* child-rearing benefits
ethnic Germans, 361, 389–90. *See also* immigration
European Coal and Steel Community (ECSC), 412, 421
European Community/Union, 100, 111, 274, 321, 407, 425, 515. *See also* European integration
  enlargement of, 166, 178–79, 473
  and foreign policy, 403, 405, 488
  German regard for, 325–28
  and nation-states, 351–52
  and women, 250
European Defense Community (EDC), 404, 412, 421, 431
European Economic Community (EEC), 165, 171, 174–78
European Free Trade Association (EFTA), 168, 175
European integration, 167–71, 422, 429, 433, 435–37, 515. *See also* European Community/Union
  and immigration, 365, 391
  and institutions, 171–74, 217–21
  and international relations theory, 476–77
European Monetary System (EMS), 191–92, 195
European Payments Union (EPU), 164, 171–74, 194
European Single Market, 167, 175
European Union. *See* European Community/Union
Eurosclerosis, 233
extraparliamentary opposition, 46, 76, 350
extremism, 7–8, 35, 38–40, 42, 44, 46–48, 50, 54, 145, 214, 329

family leave. *See* child-rearing benefits
family rights, 237
Federal Constitutional Court (FCC), 9, 344, 506–7
  and citizenship, 111–13
  and civil service, 70–71, 83
  and "guest workers," 363–64
  influence of, 97, 103, 109, 135, 349–50
  as nondemocratic, 113–14

  and political parties, 3, 7, 39, 42, 81, 98, 99, 101–4, 132–37, 104–11
federalism, 217, 340–41
five percent hurdle, 40, 45, 51, 52, 65, 99. *See also* electoral system
foreign policy, 22–27, 514–16. *See also* Bundeswehr
  change after World War II, 420–21
  and collective memory, 439–40, 451–55, 462–63, 467–68
  and domestic politics, 410, 416, 421, 427–28
  and historical memory, 410–13
  limited sovereignty of BRD, 403, 405–7, 421, 426, 431, 441
  recognition of Croatia and Slovenia, 408, 415, 433, 473–75
  role of ideas, 402, 442, 475
  since unification, 401, 404–5, 417, 431–32, 439–41, 474–77, 490
Foreign Voting Case, 100, 111–12, 332, 364
foreign workers, 361–62. *See also* immigration
Four-Power Regime, 405–7, 412
France, 421–32, 454–55
Frankfurt Assembly, 288
Free Democratic Party (FDP), 38, 40, 43, 138, 488
  dismantling welfare state, 218–19
  in role as kingmaker, 46, 50
Free German Youth (FDJ), 42
Frey, Gerhard, 49
full-employment policies, 208–9, 215, 218–19

gender, 228, 237, 250–51, 251–53, 257–59. *See also* women
General Agreement on Tariffs and Trade (GATT), 165, 171, 174, 177
Genscher, Hans-Dietrich, 331, 332, 416, 488
geographical location, 179–81, 196
geopolitics, 23–24, 274, 347, 402–5, 409–10, 413, 416, 439–40
German Federation of Unions, 42, 210
German language, 290, 296
German mark, 166–67, 191, 488, 492
German Party (DP), 38, 40
German People's Union, 49, 52, 140, 386

524   *Index*

German Right Party (DRP), 40, 41, 44, 45
globalization, 1–2, 13, 166, 212, 226, 504
Gorbachev, Mikhail, 279, 404, 444
grand coalition, 44, 46, 48, 76, 210
Grass, Günther, 76
Great Depression, 300–305
Green Party, 40, 51, 86, 99, 104, 139, 315–16
   and antimilitarism, 329–30, 333–34, 487, 491–92
   and European Community, 327–28, 515
   and immigration, 368–69, 373, 386
"guest workers." *See* foreign workers
Gulf War, 489–91

Habermas, Jürgen, 76, 461–62
Hamburg, 52, 81, 139–40
Havel, Vaclav, 272
health insurance. *See* insurance
Heidelberg Manifesto, 366–67, 385, 386
Heinemann, Gustav, 78
Herzog, Roman, 73
Hesse, 47, 52
Hindenburg, Paul, 38
historical memory, 25, 402, 411–12, 415–17. *See also* collective memory
   definition of, 410
   and foreign policy, 475, 478–81
   and unification, 413–15
   and Western integration, 412–13
Historikerstreit, 281, 331–32, 444
Honecker, Erich, 278–79

identity, 16–17, 85, 275, 281, 294–95, 332–33, 442
   east and west differences, 333, 372
   eastern, 51–52, 279, 324–25
   party, 138–39
   western, 313
ideology, 442–43, 444, 446, 448, 478
IG Metall, 11, 213, 225. *See also* industrial relations; unions
immigration, 53, 332, 361–62, 365–70, 382–87, 389–90, 392–94, 512–14. *See also* citizenship
   categories of immigrants, 361–62, 367, 389–90
   and culture, 20–21
   immigrants in schools, 311–12
   and institutions, 388, 392

   and *jui sanguinis,* 20–21, 357–61, 384–87
   labor market, 165, 358–59, 366
   public discussion of, 365–70, 382–87, 392–94
   and unification, 370–74
imperialism, 293, 297–99
industrial relations, 12–13, 207–8, 215, 424, 511
   as peaceful, 211, 234, 317
   in Weimar Republic, 302–3, 457
industrial specialization, 181–89, 196
inflation, 165, 190–95, 303
insiders vs. outsiders, 15–16, 235–36, 245–47, 250–52, 464, 509
institutional change, 38–39, 45, 48, 67, 504–5
institutional design, 3, 35, 55, 94, 96, 342, 347
institutions, 1, 7, 11–13, 15, 17–19, 76–77, 226–27, 231, 279, 294, 306–7, 510
   as ambiguous, 406–10, 415–17, 454
   and culture, 2–5, 8–10, 16, 26–28, 124, 274, 456, 479–80, 516–17
   definition of, 3, 402–3
   as discriminatory, 248, 510
   and economy, 171–74, 196, 179–81, 195, 207–8, 318–20
   and foreign policy, 24–25, 401–2, 404–5, 415, 440, 475, 488
   and historical continuity, 423–24
   and international relations theory, 476–78
   transfer from West to East, 216–17
   use of European institutions, 430, 443, 453, 456, 516
   as value-oriented, 68–70, 96, 107–9, 226
insurance, 204–5, 206, 219, 232
international relations theory, 23, 476–81, 440–44, 490–93

Jaspers, Karl, 75–78
Jesse, Eckhard, 42, 146
judicial review, 96–97, 99, 104
jui sanguinis, 111, 360, 369, 372–73, 382
Jusos. *See* Young Socialists

Kiesinger, Kurt, 78, 80
Kinkel, Klaus, 441
Kohl, Helmut, 36, 44, 50, 83, 136, 225, 252, 486

and Bundeswehr, 312
commitment to West, 401, 405, 407, 414–15, 434, 463, 488
and Gulf War, 489–91
and historical memory, 414–15
and immigrants, 385
and Ostpolitik, 432
and unification, 474
Kommunistische Partei Deutschlands (KPD). *See* Communist Party of Germany
Korean War, 404, 409, 427
Kulturkampf, 290–91, 296

labor, 208–9, 213, 219, 236
Lafontaine, Oskar, 416
learning, social, 286–87, 294, 312, 323–24, 332, 334–35
and foreign policy, 410–12, 451–52, 475–76
Liberal Party, 289–91, 293
Lower Saxony, 42, 112

Maastricht Treaty, 425, 433, 436–37, 488
Marshall Plan, 173–74, 427
memory, 273–74, 276. *See also* collective memory; historical memory; political culture
middle class, 288, 296
migration, 380–81. *See also* immigration
militant democracy, 41–42, 45, 54–55, 72–74, 96, 133, 507
Mitterand, François, 404, 414, 488
mobilization, 9, 75–76, 79, 287, 290, 301–2, 315
Modell Deutschland, 208, 216, 233–34, 251–53
monetary policy, 190–97, 298
motherhood protection, 237–38
multiculturalism, 357, 367, 368–69, 386–87, 512–14
multilateralism, 330–31, 350, 351, 403, 405, 474. *See also* European integration; foreign policy; Western integration
German commitment to, 405, 475, 491

National Democratic Party (NDP), 44–45
national identity, 17, 365–70, 393. *See also* identity; nationalism

national interest, 417, 422, 426, 474, 413, 425, 436, 491
nationalism, 18–20, 334–35, 345, 359–61, 367–69, 373–74, 412, 434. *See also* rationalized nationalism
contested nationalism, 291–92, 297
ethnonationalism, 340–42, 345–48, 357, 372, 393
and European integration, 325–28, 349, 463
lacking in GDR, 324–25
liberal nationalism, 313–21, 321–24, 329
in postwar period, 36–37, 428
racist integral nationalism, 300–308, 329, 367
synchretist German nationalism, 288–91, 294–95, 303
national security, 425, 480–81, 484–85. *See also* foreign policy
domestic debate about, 475, 483, 485–87
and Greens, 492
nation building, 343–44, 348–52, 380, 382
nationhood, 511–13. *See also* nationalism; nation-state
nation-state, 288, 324–25, 340–42, 345, 352–53, 379, 410, 430
NATO, 274, 279, 321, 403–5, 430–31, 488–89, 490. *See also* foreign policy; Western Alliance; Western integration
naturalization, 359, 364, 370–71, 390–92. *See also* citizenship; immigration
Nazis, 303–7
and collective memory, 450–51, 457–60
New Left, 46
Nolte, Claudia, 250
Non-Proliferation Treaty, 425
North-Rhine Westphalia, 130, 250
nostalgia, 273, 465
Notstandgesetze. See Emergency Laws

Official Propaganda Case, 101
Organization for Economic Cooperation and Development (OECD), 166
Organization for European Economic Recovery (OEEC), 164, 171–74
Ostpolitik, 280–81, 322–23, 324, 351–52, 485. *See also* East-West relations; foreign policy in 1980s and 1990s, 405, 414–15, 432–87

Parliamentary Council, 7, 19–20, 37–38, 129, 135, 339–40, 342–43
Parteienstaat/Party State, 65–66, 72, 125–26, 130–32
  and Federal Constitutional Court, 132–37
  origins of, 130–31
  and representation, 140–42, 149
Party of Democratic Socialism (PDS), 40, 99, 139, 217, 329, 371, 505–6
  and extremism, 51–52, 145
  and longing, 280
party system, 4, 7, 38, 40, 43–44, 298
patronage, 140–41
pensions, 204–5, 216, 232
plebiscite. *See* referendum
Poland, 276, 296, 432
political community, 73–74, 278, 345
political culture, 6–7, 10, 17–18, 20–22, 97, 128, 143, 149, 347, 505, 516. *See also* collective memory; historical memory
  and constructivism, 478–81
  definition of, 3–4
  and gender, 227–28, 232, 248, 259
  and institutions, 2–5, 8–9, 10, 16, 26–28, 274–75, 516–17
  political-military culture, 480–81, 482, 487, 490–91, 475–76
  and political parties, 124–25, 133, 137
political parties, 9–10, 38–39, 63–66, 129, 138, 146–47, 345, 383, 424, 504
  antiparty sentiment, 123, 126–27, 137–47
  "catch-all" parties, 65, 74–75, 142, 210, 311
  and civil service, 64–66, 129–30, 141, 296
  as institutions, 102, 124, 132
  as integrators, 65, 134, 217
  rehabilitation after World War II, 128–31, 309–11, 345
  state funding of, 101–4, 132, 141, 148, 162
Politikverdrossenheit, 122, 144
postmaterialism, 139–40, 145, 315–16, 349
price competitiveness, 192–95, 213
proporz. *See* quotas
protest voting, 45, 49, 53, 145
public discourse, 411, 425, 445, 513–14

quotas, 135, 141–43, 250

radical right, 42, 45, 423, 434. *See also* extremism; National Democratic Party; Republikaner (REP)
radicals decree. *See* anti-radicals decree
RAF (Baader-Meinhof group), 47, 49–50. *See also* extremism; terrorism
rationality, 22–23, 25, 477
rationalized nationalism, 286, 293–95, 308–13, 334–35
realist theory. *See* international relations theory
rearmament, 404, 482
Rechtsstaat, 9, 95–96, 382–83, 461
Reconstruction, 164, 194
reeducation. *See* denazification
referendum, 14, 39, 63, 100, 126, 131
regional trade structures, 167–71
religion, 45, 65, 290, 293, 295, 302, 306, 313
  and foreign policy, 482–83
  integrating non-Christians, 368, 374
  and longing, 275–76
  and nationalism, 289–91
representation, 98, 100, 139–40
Republikaner (REP), 50, 52–53, 55, 139, 329
  and anti–immigrant views, 386
  emergence of, 49, 386
  and unification, 99, 371
Rhineland-Palatinate, 256
Rühe, Volker, 489, 492

Saarland, 213, 353
Scharping, Rudolph, 414–15
Schäuble, Wolfgang, 373
Scheel, Walter, 79
Schleswig-Holstein, 52, 139–40
Schmidt, Helmut, 46–47, 50, 208, 215, 318, 486
Schoenhuber, Franz, 49
Schröder, Gerhard, 215
Schumacher, Kurt, 128–31, 134, 413, 428
SDS. *See* Socialist German Student Federation
single mothers, 242–43
social assistance, 232–33, 235, 252
Social Democratic Party (SPD), 37, 40, 42,

47, 220, 225, 292, 434. *See also* political parties
and Bad Godesberg, 43, 46, 210, 486
criticism of, 137–44
cooperation with CDU, 210
economic policy, 318–20
and European Community, 326–28
and foreign policy, 46, 428, 483
and foreign workers, 365
and historical memory, 414–15
and immigration, 384, 386
and imperialism, 298–99
integration of left-wing parties, 36, 46
and unemployment, 213–15
and working women, 239, 249–50
Socialist German Student Federation, 46
Socialist Reich Party (SRP), 39–40, 42, 73
Socialist University Federation (SHB), 46
socialization, 410
social market economy, 316–21
social security, 203–4, 206–7, 215–17, 219, 229, 232–33, 239, 292, 364
Soviet Union, 403, 422, 433, 434–35, 487–89. *See also* East-West relations
Sozialistische Einheitspartei Deutschland (SED), 46–47, 49, 280, 324–25
Sozialversicherung. See social security
specialization of industry. *See* industrial specialization
Standard employment relationship, 205, 213–14, 236
Standortdebatte, 163, 215, 256
Stasi, 48, 50, 84
state-society relations, 72, 101, 125, 132, 203, 211, 295, 382
Strauss, Franz Josef, 36, 41
Stresemann, Gustav, 302
student mobilization, 46, 76–77

technology, 186–89, 315
terrorism, 48, 77, 80, 312–13
Thatcher, Margaret, 431
Trümmerfrauen, 240, 460
Two-Plus-Four Treaty, 404, 425

Ulbricht, Walter, 277–78, 324
unemployment, 15, 40, 84, 163, 197–98, 209, 509–10
benefits, 206, 252
in eastern Germany, 51

and foreign workers, 364
political impact of, 13, 212–17
during Weimar, 301–2
and women, 246, 253–56
unification, 17, 84, 98, 218, 279, 383, 426, 504. *See also* Western integration
and abortion, 105–6, 108
economic effect of, 13, 166–67, 216–17, 252, 508
and immigration, 370–74
and longing, 280–82
and nation-state, 352–53
nineteenth century, 289–90
and political parties, 136–38, 143
and women, 257–59
unions, 11, 42, 45, 209, 247, 255, 292. *See also* IG Metall; industrial relations
and extraparliamentary opposition, 46, 76
and foreign workers, 364
and Nazis, 305–6
and women, 256–58

Versailles Treaty, 303–5, 413
Vertrauensschutz, 363
Vogel, Hans-Jochen, 85
Volksdeutschen, 360, 368–69
von Thadden, Adolf, 44
von Weizsäcker, Richard, 458
critique of political parties, 135–36, 143–44, 147–48

Warsaw Pact, 279, 405
Wehner, Herbert, 80
Weimar Republic, 38, 126, 300–303, 457
welfare, 14–16, 320, 380, 388, 391–94, 510–11
Western Alliance, 321–24, 401, 403–4, 484, 485, 489
Western European Union, 488
Western integration. *See also* Adenauer; East-West relations; European integration; foreign policy
vs. post–World War II reunification, 321–24, 340–43, 348, 407, 413, 427, 483–85, 486 and unification (1990), 404, 426, 433
Wirtschaftswunder. See economic miracle
women, 15–16, 229–31, 239, 510–11. *See also* gender

women (*continued*)
  and longing, 272
  and part-time work, 205, 236, 239, 241, 246, 249, 253
  and worker protection, 202, 239, 257
  in the workforce, 213–14, 219, 229, 233, 241–44
  unemployment, 246, 253–56
  and unification, 257–59
worker protection, 202–4
working class, 42, 306–7
works councils, 210–11

Young Socialists, 46, 80

Zionism, 273